# REVIEW OF SOCIOLOGY

*Analysis of a Decade*

# REVIEW

*Analysis of a Decade*

# OF SOCIOLOGY

JOSEPII B. GITTLER, Editor

CHAIRMAN, DEPARTMENT OF SOCIOLOGY AND ANTHROPOLOGY

UNIVERSITY OF ROCHESTER

NEW YORK · JOHN WILEY & SONS, INC.

London · Chapman & Hall, Limited

# *Preface*

In 1954 the editor of this volume suggested to the publisher that a regular, although not necessarily frequent, review of sociology be undertaken, similar to the volumes now being published in the fields of psychology, physiology, medicine, and a number of others. The suggestion was based on a consensus among many of my colleagues that such a volume would fulfill a fundamental need arising from the fact that the research literature in sociology proliferated at a rapid rate in the decade following the close of World War II and that the sources of publication have been diffuse. There has also been no over-all summary and evaluation of the literature for this period.

As the plan was conceived and executed by the contributors, each has presented and evaluated the significant literature in his given area of specialization for the years 1945 through the first quarter of 1955. As was inevitable in a task of this magnitude, there were many delays in its completion.

It is hoped that the *Review* will prove helpful to professional sociologists as well as to advanced students in sociology. It should also prove useful to those who are interested in the current developments in the field and who are unable to give concentrated attention to the constant flow of publications.

The editor is exceedingly grateful to the scholars who contributed to this book, and to Lami S. Gittler who assisted in the editing.

JOSEPH B. GITTLER

*Rochester, New York*
*August, 1957*

# Contents

# Contents

chapter *1*

# Sociological theory

JOSEPH B. GITTLER
*University of Rochester*

ERNEST MANHEIM
*University of Kansas City*

Theory literally means contemplation. All theories involve abstraction from concrete subject matter. To theorize is to employ concepts. Concepts are abstractions of the given. Without concepts we would have not knowledge but only sensation. Indeed, the very acquisition or assertion of facts presupposes all sorts of theoretic assumptions. All our knowledge involves construct-abstractions, formalizations, idealizations. Strictly speaking, there are no such things as facts, pure and simple; facts are always interpreted facts. The reality of the world is known only within some type of conceptual, theoretical orientation (13, 18, 19, 23). The term theory, in science, denotes that conceptual apparatus which makes explanation and prediction in an area of experience possible.

Conceptual analysis and definitional examination, therefore, occupy appropriate places in scientific theorizing. Indeed, efforts of this kind in sociology have not been lacking during the past decade.

1

The field of sociology has become increasingly diversified and complex. It is no longer a single area of inquiry—if it ever was—but rather the common universe of discourse of variously specialized facets of society. Each of these specializations tends to develop its own conceptual apparatus and its particular body of theory. The present survey does not concern itself with these more specialized phases of the theoretical literature; these will be considered in the chapters of specific concern. The aim of this chapter is to review those aspects of sociological theory which are of common concern to all sociologists and which fall within their common universe of discourse.

## CONCRETION AND ABSTRACTION AS CONCEPTUAL ALTERNATIVES

In a paper read at the 1953 annual meeting of the American Sociological Society and subsequently published in the *American Sociological Review* (12), Herbert Blumer is of the opinion that the basic concepts in sociology are vague, ambiguous, and indefinite. The attempts to overcome these shortcomings, either by introducing new terms or inventing operational techniques, Blumer claims, have been fruitless. He questions whether definitive concepts in sociology are suited to the study of our empirical social world. For Blumer, the aptness of sociological concepts depends on the insight they help to give to the distinctive empirical content of the social world. Fruitful theory seeks to uncover this distinctiveness. Its tools are "sensitizing concepts." By sensitizing concepts Blumer means "a general sense of reference and guidance in approaching empirical instances," rather than precise prescriptions of what to observe and do. "Sensitizing concepts" lack the finality and rigor of mathematical constructs. However, they guide observation toward that which is significant to the purpose of analysis and theory.

Unlike these sensitizing devices, "definitive concepts," for Blumer, are the products of unwarranted abstraction from the concrete material of experience. They are precise, as all taxonomic devices must be, because they designate classes formed of common attributes. Since these attributes are isolated from the context in which the observer finds them, "definitive concepts" are not tailored to advance the true observation and portrayal of concrete social objects.

Akin to Blumer's position is Clinard's criticism of certain research practices in the study of social disorganization (17). His strictures are directed to the taxonomic treatment of social pathology as a means of tabulating isolated traits that occur in deviant individuals. For Clinard, the study of social disorganization should concern itself with the actual subjective meaning of the world to the deviant and with the nature of the group norms and attitudes from which he deviates.

## THEORY OF DEFINITIONS IN SOCIOLOGY

Closely allied to the problem of conceptual analysis is the problem of criteria for definitions of sociological concepts. Several articles appeared during the decade on this question of definitions. This is a continuation of a trend going back many decades and including the writings of Eubank (24), L. L. Bernard (10), Kauffman (38), Chapin (16), Dodd (21), Alpert (3), and many others. In an article in the *American Journal of Sociology*, Timasheff surveys the basic types of definitions employed in the social sciences—the verbal, inductive, imposed, and operational (82). The advantages of the various procedures are analyzed and each is assigned a particular position in scientific research.

While the trend toward operational definitions in sociology continued, vigorous criticism of this movement appeared in the last decade. Blumer (13) discusses the failure of operationalism to get at the concrete social reality. Gittler (29) observes a conflict between the instrumentalism of operationalism and the need for a social ontological approach to definitions. Zetterberg (90) appeals for a close correspondence between operational and nominal definitions. Adler (2), in his attack on the inadequacies of operational definitions, calls for a specifically sociological kind of definition that would embody the subject matter of sociology.

In addition to the polemic on operationalism, sociologists' attention has been directed to a newly emerging science of signs: "semiotics." Morris (55) divides this science into three branches: semantics, which deals with the relation of signs to objects; syntactics, which deals with the relation of signs to signs; and pragmatics, which deals with the relation of signs to individuals. Morris makes out a strong case for the need of social scientists to take account of semiotic considerations in their empirical research.

## GENERAL THEORETICAL ORIENTATIONS IN METHODOLOGY

### *The naturalist and positivist versus verstehen*

Scientific theory may be viewed either in its substantive or methodological aspect. Substantive sociological theory is comprised of concepts and propositions about social reality. Methodological theory in sociology deals with the modus of sociological inquiry. Instead of concerning it-

self with the *what* (substantive theory) of sociological investigations, it
focuses on the *how* of sociological research (44). Again, the subject of
review in this section is the discussion of the last ten years in so far as it
is of common concern to all sociologists rather than a review of the literature on specific research techniques as they apply to particular areas of
sociological interest.

For more than half a century social scientists have disagreed on the
question of whether scientific procedure is universal and common to all
fields of inquiry, or whether there is a valid and fruitful method which
is peculiar to the social sciences. At a symposium held in December,
1952, at the annual meeting of the American Philosophical Association,
Ernest Nagel criticized Max Weber and his school, when he interpreted
their views to mean that the causal-functional approach of the natural
sciences was not applicable to social science (57). This inapplicability
results from the social sciences' seeking to "understand" social phenomena
in terms of "meaningful categories." These "meaningful categories" are
not accessible to sensory observation because they call for identification
by the social scientist with the human objects of study in order to get at
their attitudes, goals, and emotions.

Alfred Schutz (72, 73) takes issue with Nagel by claiming that he fails
to understand Max Weber's concept of subjective interpretation because
of Nagel's basic bias of logical empiricism, which identifies "experience
with sensory observation and which assumes that the only alternative to
controllable and, therefore, objective sensory observation is that of subjective and uncontrollable and unverifiable introspection" (72, page
261). Schutz attacks this alternative as a misinterpretation of Weber
and the phenomenologists. For him the social world, which is an inter-
subjective world, is experienced from the outset as a meaningful one.
"We normally 'know' what the other does, wherefore he does it, why he
does it at this particular time and in these particular circumstances.
That means that we experience our fellow-man's action in terms of his
motives and goals" (72, page 264). These experiences, Schutz holds,
need not be subjective and private; they can be objective and verifiable.
In answer to the question of how this can be done, Schutz suggests that

> The concepts formed by the social scientist are constructs of the constructs
> formed in common-sense thinking by the actors on the social scene. . . .
> The scientific constructs formed on the second level, in accordance with the
> procedural rules valid for all empirical sciences are objective ideal typical
> constructs and, as such, of a different kind from those developed on the first
> level of common-sense thinking which they have to supersede. They are
> theoretical systems embodying testable hypotheses . . . (72, page 270).

In the last decade the conflict of the natural science approach (including that of the positivists, neopositivists, operationalists) versus the antinaturalist approach (including the humanists, phenomenologists, intuitionists, and the followers of *verstehen*) continued with significant vigor. The antinaturalists based their major argument against the employment of natural science methods in human-social affairs on the fallacy of reductionism. They maintained that the social world is so discontinuous with the "lower" levels of nature that a common logic and method cannot be adequate to all of them. They then concluded that problems affecting human relations and social behavior must be investigated by the use of canons of validity and intelligibility differing radically from those used in the natural sciences.

Brand Blanshard adequately exemplifies this antireductionist point of view. In an essay dated 1942 he contends that the methods of natural science are unable to cope with the human mind. "With the faintest and simplest element of consciousness, natural science meets something for which it has no pigeon-hole anywhere in its system . . . (11, page 189). Mind at its best, he claims, is autonomous. Granting that it is connected mysteriously and intimately with physical processes that natural science claims as its own, it cannot be reduced to those processes, nor can it be explained by the laws of those processes" (11, page 203).

Frank Knight, although his major writings on this question date back several decades, continued to criticize the trend of positivism in the social sciences. He states that the claim or assumption of a parallelism between social and natural science is actually one of the most serious of the sources of danger which threaten destruction to the values of what we have called civilization (39, 40).

Similarities to Frank Knight's position can be found in F. S. Hayek's study of *The Counter-Revolution of Science* that appeared in 1952 (34). It is Hayek's major thesis that social science suffers greatly from its slavish imitation of the methods and techniques of natural science. This unqualified duplication he refers to as the "scientistic" prejudice.

Throughout the volume, Hayek repeatedly suggests the need for a different approach to human-social phenomena than that which is used in the natural sciences. He asserts that the methods of knowing must be adjusted to the nature of the subject matter under investigation, that empirical procedures depend on meta-empirical and ontological judgments and assumptions about social reality. Failure to recognize a unique social reality by distinguishing it from the biological and physical universes leads to a spurious reductionism of nineteenth century physical and biological determinism.

Hayek refers to three fallacies of the "scientistic" commitment: (a) objectivism, (b) methodological collectivism, and (c) historicism.

By the fallacy of objectivism, Hayek means the failure of the social scientists, such as the behaviorists, to acknowledge the subjectivity of the human mind. Their rejection has led to a denial of introspection as a possible *modus operandi* for the ascertainment of social knowledge.

The fallacy of methodological collectivism Hayek sees as the tendency to treat as wholes such things as "society," "the economy," and "capitalism." This tendency, he states, forces us to view social events from the outside instead of internally, where meanings are to be found. Hayek claims that

> it is only by the individualist or compositive method that we can give a definite meaning to the much abused phrases about the social processes and formations being in any sense "more" than "merely the sum" of their parts, and that we are enabled to understand how structures of interpersonal relationships emerge, which make it possible for the joint efforts of individuals to achieve desirable results which no individual could have planned or foreseen. The collectivist, on the other hand, who refuses to account for the wholes by systematically following up the interactions of individual efforts, and who claims to be able directly to comprehend social values as such, is never able to define the precise character of these wholes or their mode of operation, and is regularly driven to conceive of these wholes as the model of an individual mind (34, page 85).

The fallacy of historicism Hayek considers to be the new history that lays emphasis on empirical generalization rather than on the description of the specific and the unique. This tendency suffers, Hayek believes, from the "scientistic" shortcoming.

Ernest Nagel takes issue with the contention that the application of natural science methods to the study of social phenomena means reducing social phenomena to material things. Nagel, in a republished essay (first published in 1943), argues that it is untrue and a mistaken notion that natural science "reduces" everything to blind, "undifferentiated collocations of material particles," and thus fails to do justice to the distinctive traits of human behavior (56).

Nagel argues that all that science seeks to do is to determine the precise conditions under which events come into being and continue to exist. He goes on to say that

> in ascertaining those conditions the sciences do not thereby deny the existence of any traits found in nature, whether in the human scene or elsewhere. . . . Whether . . . explanations can be stated entirely in terms of a special class of entities and their relations (for example, in terms of the distribution of electrically charged particles) is a specific empirical issue which can be resolved only by detailed empirical inquiry; it cannot be settled by dialectic,

or by an a priori fiat such as that the living cannot be explained in terms of non-living (56, pages 24–25).

He therefore considers the reductionist argument against natural science methods in social science to be pointless. "The conclusion seems unavoidable that those who would exclude the logical methods of the natural sciences from fields of social inquiry, on the score that these methods commit their users to the 'reductive fallacy,' are in effect recommending the abandonment of the quest for the causal determinants of human affairs" (56, pages 22–23).

Closely akin to the antinaturalist methodological school are the partisans of *verstehen*. Reflecting a heritage from Dilthey, Weber, Cooley, MacIver, Sorokin, and others, the protagonists of *verstehen* continued to be vocal and discursive in the last decade. Thelma Z. Lavine criticizes the present philosophical trend of naturalism, especially its insensitivity to the problems of the social sciences (42). Naturalism's greatest flaw, she claims, is its failure to cope with the nonexperimental elements in scientific inquiry, peculiar to psychological and social realities. For ascertaining the nonexperimental, Miss Lavine suggests the method of *verstehen* which seeks to explain human-social action through the frameworks of understanding and meaning. These are considered necessary for the comprehension of the subjective elements of motives and intentions which are always present in human-social behavior.

In 1952 Florian Znaniecki reaffirmed his identification with the *verstehen* school through the publication of his volume *Cultural Sciences: Their Origin and Development* (93). This work brings together in systematic form Znaniecki's major reflections on the nature and possibilities of sociology as a science. Sociology is conceived of as a basic cultural science. The cultural sciences deal with a different realm of reality than do the natural sciences. Cultural reality involves human action. Human action is meaningful behavior—i.e., it is interpreted by humans who experience the behavior (Znaniecki calls this the *humanistic coefficient*).

In 1948 there appeared an article by Abel on "The Operation Called *Verstehen*" (1). Abel analyzed the concept of *verstehen* as it is used in the writings of social theorists. Abel contends that the distinct nature of social science phenomena has made many theorists search for a unique methodology necessary for the understanding of these phenomena. Many have found an answer in the operation called *verstehen*.

Abel's analysis shows that the *verstehen* procedure cannot provide new knowledge because it cannot be used as a means of verification. If this is true, questions arise about the scientific efficacy of the *verstehen* operation. Although *verstehen* may perform auxiliary functions in scientific investigations, such as providing "hunches" that are necessary in the formulation of hypotheses, as a scientific technique in itself it is highly questionable.

In the same volume of the *American Journal of Sociology* there appeared an article by Redfield which amplifies the discussion further. Without using the term, nor explicitly aligning himself with the method of *verstehen,* Robert Redfield emphasizes the role of creative thinking, insight, and art for important social science discoveries. He cites three books that are considered classics and that have influenced the course of thinking in the social sciences within the last one hundred years—de Tocqueville's *Democracy in America,* Sumner's *Folkways,* and Veblen's *The Theory of the Leisure Class.* The method of inquiry and analysis employed in them was not formally scientific; none of the books delineates and evaluates precisely the techniques used in coming to its generalizations. Yet, claims Redfield, these books must be considered works in the social sciences because of the "illumination they throw upon man's nature or upon the nature of society" (69).

Several decades ago, Max Weber suggested that the meaningful, subjective aspects of human-social phenomena could best be approached through the concept of the ideal type (87). The concept became a major device for implementing his method of *verstehen.* In the last decade, several interesting refinements of the concept have emerged.

Howard Becker, who prefers the use of the term constructed type, differentiates the ideal type from the pure fictional type of Hans Vaihinger. Pure fictional types, Becker claims, are only "logically possible," having little or no empirical probability; ideal types have "objective probability" (5, page 261). Both Becker (6) and Hempel look upon the concept of the ideal type as a scientific tool for objectifying and generalizing social phenomena. Hempel, however, claims that ideal types represent not concepts, but theories, and, as such, alleged differences between the explanatory use of ideal types and the method of explanation in the natural sciences are spurious and invalid (35).

If one were to venture a summarization of the *verstehen* position in recent years, it would consist of a recognition of the distinctive nature of human-social reality, but at the same time an acknowledgment that this reality is subject to scientific analysis and study, even if the specific techniques employed must vary from those in the natural sciences.

This last statement suggests a rapprochement between the method of *verstehen* and its frequently alleged antagonist, positivism. Nineteenth-century positivism, which found its leading exponents in Auguste Comte, Ernest Mach, and Charles Pierce, sought primarily to eliminate the "metaphysical" from scientific discussion. Contemporary positivism—neopositivism—seeks to blend the elements of quantitativism, behaviorism, and operationalism in the study of human behavior (83). George Lundberg, who epitomizes this contemporary trend in sociology, has constantly advocated the use of physical science as the model for sociological inquiry and analysis (46). The neopositivist school with its emphasis on quantitative, mathematical techniques found its major proponents in the last decade among George K. Zipf (91, 92), Nicholas Rashevsky (67, 68), Paul F. Lazarsfeld (43), Samuel A. Stouffer (79, 89), Herbert A. Simon (75), John von Neumann and Oskar Morgenstern (86), S. C. Dodd (21, 22), Jessie Bernard (9) and J. C. C. McKinsey (47).

Formal mathematical-deductive sociology should be distinguished from statistical sociology, an approach which permeates and dominates almost every empirical study of present-day sociology. The first type is a recent development and is engaged in by relatively few sociologists. Both the developments in statistical sociology and in formal mathematical sociology are treated in some detail in Chapter 2 on quantitative methods.

### The functional approach

There are many sociologists who believe that elaborate mathematical sociology at present, or in the near future, is not feasible. Although some hold that mathematical-analytical sociology (similar in form to that of analytical mechanics) is superior to the functional approach, the second, only, currently obtains in sociology (59, page 5).

In sociology, the concept of function has come to take a prominent—if not the most prominent—place in recent methodological theory. Its fitness for empirical use, therefore, has come under close scrutiny. The impetus for this interest has not been entirely theoretical; it originated in the work of Malinowski and Radcliffe-Brown, anthropologists who aimed at more than an enumerative description of customs and felt the need of some working principle for discovering the adaptive roles which given institutional practices play in a society.

Functionalism in sociological writings has been used in a variety of ways. Its most recent usage (for which the term structural-functional analysis is often employed) connotes the importance of studying the dynamic interrelations of the parts of a boundary-maintaining social system (66).

In its simplest form the functional inquiry seeks to uncover the order in which different activities traditionally performed in a group depend on each other. This inquiry need not encounter serious difficulties when it is not planned on an ambitious scale, but rather to establish relationships of single variables. The simplest pattern of these relationships may be stated as follows: activity A is a condition for B, and if B is recognized as necessary by the actors, *A* is also necessary. It may be noted that this relationship is not stated in a reversible form: *B* does not necessarily condition *A*.

In an article on "Some Social Functions of Ignorance," Wilbert Moore and Melvin Tumin propose pairs of such relationships: ignorance contributing to the preservation of a power equilibrium, to the privileged position of specialists, to inequality, to group morale, to fair competition, to bureaucratic organization, to work incentives, and to ethnic stereotypes (54). In the qualified form in which these conditional relationships are stated, they raise no serious problem. The authors suggest how one type of conduct (compliance or forbearance) that is necessary for other types of conduct (e.g., exercise of prerogatives) may be motivated, without implying that privilege necessarily engenders ignorance, or, in other words, without implying that the relationship is reversible and determinate. The authors do not bear the burden of showing whether and when ignorance becomes indispensable for a social system. In this partial or incomplete functional scheme only single pairs, and not systems, of variables are employed. In its present form, therefore, the proposition may be easily translated into verifiable terms.

Complete and systematic functional schemes are more ambitious. They seek to offer a complete account of one variable or one observed pattern of activity in terms of several or all others which may be found established within the same group. A complete functional exposition operates with the concept of an equilibrium, that is, with the interlocking system of activities in a group at a given time. In fact, the criterion of completeness is whether the assumption of an equilibrium, which depends on the performance of each constituent activity, is inescapable for the functional scheme. Once the equilibrium is assumed as given, any one of its component variables becomes determinate within certain definable limits. The position of a variable in such a scheme is reversible: activity *A* may be construed as being conditioned by *B*, *C*, and *D*, in one context while *B* may appear to be conditioned by *A*, *C*, and *D*, in another. Thus, *A* appears both as a dependent and independent variable. In a complete system whose functional components are known, any one variable may be construed through all others. The scheme follows a mathematical model, but in its actual application it often falls short of the paradigm. The fieldworker who attempts to account for what he observes and assumes that the observed items constitute a complete system is rarely in a position to witness the variation of all items, let alone their covariance, for it takes usually more than a generation until a new institutional pattern crystallizes. He can only guess at the effect of a modification of *A* on *B*, *C*, and *D*. Nor is the fieldworker in a favorable position to substantiate the assumption that the observed patterns of activities form a complete system without which his functional exposition remains incomplete, open-ended, and merely suggestive, as the hypotheses of Moore and Tumin are intended to be. Under these circumstances the attempt to construct a complete functional scheme becomes conjectural, with few opportunities for verifiable interpretations.

If the functional method of the systematic type posits difficulties to the fieldworker in preliterate and largely self-contained communities, it presents even more serious problems to the sociologist who attempts to apply the same method to segments of urban society. Understandably, functionalism has come in for much criticism. Some authors, such as, for example, Dorothy Gregg and Elgin Williams, reject the approach altogether (30, 33, 57). Most sociologists, however, seek correctives for the present shortcomings of the functional method.

Merton pointed out that the retrospective application of the concept of functional prerequisites easily becomes a source of deterministic bias. The observer who considers every item in a system as an indispensable prerequisite for an assumed equilibrium tends to overlook alternative modes of satisfying a recognized need. The temptation to ignore alternative solutions which are potential in every system is the source of another bias: the conservative tendency to construe systems statically and to rule out change. A third potential lapse of the uncritical use of the functional schema is the lack of discrimination between conscious motives and objective consequences. A functional schema which does not offer an account of how necessary performances are motivated is both incomplete and deficient. Only critical observation can tell whether an action realizes its intended purpose. If the actual effect does not motivate a necessary activity, the fieldworker must discover how the system provides an adequate motivation for the required performance. To make the observer aware of the difference between effect and conscious motive, Merton suggests the terms "manifest" and "latent functions." The first term refers to those actions the consequences of which the performer recognizes as necessary, and the second covers the actual consequences of which the participants are not even aware (49, pages 21–81).

Mannheim's theory of multiple causation has some features in common with Merton's views, particularly as it concerns the place of motives in a functional scheme (48). A plurality of causes is at work, for example, when a stabilized pattern of activities which an institution requires for its maintenance feeds on a variety of inducements. Practically all institutions offer some scope for the free play of incentives. Some are functionally irrelevant but compatible with the functional requirements of a system; others are incompatible and tend to disrupt the system; but only the functionally required—or functionally effective—motivations explain why a system maintains itself. It is not necessary, therefore, to take a complete inventory of motives to understand why a system is a going concern. Attempts to take stock of the complete array of motives at work in an institutional type of performance tend to "overexplain" the phenomenon. It is the pattern of objective requirements that provides the focus for the inquiry into motives. The dominance of the required motives over the irrelevant or incompatible ones may be the result of a trial-and-error type of adaptation and need not stem from conscious anticipation of the required consequences. Various beliefs and rationalizations which are inconsistent with each other may combine to supply an adequate motivation for an institutional pattern of conduct. The question that governs the causal inquiry is not what conceptions individual participants entertain about the effect of their actions, but what adaptations—conscious or unconscious—perpetuate the functionally required motives. Some institutions make provision for an adequate supply of inducements, while others are able to rely on the free play of random adaptations.

Bredemeyer also aims at a scheme for the study of functions in their systematic and determinate relationships (15). He incorporates Merton's distinction between effect and motivation in his recommendations for the study of functional systems. They should disclose: (a) the needed actions which maintain the system; (b) the needed motives for each type of action; (c) how these motives operate and what their sources are; and (d) to what extent the actual and the required motives diverge or coincide. A complete account, therefore, should explain both the consequences of an activity and the conditions that make it functional.

Selznick's observations on functionalism are related to his theory of organization (74). It is in this special context that he deals with the question of how a system maintains itself. The basic requirement of a system is "the maintenance of the integrity and continuity of the system itself." Applying this postulate to formal organizations, Selznick lists the following maintenance functions: (a) provisions for the security of the system as a whole in relation to its environment or to external encroachments; (b) preservation of the channels of communication through which leadership and control are exercised; (c) stable, informal relations within the organization; (d) safeguarding continuity and legitimacy in the policy-framing and decision-making process; and (e) maintenance of a common outlook concerning the purpose of the organization.

Firey's criteria for the study of schisms in social groups mark an additional step toward a complete functional schema (27). His theory of group integration employs the concepts of ends, environment, environmental resistance, and stress. His scheme is embodied in a set of theorems designed with a view to mathematical elaboration: (a) "a social system is constituted by ends which tend to maintain its identity as a system through meeting environmentally imposed resistances"; (b) every end of a social system is indispensable for its maintenance—any substitution of one end for another alters the character of the system; (c) only a limited variety of interactions can attain the ends which a system must achieve to maintain itself; (d) at the same time as the environmental resistances diminish, the utility and self-maintaining performances of the system also decline; (e) environmental resistances do not affect a system evenly as a unit; they may impose unequal stresses on different areas of the system.

Homans' explorations in the area of group structures move on a lower level of abstraction (36, 37). For heuristic purposes Homans, too, assumes that the components of a social system constitute an equilibrium which must guide the analysis toward increasing degrees of determinacy. For comparative purposes he chooses a small set of categories, simple enough so as to minimize the assumptions which enter into their empirical application. In their combined use, however, these categories take on a more complex character. In keeping with established anthropological usage, Homans distinguishes between the primacy, or external system, of a group, which centers around sustaining functions, and the secondary, or internal, system involving a derivative pattern of interaction which affects the primary functions but does not perform them. Both systems are analyzed under three aspects: (a) operations or activities, that is, pursuits described as goal-directed actions rather than in their social setting; (b) sentiments or motivations, defined broadly so as to include drives; and (c) interaction. Additional concepts which Homans introduces, such as vertical and horizontal interaction, are essentially derivatives of those listed.

The application of this scheme to five selected instances, which provide Homans with the needed case material, occasions a series of generalizations such as: a person's rank in an informal group depends upon the degree to which his behavior realizes the norms of the group; initiative in interaction with an external system correlates with initiative in interaction within a system; as the number of activities in which the members of a group engage diminishes, leadership, social differentiation, and the sway of common norms also decline; positive sentiments within a group increase with the distance of its members to outsiders; and so forth. The significance of this study, however, lies not so much in the resulting generalizations, but rather in the attempt to test a simple but systematic scheme for the study of group structure. The design of the scheme makes successive refinements possible.

Most theories which envisage structure as a comprehensive system of functions employ in some fashion the concept of equilibrium. While of unquestioned heuristic service, the construct of functional equilibrium has so far remained a postulate without ascertainable empirical criteria. It has become an increasingly frequent adjunct of systematic functional theory and, stripped of its earlier normative connotation, it has made its entry into the textbook literature (8, 41). It remains to be seen whether the theory of equilibrium will come of age in the course of continued probings.

Other criticisms of the functional approach have been of several kinds. Some have found a conflict between the functional point of view and the historical (57). The tendency of some interpretations of functionalism to replace causal analysis has also been attacked (84). A few critics have charged that functionalism is inherently static and conservative (49, page 38), and that it tends to maintain the status quo (53). Despite criticisms, structural-functional analysis represents today the major line of methodological theoretical development in sociology.

## SYSTEMATIC SUBSTANTIVE THEORY IN SOCIOLOGY

The histories of the sciences tend to show that they start at a common-sense level and then proceed in two directions: (a) upward, to empirical laws and generalizations; (b) downward, to their foundations, seeking to elaborate through criticism and analysis the logical foundations for the superstructure, i.e., the empirical laws and generalizations.

At the beginning of this chapter we stated that all scientific knowledge is theoretical knowledge. Facts are conceptual assertions of the given. The ideal of science is to achieve a systematic interconnection of propositions. Systematic science becomes equivalent, therefore, to systematic theory in a science (19). Systematic theory tends, ideally, to become "logically closed," and thus reach such a state of logical integration that every logical implication of any combination of propositions in the system is explicitly stated in some other proposition in the same system (14, 23, 28, 52, 56, 59, 85, 88, 89, 90).

Systematic theory varies in its level of integration from science to science (26, 50). Parsons and Shils (65) distinguish four different levels of theoretical systematization: (a) *ad hoc* classificatory systems, (b) categorical systems, (c) theoretical systems, and (d) empirical-theoretical systems. They believe that sociology is in the "categorical systems" stage of development.  By categorical system they mean "a system of classes which is formed to fit the subject matter, so that there are intrinsic relations among the classes and these are in accord with the relations among the items of the subject matter" (65, page 50).

Talcott Parsons' theoretical system, which is described in the next section, has been referred to as an inclusive theoretical system—that is, a system of propositions and theorems logically interrelated and deduced from an assumed set of definitions and postulates (90, page 13).  Some disagreement arose in the last decade over the readiness of sociology to develop an inclusive theoretical system.  Robert K. Merton has advocated for sociology, for the present and for the near future, a concern for middle-range theories.  He defines them as "theories intermediate to the minor working hypotheses evolved in abundance during the day-by-day routines of research, and the all-inclusive speculations comprising a master conceptual scheme from which it is hoped to derive a very large number of empirically observed uniformities of social behavior" (49, page 5).  This point of view has also been expressed by Irving Crespi (20), and in the writings of Zetterberg who prefers the term miniature theories (90).  Harry Elmer Barnes would tend to agree with Merton and Zetterberg, pointing to the end of the era of theoretical system building and prophesying that "sociological writing from this time [1948] onward promises to be mainly specialized forms of social theory . . ." (4, page x).

Some writers, however, consider theoretical system building in sociology an inevitable and desirable undertaking (58).  Indeed, in the last decade, theoretical systems have not been lacking.  In the next sections we shall outline several of these systems.

### Talcott Parsons

It appears reasonable to state that the major theoretical system of the last decade has been that of Talcott Parsons.  Other authors' systems (Becker, Znaniecki, Sorokin) have also appeared during the last decade.  However, a difference may be found in the fact that although Parsons' sociological theorizing began in the early thirties, his work and thought have gone through drastic remodelings.  The others have tended to remain with their "one" positions, involving little modification or reshaping.

Holding that the structural-functional approach is the only way for sociology to achieve systematic theory, Talcott Parsons adopts the "action" frame of reference as the major starting point for his system (60–65).  By the concept of action, Parsons means behavior that is "oriented to the attainment of ends in situations, by means of the normatively regulated expenditure of energy" (65, page 53). Action, therefore, involves actors, a situation of action, and the orientation of actors to that situation. In so far as action is organized around an individual, personality is formed. Action on a collective plane—organized around relations of actors—leads to a *social system* when the interaction involving a plurality of actors gives rise to a shared system of value-orientation standards. The basic unit in a social system is the *role*. A social system consists of a network of roles.

Now, the role of an actor in a given situation involving other actors will be determined by his *motivational* and *value* orientations. *Motivational* orientation has three modes: the *cognitive* mode, consisting of that which the actor perceives in a situation; the *cathectic* mode, whereby the actor invests an object with affective significance; and the *evaluative* mode, whereby an actor allocates his time and energy in choosing interests most gratifying to him.

The actors' value orientations are further subdivided into three modes: the cognitive, the appreciative, and the moral. In a social system the orientation of an actor to other actors will vary according to whether cathection, cognition, or morality (or combinations of these) have primacy.

Parsons contends that every role springing from these three modes of orientation, plus the two ways of estimating an object in terms of complexity and specificity or generality of interest, involves a choice among five pairs of alternative orientation. These alternatives are termed "pattern-alternatives" and include: (a) affectivity vs. affective neutrality; (b) ascription vs. achievement; (c) specificity vs. diffuseness; (d) universalism vs. particularism; (e) self-orientation vs. collective orientation.*

Parsons conceives of action as made up of three systems: (a) the personal system, (b) the social system, and (c) the cultural system. We have referred to the first two.

By the cultural system Parsons means a pattern of culture whose component parts are interrelated with form value systems, belief systems, and systems of expressive symbols. The culture system constitutes the standards and channels for conducting action; it is not action in itself. Culture systems are not systems of interactions characteristic of social systems, but, rather, the patterns of values, norms, and symbols which guide the choices of individual actors and which limit the types of interaction.

The three systems—personality, social, and cultural—are not reducible in terms of one another. However, they interpenetrate one another; each is indispensable to the other two in the concrete manifestation of action.

---

* Utility of these alternatives as variables has been questioned by many writers. See bibliographical references 7, 25, 61, 70, 71, 76, 78, 81, 84.

### Marion J. Levy, Jr.

In 1952 Marion Levy's *The Structure of Society* (45) was published. Using the Parsonian frames of reference—social action, social system, structural-functional analysis—with amplifications, Levy seeks to construct from present knowledge of empirical materials on different societies a general conceptual scheme and theoretical system for beginning the comparative analysis of societies. Elaborating on and believing that the structural-functional approach constitutes the main line of development in sociology, Levy introduced the concepts of functional and structural requisites and prerequisites.

A functional requisite is "a generalized condition necessary for the maintenance of the unit with which it is associated, given the level of generalization of the definition of that unit and the most general setting of such a unit" (45, page 62). A structural requisite "is a pattern (or observable uniformity) of action (or operation) necessary for the continued existence of the unit with which it is associated . . ." (45, page 63). By functional prerequisite Levy means "a function that must pre-exist if a given unit in its setting is to come into being" (45, page 72). The term structural prerequisite is defined "as a structure that must pre-exist if a given unit in its setting is to come into being" (45, page 72).

Levy posits the functional requisites of any society as follows: meeting biological needs, role differentiation and role assignment, communication, shared cognitive orientations, shared goals, regulation of choice of means, regulation of expressed emotions, adequate socialization, control of disruptive forms of behavior, and adequate institutionalization.

For the structural requisites Levy suggests six aspects of ubiquitous relationships: the cognitive aspect, the membership criteria aspect, the substantive definition aspect, the affective aspect, the goal orientation aspect, and the stratification aspect (45, pages 238–279).

Using these concepts Levy then discusses several major analytical structures, including role differentiation, solidarity, groups, economic allocation, and political allocation.

### Robert K. Merton

Merton, a student of Parsons, has become one of his major methodological appraisers. Although Merton's interests and activities have definitely been in theoretical analysis, it is rather difficult to find any formal theoretical system in his writings. He has been engaged about as much in empirical research as in theoretical exposition. This fact is perhaps in harmony with his view that sociology is, at present, primarily ready for "middle-range theories" rather than for an inclusive theoretical system.

In 1949 there appeared in book form (49) a volume of essays by Merton, all but one of which had been published previously. His chapter on "Manifest and Latent Functions" is of special interest for this discussion. Introducing his concepts of manifest and latent functions, he sets forth his paradigm for codifying functional analysis in sociology.

Another of Merton's major publications of the last decade (1948) is his article, "The Bearing of Empirical Research upon the Development of Sociological Theory" (51). This article emphasizes the need for a continuous reciprocal relation between theory and research. In an earlier article Merton analyzes the trends in sociological theory and evaluates the most prevalent and widely used types of sociological theorizing. He concludes with the suggestion that "codification, as a procedure complementing the formal derivation of hypotheses to be tested, will facilitate the co-development of viable sociological theory and pertinent research" (50).

### Florian Znaniecki

In 1952 Znaniecki's *Cultural Sciences: Their Origin and Development* was published (93). In this work he outlines his major theoretical system, which had been scattered throughout his multifarious writings since 1910.

Like Parsons, Znaniecki designates social action as the basic element of sociological analysis and the chief datum of all the cultural sciences. Social action is based on values and falls into three types: creative, initiative, and habitual.

All social actions are the result of interaction among conscious human agents, and they must be studied in terms of their meanings to the individuals involved in the actions. (This is Znaniecki's "humanistic coefficient.")

Social action takes place within a given set of circumstances referred to as the *situation*. The conception, attitudes, and awareness of the acting agent in the situation are known as the *definition of the situation*. All social action is based on standards of value. These standards are shared by others and become integrated to form ideological systems. Ideological systems give rise to cultural patterns and systems of action which are therefore axionormatively ordered. It is this axionormative order that enables scientists to develop systematic classification of human action.

### Pitirim A. Sorokin

In 1947 Sorokin produced a systematic treatise on sociology (77). All sociocultural phenomena can be understood through the basic concept of meaningful human interaction. Human interaction constitutes "any event by which one party tangibly influences the overt actions or the state of mind of the other" (77, page 40).

Sociocultural interaction includes three inseparable components: "*personality* as the subject of interaction; *society* as the totality of interacting personalities . . . and *culture* as the totality of meanings, values and norms possessed by the interacting personalities and the totality of the vehicles which objectify, socialize and convey these meanings" (77, page 63). Each of these constituent elements is extensively analyzed into additional subconcepts to furnish the multiple facets of this general sociological theory.

### Georges Gurvitch

Georges Gurvitch is best known for his critical analysis of Durkheim (32) and for his depth-sociology. He is sometimes classed as a phenomenological sociologist (84).

In his 1950 treatise on sociology (31) Gurvitch points to the necessity of relating sociological laws to the different spheres and levels of social reality. These levels include: (a) the ecological level, (b) the social organizations level, (c) the level of social models, (d) the collective behavior level, (e) the social roles level, (f) the attitudinal level, (g) the level of social symbols, (h) the social change-innovation level, (i) the level of collective ideas and values, and (j) the level of collective mental states.

In addition, Gurvitch distinguishes between microsociology and macrosociology. Each calls for a distinct methodology. The first studies small social systems; the second is concerned with large-scale social entities.

### CONCLUSION

From this survey, one would have to take exception to the view that the era of comprehensive systematic theory in sociology is over. However, compared to the theoretical systems of earlier years, present-day systems, even if less sanguine, aim at empirical application.

Znaniecki's admonition of several years ago that sociology seems to be disintegrating into a number of separate disciplines with little, if any, logical connection among them, appears to be only partially true. Perhaps the hope for integration is greater than the accomplishment. But the attempts and interests are not absent.

Sociological theory is facing problems which are inherent in all theorizing, not only in the field of sociology. Such problems as a common system of notation by which to distinguish variables belonging to different logical types, the problem of empirical techniques, the problem of rules governing the inference of theorem from theorem and theory from theory—these are the usual pains of a maturing discipline.

It is inevitable, therefore, that some selection be made among the sizable volume of publications which bear on sociological theory, and that some phases of the literature receive more emphasis than others. In selecting publications for the present discussion, their intrinsic merit was only one of several possible considerations. That an article or book is included in this report is not in itself an indication that the authors considered it of greater or more enduring significance than another which was left unmentioned. The major objectives in this chapter have been clarification and elucidation rather than prognostication and prediction.

## BIBLIOGRAPHICAL REFERENCES

1. Abel, Theodore, "The Operation Called *Verstehen*," *Amer. J. Soc.*, Vol. 54 (1948–1949), pp. 211–218.

2. Adler, Franz, "Operational Definitions in Sociology," *Amer. J. Soc.*, Vol. 52 (1946–1947), pp. 438–444.

3. Alpert, Harry, "Operational Definitions in Sociology," *Amer. Soc. Rev.*, Vol. 3 (1938), pp. 855–861.

4. Barnes, Harry Elmer, *An Introduction to the History of Sociology*, Chicago, University of Chicago Press, 1948.

5. Becker, Howard, *Through Values to Social Interpretation*, Durham, N. C., Duke University Press, 1950.

6. Becker, Howard, "Interpretative Sociology and Constructive Typology," in *Through Values to Social Interpretation*, Durham, N. C., Duke University Press, 1950, pp. 189–247.

7. Becker, Howard, Review of Parsons' *The Social System* and *Toward a General Theory of Action*, *Social Forces*, Vol. 30 (1952), pp. 463–465.

8. Bennett, John W., and Tumin, Melvin, *Social Life*, New York, Alfred A. Knopf, 1948, p. 499.

9. Bernard, Jessie, "The Theory of Games of Strategy as a Modern Sociology of Conflict," *Amer. J. Soc.*, Vol. 59 (1953–1954), pp. 411–424.

10. Bernard, L. L., "The Definition of Definitions," *Social Forces*, Vol. 19 (1940), pp. 500–510.

11. Blanshard, Brand, "Fact, Value, and Science," in Ruth Nanda Ashen, ed., *Science and Man*, New York, Harcourt, Brace and Co., 1942, pp. 185–203.

12. Blumer, Herbert, "What is Wrong with Social Theory?" *Amer. Soc. Rev.*, Vol. 19 (1954), pp. 3–10.

13. Blumer, Herbert, "Science Without Concepts," *Amer. J. Soc.*, Vol. 36 (1930–1931), pp. 515–533.

14. Braithwaite, Richard B., *Scientific Explanation*, Cambridge, Eng., Cambridge University Press, 1953, pp. 1–21.

15. Bredemeyer, Harry, "The Methodology of Functionalism," *Amer. Soc. Rev.*, Vol. 20 (1955), pp. 173–180.

16. Chapin, F. Stuart, "Definition of Concepts," *Social Forces*, Vol. 18 (1939), pp. 153–160.

17. Clinard, Marshall B., "The Group Approach to Social Reintegration," *Amer. Soc. Rev.*, Vol. 14 (1949), pp. 257–262.

18. Cohen, Morris R., *Reason and Nature*, New York, Harcourt, Brace and Co., 1931, pp. 76–79.

19. Cohen, Morris R., and Nagel, Ernest, *An Introduction to Logic and Scientific Method*, New York, Harcourt, Brace and Co., 1934, pp. 394–396.

20. Crespi, Irving, "Comments on Parsons' 'The Prospects of Sociological Theory,'" *Amer. Soc. Rev.*, Vol. 15 (1950) p. 432.

21. Dodd, Stuart C., *Dimensions of Society*, New York, The Macmillan Co., 1942.

22. Dodd, Stuart C., "All or None Elements and Mathematical Models for Sociologists," *Amer. Soc. Rev.*, Vol. 17 (1952), pp. 167–177.

23. Einstein, Albert, "Science, Philosophy, and Religion," in Philip P. Wiener, *Readings in Philosophy of Science*, New York, Charles Scribner's Sons, 1953, p. 603.

24. Eubank, Earle E., *The Concepts of Sociology*, New York, D. C. Heath and Co., 1932.

25. Faris, Ellsworth, Review of Parsons' *The Social System*, *Amer. Soc. Rev.*, Vol. 18 (1953), pp. 103–106.

26. Feigl, Herbert, and Sellars, W., *Readings in Philosophical Analysis*, New York, Appleton-Century-Crofts, 1949, pp. 510–514.

27. Firey, Walter, "Informal Organization and the Theory of Schism," *Amer. Soc. Rev.*, Vol. 13 (1948), pp. 15–24.

28. Gillin, John, ed., *For a Science of Social Man*, New York, The Macmillan Co., 1954, p. 260.

29. Gittler, Joseph B., "Social Ontology and the Criteria for Definitions in Sociology," *Sociometry*, Vol. 14 (1951), pp. 355–365.

30. Gregg, Dorothy, and Williams, Elgin, "The Dismal Science of Functionalism," *Amer. Anthropologist*, Vol. 50 (1948), pp. 594–610.

31. Gurvitch, Georges, *La Vocation actuelle de la Sociologie: Vers une sociologie differentielle*, Paris, Presses Universitaires de France, 1950.

32. Gurvitch, Georges, *Essais de sociologie*, Paris, Librairie de Recueil Sirey, 1936.

33. Hacker, Helen M., "Arnold Rose's 'A Deductive Ideal-Type,'" *Amer. J. Soc.*, Vol. 56 (1950–1951), p. 356.

34. Hayek, F. S., *The Counter-Revolution of Science: Studies on the Abuse of Reason*, Glencoe, Ill., The Free Press, 1952.

35. Hempel, Carl G., "Symposium: Problems of Concept and Theory Formation in the Social Sciences, II," in American Philosophical Association, Eastern Division, *Science, Language, and Human Rights*, Philadelphia, Pa., University of Pennsylvania Press, Vol. 1, 1952, pp. 65–86.

36. Homans, George C., "A Conceptual Scheme for the Study of Social Organizations," *Amer. Soc. Rev.*, Vol. 12 (1947), pp. 13–26.

37. Homans, George C., *The Human Group,* New York, Harcourt, Brace and Co., 1950.

38. Kauffman, F., "The Significance of Methodology in the Social Sciences," *Social Research,* Vol. 5 (1938), pp. 442–463.

39. Knight, Frank H., "Fact and Value in Social Science," in Ruth Nanda Anshen, ed., *Science and Man,* New York, Harcourt, Brace and Co., 1942, p. 325.

40. Knight, Frank H., Review of Hans Kelsen's *Society and Nature, Amer. J. Soc.,* Vol. 50 (1944–1945), pp. 226–227.

41. La Piere, Richard T., *Sociology,* New York, McGraw-Hill Book Co., 1946, pp. 168–174, 408–421.

42. Lavine, Thelma Z., "Note to Naturalists on the Human Spirit," *Jour. of Philos.,* Vol. 50 (1953), pp. 145–154.

43. Lazarsfeld, Paul F., *Mathematical Thinking in the Social Sciences,* Glencoe, Ill., The Free Press, 1954.

44. Lazarsfeld, Paul F., and Merton, Robert K., "Friendship as a Social Process: A Substantive and Methodological Analysis," in Morroe Berger, *Freedom and Control in Modern Society,* New York, Van Nostrand and Co., 1954, p. 19.

45. Levy, Marion J., Jr., *The Structure of Society,* Princeton, N. J., Princeton University Press, 1952, pp. 62–72, 238–279.

46. Lundberg, George, *Foundations of Sociology,* New York, The Macmillan Co., 1939.

47. McKinsey, J. C. C., *Theory of Games,* New York, McGraw-Hill Book Co., 1952.

48. Mannheim, Karl, *Essays on the Sociology of Culture,* London, Oxford University Press, 1955.

49. Merton, Robert K., *Social Theory and Social Structure,* Glencoe, Ill., The Free Press, 1949.

50. Merton, Robert K., "Sociological Theory," *Amer. J. Soc.,* Vol. 50 (1944–1945), pp. 462–473.

51. Merton, Robert K., "The Bearing of Empirical Research upon the Development of Sociological Theory," *Amer. Soc. Rev.,* Vol. 13 (1948), pp. 505–515.

52. Miller, Neal E., "Comments on Theoretical Models," in David Krech and George S. Klein, *Theoretical Models and Personality Theory,* Durham, N. C., Duke University Press, 1952, pp. 82–99.

53. Moore, Barrington, Jr., "The New Scholasticism and the Study of Politics," *World Politics,* Vol. 6 (1954–1955), p. 132.

54. Moore, Wilbert E., and Tumin, Melvin M., "Some Social Functions of Ignorance," *Amer. Soc. Rev.,* Vol. 14 (1948), pp. 787–795.

55. Morris, Charles, *Signs, Language and Behavior,* New York, Prentice-Hall, 1946.

56. Nagel, Ernest, *Sovereign Reason,* Glencoe, Ill., The Free Press, 1954.

57. Nagel, Ernest, "Problems of Concept and Theory Formation in the Social Sciences," in American Philosophical Association, Eastern Division, *Science, Language, and Human Rights,* Philadelphia, Pa., University of Pennsylvania Press, Vol. 1, 1952.

58. Nett, Roger, "System Building in Sociology—A Methodological Analysis," *Social Forces,* Vol. 31 (1952), pp. 25–30.

59. Parsons, Talcott, *Essays in Sociological Theory: Pure and Applied,* Glencoe, Ill., The Free Press, 1949.

60. Parsons, Talcott, *Essays in Sociological Theory,* 2nd ed., Glencoe, Ill., The Free Press, 1954, Chap. 11.

61. Parsons, Talcott, "Some Comments on the State of the General Theory of Action," *Amer. Soc. Rev.,* Vol. 18 (1953), pp. 618–631.

62. Parsons, Talcott, *The Social System,* Glencoe, Ill., The Free Press, 1951.

63. Parsons, Talcott, and Bales, Robert F., *Family, Socialization and Interaction Process,* Glencoe, Ill., The Free Press, 1955.

64. Parsons, Talcott, Bales, Robert F., and Shils, Edward A., *Working Papers in the Theory of Action,* Glencoe, Ill., The Free Press, 1953.

65. Parsons, Talcott, and Shils, Edward A., *Toward a General Theory of Action,* Cambridge, Mass., Harvard University Press, 1951.

66. Radcliffe-Brown, A. R., *Structure and Function in Primitive Society,* Glencoe, Ill., The Free Press, 1952.

67. Rashevsky, Nicholas, *Mathematical Theory of Human Relations,* Chicago, University of Chicago Press, 1951.

68. Rashevsky, Nicholas, *Mathematical Biology of Social Behavior,* Chicago, University of Chicago Press, 1951.

69. Redfield, Robert, "The Art of Social Science," *Amer. J. Soc.,* Vol. 54 (1948–1949), pp. 181–190.

70. Rostow, W. W., "Toward a General Theory of Social Action," *World Politics,* Vol. 5 (1953), pp. 530–554.

71. Schrag, Clarence C., Review of *Toward a General Theory of Action, Amer. Soc. Rev.,* Vol. 17 (1952), p. 249.

72. Schutz, Alfred, "Concept and Theory Formation in the Social Sciences," *Jour. of Philos.,* Vol. 51 (1954), pp. 257–273.

73. Schutz, Alfred, "Common Sense and Scientific Interpretation of Human Action," *Philosophy and Phenomenological Research,* Vol. 14 (1953), pp. 1–37.

74. Selznick, Philip, "Foundations of the Theory of Organization," *Amer. Soc. Rev.,* Vol. 13 (1948), pp. 15–24.

75. Simon, Herbert A., "A Formal Theory of Interaction of Social Groups," *Amer. Soc. Rev.,* Vol. 17 (1952), pp. 202–211.

76. Smith, M. Brewster, Review of *Toward a General Theory of Action, Amer. Jour. of Abnormal and Social Psychology,* Vol. 48 (1953), pp. 315–318.

77. Sorokin, Pitirim A., *Society, Culture and Personality: Their Structure and Dynamics. A System of General Sociology,* New York, Harper and Brothers, 1947.

78. Sprott, W. T. H., "Principia Sociologica," *British Journal of Sociology,* Vol. 3 (1952), pp. 203–221.

79. Stouffer, Samuel A., "Measurement in Sociology," *Amer. Soc. Rev.,* Vol. 18 (1953), pp. 591–597.

80. Stouffer, Samuel A., Guttman, Louis, and others, *Measurement and Prediction: Studies in Social Psychology in World War II,* Vol. 4, Princeton, N. J., Princeton University Press, 1950.

81. Swanson, G. E., "The Approach to a General Theory of Action by Parsons and Shils," *Amer. Soc. Rev.,* Vol. 18 (1953), pp. 125–134.

82. Timasheff, Nicholas S., "Definitions in the Social Sciences," *Amer. J. Soc.,* Vol. 53 (1947–1948), pp. 201–209.

83. Timasheff, Nicholas S., "Sociological Theory Today," *American Catholic Sociological Review,* Vol. 11 (1950), pp. 25–33.

84. Timasheff, Nicholas S., *Sociological Theory,* Garden City, N. Y., Doubleday and Co., 1955.

85. Verplanck, William S., "Burrhus F. Skinner," in William K. Estes, and others, *Modern Learning Theory,* New York, Appleton-Century-Crofts, 1954, p. 269.

86. Von Neumann, John, and Morgenstern, Oskar, *Theory of Games and Economic Behavior,* Princeton, N. J., Princeton University Press, 1944.

87. Weber, Max, *Gesammelte Aufsätze zur Wissenschaftslehre,* Tubingen, P. Siebeck, 1922.

88. Werkmeister, W. H., "Science, Its Concepts and Laws," *Jour. of Philos.,* Vol. 46 (1949), pp. 449–450.

89. Werkmeister, W. H., *The Basis and Structure of Knowledge,* New York, Harper and Brothers, 1948, pp. 343–365.

90. Zetterberg, Hans L., *On Theory and Verification in Sociology,* New York, The Tressler Press, 1954.

91. Zipf, George K., *Human Behavior and the Principle of Least Effort,* Cambridge, Mass., Addison-Wesley Press, 1939.

92. Zipf, George K., "The Hypothesis of the Minimum Equation," *Amer. Soc. Rev.* Vol. 12 (1947).

93. Znaniecki, Florian, *Cultural Sciences: Their Origin and Development,* Urbana, Ill., University of Illinois Press, 1952.

chapter $2$

# Quantitative methods*

SAMUEL A. STOUFFER
*Harvard University*

The advances in the development of quantitative methods since World War II and in their applications in the social sciences, including sociology, are chronicled, piecemeal, in thousands of publications. The modest aim of this chapter is to select for brief citation certain developments which seem to the writer of most present or future significance to the sociologist. Where possible, references are given to introductory expository treatments or reviews of the literature that the nonspecialist may wish to consult before digging into heavier mathematical treatises or detailed substantive studies, some of which also are cited.

First, we shall consider some developments in mathematical thinking which hold considerable promise for sociologists in the future, although current application may be scant. Second, we shall review selected

* The author gratefully acknowledges the advice of his colleague, Professor Frederick Mosteller, especially on matters dealing with mathematical statistics.

aspects of the research process in which important progress has been made directly in sociology and closely related fields.

A decade that has seen the main elaboration of game theory, decision functions, sequential analysis, information theory, and cybernetics, and that has provided new and important applications of the theory of stochastic processes, is certain to rank as a peiod of historical significance. The mathematical thinking is freighted with new concepts and new tools which some day may have considerable effect on all of the social sciences, including sociology. Likewise, a decade that has been marked by advances both theoretical and immediately practical in sample surveys, in the design of experiments, in measurement, in analysis, in official compilations of data, and in substantive model building, affords a chronicle of often exciting progress. Sociologists themselves have sometimes been the innovators of technical ideas whose uses transcend the boundaries of sociology and sister disciplines. And progress on all fronts has been speeded up by increasing utilization of new types of electronic computing machinery.

## SOME DEVELOPMENTS IN MATHEMATICS AND MATHEMATICAL STATISTICS WHICH MAY HAVE FUTURE IMPORT FOR SOCIOLOGY

### *The theory of games*

Von Neumann and Morgenstern published in 1947 *The Theory of Games* (124), a mathematical treatise with far-reaching implications.

Along with Von Neumann's earlier work on games, it had an almost immediate influence on statistical theory, leading Wald to develop the concept of *decision functions,* which will be treated briefly below. As a framework of thinking in a rigorously logical way, the models have been broadly serviceable to many diverse kinds of scholars, including those serving the planners of our national defense. How explicitly the ideas will prove fruitful in sociological thinking—even if not easily applicable in empirical research—remains to be explored. Game theory may, for example, be helpful in exploring the solutions of role conflicts or value conflicts.

*The Theory of Games* is a quite formidable book. Happily, there became available in 1954 a simple yet rigorous introduction for the non-mathematical reader: Williams, *The Compleat Strategyst* (130). A few days with this entertaining volume would be a rewarding experience to many sociologists.

No one illustration can impart the full flavor of game theory. But, as one example, consider a two-person game in which A stands to win either $4, $5 or $6 from B depending on what B does. If A and B each act to their best advantage, what will each do? (See the diagram of Game 1.) A's best strategy is to make sure of getting the highest possible

### PAYOFF TO A, AS AN OUTCOME OF INDICATED STRATEGIES

| | GAME 1 | | GAME 2 | |
| | Strategy No. 1 for B | Strategy No. 2 for B | Strategy No. 1 for B | Strategy No. 2 for B |
|---|---|---|---|---|
| Strategy No. 1 for A | $6 | $5 | $4 | $6 |
| Strategy No. 2 for A | $5 | $4 | $5 | $4 |

*minimum*, whatever B does. Hence he chooses Strategy No. 1, represented by the top row. B's best strategy is to make sure of paying the lowest possible *maximum*. Hence he chooses Strategy No. 2, represented by the right-hand column. The game costs B $5.

This is a special case where correct strategies guarantee that the payoff will be a single number. More frequently, however, somewhat more complicated *mixed* strategies will be required. Consider Game 2, in the diagram shown. In Game 2, if A plays Strategy No. 1 all the time or Strategy No. 2 all the time, then B can keep his loss to $4. But if A uses Strategy 1 in a random $\frac{1}{3}$ of the plays and Strategy 2 in $\frac{2}{3}$ of the plays he can make an average of $4$\frac{2}{3}$, no matter what B does.

The problem becomes more complex the more numerous the strategies available to each player and, especially, the more numerous the players.

Some thinking about the social sciences, which uses game theory instructively, is found in Marschak's paper in Lazarsfeld (editor), *Mathematical Thinking in the Social Sciences* (91).

### Decision functions

Here the statistician or investigator is viewed as playing a game against "nature." He must choose among alternative strategies in the absence of full knowledge of how things are in nature. It is assumed that a cost function can be assigned to the investigator's errors.

This approach, developed in Wald's treatise, *Statistical Decision Functions* (126), unified and extended all the classical notions of estimation, testing hypotheses, and, in principle at least, the design of experiments.

Other basic treatises have appeared, such as Blackwell and Girschick, *Theory of Games and Statistical Decisions* (8), and Savage, *The Foundations of Statistics* (103). These are heavily mathematical. There is a popular book by Bross, *Design for Decision* (10).

The cost functions are likely to be quite complicated and needed data are not readily available. Nevertheless, the mode of thinking, like that in game theory more generally, may be important to sociologists even if some crucial data are lacking.

An illustration of a direct application of decision theory in a parole prediction problem has been offered by Goodman (47). To the usual data on violation rates he attaches arbitrary numbers representing the estimated "social cost," respectively, of paroling a man who will violate, of not paroling a man who will not violate, etc. Even if the numbers are arbitrary, some rather intriguing findings ensue which can hardly fail to sharpen one's thinking as to the alternative courses of action faced by a parole board.

In statistical operations, generally, there has been increasing concern with the decision between alternatives, even where some of the new ideas of Wald, including the cost function, are not immediately usable. From classical theory we have the notion of power functions or sensitivity of tests of significance, but not always in a form useful to the elementary student. Mosteller and Bush, in Lindzey (editor), *Handbook of Social Psychology* (94), present a lucid exposition of operating characteristics or power curves for the common tests of significance. The problem is to compare and evaluate in any given case the probabilities of two types of error: Type I, rejecting the null hypothesis when it is true, and Type II, accepting the null hypothesis when it is false. The paper makes available a series of charts and tables for quick computation. In addition, Mosteller and Bush discuss, in nontechnical language with numerous illustrations, a variety of other problems involving tests of significance which have as yet received little attention in the elementary textbooks but already have an important place in social science, including sociology. Among accepted techniques are (a) short-cut allowances in the analysis of variance, (b) the matching problem, (c) nonparametric methods, (d) quick methods (such as substitution of the range for the standard deviation), (e) transformations and (f) combining tests of significance.

### Sequential analysis

This is a method of testing hypotheses when the information comes in successive small bits. At each stage we decide to accept a hypothesis or to reject it or to get some more information before deciding. The notions involved in sequential analysis should eventually be of much interest to sociologists working in experimental studies. How many sessions of a small group, for example, are necessary, before we call it quits? It also could apply to surveys. Suppose $n$ cases are studied; is this quantity enough? Or should we get $2n$ cases?

The ideas that are organized systematically in Wald's *Sequential Analysis* (125), have some rather severe limitations in sociological research. Often we are studying several different variables at the same time. For one variable we may need $n$ observations, for another $2n$. Moreover, if the investigation deals with more than two alternative hypotheses, one may require different timing points for each hypothesis. Finally, it should be noted that one can never do as well, estimation-wise, *on the average*, with sequential sampling as one can do with a fixed-sized sample which has the average size of the sequential sample.

Nevertheless, there are clear advantages for study design in taking into account the idea of sequential analysis. Sometimes it reduces the cost of a study substantially if intelligently applied—even by as much as a factor of 50 per cent. But it may increase the cost.

The Statistical Research Group at Columbia University has published a practical handbook, covering a variety of statistical problems in which sequential analysis may be applicable (109).

### Stochastic processes

By stochastic processes we mean systematic changes in the probability of an event through time. Formally, stochastic processes can be conceived more generally, but most of the work done has involved time sequences. The basic idea is that the behavior of an organism, a person, or a society at time $t_i$ is some probability function of its behavior at time $t_{i-1}$ and still earlier periods. If at each time we ignore all earlier periods except the one immediately previous and simply assume that there is some structured sequence such that the behavior at $t$ is a probability function of the state of affairs and behavior at $t - 1$, we have what is known as a Markov process—a model of increasing importance in psychology and the social sciences.

A comprehensive mathematical treatment will be found in Bartlett, *Introduction to Stochastic Processes* (3). A clear introduction to the theory of stochastic processes with concrete adaptation of the theory in models of interest to students of learning theory and of socialization is available in Bush and Mosteller, *Stochastic Models for Learning* (11). This recent book is likely to have a considerable impact on psychology and the social sciences, not only because of its rigor in the formulation of working models, but also because of its concern with specifying parameters which are measurable and which can be shown empirically to behave in ways postulated. Too much of what passes for mathematical model building in the social sciences—econometrics affords numerous examples—seems to be an exercise in equation writing with little or no concern over the ways and means of relating the models to empirical phenomena.

Other recent applications of the idea of stochastic processes in areas of interest to sociologists may be found in Anderson's chapter on panel studies (repeated interviews of the same person) in Lazarsfeld (editor), *Mathematical Thinking in the Social Sciences* (81), and in a recent monograph by Blumen, Kogan, and McCarthy, *Industrial Mobility of Labor as a Probability Process* (9). Using a sample of actual Social Security records, Blumen and his colleagues develop and test a stochastic model to account for movement of workers from one group of industries to another. See especially Chapters 4, 6, and 7.

### Information theory

Like a good many other mathematical developments of recent years, mathematical communication theory cannot yet be said to have had much impact on sociology. But the potential is not to be disregarded. The principal treatise is Shannon and Weaver, *The Mathematical Theory of Communication* (104). The second part of this book, written in popular style by Weaver for the *Scientific American,* is a nontechnical introduction to the central ideas, which relate to the accuracy with which symbols of communication can be transmitted. Such concepts are used as "noise," namely, disturbances like radio static which introduce errors in communication, and "redundancy," which measures the fraction of a message which is unnecessary in the sense that if it were missing the message would still be essentially complete. The theory is mainly the work of Shannon, who organizes the mathematical postulates and proofs in the first part of Shannon and Weaver. Eventually, it is thought, information theory can study with elegance and rigor such linguistic and semantic problems as "How do transmitted symbols convey the desired meaning?" and perhaps, even further, can contribute to answering the question "How effectively does the received meaning affect conduct in the desired way?" Incidentally, the concept of stochastic processes plays a central role in the relevant mathematical formulations. For a bibliography of experiments of particular interest to psychologists, see Luce (86).

### Cybernetics

This widely discussed topic is best known to the public through Wiener's book, *Cybernetics* (128). It involves ideas of information theory but is concerned especially with "feed back." As a model for the development of weapons' systems, for example, which can automatically change course when a moving target changes, it is of central importance. Social interaction would seem to find use for many kinds of analogues of such themes. The equations of Richardson—though now nearly two decades old—as to the reaction of a government, in its expenditures, to the suspected armament of a potential enemy in an arms race, contain a feed-back idea (2). One of the most promising places for sociological use of mathematical feed-back concepts may be in small group research. But this work lies largely in the future.

### General comments

Much of the thinking cited above involves relatively abstruse mathematics. It may be many years before those ideas which are important to sociological research take hold. The process will be speeded up as the number of sociologists literate in mathematics increases. The number still being distressingly small, there is present a great challenge for youth with mathematical aptitude who become interested in working on sociological problems. Meanwhile, there is some danger of superficial or even meretricious use of some of these concepts, merely because they are esoteric and fashionable.

In the past decade many new general treatises on mathematical statistics have appeared. Quite high-powered and difficult are Cramer, *Mathematical Models of Statistics* (25), Kendall, *The Advanced Theory of Statistics* (73), and Wilks, *Mathematical Statistics* (129). At a more elementary level one may cite textbooks by Hoel (61), and by Mood (93).

Some other contributions of mathematical thinking are cited below in the contexts of more specifically sociological quantitative studies.

Among Americans responsible for the dissemination of modern thinking in mathematical statistics and its applications, one should mention Walter A. Shewhart, who long before World War II led the movement to introduce sampling inspection and quality control in industrial production. His major contribution in the past decade has been to edit the *Wiley Publications in Statistics*, several of which are included among the works cited above.

## SAMPLING SURVEYS

Few developments differentiate the era in which sociological research
is now engaged from earlier periods more distinctively than the extensive use of sampling surveys, often of entire cross sections of the national
population.

Theory and practice have improved simultaneously.

The outstanding theoretical contribution is perhaps that of the probability sample, which has been made sufficiently practicable to replace
quota sampling for many kinds of inquiries.

The idea behind the probability sample is that every individual in the
population has a known probability of entering the sample. Only if
this can be brought about, or if it can be shown to be satisfactorily ap-
proximated, is it strictly justifiable to use the methods of estimation and
tests of significance available from mathematical statistics.

There are many methods of obtaining a probability sample. Usually
a population is divided by geographical areas into $n$ primarily sampling
units. From these a sample of $m$ is drawn at random, perhaps by the use
of random numbers. A map may be used to designate $k$ subunits within
one of these $m$ units, such as city blocks or street segments or, in rural
territories, highway segments. From these $k$ subunits a sample is again
drawn at random. Within a subunit every household is prelisted. Finally, from this prelisting specific households are drawn at random to
constitute the sample to be interviewed or enumerated. Further specifications are necessary if the sample is to comprise not households as a
whole but one individual within each houehold.

There is no discretion left to the interviewer in selection of respondents.
He or she must make every effort to contact the predesignated household
or person and complete the interview even if this entails numerous calls.
Even the most persistent and expensive efforts seldom succeed in achieving higher than a 90 per cent completion rate. However, further study
of partial data which may be available on nonrespondents often enables
an analyst to make estimates of the range of probable bias and to show
that its effect on the total outcome may be negligible.

Until about a decade ago, the method of sampling conventionally used
was the quota method. Geographical subunits may be randomly chosen
as described above, but the selection of the ultimate household or respondent is left to the discretion of the interviewers. They can select
the individuals available and willing to cooperate, subject only to the
requirement that their total list include predetermined proportions within
certain groupings by age, sex, color, socioeconomic status, etc. Public

opinion polls and most market research studies have usually relied on the quota method.

The quota method is much the cheaper, costing perhaps from only a fifth to a third as much as the probability method. The quota method is also much faster, since a sequence of recalls upon people not at home or not willing to respond when first approached takes a great deal of time, not to mention ingenuity and patience. For quick results—for example, a study which must be completed within a few hours or a few days—the quota method may be the only feasible procedure. But it is subject to obvious biases which can be of critical significance in many kinds of studies, and, even more important, it does not lend itself to adequate internal checks on the nature or degree of these biases.

The pioneer work in developing the theory of the probability method and working out ways of making it practically useful was done in Washington, where especially key roles were played by Deming in the Bureau of the Budget and Hansen in the Bureau of the Census. Each has contributed book-length treatises dealing both with theory and applications. Deming's *Some Theory of Sampling* (27) provides a concise mathematical treatment, numerous numerical illustrations, and one elaborate example. His Chapter 12, describing in complete detail the design and execution of a population sample for Greece, is a model of exposition. Hansen, Hurwitz, and Madow, in *Sample Survey Methods and Theory* (58), have given the most complete mathematical treatment of sampling problems as they apply to a wide variety of special situations. Volume I deals with a wealth of applications; Volume II is theoretical.

A forthcoming volume by Stephan and McCarthy (110), which the writer has seen in manuscript, is written for the reader with less mathematical training and uses a large variety of data from actual surveys to compare probability and quota methods of sampling. It does not always follow, for reasons cited above among others, that the probability method is the only procedure which should be used.

Some studies use sampling procedures much less defensible than either the probability method or the quota method. A case in point is the Kinsey reports (75, 76). Because of the sensitive nature of the inquiry, Kinsey was understandably willing to sacrifice sampling niceties in order to locate respondents who could be depended on to cooperate conscientiously. The monographic study by Cochran, Mosteller, and Tukey, *Statistical Problems of the Kinsey Report* (19), is more than just a critical review of Kinsey's procedure. It presents a concise reformulation of the central problems of survey sampling theory and can well serve as an introductory guide for the student wishing to cope with the major issues. See especially Appendix D, "Probability Sampling Considerations."

Sampling is, of course, only one aspect of the survey procedure into which error or bias can enter. Questionnaire construction, interviewing, editing and coding, and analysis all have their perils. An excellent summary and analysis of the kinds of errors is available in Chapter 2 of Deming (27), entitled "The Various Errors of a Survey." A critical treatment of several of these types of errors as they enter into election polling appears in Mosteller, Hyman, McCarthy, Marks, and Truman, *The Pre-Election Polls of 1948* (95).

Considerable attention has been given to the subject of the interviewer. Hyman's volume on *Interviewing in Social Research* (65) formulates many of the issues and presents a body of evidence, some of it experimental, as to differential interviewer effect. Chapter 12 by Eleanor and Nathan Maccoby in Lindzey (editor), *Handbook of Social Psychology* (84, 88) provides a review of the literature and brief critical analysis of the main issues.

Several of the handbooks on social research in general treat problems of the sampling survey at greater or less length. A useful elementary guide to surveying is that of Parten, *Surveys, Polls, and Samples* (97). The most recent handbook and, for some aspects of the research process, one of the best for the practical researcher, is that by Hyman, *Survey Design and Analysis* (66). Good summaries by Campbell and Katona (12) and by Katz (71) appear in Leon Festinger and Daniel Katz (editors), *Research Methods in the Behavioral Sciences* (37).

## EXPERIMENTAL DESIGN

In contrast with psychology, sociology has not been distinguished by reliance on controlled experiments for the testing of hypotheses. This situation is changing—and perhaps the greatest single impetus for change is the discovery of the possibilities of experimental studies of social structure and of interaction in small groups. As described in chapter 12 of this volume, there are two objectives of such research: the understanding of processes within small groups *per se*, and the use of the small group as a microscopic model for larger social organizations. The reader is referred to chapter 12 for the principal bibliography on small-group research problems.

The mathematical statistician has fundamental contributions to make with respect to experimental design. The central problem is to get the most information out of a design for the least cost, and the power of statistical models to help accomplish this has been appreciated ever since the early work of Fisher three decades ago. Fisher's textbook, *Statistical*

*Methods for Research Workers* (39), and his little volume on *The Design of Experiments* (40) are much used classics. More recently, the mathematical literature has been enriched with a treatise by Kempthorne, *The Design and Analysis of Experiments* (72) and at a less technical level by Cochran and Cox, *Experimental Designs* (18). Helpful introductions to the problems and summaries of bibliography have been contributed by Festinger, in Festinger and Katz (editors), *Research Methods in the Behavioral Sciences* (37, 38), Edwards, in Lindzey (editor), *Handbook of Social Psychology* (35, 84), and in *Experimental Design in Psychological Research* (34).

In the study of communications, controlled experiments are helping to test hypotheses about conditions that make for attitude change. The volumes by Hovland, Lumsdaine, and Sheffield, *Experiments on Mass Communication* (62) and by Hovland, Janis, and Kelley, *Communication and Persuasion* (63), provide instructive examples of such experiments. The appendixes to the former book make some needed methodological contributions, with respect to the base line for computing percentage change, "marginal" vs. "internal" effects, comparison of the "before-after" and the "after-only" design of experiments, and the analysis of regression effect.

Another type of experimental study is illustrated by the work of Bavelas on the variation in accuracy of information transmitted where the chains of communication through various individuals are changed by altering the structure of a group experimentally. See the paper by Bavelas in Lerner and Lasswell (editors), *The Policy Sciences* (4).

Full-scale experimental studies performed outside of the laboratory are rare. This makes all the more noteworthy the series of ingenious field experiments conducted by Dodd (29) and the staff of his Public Opinion Laboratory at the University of Washington, under contract with the Air Force. Some of this work has been reported in individual papers, and a complete monographic analysis of "Project Revere" is awaiting publication. Examples describing the diffusion of information throughout a city following leaflet drops from the air are reported by Dodd (32) and DeFleur (26). The "Revere" studies take on additional significance because they are not merely *ad hoc* statistical reports, but represent empirical tests of mathematically formulated a priori propositions, deriving from Dodd's general theory of "interactance." Diffusion of information throughout a community has some remarkable and predictable uniformities. Even skeptics who may have been unhappy about some of Dodd's earlier conceptualization, including his rather special notation,

must recognize in these studies refreshing evidence of sociology's maturing as a natural science.

Another example of a field experiment is reported by Hughes and Star
(64), measuring the effectiveness of a systematic effort to inform the
people of Cincinnati about the United Nations.

The model of a fully controlled experiment, in which the experimenter
himself supplies the stimulus, is important to sociologists for two reasons.
One, it shows the *price of proof,* which comes high because of the intricate
care that must go into a foolproof design.   Two, it serves as an ideal
against which to evaluate the shortcomings of quasi-experimental methods, like the panel technique or ordinary correlational analysis.   This
subject is outlined simply in a paper by the writer (116).   More detailed
analysis of the use of various approximations to controlled experiments
in sociology, including what has been called the *ex post facto design,*
appears in volumes by Greenwood (49) and Chapin (15).

Inadequate though they are, when compared with a controlled experiment, panel techniques using repeated interviews of the same individuals
yield much information as to process which cannot be found through
comparisons of different sets of individuals.   Such panel studies are becoming more numerous in the field of voting behavior and in research on
consumer attitudes and actions.   Especially noteworthy is the work of
the University of Michigan's Survey Research Center, under the direction
of Rensis Likert, whose studies of consumer finances have been made
regularly for the Federal Reserve Board (70).   Panels are used frequently.   These studies are notable also because of their employment of
theoretical models of economic behavior, due mainly to Katona.   This
operation recently received a methodological review in a report to a
Congressional committee (108).   Before and after the first atom bomb
was dropped at Bikini, Cottrell and Eberhart (24) charted public attitudes.   On voting behavior, two out of several panel studies which are
especially noteworthy for their detailed analysis of the influences con-
verging on the voter and the process of making up his mind are Lazarsfeld, Berelson, and Gaudet, *The People's Choice* (77), and Berelson,
Lazarsfeld, and McPhee, *Voting* (7).   Another kind of example, with emphasis on prediction, is Clausen's report (17) on what jobs veterans took
after World War II compared with their expressed plans while still in
the Army.   Section III of Lazarsfeld and Rosenberg (editors), *The
Language of Social Research* (82) excerpts a number of panel studies.
There is need for a systematic methodological handbook on panel studies
and such a volume is nearing completion in the department of Sociology
at Columbia.

## MEASUREMENT

This has been a decade of very important developments, both theoretical and practical, in certain areas of measurement. Perhaps most notable for sociology has been the work on scaling of qualitative responses.

A general introduction to measurement and a review of the literature with special emphasis on psychophysics is presented by Stevens in Chapter 1 of his *Handbook of Experimental Psychology* (111). The conventional psychometric work on scaling is receiving thorough treatment by Torgerson in a forthcoming monograph for the Social Science Research Council. Some of these areas also are covered well in textbooks by Guilford (50) and Gulliksen (51). The newer work, particularly by Guttman and Lazarsfeld, is seen usefully in the perspective of scaling in general in Green's summary in Lindzey (editor), *Handbook of Social Psychology* (48); see also Coombs (22).

Before the war, the main direction in attitude measurement was probably that initially taken by Thurstone and many of his students. This work involved an adaptation of psychophysical techniques, such as the methods of paired comparisons, equally appearing intervals, and successive intervals.

A fresh approach to scaling was introduced by Guttman and developed during and immediately after the war by him and various associates. His basic ideas involved several major departures from current practice. He dispensed with the idea of a hypothetical underlying attitude continuum, he treated qualitative data *as* qualitative, and he introduced a model involving a system of components. The first of the components he identified as a simple ranking of respondents by content, the second as an ordering on the dimension of "intensity," the third as an ordering on the dimension of "closure," and the fourth as an ordering on the dimension of "involution" or "involvement." The main ideas are described and illustrated with numerical examples in chapters by Guttman, Suchman, and Stouffer in *Measurement and Prediction* (52), and by Guttman in Lazarsfeld (editor), *Mathematical Thinking in the Social Sciences* (53).

Guttman's model has been used widely, especially in the simple ranking of respondents on the content of attitudes. Techniques for rapid machine computation have been developed, for example, by Ford (41); new methods for allocating error, for example, the "image technique," proposed by Guttman (54); and new methods for reducing error, for example, the H-technique introduced by Stouffer, Borgatta, Hays, and Henry (117). The Guttman scale is essentially a "cumulative" rather than an "interval" scale and some of the failures to obtain satisfactory results have occurred because of misuse of items lacking this cumulative property. ("Are you over six feet tall?" is a "cumulative" item, as contrasted with "Are you between 5 feet 10 inches and 6 feet tall?".) Mosteller has shown how a model analogous to Guttman's can be constructed with items of the "interval" type (115, pages 11–12). A new use of the Guttman technique to construct an "object scale" is described in Riley (101).

Differing from Guttman's in basic assumptions is the latent structure model introduced by Lazarsfeld. A simple description is given by Green (48); Lazarsfeld's main expositions appear in *Measurement and Prediction* (48, 78) and in *Mathematical Thinking in the Social Sciences* (80, 81). Lazarsfeld's method postulates a simple latent variable that accounts for all the interrelationships among items except for random error. The idea is analogous to Spearman's single-factor theory of factor analysis, except that Lazarsfeld deals with qualitative data, not quantitative. Although the theory is quite general, it has been proposed for practical use in a number of special cases. For example, being essentially a probability model, it makes possible a theoretical accounting system for errors in the special case where cumulative items are used as in the Guttman scale. As yet there has been relatively little substantive use of Lazarsfeld's scaling model, partly because of the computations involved and partly because of the instability of calculated estimates of parameters when samples are small. Similarly, not too much use has been made of another and quite different approach introduced by Coombs (21, 23)—an "unfolding technique" which seeks not only to rank items but also to determine the rank order of magnitudes of intervals between items. The concept of intervals which have a rank but not a metric order has challenging theoretical possibilities.

An impetus for developing most of these new models has been the desirability of maximizing the information that can be had from a relatively small number of test items. This is necessary if the data are to be obtained in a door-to-door survey, or if many different variables are to be measured at a single sitting. If one has the time to administer a test with a large number of items—say twenty or more—the older psychometric methods, usually based on one form or another of item analysis, may be quite adequate.

None of the methods described above provides a guarantee, however, of accuracy or validity of response in situations where the respondent has something to conceal—sometimes, even, something to conceal from himself. Projective tests, by providing unstructured or semistructured stimulus material, seek to entice the subject into revealing wishes or needs inadvertently. By describing what he sees in an ink blot (Rorschach test), or telling a story about a picture (Thematic Apperception test), or filling in a "balloon" in a cartoon (Rosenzweig test), or drawing a figure of a person (Zondi test), or completing half-finished sentences (Sentence Completion test), he sometimes gives himself away. The earliest device of this type was the Word Association test, first suggested by Francis Galton many decades ago and popularized by Jung.

Increasing use of such devices is being made by sociologists and anthropologists, as well as by clinical psychologists who are the leaders in such test development. Evidence is submitted that many of these tests do succeed in tapping domains of personality and attitude inaccessible to direct and overt questioning. But most of the instruments, in spite of hundreds of uses reported in a vast and growing literature, seldom prove themselves as general research tools under rigorous statistical tests of validity, and research claims must be scrutinized with caution unless statistically documented. For a summary of what the tests seek to accomplish and how they do it, see Chapter 8 in Rotter, *Social Learning and Clinical Psychology* (102), and Chapter 7 in Jahoda, Deutsch, and Cook, *Research Methods in Social Relations* (69). Much more detailed summaries, although older, appear in Rapaport (98). As one of several examples, a rather well-documented use of the method one may cite is McClelland's *Achievement and Motive* (87).

The adaptation of projective tests to general research use, as distinguished from their initial objective of serving as a tool for clinical diagnosis, is one of the most challenging tasks ahead and calls for intensive cooperation between substantive specialists and experts in statistics and experimental design. "Visceral certitude" will not do as a criterion. The perils of intuitive analysis or prediction as contrasted with actuarial analysis have seldom been better analyzed than in a monograph by Meehl (92).

Hand in hand with the increasing number of formal measuring devices has gone an increasing use of informal and relatively unstructured interviewing. Guttman's models for components give promise of further systematic conceptualization and measurement, but after several years are still largely in the blueprint stage. The sociologist who wants to investigate the salience, intensity, etc., of attitudes still needs to use the unsystematic procedures which go by the name of the "depth interview." Because of its undisciplined character and the subjectivity and judgment involved in interpretation, the so-called depth interview can easily become a specious performance. Currently it is enjoying a vogue in market research, accompanied by too pretentious claims. If, however, the data are treated modestly and carefully, they can be of much importance in throwing further light on the meaning of those aspects of a survey which can be systematically quantified. In the use of such informal methods, increasing attention has been given to the logic of classifying "free answers"—for example, "reasons why." There is an introduction to the problems involved by Lazarsfeld and Barton in Lerner and Lasswell (editors), *The Policy Sciences* (79, 83), and a good popular treatment in Zeisel's *Say It With Figures* (133). See also Cartwright, in the Festinger and Katz handbook (13, 38).

Thus far this discussion has concerned mainly problems involved in the interpretation and measurement of individual verbal responses. The past decade also has seen notable progress in observation and measurement of behavior in situations of social interaction. Indeed, this has been a necessary condition for the development of small-group research, much of it experimental, which has been reported in numerous publications. This material is covered in chapter 12 of the present volume. Useful summaries of the measurement problems appear in Lindzey (editor), *Handbook of Social Psychology* (84), in the chapters by Heynes and Lippitt (60) and by Lindzey and Borgatta (85).

Another area of importance in sociological research is that of content analysis, involving systematic classification and counting of information contained in written communications, pictures, or speech. Methodological problems recently have been reviewed by Berelson in the Lindzey *Handbook* (6). He has assembled examples of a variety of substantive studies in a volume of readings, *Content Analysis in Communication Research* (5). One of the developments to be anticipated in the future may be a closer meshing between this type of content analysis and mathematical information theory.

## OFFICIAL STATISTICS AND OTHER COMPILATIONS

With the increase in sampling surveys and experimental studies designed for the specific purposes of the investigator, a decreasing proportion (though perhaps not a decreasing amount) of sociological studies are based on secondary analyses of official bodies of statistics, such as the U. S. Census. The pendulum may have swung too far and it might be desirable for sociologists to do much more than they now do with public data before embarking on private collections on their own. This thought is fortified by the fact that public data have improved so much both in quality and quantity. A statistician familiar with government statistics in the early 1930's would find many of the bureaus in Washington almost unrecognizable today. The Division of Statistical Standards in the Bureau of the Budget has had an important part in elevating such standards throughout the government. In various agencies, notably the Bureau of the Census, professional social scientists with Ph.D.'s are occupying key analytical posts.

Three developments, largely though not wholly of the past decade, are especially notable. One is the use of sample surveys, either as an integral part of a complete enumeration as in the Census or as a device to obtain information at short periodic intervals. Another is the use of quality checks to evaluate the accuracy of reported responses. The third is the use of new high-speed computers to accelerate tabulation and vastly increase the detail with which findings may be reported.

Thus, to cite only one of numerous examples, our knowledge of the American labor force, both at decennial Census periods and at frequent interim points, is enormously increased. Studies of internal migration of this labor force, which in an earlier period could not even have been contemplated, are now possible in much detail. These data can enrich a considerable range of sociological research, not only in demography, but also in any studies where class structure, or urbanization, or mobility enter as important variables.

Government agencies have pioneered in improving methodology, not only of sampling surveys, as described earlier in this chapter, but also in studies of the quality of responses. As a planned part of the 1950 Census, for perhaps the first time, a staff was set up with the responsibility of ascertaining the magnitude of response errors. See papers by Hansen, Hurwitz, Marks, and Mauldin (56), Marks and Mauldin (89), Marks, Mauldin, and Nisselson (90), and Hansen, Hurwitz, and Pritzker (57).

One of the notable advantages of the new high-speed computers is the speed with which they can perform analyses of time series. For example, from the Bureau of the Census, is a paper by Shiskin (105).

Among publications useful to the student seeking broad acquaintance with current government statistics one may note Hauser and Leonard, *Government Statistics for Business Use* (59), and Jaffe and Stewart, *Manpower Resources and Utilization* (68). A methodological publication, oriented primarily but not exclusively to demography, which provides a critical background for the user of official statistics, has been edited by Jaffe, *Handbook of Statistical Method for Demographers* (67).

This section would not be complete without reference to the new richness of international statistics made available with the establishment of the Statistical Offices of the United Nations. Never before were such thorough and comprehensive compilations made available as in such publications as the *Statistical Yearbook* and *Demographer's Yearbook*. The best bibliographical source is, of course, the current listings in *Population Index*. Among important secondary compilations of international data of concern to the sociologist is the Woytinskys' mammoth volume, *World Population and Production* (131).

Though not collected directly under governmental auspices, there are other large compilations of source material for sociological research which should be noted. An example is the large body of basic data on public opinion assembled and catalogued at Princeton under the direction of Hadley Cantril. Data for the years 1935–1946 are summarized in Strunk, *Public Opinion* (118). Of very great potential importance for sociology as well as anthropology are the Human Relations Area Files at Yale, under the direction of Clellan S. Ford. Ethnological, historical, geographical, and other data from several hundred societies throughout the world have been assembled, indexed, and photoreproduced for cross-filing under multiple rubrics. Several major universities are now repositories for these Files, which enable a scholar to do in a few hours what otherwise might take several years of library research. The production of new material has been stepped up in the last few years by very large government contracts. To give just one illustration of the usefulness of this remarkable new research tool, one may cite Murdock's *Social Structure* (96), which uses statistical tables to test hypotheses about kinship structure, kinship terminology, and other aspects of social organization in 250 societies. The very accessibility of such rich data raises some tricky problems in the applicability of statistical theory—especially in handling situations where societies are not independent and in interpreting tables where the apparent absence of a practice or trait may be due merely to inadequate reporting.

## ANALYSIS OF DATA

Any comparison with earlier work of the sociological literature as published in books and journals over the past decade would hardly fail to register several points with respect to analysis of data:

1. There are more studies involving the simultaneous treatment of several variables.

2. There is more careful and critical use of appropriate tests of significance.

3. There is a healthy and growing body of criticism of published work, oriented toward improving and promoting technical as well as substantive competence.

### Multivariate analysis

While, as indicated, the simultaneous analysis of several variables and attributes is surely on the increase, the kind of analysis made is changing also. This is a direct outgrowth of the fact that sampling surveys and experimental studies lend themselves to subdividing the data so that several variables can be held *experimentally* constant—as frequently cannot be done with secondary analyses of Census and other official statistics, in which variables may have to be held constant mathematically, if at all. Hence, partial- and multiple-regression analysis may not be needed to quite the same extent as in an earlier period. Most of the publications based on polling—such as the Indianapolis study of fertility (127), the Kinsey Reports (75, 76), the analysis of voting decisions by Lazarsfeld and Berelson (7), and the variety of studies reported in *The American Soldier* (114)—are of the kind which can be analyzed by subdividing the data directly to take into account a variety of variables. Moreover, the resources behind many of these studies have provided large enough samples, or the design has called for enough successive observations in time, so that replications are possible. *The American Soldier* in a single table (I, page 228) summarized matched comparisons of 8,554 pairs of percentages, each percentage in turn being based on the responses of from forty to several hundred soldiers.

While the student now has available in published form numerous examples of what can be accomplished, with the aid of IBM machines, by way of elaborate analysis, there has not been much systematization of some of the methodological problems implied. Kendall and Lazarsfeld, in *Continuities in Social Research* (74), provided an example of such treatment, which is only a beginning of what needs to be done. We are not speaking here of conventional statistical treatment, such as that involved in the selection of appropriate summary measures, but rather the analysis of what logically is involved when certain classes of variables or attributes in a given type of problem are "held constant."

Also important are handbooks on analysis. The recent manual by Hyman, *Survey Design and Analysis* (66), treats practical analysis problems more systematically and in more detail than the usual elementary textbooks on statistics. See also Ackoff, *The Design of Social Research* (1). Particularly useful by way of exemplification is the reader edited by Lazarsfeld and Rosenberg, *The Language of Social Research* (82).

There has been considerable use of multiple-regression analysis and an increasing interest in the properties of the discriminant function, which is multiple-regression analysis appropriate to situations where the dependent variable is qualitative. This is a particularly efficient device for many classes of prediction problems, in which attention is focused mainly on maximum predictability rather than on a detailed understanding of the prediction variables. See Tiedeman and Bryan (123) and Tatsuoka and Tiedeman (120). One of Tiedeman's important contri-

butions is the extension of earlier techniques to permit the prediction
of a criterion containing more than two categories.

With increasing frequency one now finds factor analysis used in sociological studies. New electronic machines, especially the digital computer,
are revolutionizing computation in factor analysis, making feasible the use
of matrices of more than a hundred tests or test items if desired.

The literature on factor analysis now runs into thousands of titles.
The past decade has seen the publication of many treatises, textbooks,
and handbooks. One of the best elementary texts is by Fruchter, *Introduction to Factor Analysis* (45). Thurstone's Multiple-Factor Analysis
(122) and Thomson's *The Factorial Analysis of Human Ability* (121)
are major treatises, with emphasis on measurement of intellectual abilities.
French has summarized many factorial studies of aptitude and achievement (43) and of personality (44). Factor analysis of sociopsychological and sociological material is extensively treated in Cattell's *Factor
Analysis* (14), in Stevenson's *The Study of Behavior* (112), and in
Eysenk's *The Structure of Human Personality* (36). Perhaps the best
quick introduction to the techniques is found in Chapter 16 of Guilford's
revised *Psychometric Methods* (50).

The purpose of factor analysis, speaking most generally, is to reduce a
large number of individual tests (or test items) to a small number of
types. These types are independent if the axes are orthogonal, are correlated if the axes are oblique.

There are still areas of controversy, both with respect to the kind of
model and with respect to the purpose of factor analysis. Criticisms of
the kind of model usually turn on the issue of rotation of axes. Rotation
seeks to minimize the number of tests, with approximately zero loadings
on a given factor. Because it involves arbitrary subjective judgment it
has been as distasteful to some mathematicians as it has been acceptable
to most psychologists. Criticisms of the purpose of factor analysis turn
on the degree of empiricism involved. Differences of opinion arise as to
whether or not one is justified in throwing into the hopper a miscellaneous
assortment of tests or test items in the hope that some previously unspecified types of factors will emerge. There are many factor analysts, among
them Thurstone, the father of multiple-factor analysis, who have looked
askance at this sort of raw empiricism. They think that one should have
some pretty good guesses in advance as to the major factors that are
likely to emerge and, if necessary, build additional tests, as pure as
possible in the anticipated factors, for inclusion in the original matrix.
However, the revolution in computing ease that has been wrought by the
digital computer is likely to encourage relatively blind analyses of scores
or even hundreds of items. When factors emerge, especially if there are

many of them, it is not always easy to assign substantive meaning to the factors. Moreover, the system may be unstable and stand up badly upon replication over a new sample of persons or a new sample of test items. Replication seems almost compulsory before solid conclusions are reached.

Note should be taken of a challenging new approach to the factor problem proposed by Guttman (54) in what he calls *radex analysis,* which opens up a new vista of thinking. He conceives of models of factors which are *ordered* in complexity. One such model is the *simplex.* A test of addition may involve only a simple factor, but a test of multiplication may involve that same factor plus something more complex, while a test of numerical reasoning may involve both of these and a third factor still more complex. The ideas are too new to have been tested beyond the illustration stage.

Some criticism has been directed at factor analysis because of its assumptions of linearity and its quantification of essentially qualitative items. Latent structure analysis, described above under Measurement, in its most general formulation may be thought of as a model for factor analysis free of some of these limitations. But practical computations for multiple-factor cases have not yet been devised.

### Use of tests of significance

A comparison of statistical reports today with those of a decade ago in such publications as the *American Sociological Review* and the *American Journal of Sociology* cannot fail to reveal an increasing sophistication in the use of tests of significance. This reflects the influence of courses in statistics and graduate training in all of our major university centers.

While more and more sociologists are learning how to use an analysis of variance appropriately, increased knowledge of statistical theory need not lead to pedantry. Papers need not be cluttered up with $\pm$ signs or $\chi^2$ or F-tests for every computation reported in a table. In fact, some of the best studies of the past decade tend to confine tests of significance to a few critical points at issue.

Moreover, there is increasing use of simple order statistics, described earlier in this chapter. If one has ten tables all showing differences in the same direction, the probability of getting such a result on a null hypothesis of no difference is so small (1 in 1,024) that no elaborate tests may be called for. Consistency among numerous small subsamples, found through cross-tabulation, is increasingly used as a criterion of significance.

It is regrettable that elementary textbooks in statistics for sociologists have not given these kinds of analysis much more extensive treatment.

For elementary discussions see Mosteller and Bush in the Lindzey handbook (94), and Smith in the Festinger and Katz handbook (107).

### Criticism of published work

It is a sign of coming of age of a discipline when the criticisms of published work take a close look at the technical operations. Too often in the past, sociological criticism has been directed at the substantive conclusions only, judging them in accord with the critics' own preconception of what the conclusions should have been. This is legitimate, of course, but may make no constructive contribution toward raising the standards of research and scholarship.

In the past decade, reviews in sociological journals have focused increasingly on critiques of the techniques used and it is to be hoped that this practice will increase without, however, any diminution of substantive evaluation. Sometimes the critiques are brought together in monographic form. Examples of such work are the critique by Mosteller, Hyman, McCarthy, Marks, and Truman, of the pre-election polls of 1948 (95), the critique by Cochran, Mosteller, and Tukey of the Kinsey report (19), and two volumes on "continuities in social research" (16, 74).

## MATHEMATICAL MODELS IN SOCIOLOGY

Here we are not concerned with models that specify a methodological operation irrespective of the subject matter, like the binomial expansion as a probability function, or like a system for multiple-factor analysis. We refer rather to efforts to formulate in mathematical language hypotheses or sets of hypotheses about *social behavior,* which will have considerable generality.

Such endeavor plays a relatively small part in the total body of sociological theory as of today. But interest is growing, as is evidenced by several of the papers in Lazarsfeld (editor), *Mathematical Thinking in the Social Sciences* (80). Work of men like Dodd (28, 30, 31, 32), Rashevsky (99, 100), Zipf (134), Stewart (113), and Simon (106), much of which has appeared since World War II, is a sufficiently promising beginning to justify a prediction of increased attention in the years immediately ahead. Particularly, it is likely that some of the new mathematical concepts cited at the beginning of this chapter will be incorporated in specifically sociological models.

In this context, it is valuable to consider a thoughtful paper by Arrow (2), which makes a case for mathematical models on two grounds, (a) in contributing to *clarity* of logical deductions, and (b) in formulation of theory such that it can be tested empirically by tapping the great resources of modern statistical induction. He points out that such models, though mathematical, may be essentially qualitative—as in dealing with such questions as whether the occurrence of one event implies the occurrence of another. Quantitative considerations may enter in even when the data are essentially qualitative—the Mendelian theory of inheritance is a prototype of the transformation of qualitative into quantitative analysis via the probability calculus.

Mathematical models in sociology, like verbal theorizing, may be useful as direction finders or clarifiers even if they are at too abstract a level to come closely to grips with empirical data. But the best of such models will be those which, though possessing considerable generality, specify measurements which can be made and operations which in fact can be performed. It is not necessarily a difficult achievement for a person with some mathematical sophistication to write out a system of differential equations or to specify a particular stochastic process. But to select out of the multiplicity of such possibilities those particular models which are most likely to square with empirical reality may take years of ingenuity, as well as, perhaps, luck. The sociologist who wants to get an intimate feeling for the points just made can profit by reading not only some of the sociological references cited above but also a psychological exercise in model building like that of Bush and Mosteller (11), which, as noted earlier, is singularly respectful of the needs of squaring mathematical concepts with observed events in the empirical world.

An augury of the concern with mathematical formulations in sociology is the fact that the compilation edited by Lazarsfeld, *Mathematical Thinking in the Social Sciences* (81), though quite expensive, was sold out within a year and has gone into a second edition.

## ORGANIZATION FOR TRAINING AND RESEARCH IN USE OF QUANTITATIVE METHODS

As the years move on, it becomes increasingly apparent to successive new generations of university students of sociology that literacy in their discipline requires at least an elementary knowledge of quantitative methods, and that research creativity in any area where numbers are used requires considerably more than an elementary knowledge.

Some of the elementary knowledge can be acquired in formal courses in statistics, aided by textbooks in social statistics such as Hagood and Price (55), Cohen (20), or Dornbusch and Schmid (33). Indispensable know-how can be acquired vicariously by courses in research methods using handbooks like those of Young (132), Jahoda, Deutsch, and Cook

(69), Goode and Hatt (46), Ackoff (1), Festinger and Katz (37), Hyman (66), as well as texts in methodology like Lazarsfeld and Rosenberg (82). Almost all of these publications are recent and provide the teacher of such courses with excellent material. But it is idle to pretend that such courses or such reading alone will do the training job, beyond the most elementary level.

The student who is to use quantitative methods creatively must have a better basic knowledge of statistical models than ordinarily can be acquired in a beginning course. The price he must pay to master some of the thinking which is the staple of current statistical theory is at least elementary college mathematics, including not only elementary algebra but some matrix theory and integral calculus. If the student comes to his graduate work, as is so often the case, without these preparations, he had better resign himself to an additional year in residence. Of course, if he is to be a creative fashioner of new statistical concepts, not merely a user in sociological research of those already available, he will need much more mathematics and more advanced study in probability and statistics. Several sociology departments now have on their faculty someone with a Ph.D. in mathematics.

But technical knowledge of statistical theory is not enough. The student needs to get immersed in practical research experience. Every science is in part an *art*, which is learned by doing just as one learns to paint. This is true of chemistry, much of which is learned through the finger tips in the laboratory, and it is true of sociology.

Recognizing this fact, many of the large universities that are training graduate students in sociology have research centers, institutes, or laboratories attached to the department or readily available. This is largely a development of the postwar period and may be one of the most significant of all the advances to be noted in this review of progress. Michigan has its Survey Research Center, Chicago its National Opinion Research Center, North Carolina its Institute of Statistics, Columbia its Institute of Applied Social Research, Harvard its Laboratory of Social Relations, Washington its Public Opinion Laboratory, Minnesota its Laboratory for Research in Social Relations—to cite only a partial list of the examples. These research facilities, in conjunction with graduate research seminars, are in many instances able to provide a richness of practical experience not previously available. Often they are working on large-scale research projects in which the younger person can come to play a responsible as well as a routine part.

Large-scale organized research usually requires centers such as those named above for direction and staffing. Such projects not only serve as a training ground but also represent the only way certain kinds of mass data can be collected and analyzed.

But it would be a mistake to conclude that large-scale organized research is in danger of replacing the individual worker and of driving him into a second-rate position. Some sociologists fear just that. They need have no such fear. Most of the research, quantitative as well as qualitative, reviewed in the various chapters of this book is by individual scholars working with limited resources. So will be most of the research of the future. Contributions that represent turning points in thought come from disciplined imaginations, which reside in individuals, not in organizations as such.

## BIBLIOGRAPHICAL REFERENCES

1. Ackoff, Russell L., *The Design of Social Research,* Chicago, Univ. of Chicago Press, 1953.

2. Arrow, Kenneth J., "Mathematical Models in the Social Sciences," in Daniel Lerner and Harold D. Lasswell, *The Policy Sciences,* Stanford, Calif., Stanford Univ. Press, 1951.

3. Bartlett, Maurice S., *Introduction to Stochastic Processes,* London, Cambridge Univ. Press, 1955.

4. Bavelas, Alex, "Communication Patterns in Task-Oriented Groups," Chap. 10 in Daniel Lerner and Harold D. Lasswell, *The Policy Sciences,* Stanford, Calif., Stanford Univ. Press, 1951.

5. Berelson, Bernard, *Content Analysis in Communication Research,* Glencoe, Ill., The Free Press, 1952.

6. Berelson, Bernard, "Content Analysis," Chap. 13 in Gardner Lindzey, *Handbook of Social Psychology,* Cambridge, Mass., Addison-Wesley, 1954.

7. Berelson, Bernard, Lazarsfeld, Paul F., and McPhee, Wilson, *Voting: A Study of Opinion Formation in a Presidential Campaign,* Chicago, Univ. of Chicago Press, 1954.

8. Blackwell, David, and Girshick, M. A., *Theory of Games and Statistical Decisions,* New York, Wiley, 1954.

9. Blumen, Isadore, Kogan, Marvin, and McCarthy, Philip J., *Industrial Mobility of Labor as a Probability Process,* Cornell Studies in Industrial and Labor Relations, Vol. 6, Ithaca, N. Y., Cornell Univ. Press, 1955.

10. Bross, Irwin D. J., *Design for Decision,* New York, Macmillan, 1953.

11. Bush, Robert R., and Mosteller, Frederick, *Stochastic Models for Learning,* New York, Wiley, 1955.

12. Campbell, A. A., and Katona, George, "The Sample Survey," in Leon Festinger and Daniel Katz (editors), *Research Methods in the Behavioral Sciences,* New York, Dryden Press, 1953.

13. Cartwright, Dorwin P., "Analysis of Qualitative Material," in Leon Festinger and Daniel Katz (editors), *Research Methods in the Behavioral Sciences,* New York, Dryden Press, 1953.

14. Cattell, Raymond B., *Factor Analysis. An Introduction and Manual for the Psychologist and Social Scientist,* New York, Harper, 1952.

15. Chapin, F. Stuart, *Experimental Designs in Sociological Research*, New York, Harper, 1947.

16. Christie, Richard, and Jahoda, Marie (editors), *Studies in the Scope and Method of the Authoritarian Personality*, Glencoe, Ill., The Free Press, 1954.

17. Clausen, John A., "Studies of the Post-War Plans of Soldiers," Chaps. 15 and 16 in Samuel A. Stouffer, *et al.*, *Measurement and Prediction*, Princeton, N. J., Princeton Univ. Press, 1950.

18. Cochran, William G., and Cox, Gertrude M., *Experimental Designs*, New York, Wiley, 1950.

19. Cochran, William G., Mosteller, Frederick, and Tukey, John W., *Statistical Problems of the Kinsey Report*, Washington, D. C., Amer. Statistical Assn., 1954.

20. Cohen, Lillian, *Statistical Methods for Social Scientists*, New York, Prentice-Hall, 1954.

21. Coombs, Clyde H., "Psychological Scaling without a Unit of Measurement," *Psychological Review*, Vol. 57 (1950), pp. 145–158.

22. Coombs, Clyde H., "Theory and Methods of Social Measurement," in Leon Festinger and Daniel Katz (editors), *Research Methods in the Behavioral Sciences*, New York, Dryden Press, 1953.

23. Coombs, Clyde H., "A Theory of Psychological Scaling," *Engineering Research Institute*, Bulletin No. 34, Ann Arbor, Mich., Univ. of Michigan Press, 1951.

24. Cottrell, L. S., Jr., and Eberhart, S., *American Opinion on World Affairs in the Atomic Age*, Princeton, N. J., Princeton Univ. Press, 1948.

25. Cramer, Harold, *Mathematical Models of Statistics*, Princeton, N. J., Princeton Univ. Press, 1946.

26. DeFleur, Melvin L., "A Mass Communication Model of Stimulus Response Relationships," *Sociometry*, Vol. 19 (1956), pp. 12–25.

27. Deming, William Edwards, *Some Theory of Sampling*, New York, Wiley, 1950.

28. Dodd, Stuart C., *Dimensions of Society*, New York, Macmillan, 1942.

29. Dodd, Stuart C., *Systematic Social Science*, Seattle, Seattle University Bookstore, 1947.

30. Dodd, Stuart C., "The Interactance Hypothesis—A Gravity Model Fitting Physical Models and Human Groups," *Amer. Soc. Rev.*, Vol. 15 (1950), pp. 245–256.

31. Dodd, Stuart C., "All-or-None Elements and Mathematical Models for Sociologists," *Amer. Soc. Rev.*, Vol. 17 (1952), pp. 167–177.

32. Dodd, Stuart C., "Diffusion is Predictable: Testing Probability Models for Laws of Interaction," *Amer. Soc. Rev.*, Vol. 20 (1955), pp. 392–401.

33. Dornbusch, Sanford M., and Schmid, Calvin F., *Primer of Social Statistics*, New York, McGraw-Hill, 1955.

34. Edwards, Allen L., *Experimental Design in Psychological Research*, New York, Rinehart, 1950.

35. Edwards, Allen L., "Experiments: Their Planning and Execution," Chap. 7 in Gardner Lindzey (editor), *Handbook of Social Psychology*, Cambridge, Mass., Addison-Wesley, 1954.

36. Eysenk, H. J., *The Structure of Human Personality*, London, Methuen, 1953.

37. Festinger, Leon, and Katz, Daniel (editors), *Research Methods in the Behavioral Sciences*, New York, Dryden Press, 1953.

38. Festinger, Leon, "Laboratory Experiments," in Leon Festinger and Daniel Katz (editors), *Research Methods in the Behavioral Sciences*, New York, Dryden Press, 1953.

39. Fisher, R. A., *Statistical Methods for Research Workers*, 11th edition, Edinburgh, Oliver and Boyd, 1950.

40. Fisher, R. A., *The Design of Experiments*, 6th edition, Edinburgh, Oliver and Boyd, 1951.

41. Ford, Robert N., "A Rapid Procedure for Scaling Attitude Questions," *Public Opinion Quarterly*, Vol. 14 (1950), pp. 507–532.

42. French, John R. P., Jr., "Experiments in Field Settings," in Leon Festinger and Daniel Katz (editors), *Research Methods in the Behavioral Sciences*, New York, Dryden Press, 1953.

43. French, J. W., *The Disruption of Aptitude and Achievement Tests in Terms of Rotated Factors*, Psychological Monograph No. 28, Chicago, Univ. of Chicago Press, 1951.

44. French, J. W., *The Description of Personality Measurements in Terms of Rotated Factors*, Princeton, N. J., Educational Testing Service, 1953.

45. Fruchter, Benjamin, *Introduction to Factor Analysis*, New York, Van Nostrand, 1954.

46. Goode, William J., and Hatt, Paul K., *Methods in Social Research*, New York, McGraw-Hill, 1952.

47. Goodman, Leo A., "Generalizing the Problem of Prediction," *Amer. Soc. Rev.*, Vol. 17 (1952), pp. 609–612.

48. Green, Bert F., "Attitude Measurement," Chap. 9 in Gardner Lindzey (editor), *Handbook of Social Psychology*, Cambridge, Mass., Addison-Wesley, 1954.

49. Greenwood, E., *Experimental Sociology*, New York, Kings Crown Press, 1945.

50. Guilford, J. P., *Psychometric Methods*, 2nd edition, New York, McGraw-Hill, 1954.

51. Gulliksen, Harold, *Theory of Mental Tests*, New York, Wiley, 1950.

52. Guttman, Louis, Chaps. 2, 3, 6, 8 and 9 in S. A. Stouffer *et al.*, *Measurement and Prediction*, Princeton, N. J., Princeton Univ. Press, 1950.

53. Guttman, Louis, Chap. 5 in "The Principal Components of Sociable Attitudes," in Paul F. Lazarsfeld (editor), *Mathematical Thinking in the Social Sciences*, Glencoe, Ill., The Free Press, 1954.

54. Guttman, Louis, Chap. 6 in "A New Approach to Factor Analysis: The Radex," in Paul F. Lazarsfeld (editor), *Mathematical Thinking in the Social Sciences*, Glencoe, Ill., The Free Press, 1954.

55. Hagood, Margaret J., and Price, Daniel O., *Statistics for Sociologists*, New York, Holt, 1952.

56. Hansen, Morris H., Hurwitz, William N., Marks, Eli S., and Mauldin, W. Parker, "Response Errors in Surveys," *Jour. Amer. Statistical Assn.*, Vol. 46 (1951), pp. 147–190.

57. Hansen, Morris H., Hurwitz, William N., and Pritzker, Leon, "The Accuracy of Census Results," *Amer. Soc. Rev.*, Vol. 18 (1953), pp. 417–423.

58. Hansen, Morris H., Hurwitz, William N., and Madow, William G., *Sample Survey Methods and Theory*, Vols. 1 and 2, New York, Wiley, 1953.

59. Hauser, Philip M., and Leonard, William R., *Government Statistics for Business Use*, New York, Wiley, 1946.

60. Heyns, Roger W., and Lippitt, Ronald, "Systematic Observation Techniques," Chap. 10 in Gardner Lindzey (editor), *Handbook of Social Psychology*, Cambridge, Mass., Addison-Wesley, 1954.

61. Hoel, Paul G., *Introduction to Mathematical Statistics*, 2nd edition, New York, Wiley, 1954.

62. Hovland, Carl I., Lumsdaine, Arthur A., and Sheffield, Fred D., *Experiments on Mass Communication,* Princeton, N. J., Princeton Univ. Press, 1949.

63. Hovland, Carl I., Janis, Irving L., and Kelley, Harold H., *Communication and Persuasion,* New Haven, Conn., Yale Univ. Press, 1953.

64. Hughes, Helen M., and Star, Shirley A., "Report of an Educational Campaign: The Cincinnati Plans for the United Nations," *Amer. Jour. Soc.,* Vol. 55 (1950–1951), pp. 389–400.

65. Hyman, Herbert, *Interviewing in Social Research,* Chicago, Univ. of Chicago Press, 1954.

66. Hyman, Herbert, *Survey Design and Analysis,* Glencoe, Ill., The Free Press, 1955.

67. Jaffe, A. J., *Handbook of Statistical Method for Demographers,* 2nd edition, Washington, D. C., U. S. Government Printing Office, 1951.

68. Jaffe, A. J., and Stewart, C. D., *Manpower Resources and Utilization: Principles of Working Force Analysis,* New York, Wiley, 1951.

69. Jahoda, Marie, Deutsch, Morton, and Cook, Stuart W., *Research Methods in Social Relations,* 2 volumes, New York, Dryden Press, 1951, 1952.

70. Katona, George, *et al., Contributions of Survey Methods to Economics,* New York, Columbia Univ. Press, 1954.

71. Katz, Daniel, "Field Studies," in Leon Festinger and Daniel Katz (editors), *Research Methods in the Behavioral Sciences,* New York, Dryden Press, 1953.

72. Kempthorne, Oscar, *The Design and Analysis of Experiments,* New York, Wiley, 1952.

73. Kendall, Maurice G., *The Advanced Theory of Statistics,* London, Griffin, 1946.

74. Kendall, Patricia L., and Lazarsfeld, Paul F., "Problems of Survey Analysis," in *Continuities in Social Research: Studies on the Scope and Method of "The American Soldier,"* Glencoe, Ill., The Free Press, 1950, pp. 133–196.

75. Kinsey, Alfred C., Pomeroy, Wardell B., and Martin, Clyde E., *Sexual Behavior in the Human Male,* Philadelphia, Saunders, 1948.

76. Kinsey, Alfred C., Pomeroy, Wardell, B., Martin, Clyde E., and Gibhard, Paul H., *Sexual Behavior in the Human Female,* Philadelphia, Saunders, 1953.

77. Lazarsfeld, Paul F., Berelson, Bernard, and Gaudet, Hazel, *The People's Choice,* 2nd edition, New York, Columbia Univ. Press, 1948.

78. Lazarsfeld, Paul F., Chaps. 11 and 12 in S. A. Stouffer, *et al., Measurement and Prediction,* Princeton, N. J., Princeton Univ. Press, 1950.

79. Lazarsfeld, Paul F., and Barton, Allen H., "Qualitative Measurement in the Social Sciences: Classification, Typologies, and Indices," Chap. 9 in Daniel Lerner and Harold D. Lasswell (editors), *The Policy Sciences,* Stanford, Calif., Stanford Univ. Press, 1951.

80. Lazarsfeld, Paul F., "A Conceptual Introduction to Latent Structure Analysis," Chap. 7 in Paul F. Lazarsfeld (editor), *Mathematical Thinking in the Social Sciences,* Glencoe, Ill., The Free Press, 1954.

81. Lazarsfeld, Paul F. (editor), *Mathematical Thinking in the Social Sciences,* Glencoe, Ill., The Free Press, 1954.

82. Lazarsfeld, Paul F., and Rosenberg, Morris (editors), *The Language of Social Research,* Glencoe, Ill., The Free Press, 1955.

83. Lerner, Daniel, and Lasswell, Harold D. (editors), *The Policy Sciences,* Stanford, Calif., Stanford Univ. Press, 1951.

84. Lindzey, Gardner (editor), *Handbook of Social Psychology*, Cambridge, Mass., Addison-Wesley, 1954.

85. Lindzey, Gardner, and Bogatta, Edgar F., "Sociometric Measurement," Chap. 11, in Gardner Lindzey (editor), *Handbook of Social Psychology*, Cambridge, Mass., Addison-Wesley, 1954.

86. Luce, R. D., "A Survey of the Theory of Selective Information and Some of Its Behavioral Applications," Bureau of Applied Social Research, Columbia Univ., Technical Report No. 8, 1954.

87. McClelland, David C., *Achievement and Motive*, New York, Appleton-Century-Crofts, 1953.

88. Maccoby, Eleanor E., and Maccoby, Nathan, "The Interview: A Tool of Social Science," Chap. 12, in Gardner Lindzey (editor), *Handbook of Social Psychology*, Cambridge, Mass., Addison-Wesley, 1954.

89. Marks, Eli S., and Mauldin, W. Parker, "Response Errors in Census Research," *Jour. Amer. Statistical Assn.*, Vol. 45 (1950), pp. 424–438.

90. Marks, Eli S., Mauldin, W. Parker, and Nisselson, Harold, "The Post-Enumerative Survey in the 1950 Census: A Case History in Survey Design," *Jour. Amer. Statistical Assn.*, Vol. 48 (1953), pp. 220–243.

91. Marschak, Jacob, "Probability in the Social Sciences," Chap. 4, in Paul F. Lazarsfeld (editor), *Mathematical Thinking in the Social Sciences*, Glencoe, Ill., The Free Press, 1954.

92. Meehl, Paul E., *Clinical vs. Statistical Prediction: A Theoretical Analysis and Review of the Evidence*, Minneapolis, Minn., Univ. of Minnesota Press, 1954.

93. Mood, Alexander F., *Introduction to the Theory of Statistics*, New York, McGraw-Hill, 1950.

94. Mosteller, F., and Bush, R. R., "Selected Quantitative Techniques," Chap. 8 in Gardner Lindzey (editor), *Handbook of Social Psychology*, Cambridge, Mass., Addison-Wesley, 1954.

95. Mosteller, F., et al., *The Pre-Election Polls of 1948*, New York, Social Science Research Council, 1949.

96. Murdock, George Peter, *Social Structure*, New York, Macmillan, 1949.

97. Parten, Mildred B., *Surveys, Polls, and Samples*, New York, Harper, 1950.

98. Rapaport, David, *Diagnostic Psychological Testing*, Chicago, The Year Book Publishers, 1945.

99. Rashevsky, Nicholas, *Mathematical Theory of Human Relations*, Mathematical Biophysics Monograph Series No. 2, Bloomington, Ind., Principia Press, 1947.

100. Rashevsky, Nicholas, "Two Models: Imitation Behavior and Distribution of Statute," Chap. 2 in Paul F. Lazarsfeld (editor), *Mathematical Thinking in the Social Sciences*, Glencoe, Ill., The Free Press, 1954.

101. Riley, Matilda, W., et al., *Sociological Studies in Scale Analysis*, New Brunswick, N. J., Rutgers Univ. Press, 1954.

102. Rotter, Julian B., *Social Learning and Clinical Psychology*, New York, Prentice-Hall, 1954.

103. Savage, Leonard J., *The Foundations of Statistics*, New York, Wiley, 1954.

104. Shannon, Claude E., and Weaver, Warren, *The Mathematical Theory of Communication*, Urbana, Ill., Univ. of Illinois Press, 1949.

105. Shiskin, Julius, "Seasonal Computations on the Univac," *Amer. Statistician*, Vol. 9 (1955), pp. 19–23.

106. Simon, Herbert A., "Some Strategic Considerations in the Construction of

Social Science Models," Chap. 8 in Paul F. Lazarsfeld (editor), *Mathematical Thinking in the Social Sciences*, Glencoe, Ill., The Free Press, 1954.

107. Smith, Keith, "Distribution-Free Statistical Methods and the Concept of Power Efficiency," in Leon Festinger and Daniel Katz (editors), *Research Methods in the Behavioral Sciences*, New York, Dryden Press, 1953.

108. Smithies, Arthur, *et al.*, "Consumer Survey Statistics," in *Reports of Federal Reserve Consultation Committees in Economic Statistics,* Hearings before the Subcommittee on Economic Statistics of the Joint Committee on the Economic Report, 84th Congress, Washington, D. C., U. S. Government Printing Office, 1955.

109. Statistical Research Group, Columbia University, *Sequential Analysis of Statistical Data: Applications*, New York, Columbia Univ. Press, 1953.

110. Stephan, Frederick F., and McCarthy, Philip J., Manuscript of *Sampling Opinion—An Analysis of Procedure* (in press).

111. Stevens, S. S., "Mathematics, Measurement, and Psychophysics," Chap. 1 in S. S. Stevens (editor), *Handbook of Experimental Psychology*, New York, Wiley, 1951.

112. Stevenson, W., *The Study of Behavior*, Chicago, Univ. of Chicago Press, 1953.

113. Stewart, John Q., "Demographic Gravitation: Evidence and Application," *Sociometry*, Vol. 11 (1948), pp. 31–58.

114. Stouffer, Samuel A., Suchman, Edward A., DeVinney, Leland C., Star, Shirley A., and Williams, Robin M., *The American Soldier*, Vol. 1; Stouffer, Samuel A., Lumsdaine, A. A. and Marion H., Williams, Robin M., Smith, M. Brewster, Janis, Irving L., Star, Shirley A., and Cottrell, Leonard S., Jr., *The American Soldier*, Vol. 2, Princeton, N. J., Princeton Univ. Press, 1949.

115. Stouffer, Samuel A., "An Overview of the Contribution to Scaling and Scale Theory," Chap. 1 in S. A. Stouffer, *et al.*, *Measurement and Prediction*, Princeton, N. J., Princeton Univ. Press, 1950.

116. Stouffer, Samuel A., "Some Observations on Study Design," *Amer. J. Soc.*, Vol. 55 (1950), pp. 355–361.

117. Stouffer, S. A., Borgatta, E. F., Hays, D. G., and Henry, A. F., "A Technique for Improving Cumulative Scales," *Public Opinion Quarterly*, Vol. 16 (1952), pp. 273–291.

118. Strunk, Mildred, *Public Opinion 1935–1946*. Prepared under the editorial direction of Hadley Cantril, Princeton, N. J., Princeton Univ. Press, 1951.

119. Suchman, Edward A., Chaps. 4, 5, and 7 in S. A. Stouffer, *et al.*, *Measurement and Prediction*, Princeton, N. J., Princeton Univ. Press, 1950.

120. Tatsuoka, M. M., and Tiedeman, D. V., "Discriminant Analysis," *Review of Educational Research*, Vol. 24 (1954), pp. 402–420.

121. Thomson, G. H., *The Factorial Analysis of Human Ability*, 5th edition, Boston, Houghton Mifflin, 1951.

122. Thurstone, L. L., *Multiple-Factor Analysis; a Development and Extension of the Vectors of Mind*, Chicago, Univ. of Chicago Press, 1947.

123. Tiedeman, David V., and Bryan, Joseph G., "Prediction of College Field of Concentration," *Harvard Educational Review*, Vol. 24 (1954), pp. 122–139.

124. Von Neumann, John, and Morgenstern, Oskar, *The Theory of Games and Economic Behavior*, Princeton, N. J., Princeton Univ. Press, 1947.

125. Wald, Abraham, *Sequential Analysis*, New York, Wiley, 1947.

126. Wald, Abraham, *Statistical Decision Functions*, New York, Wiley, 1950.

127. Whelpton, P. K., and Kiser, Clyde V. (editors), *Social and Psychological Factors Affecting Fertility*. Reprinted from the *Milbank Memorial Fund Quarterly*, Vol. 1, 1946, Vol. 2, 1950, Vol. 3, 1952.

128. Wiener, Norbert, *Cybernetics*, Cambridge, Technology Press, and New York, Wiley, 1948.

129. Wilks, Samuel S., *Mathematical Statistics*, Princeton, N. J., Princeton Univ. Press, 1943.

130. Williams, J. D., *The Compleat Strategyst, Being a Primer on the Theory of Games of Strategy*, New York, McGraw-Hill, 1954.

131. Woytinsky, W. S., and Woytinsky, E. S., *World Population and Production, Trends and Outlook*, New York, Twentieth Century Fund, 1953.

132. Young, Pauline V., *Scientific Social Surveys and Research*, New York, Prentice-Hall, 1949.

133. Zeisel, Hans, *Say It With Figures*, New York, Harper, 1947.

134. Zipf, George Kingsley, *Human Behavior and the Principle of Least Effort*, Cambridge, Mass., Addison-Wesley, 1949.

# chapter 3

# Population research

CLYDE V. KISER
*Milbank Memorial Fund*

The decade since the close of World War II has been an eventful one for population trends and for research in population problems. With respect to trends the period has been notable for what Joseph S. Davis called the "population upsurge." Within the more industrialized areas, particularly in the United States and Canada, birth rates increased rapidly after the war (12, 130, 133). An all-time peak in the marriage rate for the United States was reached in 1946 and the next year (1947) witnessed the largest number of births on record up to that date and the highest *birth rate* since that of 1921 (130). Although the current birth rate for the United States is a little lower than that for 1947, new records on numbers of births were established annually during 1951–1954. In 1954 over four million births occurred in this country.

The unanticipated flood of births brought rapid population growth to most of the countries that had been labeled as those of "incipient population decline." However, the label still appears appropriate for most countries of Northern and Western Europe because in those places there has been considerably less persistence of the high birth rate than in the United States and Canada. Some of the less-developed countries have experienced rather sudden spurts of growth since 1945 because of declines in death rates.

### Background

In order to secure a better appreciation of the nature of research in population since World War II, a brief sketch of earlier developments in this field may be helpful. Although the science of demography has its roots in the ancient censuses, Malthus is generally regarded as the "father" of the scientific study of population and it was not until 1855 that the term "demography" was coined by Achille Guillard (31).

Although the United States can claim the oldest uninterrupted chain of decennial Census data, it was a latecomer among modern nations in the development of vital statistics. In most Western countries registration data and census data developed simultaneously at common national levels. However, whereas there is constitutional provision in the United States for a decadal federal census, the registration of births, deaths, and other vital events remains the ultimate prerogative and responsibility of the several states. It was not until 1900 and 1915, respectively, that death and birth "registration areas" were established in the United States as the beginnings of a national system of vital statistics. It was not until 1933 that the death and birth registration areas covered the total area of continental United States.

As in most social sciences, the subject matter for research in demography is greatly influenced by the types of materials available and by the nature of existing problems. Thus, during the approximate period 1875–1920 the treatises on demography were based largely upon census and immigration materials and they were concerned with the "dangers" of overpopulation and unrestricted immigration.

When the problem of immigration was "settled" by passage of the Quota Acts of the twenties, the attention of the students in this country correspondingly turned to the problem of natural increase. By that time, too, the birth registration area had expanded sufficiently to permit treatment of the data on something approximating a national basis.

In 1925 Dublin and Lotka published "On the True Rate of Natural Increase" (22) and demonstrated that the age-specific fertility of native-white women in the United States was scarcely sufficient, at that time, to yield permanent replacement of the population through births. This article and ensuing ones on the aging of the population cast an entirely different light on the nature of our national population problems and colored the thinking of demographers for a quarter of a century.

The first United States population projections from the Scripps Foundation for Research in Population Problems were published by Whelpton in 1928 (137). These were based upon given assumptions regarding trends of age-specific birth and death rates and immigration. The "medium" estimates indicated a population of 151.6 million in 1950 and 171.5 million in 1975, and a leveling off at about 186 million by the year 2000. These results were similar to those derived by Pearl and Reed (82) in their first [1920] effort at fitting the logistic curve to the population growth of the U. S.* In both cases the estimates for 1950 proved to be remarkably accurate. However, long before 1950 Pearl and Reed had revised their estimates downward and Whelpton had done this several times (21). The "medium" Scripps Foundation estimates that were published in 1935 indicated a population of 141.6 million for 1950, a near-maximum of 158.3 million for 1980, and declines thereafter (21).

Whereas the outlook during the thirties was for declines in the total population, there were marked differentials in fertility by rural-urban, regional, and socioeconomic status. The rural-urban and regional differences in fertility in particular impinged upon a wide variety of social problems associated with the economic depression. Studies indicated that the areas of highest fertility tended also to be characterized by lowest levels of living, poorest facilities for child health, and poorest educational facilities. The "rural problem areas" were given prominence in *The Problems of a Changing Population* published by the National Resources Committee in 1938 (131). They also figured prominently in the report *Foundations of American Population Policy,* which was sponsored by the National Economic and Social Planning Association in 1940 (62). Goodrich's *Migration and Economic Opportunity* (29) is a thorough study of internal migration in relation to levels of living and employment. The coexistence of high fertility and poor schools underlay the work and recommendations of the [President Roosevelt's] Advisory Committee on Education (1) and helped to stimulate the program of federal grants-in-aid for education and health. Perhaps partly for the same reason, several Southern states also became the first to institute contraception in the State and County public health programs.

In general, therefore, the decade of the thirties was one in which popu-

---

* According to the first Pearl-Reed curve, the indicated population for 1950 was 148.7 million and that for the year 2000 was 184.7 million with an ultimate of 197.3 million. It is recognized, of course, that in fitting the logistic, one must make initial assumptions regarding the upper asymptote.

lation research was closely identified with the social and economic problems of the depression. In the United States, studies were directed to the demographic bases of poverty, ill-health, and illiteracy in the rural areas. Prominent in the population theory of the decade was the work of Alvin Hansen (34) of this country and W. B. Reddaway (90) of England on the economics of a declining population.

The decade of the thirties also ushered in the first really comprehensive study of differential fertility by socioeconomic status within the United States (106). This work was followed by the well-known series of studies of the prevalence and effectiveness of contraception (3, 84, 103, 104). During the closing years of the decade plans were developed for the study of social and psychological factors affecting fertility (142).

In other Western countries, demographic developments of significance during the thirties were the efforts at pronatalist legislation. In Germany and Italy these efforts were attuned to Nazi and fascist philosophies of expansion; in France they appeared to be motivated by needs for national defense; and in Sweden they were part and parcel of a large program of social welfare (116).

Despite the emphasis on national population problems, some of the research effort of the thirties was devoted to international or world population problems (86, 113). The International Union for the Scientific Investigation of Population Problems, founded in 1928, held a relatively small meeting in London in 1931 and a larger one in Paris in 1937. However, it was not until the forties that a really pronounced shift from national to international emphasis on research in population occurred.

### Defense and wartime forties

The first half of the forties (1940–1945) was marked by several important developments. Apparently as a result of defense and wartime prosperity, and partly as a result of selective service calls, marriage rates increased sharply during the early forties and so did the birth rates. The significance of the increase in the birth rate was discounted in several of P. K. Whelpton's early analyses of natality data by parity (138, 140). Although Whelpton's diagnosis of this particular problem proved to be incorrect, his work during this period led him to a discovery of a fundamental weakness of the net reproduction rate (138).

An important characteristic of the 1940–1945 period was the transition from national to international orientation of population research. A beginning in this direction was made by the League of Nations shortly after the outbreak of the war in Europe in 1939. After the outbreak of the war, the Economic, Financial, and Transit Section of the League of Na-

tions moved to Princeton, New Jersey. Mr. Alexander Loveday, head of
the Section, became convinced that the collecting and correlating of a
series of social, economic, and demographic data about various countries
of Europe would be of value in the postwar construction in Europe. The
Office of Population Research of Princeton University agreed to undertake the collection and analysis of data and this study resulted in a series
of volumes on Europe (53, 60, 73, 76).

That the war would not be contained in Europe was made abundantly
clear by Pearl Harbor. After the United States entered the war in
December, 1941, the Geographic Division of the Department of State
also entered into an agreement with the Office of Population Research
wherein the Office would supply the State Department with data about
selected countries of the world (19, 65, 109). These developments probably helped to channel the interests of the Office of Population Research
toward comparative international demography.

Government and military agencies needing "area" studies of different
types also served to stimulate research on population problems in various
areas of the world. In a summary of demographic research during the
early part of the forties, Irene Taeuber suggests that because of the dearth
of trained demographers much of the "area" research of that period probably was of inferior quality (108). Whatever this case may be, "area"
research did, in all likelihood, a great deal to demonstrate the close relation of population to the economic and military potentials of given areas.

THE POSTWAR PERIOD (1945–1955)

*Role of the United Nations*

The general postwar climate and nature of the peace favored increased
interest in world population problems. Prominent in this connection is
the role of the United Nations and its specialized agencies. The United
Nations has stimulated interest and research in world population in a
variety of ways. Recognizing the basic importance of population to social,
economic, and political problems of the world, the United Nations provided for the establishment of a Population Commission within its Social
and Economic Council.

The Population Commission, which was organized in 1946 and held its
first meetings in 1947, is charged mainly with providing certain types of
information on population problems. Its servicing agency is the Population Branch, Bureau of Social Affairs. The research that has been carried out or sponsored by the Population Branch (or, as previously named,
the Population Division) forms an important segment of the research in
demography of the past decade (120–123). One of its most ambitious

research projects resulted in the recent report, *The Determinants and Consequences of Population Trends* (123).

Working in close relationship with the Population Branch is the Section on Demographic and Social Statistics within the Statistical Office. The Section on Demographic and Social Statistics is chiefly responsible for *Demographic Yearbook,* which has been a great boon to students of demography throughout the world (124).

One of the aims of the United Nations as expressed in the preamble of its charter, "To employ international machinery for the promotion of the economic and social advancement of all people," also has done a great deal to stimulate interest and research in world population problems. The Technical Assistance Administration and the specialized agencies of the United Nations have attempted to implement this goal and in doing so they have fostered interest in world population problems (119). These agencies have directed attention toward the massive problems of poverty, illiteracy, ill-health, and overpopulation in large areas of the world. To some extent, the success of these agencies, at least in the initial stages, helps to point up and even to enhance the population problem. The very success of the World Health Organization, for instance, is directly measured by reductions in the death rate. The population problem that arises from this situation is that high birth rates are more resistant to change than are high death rates. The consequence is that reductions in death rates tend to be followed by rather immediate rises in population and this increase in population tends to retard advances in average levels of living.

The United Nations and its specialized agencies not only direct attention to the problem areas of the world, they also facilitate research by helping to collect data from various countries of the world. Thus, *Statistical Yearbook, Demographic Yearbook,* and *Monthly Bulletin of Statistics* are made possible by the United Nations' regular solicitation of demographic, social, and economic statistics from the member states. Most of the specialized agencies also provide regular statistical data bearing on one or more facets of demography. Outstanding among these is *Annual Epidemiological and Vital Statistics,* published by World Health Organization (143). It is true that some of the data are meager and unreliable. Here again, however, the United Nations has a significant role in stimulating the improvement of national statistics.

### National governments

During the past decade national governments at various levels of demographic advancement have taken an increased interest in population problems and population research. In England, a Royal Commission on

Population was appointed in 1945 to study population trends in that country and to make recommendations regarding them. The result is a series of reports that proceed from scientific analyses based upon field studies to the recommendations regarding population policy (117, 118).

In France, an Institut National d'Études Démographiques was organized in 1945. The Institute has a sizable and capable research staff. It is directed by Mr. Alfred Sauvy and it publishes *Population*.

In Japan, a Population Policy Committee, with a membership that cuts across several government agencies, has been active in sponsoring research on a variety of demographic problems, including the economic aspects, contraceptives, and sterilization (49, 50).

The Social Science Research Center at the University of Puerto Rico (a national University) has sponsored research in contraception and fertility for several years (40). Similarly, national awareness of the population problem of India has been enhanced by Nehru's public statements on this question (100).

In the United States increasing official interest in population is manifested by the spread of population research to agencies other than the Bureau of the Census and the National Office of Vital Statistics. These include the Department of State, Department of Agriculture, Social Security Administration, and various military agencies.

### Private agencies in demography

There has been a marked proliferation of interest in demography among private agencies during the past decade. The first foundation to engage in serious population research in this country was the Scripps Foundation for Research in Population Problems, organized in 1922. The Milbank Memorial Fund itself antedates the Scripps Foundation, but its work in population did not begin until 1928 when its Division of Research was organized. Population research was included in the Fund's program largely at the behest of Edgar Sydenstricker, who believed strongly in the interrelation of problems of public health and problems of population.

Several other foundations have given occasional support to specific research in population for many years. Thus, in the late thirties the Carnegie Corporation of New York agreed to support the Study of Social and Psychological Factors Affecting Fertility. It gave the chief support to the Office of Population Research during 1942–1947.

The Rockefeller Foundation has been the chief support of the Office of Population Research since 1947. With a long history of international health work, the Rockefeller Foundation has been in position to observe the close relation of population problems to health problems in the Orient and other underdeveloped regions. It supported the recent study (71) of fertility and expectations regarding family size among a presumably representative group of 3,000 white women that is described elsewhere in this chapter.

The Population Council was established in 1953 under a grant from John D. Rockefeller, III. Under the direction of Frederick Osborn, the Population Council appears to be concerned mainly with population problems in underdeveloped areas. As first steps it has undertaken a rather extensive program of fellowships with some stated preference for applicants from such areas. The Population Council also has supported a series of research efforts of relatively small scope within the United States.

The Ford Foundation helped to support the World Population Conference in Rome and it has cooperated with the Population Council in various projects. The Giannini Foundation helped to support Thomas' study resulting in *The Spoilage* and *The Salvage* (111, 112). In England, the Nuffield Foundation has provided assistance to demographic research. Also in England, the organization PEP (Political and Economic Planning, an independent nonpolitical organization) has recently published articles on world population and resources (81).

## SUBSTANTIVE RESEARCH SINCE 1945

### Fertility

During the past ten years striking developments have occurred in research in fertility. Prominent in this connection have been the efforts to improve the measures of replacement. The net reproduction rate and the true rate of natural increase were the widely used measures of replacement for about two decades following their presentation in this country in 1925 (22). As early as 1944, P. K. Whelpton presented a paper at a New York meeting of the American Public Health Association in which he pointed up a logical deficiency of the net reproduction rate (138). As is known, the net reproduction rate ($R_o$) is derived by summation of single-year, age-specific fertility rates for all ages of the child-bearing span (e.g., 15–49). The summation is designed to indicate the meaning or significance of age-specific fertility during a given period in terms of self-replacement potentialities of a population over a generation. Like the life table, the reproduction rate is based on the assumption that the age-specific vital rates of a population at a given period of time can represent those of a cohort passing through life. Since the convention is to consider female births alone, the net reproduction rate may be conceived as the average number of daughters per woman that is implicit in given schedules of age-specific fertility and mortality. The average number of daughters per woman, of course, is equivalent to the ratio of females in one generation to those in the succeeding generation.

The sharp upturn in marriage and birth rates during the early forties led Whelpton to a consideration of the relevance of these increases to size of future population. In the paper mentioned above, he computed reproduction rates by order of birth and uncovered a logical inadequacy of the net reproduction rate. Computing age-specific fertility rates for 1943 by order of birth, Whelpton found that if a cohort recapitulated the age-specific rates for first births observed in 1943, something like 108 per cent of the women eventually would have first births. This, of course, is a logical absurdity because no one can have more than one "first" birth or more than one "first" article of any kind. The explanation was that an abnormal number of first births had been crowded into the year 1943. Situations of this type continued during the war and early postwar years. This condition arose both from the eventuation of marriages that had been postponed because of the economic depression and from a trend toward earlier marriage.

Although the net reproduction rate is more sensitive than the crude birth rate and although it serves in a sense the function of a speedometer, it has definite limitations. The assumption that an actual cohort of females will recapitulate the age-specific fertility and mortality experience of a cross section of the population at any given time carries with it the implicit assumption that age is the only variable in fertility that matters. It implies that other factors, such as marital status and number of children the women already have at a given age, will remain the same over the next generation.

The effort to improve measures of replacement and fertility led Whelpton into attempts to "adjust" net reproduction rates (139) and to study cohort fertility (141). Henry, Hyrenius, Quensel, and others have taken up the quest for better methods (39, 42, 89). Finding a gap between reproduction rates based upon female births and those based upon male births, Karmel examined the mathematical relationship between these rates in a stable population and computed the conditions under which the same true rate of natural increase would be yielded by both the male and female rates (51). According to his results, the differences may be reduced ultimately to male-female differences in marriage rates by age.

Hajnal pointed up the importance of studying fertility trends in relation to changes in proportions married and distibutions of women by duration of marriage. He recommended an analysis of trends in fertility among successive cohorts of marriages that relates yearly fertility rates to the number of children already born to the marriages studied (33).

### Differential fertility

The spectacular increase in the birth rate during the forties raised questions as to its implications for differential fertility. Data collected by the Current Population Survey as well as by the preliminary data for a *1950 Census Monograph on Fertility* testify to a narrowing of differentials in fertility rates during the 1940–1950 period (54, 125–129, 136). This has come about by virtue of much sharper increases in fertility ratios among the "upper" than among the "lower" classes by occupation or education. In general, the percentage increases in fertility ratios have been greatest among classes that formerly were characterized by the lowest levels of fertility. Studies indicated that the relative increases in fertility ratios tended to be higher among the urban than among the rural population, higher in the Northeast than in the South, as well as higher in the "upper" than in "lower" socioeconomic groups.

### Social and psychological factors affecting fertility

The Indianapolis Study (142) was oriented to problems of low fertility in cities. It was designed to carry a step further the studies of differential fertility. Previous studies of contraception had indicated that class differences in fertility could be accounted for in the main by class differences in contraceptive practice. There remained the problem of *why* some classes more than others were prompted to utilize the means of family limitation.

Several summaries of the Indianapolis Study, including appraisals of its strengths and weaknesses, have been published during the past few years (55). Some of the outstanding findings were those concerning (a) the relation of religion to fertility, (b) the relation of "relative sterility" to socioeconomic status, (c) the relative influences of impairments of fecundity and of contraception in lowering fertility below assumed "biological potentials," (d) patterns of fertility planning within a population unselected with reference to prior attendance at a birth control clinic, (e) the patterns of differential fertility within groups of specific fertility-planning status, and (f) the role of economic security in relation to size of planned family (142).

Methodologically, the Indianapolis Study pointed up the difficulty of separating cause from effect in ex post facto data. It emphasized the desirability of a longitudinal study and one in which data would be collected for the necessary classifications *before* rather than *after* the event of pregnancy.

The Indianapolis Study also provided a methodological lesson regarding the type of couples selected for study. The restriction of the Indianapolis Study to a highly homogeneous group narrowed the range of fertility variations and possibly also narrowed the range of the variation of social and psychological characteristics and attitudes. Furthermore, the measures of psychological characteristics were rather crude. Probably largely for these reasons the Study failed to uncover important relationships of fertility to psychological characteristics, especially after socio-economic status was held constant.

### Plans for a new study of social and psychological factors affecting fertility

With grants from the Population Council the Milbank Memorial Fund is sponsoring the work of a committee on the development of plans for a new study of social and psychological factors affecting fertility (71). Attempting to profit from the experience of the Indianapolis Study, the committee has made the following tentative plans: Instead of selecting one city and homogeneous couples, effort will be made to have the sample representative of native-white married women under thirty-five years of age and of similar parity in some large segment of the urban population.

Instead of using total past fertility as a dependent variable, the new study may be concerned with factors affecting *the eventuation of and the length of time required for the third birth.* More specifically, the sample may be restricted to couples who recently had their second birth. Data regarding past fertility and contraceptive history and data regarding the independent variables are to be collected at the first visit. Eighteen months later a second visit will be made to ascertain which couples had a third birth during that interim. After another interval of eighteen months, a third visit will be made. When this work is completed, decision will be made as to the continuation of the study another five or ten years for the investigation of factors related to later orders of birth.

As in the Indianapolis Study, some type of classification by fertility-planning status will be used as a dependent variable. In addition, an index of "psychological availability of contraception" may be developed on the basis of the respondents' expressed attitudes toward contraception.

### A current study of fertility and fertility expectations

A companion study to the prospective one just described is currently under way. With a grant from the Rockefeller Foundation, the Social Science Survey Center of the University of Michigan and the Scripps Foundation for Research in Population Problems are jointly conducting a study of fertility and fertility expectations among a nationally representative sample of white married women in the United States. Of significance in itself is the fact that data on contraceptive practice were secured from a cross section of the population without encountering any objections. The design calls for repetition within five years (but not a follow-up of the same couples). One of the ultimate aims is the improvement of bases for population projections. The collection of data has been completed and the processing of data in this study is under way (71).

### Role of contraception

Before 1930 little was known about the actual impact of contraceptive practice on fertility trends and differentials. In fact, during the twenties there were two opposing schools of thought regarding reasons for the declining birth rate and the existing differentials in fertility according to rural-urban and socioeconomic status. These were the "biological" and the "cultural" schools. According to the "biological" interpretation fertility rates were relatively low in the "upper" urban classes because reproductive capacity was relatively low. The general decline of the birth rate was also attributed to a gradual weakening of reproductive capacity due in part to the transition from rural to urban economy. Notable exponents of this "school" were Corrado Gini (27) of Italy and Raymond Pearl of the United States (83). Most of the students of population, however, were inclined to regard group differences in fertility as being of voluntary origin and as being implemented by contraception.

During the thirties several large inductive studies of the use and effectiveness of contraceptive practice were carried out. These included Pearl's study of 30,000 women in maternity hospitals east of the Mississippi (84), Stix's and Notestein's study of about 1,000 former patients of Margaret Sanger's Birth Control Clinic in New York City (103), Stix's study of relief referrals and low-income patients of a birth control clinic in Cincinnati, Ohio, and her study of white and Negro recipients of birth control services in the Spartanburg (S. C.) County Hospital (104), and Beebe's study of the acceptability and effectiveness of contraceptive jelly among wives of coal miners in Logan County, West Virginia (3).

As perhaps is apparent even from the brief description, each set of data mentioned above has some special weakness or limitation. However, despite the variety of conditions under which the data were collected and despite the variety of their limitations, all of the studies mentioned above had in common one type of result. They all indicated that class differences in fertility could be accounted for almost entirely by class differences in the prevalence and effectiveness of contraception.

As for the period since 1945, the research on contraception has included a number of contributions.

Two studies were based upon the Indianapolis Study materials. In one of these, Whelpton and Kiser attempted to compare the relative influence of contraception and "impairments of fecundity" in the reduction of fertility below assumed "biological norms." "High, medium, and low estimates of *normal* fecundity are obtained by utilizing, respectively, the experience of the most fecund 60 per cent, 75 per cent, and 85 per cent of the couples" (142, page 340). On the basis of the medium assumption, impairments in fecundity alone (in the absence of contraception) serve to lower the fertility rate by about 27 per cent. In contrast, voluntary control alone (i.e., under assumed absence of impairments) reduced the fertility rate by about 67 per cent (142, page 334).

In the other analysis of Indianapolis Study materials, Westoff, Herrera, and Whelpton compared the use, effectiveness, and acceptability of various methods of fertility control reported in the Indianapolis Study. According to the authors, "Individual methods of contraception vary widely in their effectiveness. They range from the highly effective methods of diaphragm and jelly, condom, and condom combined with douche to the least effective methods of the safe period, suppository, and douches. These differences support, in general, the results of previous studies on this subject" (142, page 943).

Materials regarding contraception were also basic to the classification of Indianapolis Study couples by "fertility-planning status." It will be recalled that most of the hypotheses in the Indianapolis Study are concerned with the relation of given independent variables to the "proportion of couples practicing contraception effectively" as well as to "size of the planned family." * As in other investigations, a strong direct relation of fertility-planning status to socioeconomic status was found. Hence, in the sample as a whole, fertility rates were, in general, *inversely* related to socioeconomic status. However, when the analysis was restricted to the "number and spacing planned" group alone, the fertility rates (although, in general, relatively low) were *directly* rather than *inversely* re-

---

* For purposes of the Study "couples practicing contraception effectively" and the "planned families" were synonymous. In each case they were composed of the "number and spacing planned" and the "number planned" couples.

lated to fertility. Also, within the "number and spacing planned" group, fertility was found to be directly related to feeling of economic security as measured in the Study.

The interest in underdeveloped areas has stimulated research into the cultural barriers against contraception in such areas. It has stimulated the study of the closely related problems of value systems favoring high fertility in underdeveloped areas. Studies of these types have been made for Ceylon, India, Puerto Rico, Taiwan, Malaya, Egypt, Africa, and many other areas (2, 16, 36, 61, 64, 65, 68–70, 99). Of particular interest are the studies that have been conducted in India under the joint aegis of the government of India and the United Nations (70, pages 11–23).

### Mortality

It is perhaps fair to say that since 1945 statistical research in mortality has lagged behind that in fertility and that research in mortality has not been commensurate with the importance of downward trends in mortality in the underdeveloped areas since 1945.

The case of Ceylon is frequently cited as one in which dramatic declines in mortality have occurred as a result of D.D.T. spraying and other forms of disease prevention and health promotion. Until 1947, the death rate in Ceylon was 20 or higher. In 1947 it dropped to 14.3 and it was 10.9 in 1953. Dramatic declines in mortality also have been achieved in Japan and Puerto Rico. There is much need for research regarding the causes, mechanics, and probable permanence of the declines in mortality in underdeveloped countries in recent years. The suggestion has been made by some that mosquitoes are developing immunity to D.D.T. and that in some areas constantly stronger solutions are required. However, in view of the broad scope of health work being carried on by the World Health Organization in underdeveloped areas all over the world and in view of the attacks of the Food and Agriculture Organization on problems of hunger and malnutrition, one sees the lack of wisdom in attributing all of the declines in mortality, even in Ceylon, to a single factor such as spraying with D.D.T.

Among the significant studies in mortality during the past decade are those that have been carried out at the United Nations by the Population Division and by the Demographic Section of the Statistical Office of the United Nations (71, 123). The 1951 issue of the *Demographic Yearbook* gave especial emphasis to data on mortality in a world setting.

Valaoras (24), Sauvy (95), and Coale (14) have written recently on the relation of declining mortality to age distribution. Contrary to popular assumption, declines in mortality have contributed very little to changes in the percentage age distribution of populations (see also 122). Actually, to the extent that declines in mortality have been greatest among infants and children, they have tended to minimize rather than to accentuate percentage shifts toward the older age groups. The lack of vital statistics in underdeveloped areas has stimulated some to devise ways and means of estimating mortality and life-table values for such areas.

There has been a dearth of research on differentials in mortality and morbidity in this country, but research is now under way in the National Office of Vital Statistics on occupational and social class differentials in mortality (72). There have been some recent studies in differential mortality and morbidity in European countries, especially England (71, 105, 123).

Some research has been devoted to historical aspects of mortality. Several historians have attempted to assess health conditions in various European countries (38, 40, 85, 91). Stolnitz has recently compared the recent declines in mortality in underdeveloped countries with historical trends in the West (72).

Despite the lack of research, the period since World War II has been notable for the improvement of mortality data, which represents an increasing world coverage as well as a constant bettering of the data. There have also been important revisions in the international list of the causes of death. These were made at an International Conference, held in Paris in 1948 under the auspices of the World Health Organization. The latest revisions are notable for their unification of the classification of causes of death and morbidity (67, pages 115–124).

The role of mortality in the demographic revolution has been studied intensively because of its practical implication for programs of modernization. The preliminary work for *The Future Population of Europe and the U.S.S.R.: Population Projections, 1940–1970* disclosed that among European countries, the height-slope relation [of mortality rates] was substantially independent of time. That is, "mortality rates of any given height tended to have a characteristic downward slope . . ." (76, page 22). However, this empirical finding related only to Europe and for the past up to 1940. In the book itself, the authors emphasized the, importance of testing the finding in other populations and for periods subsequent to 1940. It seems highly likely that the recent spectacular declines in mortality in areas such as Ceylon do not conform to the Western patterns of declines in mortality.

One of the highly practical implications of patterns of mortality trends is that if the underdeveloped countries follow the same pattern as the Western countries with respect to time required to complete the transition from high to low birth and death rates, the underdeveloped countries would require a century or more to make this change. Furthermore, the Western pattern of this transition is that of heavy population growth because of the tendency for declines in birth rates to lag behind declines in death rates.

Until fairly recently Japan was about the only Oriental country that afforded any basis for judging whether the countries of the Orient would recapitulate the experience of the Western countries with respect to the demographic revolution. Kirk once pointed out that the 1920–1940 levels and trends of birth and death rates in Japan corresponded closely to those existing in England during 1880–1900 (52). This suggested that Japan would need approximately the same length of time that England had required to complete the demographic transition. Since the last war, Japan has experienced still further sharp declines in both mortality and fertility. Having now a population of about 90 million, she probably will reach the 100 million mark much earlier than was forecast ten years ago. However, she probably also will attain a stationary population earlier than was anticipated. This is not intended to minimize the economic difficulties that may be in store for Japan. It is rather to indicate that apparently the time requirements for the demographic transition in the West will not necessarily be those of the underdeveloped areas that are now on the threshold of at least some modernization.

### Migration

Lacroix once described migration statistics as the "poor cousins" in demographic data (67, pages 71–105). One of the reasons for this state of affairs is the lack of uniformity in the definition of migration. Thus, one student may define any physical movement as a migration. Others may insist that migration implies at least the intention of a rather permanent change of residence, which, in turn, implies some minimum criteria regarding both time and distance.

Another difficulty is the lack of systematic compiling of migration statistics in most countries of the world. A faithfully kept permanent population register, such as that in Sweden, automatically yields migration statistics and such data have been utilized for studies of both internal and international migrations involving Sweden (110).

### International migration

Most sovereign countries make some effort to count the number of people entering and leaving their borders. However, the task is complicated by the wide variety of arrivals and departures—ranging as they do from persons crossing national boundaries for a few hours of work or visiting to those leaving their homeland to reside elsewhere.

Although one of the traditional effects of war is to cast families and individuals adrift, perhaps this was never done before on so large a scale as during the incumbency of Hitler, i.e., the twelve years from 1933 to 1945. During the thirties, immigration from Europe to the United States was weighted heavily by the refugees. This small avenue of escape was sealed off by the war.

We knew in a general way that much in the way of forced migrations, population transfers, concentrations, and mass killings occurred during the war, but there has been little in the way of reliable statistical data on the problem. However, among the first demographic analyses of Europe after VE day were those directed to the movements of refugees and displaced persons. There were independent studies by Schechtman and Kulischer—both of whom were well qualified for studies of this type (56, 97). Later, Frumkin (26) attempted to reconstruct for each European country a population balance sheet for the years 1939–1947. Although much of his work must be taken on faith, probably no other person could have done a better job. Frumkin's task was the difficult one of reconstructing for each country of Europe the existing population in 1939 and by addition of births and in-migrants and by subtraction of deaths and out-migrants during the years 1939–1947 arriving at population figures for 1947. Furthermore, he attempted a classification of the deaths by whether they were war losses. Within the United States the problems of the refugees and their adjustment to this country have been studied by Davie (66, pages 110–123).

However serious may be the cases of displaced persons, they are perhaps *social* rather than *demographic* problems. The research during the past decade on the more normal type of international migration has included the work of Kirk (53, 66), Isaac (45–48), and the staff of the Population Branch of the United Nations (121, 122). In tracing the overseas migration from Europe to other parts of the world, Kirk states: "The peopling of other continents by Europeans is the largest and most spectacular migration in human history. Over 60 million Europeans have sought new homes overseas since the first colonization movements of the Sixteenth Century" (66, page 53).

The peopling of other continents by Europeans was part and parcel of the vast expansion of population following the commercial and industrial revolutions and the discovery of new lands. It would be difficult to assign degrees of importance to the various factors which happened to coincide in time. The Europeans chanced to be at a stage of cultural development following explorations that led to the discovery and acquisition of new lands, to advances in agriculture and manufacturing, and to colonization. Increases in population came at a time when new lands were available to help accommodate the increases. Kirk states that Europe has since "dried up" as a source of population for settlement because her birth rates have declined, because the empty lands have been settled, and because national regulations in both emigration and immigration now exist.

Although Isaac apparently agrees that the long-time demographic trends have served to diminish migration potentials in Europe, he is nevertheless much concerned about the practical problems of "surplus population" that have confronted Western Europe since World War II. He points out that countries of Eastern and Southern Europe still have a period of heavy growth ahead of them. Some of these countries, of course, have subsequently entered the Soviet orbit and in this manner have "solved" their population problems. Other countries still face the conventional problem of too little industrialization and too many people on too small farms. Furthermore, even the most advanced countries of Europe, such as England and France, have experienced postwar increases in birth rates of unexpected magnitude (46).

In addition, there is the whole problem of refugees and displaced persons. As already noted, Kulischer and Schechtman wrote books centering exclusively on migration of this type. Isaac attempts to view the problems faced by the International Refugee Organization, the International Labor Office, and the Intergovernmental Committee on Migration in the light of long-time demographic trends, but he is also concerned with concrete problems being faced by these agencies. He has been concerned with the economic, social, and psychological factors affecting the postwar migration from England to Australia and other countries. In a report written under the auspices of the Research Group for European Migration, Isaac and Van den Beld discuss the problem of planned migration from the standpoint of sending and receiving countries (48).

Careful studies have also been made during the past decade of migration in other parts of the world (11, 44). Irene Taeuber has written on migration and the population potential of Monsoon Asia (66, pages 7–29), Kingsley Davis has studied the prospects for future migration into Latin America (66, pages 30–48, and the Population Branch of the United Nations has prepared a series of studies on migration problems in various parts of the world (120, 121).

Although the need for some type of international cooperation on problems of migration is rather apparent, few of the students of migration go so far as to recommend anything like international control of migration. Goodrich's summary of the case probably will be disputed by few.

> The most cursory examination of the question shows how far we are from "One World" in any literal sense of the phrase. If the United Nations were really One World, we might expect that the movement from one nation to another would be as free from restrictions as movements from one to another state of the United States. Or alternatively, if migration were not to be entirely free, we might expect that, in a One World, it would be a world body which decided which regions should be open to immigration and on what terms. Obviously we are far from any such situation. . . . For the foreseeable future, migration between nations will not be free and unrestricted; it will continue to be the Congress of the United States and not the Assembly of the United Nations which determines who may enter the United States (30, page 74).

In later sections of the same article, however, Goodrich emphasizes that a great deal can be done on a voluntary basis at the international level by way of assisting intelligent approaches toward the problem of international migration. Recent years, for instance, have witnessed marked advances in the principle of bilateral agreements. The Population Commission of the United Nations has chosen migration as one of its areas of concern and it hopes to stimulate international cooperation in the approaches to this problem.

The International Labor Office is also much concerned about international migration, especially as a means of maximizing employment. It has already demonstrated that a private or semiofficial international organization can render much service in publishing up-to-date news regarding immigration laws in various countries and the needs and wishes of the various countries regarding immigration and emigration. Information of this type is disseminated by the ILO not only through its official organ *International Labour Review*, but also through *Migration*, a mimeographed bimonthly which was initiated in 1952.

### Internal migration

Studies of internal migration have been carried on in many countries. Within the United States an important part of the research on this problem during the past decade has been based upon the 1940 Census question regarding place of residence five years previously, i.e., April 1, 1935. A series of special reports on these data, analyzed by states, has appeared (cf. 7, 32, 37, 87, 88, 115). Studies of migration that are based upon the 1950 Census data regarding place of residence *one year* previously have been planned by the Census Bureau.

The works of Bogue (6–8), and Price (58, 87, 88) deserve special mention because of their application of newer techniques of analysis.

During the war special censuses and studies based upon school registrations, draft data, sugar-rationing books, etc., were made in order to assess the population of given areas. Thus, at least indirect evidence could be secured regarding population shifts from rural to urban areas and regarding the growth of particular boom areas (98, 107, and 66, pages 124–158). These studies, as later confirmed by the 1950 Census reports, indicated heavy movements to war-boom cities, and relatively heavy movements of Negroes to the West Coast. Significant works have also appeared on particular ethnic groups involved in migration, such as the Puerto Ricans (96) and the Japanese (111, 112).

### Population theory

In his presidential address at the 1952 meeting of the Population Association of America, Vance stated:

> Demography, on the whole, is doing very well these days. We have facts, we have the techniques and we are neatly polishing up our concepts. But there is one area where demography is getting rather poverty-stricken and frayed at the edges. In the realm of high theory we have been living off our capital and borrowing from our associates. It seems some time since we have made any investment of our own in basic theory (134).

It is true that, in the United States at least, there has been some reaction against population theory for the past twenty-five years. In fact the growth of interest in demography since the early thirties, when the Population Association of America was started, is sometimes described as a reaction against academic discussion of such topics as Malthus and the optimum population.

As the situation was analyzed by Sydenstricker and Notestein in 1930:

> A change in emphasis in the study and discussion of population problems seems to be evident in the growing tendency to question some of the assumptions that constitute the premises in our reasoning, in an impatience with mere generalizations from trends of birth and death rates only, and in an increasing desire to collect more adequate data (106).

It is also known, however, that data-gathering in the absence of theory can be as fruitless as theory in the absence of data. As Vance has stated, "There is such a thing as an excess diet of raw data. Undigested, it is very bad for the development of the theoretical muscles" (134).

Most of the existing population theory is concerned with population growth or size in relation to such economic factors as food, level of living, employment, income, and resources. Some of the writings of Hansen

(34), Kuznets (57), Penrose (86), Spengler (101, 102), and Sauvy (93, 94) fall into this general category.

The increasing attention to underdeveloped areas during the past For the so-called "demographic dilemma" of underdeveloped areas impinges upon a number of aspects of population theory, including the Malthusian hypothesis, the optimum population, the demographic transition, the size of the labor force, economic development, and food and decade probably accounts for the renewal of interest in population theory. resources in relation to population.

The revival of interest in Malthus' theory is evinced by the recent articles and books on this subject (28, 63).

### The demographic transition

Briefly described, the "demographic transition" is the transition from high to low birth and death rates that countries undergo following modernization. In the past at least, the transition has been accompanied by a period of rapid population growth because the decline in the death rate tends to precede the decline in the birth rate. The lag in the decline of the birth rate has been designated as the "demographic gap."

No single person can be credited with the development of the theory of the demographic transition. In 1928, Thompson discussed the possibility of classifying countries into three types on the joint bases of demographic and economic development (114). In 1935, Himes wrote an article entitled "The Vital Revolution" (41). In 1936, Carr-Saunders discussed the tendency for modernization to bring declines in mortality before it brings declines in fertility and he presented the well-known chart concerning trends in crude birth and death rates in England and Wales since about 1740 (10). Notestein and his associates helped to popularize the concept of the demographic transition and especially the threefold division of countries on the basis of their stage of demographic development (77, 78). Blacker described five "types" in 1947 (5). Davis (17, 18) and Cowgill (15) have suggested the need for certain revisions implicit in more recent trends.

The demographic transition has close relevance to problems of economic development. Students of population urge that such organizations as those for World Health, Food and Agriculture, and Technical Assistance give attention to ways and means of hastening declines in the birth rate in order to narrow the "demographic gap" and to minimize population growth in the areas concerned. There have been several empirical and descriptive studies of the processes of economic development

(2, 68, and 69, pages 9–54). A purely theoretical approach has been made by Leibenstein (59).

### Future population and resources

Probably no subject in the domain of population problems has aroused more controversy and emotion during the past decade than has the old question with which Malthus was concerned over a hundred and fifty years ago. As has been suggested, the interest in underdeveloped areas, the activity of international agencies, and the recent examples of the potentiality of heavy population are factors that have served to renew interest in Malthus and the general question of food and population.

There have been some attempts to analyze the factors on a strictly objective basis (4, 25, 35, 64, 92, 144). However, the argument over food versus population has become one of the "great debates," and many of the books and articles on the subject are highly partisan and can readily be characterized as "optimistic" or "pessimistic." Thus, in the former group have been Orr (79), de Castro (20), and Clark (13); in the latter, Osborn (80), Vogt (135), and Burch and Pendell (9).

The population resource controversy cuts across vested interests in fields of religion and political economy. It embraces the Catholic-non-Catholic cleavage on contraception and the Communist-non-Communist divergence on the causes of unemployment and hunger. Thus, for entirely different reasons the Catholics and the Marxists happen to fall in the same camp (optimists) on the question of future population in relation to food.

Some of the students who have attempted to analyze the issues dispassionately point out the importance of distinguishing between what is possible in the way of food production from a purely technical standpoint and what is possible in the light of both technical knowledge and cultural factors.

### Aging of the population

The many articles, symposia, and books on the aging of the population is a measure of the growing importance of this problem (24, 43, 75, 95). As these works have indicated, age composition is related to many social and economic problems such as those of education (1), size of labor force (23), pensions and patterns of employment, consumption, and recreation. There are few aspects of community life that are not affected by the changing age structure of the population.

Some recent research has been done regarding the factors responsible for the changing age distribution of a population. Previously, even professional demographers have in most cases ascribed the shift to the joint factors of changing fertility and mortality rates. For some time demographers have been aware that varying fertility wields the major influence. Writing in 1924, Newsholme stated, "These changes [in the age distribution of the population] have been brought about chiefly by the fall in the national birth rate since 1877" (74). Not until very recently, however, have the independent researches of Sauvy, Valaoras, and Coale demonstrated that the increasing proportion of aged persons in the past has been almost wholly a function of declining fertility (95, 132, 14).

At the other extreme, some of the medical and public health people have tended to attribute virtually all of the responsibility for the aging of the population to declines in mortality. Some of the confusion in this instance arises from semantics. If by "aging" one means increase in the expectation of life, these increases are properly attributed to declines in mortality. (Even in this instance, however, much of the decline in mortality has resulted in saving of lives of infants and this has been facilitated in part by spacing of babies.) Also, if by aging one means increase in *number* of old people, the process is properly attributed to decline in mortality. However, if by aging one means the increase in proportion of old people the declines in fertility have been much more important than declines in mortality. One reason for this is that the declines in mortality in the past have occurred largely as a result of the saving of lives of babies. This is demographically the equivalent of increasing the birth rate, which serves to minimize and to delay rather than to accentuate and to initiate percentage shifts toward older ages.

### International Union for the Scientific Study of Population

As previously indicated, the International Union for the Scientific Investigation of Population Problems was organized in 1928. Its form was that of national committee membership. In 1947 it was reorganized under the name International Union for the Scientific Study of Population. The new Union differs from its predecessor in that it was organized under an individual membership basis. A related difference is that many more countries are represented in the membership of the new Union. This arises partly from the special efforts to enroll qualified members from underdeveloped areas of the world. The International Population Union and the United Nations were sponsors of the World Population Conference described in previous pages of this chapter. Through its assemblies, its periodic scientific meetings, and distribution of publications, the Union serves an important function to students of demography throughout the world.

## SUMMARY

The period since World War II has been one of great changes in population trends and of sharp increase of interest in population problems and population research.  True, the trade of demography suffered a severe jolt when the unexpected increases in marriages and births led to population growth far exceeding that postulated in population projections for the United States.  Demographers have been chided about this, and doubtless some of them have done a great deal of soul searching to see whether or not the truth is in them.  However, they have not been allowed to meditate long, for the services and skills of the trained demographer have been in demand in many quarters.

The expansion of research in demography during the past decade may be seen in the establishment of a United Nations Population Commission and its servicing agency, the Population Branch.  It may be seen also in the demographic activity of the Statistical Office of the United Nations and in several of the specialized agencies of the United Nations.

The activities of the international agencies, and particularly the new interest in underdeveloped areas, have served to enhance interest in world population problems and in the demographic implications of modernization programs.

The new interest in population is by no means confined to the highly developed countries.  Many of the underdeveloped countries are taking stock of their demographic positions.  This work is being done by official bodies as well as by the social scientists.

The period was characterized by a large increase of interest in population in government and private agencies and in the universities.  It marked the first attempt at inter-American coordination in census taking. It witnessed the inauguration of a *Demographic Yearbook*.  It saw several countries seek the help of the United Nations in connection with special demographic surveys.

The existence of a strong and world-wide interest in population questions was demonstrated at the World Population Conference, held in Rome in 1954.  Some five hundred persons, representing all except very few countries, participated.  The papers were concerned with the components and results of population change in both underdeveloped and highly developed countries; they were concerned with methods and with substantive data; they were concerned with problems and with policy. The Conference was an appropriate testimony to the shift from national to international orientation in demography.

Probably the primary need for future advancement in population research is the improvement of vital statistics and census data.  China, standing at the top in size of population, has no adequate census or vital statistics system. A second need is for studies of the value systems that sanction and perpetuate large families in the underdeveloped areas of the world. A third need is the development of methods for the study of attitudes and psychological variables in relation to contraception and fertility in the highly developed areas. A fourth need is the development of population theory. This does not mean that the search for "the law" of population should be continued. However, as Vance has stated "demography remains relatively unstructured. It lacks, shall we say, a binder for its diverse findings" (134).

Finally, the writer wishes to state that after reviewing the literature of the decade from 1945 to 1955, he believes strongly that the next ten years will witness a continued rapid development in demography. In each area of "need" mentioned above, some research is already in progress. With the backing of the United Nations, national governments, and private agencies, and with the attraction of demography for able students, the future looks bright indeed.

## BIBLIOGRAPHICAL REFERENCES

1. Advisory Committee on Education, The, *Report of the Committee,* Washington, D. C., U. S. Government Printing Office, February, 1938.

2. Barclay, George, *Colonial Development and Population in Taiwan,* Princeton, Princeton University Press, 1954.

3. Beebe, Gilbert W., *Contraception and Fertility in the Southern Appalachians,* Baltimore, Williams & Wilkins Co., 1942.

4. Black, John D., "The Economics of Freedom from Want," *Chronica Botanica,* Vol. 11 (1948), pp. 259–270.

5. Blacker, C. P., "Stages in Population Growth," *Eugenics Review,* Vol. 39 (1947), pp. 88–102.

6. Bogue, Donald J., *A Methodological Study of Migration and Labor Mobility in Michigan and Ohio in 1947,* Oxford, Ohio, Scripps Foundation, 1952.

7. Bogue, Donald J., and Margaret J. Hagood, *Subregional Migration in the United States, 1935–40,* Vol. II, Oxford, Ohio, Scripps Foundation, 1953.

8. Bogue, Donald J., and Dorothy L. Harvis, *Comparative Population and Urban Research Via Multiple Regression and Covariance Analysis,* Oxford, Ohio, and Chicago, Ill., Scripps Foundation and University of Chicago, 1954.

9. Burch, Guy I., and Elmer Pendell, *Human Breeding and Survival: Population Roads to Peace and War,* New York, Penguin Books, 1947.

10. Carr-Saunders, Alexander M., *World Population,* Oxford, Oxford University Press, 1936.

11. Carter, Hugh P. (ed), "Reappraising Our Immigration Policy," *Annals of the American Academy of Political and Social Science,* Vol. 262 (1949), pp. 1–192.

12. Charles, Enid, *The Changing Size of Family in Canada,* Canada, Dominion Bureau of Statistics, Eighth Census of Canada, Census Monograph No. 1, Ottawa, 1948.

13. Clark, Colin, *World Resources and World Population, Proceedings of the United Nations' Scientific Conference on the Conservation and Utilization of Resources*, Vol. 1, New York, United Nations, 1950, pp. 15–28; "New Light on Population," *The Listener* (1953), pp. 503–504.

14. Coale, Ansley J., *The Effect of Declines in Mortality on Age Distribution*, in preparation; *see* (72), pp. 125–132.

15. Cowgill, Donald O., "The Theory of Population Growth Cycles," *American Journal of Sociology*, Vol. 55 (1949), pp. 163–170.

16. Dandekar, V. M., and K. Dandekar, *Survey of Fertility and Mortality in Poona District, Poona*, Poona, India, Gokhale Institute of Politics and Economics, 1953.

17. Davis, Joseph S., "Population and Resources," *Journal of the American Statistical Association*, Vol. 45 (1950), pp. 346–349.

18. Davis, Joseph S., "The Population Upsurge and the American Economy, 1945–80," *Journal of Political Economy*, Vol. 61 (1953), pp. 369–388.

19. Davis, Kingsley, *The Population of India and Pakistan*, Princeton, Princeton University Press, 1951.

20. de Castro, Josue, *The Geography of Hunger*, Boston, Little, Brown & Co., 1952.

21. Dorn, Harold F., "Pitfalls in Population Forecasts and Projections," *Journal of the American Statistical Association*, Vol. 45 (1950), pp. 311–334.

22. Dublin, L. I., and A. J. Lotka, "On the True Rate of Natural Increase," *Journal of the American Statistical Association*, Vol. 20 (1925), pp. 305–339.

23. Durand, John D., *The Labor Force in the United States, 1890 to 1960*, New York, Social Science Research Council, 1948.

24. Eastern States Health Education Conference, *The Social and Biological Challenge of Our Aging Population*, New York, Columbia University Press, 1950.

25. Food and Agriculture Organization of the United Nations, *The State of Food and Agriculture, 1953. Part II. Longer Term Prospects*, Rome, U. N. Food and Agriculture Organization, 1954.

26. Frumkin, Gregory, *Population Changes in Europe Since 1939*, New York, Augustus M. Kelley, 1951.

27. Gini, Corrado, "The Cyclical Rise and Fall of Population," in *Population*, Lectures on the Harris Foundation, Chicago, University of Chicago Press, 1930, pp. 1–140.

28. Glass, D. V. (ed.), *Introduction to Malthus*, London, Watts & Co., 1953.

29. Goodrich, Carter, *Migration and Economic Opportunity*, Philadelphia, University of Pennsylvania Press, 1936.

30. Goodrich, Carter, "Possibilities and Limits of International Control of Migration," in *Postwar Problems of Migration*, New York, Milbank Memorial Fund, 1947, pp. 74–81.

31. Guillard, Achille, *Elements de statistique humaine ou démographie comparée*, Paris, Guillaumin et Cie, 1855.

32. Hagood, Margaret J., and Emmet F. Sharp, *Rural-Urban Migration in Wisconsin, 1940–1950*, Madison, Wisconsin Agricultural Experiment Station, 1951.

33. Hajnal, J., "The Analysis of Birth Statistics in the Light of the Recent International Recovery of the Birth Rate," *Population Studies*, Vol. 1 (1947–1948), pp. 137–164.

34. Hansen, Alvin H., "Economic Progress and Declining Population Growth," *American Economic Review*, Vol. 29 (1939), pp. 1–5.

35. Hatt, Paul K. (ed.), *World Population and Future Resources*, New York, American Book Co., 1952.

36. Hatt, Paul K., *Backgrounds of Human Fertility in Puerto Rico*, Princeton, Princeton University Press, 1952.

37. Hawley, Amos H., *Intra-State Migration in Michigan, 1935–1940*, Ann Arbor, University of Michigan Press, 1953.

38. Helleiner, K. F., "Population Movement and Agrarian Depression in the Later Middle Ages," *Canadian Journal of Economics and Political Science*, Vol. 15 (1949), pp. 368–377.

39. Henry, Louis, *Fécondité des mariages*, Paris, Institut National d'Études Demographiques, Travaux et Documents, Cahier No. 16, 1953.

40. Hill, Reuben, Kurt Back, and J. Mayone Stycos, "Family Action Potentials and Fertility Planning in Puerto Rico," in *Current Research in Human Fertility*, New York, Milbank Memorial Fund, 1955, pp. 42–64.

41. Himes, Norman E., "The Vital Revolution," *Survey Graphic*, Vol. 24 (1935), pp. 171–173.

42. Hyrenius, H., "Reproduction and Replacement," *Population Studies*, Vol. 4 (1951), pp. 421–431.

43. Industrial Relations Research Association, *The Aged and Society, A Symposium on the Problems of an Aging Population*, Champaign, Illinois, Twin City Printing Co., 1950.

44. International Union for the Scientific Study of Population. *Cultural Assimilation of Immigrants*. Papers presented under the Auspices of UNESCO. Supplement to *Population Studies*, March, 1950.

45. Isaac, Julius, *Economics of Migration*, New York, Oxford University Press, 1947.

46. Isaac, Julius, "European Migration Potential and Prospects," *Population Studies*, Vol. 2 (1949), pp. 379–412.

47. Isaac, Julius, "International Migration and European Population Trends," *International Labour Review*, Vol. 66 (1952), pp. 185–206.

48. Isaac, Julius, and C. A. Van den Beld, *The Effect of European Migration on the Economy of Sending and Receiving Countries; An Interim Report*, The Hague, Research Group for European Migration Problems, IV, 1953.

49. Japan, "Council for Population Policies Newly Created in the Foundation Institute," *Jinkō Monda Kenkyū*, Vol. 9, Nos. 1–2, November, 1953, pp. 68–70.

50. Japan, Population Problems Research Council, The Mainich Newspapers: *The Future of Japan—Her Population and Natural Resources*, Population Problems Series No. 11, Tokyo, 1955.

51. Karmel, P. H., "The Relations Between Male and Female Reproduction Rates," *Population Studies*, Vol. 1 (1947–1948), pp. 249–274, 352–387.

52. Kirk, Dudley, "Population Changes and the Postwar World," *American Sociological Review*, Vol. 9 (1944), pp. 28–35.

53. Kirk, Dudley, *Europe's Population in the Interwar Years*, Geneva, League of Nations, 1946.

54. Kiser, Clyde V., "Fertility Trends and Differentials in the United States," *Journal of the American Statistical Association*, Vol. 27 (1952), pp. 25–48.

55. Kiser, Clyde V., and P. K. Whelpton, "Résumé of the Indianapolis Study of Social and Psychological Factors Affecting Fertility," *Population Studies*, Vol. 7 (1953), pp. 95–110.

56. Kulischer, Eugene M., *The Displacement of Population in Europe*, Montreal, International Labour Office, 1943.

57. Kuznets, Simon S., *Economic Change; Selected Essays in Business Cycles, Natural Income, and Economic Growth*, New York, W. W. Norton & Co., 1953.

58. Lee, Everett S., and Daniel O. Price, *Net Intercensal Migration, 1870–1940*, 3 vols., Philadelphia, University of Pennsylvania Press, 1953.

59. Leibenstein, Harvey, *A Theory of Economic-Demographic Development*, Princeton, Princeton University Press, 1954.

60. Lorimer, Frank, *The Population of the Soviet Union: History and Prospects*, Geneva, The League of Nations, 1946.

61. Lorimer, Frank (ed.), *Culture and Human Fertility*, New York, International Documents Service, Columbia University Press, 1955.

62. Lorimer, Frank, Ellen Winston, and Louise K. Kiser, *Foundations of American Population Policy*, New York, Harper and Brothers, 1940.

63. McCleary, George F., *The Malthusian Population Theory*, London, Faber & Faber, Ltd., 1953.

64. Mair, George F. (ed.), *Studies in Population*, Princeton, Princeton University Press, 1949.

65. Milbank Memorial Fund, *Demographic Studies of Selected Areas of Rapid Growth*, New York, 1944.

66. Milbank Memorial Fund, *Postwar Problems of Migration*, New York, 1947.

67. Milbank Memorial Fund, *Problems in the Collection and Comparability of International Statistics*, New York, 1949.

68. Milbank Memorial Fund, *Modernization Programs in Relation to Human Resources and Population Problems*, New York, 1950.

69. Milbank Memorial Fund, *Approaches to Problems of High Fertility in Agrarian Societies*, New York, 1952.

70. Milbank Memorial Fund, *The Interrelations of Demographic, Economic, and Social Problems in Selected Underdeveloped Areas*, New York, 1954.

71. Milbank Memorial Fund, *Current Research in Human Fertility*, New York, 1955.

72. Milbank Memorial Fund, *Trends and Differentials in Mortality*, New York, 1956.

73. Moore, Wilbert E., *Economic Demography of Eastern and Southern Europe*, Geneva, The League of Nations, 1945.

74. Newsholme, Arthur, *The Elements of Vital Statistics*, New York, D. Appleton and Co., 1924.

75. New York State, Joint Legislative Committee on Problems of the Aging: *Birthdays Don't Count*, Legislative Document No. 61, Albany, Fort Orange Press, 1948.

76. Notestein, Frank W., Irene B. Taeuber, Dudley Kirk, Ansley J. Coale, and Louise K. Kiser, *The Future Population of Europe and the U.S.S.R.: Population Projections, 1940–1970*, Geneva, League of Nations, 1944.

77. Notestein, Frank W., *Population—The Long View*, in Theodore W. Schultz (ed.), *Food for the World*, Chicago, University of Chicago Press, 1945, pp. 36–57.

78. Notestein, Frank W., "The Population of the World in the Year 2000," *Journal of the American Statistical Association*, Vol. 45 (1950), pp. 335–345.

79. Orr, John B., "World Resources," in Proceedings of the International Congress in Population and World Resources in Relation to the Family, London, 1948, pp. 8–18.

80. Osborn, Fairfield, *Our Plundered Planet*, Boston, Little, Brown & Co., 1948.

81. Political and Economic Planning (PEP), *World Population and Resources, Planning* (London), Vol. 20 (1954), pp. 45–72.

82. Pearl, Raymond, and Lowell J. Reed, *On the Rate of Growth of the Popula-*

*tion of the United States Since 1790 and Its Mathematical Representation,* Proceedings of the National Academy of Science, Vol. 6 (1920), pp. 275–288.

83. Pearl, Raymond, *The Biology of Population Growth,* New York, Alfred Knopf, 1925.

84. Pearl, Raymond, *The Natural History of Population,* New York, Oxford University Press, 1939.

85. Peller, S., "Mortality, Past and Future," *Population Studies,* Vol. 1 (1947–1948), pp. 405–456.

86. Penrose, E. F., *Population Theories and Their Application: With Special Reference to Japan,* Stanford, Food Research Institute, 1934.

87. Price, Daniel O., "Distance and Directions as Vectors of Internal Migration, 1935 to 1940," *Social Forces,* Vol. 27 (1948), pp. 48–53.

88. Price, Daniel O., "Estimates of Net Migration in the United States, 1870–1940," *American Sociological Review,* Vol. 18 (1953), pp. 35–39.

89. Quensel, Carl-Erik, "Some Critical Remarks on the Concept of the Net Reproduction Rate," *Ekonomisk Tidskrift,* Vol. 43 (1941), p. 227.

90. Reddaway, W. B., *The Economics of a Declining Population,* London, G. Allen and Unwin, Ltd., 1st edition, 1939; 2nd edition, 1946.

91. Russell, Josiah C., *British Medieval Population,* Albuquerque, University of New Mexico Press, 1948.

92. Salter, Robert M., "World Soil and Fertilizer Resources in Relation to Food Needs," *Chronica Botanica,* Vol. 14 (1948), pp. 226–235.

93. Sauvy, Alfred, *Richesse et population,* Paris, Payot, 1944.

94. Sauvy, Alfred, *Théorie générale de la population,* Vol. 1, *Economic et population,* Paris, University of Paris Press, 1952.

95. Sauvy, Alfred, "Le Vieillissement des populations et li'allongement de la vie," *Population,* Vol. 9 (1954), pp. 675–682.

96. Senior, Clarence, "Migration and Puerto Rico's Population Problems," *Annals of the American Academy of Political and Social Science,* Vol. 285 (1953), pp. 130–136.

97. Schechtman, Joseph B., *European Population Transfers, 1939–1945,* New York, Oxford University Press, 1946.

98. Shryock, Henry S., Jr., "Wartime Shifts of the Civilian Population," *Milbank Memorial Fund Quarterly,* Vol. 25 (1947), pp. 269–283.

99. Smith, T. E., *Population Growth in Malaya,* London, Royal Institute of International Affairs, 1952.

100. Sovani, N. V., "The Problem of Fertility Control in India: Cultural Factors and Development of Policy"; *see* (68), pp. 62–73.

101. Spengler, Joseph J., "Aspects of the Economics of Population Growth—Parts I and II," *Southern Economic Journal,* Vol. 14 (1947–1948), pp. 123–147, 233–265.

102. Spengler, Joseph J., "Economic Factors in the Development of Densely Populated Areas," *Proceedings of the American Philosophical Society,* Vol. 95 (1951), pp. 20–53.

103. Stix, Regine K., and Frank W. Notestein, *Controlled Fertility,* Baltimore, Williams & Wilkins Co., 1940.

104. Stix, Regine K., "Comparative Appraisal of Three Contraceptive Services," *Journal of the American Medical Association,* Vol. 118 (1942), pp. 283–290.

105. Sutherland, Ian, "Variations in Occupational Mortality Between and Within Social Classes," *The British Journal of Social Medicine,* Vol. 1 (1947), pp. 126–134.

106. Sydenstricker, Edgar S., and Frank W. Notestein, "Differential Fertility Ac-

cording to Social Class," *Journal of the American Statistical Association*, Vol. 25 (1930), pp. 9–32.

107. Taeuber, Conrad, "Wartime Population Changes in the United States," *Milbank Memorial Fund Quarterly*, Vol. 24 (1946), pp. 235–250.

108. Taeuber, Irene B., "Population Studies in the United States [1939–1945]," *Population Index*, Vol. 12 (1946), pp. 254–269.

109. Taeuber, Irene B., "Demographic Transitions in Japan: Omens for the Future of Asian Populations"; see (70), pp. 9–31.

110. Thomas, Dorothy S., *Social and Economic Aspects of Swedish Population Movements, 1750–1933*, New York, Macmillan Co., 1941.

111. Thomas, Dorothy S., and Richard Nishimoto, *The Spoilage*, Berkeley, University of California Press, 1946.

112. Thomas, Dorothy S., *The Salvage*, Berkeley, University of California Press, 1952.

113. Thompson, Warren S., *Danger Spots in World Population*, New York, Alfred A. Knopf, 1929.

114. Thompson, Warren S., "Population," *American Journal of Sociology*, Vol. 34 (1928), pp. 959–975.

115. Thompson, Warren S., *Migration Within Ohio, 1935–40*, Oxford, Ohio, Scripps Foundation, 1951.

116. Thompson, Warren S., *Population Problems*, 4th edition, New York, McGraw-Hill Book Co., 1953.

117. United Kingdom, Royal Commission on Population, *Report*, Parliament, Command Papers, No. 7695, London, H. M. Stationery Office, 1949.

118. United Kingdom, Royal Commission on Population, *Papers*. Vol. I. Family Limitation and Its Influence on Human Fertility During the Past Fifty Years, 1949; Vol. II. Reports and Selected Papers of the Statistics Committee, 1950; Vol. III. Report of the Economics Committee, 1950; Vol. IV. Reports of the Biological and Medical Committee, 1950; Vol. V. Memoranda Presented to the Royal Commission, 1950; London, H. M. Stationery Office.

119. United Nations, Secretary-General (in consultation with executive heads of interested specialized agencies), *Technical Assistance for Economic Development*, New York, 1949.

120. United Nations, Department of Social Affairs, Population Division [Reports on demographic aspects of migration—numbers relate to ST/SOA/Series A]. No. 5. *Problems of Migration Statistics*, 1950; No. 11. *Sex and Age of International Migrants: Statistics for 1918–1947*, 1953; No. 12. *Economic Characteristics of International Migrants: Statistics for Selected Countries, 1918–1950*; No. 16. *Elements of Immigration Policy*, 1954; No. 18. *International Research on Migration*, 1953.

121. United Nations, Population Division, "Internal Migrations in the Far East During Recent Times: The Countries of Emigration," *Population Bulletin*, No. 1 (December, 1951), pp. 13–30; "The Countries of Immigration," *Population Bulletin*, No. 2 (October, 1952), pp. 27–58.

122. United Nations, Population Division, "Some Quantitative Aspects of the Aging of Western Populations," *Population Bulletin*, No. 1 (December, 1951), pp. 42–57; No. 4 (December, 1954), pp. 30–38.

123. United Nations, Department of Social Affairs, Population Division, *The Determinants and Consequences of Population Trends*, New York, 1953.

124. United Nations, Department of Economic Affairs, Statistical Office, *Demographic Yearbook, 1954*, 6th issue, New York, 1954.

125. United States, Bureau of the Census, *Population: Fertility, 1950 Population Census Report P-E No. 5C,* Preprint of Vol. IV, Part 5, Chapter C, Washington, U. S. Government Printing Office, 1955.

126. United States, Bureau of the Census, *Population, Differential Fertility, 1940 and 1910, Women by Number of Children Under 5 Years Old,* Washington, U. S. Government Printing Office, 1945.

127. United States, Bureau of the Census, *Population, Differential Fertility, 1940 and 1910, Women by Number of Children Ever Born,* Washington, U. S. Government Printing Office, 1945.

128. United States, Bureau of the Census, *Population, Differential Fertility, 1940 and 1910, Fertility by Duration of Marriage,* Washington, U. S. Government Printing Office, 1947.

129. United States, Bureau of the Census, *Current Population Reports*—Population Characteristics, Series P–20, No. 18, June 30, 1948; Series P–20, No. 27, February 3, 1950; Series P–20, No. 46, December 31, 1953.

130. United States, National Office of Vital Statistics, *Summary of Natality Statistics, United States, 1952,* Vol. 40, No. 8, January 27, 1955.

131. United States, National Resources Committee, *The Problems of a Changing Population,* Washington, U. S. Government Printing Office, 1938.

132. Valaoras, Vasilios G., "Patterns of Aging of Human Populations"; *see* (24), pp. 67–85.

133. Van den Brink, T., "Birth Rate Trends and Changes in Marital Fertility in the Netherlands After 1937," *Population Studies,* Vol. 4 (1950), pp. 314–332.

134. Vance, Rupert B., "Is Theory for Demographers?" *Social Forces,* Vol. 31 (1952), pp. 9–10.

135. Vogt, William, *Road to Survival,* New York, William Sloane Associates, 1948.

136. Westoff, Charles F., "Differential Fertility in the United States: 1900 to 1952, *American Sociological Review,* Vol. 19 (1954), pp. 549–561.

137. Whelpton, P. K., "Population of the United States, 1925–1975," *American Journal of Sociology,* Vol. 34 (1928), pp. 253–270.

138. Whelpton, P. K., "Effect of Increased Birth Rate on Future Population," *American Journal of Public Health,* Vol. 35 (1945), pp. 326–333.

139. Whelpton, P. K., "Reproduction Rates Adjusted for Age, Parity, Fecundity, and Marriage," *Journal of the American Statistical Association,* Vol. 41 (1946), pp. 501–516.

140. Whelpton, P. K., "The Meaning of the 1947 Baby Boom," *Vital Statistics—Special Reports,* Vol. 33 (1948), pp. 1–10.

141. Whelpton, P. K., *Cohort Fertility: Native-White Women in the United States,* Princeton, Princeton University Press, 1954.

142. Whelpton, P. K., and Clyde V. Kiser (eds.), *Social and Psychological Factors Affecting Fertility.* Vol. 1. *The Household Survey,* 1946; Vol. 2. *The Intensive Study: Purpose, Scope, Methods, and Partial Results,* 1950; Vol. 3. *Further Reports on Hypotheses in the Indianapolis Study,* 1952; Vol. 4. *Further Reports on Hypotheses and Other Data from the Indianapolis Study,* 1954. New York, Milbank Memorial Fund.

143. World Health Organization, *Annual Epidemiological and Vital Statistics, 1947–1949,* Geneva, 1952.

144. Woytinsky, W. S., and E. S. Woytinsky, *World Population and Production,* New York, The Twentieth Century Fund, 1953.

chapter 4

# Personality and social structure*

BERT KAPLAN

*University of Kansas*

One of the more dramatic phenomena in social science during the past decade has been the tremendous development of interest in the field of research and theory concerning the relationships between personality and social systems. Although sociologists like G. H. Mead, E. W. Burgess, and C. H. Cooley, to mention only a few, made significant contributions in this field, it was not until recent years that interest in it became general. The main theoretical and empirical issues within it are not easy to determine and the fact that a great many sociologists as well as anthropologists and psychologists are concerned with this area does not mean that they are all focused on the same issues. Probably the main sub-area is what has come to be known as the culture and per-

* I wish to acknowledge the helpful criticisms and suggestions of Harry Basehart, William Delaney, Jean and John Gullahorn, Alex Inkeles, Gardner Murphy, and Benjamin Paul who have read parts or all of the manuscript.

sonality field. This field has been mainly dominated by anthropologists and by studies of national character and of modal personality in non-literate societies (47, 58, 41). Both sociologists and psychologists, however, have recognized its relevance for their problems and have not only applauded from the sidelines, but have integrated its empirical findings and conceptions into their own theories and teaching. However, the culture and personality area does not encompass the whole field. Since sociologists have tended to define the term personality rather broadly, frequently as being synonymous with the individual, and there has been little clear consensus as to the meaning of social structure, the writings under the heading of personality and social structure have ranged widely, going from such broad problems as the relationship of the individual to society to more narrow ones involving specific kinds of behavior and small-group structure. One result is a considerable amount of misunderstanding and faulty communication, especially when the parties to the discussion are from different disciplines.

In the present chapter no attempt will be made to consider all of the different frameworks which have been utilized, nor shall research under any particular framework be reviewed comprehensively. Instead, attention will be focused on a limited number of issues which are believed to have been of special importance during the past decade. The concept "personality" will be used throughout in a more narrow sense than is frequently the case, and will in general coincide with the implicit definitions of the psychiatrist, the psychoanalyst, and the clinical psychologist in which the idea of motivation or of need-disposition is central. The term social structure will also be assigned a relatively narrow meaning and will be used to indicate the over-all organization of social institutions and other components of the social system. In other words, we shall be concerned with "the social structure" rather than with specific kinds of "social structuring." In addition no systematic distinction will be maintained between social and cultural systems, and social and cultural components will be regarded as elements of a single system.

The main focus of this chapter will be on the role of personality in the maintenance and proper functioning of social systems. This focus may be distinguished from the more usual one of the impact of the social system on personality, although, as we shall see, they are not completely separate. We shall consider first a number of conceptions concerning the part which personality plays in social systems; secondly, some of the ways in which it is thought that personality acquires a shape that is appropriate to the role it plays; and, finally, we shall discuss a number of empirical and methodological issues which are relevant to these and other questions in the culture and personality area.

## THE PLACE OF PERSONALITY IN SOCIAL FUNCTIONING

It seems possible to distinguish three ways in which personality has been thought to function in or influence social systems: as a determinant of social institutions, as an integrating link between social institutions, and, finally, as a support for social institutions by guaranteeing appropriate behavior and minimizing disrupting deviant behavior.

### *Personality as a determinant of social institutions*

At present this viewpoint is in general disrepute among social scientists. Geza Roheim has perhaps been the principal exponent of Freud's primal-horde theory in which society, represented by the totem, emerged as a result of the rebellion of the sons against their father. In killing him, however, they introject his image which becomes, as the superego, the basis for law and order. Roheim (96, 97) gave rich documentation to the belief that religious ritual and mythology received their form and content from variants of the childhood neurosis surrounding the Oedipus complex. In this respect he and a host of other psychoanalytic writers have anticipated Kardiner when he suggests that the secondary institutions of a culture are determined by basic personality constellations. The difference is that Roheim and the early psychoanalytic writers emphasized the universality of the personality processes involved, i.e., the Oedipus complex, while Kardiner introduced the idea that these processes varied from group to group. Roheim undoubtedly had an important point when he sought to demonstrate the existence of panhuman personality processes. However, it would seem difficult to derive the astonishing diversity of cultural forms from these basically similar processes. In addition it is possible that myths and religious rituals might reflect key personality processes but that components of other social institutions would not.

A number of writers on the subject of national character have suggested, although often not explicitly, that important social institutions are reflections of personality forces. Thus in Gorer's analysis of Americans (26), political systems, dating patterns, and certain economic practices are regarded as emerging from feelings about authority, uncertain self-esteem, and the need for love, respectively. Similar interpretations are made for the Great Russians (27) and the Japanese (25). The same kind of analysis is to be found in the writings of Mead (76), La Barre (61), and others.

Although, as Inkeles and Levinson (47) point out, many social institutions are historical residues from periods long past and it is therefore not possible to establish causal connections with any assurance, it does not seem necessary to exclude the possibility that modal personality processes do have a dynamic role, taken together with other forces, in determining the form of particular institutions. Fromm (20, 21) in his analysis of "character" in our own society has discussed the situation in which large numbers of individuals transcend the values of their society and become "free and productive" in influencing "morality" so that it reflects their own nature and potentialities. Lynd (67) takes a similar view, emphasizing that man's biology imposes certain needs and rhythms on him, and that he consequently must shape social institutions which will be congenial rather than alien to them. Riesman's "autonomous" man (95) is also independent and value producing.

Barnouw (6) has given an interesting analysis of the part which personality can play in historical processes. By contrasting the course of acculturation of the Wisconsin Chippewa with that of neighboring tribes such as the Dakota and Cheyenne he attempts to show that differences were related to personality differences among the groups. Although the brief personality analyses presented are not particularly convincing, the theory that modal personality patterns play a significant role in historical events seems important and one wishes that historians would take note of it.

### Personality as a factor in the integration of social institutions

The principal exponent of this point of view has been Abram Kardiner (53, 54, 55). He theorizes that certain aspects of a culture which he calls "primary institutions," and which consist for the most part of child rearing practices, exercise a crucial role in the formation of the personality characteristics of members of the group. Since the effect of these primary institutions is felt by all children in the group, the resulting adult patterns will be shared ones. These shared personality characteristics, known as the basic personality structure, in turn have a crucial effect on certain other aspects of the culture, namely, the secondary institutions. The basic personality structure serves as a link between different social institutions and is regarded as one of the main bases for the integration of culture. This theory has been subjected to a number of tests, the main ones being the Alorese study reported by Du Bois (18) and the research of Whiting and Child (114). The Kardiner-Du Bois study actually provided a test for only the first part of the theory, namely, that adult personality constellations are caused by child rearing practices. This study is discussed below (page 112).

The Whiting and Child research constitutes a more direct test of the "personality integration of culture" theory. This study attempted to test the theory that a relationship existed between culturally patterned child rearing practices and personality. Instead of making direct observation of personality characteristics, Whiting and Child considered that belief systems relating to illness and death could be regarded as indices of these characteristics. In a sophisticated and relatively precise way these writers described a number of variations in each of five areas of child training, those dealing with oral, anal, and sexual behavior as well as dependence and aggression. It was hypothesized that particular kinds of training in each of these areas would lead to certain personality characteristics which in turn would be reflected in the belief systems. For example, especially gratifying or frustrating experiences in any of these areas would lead to "fixations," or lifelong preoccupations that would influence the belief systems. Child-rearing practices and belief systems were examined in 75 cultures, a work constituting one of the first major uses of the Cross-Cultural Files (for others, see Murdock, 82, and Horton, 43). The authors conclude that there was confirmation of the general hypothesis that child training practices are related to explanations of illness and therapeutic practices. Although their argument that this relationship occurs through the mediation of personality variables is convincing, the possibility exists that the basis for this relationship lies in some third factor. However, the conclusions are quite startling and suggest that the more usual theory of social integration in which social institutions are thought to be related to each other in terms of the functions of each in the maintenance of the whole may not be the only or even the best model for understanding social integration. Sapir (99) has suggested that the relationship between various aspects of a social pattern are frequently of an unexpected, subtle, and symbolic nature and are not comprehended by any single theoretical scheme. It seems possible, then, that there is more than one basis for social integration and that some institutions are connected to each other in a totally different way than others are. Thus the theory of personality integration of cultural institutions need not be regarded as contradicting the structural-functional approach.

### Personality as a support of the social system

Since sociocultural systems can be said to exist concretely only in individuals (100, 15, 58) their maintenance is dependent on the support and compliance of individuals. That is, the individuals who are the carriers of culture must perform willingly. The development in a group's mem-

bers of personality characteristics which insure this willingness to participate may be regarded as the primary task of the socialization institutions.
Inkeles and Levinson (47) speak of the situation of "ideal congruence"
as involving the maximum degree of compatibility between personality
traits and social requirements. They say that:

> Insofar as the relevant traits of character are modally present in the popula-
> tion of any society, the chances are increased that culturally and structurally
> important goals will be aspired toward and implemented by the society's
> members, thus in significant degree ensuring the continued effective func-
> tioning of the social system (page 1006).

Inkeles and Levinson emphasize the importance of "modal" personality,
that is, of the regularities in the personalities of members of a group
which can be ascribed to the sociocultural system pattern. In their discussion of congruence they focus for the most part on the relation of those
modes to societal functioning.

It is obvious, however, that "ideal" congruence does not always exist
and perhaps never does. Inkeles and Levinson speak of two types of
noncongruence, that induced by institutional change when relatively well-
established modal personality types exist and that occurring in a stable
society when there is a large influx or immigration of a personality type
different from the ones most prevalent in the society. Both of these situations present opportunities for crucial empirical research to determine
the extent to which either character type or institutional pattern changes
radically. That is, when there is noncongruence of either type it becomes
possible to follow, although it may take a number of years or even generations, the vicissitudes of change in either social system or personality
types or both. Present-day Soviet Russia is a good example of noncongruence and a number of workers have been studying it.

Dicks (16, 17) has contributed important empirical findings which
demonstrate this noncongruence in Soviet Russia. He finds that the traditional Russian oral personality traits are not appropriate to the Soviet
system and that important strains result. He notes, however, that a new
personality type has emerged which is characteristic of the leaderships
and is predominantly "anal." This "type" appears to be an overreaction,
or a swing which is too far in the opposite direction and is also noncon-
gruent. The two prevalent personality types exert opposing influences on
the social system and both appear to give rise to chronic tension, frustration, and malaise.

Inkeles (46) has described changes of child-rearing values in three
generations of Russians in the direction of providing more appropriate
adaptations to the changed social conditions and suggests that similar
changes probably operate at the personality level. One interesting con-

clusion which can be drawn from observations of noncongruence such as that existing in the Soviet Union is that the social system as a whole nevertheless persists. Even drastic noncongruence does not seem to disrupt the society's functioning. This should warn us against being too certain of the dependence of societal functioning upon the support of particular personality characteristics. Noncongruence undoubtedly results in strain among individuals, and in inefficiency in the social system, but so long as the necessary tasks get done it is not fatal or perhaps even serious. As Parsons suggests (92) the system of positive and negative sanctions stands as a second line of defense when appropriate motivations fail to develop, and the required behavior can be elicited by these mechanisms. Although Inkeles and Levinson point out that the effectiveness of sanctions can be increased by certain personality characteristics, it is probable that sanctions do not depend entirely on the existence of such characteristics.

### Role and personality

One of the most significant theoretical trends in sociology during the past decade has been the concentration on the concept of role as the mediator between societal requirements and individual behavior. This concept has in most serious theoretical attempts come to assume the position of a cornerstone without which many conceptual structures would be unstable. This is primarily because of the importance of the role for the social system. To quote Parsons (88)

> Roles are from the point of view of the functioning of the social system, the primary mechanisms through which the functional prerequisites of the system are met. There is the same order of relationship between roles and functions relative to the system in social systems as there is between organs and functions in the organism (page 115).

Baldwin (5) has suggested that for many "role" is a descriptive concept and refers simply to certain uniformities of behavior in a particular class of individuals, i.e., "the cowboy" or "the Bostonian." Used in this sense the "role" does not have any functional significance in maintaining the social system. The concept has also been used in an explanatory sense, as, for example, when it defines the expectations of people in general about appropriate behavior for individuals occupying a certain position. We follow the second usage.

While appropriate role behavior can be elicited through the operation of a system of positive and negative sanctions or rewards and punishments, it may also be encouraged by the development of motivations that will guarantee proper behavior without the application of external sanctions. We have suggested above that in the absence of relevant motivations external sanctions may insure the requisite performances. One thinks of a society in which slaves do most of the necessary jobs under threat of punishment. However, this does not seem to be the typical situation. In most known societies participation is voluntary and individuals seem predisposed to fill the available roles. External sanctions, it seems, are of secondary importance in behavioral conformity and come into force mainly in relation to deviance and in cases where some kind of failure of the socialization process has occurred.

American social scientists have placed great emphasis on the theory that a role, once occupied, exerts a strong formative influence on its occupant. Newcomb (85), for example, has taken the position that many role assignments are made on the basis of visible characteristics which individuals possess but that once the role has been assigned its occupant usually acquires still other characteristics which add to his fitness. These new characteristics, or "acquired motive patterns" as Newcomb calls them, develop chiefly because the role becomes an important element in the individual's self picture (23). Thus the new boss comes after a short time to think of himself as a boss and a new ego-identity, to use Erikson's term, is established. Subsequently, the need to maintain this new self picture involves a host of new goals or motives. Waller's study of the teacher (112) provides a good example of this process (68).

Merton's (79) analysis of the bureaucratic personality provides an excellent illustration of the way in which tendencies which may be only slight when the individual first assumed a role become important after he has been in it for a number of years. The "personality" pattern of the bureaucrat thus comes to be, in an important sense, organized around his role in the bureaucracy. However, the increased fitness of the individual for his role is not the only consequence of this development. It has negative effects as well. Using Veblen's term "trained incapacity" and Warnotte's "professional deformation," Merton describes the way in which the bureaucrat because he becomes *too* "methodical, prudent and disciplined," actually is *unfit,* to a certain degree, for his office. In the process of leaving a margin of safety and becoming specially efficient there is a transference of focus from aims to means, the latter becoming ends in themselves. It is clear from this example that the influence of role on personality is not necessarily in the direction of creating increased fitness. The effect may be just the opposite. In addition it is probable that some of the effects of role have little or no relevance to the dimension of "fitness." The main point is that it seems likely that many of the influences roles exert on personality are random to the idea of efficiency in role performance. In the present climate of opinion in the social sciences, which tends to assume that there is a rather close fit between personality and social structure, this is a somewhat radical hypothesis. Gerth and Mills (23), for example, express the common viewpoint that although character structure is anchored in the organism, "it is formed by the particular combination of social roles which the person has incorporated from out of the total roles available to him in his society." The view we have suggested is that the fit is less close than is generally thought and occurs through a few main links rather than through myriad minor ones.

A second reason that individuals are frequently found to have personality traits which are appropriate to the roles they occupy resides in the fact that there is a considerable amount of role recruitment and self-recruitment. To some degree individuals seek roles that are most congenial to them. Henry's (38) study of the personality characteristics of successful American business executives is relevant to this point. Using interviews and projective tests, principally the Thematic Apperception Test, he found that to a remarkable degree the one hundred individuals studied had certain characteristics in common. It seemed to Henry that these characteristics were a minimum requirement for success and that the absence of them was coincident with failure within their organizations.

The characteristics found by Henry were strikingly appropriate to the requirements of the executive position. However, as Henry points out:

> The extent to which such reshaping of the adult personality is possible, however, seems limited. An initial selection process occurs in order to reduce the amount of time involved in teaching the appropriate behavior. Those persons whose personality structure is most readily adaptable to this particular role, tend to be selected to take this role. Whereas those whose personality is not already partially akin to this role are rejected (page 286).

To this we would add that it is obvious that individuals with the above-described characteristics would seek executive positions and would be relatively successful in doing so. Newcomb's suggestion (85) to the effect that, "we should expect to find more uniformity in personality on the part of those holding the same achieved positions, than on the part of those holding the same ascribed position," is applicable here, as is the concept of "anticipatory socialization."

From the point of view of a systematic theory of the formative influence of roles or social systems on personality, however, the two kinds of relationships just discussed, namely, those resulting from random effects of role and those resulting from recruitment and self selection, are of only secondary interest. These relationships do little to clarify the mechanism by which personality is systematically shaped into socially appropriate patterns.  The question of chief theoretical interest in the present chapter is not whether role influences personality or the behavior of individuals but whether the role or other units of the society systematically produce in individuals particular motivational and other components of personality which induce conformity to role and societal requirements.  There is an implication in much theoretical work in this field of study that since role behaviors vary widely, there is a corresponding variability at the personality level which serves to explain the behavioral differences.  The most usual statement is that role requirements become "internalized" and are transformed into individual motives.  Thus what was originally a unit of the social system, the role expectation, becomes a component of the personality or self system.  This view is reflected in the expectation that particular personality patterns will be found among individuals in various roles.  Linton (66) has introduced the concept "status personality" to indicate this idea.  He says that "all societies assume that the individuals who occupy certain positions in their systems of organization, will as a group, show personality norms differing from those of individuals in certain other positions."  Although Linton does mention the possibility that the "status personality" is a cultural fiction which results from the confusion of similarities in role *behavior* with similarities in *personality*, and treats the matter as an open question to be clarified by empirical research on the personalities of individuals in various status groups, the concept has received widespread and somewhat uncritical acceptance.

Parsons has suggested in his analysis of the American professional (87) that the same motives are not necessarily present in all individuals who are playing the same role.  He states, although it is not clear whether it is on the basis of any empirical study:

> Indeed there is little basis for maintaining that there is any important broad difference of typical motivation in the two cases (doctors and businessmen), or at least any of sufficient importance to account for the broad differences of socially expected behavior (page 196).

Also the recurrent patterns of behavior which are required for institutional functioning may have different meanings in different personalities.

> The social problem is to get the patterns (of behavior) whatever their functional significance to the person. . . . It does not matter whether there are important differences among types of personality possessing this need-disposition as long as it exists.  Moreover it does not even matter greatly whether the dominant sub-integrations of need-dispositions are not directly gratified . . . as long as the personality systems allow them to carry out the action without more than a certain amount of strain and as long as there are . . . institutions capable of absorbing and tolerating the repercussions of the strain (93, page 158).

Parsons suggests that the crucial personality variables underlying role behavior are an identification with the moral order, a respect for legitimate authority, and a feeling of "disinterested" obligation to live up to expectations in his variously defined roles. This is a crucial idea that has general applicability for the whole culture-personality field. Thus, for example, if the Zuni "ideal personality" requires nonaggressive behavior, the motivational component involved in nonaggressive behavior which conforms to this pattern is not necessarily "lack of aggression," but rather may be compliant and conforming tendencies in the individual. With this possibility it is not necessary that the social system create different motivational patterns for each of the roles contained within it. It suggests instead that the motivations toward conformity and toward acquiescence to legitimate authority are among the chief points of contact between social structure and personality.

As Parsons and Shils say (93):

> In most cases, individuals perform role functions in the division of labor which do not, as such, completely and directly gratify any specific need-disposition or any set of the need-dispositions of their personality system. It is the nature of instrumental action that it should be this way. Conformity with the role-expectations is possible, however, either through a generalized need-disposition to conformity or through instrumental orientations (page 152).

It is possible to inquire more closely into the nature of personality characteristics upon which conformity is based. The "respect for legitimate order" seems to be just one of such characteristics. It may itself be divided into two types, that which derives from the "internalization" of a more or less stable set of traditional values and that which involves simply the moral orientation, that is, the desire to do what is good and right without, however, the commitment to any particular set of ideas about what is good or right. From the first of these ideas we derive our theories of the superego; the second is closer to what White (113) has called "the mature conscience" and Erikson (19) has called the "humanization of conscience." It is clear that both types sustain conformity.

For the most part, social scientists have accepted the theory of the psychoanalysts that the value system internalized as the superego forms the chief basis for conformity. In recent years it has become apparent that a second main basis exists as well. We refer to what Riesman (95) has called "other directedness." In a society which is becoming increasingly characterized by normlessness, sociability and the orientation toward acceptance and popularity have become important bases for conformity. Here also the orientations provided by the group become coercive in their influence.

The "marketing orientation" described by Fromm (21) is a related personality trend. Individuals with this orientation are dependent upon others for acceptance and status. In order to win the acceptance the individual "becomes" the kind of person who is in the greatest demand. He tries to be as "attractive" as possible and in Fromm's terms says, "I am as you desire me." This behavior is extraordinarily plastic and flexible, shifting with the "requirements of the market." As Fromm says:

> . . . its very nature is that no specific and permanent kind of relatedness is developed, but that the very changeability of attitudes is the only permanent quality of such orientation. In this orientation those qualities are developed which can best be sold . . . the premise of the marketing orientation is emptiness, the lack of any specific quality which is not subject to change since any persistent trait of character might conflict someday with the requirements of the market (page 77).

Since for the most part role requirements specify desirable behavior but do not specify the motivations for it, this arrangement works well in insuring conformity. However, this concept is more applicable when the roles are functionally specific than when they are functionally diffuse, to use Parsons' terms (88).

Baldwin (5) in his analysis of the psychological mechanisms underlying behavioral uniformities distinguishes two types of compliance. In one of these the compliant behavior is instrumental to the achievement of some reward or avoidance of a punishment. Baldwin, however, believes that the two bases for compliance which we have discussed above, that is, compliance out of a sense of duty and compliance to fulfill the expectations of some other person, are consummatory in nature and require no cognition of reward in order to be executed. He says:

> Compliance to a cognized rule is a general mechanism permitting very great flexibility. The rule may change, it may hold only on odd numbered weeks, it may hold only when one is elected to a role. If it is intellectually clear, then compliance can occur. This mechanism is therefore most suitable for those social uniformities which require flexibility (page 23).

Baldwin suggests that compliance is possible only for voluntary behavior and cannot be elicited against the will of the actor; hence the special requirement that it be based on the motivational dispositions of the actor. Parsons and Shils (93) make the related point that the

> . . . need to be approved and esteemed is . . . a fundamental motivational basis for the acceptance of socially necessary disciplines. There is a sense in which, paradoxical as it may seem, the core of the reward systems of societies is to be found in the relevance of this element of the motivation of individuals. What people want most is to be responded to, loved, approved, and esteemed. If, subject, of course, to an adequate level of physiological

need-gratification, these needs can be adequately gratified, the most important single condition of stability of a social system will have been met (page 150).

These bases of conformity are related in various ways to the systems of positive and negative sanctions operating in a society. The latter may be regarded as direct social mechanisms for inducing appropriate role behavior. Their success, however, as Inkeles and Levinson (47) suggest, is dependent upon the responsiveness of individuals to them. In discussing the relationship of personality to *positive* sanctions, which are defined as the rewards offered for effective behavior, they suggest that the effectiveness of such sanctions depends on the motivations of individuals to attain them.

In our own society a major *positive* sanction is money, which may be regarded as an all-purpose reward capable of satisfying a wide variety of different needs for gratification. Most frequently, however, it is regarded as a means of attaining "success." Financial and social success as rewards can be most meaningful when the main basis for conformity is of the "other directedness" or "market orientation" variety but will probably not be relevant if the moral orientation is prevalent. Inkeles and Levinson distinguish congruence between motivational trend and sanction from a second type of congruence in which other psychological traits affect the "instrumental adequacy" of the individual. Thus in a society where accumulation of wealth is rewarded by recognition, the "tendency to be penurious" increases one's chances of achieving the proffered reward. While such characteristics undoubtedly help explain individual differences in achieving rewards, it does not seem necessary that they be modal in a group, for the reason that the proffered rewards do not actually have to be achieved in order to function as motivators. In fact if everyone in the group could actually reach them, their attraction would probably be much diminished. The fact that rewards are partly out of the reach of most of those striving for them may result in strain, but this does not necessarily interfere with the efficient functioning of the social system.

It is more difficult to say what type of positive sanction is most closely associated with the moral orientation we described above since moral behavior does not require an extrinsic reward. As Baldwin (5) says: "There may be people who want to comply with a rule. For them the reward or sanction is psychologically unnecessary." It seems likely that negative sanctions are most important here. A number of writers have classified cultures as "guilt" or "shame" cultures (94) according to whether the main nonphysical sanctions are aimed at one or the other of these feelings. Although in actual practice it is sometimes rather difficult to make a sharp distinction between these two processes (42), one might expect that the moral orientation would fit the traditional society in which the member's own guilt over real or imagined deviancy would serve as the main sanction. The term "sanction" has a somewhat different meaning when used in this way since it stems from the individual rather than from others. In the society in which "other directedness" or the "marketing orientation" is the chief motivation for conformity we might expect that "exposure" and shaming along with rejection, failure, and withdrawal of love would serve as the most important sanctions.

The principal point made here is that a few types of motivational dispositions can provide the impetus for a wide variety of role behavior. Where most contemporary theorists have emphasized the formative effects of a particular set of role expectations and have suggested that a high degree of role differentiation results in a similar degree of differentiation at the personality level, it seems possible that adequate fulfillment of role expectations does not require this differentiation. This is not to deny the fact that such personality differentiation takes place. Roles undoubtedly do exert an influence on personality in the way Newcomb and others have indicated. This influence, however, is largely an accidental by-product rather than a crucial dynamic force explaining conformity, and it may or may not have functional consequences. While such by-products may have an important positive or negative effect on the ways in which roles are played, from the point of view of a theory dealing with the shaping of personality by society so that it will have an appropriate form, the direct influence of role on personality seems largely nonsystematic and secondary in importance. One might speak of the "unanticipated consequences" of role participation. The same thing might be said about role conflict. From the point of view of understanding mental health problems, role conflicts are undoubtedly of great importance. Most writers on the subject of personality and social structure have inclined toward the position that personality "strains" are "undesirable," functionally speaking. Except when the strains are very extreme it is unlikely that this is true. Social systems function by and large with little regard to the strain or comfort of their members so long as appropriate behavior is forthcoming. This opinion applies to strain resulting from role conflict (105, 22, 44, 4), to strain arising from the lack of congruence between role expectations and personality dispositions (106, 101, 3), and to strain resulting from the futile striving for proffered rewards. As Parsons (88) says:

> From the point of view of functioning of the social system it is not the needs of all the participant actors which must be met nor all the needs of any one but only a sufficient proportion of a sufficient fraction of the population. It

is indeed a very general phenomenon that social forces are directly responsible for injury to or destruction of some individuals and some of the wants or needs of all individuals and though this may be reduced it is highly probable that it cannot be eliminated under realistic conditions (page 28).

### The development of socially appropriate motivations

Our problem here is somewhat more limited than that usually proposed. Instead of being concerned with the effect of social institutions on personality we shall be interested only in those systematic effects which foster efficient institutional functioning. We have suggested the theory that a very small number of powerful and widespread motivational patterns serve to explain conformity to a great variety of role requirements. These may be regarded as the absolutely necessary and minimum requirements for institutional functioning. A large number of other personality characteristics may contribute to the niceties of the situation but are perhaps dispensable.

The process by which personality comes to have this appropriate shape is ordinarily referred to as socialization. The most prevalent theory of socialization is that the early care of children is socially patterned in such a way that the appropriate adult personality characteristics are produced (19). This belief rests heavily on the psychoanalytic theories which hold that the early years of life are crucial in personality development. To a very large extent research in the field of culture and personality has been focused on the problem of linking child-rearing practices to adult personality patterns. This focus has been deplored by many (86, 41) who suggest that decisive influences may come in middle childhood and later.

Our concern here is with the extent to which these socialization practices have as their manifest or latent function the creation of personality characteristics that produce conformity to desired norms and role requirements. While most culture-personality studies have attributed such a function to child-rearing patterns, actual empirical demonstrations or convincing theoretical expositions are rare. Of the empirical studies the work of Allison Davis and his colleagues (14) is most germane. These writers have documented in convincing fashion the existence of different patterns of child rearing in two social classes among American Negroes. A number of aspects of the child-rearing patterns they described can be interpreted as helping to develop personality characteristics which will fit the social institutions and normative expectations of the society. Merton and Kitt (80) have referred to the kind of training in which parents prepare their children for membership in groups that are somewhat higher on the hierarchical social scale than their own groups as "anticipatory socialization."

Aberle (2) has recently discussed the question of the child-rearing practices. He makes a plea for research which will show how the pattern of socialization is related to the configuration of other social institutions and rejects the view that socialization practices aim simply at reproducing the personality characteristics of the socializing agents. Aberle explores the relations of these practices to various aspects of the social system, and also of various aspects of the socialization pattern to the social system. He concludes that there may be a broad network of relationships among a number of different aspects of the social system and socialization practices. At a number of points the type of relationship he suggests involves the training of children for adult roles. On the other hand components of certain institutions such as religious rituals seem to reinforce socialization patterns. Erikson (19) makes a similar point when he states "child training to remain consistent must be imbedded in a system of continued economic and cultural synthesis."

Murphy (83) has addressed himself to the problem of how social uniformity is created. He rejects as "naive" and simplistic the view that the child "takes over" the culture from his parents and suggests that certain processes in the child such as the demand to be admitted, to be loved and respected as a member of the group, the protest against exclusion on the grounds of immaturity and the rebellion against interference with his primitive impulses indicate that the "young absorb a good deal of their familial culture" partly because they want to, partly because they have to. "There is no simple osmosis of the prevalent social usages from old to young; there is a mixture of love-feast and battle royal." While indicating that the young learn to act, perceive, and value as their elders do, Murphy suggests that we still have only the vaguest understanding of *how* this learning takes place. In his analysis of the *how* of socialization he emphasizes the principle of "anchorage" of perceptions to what is pleasing and satisfying. To the developing child it is most satisfying to do, see, and value as others around him are doing. Thus socialization is in part based on "collectively experienced and collectively reinforced autisms." In addition a secondary set of controls in the form of "conscience" comes about through the child's identification with the strong and authoritative figures in his life. Finally, external controls reinforce the two bases of social conformity when the purely personal autisms become too prominent. Conformity thus depends "partly on authority and partly on eager acceptance."

One of the main foci of the vast and complex theoretical systems that have been built by Talcott Parsons and his collaborators (87, 88, 89, 90, 91, 92) has been analysis of the socialization process. This theory which is perhaps the most elaborate and sophisticated analysis of the relationship between personality and social structure to date has not yet been completely absorbed by workers in the social sciences. Our treatment here is intended to present only a few elements of the theory and does not make any pretense of being a systematic account of the whole.

Parsons suggests that personality and society may be regarded as independent systems, neither of which "provides the premises from which the major characteristics of the other, or of action in general, can be derived." The individual is therefore not the unit of the social system, but a separate system which interacts with it, the basic unit of the former being the status-role. Parsons distinguishes a third system, the culture, which refers to the system of meanings that give the individual a stable orientation to the objects with which he is interacting. Action is understandable only when all three systems are involved, the personality system providing the motivational energy and orientation, the cultural system providing the value orientation, and the social system the structure of the situation. These three kinds of orientations of the actor to the situation of action allow us to understand the modes of action which he selects.

The participation of the individual in the social system is organized and structured by certain role-status positions or sets of expected behaviors and must be regularized through the development of appropriate and stable motivations. These role units, which on the one hand are parts of the social system, may also become parts of the personality. This is referred to as the interpenetration of the two systems. The penetration of the third system, the cultural, subjects the other two to certain constraints and adds stability to the interactive process. The three components of the cultural system are the cognitive, cathectic, and evaluative. The concept of internalization has been somewhat broadened so that cognitive and cathectic orientations as well as moral standards are considered to be incorporated into the personality. This has the effect of viewing self-object images and characteristic affective modes as emerging from the social situations in which the individual participates. As Parsons points out, this represents a more comprehensive treatment of what the personality takes over from the outside than is given in psychoanalytic theory, where only the internalization of moral standards is given conceptual status.

The relationship between personality and social systems is seen to reside in the fact that the need-dispositions of the former and the role expectations of the latter were both derived from the same patterns of value orientation. The cultural system is on the one hand internalized and becomes a main part of the personality and on the other hand is institutionalized and becomes part of the social system. This development leads to a certain degree of structural isomorphism between personality and the social system which makes it possible for many analytic categories, i.e., the pattern variables, to be applied to both, and is the basis for the compatibility of action to both systems simultaneously. Internalization, or socialization as it is frequently referred to, consists of the acquisition of new patterns of orientation. These patterns, which emerge from the successive interactive systems in which the individual participates, consist primarily of the reciprocal role relationships which were stabilized in the interactive systems.

The crux of the Parsons theory, insofar as it concerns relations between personality and social structure, appears to reside in the concept of the penetration of the cultural system into both the personality and social systems. It is this concept which we wish to examine critically. Parsons (92) considers internalization as a process by which cultural elements can be transmitted with minimal change from one system to another. This transmission is regarded as basic. "Only in a figurative sense does an actor *have* patterns of value-orientation. In a strict sense he *is,* among other things, a system of such patterns" (93). Parsons addressed himself to the question we have raised in his paper, "The superego and the theory of social systems" (89). There, discussing Freudian theory, he states:

> . . . the cognitive definition of the object world does not seem to have been problematical for Freud. He subsumed it under external reality in relation to which ego functions constitute a process of adaptation. He failed to take explicitly into account the fact that the frame of reference in terms of which objects are cognized and therefore adapted to, is cultural and thus cannot be taken for granted as given but must be internalized as a condition for the development of mature ego functioning (page 18).

It is the broadness of the way the concept of internalization is used about which we have strong reservations.

Can values have potent influences on behavior even if they are not internalized? It does seem possible to go a very long distance toward explaining behavior which is congruent with the sociocultural system without invoking the concept of internalization. Given an individual who has developed either of the two main motivational tendencies we have discussed above, the desire to behave morally or the desire to please others, we can see that he has the problem of knowing what behavior will be satisfactory. The cultural orientations will serve as quite elaborate guides detailing what is good or bad, and what kinds of behavior are generally regarded as pleasing. The individual need merely act in terms of these orientations. Conformity involves an *acquiescence* in and *approval* of the validity of the value orientations and belief systems and an acceptance of the desirability of acting according to them. We do not believe that such acquiescence necessarily involves "internalization." Spiro (104) has said that "once something is learned it is no longer external to the organism but it is 'inside' the organism and once it is 'inside,' the organism becomes a biosocial organism determining its own behavior as a consequence of the modifications it has undergone in the process of learning."

We believe that this view of learning fails to distinguish between learning to *do* something and learning *about* something. The learning of cognitive and evaluative orientations may involve the development of representations or maps of the cultural state of affairs. These are not tendencies to action but simply guides to the nature of the world in which one lives that one may or may not act in terms of. What is learned is not, for example, the value itself but simply that the value exists and that it is deemed important by respected members of the group to which one belongs.

Lewis (65) has called attention to the fact that his distinction between the private and public aspects of personality is related to Mowrer's two-factor theory of learning (81). Mowrer's sign learning is thought to be relevant to the "private" personality while solution learning leads to either "private" or "public" personality.

The crucial situation for determining whether cultural orientations are internalized or not occurs when the individual changes his allegiance from one group to another. If, for example, the value orientations of the first group persist in the individual and continue to determine his behavior we can agree that internalization has occurred. If, however, he is able to renounce, in a real sense as well as verbally, his former values along with the group, and accept a new and perhaps contrasting set as binding on his behavior, it seems appropriate to question whether there has been any real internalization. It would perhaps be more correct to apply the concept of "reference group behavior" (80) and predict that the values which will be most significant for the behavior of an individual are those of the group to which he belongs, of which he identifies himself consciously or unconsciously as a member. We do not wish to imply that internalization does not take place nor that it is unimportant. It does seem, however, that its scope may be limited and that some values remain "external" at least in the sense that when the individual changes his group identification he abandons them. In addition the fact that actual internalization occurs and is important does not signify that the whole of the cultural pattern is internalized. The actual extent to which it is is a matter for empirical investigation. Bettelheim's observations (10) of inmates of Nazi concentration camps gives some relevant evidence. He noted that most of the older prisoners abandoned the aim of maintaining themselves as the same kind of persons they were when they entered the prison camp. They accepted the reality of the prison camp and tried to adapt to it, behaving in terms of the values of the prison camp, identifying with their guards and actually adopting their attitudes toward other prisoners.

## SOME EMPIRICAL AND METHODOLOGICAL ISSUES

In the remainder of this chapter our attention will be turned to what has become known as the field of "culture and personality." After a brief attempt at providing the immediate historical context we shall discuss some representative empirical studies and theoretical analyses with respect to three issues which we believe have been of salient importance in the work of the last decade. The three issues are: (a) how is personality to be studied in cultures other than our own, (b) how are the culture and personality concepts best defined and what order of relationship is conceived to exist between the two concepts, and (c) to what extent is the modal personality approach justified and adequate. We do not suggest that these issues comprehend all of the research in the culture-personality area. One or the other of them, however, is involved in almost every culture-personality study.

### *The historical background*

The most significant influences of the last decade in the culture-personality field came through the work of Ruth Benedict, Margaret Mead, and Abram Kardiner. Benedict's *Patterns of Culture* (9) was perhaps the single most influential work and has dominated the thinking about culture-personality relations of the great majority of sociologists, psychiatrists, psychologists, anthropologists, and educated laymen, and to a considerable extent continues to do so at the present time. The entire work pointed in impressive fashion to the diversity of cultural forms and the plasticity of human nature and also pointed out the fallacy of ethnocentrism.

Margaret Mead's work during the 1930's also was tremendously effective in documenting the astonishing extent of cultural diversity (72, 73, 74, 75). She suggests that this cultural diversity is accompanied by a similar diversity of personality traits of a very fundamental nature.

Abram Kardiner (53, 54, 55) was the third great influence on the culture-personality field. In addition to the theory of cultural integration through personality structure which we have discussed above, Kardiner introduced the concept of basic personality structure and it is through this concept that he has had his greatest influence. This concept came to be very widely used, although without the specific theoretical meanings assigned to it by Kardiner. Instead it stood for the belief that individuals in a society, with the exception of a few deviants, would have a particular constellation of personality traits in common by virtue of their exposure to similar experiences as young children. This shared personality constellation also was known as the "modal personality" and in an important sense the two terms came to dominate the culture-personality scene. This concept achieved such overwhelming acceptance that most workers in the field defined their research task as the discovery of the "basic" or "modal" personality constellations and their relationship to the child-rearing institutions in the culture under study.

The conceptions of Benedict, Mead, and Kardiner emphasizing the plasticity of human nature dominated theories and research to an amazing extent and had almost complete and universal acceptance. They provided the unified and simplified conceptions which made it possible for large numbers of people to understand the importance of cultural factors in personality development and to initiate a large quantity of important research on personality in every part of the world. Yet one cannot help feeling that the very forcefulness and appeal of their arguments led to a premature stabilization of culture-personality theory. Their theories became a kind of orthodoxy which tended to prevent the development and presentation of alternate points of view.

### How is personality to be studied

The past decade has seen the flowering of a completely new kind of study in the social sciences, the empirical study and description of personality in nonliterate and non-Western societies. Under the influence of pioneer studies by Du Bois (18), Hallowell (29, 30, 31), and J. Henry (34) the attention of anthropologists and psychologists turned to the determination of the personality characteristics of various exotic peoples, not by inference from cultural institutions, nor by observation of behavior, but through the use of the standard techniques in the armamentarium of the clinical psychologist and the psychiatrist.

A number of studies, including those by Gladwin and Sarason (24), Lessa and Spiegelman (64), W. E. Henry (37), and Mead (77), have sought to investigate the usefulness of these techniques in ethnographic work although from our point of view in an inappropriate manner. Lessa and Spiegelman, for example, present an analysis of a series of Ulithian Thematic Apperception Tests with the aim of judging the proposition that "thematic test material can reflect the culture as a whole and specifically that it can shed light on the nature of the basic personality structure of the people of Ulithi Atoll." One wonders why a procedure for study-ing personality should be used to learn about the culture and evaluated in terms of this criterion. The authors ask: "From the point of view of the anthropologist . . . how useful is the method? Is it worth the eth-nographer's time to gather test material routinely . . . ?" They conclude that "Little new was added to what the ethnographer already knew about the culture, yet the test results seemed to provide an independent veri-fication of what was observed in the field. Using different materials and separate approaches it was possible to arrive at essentially similar conclusions."

In general, there is little excuse for the psychologist to abandon his own task, that of personality description, and use his materials for cultural analysis. In this case the description of personality suffers by being vague and undifferentiated and the description of the cultural pattern is equally diffuse and stereotyped. As Wallace (111) points out, "The results well illustrate the principle that the best way to describe a culture is the old-fashioned ethnographic way. . . ."

The somewhat violent controversy over whether projective tests are useful to the anthropologist, which was the topic of a symposium in the *American Anthropologist* (35), can be simply resolved by asking what the purposes of the anthropologist are (78, 32, 39). If one of his purposes is to describe the prevalent personality characteristics of the people he is working with, he cannot avoid considering how he can do this. There can be little doubt that, at least in our own culture, projective tests have an important role to play in the comprehensive personality study, and evidence is accumulating that they work in a similar way in many other cultures as well. We can only agree with Jules Henry when he states that "Were I to go into the field tomorrow to study a culture, I would not use the Rorschach test." However, if one of Henry's purposes in going into the field was to study personality he would be very foolish not to consider seriously, at least, whether projective techniques could help him in his task.

William Henry attempted as one of the Studies in Indian Education a similar evaluation of the Thematic Apperception Test. His study is worthy of note because it constitutes one of the first applications of the test in nonliterate societies. He was able to show quite conclusively that it gave very similar results to those of the Rorschach, Life History, figure drawing, and a battery of other tests. In addition, on the basis of The-matic Apperception Tests, Henry attempted a description of certain as-pects of Hopi and Navaho society, especially those which were relevant to the personality development of children. He found that his descrip-tions were in essential agreement with the published materials on the two societies and that experts, familiar with the cultures and the literature describing them, were of the opinion that his inferences were essentially correct. Here again we must question the appropriateness of evaluating the TAT in terms of its ability to develop correct pictures of the culture.

Henry's development of a special set of TAT cards set a trend in the use of TATs that is now widely followed. He believed, and others did after him, that the Murray TAT provided scenes which were too exotic, strange, and incomprehensible for subjects in nonliterate societies to utilize for the purpose of self-expression and projection. Our own experience indicates that this is not necessarily the case. In a study of Navaho and Zuni young men (50, 109) both the Murray pictures and a specially designed set of pictures drawn by Indian artists were administered to about thirty subjects. Contrary to expectations, the Murray set yielded stories which were far superior in interest and psychological significance to those elicited by the specially designed Indian set. While one would not wish to generalize from this one piece of research, it does suggest that stimulus materials coming from another culture, which are only partly understood, may be helpful in breaking down the concrete attitudes that are so fatal to the operation of projective techniques.

Mead (77) presents and discusses the analyses by five Rorschach workers of a record of an Arapesh man collected in the early 1930's. Mead states that the Rorschach did not reveal anything about the culture which she did not already know. She does say, however, that its contribution was much greater when she turned "from the question of cultural illumination to the question of individual character formation" and since this is, as we have suggested, the test's appropriate area of application, we can regard her judgment about the test as positive. However, as we compared the Rorschach protocol with the rich life history and interview materials which are presented in the same volume, it seemed justifiable to question the usefulness of the test. The Arapesh Rorschach protocol was a lengthy document apparently rich in symbolic and expressive content. Nevertheless, the meaning of the responses is cryptic and difficult to comprehend, although they give one the strong conviction that important areas of personality are involved in them. We feel about the record much as we do about cryptic records in our own society, namely, that they are extremely personal documents in which many of the responses have quite private meanings or emotional contexts which are only incompletely indicated in the responses themselves. In consequence some further exploration with the subject himself is necessary, much in the manner in which the psychoanalyst explores the meaning of a dream. This approach seems especially important in exotic cultures where the actuarial approach used by most present-day Rorschach workers breaks down completely in the absence of extensive norms.

The difficulty of adequately interpreting the Arapesh Rorschach raises the general problem of whether collecting Rorschachs in nonliterate societies really meets a serious need in the important business of personality study or is merely a form of boondoggling which satisfies a relatively idle though by no means culpable curiosity about what Rorschachs in exotic cultures look like. We have a certain amount of faith that the former is the case at least in some societies, although on the whole we believe that there is a considerable variation from culture to culture in the optimal approach to the study of personality. The understanding of this variation is an extremely important problem for culture and personality workers. In this connection the writer's project of assembling, reproducing on Microcards, and distributing personality materials which have been collected in nonliterate and non-Western societies offers the promise of being useful.

The majority of studies in the culture and personality area have been concerned with exploring the sociocultural determinants of personality in particular societies. For the most part this work has required the delineation of modal personality trends, although in some instances particular isolated personality characteristics were studied (29). Inkeles and Levinson (47) have discussed the methodology of modal personality studies in detail and have described three typical procedures: the personality assessment of individuals, the study of collective adult phenomena, and the study of child-rearing systems. For the first type they point out the dilemma created by the need for studies of large representative samples, even in relatively small societies, and the need for "clinical" studies in depth which ordinarily require many hours of work. They suggest that brief clinical-assessment procedures such as projective techniques and semistructured clinical interviews provide partial solutions which permit moderate-sized samples of about fifty to a hundred cases but which achieve considerable penetration in depth. Henry and Spiro (36) have recently reviewed projective test studies and Gottschalk, Kluckhohn, and Angell (28) have reviewed the use of personal documents in social science.

The chief problem, however, is not the collection of adequate personality materials but their analysis and conversion into modal personality statements. It is probably correct to say that psychologists can collect more data than they can reliably and validly interpret. Two approaches seem possible. One is the scoring of protocols in terms of a number of predetermined categories; the other is the development of separate personality descriptions of each subject followed by an attempt to determine the elements which are common to all or most of the individual studies (13, 56, 50, 52). As one who has worked extensively with the second method, the writer can testify to its difficulty. In both the Hutterite and the Navaho-Zuni studies extensive case descriptions were constructed, but the very rich characterizations of the separate individuals dwindled to a very small number of relatively uninteresting modal statements. One gained the impression that more could be learned about the personality of the Hutterites, Navaho, or Zuni from any one of the case records than from a summary of a hundred and twenty case records. For example, (50) of 280 separate themes in the personality descriptions of 14 Navaho young men, only 15 themes were found in more than one third of the individual cases while 181 themes were found to hold for only one person. Only four themes held for more than half of the sample. The main difficulty with this kind of analysis is that we cannot be certain about the independence of the 280 themes. If some of them had been combined, as they might very well have by another worker, the number of modal themes might have been different.

These difficulties are not insurmountable. They simply require that substantial resources of time and talent be mobilized at the analysis of data phase of the culture-personality study. In fact, substantial resources are needed in every phase of studies of modal personality. The data collection phase should provide for twelve to twenty hours of study with each subject if there is any intention that the studies be comprehensive. Personality data can be collected in much less time, but it is a misapprehension that anything resembling a complete picture can be gained by the administration of a single projective test. Projective tests have an important, perhaps essential, role in personality studies, but they do not necessarily play the most important role and certainly the data they yield can be understood properly only in the context of the life history and information about the actual functioning of the individual in the social groups to which he belongs. Incomplete personality pictures may in some cases be worse than none at all if they are misleading and their meaning is misinterpreted.

The problem of what procedures are most fruitful in other societies is one which has barely been studied but which is absolutely basic for the culture-personality field. On the basis of materials which have been collected in perhaps thirty cultures, it is possible to say that techniques like the Rorschach, the TAT, and the life history work better in some groups than in others, and that in some they seem to be almost useless.

The greatest part, by far, of the personality studies in nonliterate societies have been conducted by anthropologists, although some psychologists have participated in them at the stage of data analysis. In one sense this has been unfortunate since the study of personality is a vastly complicated and difficult business, calling for the utmost in interpersonal skills, psychological sophistication, and creativity. Although anthropologists have very often been able to collect quite interesting materials on personality, they have by and large functioned very much at the level of the psychological technician, who can collect very valuable materials if he is told what to do but whose work frequently lacks understanding, flexibility, and depth. This is not meant as a criticism of anthropologists who have worked in the culture-personality field. The problems of discovering how to do adequate personality studies in a wide range of sociocultural systems are so difficult, however, that they require the concerted efforts of a large number of highly trained and creative specialists in personality study.

The second kind of procedure frequently used for the delineation of the modal personality is the study of collective adult phenomena. This method involves the analysis of materials such as myths, folk tales, literary works, and folk products like popular songs and movies regarded as deriving from modal personality patterns. The analyses by Bateson (7) and Kracauer (60) of German movies, by McGranahan and Wayne (69) of German and American plays, by Wolfenstein and Leites (115) of American movies are a few examples of such studies. In discussing these and other ethnographic materials, including rituals and ceremonial dances as well as some observed regularities in collective behavior which are frequently called cultural themes or "plots," Inkeles and Levinson say that there is often good reason to believe that these materials do reflect modal personality trends. They raise the question, however, of the representativeness of the particular sample of data which is being studied and say that this method cannot tell with any conclusiveness what range and varieties of modal personalities actually exist in a society. The additional point may be made that this kind of analysis often involves circularity, since the modal personality characteristics are supposed to explain the ethnographic materials from which they were inferred.

These points would seem to hold also for the method of inferring personality patterns from a knowledge of child-rearing patterns (8, 54, 55, 27). In all but a very few of these studies the confidence in such inferences has been so great that no studies of individuals have been thought necessary. Kardiner's analysis of the Alorese materials is a notable exception, but even here Kardiner gives the empirical materials much lower status than the inferred characteristics. It is obvious that this method is prejudicial to the question of whether a modal personality does indeed exist since it allows no other possibility. Both Klineberg (57) and Inkeles and Levinson (47) have emphasized the importance of the study of individuals in research on modal personality.

### Some problems of definition and methodology

The avowed purpose of most culture and personality studies during the past decade has been the illumination of the relationship between them. The achievement of this aim has been seriously hindered by a considerable degree of confusion and disagreement about the meanings of these two terms and the kind of relationship between them which is contemplated. In this section we shall discuss a number of definitional and conceptual issues which we believe have been implicitly involved in almost every theoretical and empirical work in this field during the last several years.

Perhaps the most important of these issues concerns the distinctions or the lack of them between the terms culture and personality. The most prevalent viewpoints seem to de-emphasize any distinctions. Culture and personality are thought to be so intimately related and so interdependent that the use of the two terms implies a false and artificial dichotomy. Spiro, for example, entitles his paper (104) "Culture and Personality: The Natural History of a False Dichotomy," being critical of the idea that the terms culture and personality refer to different kinds of phenomena, and also of the notion that the purpose of research and theory in this field is to build conceptual bridges between the two (11). He believes that the culture and personality "problem" is created by this false dichotomy. Spiro states that culture exists within individuals and is the product of the individual's interaction with his fellows. Since he also defines personality as the product of one's interactions with other individuals it is not surprising that he speaks of the "personality-culture" and concludes that the term personality can be substituted for the term culture in certain kinds of analysis.

It is clear that definitional problems are of key importance in these matters. Perhaps a more fundamental matter, however, is whether the worker wishes to make a distinction between the two concepts or not, for it seems that there is enough variability of definitions among authorities in these fields that each worker can choose the ones which best suit his purposes. Our own belief in this matter is that dedifferentiation serves no useful purpose but on the contrary makes it very difficult to formulate meaningful empirical research. The refusal to distinguish clearly between culture and personality leaves research with no immediate aim, since if one is not dealing with two distinguishable entities or systems there is no possibility of studying the extent or nature of their relationship. The fact that there can be no personality apart from human society does not mean that it may not be valuable for some purposes to study them as separate systems. Certainly one would not wish sociologists to abandon their focus on social systems or psychologists their focus on the individual.

Hand in hand with the "culture-in-personality" approach has gone the often stated belief that both culture and personality are abstractions from the same behavior and are, at most, two different ways of looking at the same thing (58). If such be the case the two terms and the distinctions between them are, as Smith (103) puts it, "figments of the scientific imagination." The distinction to us is not an arbitrary one but arises out of the fact that some behavior requires the culture concept for its explanation while other behavior requires the personality concept. It is probably true that almost all behavior must in some sense be explained by the interactions of both sociocultural and personality systems. However, what is significant is not that both systems participate, but that in most behavior the influence of one or the other is preponderant and in some the influence of one or the other is almost imperceptible. It is, as we understand it, one of the main tasks of culture-personality inquiry to determine the extent of overlapping influence by both systems and the particular areas in which it occurs.

One of the most confusing consequences of the failure to distinguish between the behavioral referents of the two concepts has been the discussion of certain cultural phenomena as if they were personality characteristics. This makes most of the questions with which culture-personality workers have been concerned both meaningless and tautological. As Inkeles and Levinson say: "To define national character as more or less synonymous with the sum of learned cultural behavior makes any effort to relate culture to character largely an effort to relate culture to itself."

The logic of this situation is closely dependent on the way in which the concepts are defined. Many social scientists tend to expand the meaning of personality so that it becomes roughly synonymous with the individual. The same writers frequently complain that the personality concept is too "global" and should be replaced by sub-concepts with more precise meanings. It is probably not feasible to set any exact limits on what we will regard as personality. However, one can apply to certain processes such as belief systems, attitudes, values, and sentiments, which Inkeles (45) has termed the "social personality," the terms peripheral, outer (in the sense of Lewin's onion model), temporary, and phenotypic. It seems incorrect and unsound to emphasize these processes when discussing personality but to ignore the genotypic, central, inner processes which psychologists whose specialty is personality study ordinarily regard as the "core" of personality. Sanford (98) has recently said:

> . . . with respect to the kind of motives I have called most interesting and particularly important one might say that they tend to be deep, inner, hidden, basic, central, genotypic, resistant to change, and originating early in the life of the individual.

With respect to the Parsons and Shils (93) definition of personality as the "organized system of the orientation and motivation of one individual actor" we might suggest that the "orientation" aspects of personality may be characterized as peripheral while the "motivational" aspects are central. The point is not that the former are unimportant but that it is useful to distinguish them from the motivational processes and that this distinction tends to break down if both are subsumed under a single heading. Lewis' distinction (65) between private and public personality is relevant. He indicates that much misunderstanding arises out of the fact that the anthropologist is interested primarily in the relations between the public personality and culture while the psychologist is mainly concerned with private personality.

One other definitional problem deserves some attention. Personality may be defined in terms of patterns of behavior or in terms of patterns of inner processes (71, 65). Since the proponents of the inner processes type of definition tend to agree that the inner processes are known only insofar as they are inferred from observed behavior, and the proponents of the behavioral definition for the most part accept the existence of the inner processes as intervening variables which are required to explain observed behavior, it would appear that the differences between the two viewpoints might be of only minor importance. It seems to us, however, that the possibility of making an adequate distinction between the concepts of personality and culture is dependent on defining the former in terms of inner processes rather than behavior. When the latter type of definition is used, personality tends to become synonymous with culture since there is usually no criterion available for the isolation of those behaviors which are most relevant to personality from those which refer primarily to culture. Thus the behavioral definition best suits the purposes of workers who prefer to break down the conceptual distinctions, while the inner processes definition helps those who would sharpen the distinctions.

### Studies of modal personality

To a very considerable extent studies of modal personality and national character have proceeded under the assumption that something like a modal personality does exist and that the main tasks of the researcher are to describe the modal constellation and discover its genesis in the social pattern or, more usually, in the child-rearing institutions. This research model has, as we have suggested above, been somewhat confused by the failure of many workers to maintain the distinction between personality and cultural processes. When modal personality is defined as synonymous with the sum total of learned cultural behavior there can be no question of its "existence." Smith (103) expresses this when he says:

> If in fact the members of a definable social group share a set of traditional behavior patterns that warrant designation as a culture or sub-culture, by the same token these patterns (having no existence apart from behaving persons) cannot fail to be integrated into the personalities of the members. . . . The "existence" of modal personality and status personality is no more controversial than the existence of culture and statuses. At most these are merely alternatives of organizing the same data (page 60).

Since we have maintained that personality should be regarded as a separate system which is not synonymous with nor reducible to the cultural system, the existence of modal personality constellations is for us a real problem that is not solved automatically by the knowledge of the existence of cultural regularities. Two main criteria for the acceptance of the existence of a modal personality pattern may be applied. One is that some degree of homogeneity within the group is required, and the second is that the characteristics with respect to which there is homogeneity should vary from group to group.

The Alorese study reported by Du Bois (18) and Kardiner (54, 55) which was described above is, in many respects, the most important study of modal personality that has been done. Although Kardiner claimed that the personality constellation which he derived from Alorese child-rearing patterns was found in the seven autobiographies he examined and was "almost identical in essence" to the conclusions that Oberholzer derived from the Rorschach data, he failed to support these judgments with the appropriate objective analyses. At a number of points at which Kardiner or Oberholzer claimed to find close agreement, we could only with great difficulty see any similarity whatsoever, and a number of the successes claimed by Kardiner were instances in which the adult constellations noted in the Rorschach test could be explained by the personality dynamics inferred by Kardiner. Since the chief dynamic factor was maternal deprivation, it would undoubtedly be possible to link a wide variety of adult constellations to it. In addition there was considerable variation among both the autobiographies and the Rorschachs. It seems to us that the issue which Kardiner closed so finally was not really decided by this study and that it requires replication, with the same data but using the more rigorous methods which are easily available in present-day social science. Kardiner said that "We may not in the future be obliged to study each culture with the thoroughness that we did the Alorese. The conclusions reached there will stand." In our opinion the Alorese study was only a beginning. Although it pointed the way by being the first serious well-conceived culture-personality study, and substantial resources and energies went into its consummation, these were but a fraction of those needed for an adequate study.

The Indian Education Research Project conducted jointly by the Committee on Human Development of the University of Chicago and the Bureau of Indian Affairs, in which studies of children were carried on in five cultures, is perhaps the most extensive of all of the culture-personality projects during the past decade. The five cultures studied were the Sioux by MacGregor (70), the Hopi by Thompson and Joseph (107), the Navaho by Kluckhohn and Leighton (59) and Leighton and Kluckhohn (63), the Papago by Joseph, Spicer, and Chesky (49), and the Zuni by Adair and Leighton in a still unpublished report. In addition Thompson (108) and Havighurst and Neugarten (33) have made some cross-cultural comparisons. It is not possible to deal adequately with this extensive series of studies in a few paragraphs. Methodologically, however, the studies all involved more or less orthodox ethnographic descriptions and in addition quite lengthy series of personality materials, including projective tests, autobiographies, and a number of miscellaneous tests designed to tap values and attitudes. These materials were used first to develop an over-all characterization of the personality of children in the society and second, a series of descriptions of individual children. Finally, in a relatively unsystematic way certain connections between the societies and the personality traits were made. With a few exceptions this procedure was less productive than might have been hoped. In part this was the result of a paucity of theoretical orientation; in part the relative sparseness of the personality findings was involved. Thompson's comparison (108) of the Rorschach perceptions of the Hopi, Navaho, and Papago does provide valuable evidence of the diversity of the three groups in this area, and the still unpublished comparison of the Rorschach findings in the five societies should add to the contribution of the project. In general we might say that the Indian Education studies do not add appreciably to our knowledge of the homogeneity or diversity of personality characteristics within societies but do suggest while not being completely convincing that personality differences between societies do exist.

Another typical culture-personality study is that of Gladwin and Sarason, *Truk: Man in paradise* (24). Gladwin described his purpose as that of determining whether two orders of data (psychological and ethnographic) were congruent. The conclusion was that on the whole the two pictures were congruent and that where discrepancies existed they could be explained by Sarason's ignorance of certain facts about the culture, without which it was not possible to understand the response.

How may this congruence be interpreted? The most likely explanation is that Gladwin was a keen enough observer to note the same personality characteristics reflected in everyday behavior which Sarason saw in the projective test material. Gladwin, however, focused primarily on an ethnographic description and it seems likely that the congruence also means that Sarason's personality descriptions fit the cultural facts as Gladwin knew them. Because both of these factors entered into the congruence it is difficult to say whether this study has actually demonstrated anything of importance for culture-personality theory, even though it makes a creditable contribution to a better understanding of the technique of personality study in nonliterate societies.

Since Gladwin set out to do a culture-personality study, it is appropriate to ask how he got off the track. Very early in his discussion (page 22), Gladwin equates "cultural determinants" with "life experience" and defines his task as exploring the relationship between "personality" and the "life experience." In a review of this work, Schneider (102) has made the point that the focus on "proximal" events in the life experiences of the Trukese makes it impossible to "sort the temporally stable and structurally crucial determinants (of personality) from those which are transient and, from the point of view of the culture, peripheral."

One of the most original and methodologically sophisticated attempts to delineate modal personality characteristics in a rigorous way was Wallace's (110) study of the Rorschachs of the Tuscarora Indians. In a more or less arbitrary way, he established limits (one standard deviation on either side of the mode) around the central tendencies of scores of Rorschach variables. He asserted that those subjects who fell within those limits on all 21 of the variables could be said to possess the Tuscarora "modal personality." Wallace was then able to compare the number of Tuscarora Indians who had the Tuscarora "modal personality" with Ojibwa Indians who did. He found that 37 per cent of the Tuscarora were "modal" and that only 5 per cent of the Ojibwa fell within the Tuscarora mode. This difference is a statistically significant one. Twenty-eight per cent of the 102 Ojibwa Rorschachs fell in the Ojibwa modal class. Although the definition of the limits of the modal class was somewhat arbitrary and a shift in those limits would cause a different number of individuals to fall in the modal class, the evidence does indicate rather conclusively that the Rorschachs of the two groups are different. It is difficult to decide whether the limits of the modal class which were set by Wallace are too wide or too narrow. However, if the present figures are accepted as representing something like the actual situation the relatively small percentage of cases in the groups which were found to be modal is of great interest. They seem to call for a new variety of theory that could explain how only a minority of individuals in a society, *rather than a majority,* comes to respond positively to the cultural pressure toward uniformity of personality.

The cross-cultural study occupies an important place in the culture-personality field since it offers possibilities of control of variables analogous to those of the laboratory experiment. For example, we could not really be convinced that a personality trait or pattern found commonly in a particular group was related to sociocultural factors unless it was also shown that the same trait or pattern was not found in the absence of these factors. By implication all studies of modal personality fall into the category of cross-cultural research since they suggest that the resultant personality picture is different from that found in other societies. However, it is very rare to find a research report that makes explicit comparisons. A number of cross-cultural studies have been conducted (12, 48, 1, 51, 111), but the research possibilities have only been touched on.

In general these studies reveal a number of moderately sized differences which may be taken as evidence for the existence of a cultural influence on personality. However, one is struck by the fact that in almost every case reactions within the groups were quite variable. Kaplan (50, 51) attempted to set up a direct test of the modal-personality thesis, utilizing projective test materials from four cultures in the American Southwest, the Navaho, Zuni, Mormon, and Spanish-American. He described the variance of Rorschach scores both within and among the four cultures and set up several sorting tests to see whether test protocols could be sorted into four appropriate groups and then whether they could be matched to protocols which had already been sorted. The results indicated that differences in Rorschach scores among the four groups were present although in every case the variability within the groups was large and the overlap between the groups very great. In his comparison of Navaho and Zuni TATs (unpublished manuscript) he found that

> in these two relatively small samples we find considerable variability of personality, with only a few characteristics being really widespread in the groups. However, there are many small clusters of individuals within each of the cultures which have characteristics in common. In many of these cases no similar clusters are found in the other cultures. Differences between the

cultures do exist and are fairly numerous, demonstrating the effect of culture on personality quite conclusively. However, the differences are far out-numbered by the similarities, so that we may justifiably conclude that the two cultures were more alike than different with respect to personality.

The influence of culture on personality does not appear to create a common personality configuration in its members, but instead tends to foster a variety of personality tendencies in small groups or clusters of individuals while leaving many aspects of personality free to vary without respect to group membership.

The studies reviewed above and others, such as those of Lantis (62), Lewis (65), and Honigmann (40), do not in general provide conclusive evidence with regard to the modal-personality hypothesis. They do in-dicate that societies differ somewhat in the personality characteristics that are found most frequently in them but in the absence of adequate cross-cultural studies it is difficult to say how great these differences are. In addition, most of the studies suggest that personality variability within societies is very large. This heterogeneity indicates that the very simple model which has been utilized in the culture and personality field of a modal type around which all but a few deviants tend to cluster may be an incorrect one and that simplistic theories which are closer to the actual empirical findings will have to be developed. The past decade in the culture and personality field may in one sense be regarded as a moving away from the simple theories of cultural determinism to more sophisti-cated and elaborate as well as less confident theories about the nature and extent of personality diversity in different societies and of homoge-neity within societies. The suggestion of Inkeles and Levinson (47) that societies may have multiple modes rather than a single one is a move-ment in this direction. Gardner Murphy's statement (84) perhaps best sums up the situation:

> The conception of the almost limitless flexibility of human nature has been encouraged greatly by the observations of anthropologists, who have taught us to be skeptical regarding the picture of a uniform essential nature. Our psychological methods of analysis have arisen in the western world; anthro-pologists offer observations which appear to suggest that very different kinds of human nature can be organized and cultivated in different cultural areas. Quite aside from what the anthropological observers themselves have to say, which is often more cautious and critical than what their readers have to say, there seems to be much to suggest that people may become almost anything. Human beings may be essentially gentle and cooperative, like the mountain Arapesh described by Margaret Mead (1937), or savagely competitive, like the Manus of the Admiralty Islands; they may be intensely individualistic, like the plains Indians described by Ruth Benedict (1934), or intensely group minded, like the Pueblo Indians of the Southwest. . . .
>
> Actually, it seems from the vantage point of 1954 that these anthropo-

logical studies have been much overinterpreted. . . . As in so many other cases, many psychologists were caught for a while in a dream induced by the fascinating nature of the new material, for which they had no adequate conceptual framework, and sometimes by the desire to separate the social life of man as widely as possible from the life of his humbler brethren of the mammalian genera. . . . Men do not behave like cedars, earthworms, cats, or elephants; they behave like men. All cultures work with raw human material; in every culture the educative process fails when it stretches human nature too far. We are very flexible, but not putty for the window mender, nor clay for the potter (pages 628, 629).

## SUMMARY AND CONCLUSIONS

This paper has been concerned mainly with two different but related issues that may be said to dominate the field of personality and social structure at the present time. One of these issues, which has been the principal focus of the second part of the chapter, is the nature of the relationships between societal systems and personality. While methodological problems occupied most of our attention, the issue behind them had to do with the extent of the influences of sociocultural systems on personality. The empirical question which has still to be investigated adequately is whether essentially different kinds of "human nature" are created either as a result of the varying conditions of development and existence in the world's societies or in order to satisfy the diverse requirement for participation in and support of these societies. It has undoubtedly been clear that our prejudices in this matter are in favor of the view that human nature is solidly anchored in a biological organism and that personality characteristics resulting from human biology overshadow in importance the special characteristics attributable to the particular social patterns in which development occurs. According to this view the study of the characteristics of the species, man, is a primary task which can, however, be accomplished only when the exact nature and extent of the variability of personality according to social patterns is understood.

The first part of the paper was concerned with the requirements sociocultural systems make on personality. The necessity that conformity and compliance to differing social requirements be voluntary and individually motivated appears to be at odds with the above conception. It was shown, however, that the quite diverse behaviors of individuals in different societies do not necessarily have their basis in similarly varying personality characteristics. Instead, the key to the diversity of behavior was seen to lie in the existence of any one of a small number of motivational tendencies which could be found in any society in the world.

## BIBLIOGRAPHICAL REFERENCES

1. Abel, Theodora M., and Hsu, F. L. K., "Some aspects of the personality of Chinese as revealed by the Rorschach Test," *J. Proj. Techniques,* Vol. 13 (1949), pp. 285–301.

2. Aberle, D. F., "Social system and socialization," Paper delivered at Conference on Cross-Cultural Research on Personality Development, Kansas City, Mo., May, 1955.

3. Aberle, D. F., and Naegele, K. D., "Middle-class fathers' occupational roles and attitudes toward children," *Amer. J. Orthopsychiat.,* Vol. 22 (1952), pp. 366–378.

4. Ackerman, N. W., "Social role and total personality," *Amer. J. Orthopsychiat.,* Vol. 21 (1951), pp. 1–17.

5. Baldwin, A. L., *The psychological process underlying behavioral conformity,* Paper delivered at Conference on Cross-Cultural Research on Personality Development, Kansas City, Mo., May, 1955.

6. Barnouw, V., "Acculturation and personality among the Wisconsin Chippewa," *Amer. Anthrop.,* Vol. 52 (1950), Pt. 2, Memoir 72.

7. Bateson, G., "Cultural and thematic analysis of fictional films," *Trans. N. Y. Acad. Sci.,* Ser. II, Vol. 5 (1943), pp. 72–78.

8. Bateson, G., and Mead, Margaret, *Balinese character: A photographic analysis,* New York, N. Y. Acad. of Sci., 1942.

9. Benedict, Ruth, *Patterns of culture,* Boston, Houghton Mifflin, 1934.

10. Bettelheim, B., "Individual and mass behavior in extreme situations," in T. M. Newcomb and E. L. Hartley (eds.), *Readings in social psychology,* New York, Henry Holt, 1947, pp. 628–638.

11. Bidney, D., "Toward a psychocultural definition of the concept of personality," in S. S. Sargent, and Marian W. Smith (eds.), *Culture and personality,* New York, The Viking Fund, 1949, pp. 31–52.

12. Billig, D., Gillin, J., and Davidson, W., "Aspects of personality and culture in a Guatemalan community: Ethnological and Rorschach approaches," *J. Personal.,* Vol. 16 (1947–1948), pp. 153–187, 326–368.

13. Caudill, W., "Japanese American personality and acculturation," *Genet. Psychol. Monogr.,* Vol. 45 (1952), pp. 3–102.

14. Davis, A., and Havighurst, R. J., "Social class and color differences in child rearing," *Amer. Soc. Rev.,* Vol. 11 (1946), pp. 698–710.

15. de Laguna, Grace A., "Culture and rationality," *Amer. Anthrop.,* Vol. 51 (1949), pp. 379–391.

16. Dicks, H. V., "Personality traits and national socialist ideology," *Hum. Relat.,* Vol. 3 (1950), pp. 111–154.

17. Dicks, H. V., "Observations on contemporary Russian behaviour," *Hum. Relat.,* Vol. 5 (1952), pp. 111–175.

18. Du Bois, Cora, *The people of Alor,* Minneapolis, Univ. of Minn. Press, 1944.

19. Erikson, E. H., *Childhood and society,* New York, Norton, 1950.

20. Fromm, E., *Escape from freedom,* New York, Farrar and Rinehart, 1941.

21. Fromm, E., *Man for himself,* New York, Farrar and Rinehart, 1947.

22. Gardner, B. B., and Whyte, W. F., "The man in the middle: Position and problems of the foreman," *Appl. Anthrop.,* Vol. 4 (1945).

23. Gerth, H., and Mills, C. W., *Character and social structure,* New York, Harcourt, Brace, 1953.

24. Gladwin, T., and Sarason, S. B., *Truk: Man in paradise,* New York, The Viking Fund, 1953.

25. Gorer, G., "Themes in Japanese culture," *Trans. N. Y. Acad. Sci.*, Ser. II, Vol. 5 (1943), pp. 100–124.

26. Gorer, G., *The American people*, New York, Norton, 1948.

27. Gorer, G., and Rickman, J., *The people of Great Russia*, London, Crosset Press, 1949.

28. Gottschalk, L., Kluckhohn, C., and Angell, R., *The use of personal documents in history, anthropology, and sociology*, New York, Soc. Sci. Res. Council, Bull. 53, 1945.

29. Hallowell, A. I., "Aggression in Salteaux society," *Psychiatry*, Vol. 3 (1940), pp. 395–407.

30. Hallowell, A. I., *The Rorschach Test as a tool for investigating cultural variables and individual differences in the study of personality in primitive societies*, Rorschach Res. Exch., Vol. 5 (1941), pp. 31–34.

31. Hallowell, A. I., "The Rorschach technique in the study of culture and personality," *Amer. Anthrop.*, Vol. 47 (1945), pp. 195–210.

32. Harding, C. F., "A plea for an anthropological approach to the study of personality," *Human Org.*, Vol. 12 (1953), pp. 13–16.

33. Havighurst, R. J., and Neugarten, Bernice L., *American Indian and white children: A sociopsychological investigation*, Chicago, Univ. of Chicago Press, 1955.

34. Henry, J., "Rorschach techniques in primitive cultures," *Amer. J. Orthopsychiat.*, Vol. 11 (1941), pp. 230–234.

35. Henry, J. "Symposium on: Projective testing in ethnography," *Amer. Anthrop.*, Vol. 57 (1955), pp. 245–247.

36. Henry, J., and Spiro, M. E., "Psychological techniques: Projective tests in field work," in A. L. Kroeber (ed.), *Anthropology Today*, Chicago, Univ. of Chicago Press, 1953, pp. 417–429.

37. Henry, W. E., "The thematic apperception technique in the study of culture-personality relations," *Genetic Psychol. Mono.*, Vol. 35 (1947), pp. 3–135.

38. Henry, W. E., "The business executive: The psycho-dynamics of a social role," *Amer. J. Soc.*, Vol. 54 (1949), pp. 286–291.

39. Henry, W. E., "Psychological tests in cross-cultural research," Paper delivered at Conference on Cross-Cultural Research on Personality Development, Kansas City, Mo., May, 1955.

40. Honigmann, J. J., *Culture and ethos of Kaska society*, New Haven, Yale Univ. Publications in Anthrop., No. 70, 1949.

41. Honigmann, J. J., *Culture and personality*, New York, Harper, 1954.

42. Horney, Karen, *New ways in psychoanalysis*, New York, Norton, 1940.

43. Horton, D., "The functions of alcohol in primitive societies: A cross-cultural study," *Quart. J. Stud. Alcohol*, Vol. 4 (1943), pp. 199–320.

44. Hughes, E. C., "Dilemmas and contradictions of status," *Amer. J. Soc.*, Vol. 50 (1945), pp. 353–359.

45. Inkeles, A., "Some sociological observations on culture and personality studies," in C. Kluckhohn, H. A. Murray, and D. M. Schneider (eds.), *Personality in nature, society, and culture*, 2nd ed., New York, Knopf, 1953, pp. 577–592.

46. Inkeles, A., "Social change and social character: The role of parental mediation," *J. Soc. Issues*, Vol. 11 (1955), pp. 12–23.

47. Inkeles, A., and Levinson, D. J., "National character: The study of modal personality and sociocultural systems," in G. Lindzey (ed.), *Handbook of social psychology*, Cambridge, Addison-Wesley, 1954, pp. 977–1020.

48. Joseph, Alice, and Murray, Veronica F., *Chamorros and Carolinians of Saipan: Personality studies*, Cambridge, Harvard Univ. Press, 1951.

49. Joseph, Alice, Spicer, R. B., and Chesky, Jane, *The desert people: A study of the Papago Indians,* Chicago, Univ. of Chicago Press, 1949.

50. Kaplan, B., "The modal personality hypothesis tested in four cultures," Unpublished doctoral dissertation, Harvard Univ., 1949.

51. Kaplan, B., "A study of Rorschach responses in four cultures," *Pap. Peabody Museum of Arch. and Ethnol.,* Harvard Univ., Vol. 42 (1954), 2.

52. Kaplan, B., and Plaut, T., *Personality in a communal society: An analysis of the mental health of the Hutterites,* Lawrence, Social Science Studies, Univ. Kansas, 1956.

53. Kardiner, A., *The individual and his society. With a foreword and two ethnological reports by R. Linton,* New York, Columbia Univ. Press, 1939.

54. Kardiner, A., "The concept of basic personality structure as an operational tool in the social sciences," in R. Linton (ed.), *The science of man in the world crisis,* New York, Columbia Univ. Press, 1945, pp. 107–122.

55. Kardiner, A. (with the collaboration of R. Linton, Cora Du Bois, and J. West), *The psychological frontiers of society,* New York, Columbia Univ. Press, 1945.

56. Kardiner, A., and Ovesey, L., *The mark of oppression: A psychological study of the American Negro,* New York, Norton, 1951.

57. Klineberg, O., *Tensions affecting international understanding,* New York, Soc. Sci. Res. Council, Bull. 62, 1950.

58. Kluckhohn, C., "Culture and behavior," in G. Lindzey (ed.), *Handbook of social psychology,* Cambridge, Addison-Wesley, 1954, pp. 921–976.

59. Kluckhohn, C., and Leighton, Dorothea, *The Navaho,* Cambridge, Harvard Univ. Press, 1946.

60. Kracauer, S., *From Caligari to Hitler,* Princeton, Princeton Univ. Press, 1947.

61. La Barre, W., "Some observations on character structure in the Orient: The Chinese," *Psychiatry,* Vol. 9 (1946), pp. 375–395.

62. Lantis, Margaret, "Nunivak Eskimo personality as revealed in the mythology," *Anthrop. Pap. Univ. Alaska,* Vol. 2 (1953), pp. 109–174.

63. Leighton, Dorothea, and Kluckhohn, C., *Children of the people,* Cambridge, Harvard Univ. Press, 1947.

64. Lessa, W. A., and Spiegelman, M., *Ulithian personality as seen through ethnological materials and thematic test analysis,* Berkeley, Univ. of Calif. Publications in Culture and Society, 2, 1954.

65. Lewis, O., *Life in a Mexican village: Tepoztlan restudied,* Urbana, Univ. of Illinois Press, 1951.

66. Linton, R., "Problems of status personality," in S. S. Sargent and Marian W. Smith (eds.), *Culture and personality,* New York, The Viking Fund, 1949, pp. 163–173.

67. Lynd, R. S., *Knowledge for what,* Princeton, Princeton Univ. Press, 1946.

68. McClelland, D. C., *Personality,* New York, Dryden Press, 1954.

69. McGranahan, D. V., and Wayne, I., "German and American traits reflected in popular drama," *Hum. Relat.,* Vol. 1 (1948), pp. 429–455.

70. MacGregor, G., *Warriors without weapons,* Chicago, Univ. of Chicago Press, 1946.

71. MacKinnon, D. W., "The structure of personality," in J. McV. Hunt (ed.), *Personality and the behavior disorders,* New York, Ronald Press, 1944, pp. 3–48.

72. Mead, G. H., *Mind, self, and society,* Chicago, Univ. of Chicago Press, 1934.

73. Mead, Margaret, *Coming of age in Samoa,* New York, Morrow, 1928.

74. Mead, Margaret, *Growing up in New Guinea,* New York, Morrow, 1930.

75. Mead, Margaret, *Sex and temperament in three primitive societies,* New York, Morrow, 1935.

76. Mead, Margaret, *And keep your powder dry: An anthropologist looks at America,* New York, Morrow, 1942.

77. Mead, Margaret, *The Mountain Arapesh.. Vol. V: The record of Unabelin with Rorschach analysis,* New York, Anthrop. Pap. Amer. Mus. of Nat. Hist., 1949.

78. Mensh, I., and Henry, J., "Direct observation and psychological tests in anthropological field work," *Amer. Anthrop.,* Vol. 55 (1953), pp. 461–480.

79. Merton, R., *Social theory and social structure,* Glencoe, Ill., The Free Press, 1949, pp. 151–160.

80. Merton, R., and Kitt, A. S., "Contribution to the theory of reference group behavior," in R. Merton and P. F. Lazarsfeld (eds.), *Continuities in social research,* Glencoe, Ill., The Free Press, 1950, pp. 40–105.

81. Mowrer, O. H., *Learning theory and personality dynamics,* New York, Ronald Press, 1950.

82. Murdock, G. P., *Social structure,* New York, Macmillan, 1949.

83. Murphy, G., "The internalization of social controls," in M. Berger, T. Abel, and C. H. Page (eds.), *Freedom and control in modern society,* New York, D. Van Nostrand, 1954, pp. 3–17.

84. Murphy, G., "Social motivation," in G. Lindzey (ed.), *Handbook of social psychology,* Cambridge, Addison-Wesley, 1954, pp. 601–633.

85. Newcomb, T. M., *Social psychology,* New York, Dryden Press, 1950.

86. Orlansky, H., "Infant care and personality," *Psychol. Bull.,* Vol. 46 (1949), pp. 1–48.

87. Parsons, T., *Essays in sociological theory,* Glencoe, The Free Press, 1949, pp. 185–100.

88. Parsons, T., *The social system,* Glencoe, Ill., The Free Press, 1951.

89. Parsons, T., "The superego and the theory of social systems," *Psychiatry,* Vol. 15 (1952), pp. 15–25.

90. Parsons, T., "Psychology and sociology," in J. Gillin (ed.), *For a science of social man,* New York, Macmillan, 1954, pp. 67–101.

91. Parsons, T., Bales, R. F., and Shils, E. A., *Working papers in the theory of action,* Glencoe, Ill., The Free Press, 1953.

92. Parsons, T., Bales, R. F., and collaborators, *Family, socialization and interaction process,* Glencoe, Ill., The Free Press, 1955.

93. Parsons, T., and Shils, E. A., *Toward a general theory of action,* Cambridge, Harvard Univ. Press, 1951.

94. Piers, G., and Singer, M. B., *Shame and guilt: A psychoanalytic and a cultural study,* Springfield, Ill., Charles C Thomas, 1953.

95. Riesman, D., *The lonely crowd,* New Haven, Yale Univ. Press, 1950.

96. Roheim, G., "The origin and function of culture," *Nervous and Mental Disease Mono.,* Vol. 63 (1943), pp. 1–107.

97. Roheim, G., *Psychoanalysis and anthropology,* New York, International Univ. Press, 1950.

98. Sanford, N., *Surface and depth in the individual personality,* Presidential address, Div. Eight of the Amer. Psychol. Assoc., San Francisco, Sept., 1955.

99. Sapir, E., "The emergence of the concept of personality in the study of culture," *J. of Soc. Psychol.,* Vol. 5 (1934), pp. 408–415.

100. Sapir, E., "Cultural anthropology and psychiatry," in D. G. Mandelbaum

(ed.), *Selected writings of Edward Sapir in language, culture and personality,* Berkeley, Univ. of Calif. Press, 1949.

101. Schneider, D. M., "Social dynamics of physical disability in army basic training," *Psychiatry,* Vol. 10 (1947), pp. 323–333.

102. Schneider, D. M., "Review of T. Gladwin and S. Sarason, *Truk: Man in paradise," Amer. Anthrop.,* Vol. 57 (1955), pp. 1098–1099.

103. Smith, M. B., "Anthropology and psychology," in J. Gillin (ed.), *For a science of social man,* New York, Macmillan, 1954, pp. 32–66.

104. Spiro, M., "Culture and personality: The natural history of a false dichotomy," *Psychiatry,* Vol. 15 (1951), pp. 19–46.

105. Stouffer, S. A., "An analysis of conflicting social norms," *Amer. Soc. Rev.,* Vol. 14 (1949), pp. 707–717.

106. Stouffer, S. A., Suchman, E. A., Divinney, L. C., Star, Shirley A., and Williams, R. M., *The American soldier: Adjustment during army life,* Princeton, Princeton Univ. Press, 1949.

107. Thompson, Laura, and Joseph, Alice, *The Hopi way,* Chicago, Univ. of Chicago Press, 1944.

108. Thompson, Laura, "Perception patterns in three Indian tribes," *Psychiatry,* Vol. 14 (1951), pp. 255–263.

109. Vogt, E. Z., "Navaho veterans: A study of changing values," *Pap. Peabody Museum of Arch. and Ethnol.,* Harvard Univ., Vol. 41 (1951), 1.

110. Wallace, A. F. C., *The modal personality structure of the Tuscarora Indians as revealed by the Rorschach test,* Smithsonian Inst., Bur. of Amer. Ethn., Bull. 150, 1952.

111. Wallace, A. F. C., "Review of *Ulithian personality as seen through ethnological materials and thematic test analysis," Amer. Anthrop.,* Vol. 57 (1955), pp. 392–393.

112. Waller, W., *The sociology of teaching,* New York, Wiley, 1932.

113. White, R. W., *Lives in progress,* New York, Dryden Press, 1952.

114. Whiting, J. W. M., and Child, I. L., *Child training and personality,* New Haven, Yale Univ. Press, 1945.

115. Wolfenstein, Martha, and Leites, N., *Movies: A psychological study,* Glencoe, Ill., The Free Press, 1950.

*chapter* **5**

# Collective behavior

HERBERT BLUMER

*University of California*

The field of collective behavior has not been charted effectively. The original effort to organize this area was made by R. E. Park and E. W. Burgess in their *Introduction to the Science of Sociology*. Following in their tradition is a section on "Collective Behavior" by H. Blumer in *New Outline of the Principles of Sociology*, edited by A. M. Lee. Individual chapters in several introductory texts deal with the field of collective behavior in the same line of thought. The only book to bear the title "Collective Behavior," by R. LaPiere, represents a markedly different conception of the field. Interest in the field of collective behavior is unquestionably increasing. Yet, although much has been added to our knowledge of separate topics within the last two decades no significant contribution has been made to the general analysis of collective behavior.[*]

[*] Too recent to be discussed in this chapter is a volume, *Collective Behavior* by Ralph H. Turner and Lewis M. Killian (Prentice-Hall, 1957) which presents an excellent treatment of the field of collective behavior.

Gerth and Mills made a limited attempt in this direction (50). Glick touches briefly on the matter in his article on "Collective Behavior and Race Relations" (52). Strauss calls attention indirectly to the inadequacies of development in the field (144). The field is clearly in need of systematic conceptual analysis—an analysis that will establish a basic rationale, lay out the separate areas of important interest, and show their generic relationship. In this article the author merely follows his own plan of organization and scheme of analysis.

Before surveying the literature of the past decade dealing with phases of collective behavior it is desirable to explain the nature of the field. The explanation will help to distinguish collective behavior from other major matters of sociological concern and to locate its position in the general study of human group life.

In its broad sense the term "collective behavior" refers to the behavior of two or more individuals who are acting together, or collectively. Each is under the influence of the other and fits his line of action to that of the other. Behavior is collective or concerted as opposed to a mere addition of the separate lines of individual activity. Such articulation of individual lines of action may be direct as in the case of face-to-face association or indirect as in the case of an extended division of labor.

To conceive collective behavior in this broad way would be to make it embrace all of group life. The essence of group life, whether in small groups or large societies, is precisely acting together. Nothing is gained, however, in viewing collective behavior as covering the full area of sociological interest and study. There is need of delineating collective behavior as a special and restricted field inside of the general study of human group life. This should not be done arbitrarily, but in such a way as to respect the threads of similarity running through the array of topics usually grouped under collective behavior. In my judgment the easiest way of setting the field apart is to distinguish collective behavior from (a) small group behavior and (b) established or culturally defined behavior.

The groups which we have in mind in speaking of collective behavior are sizable, as in the case of crowds, riots, panics, revolutionary movements, mass audiences, and national publics. Similarly, the kinds of activity with which we are concerned involve the participation of relatively large numbers of people, as in crazes, manias, collective enthusiasm and excitement, fashion, public opinion, revivals, and mass communication. To distinguish behavior in larger groups from that in small groups is not a mere matter of convenience or expedience. Instead, such a distinction points to a *collective* factor which comes from larger size—a factor which cumulatively assumes generic distinctiveness.

One can detect the character of this "collective" factor along three lines. First, it arises as a sense of transcending power when one identifies himself with a large group or participates wittingly in a large group enterprise. This sense of the "collective" serves to support, reinforce, influence, inhibit, or suppress the individual participant in his activity. This sense of the collective enters into the control of individual activity. In small groups the narrow sphere of action allows the individual to act with a greater sense of personal control or a fuller sense of command over the scene of operation. In the broader sphere of action in large associations the individual is subject to constriction of this personal control or command, whether in the form of inhibition that comes from the involvement of larger numbers, whether in the greater indiscriminate release that is yielded by rapport with a large number of like-minded people, or whether in the uncertainty of action in a varied and broad association. Even though operating vaguely and in largely uncharted ways the sense of the collective points to an important dimension of large group activity.

Second, association in large groups sets up forms of relations different from those in small groups. In small groups, relations of members are immediate, direct, and restricted to specific individuals. In the large group, relations tend in measure to be indirect, segmental, and orientated toward broad categories of peoples. This difference has obvious effect on the process of interaction and on forms of communication. In the immediate contacts in small groups interaction rests on personal confrontation and follows the pattern of a dialogue, with controlled interpretation by each participant of the action of the other. The shift in the larger enterprise from personal confrontation and from the dialogue pattern opens the door to new and different forms of interaction. Some of these are the uncontrolled circular reaction, such as occurs in the psychological crowd; the mediated or chainlike transmission as in a social movement; the one-way type of communication without a dialogue pattern, as in mass communication; the two-way communication without dialogue interplay, frequently apparent in the formation of public opinion. Such different forms of interaction and communication represent a social arrangement quite distinct from that of the small group. They point to an important dimension of the collective.

A third reflection of the collective factor in the case of large groups is the organization on which they must rely when mobilizing for action. A small group uses confined, simple, and direct machinery. Corporate action in a large group requires the articulation of more units which are also likely to be more diverse, more removed from each other, and related through bridging links which in themselves have a different positional and functional nature. The mobilization of this extended, diversified, and indirectly connected organization requires forms of leadership, coordination, and control which, again, differ from those in small groups. Such instrumentalities of action as incitation, agitation, gaining attention, the development of morale, the manipulation of discontent, the overcoming of apathy and resistance, the fashioning of group images, and the development of strategy are different in the large enterprise. To be successful these devices must respect the collective nature of the larger entity that has to act corporately.

These few remarks should suffice to suggest the presence of a new dimension—a collective dimension—that comes with larger acting groups. This collective dimension implies a different framework of relations between the participating members, different forms of interaction, and different ways of mobilizing for corporate activity. A major task confronting workers in the field of collective behavior is to establish the basic patterns in such relations, to delineate the major forms of interaction, and to trace the different generic ways in which collectivities become organized for action.

We may turn now to the second way in which the field of collective behavior is set apart. There is little generic difference between human groups—whether small or large—if their activity is controlled by established rules, definitions or norms, or if their organization is set by such established regulations. An understanding of human groups which are organized in this manner requires little more than an identification of the controlling cultural definitions. Most large group activity and structure in human societies is an expression of such cultural definitions. Indeed, the study of such regularized activity and structure has been the predominant concern in sociology. Collective behavior, as I see it, lies outside of this area of cultural prescription. Instead, it is concerned with large group activity that comes into being and develops along lines that are not laid out by pre-established social definitions. Such activity and the organization of people which it presupposes are formed or forged to meet undefined or unstructured situations. This is true in such typical cases of collective behavior as crowd behavior, the formation of public opinion, the shift in popular interest in music, literature, and entertainment, the operation of fashion, the generation of social unrest, and the rise of a social movement. The characteristic behavior of each such instance is not an expression of a pre-established prescription but is produced out of a forging process of interaction.

These distinctions which result from contrasting large groups with small groups, and forged activity with prescribed activity, set a framework for the field of collective behavior. The major tasks in this framework are to identify the forms of interaction in unstructured large groups, to establish a generic classification of such collectivities, to isolate the natural line of formation of each type of collectivity, and to ascertain the nature of the processes or "mechanisms" essential to the activity of the given type of collectivity.

It should be pointed out that collective behavior as I have sketched it is becoming more extended and more important in contemporary society. Modern society is moving steadily toward "large-scale" organization. Likewise, its activities and structure are ceasing to be expressions of established prescriptions and, instead, are being built up to meet a changing world. I suspect that sociologists and other students of human group life will be forced increasingly to approach the study of the contemporary world inside of a framework of collective behavior.

The report which follows seeks to depict the literature in the field of collective behavior during the past decade. It has not been possible to do this in any thorough way. First, the writing is scattered widely through all kinds of publications, without any charts which might aid one to bring them together. I am sure that I have missed many items that have merit. Second, the literature is most voluminous. To cite all of it would yield a huge tome. I have had to be very selective. In doing so, I reflect the limitations of my own assessment. Finally, there are many areas in the field of collective behavior in which little or nothing has been written in the last decade. Thus, the presentation which follows diverges considerably from an ideal full outline of the field.

## CROWDLIKE BEHAVIOR

Crowd behavior is commonly recognized as an elementary but very important form of collective behavior. Its elementary nature is suggested by its short life, its spontaneity, its simple forms of emotional interplay, its lack of the delicate and complicated alignment that occurs between self-conscious individuals, and its lack of any intricate organization. The importance of crowd behavior lies along two lines. First, the crowd has profound possibilities of dissolving individual organization, freeing individuals from the arresting hold of given group values and thus preparing them to disregard, attack, or undermine the values in given areas of the established social order. Second, the crowd is a means of energizing group action by arousing strong collective feelings as in the case of enthusiasm, courage, and glee. Latent with strong destructive and constructive potentialities the crowd is an important collectivity, particularly in societies undergoing transformation.

Despite this importance the literature of the last decade is marked by a paucity of serious analysis of the nature of the crowd, the conditions which induce it, and the manner in which its influences are exercised. Where discussion of crowd behavior is undertaken the treatment is conventional, showing little realistic understanding or insight beyond what has come to be stock knowledge, and suffering, usually, from arbitrary speculative interpretation. Somewhat typical is the account of crowd and mob behavior given by Doob (39). Swanson (145) has made the most serious effort to get at some of the mechanisms of the crowd through a simulated laboratory study. The results of his study are inconclusive in the light of the variety of crowds in actual life. Festinger, Pepitone, and Newcomb (45) have advanced an interesting thesis of the crowd from the standpoint of a process of deindividuation.

If little attention has been given to the analysis of the crowd as such, much consideration has been devoted to specific kinds of crowds or crowd behavior. One instance of this analysis is the treatment of rumor. Rumor is one form through which incipient crowd mindedness is expressed. A definitive work on rumor by Allport and Postman appeared in 1947 (3), built largely from studies undertaken during World War II but also covering much of the literature. It presented theoretical interpretations which have been adopted widely. Chorus (25) and Peterson and Gist (114) have added corrections to the Allport-Postman analysis while accepting the main tenets of these authors. Schall (127) was led through a sociometric study to discount the importance of the social position of the individual in the transmission of rumor and to lodge more importance on personality dynamics. In a study of stock market rumors Rose (124) has endeavored to isolate their role in the behavior of the market. The formidable amount of study devoted to rumor in recent years is particularly impressive in contrast to the infrequent attention given this topic before 1940. Although noteworthy advances have been made in our understanding of the mechanics of their transmission and of their transformation one must recognize that much remains to be known about their nature, particularly of their collective role and function. We have little definitive analysis of the collective conditions and preoccupations of the group that hinder or favor the occurrence of rumors. We need much more meaningful classifications of rumors. We need a fuller knowledge of the role of rumor in organizing and orienting groups to action. We need to know how individuals view, assess, and handle rumors. It is very likely that fruitful extension of our knowledge of rumor will require a significant shift in the way in which this matter is currently being studied.

Panic is another form of crowd behavior that has been given much attention in recent years. Since Strauss (143) surveyed the literature in 1944 much has been written. With the exception of studies of disaster the writings have largely lacked a basis in the empirical observation of actual instances of panic. There have been a number of studies of simulated panic situations. The high degree of controversy marking the literature indicates that treatment is still chiefly on the level of speculative interpretation. One major line of controversy is whether panic behavior is irrational ("nonadaptive") or based on reasonable individual perception. Foreman (46) presents detailed explanations of the antecedent conditions and causes of panic, based on the first of these ideas. In contrast, Mintz (108) argues that panic behavior is not a result of disorganized emotion. He contends, instead, that it represents a breakdown of cooperation in the course of which a reward structure arises which places a premium on individual efforts of self-protection. Leeper (90) has sought to develop a motivational theory of emotion to replace the idea of emotion as a disorganized response. Gilbert (51) reflects the return to a collective interpretation in ascribing panic behavior to a sudden collapse of group values. It is evident that much more groundwork is needed in the study of actual panic situations. Seemingly, the most fruitful inquiry lies along the line of how people in a panic situation regain measures of control of themselves. This indirect approach offers good possibilities of revealing the mechanisms of panic formation.

Much attention has also been given in recent years to the topic of riots, chiefly as a result of increased interest in ethnic relations and civil rights. A number of race riots have been the object of study. Best known is the study by Lee and Humphrey of the race riot in Detroit (88). Clark (27) presents an article dealing with a race riot in Harlem, New York City. Gremley seeks to explain the Cicero, Illinois, race riot (55). Dahlke (33) endeavors to construct a typology by comparing the 1943 riot in Detroit with a Russian riot against the Jews in 1903. Clark and Barker (28) present a study of a participant in "zoot-suit" riots. Interesting materials are given by Bontemps and Convoy in their book, *They Seek a City* (20). The most fruitful knowledge seems to have been yielded along the line of the control of riots. The materials prepared by Lohman (100) represent the best statement. Despite the work on riots, of which the above citations are typical, there are large gaps in our knowledge. No effort has been undertaken to study systematically the wide range of different kinds of riots. We need an effective classification of riots along generic lines. Work in this direction would also offer good prospects of yielding a more penetrating understanding of the mechanisms involved in riot formation.

Students of the crowd are aware of an assortment of crowdlike phenomena of great importance, such as so-called "mass hysteria," manias and crazes, collective excitement, collective alarms, and mass fears. In many ways these more extended, diffuse, and vague forms of collective behavior are far more important in our modern type of world than the more specific and restricted crowd phenomena considered above. Little study, however, is given to them. The recent literature on them is very sparse. A few of the more suggestive studies may be cited. Meerloo (106) has presented a monograph on mass delusion. Johnson (71) writes about a specific instance of mass hysteria—that which developed around the "phantom anesthetist" of Mattoon, Illinois. Schuler and Parenton describe an hysterical outbreak in a Louisiana high school (131). Hackett has dealt briefly with the "flying saucer" (56). Myers (111) considers anti-communist hysteria. Jeffreys has undertaken an interesting analysis of the "African Tarantual or Dancing Mania" (70). This broad area of marginal crowd behavior, just because it is studied so little in any concerted and systematic way, offers the highest possibilities of fruitful returns for study. With the increasing formation of a vast mass society the circulating and pulsating currents of crowdlike disturbance become very important in influence. They set social climates, determine institutional preoccupation, lead to shifts in the power structure, and affect vitally political decisions. Through sheer necessity they will undoubtedly come to gain in the future the degree of careful study which is so markedly absent today.

Any embracing study of the crowd should consider the general conditions conducive to the formation of crowds and the emergence of crowd-like behavior. Scarcely any serious attention has been given to this phase of the topic. While we recognize the intimate connection of crowds to conditions of social disturbance and disorganization, such conditions have not been studied carefully. Thus while we have an extensive literature on social disorganization and on the philosophical side of the crises of modern civilization this literature offers little of value for understanding the general social setting of crowd behavior. Only a few studies have, at the best, some tenuous relations to the problem. Bettelheim (14) gives an interesting account of individual and mass behavior in the tense situation of a concentration camp. Killian (72) relates the crisis situations in disaster to latent conflicts between group loyalties. Robinson (120) reports on the way in which social disorganization was reflected in the dancing and drinking patterns of middle class society. Lipset (99) has studied the opinion formation and attitudes of university students during a vivid oath controversy. The large questions of the nature of social crisis and disturbance and of how they foster different kinds of crowd mindedness and behavior have not been dealt with.

The above survey of recent literature on the crowd, while necessarily omitting a large number of bibliographical references, gives a typical picture of the character of current contributions. It is evident that little progress is being made in analyzing the generic nature of the crowd and the kinds of behavior related to it. The retarded state of our knowledge in this area seems to be caused in part by the paucity of study of actual natural instances of crowd behavior. A current trend to set up simulated instances that will lend themselves to laboratory observation merits support. As yet, however, such studies have not been very fruitful. In a measure this points to the other major source of inadequacy in our knowledge of the crowd—the absence of a well-thought-out analytical scheme which would provide fruitful hypotheses and lead to more incisive observations.

## MASS BEHAVIOR

A second large area in the field of collective behavior is constituted by mass behavior. Older writers like LeBon and even recent writers like Ortega y Gassett have shown an inclination to regard mass behavior as if it were the same as crowd behavior. Currently, there is a growing recognition that it must be taken as generically distinct. As happens so frequently in the case of major topics in collective behavior, no satisfactory statement has been made of the generic nature of mass behavior. Blumer (16) regards the mass as being a large aggregation of anonymous individuals who are otherwise highly differentiated in terms of class position, stated occupation, ethnic affiliation, religious background, etc. Essentially they do not interact and collectively have no organization. Lederer (86) regards the mass primarily as a detribalized proletariat, showing the characteristic behavior of crowds. Wirth (154) has analyzed mass society in terms of the kind of consensus which it imposes and requires. Selznick has made a noteworthy contribution (133) in showing the relatively unguarded position of organizations in mass society. Still, despite an amazing growth of concern with mass society and some accretions of knowledge of mass behavior, a clear and penetrating analysis of the mass is a task before us. It seems clear that the framework for such an analysis will be based on the recognition of the following features: (1) vast numbers of diverse individuals, unknown to one another; (2) a vast array of highly different groups and local cultures; (3) great physical and mental mobility with a contingent weakening of traditional view and of affiliation with fixed groups; and (4) the development of large-scale organizations geared to the more extended, complicated, and shifting arena of operations. The analysis will be concerned with the difficult questions of how a mass is composed, how it operates, and what kinds of influence on social life are exerted by mass behavior. Current study is guided only in limited degrees by such generic considerations.

As one would suspect, the greatest amount of contemporary study in the area of mass behavior is directed to mass media of communication. The conspicuous place of the press, motion pictures, radio, and television in contemporary life has aroused great interest in their role. We can ignore the large literature concerned with questions of public policy in the case of such media. Similarly we can discard any consideration of the vast amount of descriptive literature concerned with the structure and operation of the different media, or with diverse quantitative data on the composition of mass audiences. Such accounts are rarely written with an eye to singling out the peculiar organization that is imparted to the media and their operation by virtue of having to serve a mass audience. Such treatment, were it to be given, would be of telling value to an analysis of mass behavior.

The relevant literature is concerned chiefly with audience reaction. But even here, in spite of many disparate studies, little analytical knowledge of mass behavior has been yielded. Two good collections of readings dealing in large part with mass communication have been prepared by Berelson and Janowitz (13) and Schramm (129). Klapper (75) has written on the comparative effects of mass media, dealing nicely with the topic of mass persuasion. A few representative examples of research in the field may be cited. Hovland, *et al.* (66) present a number of studies of the effects of various media used in the instruction of American soldiers, which include interesting findings on the immediate and long-range effects of motion pictures. Warner and Henry report on a lengthy study made of daytime radio serials (150). Janowitz (69) in his study of the local community newspapers in and around Chicago shows that the image which readers have of the newspapers is of great direct importance in determining how they are influenced by the newspapers. Somewhat related to this work are the findings of Kracauer in his studies of the influence of motion pictures. He calls attention in one study (77) to the fact that in portraying foreign characters motion pictures reflect the popular attitudes of the time, but that they also turn these vague attitudes into concrete images. In a study of a particular motion picture that sought to point out the futility of intergroup prejudice, Cooper and Dinerman (31) show the diverse and sometimes unexpected and undesired changes induced by the picture, depending on the initial orientation of the viewers. In a study of another picture, Hulett (67) has noted a kind of "propaganda sophistication" carried by movie-goers which leads to a discount of the manifest content of motion pictures. In a promising study of the reception given to the telecast of the 1952 political conventions Kurt and Gladys Lang (83) deal with the influence of the interaction among the viewers. Riley and Flowerman (118) stress the fact that the member of the audience of mass media does not react as an isolated or discrete individual but as a member of the groups to which he belongs and with which he communicates. This thesis is presented further by the senior author and his wife (119). It seems correct to say that the delineation of the mass through studies in mass communication lies ahead as a major task. The initial theoretical guidance needed to undertake this task is not reflected in the welter of separate and restricted studies of the current period.

A second important area of mass behavior is constituted by popular interests—popular songs, dances, and novels, and the play of fashion. The "popular" transcends the multitudinous differentiations of local groups and status identification. It represents one of the highly important focal points of group identity and group unity in a mass society. Its shifting character reflects the dynamic social setting to which it seems to be indigenously attached. In short, the realm of the popular is one of the most symptomatic expressions of a mass society. Its analysis would undoubtedly provide crucial insight into the nature of modern societies. Very little work has been done in this area—despite an increasing interest in the study of "popular culture." This situation is in part caused by the baffling question of where and how to break into the study of this area. The relevant literature of the past decade is sparse and disconnected. In his work on *The Lonely Crowd* Riesman has developed his well-known thesis of the growth of "other-mindedness" as an explanation of many phenomena of modern people, including their interest in the popular. Spaeth has given us a valuable history of popular music in America with many suggestive possibilities (137). Harvey has made an interesting study (58) of the content characteristics of best-selling novels. Employing a somewhat different approach Austin has sought to identify the types and trends among non-fiction best sellers (5). A suggestive volume on fashion has been written by Bell (11). The literature on fashion is admittedly lacking in significant analytical leads. Cobliner (29) has sought to ascertain through questionnaires given to college women why they conform to fashion. This type of motivational study has so far thrown no light on fashion as collective behavior. The study by Barber and Lobel (7) seems more promising. They regard costume as having a "role-symbolic" function. This aspect of fashion is, however, very limited. Crucial questions, such as the symbolism of new styles in relation to changes in vague taste, have not been undertaken. One promising line of attack is through the study of the control of fashion, particularly the limitations on this control. A beginning step in this direction has been made by the Schiffers (128).

It is of some interest to note the amount of interest in the subject of popular heroes. There were a surprising large number of works, several of book length, written on this topic in the early 1940's. Best known is the work by Sidney Hook (64). Meadows has sketched some of the social psychological features of the hero (104). Gallacher compares the ideal hero of antiquity with his counterpart in today's comic strip (47). Tumin has compared actual instances of a hero and a scapegoat in a Guatemalan peasant community (149). Speier in a trenchant article (140) complains of the absence of study of hero worship by social science, and offers the thesis that modern literate masses are inclined to choose as heroes those who are bent on destroying their political freedom. His analysis of modern hero worship merits reading. Seemingly the most careful and systematic studies of the popular hero are being made by Klapp. He has given us two important articles in which the popular hero is analyzed as a collective symbol (73, 74).

In an important and discernible way diverse attention is given to mass behavior in many of the works treated in subsequent sections of this report. Yet, despite the many-sided concern with mass behavior it is clear that scientific and scholarly study in this area is only in the beginning stages. There is definite need of an imaginative framework which, in being realistically grounded, will serve as a fruitful guide to significant inquiry, and as a cadre for coherent theoretical knowledge. This need is not merely academic but vital to an understanding of the mass-structured world into which we are increasingly moving.

## THE PUBLIC AND PUBLIC OPINION

Vigorous interest in public opinion and its study remains unabated. There is a continuous flow of literature on this topic. It should be noted, however, in introducing this section, that this preoccupation with the topic of public opinion has contributed very little to the identification and understanding of the public. There is clear need for treating the public as a generically distinct kind of collectivity. It should be set apart from the crowd and from the mass. The original set of distinctions between the public and the crowd made many years ago by Robert E. Park have not been improved or added to. Similarly, the simple differences drawn by the writer in 1937 between the public and the mass still remain without significant additions. It is unfortunate that such little interest is taken in trying to identify the characterisic makeup of the public. This kind of knowledge would have undoubted value in studying public opinion and in leading to a more incisive and realistic understanding of its place in the organization of social life. Because of the limited degree to which current literature on public opinion adds to general knowledge of collective behavior this section of the paper will be brief, in contrast to the large amount of literature.

In the general area of public opinion Speier has contributed an interesting article on the historical development of public opinion (138). His thesis is that it is a product of a middle class society. Cantril presents some interesting observations on the trend of opinion during World War II (24) which are suggestive with regard to certain features of the public. A theoretical analysis of the relation of communication and public opinion is undertaken by Berelson (12). These three works are representative of the relatively small amount of more serious attention devoted to the analysis of public opinion.

As one would suspect, the vast bulk of recent literature is concerned either directly or indirectly with public opinion polling. One focal point of concern is the improvement of the techniques of the poll. Dodd (34) offers a set of twelve tentative rules which he believes will lead to more effective prediction. Haner and Meier argue for the quota sampling method as the most sound in polling (57). Gallup explains the improvements in technique that correct for deficiencies in his polls of the presidential election in 1948 (48). A second concern is the relation of polling to the functioning of a democratic society. Ranney discusses this matter specifically (116). Leiserson contends that the opinion poll can aid in the formation of public policy only if it is designed to throw light on the political process as it actually functions (92). Third, there is a literature which is critical of public opinion polling. The best-known work is that by Lindsay Rogers (122). Blumer questions whether public opinion polling is actually dealing with public opinion in any realistic sense (17). Riesman and Glazer argue for the need of finding out the meaning of the respondents' answers and for the relating of answers to character structure (117). Rose (123) suggests a number of propositions for increasing the sophistication of public opinion polling. In an effort to assess the influence of social classes on public opinion Kornhauser introduces some critical comments on how to make more adequate studies of public opinion (76).

Note should be taken also of a number of studies which sought to lay bare some of the factors seemingly influencing the formation of opinion. In a study of student reactions to the University of California oath controversy Wilner and Fearing found a close relation between opinions and expected consequences of alternative solutions of the issue (152). In a related way Janis *et al.* found through a study of opinion on atomic bombs that an earlier optimistic message has produced a set resistance to a later pessimistic communication (68). Herzog presents findings to show some patterning of reasons in the case of those people who are for or against a proposal (62).

The foregoing sample instances from current literature reflect the limited manner and extent of actual concern with the problem of the public and of public opinion. Attention has become centered primarily on polling and on quasi-experimental studies of public opinion formation. Because of the restricted extent to which the public has been singled out as an object there is a minimum of work directed to outlining its nature and the ways in which it operates. This is clearly shown in the work on public opinion. By and large it is not viewed as a social process operating in a complicated social structure. Thus, little attention is paid to such crucial questions as to how public issues arise, how an opinion process begins with regard to such issues, and how the opinion is mobilized in preparation for decisions on the issues. Until study shifts to these larger natural matters, the results from current lines of concern are not likely to contribute much knowledge in this area of collective behavior.

## PROPAGANDA, PSYCHOLOGICAL WARFARE AND COMMUNIST TACTICS

We have observed that analytic study of the mass and of the public is infrequent and weak. There is, however, a prodigious literature dealing with a special line of effort to get control of masses, publics, and, indeed, of established societies. This special line of effort is constituted by propaganda, by "psychological warfare," and by totalitarian tactics. The great amount of study devoted to these forms and instances of control is, of course, a direct consequence of their importance in the contemporary episode of world history, marked by total wars, imperialistic expansion, domination of conquered peoples, totalitarian control, and the carrying on of "cold wars." The concern devoted to these matters is a very vivid instance of how pressing political and social events may direct lines of preoccupation in the social sciences.

The huge literature which has developed in the last decade around these topics has yielded a fair sum of knowledge in the field of collective behavior, but not in proportion to the amount of study. It is interesting to note, further, that these studies of propaganda, psychological warfare, and totalitarian tactics have frequently an adverse consequence in leading to distorted images of the public, the mass, and, indeed, of society. The distortion comes from viewing the public, the mass, and society as if they had a makeup that is limited solely to what is implied in the use of propaganda, psychological warfare, and totalitarian tactics. Thus, all too frequently, the public is treated as if little or no significance was attached to the moving play of discussion or to the flexible mobilization of effective public opinion—despite the fact that these are the chief ways in which the public operates. Similarly, the mass is frequently misconceived as devoid of a process of alternative selection by its members, although telling evidence indicates that such selection is the chief line of operation of the mass. Similarly—although of no concern in this article on collective behavior—society is frequently misrepresented in ignoring or minimizing the normal processes of institutional control and social interaction. More faithful knowledge—both of the nature of mass, public, and society, and of the nature of devices such as propaganda, etc.—would be yielded by studying the failures of such devices and the resistances to them. Propaganda, psychological warfare, and totalitarian tactics, where they are brought into play, are merely parts of a far larger defining process which is shaping the activities of people.

With these introductory comments we may approach the literature of the past decade. As indicated, the literature is voluminous. Reference will be made to only a small portion of the writings.

## A. Propaganda

The better of the general treatments of propaganda are given in four works: Kris and Leites (79), Doob (36), Lasswell (85), and Lerner (95). A scrutiny of such general treatments shows a need for discriminatory classification of propaganda. There is a tendency to handle it as a homogeneous matter and characterize it in terms of more spectacular instances. Classificatory analyses in terms of tasks, tools, organization of people to be influenced, and character of the situations would be of undoubted value in introducing a higher order of understanding. Suggestions of the possibilities of such a more differential approach are given in studies by Dowd and Domenach. Dowd (40) treats the reliance on art by the leaders of the French Revolution in mobilizing sentiment, in the absence of mass media such as we are familiar with in recent times. Domenach (35) traces how Lenin developed a scheme of propagandizing Marxian doctrine in an emerging international society.

Discussions of principles and techniques of propaganda are many. On the basis of a study of Goebbels' diary Doob (38) presents nineteen principles. Lasswell (84) approaches the problem through an analysis of mass insecurity. An article by Brecker (21) gets at the matter by comparing the lines of propaganda followed by the U.S.S.R., the U.S.A., and

Great Britain. Wilson (153) describes the techniques used by British industry in opposing the nationalization program of the British Labor Party. Efforts to delineate propaganda techniques through experimental study are typified by the following references. Cromwell and Kunkel (32) studied the effect of repeating the same oral propaganda after an interval of thirty days by comparing the results of the first and second presentations. Lumsdaine and Janis (102) made an interesting experimental comparison between the presentation of a single point of view and the presentation of that point of view accompanied by indication of opposing points of view. They found the latter presentation to have a more solid and stable effect. Bettelheim and Janowitz (15) took fifty army veterans whose "tolerance attitudes" were known and exposed them experimentally to anti-Semitic propaganda. They found that such propaganda was most likely to be effective if it was authoritative and objective and if it diminished anxieties. Although not in an experimental study, Mintz analyzed the results of trying to induce consumers to reduce consumption through propaganda appeals (109). He found that these efforts were ineffective unless the consumers reinforced each other in complying with the appeals. Kriesberg (78) studied a group of union members subjected to the cross-pressure of conflicting propaganda from Roman Catholic and Communist sources and presents some interesting examples of accommodation.

It appears that the study of propaganda needs to be guided chiefly by a fuller appreciation of the particular structure of the situation in which it is to be applied. This approach means an understanding not only of the cultural background of the people but of their mobilization to their world of current events. This latter point of concern is important for it covers the direction of attention and sensitivities of people, the organization of their feelings, "what is on their mind," and the area of incipient impulses and disturbed feelings and thought. These matters should be understood in terms of the structure of interaction between the individuals—the lines of firm definition, of conflicting definition, or of apathetic definition; the breakdown of established affirmations of value and the emergence of new circles of communication, with the shifts in prestige figures that this implies. Propaganda becomes a matter of feeling out soft or weak points in the organization of thought and feeling and of detecting the emergence of areas of new sensitivity and interest. These become the focal points for the definitions which propaganda seeks to introduce. Such a framework as this would offer greater likelihood of bringing the study of propaganda inside of the context of social life, instead of continuing it as an independent and self-contained activity.

### B. Psychological warfare

The broader area of psychological warfare has been subject to a great deal of attention, following in the wake of the outbreak of World War II with the dramatic use by Nazi Germany of psychological campaigns. An impressive number of books appeared on this topic in the early 1940's. In considering the period since then, attention is called first to a general treatment by Cohen (30) and a more definitive work by Linebarger (96). Speier, who has been conducting his main studies in this area, has given us a critical and stimulating assessment of psychological warfare (139). Doob (37) has sketched a topology of the factors in psychological warfare, indicating twenty-seven logically conceivable routes which such warfare might take. White outlines the similarities and the differences in the premises of psychological warfare as contained in the prewar propaganda of Hitler and Roosevelt (151). In a careful study, Shils and Janowitz deal with the disintegration of the German army in the face of the psychological attacks on them by the Allies (135). Boehm shows how the Soviets made use of German prisoners in their psychological warfare against Hitler (18). Herz (61) draws a series of guiding principles from his analysis of the use of leaflets in World War II.

The foregoing references are only a minute portion of writings on psychological warfare. This topic obviously is very broad and has many diverse aspects. Because of the immense practical importance of psychological warfare in the actual struggle of nations and people the work done in this area benefits from a strong empirical orientation. But this practical-mindedness seems also to be the source of its major weakness. Psychological warfare does not rest on any careful set of analytical premises. It needs a well-thought-out theoretical basis to bring meaningful order and direction to its operation. Its present status gives much justification to the charge that psychological warfare is effective only in the disintegration brought about by the application of superior military might. The guiding framework needed in psychological warfare will probably have to come from the more thorough study and analysis of social crisis and collective tension. The sources of strength of psychological warfare are contained in the general state of collective tension which exists, and its opportunities are set by the real or imagined crises which develop. Analysis of these focal theoretical topics seems to the writer as the best suited to developing a good analytical basis for the guidance of psychological warfare. Such analysis would also yield contributions to the knowledge of collective behavior that are given only sparsely and disconnectedly by current studies.

### C. Totalitarian tactics

The aggressive expansion of communism with new strategies of operation has given rise to a rich literature on the description and analysis of totalitarian tactics of both undermining and controlling peoples. Much of this literature is very pertinent to the topic of collective behavior since it is concerned with efforts to restrain and corrupt existing lines of established collective action and to mobilize people collectively in new directions. The most interesting body of such literature deals with the domination established by communism in its satellites in Eastern Europe. A series of good descriptive accounts are given by Bartlett (8), Mikolajczyk (107), Ciechanowski (26), Lane (82), and Ferenc Nagy (112). More pointed analyses of this conquest and domination are given by Tomasic (147), Raditsa (115), Taborsky (146), and Slendi (136). The expansion of Chinese communism has also given rise to a similar numerous set of works. The tactics used in domestic control by established communist regimes has also been well studied. Good treatments of such control in Soviet Russia are given by Hazard (59), Towster (148), and Fainsod (44). Two appropriate articles pertaining to such control in the case of communist China are given by Steiner (141, 142).

A more analytical account of the rationale, or working philosophy, behind communist strategy and tactics is given by Scott (132). Rossi unveils a good picture in his description of communist operations in France (126). A very incisive analysis is given by Selznick with particular reference to the problems of organization (133). A good account of the strategy of infiltration in Czechoslovakia has been prepared by Duchacek (41).

The insufficiency of space in this article does not permit even the sketchiest summary of the material on totalitarian tactics. Such tactics cover a far-reaching range of matters of importance in collective behavior, such as the generation of social unrest, agitation, recruitment of followers and sympathizers, propaganda, indoctrination, intimidation, use of terror, "brain washing," development of morale, the use of the purge, the undermining of established values, the grafting on of new ideologies, infiltration, the organized seizure of strategic organizational posts, the exercise of new forms of repressive controls, and the formation of new organizational networks. I have only one concluding observation to make. In my judgment the study of such tactics should be concerned not only with identifying their mechanics but with an analysis of the structure of social life which the given tactic seeks to affect. It must be recognized that these tactics are instruments operating on social life—their efficacy demands some sort of corresponding propitious structure of the social life. Thus, the study of the fate of the tactics can become a means of forming a more penetrating analysis of the nature of social life in its varying forms. It is probable that the study of failures in the use of tactics would be most fruitful in such analysis, for such failures point to resistance. In turn, such resistance stands for something hard and tangible in the makeup of social life—the sort of solid things that give character and being to the given form of group life, whether a society, institution, a public, a mass, or a crowd.

## SOCIAL MOVEMENTS

One of the most important areas in the field of collective behavior is constituted by social movements. There are many kinds of social movements. The range of their diversity is suggested by referring to a few types: revolutionary, reform, naturalistic, revival, messianic, nativistic, religious, cooperative, ideological and ethical. Whatever be its type, a social movement signifies either a collective effort to transform some given area of established social relations, or else a large unguided change in social relations involving, however unwittingly, large numbers of participants. In either case a social movement constitutes a very important form of collective behavior—it is a large-scale social enterprise or occurrence in which the behavior of people collectively is being built up or wrought out in new forms.

The intrinsic conditions of modern life are particularly conducive to the rise of social movements; and social movements are one of the chief ways through which modern societies are remade. In the face of such pervasive conditions as increasing social contacts, extending communications, technological innovation, mobility, institutional encroachment, and the breaking down of traditional cultural forms, people in modern societies are forced to seek new ways of living and to develop new kinds of social relations. It is not surprising that a great deal of this effort should give rise to collective enterprises which seek deliberately to achieve specific goals. But in addition to such organized and consciously directed movements there is another kind that is fostered even more by the dynamic character of modern society. I refer to the relatively undirected and essentially unorganized change of people in a common direction—as in the case of an extension of a democratic philosophy or the growth of interest in science. Such diffuse movements, without a directing leadership or an organized membership, are especially likely to arise and flourish in a world marked by dislocation and the play of new currents of communication. They are probably the most important type of movement.

There is no wide realization of the importance of social movements as an intrinsic formative device in modern society. Spectacular movements of grandiose dimensions, like the Nazi movement or the communist movement, have, of course, attracted enormous attention. But there is a disappointing amount of interest in dealing analytically with the whole broad field of social movements. Consequently, while the literature of the past decade relating to social movements is bulky, it is very unbalanced and leaves broad areas of the field untouched. There is only one volume which seeks to address the field as such. This excellent book by Heberle (60) is confined to movements with political objectives and does not deal with other important classes of movements. It stands out, however, as an effort to develop a comparative and systematic theory of social movements. Another unique effort along this line is the penetrating work of Hoffer (63); this work, however, is more in the nature of a thoughtful essay on the psychology of a given type of participant in mass movements than a systematic analysis of such movements. Meadows (105) has presented a series of interesting suggestions on the nature of social movements. Scarcely any other references can be made to works which endeavor to deal with the broad topic of social movements as such. One is forced to recognize that few social scientists have got the idea that there is a *field* of social movements that merits systematic scholarly study.

As one would suspect, most contemporary concern with social movements is focused on grandiose political movements of a revolutionary or quasi-revolutionary character—such as communism, fascism, and socialism. Further, most treatments of these broad movements are not strictly analytical; they deal, instead, with programs and ideologies or construct histories of the movements. Thus, while these accounts are frequently very thoughtful they rarely make any noticeable contribution to theoretical knowledge of social movements. A good example is the excellent work edited by Egbert and Persons on *Socialism and American Life* (42). This contains first-rate accounts of American socialism—many of which, indeed, provide original data usable for formulating propositions about movements. But the analytical discussions of generic aspects of movements are sparse.

The works which attempt general analysis of the broad mass movements usually move along two lines: (1) an explanation of the "causes" of the movement, generally in terms of psychological motivation or class structure, or (2) an analysis of the personality structure of the adherents of the movement. The work of Adorno *et al.* on *The Authoritarian Personality* (1) reflects the second of these two lines of treatment. This book has had a great influence in furthering a type of analysis cast in terms of personality structure. Several trenchant criticisms of this type of thesis have appeared. Reference is made here to only one of them, by Shils (134). A favorite line of psychological analysis is through the use of psychoanalytic theory. The recent work by Leites, *A Study of Bolshevism* (93), while more tempered than many kindred works, represents this type of treatment. On a more elevated plane and showing highly respectable scholarship is the work by Arendt on *The Origins of Totalitarianism* (1). Although not doctrinaire it still typifies an approach which endeavors to account in a quasi-historical manner for the origin and rise of a broad ideology.

While not detracting from the kind of treatment represented by these various works it is necessary to note that they ignore what seems to be so essential to social movements deliberately seeking change, namely, the intricate play of factors which must be skillfully employed to forge and direct a movement, as well as the fortuitous circumstances that facilitate their use. A consciously directed and organized movement cannot be explained merely in terms of the psychological disposition or motivation of people, or in terms of a diffusion of an ideology. Explanations of this sort have a deceptive plausibility, but overlook the fact that *a movement has to be constructed* and has to carve out a career in what is practically always an opposed, resistant, or at least indifferent world. Thus, conscious movements have to depend on effective agitation, the skillful fomentation and exploitation of restlessness and discontent, an effective procedure for the recruitment of members and followers, the formation of a well-knit and powerful organization, the development and maintenance of enthusiasm, conviction, and morale, the intelligent translation of ideology into homely and gripping form, the development of skillful strategy and tactics, and, finally, leadership which can size up situations effectively, time actions, and act decisively. These are the ingredients of successful movements. To ignore them through preoccupation with the "causes" of movements leads to inadequate and distorted knowledge.

A survey of the literature shows sparse and spotty concern with the "mechanisms," such as those just mentioned, which are used to build up a movement and guide its destiny. A fair amount of attention has been given to the problem of attracting people to a movement or to its ideology. This attention is turned predominantly, however, to the appeal of communism. A general account is attempted by Brown (23). Krugman (80) studied some fifty former members of the American Communist Party in an effort to isolate the appeal of communism to middle class intellectuals and trade unions. In another paper he reports on the psychoanalytic findings concerning thirty-five patients who were members of the American Communist Party, with focus on the role of hostility in responding favorably to communist appeal (81). Ehrmann deals with the appeal of communism to the French peasants (43). McCormack reviews and analyzes the literature on the motivation of radicals (103).

A little reflection should lead one to realize that the gaining of sympathetic support and the recruitment of followers for a movement involve much more than the psychological condition of individuals on one hand and, on the other, a set of "appeals" which are supposed to fit the psychological conditions. These two factors, or so-called variables, are important, and have to be taken into account. However, the gaining of sympathizers or members rarely occurs through a mere combination of a pre-established appeal and a pre-established individual psychological bent on which it is brought to bear. Instead, the prospective sympathizer or member has to be aroused, nurtured, and directed, and the so-called appeal has to be developed and adapted. This takes place through a process in which attention has to be gained, interests awakened, grievances exploited, ideas implanted, doubts disspelled, feelings aroused, new objects created, and new perspectives developed. To repeat, this comes not from mere contact of appeal and psychological disposition; it occurs from contact of person with person, in a structured social situation wherein people are interacting with one another. The so-called appeal has to compete with other appeals and further has to contend with the resistance and indifference set by the existing social structure. These have to be overcome. Thus, realistically it is not the mere appeal that counts; instead, it is a *process of agitation* that is important.

It is peculiar that no systematic and comprehensive study has ever been made of agitation. At the best, over generations, writing dealing with this topic consists of casual observations, analyses of restricted forms of agitation, and restatements of platitudes. The literature of the past decade has not improved this picture much. The one noteworthy exception is the volume by Lowenthal and Guterman dealing with the techniques of American political agitation (101). This work presents an incisive treatment of the demagogue and expert propagandist. Yet its analysis is based on the outstanding leader—the conspicuous public figure. This higher level of agitation is important in its own right. Yet alongside of it is the vast structure of agitation on lower levels—the community agitators, the neighborhood organizers, the local officials, the zealots among the rank and file, the average party member discussing his views with friends, acquaintances, relatives, and fellow workers. Systematic knowledge of agitation on these lower levels is exceedingly limited.

Not much can be reported in the way of studies of the control and retention of members in a movement—the development of enthusiasm and zeal, the cementing of inner unity, the implanting of convictions, the fostering of allegiance, and the development of voluntary commitment. To be true, studies of communist parties like that of Selznick (133) touch on these matters, but do not deal with actual working procedures. The nearest approach to the study of group unity and tenacity is in the literature on "morale"; yet the recent literature on morale is not concerned specifically with social movements. Consequently, its value is more inferential. A few references may be given. Indirectly, Rogers deals with morale in his book, *Dealing with Social Tensions* (121). Leighton (91) treats the way in which people mobilize their resources under stress. Alexander (2) emphasizes the dependence of morale on effective leadership. Shils and Janowitz declare as a result of their studies of German army units that morale depended predominantly on the structure of the primary association of the soldiers (135). As these few references suggest, the writing on morale during the last decade has not contributed much knowledge that can be used in the analysis of morale in social movements.

The same sort of evaluation must be made with regard to the place of "ideology" in the structure of a movement. Obviously, the aims, the myths, the claims, the criticisms, the arguments, and the rationalizations which collectively constitute an ideology have a vital effect on the participants in a movement. However, questions as to how an ideology functions in the life of a movement and as to how it must be shaped and presented to be effective have been scarcely touched in the literature. Thus, although much has been written during the last decade on ideology little of this literature sheds light on the role of ideology in holding together the members of a movement and energizing their action. A similar judgment must be given in the case of the literature on leadership. The recent literature on leadership is rich, but again it contains little that contributes to an analysis of leadership as a mechanism in the life of movements. Excellent studies have been made of other aspects of leadership. Thus Schueller (130) in a study of the Politburo in Soviet Russia traces the different types of leadership required in the different stages of development of this top group. Lerner has studied the Nazi elite (94) in terms of the social classes from which they have been recruited. In another study of Nazi leadership Gerth analyzes the reliance on charismatic and bureaucratic approaches (49). These three references, which are obviously only a few among many, suffice to indicate the paucity of study of leadership as a functioning element in the inner control and direction of movements. We can conclude this lengthy paragraph by saying that the crucial factors which form and maintain unity and persistency in movements have not gained much attention from writers during the last decade.

One of the important tasks confronting study of social movements is to develop a classification of movements along generic lines, and to study each of the classes or types. To the best of my knowledge no one has ever sought to develop a systematic topology of movements. Certainly nothing has been written on this topic in the last ten years. Attention, however, has been given to the consideration of some of the types of movements. What has been written along these lines is rarely in the form of a systematic analysis of the given type; usually it is a study of an instance of the given type. As one would suspect, most attention has been given to revolutionary movements. In an incisive article Neumann discusses the structure and strategy of revolution as represented by the events of 1848 and 1948 (113). Brinton revised his well-known book on *The Anatomy of Revolution* (22). Hopper endeavors to reduce the "revolutionary process" to a series of stages based on sociological concepts (65). Lee (89) traces the influence of the agrarian situation in China as a factor in social upheavals in that country. The work of Belden (10) contains much valuable material of an analytical nature on the communist revolution in China. Enough material is on hand to allow for an effective analysis of revolutionary movements as a generic form. What is lacking is an effective scheme for handling the material.

The treatment in recent literature of other types of social movements is limited. Little attention is given to reform movements. Note may be taken of an article by Lee (87) in which he sketches techniques used in social reform, on the basis of the new drive for prohibition. While a sizable amount of writing on nationalism has appeared during the past decade, not much of it has been devoted to analytical studies of nationalist movements. The long-neglected topic of nativistic movements has gained more attention in recent years. Linton headed the work on this topic with a good article published in 1943 (97). Balandier has contributed an excellent account of the messianic form taken by such movements among native Africans, especially in the Congo area (6). His analysis is made effectively in terms of the disquietude and disorganization occasioned by missionary activities, by a new economy, and by colonial domination. The Mau-Mau trouble in Kenya has given rise to a considerable literature. An article by Rosenstiel typifies the better type of analysis of this movement (125). Finally, one finds in recent literature discussions of scattered movements. Lipset has made a careful study of the Co-operative Commonwealth Foundation, an agrarian movement in Western

Canada, and throws much light on the factors that conduce to organized radicalism (98). Wright (155) has inquired into the difficulties which block the efforts to form a syndicalist movement among present-day French peasants. Munch analyzes the contemporary peasant movement in Norway (110). Bogardus presents a brief account and analysis of the "Antigonish Movement" in Nova Scotia—an interesting self-help movement (19). Becker (9) gives a helpful account of the youth movement in Germany. Gould compares the youth movement in Hitler's Germany with that in Soviet Russia (53). Green and Melnick have assessed the feminist movement (54).

The account which has been given of recent writing on social movements reflects the scattered and spotty concern with this area of collective behavior. It highlights, above all, the urgent need for a conceptual framework that will make possible a coherent scheme of analysis and provide leads to better directed study.

## CONCLUSION

An over-all assessment of the literature in the field of collective behavior during the last decade requires a recognition of a marked increase in the amount of study being devoted to topics which it covers. This increase is not uniform—indeed, there are some topics which have remained without attention. The general picture, however, shows a steady augmenting interest. This growth in amount of concern has not been matched by development in theoretical analysis. The field remains without a unifying conceptual scheme. Indeed, there are not many signs of even tentative advances in this direction. The writer suspects, however, that the sheer increase of interest in divergent topics will lead scholars to bridge the widely dispersed and disparate treatments that make up today's literature. The development of schemes that will bring together what is now separated will have the effect of laying out problems of a deeper theoretical import. This should turn scholarly interest more definitely along generic lines and thus lead to more fruitful analytical schemes for understanding the empirical world with which collective behavior is concerned.

## BIBLIOGRAPHICAL REFERENCES

1. Adorno, L. W., *et al.*, *The Authoritarian Personality*, New York, Harper and Bros., 1950.

2. Alexander, Leo, "Morale and Leadership," in *Transactions of the Conference on Morale and the Prevention and Control of Panic*, New York Academy of Medicine, 1951.

3. Allport, Gordon, and Leo Postman, *The Psychology of Rumor,* New York, Henry Holt and Co., 1947.

4. Arendt, Hannah, *The Origins of Totalitarianism,* New York, Harcourt, Brace and Co., 1951.

5. Austin, Garry R., "Non-fiction Best Sellers: Types and Trends," *Journal of Social Psychology,* Vol. 38 (1953), pp. 141–143.

6. Balandier, George, "Messianisms and Nationalisms in Black Africa," *Cahiers de Internationaux Sociologie,* Vol. 14 (1953), pp. 41–65.

7. Barber, Bernard, and L. Lobel, "Fashion in Women's Clothes and the American Social System," *Social Forces,* Vol. 31 (1953), pp. 124–131.

8. Bartlett, Vernon, *East of the Iron Curtain,* London, Latimer House, 1949.

9. Becker, Howard, *German Youth: Bond or Free,* New York, Oxford University Press, 1946.

10. Belden, Jack, *China Shakes the World,* New York, Harper and Bros., 1949.

11. Bell, Quentin, *On Human Finery,* London, Hogarth Press, 1947.

12. Berelson, Bernard, "Communication and Public Opinion," in Wilbur Schramm, *Communication in Modern Society,* Urbana, Ill., University of Illinois Press, 1948.

13. Berelson, Bernard, and Morris Janowitz, *Reader in Public Opinion and Communication,* Glencoe, Ill., Free Press, 1953.

14. Bettelheim, Bruno, "Individual and Mass Behavior in Extreme Situations," *Journal of Abnormal and Social Psychology,* Vol. 38 (1943), pp. 417–452.

15. Bettelheim, Bruno, and Morris Janowitz, "Reactions to Fascist Propaganda— A Pilot Study," *Public Opinion Quarterly,* Vol. 14 (1950), pp. 53–60.

16. Blumer, Herbert, "Collective Behavior," in A. M. Lee, *New Outline of the Principles of Sociology,* New York, Barnes and Noble, 1946.

17. Blumer, Herbert, "Public Opinion and Public Opinion Polling," *Amer. Soc. Rev.,* Vol. 13 (1948), pp. 542–549.

18. Boehm, Eric H., "The 'Free Germans' in Soviet Psychological Warfare," *Public Opinion Quarterly,* Vol. 14 (1950), pp. 285–295.

19. Bogardus, Emory S., "The Antigonish Movement," *Sociology and Social Research,* Vol. 37 (1953), pp. 189–195.

20. Bontemps, Arna, and Jack Convoy, *They Seek a City,* Garden City, N. Y., Doubleday, Doran and Co., 1945.

21. Brecker, R. L., "Truth as a Weapon of the Free World," *Annals, American Academy of Political and Social Science,* Vol. 278 (1951), pp. 1–11.

22. Brinton, Crane, *The Anatomy of Revolution,* New York, Prentice-Hall, 1952.

23. Brown, H. G., "The Appeal of Communist Ideology," *American Journal of Economics and Sociology,* Vol. 2 (1943), pp. 161–174.

24. Cantril, Hadley, "Trends of Opinion During World War II: Some Guides to Interpretation," *Public Opinion Quarterly,* Vol. 12 (1948), pp. 30–44.

25. Chorus, A., "The Basic Law of Rumor," *Journal of Abnormal and Social Psychology,* Vol. 48 (1953), pp. 313–314.

26. Ciechanowski, Jan, *Defeat in Victory,* New York, Doubleday and Co., 1947.

27. Clark, Kenneth B., "Group Violence: A Preliminary Study of the Attitudinal Pattern of Its Acceptance anod Rejection; A Study of the 1943 Harlem Race Riot," *Journal of Abnormal and Social Psychology,* Vol. 19 (1944), pp. 319–337.

28. Clark, K. B., and J. Barker, "The Zoot Effect in Personality: A Race Riot Participant," *Journal of Abnormal and Social Psychology,* Vol. 40 (1945), pp. 145–148.

29. Cobliner, W. Godfrey, "Feminine Fashion as an Aspect of Group Psychology:

Analysis of Written Replies Received by Means of a Questionnaire," *Journal of Social Psychology,* Vol. 31 (1950), pp. 283–289.

30. Cohen, John, *Human Nature, War and Society,* London, Watts and Co., 1946.

31. Cooper, E., and H. Dinerman, "Analysis of the Film 'Don't Be a Sucker': A Study in Communication," *Public Opinion Quarterly,* Vol. 15 (1951), pp. 243–264.

32. Cromwell, Harvey, and Richard Kunkel, "An Experimental Study of the Effect on the Attitudes of Listeners of Repeating the Same Oral Propaganda," *Journal of Social Psychology,* Vol. 35 (1952), pp. 175–184.

33. Dahlke, H. Otto, "Race and Minority Riots: A Study in the Typology of Violence," *Social Forces,* Vol. 30 (1952), pp. 419–425.

34. Dodd, S. C., "Predictive Principles for Polls: Scientific Method in Public Opinion Research," *Public Opinion Quarterly,* Vol. 15 (1951), pp. 23–42.

35. Domenach, Jean-Marie, "Leninist Propaganda," *Public Opinion Quarterly,* Vol. 15 (1951), pp. 265–273.

36. Doob, Leonard, *Public Opinion and Propaganda,* New York, Henry Holt and Co., 1948.

37. Doob, Leonard W., "The Strategies of Psychological Warfare," *Public Opinion Quarterly,* Vol. 13 (1949), pp. 635–644.

38. Doob, Leonard W., "Goebbels' Principles of Propaganda," *Public Opinion Quarterly,* Vol. 14 (1950), pp. 419–442.

39. Doob, Leonard W., *Social Psychology,* New York, Henry Holt and Co., 1952.

40. Dowd, David L., "Art as National Propaganda in the French Revolution," *Public Opinion Quarterly,* Vol. 15 (1951), pp. 532–546.

41. Duchacek, Ive, *The Strategy of Communist Infiltration: The Case of Czechoslovakia,* New Haven, Yale Institute of International Studies, 1949.

42. Egbert, Donald Drew, and Stowe Persons (eds.), *Socialism and American Life,* Princeton, Princeton University Press, 1952.

43. Ehrmann, Henry W., "The French Peasant and Communism," *American Political Science Review,* Vol. 46 (1952), pp. 19–43.

44. Fainsod, Merle, "Controls and Tensions in the Soviet System," *American Political Science Review,* Vol. 44 (1950), pp. 266–282.

45. Festinger, L., A. Pepitone, and T. Newcomb, "Some Consequences of De-Individuation in a Group," *Journal of Abnormal and Social Psychology,* Vol. 47 (1952), pp. 382–389.

46. Foreman, Paul B., "Panic Theory," *Sociology and Social Research,* Vol. 37 (1953), pp. 295–304.

47. Gallacher, S. A., "The Ideal Hero of Antiquity and His Counterpart in the Comic Strip of Today," *Southern Folklore Quarterly,* Vol. 11 (1947), pp. 141–148.

48. Gallup, George, "The Gallup Poll and the 1950 Election," *Public Opinion Quarterly,* Vol. 15 (1951), pp. 16–22.

49. Gerth, Hans, "The Nazi Party: Its Leadership and Composition," in R. Bendix, *Reader in Bureaucracy,* Glencoe, Ill., Free Press, 1952.

50. Gerth, Hans, and C. Wright Mills, *Character and Social Structure: The Psychology of Social Institutions,* New York, Harcourt Brace and Co., 1953.

51. Gilbert, G. M., "Social Causes Contributing to Panic," in *Transactions of the Conference on Morale and the Prevention and Control of Panic,* New York Academy of Medicine, 1951.

52. Glick, C. E., "Collective Behavior and Race Relations," *Amer. Soc. Rev.,* Vol. 13 (1948), pp. 287–294.

53. Gould, Julius, "The Komsomol and the Hitler Jugend," *British Journal of Sociology*, Vol. 2 (1951), pp. 305–314.

54. Green, Arnold, and Eleanor Melnick, "What Has Happened to the Feminist Movement?" in Alvin Gouldner, *Studies in Leadership*, New York, Harper and Bros., 1950.

55. Gremley, William, "Social Control in Cicero," *British Journal of Sociology*, Vol. 3 (1952), pp. 322–338.

56. Hackett, Herbert, "The Flying Saucer," *Sociology and Social Research*, Vol. 32 (1947–1948), pp. 869–873.

57. Haner, C. F., and N. C. Meier, "The Adaptability of Area Probability Sampling to Public Opinion Measurement," *Public Opinion Quarterly*, Vol. 15 (1951), pp. 335–351.

58. Harvey, John, "Content Characteristics of Best-Selling Novels," *Public Opinion Quarterly*, Vol. 17 (1953), pp. 91–114.

59. Hazard, J. N., "Soviet Domestic Policy in the Postwar World," *American Political Science Review*, Vol. 40 (1946), pp. 80–89.

60. Heberle, Rudolph, *Social Movements: An Introduction to Political Sociology*, New York, Appleton-Century-Crofts, 1951.

61. Herz, Martin F., "Some Psychological Lessons from Leaflet Propaganda in World War II," *Public Opinion Quarterly*, Vol. 13 (1949), pp. 471–486.

62. Herzog, E. G., "Patterns of Controversy," *Public Opinion Quarterly*, Vol. 13 (1949), pp. 39–52.

63. Hoffer, Eric, *The True Believer*, New York, Harper and Bros., 1951.

64. Hook, Sidney, *The Hero in History*, New York, John Day Co., 1943.

65. Hopper, Rex D., "The Revolutionary Process: A Frame of Reference for the Study of Revolutionary Movements," *Social Forces*, Vol. 28 (1949–1950), pp. 270–279.

66. Hovland, Carl I., Arthur H. Lumsdaine, and Fred D. Sheffield, *Experiments in Mass Communication*, Princeton, Princeton University Press, 1949.

67. Hulett, J. E., "Estimating the Effect of a Motion Picture on Local Public Opinion," *Amer. Soc. Rev.*, Vol. 14 (1949), pp. 263–275.

68. Janis, I. L., *et al.*, "Effects of Preparatory Communications on Reactions to a Subsequent News Event," *Public Opinion Quarterly*, Vol. 15 (1951), pp. 487–518.

69. Janowitz, Morris, "The Imagery of the Urban Community Press," *Public Opinion Quarterly*, Vol. 15 (1951), pp. 519–531.

70. Jeffreys, M. D. W., "African Tarantual or Dancing Mania," *Eastern Anthropologist*, Vol. 6 (1953), pp. 98–105.

71. Johnson, D. M., "The 'Phantom Anesthetist' of Mattoon: A Field Study of Mass Hysteria," *Journal of Abnormal and Social Psychology*, Vol. 40 (1945), pp. 175–186.

72. Killian, Lewis M., "The Significance of Multiple-Group Membership in Disaster," *Amer. J. Soc.*, Vol. 58 (1952–1953), pp. 309–314.

73. Klapp, Orrin E., "The Creation of Popular Heroes," *Amer. J. Soc.*, Vol. 54 (1948–1949), pp. 135–141.

74. Klapp, Orrin E., "Hero Worship in America," *Amer. Soc. Rev.*, Vol. 14 (1949), pp. 53–62.

75. Klapper, Joseph T., *The Effects of Mass Media*, New York, Bureau of Applied Social Research, Columbia University, 1949.

76. Kornhauser, Arthur, "Public Opinion and Social Class," *Amer. J. Soc.*, Vol. 55 (1949–1950), pp. 333–345.

77. Kracauer, Siegfried, "National Types as Hollywood Presents Them," *Public Opinion Quarterly,* Vol. 13 (1949), pp. 53–72.

78. Kriesberg, Martin, "Cross Pressures and Attitudes: A Study of the Influence of Conflicting Propaganda on Opinions Regarding American-Soviet Relations," *Public Opinion Quarterly,* Vol. 13 (1949), pp. 5–16.

79. Kris, Ernst, and Nathan Leites, "Trends in Twentieth Century Propaganda," *Psychoanalysis and the Social Sciences,* Vol. 1 (1947), pp. 393–409.

80. Krugman, Herbert E., "The Appeal of Communism to American Middle Class Intellectuals and Trade Unions," *Public Opinion Quarterly,* Vol. 10 (1952), pp. 331–355.

81. Krugman, Herbert E., "The Role of Hostility in the Appeal of Communism in the United States," *Psychiatry,* Vol. 16 (1953), pp. 253–261.

82. Lane, Arthur Bliss, *I Saw Poland Betrayed,* Indianapolis, Bobbs-Merrill Co., 1948.

83. Lang, Kurt, and Gladys E. Lang, "The Unique Perspective of Television," *Amer. Soc. Rev.,* Vol. 18 (1953), pp. 3–12.

84. Lasswell, Harold, "Propaganda and Mass Insecurity," *Psychiatry,* Vol. 13 (1950), pp. 283–299.

85. Lasswell, Harold D., "The Strategy of Soviet Propaganda," in *Proceedings of the Academy of Political Science,* Columbia University, 1951, Vol. 24 (1951), pp. 214–226.

86. Lederer, Emil, *State of the Masses,* New York, Norton, 1940.

87. Lee, Alfred M., "Techniques of Social Reform, An Analysis of the New Prohibition Drive," *Amer. Soc. Rev.,* Vol. 9 (1944), pp. 65–77.

88. Lee, Alfred M., and Norman D. Humphrey, *Race Riot,* New York, Dryden Press, 1943.

89. Lee, Shu-Ching, "Agrarianism and Social Upheaval in China," *Amer. J. Soc.,* Vol. 56 (1950–1951), pp. 511–518.

90. Leeper, R. W., "A Motivational Theory of Emotion to Replace 'Emotion as a Disorganized Response," *Psychological Review,* Vol. 55 (1948), pp. 5–21.

91. Leighton, Alexander, "Beliefs Under Stress," in R. C. Snyder and H. H. Wilson (eds.), *Roots of Political Behavior,* New York, American Book Co., 1949.

92. Leiserson, Avery, "Opinion Research and the Political Process: Farm Policy an Example," *Public Opinion Quarterly,* Vol. 13 (1949), pp. 31–38.

93. Leites, Nathan, *A Study of Bolshevism,* Glencoe, Ill., Free Press, 1954.

94. Lerner, Daniel, *The Nazi Elite,* Hoover Institute and Library on War: Stanford University Press, 1951.

95. Lerner, Daniel, *Propaganda in War and Crisis,* New York, George W. Stewart, 1952.

96. Linebarger, Paul M. A., *Psychological Warfare,* Washington, D. C., Washington Infantry Journal Press, 1948.

97. Linton, Ralph, "Nativistic Movements," *American Anthropologist,* Vol. 45 (1943), pp. 230–240.

98. Lipset, Seymour M., *Agrarian Socialism,* Berkeley, University of California Press, 1950.

99. Lipset, Seymour M., "Opinion Formation in a Crisis," *Public Opinion Quarterly,* 1953, Vol. 17 (1953), pp. 20–46.

100. Lohman, Joseph D., *The Police and Minority Groups,* Chicago, Chicago Park District, 1947.

101. Lowenthal, Leo, and L. Guterman, *Prophets of Deceit, A Study of the Techniques of the American Agitator,* New York, Harper and Bros., 1949.

102. Lumsdaine, A. A., and I. L. Janis, "Resistance to Counterpropaganda Produced by One-Sided and Two-Sided 'Propaganda' Presentations," *Public Opinion Quarterly,* Vol. 17 (1953), pp. 311–318.

103. McCormack, Thelma, "The Motivation of the Radical," *Amer. J. Soc.,* Vol. 56 (1950–1951), pp. 17–24.

104. Meadows, Paul, "Some Notes on the Social Psychology of the Hero," *Southwestern Social Science Quarterly,* Vol. 26 (1945), pp. 239–247.

105. Meadows, Paul, "Theses on Social Movements," *Social Forces,* Vol. 24 (1946), pp. 408–412.

106. Meerloo, A. M., *Delusion and Mass-Delusion,* New York, Nervous and Mental Disease Monographs, 1949.

107. Mikolajczyk, Stanislaw, *The Rape of Poland: Pattern of Soviet Aggression,* New York, Whittlesey House, 1948.

108. Mintz, Alexander, "Non-adaptive Group Behavior," *Journal of Abnormal and Social Psychology,* Vol. 46 (1951), pp. 150–158.

109. Mintz, Alexander, "The Failure of a Propaganda Campaign Attempting to Influence the Behavior of Consumers in the National Interest by Predominantly Selfish Appeals," *Journal of Social Psychology,* Vol. 38 (1953), pp. 49–62.

110. Munch, Peter A., "The Peasant Movement in Norway," *British Journal of Sociology,* Vol. 5 (1954), pp. 63–77.

111. Myers, Robert C., "Anti-Communist Mob Action," *Public Opinion Quarterly,* Vol. 12 (1948), pp. 57–67.

112. Nagy, Ferenc, "Soviet Imperialism in Hungary," *Foreign Affairs,* Vol. 26 (1948), pp. 554–566.

113. Neumann, Sigmund, "The Structure and Strategy of Revolution: 1848 and 1948," *Journal of Politics,* Vol. 11 (1949), pp. 532–544.

114. Peterson, Warren, and Noel Gist, "Rumor and Public Opinion," *Amer. J. Soc.,* Vol. 57 (1951–1952), pp. 159–167.

115. Raditsa, Bogdan, "The Sovietization of the Satellites," *Annals, American Academy of Political and Social Science,* Vol. 271 (1950), pp. 122–134.

116. Ranney, John C., "Do the Polls Serve Democracy?" *Public Opinion Quarterly,* Vol. 10 (1946), pp. 349–360.

117. Riesman, David, and Nathan Glazer, "The Meaning of Opinion," *Public Opinion Quarterly,* Vol. 12 (1948), pp. 633–648.

118. Riley, M. W., and S. H. Flowerman, "Group Relation as a Variable in Communications Research," *Amer. Soc. Rev.,* Vol. 16 (1951), pp. 174–180.

119. Riley, John W., and Matilda W. Riley, "A Sociological Approach to Communications Research," *Public Opinion Quarterly,* Vol. 15 (1951), pp. 445–460.

120. Robinson, Duane, "Social Disorganization Reflected in Middle Class Drinking and Dancing Recreational Patterns," *Social Forces,* Vol. 20 (1942), pp. 445–449.

121. Rogers, C. R., *Dealing with Social Tensions,* New York, Hinds, Hayden and Eldrage, 1948.

122. Rogers, Lindsay, *The Pollsters: Public Opinion, Politics, and Democratic Leadership,* New York, Alfred A. Knopf, 1949.

123. Rose, A. M., "Public Opinion Research Techniques Suggested by Sociological Theory," *Public Opinion Quarterly,* Vol. 14 (1950), pp. 205–214.

124. Rose, A. M., "Rumor in the Stock Market," *Public Opinion Quarterly,* Vol. 15 (1951), pp. 461–487.

125. Rosenstiel, Annette, "An Anthropological Approach to the Mau Mau Problems," *Political Science Quarterly*, Vol. 68 (1953), pp. 419–432.

126. Rossi, Angelo, *A Communist Party in Action: An Account of the Organization and Operations in France*, New Haven, Yale University Press, 1949.

127. Schall, Herbert M., *et al.*, "A Sociometric Approach to Rumor," *Journal of Social Psychology*, Vol. 31 (1950), pp. 121–129.

128. Schiffer, B., and N. K. Jack, "The Limits of Fashion Control," *Amer. Soc. Rev.*, Vol. 13 (1948), pp. 730–738.

129. Schramm, Wilbur, *The Process and Effects of Mass Communication*, Urbana, Ill., University of Illinois Press, 1954.

130. Schueller, George K., *The Politburo*, Hoover Institute Studies, Stanford University Press, 1951.

131. Schuler, E. A., and V. J. Parenton, "A Recent Epidemic of Hysteria in a Louisiana High School," *Journal of Social Psychology*, Vol. 17 (1943), pp. 221–235.

132. Scott, Andrew MacKay, *The Anatomy of Communism*, New York, Philosophical Library, 1951.

133. Selznick, Philip, *The Organizational Weapon: A Study of Bolshevik Strategy and Tactics*, New York, McGraw-Hill, 1952.

134. Shils, Edward A., "Authoritarianism: Right and Left," in *Scope and Method of the Authoritarian Personality*, Glencoe, Ill., Free Press, 1954.

135. Shils, Edward A., and Morris Janowitz, "Cohesion and Disintegration in the Wehrmacht in World War II," in Society for the Psychological Study of Social Issues, *Public Opinion and Propaganda*, New York, Dryden Press, 1954.

136. Slendi, Stravo, "Albania Within the Slav Orbit: Advent to Power of the Communist Party," *Political Science Quarterly*, Vol. 63 (1948), pp. 257–274.

137. Spaeth, Sigmund, *A History of Popular Music in America*, New York, Random House, 1948.

138. Speier, Hans, "Historical Development of Public Opinion," *Amer. J. Soc.*, Vol. 55 (1949–1950), pp. 376–388.

139. Speier, Hans, "Psychological Warfare Reconsidered," in D. Lerner and H. D. Lasswell (eds.), *The Policy Sciences*, Stanford, Stanford University Press, 1951.

140. Speier, Hans, *Social Order and the Risks of War*, New York, George W. Stewart, 1952.

141. Steiner, H. Arthur, "Chinese Communist Urban Policy," *American Political Science Review*, Vol. 44 (1950), pp. 47–63.

142. Steiner, H. Arthur, "Current 'Mass Line' Tactics in Communist China," *American Political Science Review*, Vol. 45 (1951), pp. 422–436.

143. Strauss, Anselm L., "The Literature on Panic," *Journal of Abnormal and Social Psychology*, Vol. 39 (1944), pp. 317–328.

144. Strauss, Anselm L., "Research in Collective Behavior: Neglect and Need," *Amer. Soc. Rev.*, Vol. 12 (1947), pp. 352–354.

145. Swanson, G. E., "A Preliminary Laboratory Study of the Acting Crowd," *Amer. Soc. Rev.*, Vol. 18 (1953), pp. 522–533.

146. Taborsky, Eduard, "Government in the 'People's Democracies,'" *Annals, American Academy of Political and Social Science*, Vol. 271 (1950), pp. 55–63.

147. Tomasic, Dinko, "The Structure of Soviet Power and Expansion," *Annals, American Academy of Political and Social Science*, Vol. 271 (1950), pp. 32–42.

148. Towster, Julian, *Political Power in the USSR*, New York, Oxford University Press, 1948.

149. Tumin, Melvin M., "The Hero and the Scapegoat in a Peasant Community," *Journal of Personality,* Vol. 19 (1950–1951), pp. 197–211.

150. Warner, W. Lloyd, and William E. Henry, "The Radio Day-Time Serial: A Symbolic Analysis," *Genetic Psychology Monographs,* Vol. 37 (1948), pp. 3–72.

151. White, Ralph, "Hitler, Roosevelt, and the Nature of War Propaganda," *Journal of Abnormal and Social Psychology,* Vol. 44 (1949), pp. 157–174.

152. Wilner, D. M., and Franklin Fearing, "The Structure of Opinion: A 'Loyalty Oath' Poll," *Public Opinion Quarterly,* Vol. 14 (1950), pp. 729–743.

153. Wilson, H. H., "Techniques of Pressure—Anti-Nationalization Propaganda in Britain," *Public Opinion Quarterly,* Vol. 15 (1951), pp. 225–242.

154. Wirth, Louis, "Consensus and Mass Communication," *Amer. Soc. Rev.,* Vol. 13 (1948), pp. 1–15.

155. Wright, Gordon, "Agrarian Syndicalism in Postwar France," *American Political Science Review,* Vol. 47 (1953), pp. 402–416.

# chapter 6

# The urban community

NOEL P. GIST
*University of Missouri*

Urban sociology is probably the most unclearly defined of all the sociological fields.   Certainly its boundaries, if such exist, are indistinct, and
there is no universal agreement as to its substantive or theoretical character.   Unlike rural sociology, which customarily refers to the study of
almost all social phenomena relating to farm and village life, urban
sociology has emphasized certain facets of the city to the exclusion, or
at least minimization, of others.   Thus by accepted definition not all
sociologists concerned with urban phenomena are "urban" sociologists.

In the United States the publication of numerous college textbooks
in urban sociology during the postwar period under review may be taken
as evidence of increasing interest in the sociological aspects of cities.
This decade witnessed the appearance of no less than eleven new and
revised editions of texts dealing with various facets of city life.   Indeed,
more urban sociology texts were published in this period than in the entire

history of American sociology. In addition, a regional urban sociology, limited in its scope to the American South, made its appearance (108). Such extensive textbook publishing was made possible by the production of numerous research monographs and technical articles dealing with urbanism. Although the substantive content of urban sociology knows no geographical restrictions, textbook writing on the subject is distinctly an American phenomenon.

Although urban sociology may properly be considered a distinct discipline its scope has been broad, overlapping other academic subjects such as geography, political science, economics, and anthropology, and coinciding with the interest of city planners, social workers, and specialists in housing or urban rehabilitation. Geographers appear to have been influenced considerably by urban ecology, but sociologists seem to have little familiarity with the literature of urban geography. Nevertheless, there has been from the beginning a close affinity between economics and urban sociology, especially economics and human ecology.

### Widening horizons

Sociologists in the United States have tended to view urban sociology as an American development primarily. No doubt this is partly because more research has been conducted in American cities than in cities elsewhere, partly because American sociologists are not very familiar with literature on cities in other parts of the world, especially if that literature is in a language other than English. Urban sociology from the American outlook is therefore strikingly provincial in its scope and content.

But a new trend appears to be developing. Urban sociologists in this country are raising their sights, so to speak, focusing attention on sociological phenomena wherever they may be found, whether in Baghdad, Boston, or Buenos Aires. This change of focus has been facilitated by two developments: first, an increasing volume of data on world cities, representing in part the work of trained social scientists, both foreign and American; second, the growing realization that sociological theories concerning American cities are not necessarily valid for other parts of the world. The awakening interest in the spread of urbanism in underdeveloped areas of the world, such as Asia and Africa, is evidence of this trend. No doubt cross-cultural education accruing from the international odysseys of sociologists and technicians has been an important factor in this new orientation. At least it can be said that the vision of urban sociologists is less blurred by cultural myopia than it once was.

Recognition that urbanism is of paramount importance in the modern world is evidenced by several major conferences near the end of the first postwar decade, in which social scientists from various disciplines participated. One of these conferences, held at the University of Chicago in 1953, was concerned with the role of cities in economic development and cultural change (34). Among the participants were sociologists, cultural anthropologists, geographers, economists, and historians. Discussions centered on such matters as urbanization in preindustrial countries, the history of cities in economically advanced areas, the cultural role of cities, and the spatial order and economic growth of urban communities.

"The metropolis in modern life" was the theme of a conference held at Columbia University in 1954 in which scholars from Britain, France, and the United States participated (37). An even wider range of professional interests was represented, including law, economics, sociology, archaeology, art, theology, political science, engineering, architecture, geography, education, history, city planning, and housing. Much of the discussion at the conference dealt with the influence of the metropolis on social institutions and on the behavior and outlook of modern man.

A third conference, held in Abidjan, Africa, in 1954, under the auspices of UNESCO, was primarily concerned with the urbanization of Africa. As in the other conferences, the participants represented a number of professional interests, with discussions mainly about the impact of the city on the social and economic life of the African people.

In line with the study of cities in world perspective is the development of a world "Urban Resources Index" at Columbia University.* This project, started in 1951, involves the collection and classification of quantitative data for all cities of the world over 100,000 population. Designed for research purposes, the Index will include not only current information about cities in different cultural and economic areas, but also historical trends. Eventually the Index should make possible more precise and systematic cross-cultural comparisons in the study of urbanization.

Dickinson's studies of western European cities, primarily from the geographer's point of view, represent another contribution to the literature on world cities (27, 28). Redfield's extensive anthropological researches on folk communities and the changes occurring in primitive societies from the impact of urbanism have focused attention on the cultural roles of cities (96). A study by Davis and Casis of urbanization in Latin American countries is a strictly quantitative type of research on city growth in a major area of the western hemisphere (21). The publication in 1953 of an interdisciplinary prospectus for urban research in the United States is clear evidence of developing interest in this aspect

* This Index is now located at the University of California, Berkeley.

of social investigation (6). A special edition of the *American Journal of Sociology* dealing with "world urbanism" was published in 1955.

The importance of research in urban communities is indicated by the development of several foundations or bureaus organized for and directed toward the study of various aspects of city life. Some of these are closely affiliated with, or are a part of, urban universities. At the University of Michigan, for example, the Horace H. Rackham Fund was established for research in metropolitan centers in Michigan; at Tulane University, the Bureau of Urban Research for work in the cities of Louisiana; at Princeton University, the Bureau of Urban Research; and at Columbia University, the Bureau of Applied Social Research. Community Studies, Inc., was organized to conduct research in the metropolitan area of Kansas City. The Social Science Research Council, although not specifically oriented toward urban studies, does provide funds for research, much of which is conducted in cities. These enterprises indicate that the organization, direction, and financing of much urban research is "big business"; indeed, such a development is itself an aspect of metropolitanism.

### Shifting frames of reference

Social analyses based upon the familiar rural-urban dichotomy have never been wholly acceptable either to rural or urban sociologists. Such an arbitrary distinction, although convenient, patently does not allow for the fact that "rural" and "urban" cannot be so neatly dichotomized. Conventional urban sociology usually recognizes the fact that the urban community is only one part of a larger whole, the other part being represented by the rural community. But precisely how to deal with this interdependent relationship is by no means clear.

The effort by Sorokin and Zimmerman in the 1920's to present a systematic analysis of both sides of the rural-urban dichotomy was an ambitious undertaking, particularly because the analysis was not confined to the American scene (104). Although this dual framework made possible a comparative treatment of materials representing both rural and urban societies, mainly by the accumulation of comparable data, it added little to a theory of community life, nor did it offer an effective methodology for rural or urban research. Yet this approach has not been abandoned altogether. Bernard's "community approach" to the study of social problems, in which rural and urban distinctions are virtually ignored, is one variant (5). For Bernard, the community matrix is the basic framework, and whether it is rural or urban is incidental. A volume by Brunner and Hallenbeck represents another variant (9).

A rather different orientation having as its basic framework a rural-urban continuum has had limited acceptance. The application of this approach involves data which can be expressed quantitatively. Loomis and Beegle, rural sociologists with an affinity for sociometric techniques, have developed a method of measuring the degree of "urbanness-ruralness" of a community and also of testing the validity of urban or rural "ideal types" (76). Using standardized statistical procedures, Queen and Carpenter developed a formula for a rural-urban continuum involving data on such things as fertility, mortality, educational level, crime rates, and the like (93). Whatever may ultimately be the theoretical and methodological value of precision instruments for the "continuum approach," there will undoubtedly be a place for a typological approach. The work of Redfield (96) and of Miner (88, 89) in developing a theory of "folk" and "urban" society based on nonquantitative data hold considerable promise for urban sociology as well as sociology and anthropology in general.

## URBAN ECOLOGY

The founding fathers of human ecology—Park, McKenzie, Burgess—oriented their theoretical interpretations mainly toward economic competition for space in the city and economic dominance of the metropolis. Theirs was not entirely an economic determinism, however; certain allowance was made for social factors, especially those affecting residential locations and changes in a racially or culturally heterogeneous community. But the main emphasis, nevertheless, was competition for advantageous locational positions. If the psychological and cultural elements were explicitly recognized they were not assigned an important place in ecological theory by these major writers.

### Changing emphasis in ecological theory

During the decade under review there has been a shift in ecological theory toward an emphasis on social-psychological and cultural factors. Hence a distinction has come to be recognized between the "classical" and the "neoclassical" ecologists. As one might expect, such a distinction is by no means easily discernible, since a good many ecologists take an eclectic, or at least middle-of-the-road, approach to the subject.

The first major blast against the so-called classical ecology was fired by Firey (35). Classical ecological theory, according to Firey, fell into three categories: "Idealized descriptive schemes" such as the Burgess concentric zone theory of urban growth or Hoyt's sector theory of urban expansion; "empirically rationalistic theories" which posited the proposition that through competition and selection each person or group eventually gravitates to the spatial location which is most economically suitable; and "methodologically rationalistic theories" which likewise presuppose a "rational" land use pattern but in which the preoccupation is with methodological procedures. Whatever differences obtain between these theoretical approaches, says Firey, they have one thing in common: namely, the propensity to interpret the spatial order as a economic phenomenon, with little or no reference to psychosocial and cultural factors.

No doubt Firey overstated his viewpoint, just as he oversimplified the positions of certain ecologists in this respect. Whatever may be the merits of this controversy, at least Firey may be considered symptomatic of a trend. In his own monographic work on central Boston (35), Firey presents a considerable array of evidence that spatial location of people or institutions may be determined by sentimental values as well as by economic values, that people may cling to certain areas for prestige reasons even when such resistance to change may actually be irrational in an economic sense. His argument would appear to have particular merit for "residential" ecology.

Among the present-day American theorists who remain fairly closely identified with the "classical" point of view is Hawley (49). Although Hawley explicitly recognizes the importance of cultural factors when he states that "sustenance activities and relationships are inextricably interwoven with sentiments, value systems, and other ideational constructs," his writings actually show little concern for cultural and psychological elements in the spatial patterning of population or institutions. The main focus of attention is on "sustenance activities and relationships." McKenzie's intellectual influence is quite apparent throughout the work, and is so recognized by Hawley.

The only other general treatise on ecology, by Quinn (95), was published the same year as Hawley's work. There is little that is especially original in Quinn's treatment, but he does attempt to organize his materials under a set of concepts that permit the inclusion of a rather wide range of cultural, economic, and social-psychological elements. Much of his work is concerned with the application of ecological principles and concepts to the urban community and the metropolitan region. But his explicit emphasis upon the "impersonal, sub-social aspects of areal structure and change" and his attempt to distinguish between "social and ecological levels of coexistence relations" reveal the influence of earlier ecologists such as McKenzie and Park. His debt to McKenzie is considerable.

## Methodology

Some urban ecologists have been concerned primarily with methodology, especially with the development of precision instruments for the measurement of ecological patterns and processes. Perhaps nowhere is this interest more evident than in the efforts to devise mensurable techniques by means of which ecological *segregation* may be accurately gauged. Earlier ecologists employed the concept of segregation descriptively to mean a tendency for people having similar racial, cultural, or economic attributes to reside together in so-called *natural areas.* This idea was also applied rather loosely to tendencies of economic or other types of establishments to cluster together in a particular area.

But natural areas vary a great deal, even within the same city. Similarly, urban communities in the same society differ greatly as to the degree and character of segregation within them. Possibly even greater variations exist in this respect between cities in different cultures and countries. Recognition of this fact has underscored the need for measuring instruments which would allow the concept of ecological segregation to be operationally defined and uniformly used with a high degree of accuracy. Hatt's study of natural areas in Seattle was one of the first demonstrations to measure quantitatively a phenomenon that had been loosely conceptualized (48).

Using refined statistical techniques, Jahn, Schmid, and Schrag developed four indices which they considered applicable to the measurement of segregation of Negroes in American cities (64). Census tract data were utilized by the formula in such a way as to produce a single index number which would represent the degree of racial segregation in a particular city. Following a somewhat similar procedure, but with basic data derived from blocks rather than larger census tracts, the Cowgills developed a technique which they believe affords a high degree of precision in the measurement of segregation (18). These methods have been subjected to considerable criticism, either on the grounds of statistical inadequacy or because a single index cannot produce a valid picture of a highly complex phenomenon. It may be, as the Duncans point out, that no single index can sufficiently denote the variety of things that are commonly subsumed under the rather loose concept of ecological segregation (33).

An important methodological study utilizing a measure of ecological segregation was developed by Shevky and Williams and applied to Los Angeles County (103). These scientists sought to develop a procedure for the delineation of urban social areas which would transcend the usual methods of delineating ecological areas. Three indices were employed: (1) social rank, indicated by measures of occupation and education; (2) urbanization, representing measures of fertility, gainfully employed women, and single-dwelling or multiple-dwelling residences; and (3) segregation, representing measures of ecological segregation of racial or ethnic groups. More recently Shevky and Bell have refined their procedures (102). The method is designed specifically for American cities for which census tract data are available.

### Studies in ecological segregation .

Whatever may be the limitations of the concept of ecological segregation as a descriptive term, it has nevertheless proved a useful analytical tool and is frequently used, either implicity or explicitly, in sociological analysis. Mack points out, for example, how residential segregation of Swedes and Italians in an industrial port on Lake Erie is manifest in comparable social separation of the two groups in various social relationships, including the work situation in the same plant (79). Lee has indicated that American Chinatowns have undergone numerous ecological changes over the past few decades (72). Jonassen studied the Norwegians in New York, noting that this particular ethnic group, while becoming assimilated into the larger culture, retained its ecological identity, although shifting several times as a result of threatened invasions from other ethnic groups (67).

### Ecological decentralization

The monumental study of Adna F. Weber at the turn of the century pointed to the growth of suburbs resulting from the decentralization of population. That the social and economic importance of this trend has been recognized by urban sociologists and other social scientists is evidenced by extensive research undertaken during the past two or three decades. Although research in this general aspect of urban ecology during the 1945–1955 decade represented a continuation of work done earlier, it has been somewhat broader in scope and more varied as to method and focus. Queen and Carpenter analyzed census data for seven medium-sized cities and their fringe areas (94), and Beegle followed a similar procedure for ten major centers in Michigan (4). Obviously, analysis based upon combined data for a number of cities necessarily obscures the facts concerning a particular center.

The alternative has been for sociologists to conduct studies of specific urban areas. These researches, however, have had the obvious disadvantage of being so localized that generalizations derived from the data must be highly tentative. Lack of uniformity in the nature of hypotheses to be tested, in methods employed, and in the kinds of data obtained creates an additional difficulty in developing an appropriate theory broad enough to be applicable to the country as a whole, not to mention other countries whose patterns of urban decentralization have been quite different.

In his study of the area surrounding Madison, Wisconsin, Rodehaver (97) emphasized the cultural, social, and demographic characteristics of the fringe population, the reasons for movement into the interstitial zone, and the direction of the movement, whether from city outward or from the outlying areas toward the center. Firey's survey of the Flint, Michigan, fringe involved a careful study of three distinctive neighborhoods located on different sides of the urbanized area (36). Dewey's study of decentralization in the Milwaukee area was concerned primarily with the values and attitudes of the population with reference to peripheral residence (25). Gist undertook a study of the movement of population beyond the immediate suburban development of Columbia, Missouri, including in his sample families in which one or more members were employed in the city (43). A similar study was undertaken by Martin in the Eugene–Springfield, Oregon, area, with special emphasis placed on the kinds of adjustments the residents made to fringe residence (81).

That ecological decentralization has far-reaching effects on social relationships is suggested by technical and nontechnical writings. Wirth's famous phrase, "urbanism as a way of life," may well be amended to "suburbanism as a way of life." Whyte's insightful articles on suburban life strongly suggest that a new *modus vivendi* for the masses is in the process of development (116). Effects of suburban living on the American family are indicated by Jaco and Belknap (63), and several researches have emphasized neighboring and other forms of informal participation as an aspect of the suburban way of life. It is possible, although not demonstrated, that suburbs tend to attract a "neighborly" people and that "unneighborly" persons are disposed to remain in the congested or anonymous sections of a metropolis. But since suburban living has become fashionable, particularly in the United States, it is also possible that the values of the allegedly unneighborly metropolite have changed under conditions of the suburban environment.

### Ecology of institutions

The spatial patterning of urban institutions and the changes occurring in these patterns have been a matter of interest to urban ecologists, economic geographers, and land economists. Ecological studies of the central business district and of subordinate nuclei have usually interpreted spatial location in terms of functions performed by various establishments. According to this viewpoint, the functions of particular institutions or specialized personnel can be most effectively performed when they are located in close proximity to other institutions or personnel. Hence the development of commercial and industrial nuclei. Johnson appears to hold this position in an analysis of the central business district, with particular reference to Chicago (66).

Quinn attempts to develop a series of locational hypotheses concerning the ecology of institutions (95). One of these he calls the "hypothesis of median location." The most efficient location of a shop or store, he says, is at the median distance from its customers, although other factors may also be influential. A second hypothesis explored by Quinn is the "principle of intensiveness of utilization." Mass-patronized stores can use space more intensively than stores catering to a select and limited clientele. A third principle, particularly applicable to industry, is the "hypothesis of minimum cost." Because industrialists in a capitalistic society must make a profit in order to survive, they seek locations where fixed costs can be kept at a minimum. No doubt the cost hypothesis helps explain the tendency of industries to decentralize, or even to be widely dispersed from the main centers of population.

### Spatial movement

Urban ecologists have long been interested in the movement of population; indeed, such concepts as *invasion* and *succession* have by definition been concerned with spatial changes, and others such as centralization and decentralization have implied movements of people or institutions. Some of the recent researches of this type have been concerned with the daily ebb and flow of people within a given area, particularly in a metropolis. Liepmann's study of the "journey to work" in several British cities attracted considerable attention and apparently stimulated research on the daily movements of population (74). A comprehensive study of the daytime population in the business district of Chicago, by Breeze, was particularly concerned with the use of different forms of transportation (excluding walking) and the distances traveled from point of origin to the central business district (8). In a study of several large American cities, Foley found that about one person in five among metropolitan residents made at least one trip to the central business district each week day, and that about one person for every ten residents of the metropolis was to be found in the business zone each afternoon (39).

Sociological studies of the daily movements of population in cities are by no means mere accumulations of travel data. Most of them attempt to relate the incidence and character of movement with other social phenomena and to point up the social significance of the daily ebb and flow of people to various aspects of community life.

Of particular interest to urban sociologists and ecologists has been the selective character of population movement, especially rural-urban migrations. Research after World War II, as well as in earlier years, points to a selective process in which migrants from rural areas to cities tend, proportionally, to be superior intellectually to nonmigrants or those who move to other rural areas. It is likely, however, that this selection is basically occupational in character (57). What the researches have not clarified is the social effects, if any, of such selection on both urban and rural communities.

### The metropolitan region

The relationship of the city to its social, economic, and geographic hinterland has been generally recognized by urban sociologists, especially since the writings of Park, McKenzie, and Galpin. The most extensive recent analysis of regionalism in terms of metropolitan dominance was made by Bogue (7). It is Bogue's hypothesis that the economy of the United States is becoming increasingly organized by major metropolitan centers which exert a dominant influence over the subordinate hinterlands. Using 1940 census data on 67 areas around the major cities of the country, Bogue carefully traced the distributive patterns of retail, wholesale, service, and manufacturing activities in areas dominated by the metropolis. He makes it clear that his analysis applies only to metropolitan regions, not to smaller cities and their economic hinterlands. Unfortunately, use of mass data concerning a large number of regions obscures the characteristic features of any specific area.

### Ecological research in other countries

Human ecology as an aspect of urban sociology has been mainly an American development, but within the decade under review a number of ecological studies have been conducted in various cities of the world. Some of this research has been carried out by American sociologists, some by other nationals familiar with ecological theory and methods. Among the contributions of American sociologists to the literature are Hayner's ecological study of Mexico City (52), Hawthorne's description of Sucre, Bolivia (50), Dotson's study of ecological trends in Guadalajara,

Mexico (29), Leonard's ecological interpretation of La Pax, Bolivia (73), and Caplow's writings on urban ecology in France (11) and in Guatemala (12).

In Europe, sociologists, economists, and geographers have been especially concerned with phenomena which, in America, have generally been included in the broad field of urban ecology. Among the French, according to Caplow, a team of investigators has been studying the "social ethnography" of Paris (16), and studies have also been made of Parisian suburbs (42). Studies in human geography made under the auspices of the University of Lund in Sweden (105) bear a close resemblance to the ecological approach followed by American sociologists. Much of the work of such economists as Florence (38) at the University of Birmingham, England, also has much in common with urban ecology in the United States.

Such works as the foregoing present ample evidence that ecological theory based on the study of American cities is not necessarily applicable to cities in other parts of the world. The few Latin American studies, for example, clearly indicate that the prevailing ecological configurations in American cities of the United States are not characteristic of cities below the Rio Grande, although technological and other factors are tending to produce ecological patterns more nearly like those of the North. Caplow also presents evidence that ecological configurations in France are different from those in the United States.

## URBAN SOCIAL STRUCTURES AND RELATIONSHIPS

If the contents of textbooks written and used by academic sociologists are indicative of the nature and scope of urban sociology it is immediately apparent that the subject is interpreted to include a wide range of phenomena and conceptual interpretations, and often conflicting theoretical orientations. Most specialists or near-specialists in what is generally considered urban sociology subscribe, implicitly or explicitly, to a form of eclecticism; hence their interests range over whatever social phenomena may appear to be characteristic of the composite urban community. Nevertheless, the sociological approach to the study of the urban community is different from that of the political scientist, economist, and geographer, although at the same time there appears to be increasing reliance upon these and other disciplines.

### Social stratification of the urban community

Perhaps no aspect of city life has intrigued sociologists more than systems of social stratification. Until the first two or three decades of the present century European and American sociological writers were primarily concerned with building theories of stratification pertinent to entire societies. But after the Middletown studies by the Lynds (77) and the Yankee City investigation by Warner and his associates (112), interest in the social structures of particular cities grew rapidly. Aside from a few segmental studies of metropolitan communities, most of the comprehensive investigations have been conducted in towns or small cities. Indeed, the very size of the metropolis has been prohibitive for community-wide research. Whatever criticisms may be made of the Warner method and theory—and many have been made—it cannot be denied that his work has had profound influence on urban sociology in the United States, perhaps more so than in Europe.

The immediate postwar decade produced an abundance of sociological literature on urban social stratification in its multifarious aspects. Some of it has been methodological and theoretical, some has emphasized substantive findings. Perhaps the most ambitious effort to develop a methodology of research in the local community has been made by Warner (110). Others, like Kaufman (68) or Hill and Witing (55), have attempted to outline the scope of and to formulate research procedures for studying urban stratification. A systematic statement of the problem has been made by a panel of rural sociologists whose analysis is equally germane to rural and urban sociology (69).

Of pertinence to urban sociology are various studies representing systematic research on stratification in a specific city. Although these researches are varied as to substantive content, methodology, and theoretical orientation, in their totality they have provided many insights into urban structure and process as well as effective means of furthering systematic research. Of the 616 items in McCrae's bibliography, a large proportion were published in the postwar decade and particularly concern urban stratification (78). Among those representing investigations of American urban social systems may be mentioned Hollingshead's studies of "Elmtown" (58) and New Haven (59), Warner's work in "Jonesville" (111), research by Drake and Cayton on Chicago's Negro community (31), Hill's study of a small city in Georgia (54), a study by Mills of social stratification in middle-sized cities (84), and investigations by Davis and Havighurst of the relationship between social class and learning among children in urban communities (20).

During the decade under consideration a limited volume of sociological literature began to appear on social stratification in cities in other countries. Hawthorne's study of the class structure of a Latin American city (51), Hayner's analysis of social classes in a Mexican town (53), Tumin's work on the social structure of a city in Guatemala (107), Gist's research on caste in Bangalore, India (44), and the work of D. V. Glass and his associates on various aspects of social stratification in British cities (45) are representative. Variations in methods of research, however, have made intercultural comparisons difficult.

### Institutionalism, bureaucracy, and power

The institutional approach to urban sociology has commonly run the entire gamut of social organization, extending well beyond what may be considered the sociologist's proper domain. Textbooks on the subject usually include chapters on urban economic and political organization, as well as sections on the family, religion, recreation, and social welfare. Presumably this eclectic treatment is followed to provide a "rounded" picture of the urban community. Except for the urban family, on which considerable research has been done, sociologists have veered away from the traditional institutional type of analysis in their research activities. Little sociological interest has been shown in the urban church, although occasionally sociological studies of various aspects of religious organizations have been made. Sociological interest in urban recreation has been oriented toward studies of formal and informal group participation, communication, and the like.

A modification of the traditional institutional approach toward bureaucratic organization and power has provided a theoretical orientation of considerable significance to urban sociology. In this orientation the sociologist as well as the economist and political scientist may claim some professional competence. Not much systematic research has been done on bureaucratic organization and power in the city, but there is reason to believe that this field will be increasingly cultivated.

Some two decades ago the Lynds described in considerable detail the nature of bureaucratic organization and the structure of power in Middletown (77). The Lynd study represents one of the first sociological analyses of bureaucracy and power in a local community setting. Since that time several sociologists have directed their research efforts to the study of large-scale organization and its relation to the system of power. Some of them have been concerned with organization and power on a national or international scale, some with its local aspects.

Among the sociological works of the postwar decade which were addressed to this problem, the writing of Mills stands out (86). In his analysis of the white collar occupations he observes the trend toward the development of titanic bureaucracies and the concentration of power in these bureaucratic structures. Even the traditional professions such as law and medicine, he finds, are becoming bureaucratized. This trend is in line with the thinking of Drucker, who observes that the American system is moving toward what he calls an "employee society," with an increasing concentration of economic and political power in the hands of a few, who themselves may be taking orders from persons above them in the power structure (32). Mills has carried his interest in power to a study of labor union organization and leadership, primarily an urban development (85).

One of the significant studies of power in its community-wide aspect is Hunter's *Community Power Structure* (1952), an analysis of the power structure of a metropolis in the American South. Hunter is concerned with the decision-making process; more particularly with the socioeconomic positions of the major decision makers, the circumstances under which the decisions are made, and the way they are arrived at and passed on to others lower in the community power structure.

### Formal and informal groups

A crystallization of interest in formal and informal groups during the 1945–1955 decade has stimulated considerable research in this aspect of social organization. Much of this research has been carried on in an urban setting. A few studies of small urban groups have been done under highly controlled experimental conditions, but most of the investigations represent field work in the open sociological laboratory of the city. Among the important forerunners of this type of field research was Thrasher's *The Gang* (1927) and, later, Whyte's *Street Corner Society* (1943), republished in 1955 with some additional materials.

Some of the urban studies have focused exclusively on the groups selected for analysis, emphasizing particularly their structural features, their functions in the community's social system, and the patterns of social participation of city people. Komarovsky's study of voluntary associations in New York City revealed two important sociological facts: (a) associational membership and participation were much more characteristic of the upper white collar classes than of blue collar workers; (b) a large proportion of the adults, especially those on working class levels, had no associational affiliations (71). These findings are generally confirmed by other studies in cities of varying size. De A. Reid and Ehle found this general pattern in Philadelphia (22), as did Bushee in Boulder (10), Axelrod in Detroit (3), and Dotson in New Haven (30). There is clear evidence, however, that working class families, while participating much less than those on white collar levels, are not necessarily socially isolated.

An important type of association, until fairly recently virtually ignored by sociologists as an aspect of city life, is the clique. Warner and his associates, in their Yankee City and Jonesville researches, strongly emphasized the importance of informal associations in the social systems of these cities and in the lives of the people. Drake and Cayton likewise observed that the informal as well as the formal association figured importantly in the lives of Chicago Negroes. Probably equally important are the studies of formal and informal associations that exist within the framework of a large organization, such as an industrial plant. The extensive investigation by Roethlisberger and Dickson of informal associations among workers in the Western Electric Company plant in Chicago was the forerunner of numerous studies made in urban industrial organizations (98). In fact, the clique or other types of informal group in the factory or commercial establishment has become an important subject for sociological investigation. Among such investigations may be mentioned Whyte's studies of restaurant workers in Chicago (115) and Hughes' work on informal associations as a factor in race relations in industrial plants (61).

Social differentiation within the city has been illuminated by studies of associational structures. Some of these researches have revealed deep social cleavages along ethnic, racial, religious, or class lines. Membership in most associations is thus highly selective. Minnis found this to be true of New Haven (90), Hollingshead discovered the same tendency in midwestern Elmtown, and Drake and Cayton noted a similar differentiation in the voluntary groups of Negroes in Chicago (31). Although this aspect of social differentiation has been generally known, recent studies have provided more precise data on its nature.

### Urban occupational research

Recent sociological studies of occupations have special significance for urban sociology since so many aspects of city life are affected by the nature of work. Urban sociologists have been especially concerned with the broader social and psychological implications of occupational mobility, changes occurring in the occupational structure, shifting work roles of men and women, developing forms of social organization manifest in the rise of occupational associations, and the trend toward bureaucratization of work as an accompaniment of organization. There is some reason to believe that urban sociology will place increasing emphasis upon the occupational system and the way it functions in an urban milieu.

The appearance in 1954 of the first systematic textbook in a sociology of occupations was of special significance to urban sociology since the substantive materials presented in the volume were drawn mainly from cities and since the generalizations were especially applicable to an urban community (14). Except for the work of rural sociologists on farm populations, most of the empirical research on occupations has been done in cities. The analysis by Mills of urban white collar workers (86), the research by Lipset and Bendix (75) and by Rogoff (99) on occupational mobility in American cities, the writing of Hughes on racial and cultural contacts in the work situation (62), and the study by Drake and Cayton of the Negro in the occupational structure of Chicago (31) are of special significance to urban sociology.

### The urban neighborhood

Urban sociologists have frequently written about the "vanishing urban neighborhood." This point of view holds that the neighborhood in the metropolis, if not the small city, is a waning phenomenon, that it has been overshadowed by voluntary associations which channel the interests of individuals beyond the bounds of neighborhood life, and that the mass patronage of special forms of recreation has tended to attract the city dweller away from his neighborhood environs and thereby weaken the personalized ties that bind him to his locality group. Thus, according to this point of view, urban neighbors tend to become mere nigh-dwellers. In a brilliant and influential article written in the 1930's, Wirth expressed this viewpoint as follows:

> The distinctive features of the urban mode of life have often been described sociologically as consisting of the substitution of secondary for primary contacts, the weakening of the bonds of kinship, and the declining social significance of the family, *the disappearance of the neighborhood,* and the undermining of the traditional basis of social solidarity. All these phenomena can be substantially verified through objective indices (117; italics mine).

In the light of fairly recent investigations of urban neighborhood life it becomes impressively evident that Wirth's categorical pronouncement was a gross overstatement. It may well be that "the neighborhood," generally speaking, has declined in relative importance as a social unit, but with the exception of certain areas of extremely high mobility such as rooming-house districts it has not disappeared from the urban scene. In fact, there is reason to believe that patterns of neighborhood life are varied, ranging from neighborhoods in which social relationships are warm and intimate to those in which social contacts are ephemeral and without sentimental content. Furthermore, even within the same neighborhood the form and intimacy of social relationships often vary greatly. These are facts, to use Wirth's phrase, which have been "verified through objective indices."

Foley's researches in Rochester (40) and St. Louis (41), for example, indicate that while "neighboring" in the areas selected for study was probably less important than in former decades, and that neighborhood contacts tended to be superficial, there was nevertheless extensive inter-action among the residents. In the Rochester area a majority of the persons interviewed said that at least one-fourth of their best friends lived in the same area. Dotson's study in New Haven of the associa-tional affiliations and activities of working class families showed that families on this socioeconomic level depended more on neighborhood and kinship groups than upon formal associations for their social life (30). For families on certain social levels, at least, the urban neighborhood has retained much of its traditional richness and vigor. With the develop-ment of empirical research methods such as those of Shevky and Williams (103), Shevky and Bell (102), Wallin (109), Caplow and Foreman (13), and Deutschberger (24), this field of community study may be cultivated more fruitfully in the future.

### *Racial and ethnic relations in the city*

Because most cities have a polyglot population, relations between indi-viduals and groups representing diverse racial, ethnic, religious, and moral backgrounds comprise appropriate data for urban sociology. For the social structure of the city is shaped by the racial and ethnic atti-tudes of the people and the ways these attitudes affect social interaction between them. It is this fact, for example, that has led investigators of social stratification in the community to view the values attached to racial, ethnic, and religious attributes as important elements of a community's social system. It was recognition of this fact, also, that focused atten-tion on ecological segregation as one of the important aspects of city life, since segregation is in a sense a measure of the nature of racial and cultural relationships in general. Although most of the theories concern-ing racial and cultural relations have been based upon research con-ducted in urban communities, mainly in the United States, the phe-nomenon of racial and cultural heterogeneity and of the relationships between diverse groups is probably a universal feature of the metropolis.

Much of the research in this area is concerned with the nature of inter-racial and intercultural relationships in the city and the impact of city life on these relationships. By its very nature city life and labor tend to weaken or even break down the traditional patterns of interaction between people of different characteristics. Such writers as Masuoka (82), Weaver (113), and others have repeatedly pointed to the impact of the metropolis on Negro-white relations in America; how racial etiquette, commonly enforced in the rural milieu, becomes archaic under the highly competitive and often impersonal relations of the metropolis; or how an individual's relations with persons of opposite race or culture may vary with the specific situation, even in the same community—a result, apparently, of his identification with different groups that vary in their respective ideologies.

But there are many other facets of racial and cultural relations which illuminate the processes and forms of urban society. Recent studies of, say, Puerto Ricans in New York City (87), the Jews in Midwestern Metropolis (46), ethnic and racial minorities in Yankee City (112), the Negro community in Chicago (31), and the Chinese in American metropolitan communities (72) bring out, in one way or another, multifarious aspects of urban community life. In such studies as these may be found concrete materials bearing upon the whole range of social processes and social organization as manifest in the city.

### City and personality

The impact of the city on the personalities and behavior of those who come directly within its sphere of influence has always been a matter of considerable concern to urban sociologists, although much of their thinking on the matter has been speculative or hypothetical. The decade under review, however, has witnessed considerable research of a specialized nature, representing the beginning of what may eventually provide the basis for valid generalizations.

One approach is concerned with the urban class structure in its relation to personality and behavior. The writings of Green (47), Clark (17), and Hollingshead (60), for example, indicate a relationship between the social position and emotional problems of urban residents. Comparison of urban and rural people have been made by Mangus (80), Seeman (101), and others. A project sponsored by UNESCO on city life and personality in Australia emphasizes the successive roles the individual assumes from childhood to maturity in an urban milieu (91).

Some fairly effective writing has been done on the effects of occupational experiences, such as the writings of Mills (84–86). The bureaucrat as a social or occupational type has also been the subject of increasing interest to students of urban society (83). There is, of course, a vast amount of literature on crime and delinquency, much of it representing studies or observations made in an urban setting. Usually the basic assumption is that an urban environment in some way or another "causes" individuals to react as delinquents or criminals. Traditionally, attention focused on the slum as the principal causative agent, but studies of urban crime or delinquency have been given a more sophisticated theoretical orientation such as the familiar theory of differential association. Kinsey's study of sexual behavior, although not sociological in the conventional sense, casts some light on the impact of the city on personality (70). In general, however, there is lessened emphasis upon the so-called pathologies of urban society than in earlier decades.

An intriguing theory of changing personality structures resulting from sociocultural changes inherent in capitalism, industrialism, and urbanism has been propounded by Riesman in *The Lonely Crowd* (1950). He postulates three personality types: (1) the tradition-directed man, typical of a custom-oriented society in which behavioral conformity is rigorously demanded; (2) the inner-directed man whose "drive" is implanted early in life by his elders and which directs the individual toward "inescapably destined goals"; and (3) the other-directed man, who directs and is directed by contemporaries through the manipulation of words and images.

It is the third type which is the product of capitalism, industrialism, and urbanism in the "advanced" countries, not merely in America. Whereas inner-direction is typical of the "old" middle class—the banker, tradesman, small entrepreneur, and technically oriented engineer—other-direction has its prototype in the "new" middle class, in the bureaucrat, the salaried employee, the sales engineer. It is Riesman's belief that the conditions responsible for other-directed personalities exist in the metropolitan centers of the advanced industrialized countries, although his familiarity with the American scene leads him to base his analysis mainly on data from American urban society. He clearly specifies, of course, that his types are "ideal" constructs, that most individuals have attributes of both, or even all three; but it is his conclusion that the other-directed type, the cosmopolite, is emerging under modern conditions of metropolitan life.

### *"Moral integration"*

A few attempts have been made to measure operationally certain "moral" configurations of cities as ongoing social systems. An early study by Thorndike intended to develop a "goodness" score for each of 310 American cities revealed marked differences between cities (106). Thorndike was primarily concerned with what makes a city a "good" place in which to live. More recently, Angell addressed himself to a similar problem, the "moral integration" of American cities, developing a highly refined methodology for conducting such a study within a given city (2). Angell defined moral integration as the "degree to which there is a set of common ends and values toward which all the members are oriented and in terms of which the life of the group is organized" (page 115). Whatever may be the theoretical or practical value of such studies to social science or to programs of social action, this approach has appealed to a limited number of urban sociologists. There is some reason to question whether such extensive inquiries as those of Thorndike and Angell will yield results comparable to the vast amount of effort and resources necessary to carry them out.

### Social planning

Social planning of community life is probably accepted ideologically by most sociologists concerned with urban society. This is evidenced in part, at least, by the extensive amount of space devoted to such matters as planning and housing in textbooks concerned with city life. Urban sociologists are probably familiar with much of the professional literature on community planning, but they have made little contribution to this literature, except indirectly through their researches or theories relating to community process and structure. Apparently planning per se has offered little attraction as a subject of research. Indeed, most of the creative writing in this field has been done by professional planners or philosophers of planning. Urban sociologists, in the main, have confined their literary efforts to summaries or appraisals of these writings. A few practitioners of "applied sociology," however, have focused their interests in this field. Hillman's compendium of facts and theories relating to community organization and planning goes beyond the usual treatment of the subject by professional planners or social workers (56). Wirth's broad philosophical perspective of the metropolis gave full support to the concept of social planning and physical reconstruction in the community (118).

The concept of neighborhood has figured significantly in the literature on city planning, much of it controversial in nature. Perhaps the most comprehensive statement of the place of the neighborhood in city planning and housing programs was made some years ago by Perry, who conceived of the neighborhood plan as one of the essential features of the planned community (92). Perry's conception of the neighborhood, however, went beyond the usual sociological definition; to him the effective neighborhood, for planning purposes, was the area ordinarily centering around an elementary school, with a population ranging from three thousand to ten thousand persons, the actual size depending upon density. Perry's conception of the neighborhood unit in city planning and housing is a matter of considerable controversy among urban sociologists and planners (26). Even more controversial is the concept of mixed neighborhood. There are some who believe that the neighborhood, as a planning unit, should be homogeneous as to the racial, ethnic, or economic character of its residents, but others are committed to the idea that the mixed neighborhood is in accord with democratic principles and is therefore a workable concept (19).

### Social aspects of housing

Because of the crisis in housing during the postwar period and certain developments in public housing and urban rehabilitation, numerous urban sociologists addressed themselves directly to various aspects of social relationships affected by housing conditions. Sociological research interests therefore tended to be focused on such matters as housing arrangements most appropriate for family life, housing as an index of social stratification, and social interaction among neighbors in public housing projects. It is noteworthy that two distinguished sociologists, Wirth (119) and Chapin (15), in the same year published articles on sociological methods of housing research, while a social anthropologist, Warner, about the same time used housing as one of the indices of social class in a methodological treatise on research in community stratification. In 1951, a special issue of the *Journal of Social Issues* on social policy and social research in housing was edited and mainly written by sociologists and social psychologists.

Postwar housing developments stimulated considerable interest in social interaction among neighbors who differ in race, religion, or ethnic background. Research in this area has focused on various aspects of conflict arising from the movement of Negroes or other minorities into housing projects occupied predominantly by whites, patterns of adjustment when families of diverse racial and cultural backgrounds are integrated into urban housing projects, and devices designed to prevent integration, such as protective covenants and neighborhood associations. Two metropolitan studies illustrate the type of housing research that is especially significant for urban sociology. One of these, a part of the Columbia-Lavanburg researches on planned housing communities, is a study of race relations in an eastern metropolitan housing project half of whose 800 families were Negro and half white (65). The other, a study of racial relations in two integrated housing projects and in two segregated projects, was conducted by Deutsch and Collins at the Research Center for Human Relations, New York University (23). These researches indicated that attitudes toward racial integration in houses were more favorable in the nonsegregated projects than in those having segregated occupancy. Much of the literature pertinent to minorities and housing in America is summarized in a nontechnical work by Abrams having considerable significance for urban sociology (1). A few studies have been made of the social and economic costs of slums. Perhaps the best known of these investigations is the research by Rumney in which the incidence of delinquency, tuberculosis, infant mortality, fatal home accidents, and fires in slum areas was compared with the rates in public housing projects in the same city (100).

## BIBLIOGRAPHICAL REFERENCES

1. Abrams, Charles, *Forbidden Neighbors*, New York, Harper and Brothers, 1955.

2. Angell, Robert C., "The Moral Integration of American Cities," special supplement, *Amer. J. Soc.*, Vol. 57 (1951–1952), pp. 1–140.

3. Axelrod, Morris, "A Study of Formal and Informal Participation in a Large Community," Unpublished doctoral dissertation, University of Michigan, 1953.

4. Beegle, J. A., "Characteristics of Michigan's Fringe Population," *Rural Sociology*, Vol. 12 (1947), pp. 254–263.

5. Bernard, Jessie, *American Community Behavior*, New York, Dryden Press, 1949.

6. Bogue, Donald J. (ed.), *Needed Urban and Metropolitan Research*, Scripps Foundation for Research in Population Problems, Miami University, Oxford, Ohio, and Population Research and Training Center, University of Chicago, Chicago, Ill., 1953.

7. Bogue, Donald J., *The Structure of the Metropolitan Community*, Ann Arbor, University of Michigan Press, 1949.

8. Breeze, Gerald W., *The Daytime Population of the Central Business District of Chicago*, Chicago, University of Chicago Press, 1947.

9. Brunner, Edmund, and Wilbur C. Hallenbeck, *American Society: Rural and Urban Patterns*, New York, Harper and Brothers, 1955.

10. Bushee, J. A., "Social Organization in a Small City," *Amer. J. Soc.*, Vol. 51 (1945–1946), pp. 217–226.

11. Caplow, Theodore, "Recent Research in the Ecology of Paris," *Midwest Sociologist*, Vol. 16 (Winter, 1954).

12. Caplow, Theodore, "The Social Ecology of Guatemala City," *Social Forces*, Vol. 28 (1949), pp. 113–133.

13. Caplow, Theodore, and Robert Foreman, "Neighborhood Interaction in a Homogeneous Community," *Amer. Soc. Rev.*, Vol. 15 (1950), pp. 357–366.

14. Caplow, Theodore, *The Sociology of Work*, New York, Harper and Brothers, 1954.

15. Chapin, F. Stuart, "New Methods of Sociological Research in Housing," *Amer. Soc. Rev.*, Vol. 12 (1947), pp. 143–149.

16. Chaumbart de Lauwe, P. H., *et al.*, *Paris et l'agglomeration Parisienne*, Paris, Presses Universitaires de France, 1952.

17. Clark, Robert, "Psychoses, Income, and Occupational Prestige," *Amer. J. Soc.*, Vol. 54 (1948–1949), pp. 127–139.

18. Cowgill, Donald, and Mary S. Cowgill, "An Index of Segregation Based on Block Statistics," *Amer. Soc. Rev.*, Vol. 16 (1951), pp 825–831.

19. Dahir, James, *The Neighborhood Unit Plan: Its Spread and Acceptance,* New York, Russell Sage Foundation, 1949.

20. Davis, Allison, and Robert J. Havighurst, "Social Class and Color Differences in Child Rearing," *Amer. Soc. Rev.,* Vol. 11 (1946), pp. 703–710.

21. Davis, Kingsley, and Ana Casis, "Urbanization in Latin America," *Milbank Memorial Fund Quarterly,* Vol. 24 (1946), pp. 186–207.

22. De A. Reid, Ira, and Emily L. Ehle, "Leadership Selection in Urban Locality Areas," *Public Opinion Quarterly,* Vol. 14 (1950–1951), pp. 262–284.

23. Deutsch, Morton, and Mary Evans Collins, *Interracial Housing: A Psychological Study of a Social Experiment,* Minneapolis, University of Minnesota Press, 1951.

24. Deutschberger, Paul, *Interaction Patterns in Changing Neighborhoods,* Sociometry Monographs, No. 18, Beacon, N. Y., Beacon Press, 1947.

25. Dewey, Richard, "Peripheral Expansion in Milwaukee County," *Amer. J. Soc.,* Vol. 54 (1948–1949), pp. 118–125.

26. Dewey, Richard, "The Neighborhood, Urban Ecology, and City Planning," *Amer. Soc. Rev.,* Vol. 15 (1950), pp. 512–517.

27. Dickinson, Robert E., *City, Region, and Regionalism,* New York, Oxford University Press, 1947.

28. Dickinson, Robert E., *The West European City,* London, Routledge and Kegan Paul, 1951.

29. Dotson, Floyd, and Lillian Ota, "Ecological Trends in the City of Guadalajara, Mexico," *Social Forces,* Vol. 32 (May, 1954), pp. 367–374.

30. Dotson, Floyd, "Patterns of Voluntary Associations Among Working Class Families," *Amer. Soc. Rev.,* Vol. 16 (1951), pp. 687–693.

31. Drake, St. Clair, and Horace R. Cayton, *Black Metropolis,* New York, Harcourt, Brace and Company, 1945.

32. Drucker, Peter, "The Employee Society," *Amer. J. Soc.,* Vol. 58 (1952–1953), pp. 358–363.

33. Duncan, Otis Dudley, and Beverly Duncan, "A Methodological Analysis of Segregation Indexes," *Amer. Soc. Rev.,* Vol. 20 (1955), pp. 217–224.

34. *Economic Development and Cultural Change,* Vol. 3 (October, 1954; January, 1955; April, 1955).

35. Firey, Walter, *Land Use in Central Boston,* Cambridge, Harvard University Press, 1947.

36. Firey, Walter, *Social Aspects of Land Use Planning in the Country-City Fringe,* Michigan State College Agricultural Experiment Station Bulletin 339 (1946).

37. Fisher, Robert Moore (ed.), *The Metropolis in Modern Life,* New York, Doubleday and Company, 1955.

38. Florence, P. Sargant, "Economic Efficiency in the Metropolis," in Robert Moore Fisher (ed.), *The Metropolis in Modern Life,* New York, Doubleday and Company, 1955.

39. Foley, Donald L., "The Daily Movement of Population in Central Business Districts," *Amer. Soc. Rev.,* Vol. 19 (1954), pp. 314–324.

40. Foley, Donald L., *Neighbors or Urbanites?,* Rochester, N. Y., University of Rochester, 1952.

41. Foley, Donald L., "The Use of Local Facilities in a Metropolis," *Amer. J. Soc.,* Vol. 56 (1950–1951), pp. 242–248.

42. George, Pierre, *Études sur la banlieue de Paris,* Paris, Librairie Armand Colin, 1950.

43. Gist, Noel P., "Developing Patterns of Urban Decentralization," *Social Forces,* Vol. 30 (March, 1952), pp. 257–267.

44. Gist, Noel P., "Caste Differentials in South India," *Amer. Soc. Rev.*, Vol. 19 (1954), pp. 126–137.

45. Glass, D. V., *Social Mobility in Britain*, Glencoe, Ill., The Free Press, 1954.

46. Gordon, Albert, *Jews in Transition*, Minneapolis, University of Minnesota Press, 1949.

47. Green, Arnold, "The Middle Class Male Child and Neurosis," *Amer. Soc. Rev.*, Vol. 11 (1946), pp. 32–40.

48. Hatt, Paul K., "The Concept of Natural Area," *Amer. Soc. Rev.*, Vol. 11 (1946), pp. 423–427.

49. Hawley, Amos, *Human Ecology*, New York, Ronald Press Company, 1950.

50. Hawthorne, Harry B., and Audrey E. Hawthorne, "The Shape of a City: Some Observations on Sucre, Bolivia," *Sociol. and Social Res.*, Vol. 33 (1948), pp. 87–91.

51. Hawthorne, Harry B., and Audrey E. Hawthorne, "Stratification in a Latin-American City," *Social Forces*, Vol. 27 (October, 1948), pp. 19–29.

52. Hayner, Norman, "Mexico City: Its Growth and Configuration," *Amer. J. Soc.*, Vol. 50 (1944–1945), pp. 295–304.

53. Hayner, Norman, "Differential Social Change in a Mexican Town," *Social Forces*, Vol. 26 (May, 1948), pp. 381–390.

54. Hill, Mozell, and B. C. McCall, "Social Stratification in a Georgia Town," *Amer. Soc. Rev.*, Vol. 15 (1950), pp. 721–729.

55. Hill, Mozell, and A. N. Witing, "Some Theoretical and Methodological Problems in Community Studies," *Social Forces*, Vol. 29 (December, 1950), pp. 117–124.

56. Hillman, Arthur, *Community Organization and Planning*, New York, Macmillan Company, 1950.

57. Hofstee, E. W., *Some Remarks on Selective Migration*, The Hague, Research Group for European Problems, 1952.

58. Hollingshead, A. B., *Elmtown's Youth*, New York, John Wiley and Sons, 1949.

59. Hollingshead, A. B., "Trends in Social Stratification: A Case Study," *Amer. Soc. Rev.*, Vol. 17 (1952), pp. 679–686.

60. Hollingshead, A. B., "Social Stratification and Psychiatric Disorders," *Amer. Soc. Rev.*, Vol. 18 (1953), pp. 163–169.

61. Hughes, Everett C., "The Knitting of Racial Groups in Industry," *Amer. Soc. Rev.*, Vol. 11 (1946), pp. 512–519.

62. Hughes, Everett C., and Helen M. Hughes, *Where People Meet: Ethnic and Racial Frontiers*, Glencoe, Ill., The Free Press, 1952.

63. Jaco, E. G., and I. Belknap, "Is a New Family Emerging in the Suburbs?" *Amer. Soc. Rev.*, Vol. 18 (1953), pp. 550–557.

64. Jahn, J., Calvin F. Schmid, and C. Schrag, "The Measurement of Ecological Segregation," *Amer. Soc. Rev.*, Vol. 12 (1947), pp. 292–303.

65. Jahoda, Marie, and Patricia Salter West, "Race Relations in Public Housing," *Journal of Social Issues*, Vol. 7 (1952), pp. 132–139.

66. Johnson, Earl S., "The Function of the Central Business District in the Metropolitan Community," in P. Hatt and A. Reiss (eds.), *Reader in Urban Sociology*, Glencoe, Ill., The Free Press, 1951.

67. Jonassen, Christen T., "Cultural Variables in the Ecology of an Ethnic Group," *Amer. Soc. Rev.*, Vol. 14 (1949), pp. 32–41.

68. Kaufman, Harold F., "An Approach to the Study of Urban Stratification," *Amer. Soc. Rev.*, Vol. 17 (1952), pp. 430–437.

69. Kaufman, Harold F., *et al.*, "Problems of Theory and Method in the Study of Social Stratification in Rural Society," *Rural Sociology*, Vol. 18 (1953), pp. 12–24.

70. Kinsey, Alfred C., *Sexual Behavior of the Human Male,* Philadelphia, B. Saunders Company, 1948.

71. Komarovsky, Mirra, "The Voluntary Associations of Urban Dwellers," *Amer. Soc. Rev.,* Vol. 11 (1946), pp. 686–698.

72. Lee, Rose Hum, "The Decline of Chinatowns in the United States," *Amer. J. Soc.,* Vol. 54 (1948–1949), pp. 422–432.

73. Leonard, Olen E., "La Paz, Bolivia: Its Population and Growth," *Amer. Soc. Rev.,* Vol. 13 (1948), pp. 448–454.

74. Liepmann, Kate K., *The Journey to Work: Its Significance for Industrial and Community Life,* New York, Oxford University Press, 1944.

75. Lipset, Seymour, and Reinhard Bendix, "Social Mobility and Occupational Career Patterns," *Amer. J. Soc.,* Vol. 57 (1951–1952), pp. 366–374, 494–505.

76. Loomis, Charles P., and J. Allen Beegle, *Rural Social Systems,* New York, Prentice-Hall, 1950.

77. Lynd, Robert S., and Helen Merrill Lynd, *Middletown in Transition,* New York, Harcourt, Brace and Company, 1937.

78. McCrae, Donald G., "Bibliography on Stratification," *Current Sociology,* Vol. 2 (1953–1954), pp. 7–73.

79. Mack, Raymond W., "Ecological Patterns in an Industrial Shop," *Social Forces,* Vol. 32 (1954), pp. 351–356.

80. Mangus, A. R., "Personality Adjustment of Rural and Urban Children," *Amer. Soc. Rev.,* Vol. 13 (1948), pp. 556–575.

81. Martin, Walter T., *The Rural-Urban Fringe: A Study of Adjustment to Residence Location,* Eugene, University of Oregon Press, 1953.

82. Masuoka, J., "The City and Racial Adjustment," *Social Forces,* Vol. 27 (1948), pp. 39–44.

83. Merton, Robert K. (ed.), *Reader in Bureaucracy,* Glencoe, Ill., The Free Press, 1952.

84. Mills, C. W., "The Middle Classes in Middle Sized Cities," *Amer. Soc. Rev.,* Vol. 11 (1946), pp. 520–529.

85. Mills, C. W., *The New Men of Power,* New York, Harcourt, Brace and Company, 1948.

86. Mills, C. W., *White Collar,* New York, Oxford University Press, 1951.

87. Mills, C. W., *et al., The Puerto Rican Journey,* New York, Harper and Brothers, 1950.

88. Miner, Horace, "The Folk-Urban Continuum," *Amer. Soc. Rev.,* Vol. 52 (1952), pp. 292–308.

89. Miner, Horace, *The Primitive City of Timbuctoo,* Princeton, Princeton University Press, 1953.

90. Minnis, Mhyra, "Cleavage in Women's Organizations: A Reflection of the Social Structure of a City," *Amer. Soc. Rev.,* Vol. 18 (1953), pp. 47–85.

91. Oeser, O. A., and S. B. Hammond, *Social Structure and Personality,* Vol. I, New York, Macmillan Company, 1954.

92. Perry, Clarence, *Regional Survey of New York and Its Environs,* Vol. 7, New York, Regional Plan of New York, 1929.

93. Queen, Stuart A., and David C. Carpenter, *The American City,* New York, McGraw-Hill Book Company, 1953.

94. Queen, Stuart A., and David C. Carpenter, "The Rural-Urban Fringe: From the Urban Point of View," *Rural Sociology,* Vol. 12 (1947), pp. 254–263.

95. Quinn, James A., *Human Ecology,* New York, Prentice-Hall, 1950.

06. Redfield, Robert, "The Folk Society," *Amer. J. Soc.*, Vol. 52 (1946–1947), pp. 293–308; cf. *The Primitive World and Its Transformations*, Ithaca, Cornell University Press, 1953.

97. Rodehaver, Myles W., "Fringe Settlement as a Two-Dimensional Movement," *Rural Sociology*, Vol. 12 (1947), pp. 49–57.

98. Roethlisberger, F. J., and W. J. Dickson, *Management and the Worker*, Cambridge, Harvard University Press, 1941.

99. Rogoff, Natalie, *Recent Trends in Occupational Mobility*, Glencoe, Ill., The Free Press, 1954.

100. Rumney, Jay, and Sara Shuman, *The Cost of Slums in Newark*, Newark, 1946 [pamphlet].

101. Seeman, Melvin, "An Evaluation of Current Approaches to Personality Differences of Folk and Urban Societies," *Social Forces*, Vol. 25 (1945), pp. 16–65.

102. Shevky, Eshref, and Wendell Bell, *Social Area Analysis*, Stanford, Stanford University Press, 1955.

103. Shevky, Eshref, and Marilyn Williams, *The Social Areas of Los Angeles*, Berkeley and Los Angeles, University of California Press, 1949.

104. Sorokin, Pitirim A., and C. C. Zimmerman, *Principles of Rural-Urban Sociology*, New York, Henry Holt and Company, 1929.

105. *Studies in Rural-Urban Interaction*, Stockholm, Royal University of Sweden, 1951.

106. Thorndike, E. L., *Your City*, New York, Harcourt, Brace and Company, 1939.

107. Tumin, Melvin M., *Caste in a Peasant Society*, Princeton, Princeton University Press, 1952.

108. Vance, Rupert J., and Nicholas J. Demerath (eds.), *The Urban South*, Chapel Hill, University of North Carolina Press, 1955.

109. Wallin, Paul, "A Guttman Scale for Measuring Women's Neighborliness," *Amer. J. Soc.*, Vol. 59 (1953–1954), pp. 243–246.

110. Warner, W. L., *et al.*, *Social Class in America*, Chicago, University of Chicago Press, 1949.

111. Warner, W. L., *et al.*, *Democracy in Jonesville*, New York, Harper and Brothers, 1949.

112. Warner, W. L., and Leo Srole, *The Social Systems of American Ethnic Groups*, New Haven, Yale University Press, 1945. Cf. Warner, W. L., and Paul S. Lunt, *The Social Life of a Modern Community*, New Haven, Yale University Press, 1941.

113. Weaver, Robert, *The Negro Ghetto*, New York, Harcourt, Brace and Company, 1948.

114. Wheeler, Wayne, *Social Stratification in a Plains Community*, Minneapolis, [Private Printing], 1949.

115. Whyte, W. F., *Human Relations in the Restaurant Industry*, New York, McGraw-Hill Book Company, 1948.

116. Whyte, W. H., Jr., "The Transients," *Fortune*, Vol. 47 (1953), pp. 112–117, 221–226.

117. Wirth, Louis, "Urbanism as a Way of Life," *Amer. J. Soc.*, Vol. 44 (1938–1939), pp. 1–24.

118. Wirth, Louis, "Planning Means Freedom," in *Planning*, American Society of Planning Officials, Chicago, 1947.

119. Wirth, Louis, "Housing as a Field of Sociological Research," *Amer. Soc. Rev.*, Vol. 12 (1947), pp. 137–143.

chapter *7*

# The rural community

HOWARD W. BEERS
*University of Kentucky*

## THE STATUS OF THE CONCEPT

There has been some toe-stubbing and stumbling over the concept and data of the rural community in the decade under review (1945–1955). The development of understanding has required some sociologists to take detours, some to pause for works of construction, and some to be diverted to new interests under the rising hegemony of urbanism. Certainly as an object of research appeal, the rural community has declined in fascination before the threat of submergence by the new metropolis.

The generic definition (42) has not changed, unless toward simpler formulation as in Hawley's conclusion that "community refers to the structure of relationships through which a localized population provides its daily requirements" (38). Nor has the specifically rural construction of this concept changed in any fundamental feature. But the recent attitudes of rural sociologists in applying it in their studies have ranged from cautious to confident. Bowing, and not always rebounding to criticism, they have been sensitive to charges that the alleged rural (multi-bonded) community is a strained fiction with no present concrete referent; that it is an artifact of particular, and assertedly sentimental, habits of delineation (49); that at best it is impotent, nominalistic, or inconspicuous in the midst of more dominant society-wide features such as social class (35, 36); that it has little or no logical or problematic identity as an area of research (63, 64); that it represents a teleological aspiration, or perhaps a nostalgic sentiment of old people who feel guilt over the gigantism of modern society; or that it has been relegated to the archive and the museum by motorization of travel—that it has dissolved into the masses made by modern communication or that it has been swallowed by urbanism. Repudiation of the concept "rural community" in some recent writing seems theoretically naive in the sense that it follows from anticipation that each observed situation must be a perfect exemplification of the construct (model). But some sociologists have given up. They now study class instead of community. Others seek neutrality by referring to "locality groups" (1, 25). Still others are firm in their loyalty to the concept, asserting the rural community to be the most important human grouping in American life, widely extant, and normatively of paramount significance as a nursery of democratic ideals and practices (17).

### Preview of trends

Observations of rural communities in the United States actually have shown contrasting trends—one, the congealing of a natural town-country unit from previously adjacent but often nonnucleated neighborhoods; the other, a melting of the town-country unit into a regional amalgam differentiated more by interest than by locale. By the first trend, a rural community appears; by the second it disappears. During the decade under review, sociologists seem to have argued the existence of rural communities according to whether they had most recently attended a ceremony of confirmation or of burial. Research from 1945 on was against the background of controversy set up in earlier years by the rural sociologists of town-country tradition or "emergent community" tradition on the one hand and on the other by the sociologists who could no longer find multi-bonded communities in a world of rapid transit and instantaneous long-distance communication. Research to confirm both of these views has been reported, thus pointing to the simultaneous existence of both conditions and the concurrence of both trends but at different places and for

different reasons. No doubt the populations of some locales are com-
munity-less; the populations of other locales are possibly still almost com-
munity-bound.

### Aftermath of revolution in agriculture

Typically, in the United States, the rural community has had a short
history, encompassing in the West as few as two—and hardly anywhere
more than five or six—human generations. The jelling of social forms and
the accumulation of culture have been continually or intermittently stirred
or interrupted and redirected by tides of action and movement. This is
all in contrast to the centuries of history that underlie the organization
of rural life outside of the New World.

Writers about the American scene must be getting weary of putting
words to the tune of change. But Americans have become sociologists
not because they are pensive or reflective. It is because the visibility of
social phenomena has been heightened by the dynamics of rapid development. So much land was settled so fast, with such avidity, with such
dramatics of success and failure, and with such prodigious social, political, and economic consequence. Many a layman has sociological pro-
clivities; he has seen so much change that he may incline more to criticism
than to the passive transmission of traditions that would mark a peasant
society.

Here, however, there is no escape from the necessity of briefly inspect-
ing changes in the over-all context of rural life. Nearly everyone knows
now, by experience or by communication, that agriculture in the United
States underwent technical revolution after about 1910. That was the
third of four periods in which many writers compass the history of American rural life generally, and of the rural community cases they describe
(59, 82, 41, etc.). Pioneer settlement, powered by hand at axe and hoe
(to 1850 or 1860); expansion, powered by horse at plow and binder (to
1900 or 1910); transition, powered by engines and machines at combine
and cotton picker (to 1940 or 1950); and the current period (just beginning and of unpredictable duration) of chemicals and atoms.*

American rural life of song and story took form in the first two periods.
But history did not allow rural life in the United States a long succession
of generations in which to stabilize its features (a man's life seems long
to a boy—short to a historian). The transition period of rapid technological change transformed the societal context in fundamental ways in

---

* Half of the commercial farms in 1950 were horseless (59).

the time of hardly more than one generation. While the nation became urban and industrial, people on farms declined in number by one-fourth; output per man-hour in farm production more than doubled; the aggregate farm output increased by three-fourths.

Families on scattered farms were isolated in the geography and society of 1900, as much so, Mighell recalls, as in 1800 (59). The patterns of human contact and the networks of social relationship were consequences of that circumstance. With later migration from farms amounting to relative depopulation,* farmers now are farther apart in linear distance, but much closer in convenience and time. Whether they are closer in intimacy can hardly be told from available reports of research, but is to be doubted. Certainly their disadvantages in the amenities of living such as electricity and household convenience (except in the technology of plumbing and heating) are less. In 20 years (1935 to 1955) the proportion of farms with electricity has gone from 10 to 90 per cent. Nearly all farmers have radios, a majority have electric washing machines and refrigerators.

> Fifty years ago, a farm was in a separate world with infrequent communication with the "outside." The technology of communication has changed all this. Rural free delivery of mail, automobiles and improved highways, telephones, radios, television sets, and other devices keep farmers in better touch with main events than many city people. . . . Automobiles were found on 60 percent of all farms and if farm trucks are taken into account, three-fourths of all farmers had power wheeling available (59, pp. 152–153).

Even for farmers, the chief difference between night and day has been destroyed by electricity. Light joins space and time as a changing ecological factor in man's community experience. It is no longer inconvenient to project daytime activities into the night, and the astronomical determinism in the daily time schedule has been broken—but with resulting confusion. Night no longer forces rest; rest must be planned for, and since few people are good planners it may be that few people get enough rest. The old rural routine of "going to bed with the chickens" is hardly even remembered.

Nor was rural life any more the unchallenged monopoly of agriculturists (66). In 1950 only 69 per cent of all United States farms were classified as "commercial." A fourth (26 per cent) of the commercial farm family's money income came from off-farm sources. On the biggest commercial farms this was only 13 per cent; on the littlest it was nearly half (48 per cent). Twenty-nine per cent of all employed workers living on farms worked in nonagricultural pursuits. Mighell puts it this way:

---

* Nationally farm population declined 23.6%; rural nonfarm population increased 43.2% and urban population increased 19.5% from 1940 to 1950 (15).

The broad outline of the structure of agriculture that has emerged has a central core of several million competing commercial farms. At one side are the noncommercial farms, the part-time and residential farms, whose operators and families live in the country but find most of their income elsewhere. Surrounding the central core of commercial farms, is an outer envelope of related group interest—farm organizations, cooperatives, independent private businesses, and government agencies (59, page 164).

### Descriptive summary: the textbook view

Almost every recent study of rural communities recounts a list of changes in the general context, almost as though to apologize for what has happened to the community and to insist that it isn't the community's fault! From a Kansas study: decline in number of farms; increase in sizes of farms; increased variety of occupations; increase in total, urban, and rural nonfarm population; rising medians of education; diversification in sources of income; increased use of electricity (21). From a Missouri study: farm population decline, birth rate decline; increasing proportion aged; commercialization of agriculture; mechanization of farm production; decline in row crops and increase in livestock; increase in per capita production; growth of conservation farming; advent of measures of relief and security; roads, automobiles, trucks, buses; telephones, motion pictures, radio, electricity, etc. (41).

Such changes in context could only provoke structural strains in the rural community. A ship rolls and its timbers creak; a wind blows and the shanty sways; a flood rolls in and the bridge buckles; heat pours down and the highway blisters; new patterns of work make muscles ache. Nor are social structures immune to the forces that impinge upon them when surrounding features change.

But a conventional view of the rural community as it is usually discussed in the textbooks on rural sociology should here precede further summaries on change, substantive features, and theoretical consideration (18, 26, 47, 51, 53, 70). Ensminger's generalizations (in the textbook by Carl C. Taylor and his DFP * colleagues) about the rural neighborhood and the rural community in the United States present the usual description by rural sociologists of the rural community (26). His chapter is written around a set of fifty to sixty propositions such as are reformulated below.

* DFP in this chapter refers to the Division of Farm Population and Rural Life, Bureau of Agricultural Economics, later recognized as Rural Life and Farm Population Branch, Agricultural Marketing Service, United States Department of Agriculture.

The rural community is the geographic area with which most of the community's dwellers identify themselves. Asking rural dwellers their community's name brings uniform responses.

In the South, county seat towns function more and more as community centers. In the North, Middle West, and West: rural dwellers' most frequent and meaningful contacts are in the trade center. Trade center communities are modernizing education through school consolidation. The church is gradually becoming a village-centered institution. Recreation, because commercial, is provided largely by the towns.

Rural communities are the most important groupings in the nation. Of the nation's 14,000,000 rural families over half live dispersed. Neighborhoods are subgroupings—around schools, churches, general stores. Rural families live in neighborhoods that they readily identify. The degree and intensity of common life determine the community and the neighborhood for any individual.

The rural neighborhood is a socio-geographic unit of a small group of families to whom the area is a symbol of personal identity, among whom intimate, face-to-face contact contributes to a common life which signifies visiting, exchanging work, providing education, or religious worship. Neighborhoods vary in size with density of population and topography. Generalized definition of the community is less possible than of the neighborhood. The community is larger than the neighborhood in area, population and services available.

The community may be single or multi-centered. The degree of identification may be strong or weak. People of a community can act together providing needed institutions, organizations, services. Neighborhoods usually cluster around a community center. For both neighborhood and community, social unity lies in internal belonging, external recognition. The rural community usually has one major service center with population of a few hundred to over 2,500, providing a variety of services for a 10–12 mile radius. Farm and village people are beginning to work together (having discovered their common interests). Essential neighborhood-community differences are in size, population, services, intimacy. A neighborhood contains 15–30 families in the South: 20–80 families in the Great Plains. Communities have 80–500 open country families, plus the same number or more in town. Neighborhood relations revolve around families and are intimate. Community relations revolve around individuals and are more casual and impersonal.

Neighborhood is first, community is second as modes of common life beyond that of the family. Neighborhood and community are integrated systems of social interaction through associations of families. The neighborhood derives from the historical pattern of 12–40 pioneer families associating for protection and mutual aid. The neighborhood as a simple locality group may be gradually disappearing but the neighborhood pattern continues among farmers. Community life today is a combination of family-to-family association within the neighborhood, and an increasing number of personal and impersonal contacts in wider areas.

The rural community emerged with village and town service centers. The U.S.A. has 35,000 trade-center rural communities and 240,000 rural neighborhoods. Communities are regrouping into systems of larger service areas.

Rural dwellers may be reached most effectively through their neighborhoods and communities. The community has a culture. Neighborhoods and communities can be delineated by discussion in group meetings. Neighborhoods can be delineated by the "last family" method, communities by the "neighborhood cluster" method. Neighborhood and community boundaries seldom coincide with official boundaries (except for the New England town). Neighborhood and community are natural groups with natural leaders. Neighborhood influence facilitates or retards the adoption of new practices. Rural society is developing a complex and heterogeneous social organization. Trend: family to individual participation. Trend: wholeness to segmentation.

## CATEGORIES FOR ANALYSIS OF THE RURAL COMMUNITY

Analytical study of any circumstance or event depends on denotative concepts that are inclusive enough for complete description and classification. Study of the rural community has been conceptually uncertain; the nomenclature here, as in other problem areas of sociology, is varied and unsettled. The languages of biological ecology, social psychology, democratic ideology, and common parlance have intermingled. Pools of synonyms gather from the writings of observers who are not fully satisfied with the language of their colleagues, yet who are often tentative in their own choices of word and phrase. In part, also, the diversity of terms is a result of diversity in techniques of observation and the uncertainty of each scholar that he has seen the same things his peers described. A pool of names used as synonyms of, substitutes for, or types of rural community includes the following terms found in the literature of the decade:

close neighbors
geogroup
geosocial unit
home town
locality
locality group
natural group

neighbor group
neighborhood
rurban community
service area
territorial group
town-country community
trade area
trade center community

A pool of names for attributes of or of subtypes of neighborhood and community includes the following terms:

focal—nonfocal
general—special
group identification (or integration, we feeling, solidarity, togetherness, unity, community consciousness, stability)
independent—dependent

    major—minor
    mononucleated—polynucleated
    primary—secondary—tertiary
    unicentered—multicentered
    unibonded—multibonded

Perhaps there should be an even greater elaboration of terminology because different meanings attach to the uses of different authors. Writing could be more literal if there were a word for each meaning. Certainly "community" is a word of varied usage and meaning in the research literature.

The selected nouns and adjectives in the foregoing lists point out the problem of defining the rural community and of establishing a language with which to analyze it. At the same time they suggest, directly or indirectly, some of the major categories required to introduce more generality and order in observations of communities. By a system of classification analogous to that used in biological science, the construct (constructed type, ideal type; model) of the rural community may be presented as a *variety* of the *species* community, *genus* group, *division* social system, *kingdom* society. It has an indefinite number of hypothesized subvarieties, as yet officially unnamed, but classifiable according to chief attributes. All of these attributes are common to members of genus community, but each of them has rural manifestations which, taken together, specifically identify the rural community.

It is here proposed that some of the major categories necessary for description and functional (or structural-functional, if it pleases) analysis of rural communities may be developed from the following list, which has been arranged tentatively from the terminology in the literature of the decade under review.*

### Selected differentia of communities

1. *Determinateness:* the extent to which peripheries can be determined unequivocally as limiting the locale of the group and separating it from others.

2. *Area symbolization:* the significance or insignificance of the area as a meaningful symbol of common interest or commonality.

3. *Density:* the density of settlement expressed as number of persons per unit of area; one of the determinants of social density.

---

* "There apparently is slight use, explicitly or implicitly, of the structure, function or interactional role framework for studying the structure of the community or smaller social entities" (34).

4. *Centralization:* the extent to which social interaction within the group is diffuse, or is organized around a single center or multiple centers.

5. *Differentiation and autonomy:* the extent to which (a) the social system comprises subentities which are varied but interdependent and specialized "parts," and (b) the extent to which all the main functions necessary to the maintenance of the whole social system are performed by its sundry parts.*

6. *Articulation and integration:* the extent to which parts of the social system are functionally intersupporting and interdependent, hence also the extent to which the grouping is real, quasi-real, or only nominally a social system.†

The task of definition is not completed by the development of the foregoing categories, although they do make explicit the concept of a community with determinate boundaries, recognition of the area as a symbol, some yet-to-be-specified density of settlement, a center, differentiated but autonomous structure, and functional articulation and integration.

The rurality of any community will be evident (or not) in particular manifestations of these characteristics which will be recognized as "rural" in contrast to other types, such as urban, feudal, metropolitan, etc.

DETERMINATENESS: THE SITUATION WITH RESPECT TO IDENTIFICATION OF A RURAL COMMUNITY'S BOUNDARY OR MARGIN. Margin is probably a better word than periphery or boundary for defining the limits of a rural community. It has connotations from other applications in social science that are also useful here. Community theory might predict social marginality at the geographic boundary. Hence the margin might be at those "points" or locations at which any further participation in community *A* would require such time—space cost that it would begin to yield less satisfaction per participant than equivalent participation in adjacent community *B*. The community allegiance of residents immediately on both sides of the boundary would be presumed to be that of the "marginal man."

Sociologists have been ambivalent toward their failures to find boundaries that are clear and incontestable. Difficulties in mapping have not been sufficient cause to abandon the concept of the community, yet the margin has been elusive and "zonal" (38). It is small comfort to recall that kinetic theories of molecular motion make the edges of even physical bodies also difficult to determine.

Nearly 80 per cent of all farm families in the United States are within

---

* See Timasheff (77), p. 220, for statement of "the functional theorem."

† Elements of a "social system," after Loomis and Beegle (53), are roles, status, authority, rights and duties, ends, norms, and territoriality.

10 miles of their nearest trading center,* the average distance being 6 miles (59), traversable in 20 minutes at 30 miles per hour. This is much less time than many commuters spend in getting to their work. Two-thirds of all farm homes are within one-fifth mile of an all-weather road. Clearly, residence in the country area of a rural community no longer enforces isolation. To be one-fifth of a mile from an all-weather road is to have potential access to all the communities in the total society. If there are any roads with two dead ends they are very rare! The inter-dependence of communities is symbolized by any map of highways in the nation, or even the continent, and to the maps of highways can be added the maps of seaways and skyways.

But even though movement is possible to almost infinite areas and distances, there are still limits of cost and time. Certainly rural dwellers now often elect to go places not in terms of the shortest distance, but in terms of the most convenient time. But for all "practical purposes," there are effective limits to the movements of people, hence effective limits to the sizes of their communities, and at least hypothetical margins or bound-aries. There may also be hypothesized effective limits to the numbers and varieties of contacts persons may have at given levels of interaction, such as primary and secondary (43). Hawley suggests a classification by frequency: *primary* or daily, *secondary* or occasional, *tertiary*, or infre-quent (38). So even though margins may be difficult to identify and locate, there is no theoretical possibility that margins might cease to exist.

Three techniques of delineating boundaries are in common use. The survey method (via data from children in school, family visitation, etc.) inquiries of people about their identification with place names and their patronage of centers. The traffic-flow approach finds boundaries on the roads between centers at points of minimum travel. The neighborhood-cluster method, developed by Sanders and Ensminger (26), is the method now probably most widely used rurally. This identifies neighborhood limits by locating "marginal" residents, and clusters the neighborhoods by their natural directions of affiliation. A fourth procedure, that of sociometric choice to outline the ego-neighborhood (63), is used in some situations (53, 82). During World War II the United States Department of Agriculture caused thousands of delineations of neighborhoods and communities to be made in its campaign to reach "the last man on the last road" with wartime educational messages. In a sense, this resulted in overselling of and disillusionment with the neighborhood concept which was, after all, a construct or model and not an accurate repre-sentation of every empirically encountered group. Efforts to use the

* These data are for 1950.

neighborhood and community concepts where they did not describe actual situations resulted in some criticism, and occasional unwarranted rejection of the concept.

Recoiling from these experiences, rural sociologists have relaxed somewhat in their enthusiasm for delineating neighborhoods and communities. They are concluding that neighborhoods with discoverable boundaries may persist without great change, they may gain, they may lose their identity in newly formed special interest groupings, or in larger locality groupings. Each of these three outcomes has been reported. Each describes a currently observable situation at some place or other in the United States (57, 48, 1, 10, 52).

The reservations sociologists have had to admit with respect to the delineation of boundaries may be taken to some extent to reveal inadequacies in data. More than reconnaissance is required to document the presence or absence of locality groups with discoverable boundaries. Noting discrepancies between the delineations of insiders and outsiders, Slocum and Case (72) call attention to the need for data from the "cognitive behavior systems of residents."

It is a canon of natural area or locality group theory that boundaries are the consequence of free association and are not coterminous with administrative or legal delimitations. Nevertheless, neighborhood areas, where acknowledged to exist, have been reported often to coincide with present or former elementary school attendance areas (30, 50), and recently it has been proposed that in many parts of the United States the county now forms the most prominent rural community boundary (26, 1).

## AREA SYMBOLIZATION

The importance of bounded space (locality, territoriality) to a community is not physical only, as earth to stand on or distance to traverse in visiting neighbors. Nor is it biological as plant bed and field for the farmer. It is rather cultural and social. As a meaningful cultural object it is itself a part of the social system and a significant symbol of the community's identity and each of its other chief attributes: its centralization, density, differentiation, autonomy, and articulation. Consider for example the "feeling of belonging" which is basic to membership in a real group. It is a psychologically complex feeling extending even to sense-perceived physical objects such as a road to follow, corners to turn, houses and trees and hills to see and to be familiar with. One becomes habituated to them entirely apart from interhuman relations—or one may even personalize them to compensate for unsatisfying human relations. Familiar and family have the same root; a familiar object is an object of intimate belongingness. Does not neighborhood loyalty or consciousness imply a feeling of "I belong to *this place*" as much as "I belong to *these people*"?

> A rural community, or any other community for that matter, may be defined as simply that area in which a number of people hold certain things in common. These questions need to be answered to define further a particular community. First, what is the particular locality symbol which serves as a focus for community delineation? It may be a school community, a trade community, a geographic community, a church community, or, on a larger scale, a national or international community built around common interests in these larger realms (37, page 147).

It is not fair, however, to require that local space be the determinant of the community social system; it is enough that it be a codeterminant, offering some influence in the multicausational package of determinants. Even though it is only a "trace determinant," symbolized, space becomes a category of description and differentiation by which the existence of the rural community may be known. The research of the decade suggests, but does not demonstrate, that communities may be placed along continua of the extent to which area is a symbol. To the extent that meaningfulness of territory to its dwellers recedes, the rural community loses its identity.

## DENSITY OF SETTLEMENT

Density is usually expressed in terms of the number of dwellers per unit of area, such as "per square mile." Its chief sociological relevance lies in its effect upon contacts. Density, therefore, has time and cost dimensions. A mile by horseback is longer in time than a mile by car and negotiable with more effort but less money.

Settlement could be so sparse that dwellers would live in isolation, not forming communities. Settlement is often so dense, however, that it tends to generate an urban rather than a rural type of community. One consequence of changing technology is the social redefinition of propinquity (7, 8, 24). "Particular trade centers . . . no longer have exclusive claim to serving the needs of rural people. Propinquity is not now a compelling force in the relationship between the people in the open country and a specific trade center" (57).

The "volume of social contacts produced in an area of low population density," however, "is much smaller than in an area of high density" (61). There has been little explicit reference to this feature in the literature of the decade and the point that density is a major category in the analysis of the rural community is here made thus briefly merely "for the record" and not for full explication.

## CENTRALIZATION: ITS STATUS AND TREND IN THE RURAL COMMUNITY

Typically a community has a center. Early ecological theory made this center analogous to the head region of an organism, a point where metabolism (social interaction) is "mostest and fastest," a locus of dominance over interaction elsewhere in the body (community). This analogy is rarely emphasized in the most recent descriptions of the rural community, although much attention is given to centers. Social centralization, as a pervasive and rapid type of social process, has been conspicuous in all societal parts during the decade. Government, business, education, religion—all have experienced centralization. Historically, the rural community, emerging from a diffusion of free and equal neighborhoods to the status of a settlement with a center was in itself an early instance of social centralization in the United States.

Empirically in rural life it is easier to spot centers than to locate the edges of their circles. Centers are just more visible because of denser settlement for one thing and more varied interaction for another. Some rural community studies have begged the question of boundaries and have concentrated on the study of the centers. Human geographers have studied the locational patterns of trade centers by the hypothesis that their distribution would be controlled by radial movement of traffic, those with "equivalent functions" to be spaced at approximately equal distances (19). The well-known and always deterministic changes in transportation and communication have made all centers sensitive to change and have put them into competition with each other for patronage and participation * (81). It is the reorganization of centers and their changing relationships to each other that today complicate the search for the rural community's margin.

In the decade from 1945 to 1955 our social structure, both rural and urban, was quite amorphous—as always, thus far in United States history (12)! Concentrations of population (congested areas) were advancing or retreating as places of work and life relocated. The routing of railroads originally had much to do with village locations; highways now tend to exert similar influence. Settlement moves in from remote and inaccessible spots and is redistributed along highways and at intersections of highways. Many roads are becoming line villages ("string towns"). Today's low-hung automobiles are not suited to the parallel, deep-

---

* See discussion on community autonomy, below.

grooved ruts that formerly served as wagon roads. Trucks and military vehicles can traverse mud roads, tread creek bottoms, and climb the sides of hills—but the pull of the automobile is toward the hard-topped highway.

During the decade here being observed, the numerous "agencies" of government which burgeoned in the 1930's were fifteen to twenty-five years old, and their impact on centers and on rural centralization had become familiar and stabilized (1). Influences in the period after World War II, a tense international cold war, and a lively domestic political tug-of-war all seemed to aid and hasten the process of social centralization. Activities and programs that were nationally directed had to be operated from local centers, usually county-seat towns. Welfare programs, agricultural programs, defense mobilization, the training of military reserve forces, and numerous other activities were administered from towns that thereby became more important, while neighboring centers fell behind. There was a corresponding drawing together of small centers around regional and metropolitan centers.

The weakening of little rural centers is seen in the continuing decline in the number of one room schools and in the removal of small post offices. Small neighborhood churches resisted centralization more tenaciously than did schools, but in many areas responded definitely to townward forces (41, 4). A classification of centers by size, because of presumed correlation of size with social features, includes hamlets (under 250 population), villages (250–999), and towns (1,000–2,499).* But this formula assigns all places with 2,500 inhabitants to the category of city. Some writers do not make the distinction between villages and towns and use only the term village for places below 2,500 (55).

In 1940 nearly one third (30.9 per cent) of the rural population, two thirds (65.5 per cent) of the rural nonfarm population, and 13 per cent of the total population lived in places under 2,500. Recent studies indicate the persistence of these small centers, and Marshall attributes this fact to the presence there of the neighborhood store, the schools, the churches, places for informal visiting and shopping, and communication centers for rural society. Mighell writes, "Probably the strongest cohesive forces today in the mainly rural communities are schools and trading facilities" (59, page 149). Trade centers are being classified as primary, secondary, intermediate, or terminal. Only the first three can be rural in character. Anderson writes, "The centers are not only the locale of the community business and service establishment, but tend also to be the focal point of association and organized activities" (5).

Brownell reasserts the viewpoint that "the isolated farm home in Amer-

* See Trewartha (78).

ica has been a continuous deterrent to functional community development" (17). Mighell notes this point also, except in the case of New England, where "local government did not separate country from city." Smith observes with satisfaction that Brazil has not had to overcome some of the deterrents to solidification inherent in decentralized settlement patterns of the United States (73). Current centralization of the rural community conspires with technology to reduce the disadvantages of the isolated farmstead (61). But what other changes may follow?

The American's desire for privacy, his insistence on personal inviolability, his tenacity of personal possession have been nurtured in dispersed homes. As massing of population proceeds these things may change. To maintain them in the United States we have gone to considerable cost (6). We pay for dispersion, and thus prove it to be a valued feature of our past and present standard of living; however, things may change in the long future.

We maintain country roads, buy school buses, and support other rural services rather than bring people into villages where utilities can be provided cheaper. We "zone" areas for residential use and we appropriate public funds for housing to foster family-by-family dwelling; these are illustrations of the numerous policies to promote privacy for persons and families. It may be, however, that we have exaggerated the importance of the dispersal of farm homes as an influence inhibiting integration. Tropp reminds us that "In Wales . . . it is the long tradition of dispersed settlement based on kinship that has been associated with very closely integrated community life" (79). He cites Brittany as a similar instance. If the farms in a dispersed pattern are very small and their production is noncommercial, solidarity may be more pronounced than in places where farms are large and commercial. Hence it is not only the physical character of dispersion that counts; it is also the historical and present social context.

The community absorbs the neighborhood (14). A "community of mutual interests" integrates previously separated white and Negro neighborhoods (56). Anderson finds that "a mosaic of earlier communities underlies the emerging social organization" (5). Reorganization of association with regard to local space is retarded by the inevitable lags in the reattachment of sentiments (5). These and several similar general points that might be discussed here will be presented below in their relevance to the functional autonomy of the rural community.

There are ebbs and flows of localization. Changes go too far and are pulled back, as in school consolidation. Adult neighbors oppose the closure of the one room school, or the too-small high school, and they resist consolidation in central towns. They are overpowered in the early waves of centralization; then, after partial accommodation, they are later deferred to in the plan for supplementing the centrally consolidated senior high school with the subcentrally consolidated junior high school and possibly also the sub-subcentrally consolidated elementary school. This is an emerging pattern of rural school reorganization. It acknowledges and balances at different personal-maturity levels the efficiency of centralism and the security of localism.

As years pass after the consolidation of high schooling at a town center, the alumni of the school become more numerous throughout the district— and their "school spirit" becomes increasingly a strong component in community sentiment. This is such a recent occurrence in most of rural America that its eventual impact cannot yet be known. It is known, however, that many of the tensions and conflicts that develop when consolidation is planned will disappear within a few years. Gradual accommodation to the enlarged school district may be followed by the integration of a larger community. To a lesser extent the same process is at work with "alumni" of village Sunday schools. School-related organizations and activities are similarly effective. Integration via Parent Teacher Associations carries the adult citizenry along toward the larger community. The general interest in high school sports, such as basketball, is especially a community-wide force. As time passes, this fact becomes more significant, because the percentage of high school attendance has gone from half of the eligible young people to two-thirds or three-fourths or more in twenty years in many rural communities; this gives correspondingly greater weight to the high school as a community integrative force. This is not to assert, of course, that the high school community is as tightly knit as was the previous rural neighborhood, on a basis of primary interaction. Becker and Loomis, studying cleavages among pupils in a rural consolidated school, found that such cleavages as did exist did not follow the division of farm and nonfarm residence (11).

There are numerous instances of sociologically spurious consolidation in education, with town or village boundaries separating school systems whose buildings may be "within a stone's throw" of each other. An "independent" district comprising the county-seat town and a county district comprising all the rest of the county, each with its own high school system, symbolizes and fortifies a social separation or a dissociation of center from circle that counters the natural trends toward fusion of interest and integration of social structure. This perpetuates town-country conflict. Like the schizoid personality, here is a schizoid commonality.

### The county as a new product of centralization

The mantle of community meaning has come to rest on the county. Established as a political and administrative unit of government, the county has become at least a quasi-community and in many instances a real community. Forty-five per cent of the county seats in 3,072 counties of the United States are villages, having populations of under 2,500 (48). "Four generations have lived within the boundaries of Seward County" (5); they have elected their officials, paid their taxes, built some of their roads, been affected by agencies and organizations operating county-wide, maintained a fire district, a weed district, a soil conservation district, held county-wide meetings, served on county-wide committees. Community-like functions of the county have been described in several recent studies, especially the DFP-AES series. Mayo and Bobbitt wrote that ". . . a few families recognized no geo-social unit smaller or less formal than Wake County itself" (57). Alexander and Galloway wrote:

> As the county has come to depend more on the outside, the individual citizens have come to depend more on the county as an administrative unit, for the county has become an important instrument through which the outside, particularly state and federal agencies, has brought assistance to the people . . . paradoxically, out of a growing dependence on the outside has emerged a more vigorous county community that performs many new functions (2, page 404).

In the same vein, Anderson reported that "county consciousness is enhanced by the fact that people from all parts of the county combine trading and visiting with county court business" (5).

Mergers and combinations of small counties have long been advocated by proponents of efficient government, and enabling statutes have been in the law books of many states for more than a quarter of a century. The rareness of such consolidations is usually attributed to the vested interests of politicians and office holders, but a firmer sociological consideration lies in the growth of county-community consciousness. Many a rural county has passed from the stage of being merely a unit of government to that of being a social system with functions having the breadth and depth of a community. The county-community has absorbed some of the solidarity of its earlier constituent community parts, developing some of the attributes of a real social group. One measure of a county's community-like character might be its readiness to vote county-wide school consolidation (41).

## DIFFERENTIATION AND AUTONOMY

The research of the decade 1945–1955 describes the emergence of subsystems (74), often to the point of leading observers to assert that these entities severally have come nearly to supersede the community whole of which they were originally parts. Within a group—say a community—

there may be numerous instances of beginnings of subgroupings in various stages of emergence, like crystals forming in a solution until eventually there may no longer be any solution. Some, vague and tentative, may lapse into nonexistence without ever fully forming. Some may accelerate their repetitive interaction and become established conspicuously as subsystems. All conceivable stages between nonexistence and complete formation are possible.*

Selective neighboring as a form of differential participation is mentioned often as evidence of increasing social differentiation within the rural community (31, 39, 41). The multiplication of interest groups is mentioned in nearly all the studies. The present difficulty of starting farming, now that mechanization and high-priced land have greatly increased capital requirements, introduces a new socioeconomic differentiation, and displaces the old "agricultural ladder" of vertical mobility. It is observed of rural communities that leadership—like the practice of medicine—is now special more than general: it emerges within the interest group or subsystem rather than generally within the total community, another manifestation of differentiation (44).

An aspect of structural differentiation which gets frequent mention in recent research reports concerns the place of the center in the community. Selective trading here becomes another instance of selective participation. As the size of a trade center increases, it provides more specialized services, thus multiplying the possibilities for selection (13). "In most cases the expanded patterns of trading and contact seem to add a new dimension to social experience rather than subtracting from the local community life" (5, page 26). Smaller centers retain the more general products and services (gas, groceries, schools), in the sense that everybody patronizes them and little or no selectivity is involved.

Recent research on rural community differentiation has been somewhat superficial, focusing on the statistics of differential participation to the neglect of differential norms and values, or differential roles and statuses, except in an introductory, descriptive manner. Participation in categoric groupings thus is better known than participation in corporate groups (38).

Age, for example, is associated with certain differences in participation in the rural community, and aged persons are more numerous in the village and town centers than in the surrounding country. Youth of high school age "tend to break away from the family group participation in outside activities and to seek the company of their peers" (5). Occupational, educational, and status categories have also been mentioned. Full-

* See Hawley's corporate and categoric groups (38).

time farmers and younger farmers tend to shop further from home. Use of various services (except "doctors" and "going to town on Sundays") tends to decline with age. But Belcher concluded that "neither education nor socio-economic status seems to exert much influence on where a farmer goes" (13).

Important also is the nonparticipant in the rural community, the family which seems, in a sense, to have been left behind in the process of differentiating the community into functional subsystems; ". . . many farm families never leave home except to purchase the necessities of life. Many sell practically no farm products and engage in no educational, recreational, fraternal or religious activity away from home" (13). Functional consequences of differentiation will be discussed below under the topic of articulation and integration.

The self-sufficient farm family had a self-sufficient or autonomous and independent rural community that was not highly differentiated internally (59, 38). But things keep emerging in our civilization, which is itself emergent. The town emerges, the rural community emerges, the urban community emerges. (As each emerges, does its predecessor submerge or just merge?) The orientation of recent studies of the rural community, however, has had to be extended more than previously toward intercommunity relations, and toward contacts that range outward. One of the most frequently reported observations is that rural families, both farm and nonfarm, are now in contact with more centers than formerly, and that the social systems thus established are more overlapping, interlocking, and interdependent than ever before. Kolb and Day state that "Inter*group* relations have moved alongside of inter*personal* relations in level of importance to rural people within rural communities" (48; italics mine). Ensminger and Polson ". . . suggest that the future orientation be rural organization, not merely community organization. . . . In the past we have delineated communities. . . . It might be well to explore the possibilities of exploring the county as a universe of study . . ." (27). Boskoff spoke of "the futility of the current concentration on the community as the basic focus of rural sociological investigation" (16).

As people associate more according to special interest and less by adjacency in space they link themselves to corresponding groups in other communities. This is true of local interest groups, peer groups, and local class or status groups. Intercommunity connections are formed also between businesses, services, institutions, and agencies. Thus localities are drawn together into networks, and they develop those "associations of associations" and the "communities of communities" which frustrate the analytical observer by their complexity. This involves the local community in networks that reduce its autonomy. "Throughout the Western world, particularly where the isolated holding predominates, the familistic Gemeinschaft-like neighborhood is losing its functions. This is true not only of its economic functions but of its social functions as well" (53, pages 202–203).

The beginning point of an action, or a social interaction, lies in an impulse, originating within or outside of the social system in which the interaction is eventually consummated. Of an integrated neighborhood in pioneer America, it may have been true that most impulses to inter-action were of internal or local origin. To a lesser extent, the internal origin of most impulses would characterize an "early American" rural community.

Whether or not there are now fewer local impulses to action, it is conspicuously true that multitudes of impulses are of outside, nonlocal, even remote origin. They are felt through the lines of communication in intercommunity chains of affiliation in business and social organization, through federations of interest groups, through mass media, through in-stitutional hierarchies and bureaucratic agencies. Interaction in the autonomous community was locally generated; interaction in the rural community today is a mixture of unknown proportions of local and non-local initiation. Locality determinism, though present, is weaker now than once; the influences of nonlocal pressures are often stronger.

All rural studies of the 1945–1955 decade recount the impact of outside agencies on the rural community: these are the agencies of agricultural production control, conservation, credit, adult and vocational education, welfare and social security, and many more (DFP-AES). A conspicuous case of nonautonomy or dependence is that of the curriculum of the rural community's school, which has adopted a state's prescribed course of study out of dependence on state financial aid (38, 41).

The larger the town, some studies indicate, the greater the autonomy of the community it centers, and "the greater is the area in which people consider it as their home town" (13). But not all centers are large: many are quite small. A sample of excerpts tells the story: "The automobile reduces the villages to the role of convenience centers . . ." [lessening their autonomy] (5). "Today farm people must travel considerable dis-tances . . . must trade at several centers not limited to neighboring vil-lages or even to larger centers . . ." (13); "the rural town must adapt itself to the newer conditions . . ." (5).

The decline of local autonomy may be associated, however, with a certain kind of rise in the level of living. Sometimes intercommunity contact may replace (displace) intracommunity contact. This weakens community integrity and strengthens correspondingly the larger area grouping. But the use of many centers rather than one requires more

and wider travel, more and wider communication. To patronize more
services and more centers is thus to have a "higher" level of living.
Travel is not without cost per mile and per minute, but its costs may yield
"high returns." To have access to more centers and more services is to
have a higher level of living.

Speaking also of contacts, relationships, friendships, etc., as acts of consumption, the level of social consumption has gone up. The total volume
of participation, at least potentially, has increased—and this is an important component of the level of living. Social participation is a fulfillment
of the needs of a person, and too little of it may constitute deprivation.
Incidentally patronage of stores and businesses is a form of social participation as well as an act of economic exchange. Increase in trading contacts and a complication of the number of services may be taken to be a
part of an enlargement of social relations and a rising standard of living.
Generally, the more choices one has, whether of goods or friends, the
better one may live. Hence, the decline in functional autonomy of a
particular community may enhance for its members their gain from living
there.

Data on social participation provide evidence related to several of the
traits of a rural community: differentiation, autonomy, and articulation
in particular. The extent to which a neighborhood or community accounts for all of the participation of all of its members is one criterion
of autonomy. Christiansen (20), working under Kolb's guidance, has
analyzed the most recent data on neighborhoods in Dane County, Wisconsin, to test the hypothesis of Mayo and Marsh (58), that participation
is greater within neighborhoods than elsewhere. Studying a sample of
731 families outside of plotted and incorporated areas and selecting 12
items of participation generally asserted to be part of or closely related
to neighborhood phenomena, he tested the significance of the differences
between neighborhood and nonneighborhood residents. Of course he
had to deal equally with items of unknown relative weight. Furthermore,
neighborhoods were treated without weighting for intensity of neighborhood solidarity.

His items in one set of problems were:

1. Church attendance
2. Grocery purchases
3. Participation in school-related activities
4. Participation in church-related activities
5. Ball game attendance
6. Participation in picnics
7. Family visiting
8. Mutual assistance

    9. Attendance at parties

  10. Attendance at dances

  11. Participating in organizations (other than church and/or
        school-related)

  12. Work exchange

He concluded that "the theoretical writings which indicate the relation-ship between neighborhood membership and various forms of social participation were generally supported by the results of these tests" (20, page 30).

Partial correlation tests showed that one by one, 13 factors such as age and education (often thought to be associated with participation) did not account for the differences between neighborhood members and nonmembers.

Of the 13 participation variables with which neighborhood membership was found to be associated, the following 6 were incorporated into an index (through factor analysis) and proposed as a tool for use in other studies:

    1. Number of service centers patronized

    2. Church attendance

    3. Grocery purchases

    4. Number of church-related organizations

    5. Number of school-related organizations

    6. Number of parties attended

The Christiansen study is an ingenious quantitative test of an old hypothesis, and it bears on several problematic aspects of rural communities. It reveals the presence of some local community autonomy insofar as social participation is concerned.

## ARTICULATION AND INTEGRATION

The complex of social relationships and systems that compose a community may or may not be functionally articulated in the sense that they do or do not reciprocally support each other and enhance the functioning of the whole system. Complete and perfect articulation is integration, so the former word applies to more cases than the latter. Several studies during the decade have been directed, to some extent at least, toward the problem of describing and perhaps even measuring articulation and integration. These studies have been concerned also with the question of whether or not a rural community constitutes a *real* group, and not merely a quasi- or nominal group.

A distinction may be made here between a *grouping* and a *group*, the latter meaning a *real group* and the former a gathering or collection or enumeration of persons of similar characteristics, sometimes potentially a real group—but perhaps never to get further in the process of group formation than the statistical condition of similarity—belonging to a common category but lacking the interactive structure of a social system.*

Integration is not uniquely a sociological concept, and its application in sociology is an extension of its more general reference to any occurrence of wholeness formed of constituent parts. Integration is then a prominent identifying feature, a *sine qua non* of any system, whether a social system, a system of thought, a system of water supply, or a system of farming. Integration is a "matter of degree," however. The degree of its intensity may be known by the extent to which the parts of the given whole or system have no separate identity and exist only as parts or members.

Integration and differentiation thus become to some extent antonyms, or the polar extremes of a continuum. If there is complete differentiation we find only the several disparate phenomena which, although they may once have been parts of a whole, have now only independent existence. On the contrary, if there is complete integration, the identity of the parts is all but lost in the identity of the system—the Gestalt.

To discover the intensity of integration of a system we must take two steps:

1. Seek out and name those phenomena identifiable as parts.

2. Measure the separateness versus the inclusion of these parts (intensity of membership).

Differential social participation is a frequent focus of research, and numerous studies reveal the presence in rural communities of nonparticipants as well as very active participants (65). Social class differences afford special problems of articulating social participation. An outstanding instance of this is to be found in the home demonstration clubs that are widespread among the rural communities of the United States. Women of low class position are quite unlikely to take part in clubs that meet in homes of middle or upper class women. The circumstance that proffered services do not reach those who are in greatest need points to some lack of functional articulation within the community. However, school centralization as discussed above tends often to be an articulating influence, as are also such general associations as those of veterans which are cross-class and community-wide in scope. Cleavages (discussed in all the best-known textbooks), such as those between town dwellers and

---

* Cf. Hawley on corporate and categoric groups (38).

country dwellers, age cohorts, sectarian churches, churches and schools, political factions, cooperatives and merchants, may be so marked in a particular community as to completely sunder the system, thus exhibiting an extreme variety of nonarticulation. One might argue that cleavage and conflict are functional in their stimulation of progress and development and are thus preferable to placidity, so the point of articulation is a relative one.

On the other hand, there are important examples of rapprochement and accord among groups and institutions. One case that has been interesting to watch has been the functional (although not administrative) absorption in the rural United States of the 4-H Clubs, which seem to be becoming adjuncts of the public schools.

Free mobility both enhances and inhibits the functional articulation of a rural community. It makes for potentially rapid adjustment; it also may make for the "confounding" of confusion. There does not seem to be a satisfactory concept in use to specify the mobility within a community, the active participation in many groups and events: let it be known here temporarily as personal or social "motility." Perhaps "circulation" has a similar connotation. The term is needed to indicate local mobility, or "running around," without the changes in residence or social position to which the phrase "social mobility" conventionally refers. The significance of "going to town" is an instance of it. By older rural inhibitions going to town except on Saturday was extravagance, profligacy, and at best, neglect of duty! Only the ne'er-do-well would be guilty. The compulsion to "stay home and work" was controlling over the desire to "go places." Time and energy were not to be wasted. But now the farmer is motorized and goes to town on slightest provocation. Elders will sometimes make sardonic comments on this, observing of a given farmer that "he even drives his car to the pasture to get the cows up for milking." Incidentally, Belcher finds that full-time farmers go to more places for more reasons than do part-time farmers or nonfarmers who live in rural communities (13). In an important sense, this is another instance of differential participation.

The status of communication in the rural community reveals the character of its articulation, and the loss of local autonomy is related to the mass quality of contemporary communication. Primary contacts were basic in the structure of the early rural community, and their essence is in their direct reciprocity. Secondary contacts bulk larger in the later rural community, supplementing but not (as is often feared) entirely supplanting primary contacts. The secondary contact also has an important feature of reciprocity, although it is indirect, involving intermediaries. Both primary and secondary contacts involve two-way communication, but not so with mass communication. A person's response to a radio broadcast, newspaper, movie, or television, etc., is in no sense a return message. This is illustrated by the movie goer who neither cries at tragedy nor laughs at humor on the screen, but sits in well-schooled restraint. Mass communication is messages *to*—not messages exchanged. It is one-way action, not interaction (with apologies to Newton's "laws of motion").

The coming of mass communication to the rural community creates new problems of articulation. The older structure of primary and secondary relationships is crowded for time and attention. Persons become receivers of messages rather than participants in interaction. Rearticulation involves the formation or use of primary groups and secondary groups in which mass-received messages may be socially exchanged, and the individual receiver may become again a participant.

A related, and probably not contradictory, line of reasoning appears in recent studies. It is, as Anderson (5) expresses it, that "variations in response to county-wide or community programs are often due to poor communications." Intravenous feeding, blood transfusions, and injections would be of little effect if they did not get into the natural circulatory system, the active blood stream of the body. Similarly, messages are conveyed most effectively when they get into the natural channels of communication, as they circulate within each important social subsystem comprised in the largest relevant social system.

Anderson has used an interesting metaphor: "Recognition of local group relations by agencies serving farm people provides the best assurance of democratic action and tends to maximize participation of all rural families. Organizations set up on such lines might be called the social equivalent of contour farming" (5, page 36). One interesting study examines "the differential distribution of community knowledge," finding quantity of knowledge about local government, welfare, and education to be correlated with status, and the inward rather than outward orientation of local persons (75).

An implication of the foregoing comments on articulation is that communities undergoing the stresses of change might become self-conscious of trouble, and make efforts to "harmonize" their nonarticulated parts. In this connection it must be mentioned that much of the literature of the decade on rural communities has dealt with community organization, improvement, or development. In the main it has been "action" literature rather than research literature (46). Green and Mayo have proposed a frame of reference for predicting the action of organized groups within communities—either the total community or some of its parts—but one does not find research reports on the topic (32). In a sense, the "delineation movement" of the early 1940's was action oriented, and in fact one of the major criticisms that has been made of the whole body of rural community research (49) is that it has been for purposes of amelioration rather than the building of science.* A study of 164 "organized" communities in Mississippi was reported by Fanelli and Payne (28). A type of community reconnaissance, embracing certain researchlike features, has been developed by Sanders, yielding "community profiles" which he and his associates have prepared for several rural and town communities. The work of Sanders (67, 68, 69), Poston (62), Brownell (17), and many others represents a movement to promote community articulation, and their activity sets the stage for much important research (45). Interest in rural community development by 1955 had become in some places a preoccupation of chambers of commerce, industrialists, farmer organizations, agricultural extension services, and others. A quantity of "how-to-do-it" materials was becoming available, some of them representing very sophisticated applications of hypotheses and generalizations from community research (80).

A tentative evaluation of the enlarged rural community and its potential articulation is expressed by Schultz:

> The larger community is a more desirable area for rural organization than the neighborhood or the small community because it provides: (1) sufficient population to maintain the improved institutions and special interest groups now demanded; (2) sufficient wealth to support improved institutions; and (3) more adequate leadership (71, page 35).

Data have been sought during the decade on attributes variously called group identification, integration, we-feeling, solidarity, togetherness, unity, community consciousness, stability, cohesiveness, and similar terms. Progress has been made in the development of indexes and other devices by which to describe the attributes of communities and other social systems. The socioeconomic status scale, the participation index, the level of living index, the map delineation, attitude scales, the demographic ratio, ratings by judges, etc., were all in use before 1945. These were applied both intensively and extensively as tools of observation and analysis in rural communities during the decade that followed. An important trend in recent research has been an effort to explore these fea-

---

* As this chapter is written, rural sociologists in agricultural experiment stations (and that is where most of them are) are revising their project statements to put them in language "intelligible to laymen," and to show their practical importance to agriculture. This is a defense necessitated by a statement put into the Congressional Record by the joint committee on Agricultural Appropriations urging that federal appropriations not be used for research in rural sociology and certain other fields such as the study of "orchids in Guatemala."

tures of internal integration of the rural community as a social system. Devices have been contrived in an attempt to get past the single observer's impressionistic and subjective rating. Fessler (29) and Davies (22) have worked on scales of community consciousness and community satisfaction. The DFP-AES studies have used an A (for services) and B (for integration) rating (3). Hanna has tried judges' ratings and objective scaling (37).

The reports of such studies are leading students (but only very gradually) out of a jungle of unclear assumptions, vague hypotheses, crude instruments of observation, uncertain methods of analysis, and severely qualified and tentative findings. These, of course, are the same encumbrances that face research on other problems of social science, but they are particularly vexing in the study of the rural community. The research of 1945–1955 was clearly advanced in comparison with earlier work, but too few replications of promising and inconclusive studies are reported.

Fessler developed a "solidarity index," measuring the noncorrespondence of an eight-sided community profile with a regular octagon representing symmetrical solidarity (29). Testing how persons rate their community and the degree of consensus therein, forty statements are used. Each triangle in the octagon symbolizes integration in one of the following eight areas of community life: community spirit, interpersonal relations, family responsibility, schools, churches, economic behavior, local government, and "tension areas." He applied the test to high school juniors and seniors in "primary" rural communities. The study is clearly ingenious and important, but it stands pretty much alone without validation against other measures and as yet without reported replication. There is too much still of arbitrary and a priori designation of "areas" of community life and of conditions constituting integration. Fessler's beginning, together with the possibility of supplementation by Angell's and Thorndike's techniques of urban study and by Guttman-scale approaches to consensus open a challenging direction for further exploration.

The most recently developed measure to be applied in several studies is that developed under Carl C. Taylor's leadership and appearing as the "AB" index of community services and consciousness (3). The DFP-AES bulletins presenting this index are the salvage of an ambitious research operation conceived by Taylor and his colleagues to establish a national panel of rural counties for repetitive studies of social and cultural change (76). Bureaucratic curtailment (see C. M. Hardin: *Freedom in Agricultural Education,* 1955) brought the project down to a survey of each of twenty-four counties, reported mainly as research bulletins of the agricultural experiment stations in the states in which the counties were located (e.g., 3, 5, 7, 9, 33, 37, 39, 40, 44, 45, 60). A sample of Taylor's prefaces to the reports is:

> The purpose of this and other studies of the series has been (a) to analyze the types of groups in which rural people are organized and the patterns of group relationships through which they participate in local and nonlocal programs and services, (b) to analyze the ways in which agencies relate themselves and their programs to these types of organizations and patterns of group relationships, (c) to provide a comparison by types of farming areas, of trends in different types of organizations—formal and informal, local and nonlocal, etc., and (d) to interpret the findings for farm people and for action and educational agencies (3, page 4).

These studies of twenty-four counties probably yield more substantive knowledge of rural community life in the United States than can be found in any other set of reports.

In the community "AB" index, used in approximately the same manner in each of several studies, a superior number following the letter A (as in $A^{5-1}$) designates the number of types of business and trade services plus schools, doctors, dentists, movies, and local newspapers (5). The superior number following the letter B (as in $B^{1-3}$) indicates ratings of community consciousness assigned by observers, seeking to be objective in viewing certain "primary" and "secondary" behavior (44). Among the primary types are visiting, mutual aid, neighborly recreation, trust and confidence, and expressions of in-group feeling. Among secondary types are: live locality spirit, open-country and village cooperation, cooperation among organizations, the strength of organizations and effectiveness of leadership, the success and adequacy of local activities, and ability to adjust to change. Although the concepts "neighborhood" and "community" were used in the specifications for observing AB factors, both terms were laid aside in the analyses to be superseded by the more neutral and general designation "locality groups."

The "AB" index is a stimulating advance toward objectification, but its flaws must be recognized. Its "A" component assumes correlation, as yet largely untested, of patterns of services with unspecified other attributes of the reality of locality groups. It treats each "kind of service" as though it were of equal significance with every other type, ignoring possible needs for differential weighting, which might be discovered by some application of factor analysis. Its "B" component relies on subjective ratings, variable not only among communities but also with the idiosyncrasies of different "raters" or observers. The partially objectified items merged into the "B" summary rating are of unknown comparability with each other. They may, or may not be, intercorrelated. Then too, the A and B components, treating of services and group identification respectively, may not belong together in the same index. Finally, both the reliability and validity of the index remain to be tested. The experience of the DFP-AES sociologists with this "AB" rating will aid their successors in further efforts to develop summary indexes of community attributes.

Mayo has tried a similar method of study but has grouped the types of services (55). He devised indexes of (a) transportation and communications services, (b) professional services, (c) commercial services, and (d) institutional and organizational services. The service indexes were highly intercorrelated, but he found only slight correlation of these indexes with a rating of group identification (high, medium, low) as determined subjectively by field observers, and with an index of "awareness of locality group names."

In another report, Mayo (with Bobbitt) proposes a code designation for a "locality group" in which a succession of digits reports the combinations of services and degree of integration, as in the hypothetical case of community X 4 3 8 2 1, with 4 indicating the number of kinds of transportation and communication services, 3 the number of kinds of professional services, 8 the kinds of commercial services, 2 the kinds of institutions and organizations, and 1 the rated degree of group identification, low in this case (56).

Hanna used a panel of judges, after the pattern used in studies of prestige, to study "locality group" integration (37). By answering two questions, "Do the people have good (fair, poor) community spirit?" and "Do they stick together most of the time (some of the time, hardly ever)?" his ten judges in Magoffin County placed the cards, one for each of seventy localities, in four piles (the fourth to indicate insufficient familiarity to justify rating). He found the ratings neither reliable nor valid when checked against interviews using a schedule-test of neighborhood solidarity, or a scale of objective indexes. He accepts the rating by judges as useful to measure "action-readiness," or as a useful first approximation in sampling for further study.

Hanna's objective factor indexes are:

1. Accessibility: distance, proportion of roads improved, accessibility of improved road, traffic flow (correlation with integration rating = 0.59).
2. Population size and density: (correlation of size with integration rating = 0.3; correlation of density with integration rating = 0.24).
3. Level of living: land type (correlation with integration rating =

0.53); high school attendance rate (correlation with integration rating = 0.42).

4. Services: commercial (correlation with integration rating = 0.36); post office (no correlation); organizations (no correlation); church groups (correlation with integration rating = 0.36).

Asserting a need to distinguish three types of integration (interpersonal, normative, and functional), Hanna suggests that the greatest possibilities for determining locality group integration lie in the use of schedules for measuring solidarity (1, 29). As to objective indexes, he says "what is needed is some kind of measure of the impact of objective factors" (37).

Hanna's major conclusion, after his efforts to study integration or the "reality" of locality groups, takes the form of a recommendation on terminology:

> It is suggested that the term neighborhood be dropped from the locality group terminology and that in its place be substituted a classification of either communities or locality groups based on their primary or secondary level of association and their focus or dominant factor of integration.
>
> There is always need for simplicity in definitions and the term *locality group* is not only awkward, but it covers a very broad range of phenomena. It is suggested that we drop the use of this term and return to the use of the term *community*. As we have already suggested there need be no dichotomy of community and neighborhood.

## SUMMARY

Sociologically rurality is inherent in either the presence or absence of each community characteristic or attribute discussed above, and thus is the rural community distinguished from other types. The conventional connotation requires that the rural community be relatively determinate as to boundary, that its area be a significant symbol of commonality, that it be sparsely settled, noncentralized, undifferentiated, autonomous, articulated, and integrated. In a sense, then, rurality is a summary of characteristics rather than a separate feature in itself.

Rurality is usually considered to inhere in agriculture, with farming a pivotal activity in the rural community. However, the social features of rurality derive not so much from farming per se as from settlement and its consequences:

> . . . agriculture may prove to be an archaic mode of production. If in addition to industrialized agriculture, food and fiber come to be increasingly produced by manufacturing processes using materials that utilize the sun's energy more efficiently than plants do, there is no technological reason why nearly all of mankind could not live in conurbations of large size (23, page 434).

If agriculture were to be displaced as an occupation, would rurality cease to exist? The presumption is that it would no doubt endure in some places dominantly, in some places vestigially.

The rejection of the rural-urban dichotomy usually takes the form of a substitute proposal for continua of sociological variables, such as "cultural isolation" (34). One of the most interesting criticisms (49) argues for the rejection of "rural community" and community delineation for "profiles" determined by twelve polarities: sacred—secular; irrational—rational; group conscious—individualistic; leaders—managers; community—collectives; final answers—relative answers; fixed—fluid stratification; government by philosophy—government by substance; centripetal—centrifugal; unity of man and nature—man versus nature; production for use—production for sale; morals—techniques.

These authors wave aside the rural sociologist as naive, then perform an error of comparable magnitude—delineating a profile of several polarities that have unequal distance, unequal weight, and nonmeasurable units. They may be sound in rejecting the sentimentality, but unsound in rejecting the hypothesis of a community context of the embraced functional associations. To say something does not exist because it cannot be seen without an X ray is to utter a hasty falsehood.

Rurality and urbanity can be defined only in comparison with each other, and whether by dichotomy or continuum is logically of little importance so long as the error of trying to include all human communities is not committed. Feudal communities and plantations, for example, have been proposed as types outside the rural-urban orbit.

The research of the decade, published mainly but not entirely in the bulletins of agricultural experiment stations and in the professional journal of the rural sociologists, is not to be taken as a monument to a past feature of American rural life, only recently buried under an avalanche of urbanism. Rather it describes, with more scientific sophistication than did research in former periods, the circumstances of a changing milieu and the persistence therein of rural forms of communities in the United States.

The dominance of locality as a determining factor in social relationships is being restructured. Every new complexity of culture—whether it be a technique of hybridizing corn or television at the village high school—introduces a new complexity in the causality of sociological events. It is hardly reasonable to expect any more in sociological problems the simple one-to-one relationship that we call correlation between two variables. There are always inextricable factors in the situation that strengthen or weaken whatever relationship might have prevailed without them. The rural community may once have been a simple product of simple settlement, commensalistic at first because its dwellers "ate at the same table" so to speak, and collective later, as networks of interaction developed.

Now its peripheries are concealed by the overlaps of approaching areas around the cities. Area symbols have been modified; they are indirectly mediated, or presented as symbols of symbols. Density of settlement per se recedes in its influence on density of contacts and interaction as the technology of controlling space and time develops. Centralization becomes more conspicuous, and intercommunity relations reveal specialization of centers with division by patronage, and with primary, secondary, and tertiary levels of service. Differentiation within the community whole increases, and the autonomy or independence of the community in relation to its surrounding society yields to dependence—and interdependence. Becoming somewhat less articulated and integrated within itself the rural community is more articulated than before with the larger society. To conclude, however, that the rural community in the United States is passé would be as wrong as to conclude that the American family no longer exists because its 1875 version is no longer the prevailing form.

## BIBLIOGRAPHICAL REFERENCES

(The abbreviation AESB refers to Agricultural Experiment Station Bulletin.)

1. Alexander, Frank D., "The Problem of Locality Group Classification," *Rural Sociology*, Vol. 17 (1952), pp. 236–244.
2. Alexander, Frank D., and Robert E. Galloway, "Salient Features of Social Organization in a Typical County of the General and Self-Sufficing Farm Region," *Rural Sociology*, Vol. 12 (1947), pp. 395–405.
3. Alexander, Frank D., and Lowry Nelson, "Rural Social Organization in Goodhue County, Minnesota," *Minnesota AESB 401* (1949).
4. Almack, R. B., and Lawrence Hepple, "Rural Social Organization in Dent County," *University of Missouri AESB 458* (1950).
5. Anderson, A. H., "A Study of Rural Communities and Organizations in Seward County, Nebraska," *Nebraska AESB 405* (1951).
6. Anderson, A. H., "Space as a Social Cost," *Journal of Farm Economics*, Vol. 32 (1950), pp. 411–430.
7. Anderson, A. H., and Randall C. Hill, "Rural Communities and Organizations: A Study of Group Life in Ellis County, Kansas," *Kansas AES Circular 143* (1948).
8. Anderson, A. H., and C. J. Miller, "The Changing Role of the Small Town in Farm Areas," *Nebraska AESB 419* (1953).
9. Anderson, A. H., and Glenn V. Vergeront, "Rural Communities and Organizations," *North Dakota AESB 351* (1948).
10. Barnett, W. E., and Selz C. Mayo, "Neighbor Groups," *North Carolina AESB* (mimeo.; 1952).
11. Becker, M. G., and C. P. Loomis, "Measuring Rural, Urban and Farm and

Non-Farm Cleavages in a Rural Consolidated School," *Sociometry,* Vol. 11 (1948), pp. 246–261.

12. Beers, Howard W., "American Communities," *The Community School: National Society for the Study of Education, Fifty-Second Yearbook, Part 2,* ed. by Nelson B. Henry, Chicago, Univ. of Chicago Press, 1953, pp. 15–30.

13. Belcher, John C., "Service Relationships of Farmers in Lincoln County, Oklahoma," *Oklahoma AESB No. 1 B–383* (1952).

14. Bertrand, Alvin L., "Rural Locality Groups: Changing Patterns, Change Factors, and Implications," *Rural Sociology,* Vol. 19 (1954), pp. 175–179.

15. Bogue, Donald J., "Urbanism in the United States," *Amer. J. Soc.,* Vol. 60 (1954–1955), pp. 471–486.

16. Boskoff, Alvin, "An Ecological Approach to Rural Society," *Rural Sociology,* Vol. 14 (1949), pp. 306–316.

17. Brownell, Baker, *The Human Community,* New York, Harper, 1950.

18. Brunner, Edmund de S., and W. C. Hallenbeck, *American Society: Urban and Rural Patterns,* New York, Harper, 1955.

19. Brush, John E., "The Hierarchy of Central Places in Southwestern Wisconsin," *Geographical Review,* Vol. 18 (1953), pp. 380–402.

20. Christiansen, John R., "The Relation Between Neighborhood Membership and Social Participation," Unpublished doctoral dissertation, Univ. of Wisconsin, 1955.

21. Clover, Vernon T., "An Economic and Sociological Study of a Kansas Community," *Fort Hays, Kan., Kansas State College Studies, Econ. Series No. 2, Gen. Series No. 8* (1945).

22. Davies, Vernon, "Development of a Scale to Rate Attitude of Community Satisfaction," *Rural Sociology,* Vol. 10 (1945), pp. 246–255.

23. Davis, Kingsley, "The Origin and Growth of Urbanization in the World," *Amer. J. Soc.,* Vol. 60 (1954–1955), pp. 428–437.

24. Draper, C. R., and Daniel Russell, "Rural Organization in Val Verde Co., Texas," *Texas AES Misc. Pub. 71* (1951).

25. Edwards, Allen D., "Ecological Patterns of American Rural Communities," *Rural Sociology,* Vol. 12 (1947), pp. 150–159.

26. Ensminger, Douglas, "Rural Neighborhoods and Communities," Chap. 4 in C. C. Taylor, *et al., Rural Life in the United States,* New York, Knopf, 1949.

27. Ensminger, Douglas, and Robert A. Polson, "The Concept of the Community," *Rural Sociology,* Vol. 11 (1946), pp. 43–51.

28. Fanelli, A. Alexander, and Raymond Payne, "A Study of Organized Communities in Mississippi," *Community Studies No. 1,* Miss. State College, Soc. Sci. Res. Center, 1953.

29. Fessler, Donald R., "The Development of a Scale for Measuring Community Solidarity," *Rural Sociology,* Vol. 17 (1952), pp. 144–152.

30. Gallien, Glenn S., "Natural Neighborhoods, Wayne County, Tennessee," *Tennessee AES Rur. Res. Series Monograph* (1949), p. 193.

31. Galloway, Robert E., "A Contrast in the Rural Social Organization of Rabun County, Georgia, and Franklin County, Washington," *Rural Sociology,* Vol. 13 (1948), pp. 384–400.

32. Green, James W., and Selz Mayo, "A Framework for Research in the Actions of Community Groups," *Social Forces,* Vol. 31 (1953), pp. 320–327.

33. Grigsby, S. Earl, and Harold Hoffsommer, "Rural Social Organization in Frederick County," *Maryland AESB 451* (1949).

34. Gross, Neal, "Cultural Variables in Rural Communities," *Amer. J. Soc.,* Vol. 53 (1948), pp. 344–350.

35. Gross, Neal, "Review of Current Research on the Sociology of Rural Life," *Amer. Soc. Rev.*, Vol. 17 (1952), pp. 83–90.

36. Gross, Neal, "Sociological Variation in Contemporary Rural Life," *Rural Sociology*, Vol. 13 (1948), pp. 256–273.

37. Hanna, Edwin B., "The Integration of Locality Groups in an Eastern Kentucky County," Unpublished M.S. thesis, Univ. of Kentucky, 1954.

38. Hawley, Amos, *Human Ecology*, New York, Ronald Press, 1950.

39. Hay, Donald G., and M. E. John, "Rural Organization of Bradford County, Pennsylvania," *Pennsylvania AESB 524* (1950).

40. Hay, Donald G., and Robert A. Polson, "Rural Organizations in Oneida County, New York," *Cornell AESB 871* (1951).

41. Hepple, Lawrence M., and Margaret L. Bright, "Social Changes in Shelby County, Missouri," *Missouri AESB 456* (1950).

42. Hiller, E. T., "The Community as a Social Group," *Amer. Soc. Rev.*, Vol. 6 (1941), pp. 189–190.

43. Hoffer, Charles R., "The Changing Ecological Pattern in Rural Life," *Rural Sociology*, Vol. 13 (1948), pp. 176–180.

44. Jehlik, Paul J., "Rural Social Organization in Henry County, Indiana," *Purdue AESB 568* (1951).

45. Jehlik, Paul J., and Ray E. Wakely, "Rural Organization: A Case Study of Hamilton County, Iowa," *Iowa AESB 365* (1949).

46. Kimball, Solon T., "Some Methodological Problems of the Community Self Survey," *Social Forces*, Vol. 31 (1952), pp. 160–164.

47. Kolb, J. H., and E. de S. Brunner, *A Study of Rural Society*, 4th ed., Boston, Houghton Mifflin, 1952.

48. Kolb, John H., and LeRoy J. Day, "Interdependence in Town and Country Relations in Rural Society," *Wisconsin AESB 172* (1950).

49. Kollmorgen, Walter M., and Robert W. Harrison, "The Search for the Rural Community," *Agricultural History*, Vol. 20 (1946), pp. 1–8.

50. Lindstrom, David E., "The Rural Community and School District Reorganization," *Rural Sociology*, Vol. 17 (1952), pp. 171–172.

51. Lindstrom, David E., *American Rural Life*, New York, Ronald Press, 1948.

52. Lionberger, H. F., and E. Hassenger, "Neighborhoods as a Factor in the Diffusion of Farm Information in a Northeast Missouri Farming Community," *Rural Sociology*, Vol. 19 (1954), pp. 377–383.

53. Loomis, C. P., and J. Allan Beegle, *Rural Social Systems*, New York, Prentice-Hall, 1950, Chap. 6.

54. Marshall, D. G., "Hamlets and Villages in the United States: Their Place in the American Way of Life," *Amer. Soc. Rev.*, Vol. 11 (1946), pp. 159–165.

55. Mayo, Selz C., "Testing Criteria of Rural Locality Groups," *Rural Sociology*, Vol. 14 (1949), pp. 316–325.

56. Mayo, Selz C., and Robert McD. Bobbitt, "Biracial Identity of Rural Locality Groups in Wake County, North Carolina," *Rural Sociology*, Vol. 15 (1950), pp. 365–366.

57. Mayo, Selz C., and Robert McD. Bobbitt, "Rural Organization: A Restudy of Locality Groups in Wake County, North Carolina," *North Carolina AES Tech. Bul. No. 95* (1951), p. 46.

58. Mayo, Selz C., and C. Paul Marsh, "Social Participation in the Rural Community," *Amer. J. Soc.*, Vol. 57 (1951–1952), pp. 243–247.

59. Mighell, Ronald L., *American Agriculture: Its Structure and Place in the Economy*, New York, Wiley, 1955.

60. Miner, Horace, *Culture and Agriculture: An Anthropological Study of a Corn Belt Community*, Ann Arbor, Univ. of Michigan Press, 1949.

61. Nelson, Lowry, *The Mormon Village*, Salt Lake City, Univ. of Utah Press, 1952.

62. Poston, Richard W., *Democracy Is You*, New York, Harper, 1953.

63. Reiss, Albert J., Jr., "A Review and Evaluation of Research on the Community: A Working Memorandum Prepared for the Committee on Social Behavior of the Social Science Research Council" (mimeo.; Nashville, Tenn., 1954).

64. Reiss, Albert J., Jr., "Some Logical and Methodological Problems in Community Research," *Social Forces*, Vol. 33 (1954), pp. 51–57.

65. Richardson, Paul D., and Ward W. Bauder, "Participation in Organized Activities in a Kentucky Rural Community," *Kentucky AESB 598* (1953).

66. Riecken, Henry W., Jr., and Nathan L. Whetten, "Rural Social Organization in Litchfield County, Connecticut," *Storrs AESB 261* (1948).

67. Sanders, Irwin T., "The Individual's Sense of Community in Industrial Civilization," *A Report on the Corning Conference: Creating an Industrial Civilization*, New York, Harper, 1952, pp. 114–151.

68. Sanders, Irwin T., *Making Good Communities Better*, Lexington, Univ. of Kentucky Press, 1953.

69. Sanders, Irwin T., "Preparing a Community Profile: The Methodology of a Social Reconnaissance," *Kentucky Community Series: No. 7*, University of Kentucky (mimeo.; 1952).

70. Sanderson, Dwight, *Rural Sociology and Rural Social Organization*, New York, Wiley, 1942.

71. Schultz, Gerard, "Some Effects of the War on Rural Life in Missouri, 1939–1945," *Missouri AESB Res. Bul. 401* (1946).

72. Slocum, Walter L., and Hermann M. Case, "Are Neighborhoods Meaningful Social Groups Throughout Rural America?" *Rural Sociology*, Vol. 18 (1953), pp. 52–59.

73. Smith, T. Lynn, "The Locality Group Structure of Brazil," *Amer. Soc. Rev.*, Vol. 9 (1944), pp. 41–49.

74. Sutton, Willis A., Jr., "Developing a Community Orientation as a Tool for Research," *University of Kentucky, Bureau of School Service Bulletin*, Vol. XXVI: No. 2 (1953), pp. 39–45.

75. Sykes, Gresham M., "The Differential Distribution of Community Knowledge," *Social Forces*, Vol. 29 (1951), pp. 376–382.

76. Taylor, Carl C., "Techniques of Community Study and Analysis as Applied to Modern Civilized Societies," in Ralph Linton (ed.), *The Science of Man in a World Crisis*, New York, Columbia Univ. Press, 1945.

77. Timasheff, Nicholas S., *Sociological Theory, Its Nature and Growth*, New York, Doubleday, 1955.

78. Trewartha, Glenn T., "The Unincorporated Hamlet—One Element of the American Settlement Fabric," *Annals of the Association of American Geography*, Vol. 33 (1943), pp. 35–37.

79. Tropp, E. H., "Dispersed Settlement and the Rural Community," *Rural Sociology*, Vol. 18 (1953), pp. 338–344.

80. Watrous, Roberta C., and J. M. McNeill, *Rural Community Organizations: A List of References*, Washington, D. C., U.S.D.A. Library List No. 46, 1949.

81. Wattenberg, William W., "Attitude Toward Community Size as Evidenced by Migratory Behavior," *Social Forces*, Vol. 26 (1948), pp. 437–442.

82. West, James, and Carl Withers, *Plainville: U.S.A.*, New York, Columbia Univ. Press, 1945.

chapter *8*

# The study of social stratification

W. LLOYD WARNER
*University of Chicago*

## The problem

The contemporary study of the several varieties of social stratification is blessed (although at times confused) by an increasing use of evidence directly derived from field researches on human behavior and by the steady accumulation and use of statistical facts. These test theory, develop methods and techniques, and help establish the empirical foundations for understanding how the varying orders of rank operate in the lives of individuals in all types of society. Territorially, these studies range throughout the world, through the literate and nonliterate societies. The present chapter gives considerable attention to some of these studies but cannot cover them sufficiently for systematic comparison, something that is now possible and very much needed for the advancement of a balanced understanding of the scientific problem of rank, as well as to put the study of our own forms of social stratification in their proper perspective (114, 138, 153, 251). Conceptually these works vary from doctrinaire Marxism and other forms of economic determinism to structural analysis and psychological interpretations of behavior (16, 154, 173, 192, 242).

Disciplines and methods involved represent greatest diversity. In sociology occupational and organizational approaches predominate. The community research approach is essentially a methodological device to use present (structural) procedures for the study of the structure of status in contemporary society. Methodologically, the occupational approach can disregard the values and organization of the local community (60, 104, 198, 199, 211, 212). But in so doing it delimits the field of interest and understanding of what the human behavior, beliefs, and values are which compose some of the more important aspects of status research. Obviously both approaches and their integrated combinations are necessary (52, 125, 256, 261).

In social anthropology work now being published about Africa (20, 32, 174, 175), China (85, 86, 87, 166, 171), India (188, 189), Ceylon (228), Burma (165), and elsewhere greatly contributes to our knowledge about stratification.*

Reference group theory and method have contributed to more effective collaboration among social psychologists, psychologists, and "organizational" sociologists on the problems about the meaning of class. The use of the small group and the clique by the individual in social-class contexts to identify and place himself and communicate to others about what it is that he is, has been, and wishes to be or not be, has been studied with notable advances (36, 149, 209).

Some of the more interesting studies of communication concern the use of mass media in small groups as they are related to class levels (95, 96).

The reference group approach is but one of the many contributions by social psychology to our understanding of rank (8, 9, 52, 94).

Several varieties of psychology, including stimulus-response and psychoanalysis, have also contributed to the study of social stratification (44, 53, 58, 117). The latter comes particularly through the use of projective techniques (133). The earlier studies of John Dollard and Allison Davis gave us many of the leads now being exploited (252).

Other disciplines which have made major contributions are economics (19, 74, 115, 194, 195), political science and history (14, 22, 73, 112, 185), and education (67, 130, 131).

* I wish to thank McKim Marriott and Yung-Teh Chow for their expert assistance.

The behavior examined and the parts of society studied range from social-class systems,* castes,† occupations (21, 123, 125), occupational and social mobility,‡ age and sex divisions (32, 220), political, economic, educational, and ecclesiastical and other institutional hierarchies to the relations of these institutions to the general social structure (218, 255, 262). For example, voluntary associations, as organizations operating in American life that both close mobility for many and open and encourage it for others, have been studied indicating how they validate the status claims of some and refuse them to others. Research on associations shows how they help structure the class alignments and regulate participation, how they organize some of the ethnic and interest groups of various levels, as well as how they function to relate other hierarchies into the larger community (for example, factories, churches, and schools). See (55, 76, 193).

Present studies also include the personalities sometimes found at different status levels (126, 141, 254), the effects of status on the mental life of individuals at different status levels, the social psychological processes of the socialization of the young by the old into the status order (129, 132, 141), thus often giving precedence to the roles of family members

---

* Class studies are being pursued throughout most of the western world, particularly in the United States (7, 18, 47, 49, 75, 106, 128, 136, 159, 176, 221, 248, 249, 261) and in England and the Commonwealth (100, 215). Other areas that might be mentioned are Burma (165), Africa (174), India (188, 189, 228), and Latin America (23).

The recent literature on social mobility and stratification on China and Japan provides valuable comparative material. Several studies on social mobility and the play of such factors as education, the acquisition of property, political achievement, and personality have been examined (87, 145, 147). Studies of the gentry, peasantry, and other ranks now make it possible to substitute evidence for speculation and doctrine for the comparative analysis of stratification (56, 268). Social change, conflict, and co-operation have been treated (235).

† The study of the varieties of caste ranges over major areas of the earth and many of the major civilizations. In the United States, Hill and McCall have recently published a study of color caste and class in Georgia (15, 61, 93, 136, 138). The differences between the systems in the South and North and the effects of social change and urban life are reported on (77). Tumin has provided a detailed study from Latin America (246). The whole body of knowledge about Indian caste is now being re-examined, indicating that what has been called Indian caste varies enormously and ranges through a great variety of forms, most not conforming to the classical definitions (188, 189). The larger comparative perspective for literate and nonliterate societies is given by Murdock (206).

‡ Some of the principal issues about vertical mobility in the United States are argued in the recent studies of Warner and Abegglen (252, 253), Sjoberg (237), Rogoff (222), Hatt (125, 127), Centers (48, 51), Adams (5), and many others (10, 57, 190, 267). Those for England are (100, 101, 102, 120, 123, 201, 202, 203, 215).

(1, 80, 82, 191) and the school (2, 67, 68). The relations of status systems to problems of communication and the use of sacred and secular symbols have been given considerable attention (46, 103, 251).

The depth and lasting psychological effects of rank in American life are nowhere more clearly demonstrable than in the studies of illness and the psychobiological effects on the individual (224, 225, 226, 227). Unfulfilled status aspirations, blocked mobility, the overstriving of the very successful, the feelings of rejection of family members by those who are mobile appear as factors in the psychosomatic effects of social class (227). Many of these studies further document Durkheim's social psychological thesis having to do with *anomie.*

Any casual inventory of the recent literature also reveals theoretical interest and research on problems of power and prestige (64, 73, 105, 161, 162), on leadership (260), on social and status change. The problem of change and of change as class conflict is central to the Marxian thesis, where the structuralists are accused of being blind to the significance of change (28, 173). It is perhaps true that the structuralists have understated the role of change, yet even this is debatable. The chart showing the relations of caste and class, originally published in 1941, and used in many other recent studies (77, 251), is based on a time dimension (caste and class changing through time and in conflict as a consequence). The study of class conflict in a strike (255) and ethnic and class and ethnic changes (259), as well as other writings, all emphasize social change.

There is also concern about the advantages and disadvantages of the several methods for the study of the various aspects of stratification. The technical and methodological literature is very great, perhaps too much so, in proportion to the amount of space given to understanding the different systems of rank, the role they play in collective life, and the functions they perform. Characteristically, our understanding of the nature of such systems in certain other societies (where less attention is given to what the investigator is doing and more to learning about the nature of the system) is clearer (26, 45, 54, 111, 144, 154, 233, 234, 250).

Some of the methods used for stratifying the members of a community include the use of interviews, participant observation, and structural analyses (54, 79, 136, 257). Hollingshead uses both structural and informed panels of judges (142) for class stratification.

Occupation has been one of the principal and, at times, the only criterion used for ranking (9, 50).

Education, house typing, source and amount of income, the social register, residential area, rent, and other so-called "objective" criteria have been used (17, 35, 80).

Some have been used in combination, such as the present writer's Index of Status Characteristics (255, 257). This instrument allows for characteristics to be used other than the original ones (1, 80, 183).

Although Centers' (52) method is referred to as subjective because it uses the informant's own conception and evaluation of his class, actually, since the method is dependent on the use of objective occupations previously chosen by the researcher, it is a combination of subjective and objective methods. Except for purposes of rough classification, this division into objective and subjective is misleading. Hatt's studies of occupational ranking and class (125) clearly indicate this as do those of Warner (257).

Clearly it will be impossible to so much as pretend to cover such a vast amount of material in the brief limits of this essay. Rather, the task as defined by the writer will be to state some of the broader generalizations that now seem possible because of the recent research advances in the whole area of social stratification. These will be given in terms of descriptive and explanatory principles to advance a general theoretical and methodological framework for relating many varieties of status research to one conceptual scheme. The body of the text ordinarily will be used for this purpose. Since many will be interested in the more limited generalizations or issues that are confined to particular researches, these have been treated in extensive footnotes that follow the continuity of the text. It is hoped that this form of presentation will not allow the treatment of the general or particular to interfere with each other. Finally, the text and footnotes are referred to a selected bibliography at the end. There are thus three levels of abstraction, the most abstract being the text, the footnotes next, followed by the references indicating where the reader may go for more evidence.

The Marxian writings will not be treated here. Although the Marxians continue to develop a vast body of literature, the Communists with their variety, the Socialists with theirs, more often than not they are less research-minded and more given to the exposition of doctrine where concrete facts are likely to be convenient illustrations. Moreover, they have their own eager compilers, commentators, and polemicists. Such writings, having been dealt with elsewhere, will be largely eliminated from the present statement.

The non-Marxian economic determinists have their own theories of rank. Lineal descendants from earlier English and American theorists, in making assumptions about men as social beings they tend to see the whole problem of status and rank in purely economic terms. Moreover, following the assumptions of their progenitors, they often view *social and group* behavior in *individual* terms (5, 10, 48, 222). Individuals are not seen as interconnected parts of a social web of super- and subordinate relations, but as separate economic units to be reassembled by the investigator into economic categories which are evaluated as superior or inferior. Such studies are valuable and necessary, but they are not sufficient. They do not cover the whole area of man's group life in a status order, although many try to make them do so. Economic stratification is of first importance in any complex social system, and understanding it as such is of equal importance, but such behavior must also be examined as *one* part of the larger system of rank. Occupational studies can be treated separately, but ultimately to understand their social place they must be related by structural studies to the structure of collective life.

Although there have been a number of recent investigations of the social and status structures of communities * (136, 249, 260) and still others on the hierarchies of institutions in this and other societies (86, 87, 268), there has been no general statement about the assumptions, the methodology and theory of *structural* and comparative analysis of the forms of social stratification or of its relation to the study of occupational stratification. With the results of present and previous research on which to build, it is now possible to present some of the basic principles involved. While examining the results of contemporary research, the present enterprise will do no more than make a beginning at such an undertaking.

We may say briefly what is meant by structural studies and comparative analysis. The work of the structural analyst is similar to that of the biologist. The biologist studies the characteristics of an animal species as they are found in the animals themselves; he observes the relations of the characteristics to each other (taxonomy). He examines the genetic relations of the generations of animals and learns about the modifications and persistence of the several forms. The structural student of rank does likewise. He investigates the words and acts of men in relation to each other and observes uniformities and differences in these relations. He determines norms and modalities of behavior about what does happen and "ideally" what "ought" to happen, while learning the extent of the variations. Where possible he studies persistence and change (214).

For the structural analyst, "status is the most general term used to refer to the location of the behavior of individuals or the social positions of individuals themselves in the structure of any group. It is a defined social

* The limitations of community analysis are numerous, including the difficulty of determining how represensative the communities are of the national community (77, 79, 251, 259). Occupational studies are more easily used for national analysis, but this raises other problems, since they lose or disregard much of the significant life of the people at all levels of rank (163).

position located in a social universe. The term is synonymous with social position, social place, or social location. Statuses may or may not be ranked as superior or inferior." Therefore, they fall into two general types—the ranked and nonranked (251). We are dealing with the former only.

The form of a particular status in a rank order is defined operationally by answering the following questions: What are the rights and privileges enjoyed by those who occupy it? What are the rights and privileges of members of *other* statuses that are directly or indirectly related to it? What are the duties and obligations of those who occupy a given status and what are the duties and obligations of others who are in statuses which are related to it? To restate this in somewhat different terms, we need to know the rules of conduct and the appropriate symbols used by those who are in, or implicated with, a given status.

Status always implies and implicates the larger social universe in which it has its place. It is definable in large part explicitly or implicitly by reference to its relations with other parts of the social system. Ultimately, full understanding of a particular status can be gained not only by knowing what it is as a social object and how it is interrelated with other statuses but by understanding its relation to, and place in, the whole society (40, 108, 148, 218, 253, 256).

The comparison of particular status systems studied by this method reveals general types (class, for example), varieties of the type (open and "closed" varieties of class systems), and particular instances (the class system of a community). The latter can be "broken down" into the observed acts of behavior out of which the status norms were built by the researcher. Thus, type, variety, the particular case and the observed acts of behavior, represent various levels of abstraction and generality. In discussions about status, not recognizing this fact has caused much difficulty and several needless controversies. If a *type* of status system such as caste is taken to mean, and is equated with, a *variety* or an *instance* or one observed bit of behavior, erroneous and improper comparisons are certain to be made. For example, if American Negro—white status relations are *typed* as caste (65, 77), it does not mean that they are necessarily the same as the several varieties of Indian or African caste (39, 63) or the classical type of Indian caste,* any more than when

* The study of caste in India is being pursued by the several social sciences. Some of the problems examined and the issues now in debate are: What the roles of economic and ritual factors are in caste as a system of Indian ranking (188); how far social and economic class rather than caste determine a man's prestige and power; the degree to which tradition and social and economic change influence contemporary caste organization and behavior (189); what similarities and differences exist between Indian and other forms of caste (138). The comparative study of caste as a *type* of rank and all of its varieties has also been given attention (251).

the biologist calls St. Bernards and Pomeranians dogs, he is saying they are identical. They are alike by the criteria of taxonomy.

Each of the several forms to which social stratification or the term rank refers is composed of interconnected statuses in relations of superordination and subordination and of superiority and inferiority. Power or prestige, or power and prestige are unequally distributed among the several statuses whose entirety comprises any given system (105, 162). All orders of rank distribute unequally the highly valued material and immaterial social objects as facts of power and symbols of prestige among the superior and inferior statuses. These systems persist and are modified through time, incorporating the members of each generation into their orderings of status. The methods by which forms of rank are transferred or not from generation to generation and the rules governing the relations of the generations constitute important parts of any of these orders.* The processes which accomplish the task of socializing the young by the older with the status belief, values, and behavior of any given status system provide one of many places where structural and psychological analysis works effectively. The studies of the psychological effects of status on the learning abilities of the young and the research on performance by students at the different grade levels from different social classes have added much to our knowledge of how social class in America and Britain affects the lives of individuals and functions as a system of rank.

The public school as a structural system, its control, the place of the school in the life of the community, the recruitment of teachers in grade and high schools, the treatment of children of "higher and lower" families, and the performance and achievement of children in the schoolroom and playgrounds at different grade levels have had noteworthy treatment as partial products of class influence (15, 205, 230, 238). Perhaps no two social scientists have done more to advance our knowledge than Allison

---

* The many researches in the relation of status and class to mental performance in school clearly demonstrate the living reality of the differential effects of class levels on the individuals of the new generations. The effects of class on performance in school and the I.Q. have been well documented (42, 43, 81, 119).

The child training and infant care on the several levels show how their children are inducted into the system and by experience learn their place (83). On the other hand, the differential effects of class on individuals' learning and aspirations also have been examined and valuable results obtained, showing how some become ambitious and socially mobile and others remain "stable and immobile" (251).

Adolescence and its place in the school system as related to social class and age grading have been well documented. All studies show how previous training in childhood and infancy affect the adolescent (151) and how present experiences of the young person are greatly influenced by status (180, 207, 262).

Davis and Robert Havighurst (69, 132). Hollingshead (141), McGuire (181, 183), Neugarten (208), Taba (132), Eells (81), Stendler (241), White (262), as well as Haggard (119), Becker (25), Himmelweit (137), Kahl (153), and many others have contributed to a solid body of knowledge on class, mentality, and learning.

Since the varieties of rank differ in form (28, 29, 38, 109, 168) and function (23, 245, 246), and in their relations to the larger social systems in which they exist, all can be profitably compared and classified, and inferences drawn about the nature of the forms studied and the values they express. Fortunately a solid body of literature is now developing about the workings of status systems throughout the "civilized" and "primitive" societies of the world. The descriptive and explanatory generalizations about rank in the present chapter are built upon it.

Social stratification is a *type* of subsystem which exists in most, if not all, literate and nonliterate societies, whether in all or not is largely a matter of definition. Since the distinctions involved in the differences in definition are important, they need to be examined to help us better understand the principles involved in stratification. Stern's (242) recent paper (following similar distinctions of Hobhouse, Wheeler, and Ginsberg), as well as the publications of most anthropologists and sociologists, is not in accord with the position taken by writers like Sorokin. The latter includes such social systems as age and sex divisions among the forms of social stratification; the others do not. He declares in *Social Mobility* that "Any organized social group is always a stratified social body. There has not been and does not exist any permanent social group which is 'flat,' and in which all members are equal. Unstratified society, with a real equality of its members, is a myth which has never been realized in the history of mankind" (240, page 12).

Stratified society is manifested in various forms: "First, in the existence of the sex and age groups with quite different privileges and duties . . ." (240, page 13).

While it is true that age divisions place their members in super- and subordinate positions (32, 143, 220), the rules and principles involved are quite different from such forms of rank as social and economic class, or political, military, or ecclesiastical hierarchies, and others. Although they are socially defined and evaluated, age categories are essentially biologically founded and "fit" *everyone* during lifetime, the grades of age being statuses through which *all* maturing individuals must pass. There are no necessary invidious discriminations; age is a form that can be *commonly* shared at least by all those of the same sex. During their life development, members of the other systems of rank do not move inevitably through the higher and lower levels.

Because age grades do place people in orders of prestige and power, for our purposes they are treated as a major subtype of rank, rudimentary and nonspecialized, to be distinguished from all specialized and developed forms. They divide clearly into two basic varieties, those age divisions which are based entirely on social definitions of the aging processes and those which include other evaluative principles, such as economic, political, and birth distinctions. The second type of system is of particular importance in Africa which, with other status systems, is now being studied.

The literature on hierarchies and stratification in Africa grows rapidly. Studies of political and social systems and their relation to power and stratification have been reported (20, 32, 174). A large number of excellent monographs and papers on status systems among the different groups are regularly appearing (too numerous for discussion here). The changing stratification caused by culture contact with European systems and indigenous developments have been well studied.

This literature and the older studies of such systems as caste in East Africa need to be comparatively analyzed. Comparative studies of political hierarchies (see above) and of age grades have been successfully undertaken.*

### Criteria for the study of rank

Since the diversity of the forms of rank, even when limited to the specialized ones, is very great and, when taken on a world-wide basis, bewilderingly so, the question arises whether it is possible to make scientific sense out of the diversity and establish valid uniformities by use of classifications founded on criteria and principles basic to the behavior of men living in groups. Since all humans live in societies and since the societies are diverse in range and type, criteria adequate for this culture may not be so for others. The criteria used necessarily must be relevant to all systems of social stratification; they must be "culture free." Such criteria can only be said to be scientifically valid when founded on basic principles of human behavior and applicable at all times and places, including the *known* past of our own and other societies.

The *tests* for such guiding criteria are

a. They should be founded primarily on human adaptive behavior necessary everywhere for the maintenance and persistence of the social and biological life of all men in all groups.

b. They should be of vital significance to the life careers of individuals.

* I am particularly indebted for guidance and information about African status systems to Alfred Harris, of the University of Cambridge, who has done research in the area and on these problems.

c. They should apply to all societies and all forms of rank.

d. They should come from, and be subject to, the evidence of actual observed behavior and not the armchair theories of ideologists or those primarily interested in constructing abstract philosophical theories.

e. From them and the evidence it should be possible and scientifically necessary to establish types of rank capable of testing by further evidence and analysis, which thus begin to assume a general and more abstract and less individual and unique conceptual character and are therefore subject to further analysis and testing.

f. From the several types it should be possible to build a coherent system incorporating the uniformities and the varieties into a conception of rank that comprehends the whole diversity yet refers to and places each individual form.

g. The taxonomic system of rank, consisting of interdependent logical categories referring to empirically derived individual systems, must be capable of yielding propositions about the nature of rank, its several forms, the conditions under which they exist, and the relations between the diverse forms and their surrounding conditions.

Two *kinds* of basic questions about the access to each other of the members of the species of any given group help us meet the demands of the several tests: First, are the statuses (or a status) within a system of rank open to movement to and from them so that those who might seek access or seek to leave them may do so? Is the system of assignment of status such that each individual's position is free so that he can move vertically or horizontally toward others and they to him? Can he and they compete for higher status or strive to maintain their own? Or is the status system closed so that men cannot move from status to status, their own individual positions thus being so fixed that their careers are confined to one status (or level of rank) and competition for any other status not possible? Some systems of rank conform to the first and some to the second type. In the first, individuals, families, and other groups through time move up or down from one status to another. Vertical mobility, social and occupational, are forms of this movement. Such a type can be called an open status system, subject to free competition. The second type is a system of closed status with the individual's life chances controlled by the rules governing the status he was assigned at birth. The principles of open and restricted competition for individuals and families and of free movement as well as social control over ingress and egress from ranked statuses are involved. Obviously these two are extreme polar forms; numerous mixed types intervene along the range between the two.

The second kind of basic question may be stated: To what extent is

the life of a society and the activities of each individual controlled by
any order of rank? Is the order's province *limited* to certain activities and
not others? Is it limited to particular periods and times? Is it limited to
certain individuals and not others? Does it regulate part of the lives of
some people for part of the time but not all of it? What and how much
does it control? In brief, and to apply terms, is it a *limited* hierarchy
segmenting the membership and activities of the group, or is it inclusive,
generally comprising everyone and all or most of the activities that make
up the round of life of the group and each individual?

These two principles when used as criteria, the restriction of movement to and from statuses and the limitation and extent of the social and
individual activities, are applicable to all systems and are of significance
to each. Since systems of rank conforming to them order the several
varieties of *status* which function to control the basic activities of man
and determine who shall have or not have access to them, who shall have
power and prestige or not, they clearly meet the demands of the tests
previously set.

### The several types of rank

When the two polar types of status control, the closed form (not accessible to free competition) and the open (accessible to movement into
it and allowing movement out) are combined with the two polar types
of hierarchy (the general and all-inclusive one, which covers most or all
of the activities of the individual and the society, and the segmentary
or limited one whose controls are confined to a limited part of the society
and its behavior) four basic forms of rank are logically recognizable.
Each of the four logical types is now satisfied by empirical reality, there
being numerous documented cases from contemporary research on civilizations and on the unlettered cultures of primitive society. Many varieties exist in the middle distances which can be arranged scientifically
according to the two principles, the amount of control exercised over the
free movement of peoples, and the extent of the control exercised over
the total social activities.

The four extreme types are:

a. The inclusive (or general) system with open statuses where free
competition prevails among individuals (and families) for position.
Social class in the United States is but one variety.* Successful competition is expressed in social mobility (31, 48, 123, 202, 204).

* Several issues about social and occupational mobility are now being profitably
debated. Some of the principal ones are: How much movement is there (5, 17, 237)?
Is there more or less than previously (252, 253)? Is American society becoming less

b. The limited (segmentary) system within which the ranked statuses are open to free competition and there is movement in and out of the available statuses.

c. The inclusive (general) system whose statuses are closed and not open to competition. The position of the individual is fixed.

d. The *limited* (segmentary) system closed to free competition where, for the purposes of the hierarchy, the position of the individual is fixed and there is no movement from status to status.

The several types range from a high degree of freedom for the individual, with great fluidity of status, to a rigid, inflexible system with fixed life chances for the individual and his family.* The intermediate distances, ranging between the two extremes of the extent of the control of the variety of activities and the degree of closure of status, make it possible to recognize and place a number of intermediate or subtypes corresponding with the variations found by research in this and other societies. However, for our present purposes, only one intermediate type for each dimension will be introduced.

Each system may be in a state of equilibrium, with opposition between the ranks organized or in a state of conflict. Partly as a result of the long reign of Marxian ideology among social scientists, the literature on class conflict is far greater than that on the study of cooperation among all levels on the common tasks of society, or than on organized opposition (in Simmel's sense) among those who collaborate. In fact, some writers would define the task of the analyst of rank as the study of the history of class conflict. Structural analysis disagrees; the histories of class and other forms of rank necessarily record periods of conflict and the nature of it, but such studies will be founded on the larger problem of status opposition where cooperation is an essential part of the class relations.

or more rigid (134)? What are the factors involved in contemporary mobility: education, acquisition of skill, social and occupational imitation and modeling? Or are they personal and psychological (66, 133)? Do members of certain classes, the middle as compared with the upper or lower, move more (251)?

* Since in all or most societies there is a variety of ranked statuses, each with its own power and prestige, the same individual may be ranked differently. In some hierarchies he may have high status (a Brahmin) and in others low or high (economically or politically). For a discussion of the relation of an individual's status ratings in India see Marriott (188). By a careful study of the ratings of men of several castes by members of the community, he shows that different criteria are used by the villagers who evaluate them. Caste is but *one* system of rating. There was more disagreement about the prestige of the different men among the raters than among the members of the New York village studied by Kaufman (156, 157). *The Status System of a Modern Community* attacked the same problem (256).

Inspection of Chart I shows that the degrees of inclusion of activities have been arranged horizontally and the degrees of closure or openness of status vertically. The general and more inclusive type is at the upper

### CHART I. TYPES OF SOCIAL STRATIFICATION

The Degree of the Inclusion of Activities Controlled by a Rank Order

| | | General and Inclusive | Mixed | | Limited and Segmentary |
| --- | --- | --- | --- | --- | --- |
| | | | To General | To Limited | |
| Open With Free Competition | | General and free (certain social classes and age grades) 1 | Neither inclusive nor entirely limited, but free competition (ethnic group, certain occupations and professions) 8 | | Segmentary and free (certain factories, various military hierarchies, churches, etc., political) 3 |
| Mixed Neither Open nor Closed | Open | General extension and with intermediate rules of closure | Neither inclusive nor limited, partly open | | Segmentary, partly open |
| | Closed | (Certain ethnic groups. The middle classes more open, upper more closed) 5 | (Certain occupations and professions; certain ethnic groups; degree of assimilation) 6 | | (Certain ethnic groups; degree of assimilation; certain factories, unions, associations, churches, etc.) 7 |
| Status Closure With No Status Competition | | General with status closure, no competition (color caste, certain castes in India, sex divisions) 2 | Neither inclusive nor limited. Closed to competition (certain occupations and professions) 9 | | Segmentary with status closure. No competition (certain factories, unions, associations, etc.) 4 |

*The degree of Openness or Closure of the Status Controls*

left combined with free competition and the other extreme types (so numbered in one of the four corners) at the right; the mixed types are between them.

It will be noted that social class, which allows competition for the more prestigeful and powerful positions, is in the upper left (1) and that color caste, at the other extreme in status closure, which prohibits movement and competition, is in the lower left (2). The position of the individual and his family is *not* fixed in social class, for his life chances and those of his family can be (by the nature of the system) improved by competing freely (51) for higher position. The position of the individual and his family in a (classical) caste system is fixed and determined by birth. He is not free to compete for all or some of the prestige and power of the higher caste. His life chances (so far as caste is involved) are limited. The two forms of rank, however, are alike inasmuch as each covers the whole or most of the activities of those who are members of either system (246, 247, 266).

The literature on American, English,* and European † social class and the issues being debated are endless. Some of them are methodological (4, 71, 109, 110, 118, 191, 217, 236). Is American class no more than a statistical construct? Or is it a reality in group life (167, 239, 257)? The number of classes (109) has been discussed (251). The degree to which they exist and how they do (142) in great metropolitan centers and the smaller cities and rural areas have been issues (79, 217). Research on the varying meanings of words, objects, and symbols as they are used in the different media by different kinds of people at the several status levels in a mass society has led to many fruitful results and leads for future work (34, 35, 160). The newspapers, books (113), magazines, television, and radio (254), motion pictures, as well as rumor and gossip (229) have been given considerable attention. All show the strong influence of status in giving multiple meanings to common symbols and increasing the problem of communication within a total group. Questions about the objective and subjective aspects of class and the methodological problems involved are problems of concern to many (216). Others see the subjective and objective characteristics of class as parts of one system and possibly a false dichotomy (249, 261).

How sharply delineated or not the several levels are and the number involved in fact are interrelated problems. The present writer and those

---

* English sociologists are rapidly developing a large body of literature on social class, social mobility, and other aspects of social stratification. The several classes and their composition have been recently reported on (3, 11, 37, 88, 89, 100, 169, 170). Occupational grading and succession are now being studied (52, 253). The relation of recent political, economic, and social change to changes in the status structure has been treated (215). The broad generalities of occupational grading in English-speaking culture now seem clear (59, 152, 186).

† Studies of stratification and social mobility in other European countries, including France, Italy, Russia, the Netherlands, and the several Scandinavian countries, are being conducted and published (99, 120, 150, 177, 245).

colleagues he has had the satisfaction of working with have at no time believed they were sharp and clearly distinct (251, 257). Nor has it been believed that everyone in a community sees them alike (251). In fact, the structural type of analysis (like the occupational one) depends on the analyst's examining his data and judging where the break-points are (for purposes of analysis and scientific representation of communicable reality). The technique of "matched agreement" (251) clearly indicates that the scientific class construct refers to the norms of social reality. The class variations in an *open* system (with social mobility) necessarily make class "boundaries" indistinct. Only a classically defined caste system sharply separates two or more levels of rank.

The issue on the exact number of social classes existing in American (or English) society seems a false one. For some purposes there may be only three recognized by the participant or the informant, for example, the "Common Man Level" and those above and below it. The participant-informant may then redivide them in four, five, or six levels, running from upper down through the middle levels to the lowest class. Or he may see them as simply upper, middle, and working classes. Each system of classification exists in his mental life (beliefs and values) and behavior and among other members of the society. Analogous to these several divisions of class are those of age grades. The old, mature, and the young may be further divided or collapsed into the adult and sub-adult levels. Each is a reality.

The interrelations of the social classes have not had sufficient and proper attention. If they had, many of the false problems about the nature of American class would disappear. McCall's paper showing the amount of interaction of people in small groups among different class levels is most important (179). It indicates that for some purposes members of different classes are sometimes closer than those of the same level. This follows the approach set forth in the second volume of the Yankee City Series (256) where the interactions and relations of the six classes were measured for family, clique, and association.*

* Unfortunately for purposes of sensible debate of the real issues, this volume has not been given the same attention as Volume I. On page 12 of the second volume it is said, "When the several internal structures of the community of Yankee City had been analyzed to determine the number and kind of positions [statuses] and relations, we sought to convert all the relations and positions of the separate structures into one general positional [status] system. If this were possible [as it was] we could dispense with the older class and structural analysis and depend entirely on the positional and relational system."

In brief, each class becomes a series of multiple statuses, and they are part of an interactive totality of statuses. All of them, for the individuals who participate in them, are as contexts of behavior "reference groups."

Forms of rank in the segmentary positions are quite different from the general types (see chart, Positions 3 and 4). They are alike in so far as the control is limited; they are different since in the one the system is open, and in the other, closed to competition. The segmentary hierarchies, including political,* economic,† ecclesiastical,‡ military, and the like, in America (70, 78, 107) and many parts of Europe (231) may be open for competition for power and prestige to all those who enter them, or they may be partly closed or entirely so. The *accessibility* to the highly valued things and symbols of a society may be controlled by the rules governing such hierarchies. Salaries, wages, and other economic differences can be determined by such social rules governing movement. The distribution of goods and services and wealth is partly a function of position in the segmentary and general hierarchies.

An inspection of the cases of rank in the mixed types is revealing. The American ethnic groups are not found in any of the polar types, but primarily in the three mixed types, according to their degree of assimilation (259, 266). They are not in Position 1 with social class because, although for a brief time the ethnic subsystem covers almost all or most of the activities of the individual and his family as does class, the system itself is a subsystem that does not include everyone in the society or all

---

* Political hierarchies have their own separate bodies of literature. However, certain of them in the past have been of great influence in sociology and some in the present are of direct sociological significance. The nature of power in the hierarchy with its relation to community and individual affairs is one of them (27, 158, 185, 187, 223). The relation of the different kinds of personality to political behavior in hierarchical structures is another (161, 162). The study of the meaning of voting behavior, political parties, political attitudes, and socioeconomic and class levels and their significance for understanding national and community life is yielding valuable knowledge on which the sciences having to do with status can now depend (6, 12, 23, 30, 33, 84, 164).

† The literature on industrial hierarchies, including factories, corporations, and industries, as well as unions and other employer and employee groups, is exceedingly large and beyond the compass of this chapter. However, certain writers have emphasized the structural as well as the economic characteristics of these organizations. A few must be mentioned (19, 97, 98, 116, 196, 197, 244, 264). Others have stressed the personality as it functions in business enterprise (252).

The literature on industrial conflict has been examined in the history of structural change (115, 255).

‡ The varying ideologies of the church (218), the membership of the church (40, 41, 219, 266), and the place of churches in the class structure in the United States (219) have been studied. All show strong status relations, but they indicate that the effects of the entire community and democratic values are strongly felt by this institution (249). However, certain churches are heavily class-defined and are "store front," "middle-class," or "society" (77).

its activities. Only part of the society is involved. Yet, except in the broadest sense of the term, an ethnic group cannot be typed as segmentary since (unlike a job in a segmentary factory) most of the individual's and family's activities are ordered by it. Although in some respects certain American ethnic systems are like a caste (Position 2) in regard to closure, in fact there is always some movement and the group's ambivalent values partly encourage movement up and out. Consequently by *extent* it belongs in the mixed types. Most ethnic groups of two or three generations belong in the central position (6). They are partly general in their application of control but not entirely; they are partly open, yet there is a degree of closure beyond the rule of social class and the position of an individual is more often fixed than in an (open) social class. As an ethnic group such as the Irish Catholic becomes more assimilated, its members largely enter the general social system and confine their remaining ethnic activities (if any) to the hierarchy of the church (Position 7). Some of the members of ethnic groups who refuse to assimilate may become sects and develop a closed system (266).

When the two basic types of rank are combined, the rudimentary, universal one to which age grading belongs and the differentiated, specialized type in which social and economic class are varieties, it is then possible to cover all forms of rank existing in this and all societies. They all distribute power and prestige through the controls of the statuses which compose them.

The nature of power and its sources are concerns of fundamental importance and of necessary interest to contemporary students of rank. We need now to turn our attention to them.

### Power, prestige, and the human adaptive controls

Power may be simply defined for our immediate purposes as the possession of control over other beings and objects in the social and natural environments, making it possible to act on them to achieve outcomes that would not take place if control were not exerted. Prestige is the kind and amount of value socially attributed to objects, activities, persons, and statuses (135, 155). The two are usually interrelated; power can derive from prestige and prestige from power. However, a man may have power with little prestige or high prestige with little power.* The

---

* The problem of power and rank is of almost obsessive concern to Marxians. The followers of Max Weber are also greatly concerned with it, but conceive it more broadly and are less inclined to derive it entirely from one source (62, 187, 213, 214, 231). Others view it more in classical, political terms and with the ultimate use of force (73).

Lasswell, influenced by Freud and Pareto, as well as other psychologies and

kinds and amount of power and prestige vary from one territorial group to another. They also differ among the several forms of rank and status. The problem of how forms of rank are related to prestige and power as well as the nature of sources of power and prestige must be considered.

The Marxians and others have founded their system of class analysis on the assumption that power is *only* a product of *one* kind of status control over *one* kind of environment; that the statuses which control the means of production and the distribution of their products hold the power and are thus given the prestige which determine class alignments (61, 172); it is argued that since the technological adjustments to the natural environment are moving in a given, predetermined direction, the dependent society, its mental and cultural life, the class forms, their composition and relations are perforce moving in a predictable sequence to a classless society (28).

Clearly such economic determinists are correct in pointing out the importance of the statuses which control the natural environment and the real power inherent in such statuses or those superordinate statuses which control them. They are wrong, however, in assuming that technological control is the *only* source of power. The sources of power are *multiple,* not one. To properly understand the problems of power and prestige we must use the knowledge of sociology, social anthropology, and the psychological sciences that has accumulated since Marx and Engels. We must re-examine the whole question of the relation of power to the human adaptive controls of the several environments, and man's dependence on them.

Human survival universally *depends* on two and, it is believed, three environments. The first is the so-called natural environment which in varying degrees is controlled by the technology; the second, the human species environment which is controlled by (part of) the moral order, a system of social organization; and the third, real or not, the supernatural environment, ordered and controlled, it is believed, by the "myths" and rituals of religion and magic, a system of sacred symbols.

The very presence of these adaptive controls demonstrates: (a) that men are *dependent* on an adequate use of them for survival, each having the power of life and death over them; (b) that the controls exercised over the environments to reduce their control *over* men involve the use of several forms of power by individuals and groups; and (c) that, in exercising control, each adaptive mechanism employs real power. The tools and skills of the technology transform the natural world sufficiently

sociologies, views power broadly; but essentially he is concerned with the moral aspects of power as they are felt and expressed in the rewards and deprivations of the organism living in society (161, 162).

to aid men in acquiring and producing food, shelter, and the other creature needs and comforts which increase the life chances (Weber's term
more broadly used) of the adult individual, of the young to grow into
maturity, and in a given group of the species to survive.

The second, the control over the species, by imposing the pressures of
moral forms on animal behavior, regulates the discharge of species energy;
it controls the interactions of individuals and structures their access to
each other. Thus it orders the basic life-flow of the species and of each
individual, including the procreative processes and the relations of the
adult and immature; it orders the expression of hostility, aggression, and
violence, the disposition of prized objects, and the imposition of unpleasant tasks among the members of the group. Control over the species
environment means an exercise of real power; it also means the presence
of power in every socially organized species group and a *sense* of social
power (in Durkheim's sense) within the group among those who live in
it. The meanings and social representations of what social power is vary
from group to group; the forms by which it is utilized and expressed also
vary enormously. The violent, not to say explosive, power of the emotions generated by the moral order's control over sexuality, individual
growth and development, adult deterioration, and senility among the
several family statuses has been given much attention. This focus, under
the conceptual schemes of the psychoanalyst, has helped us understand
emotion's great force but has tended to lose some of its deserved strength
for status and power analysis because of too great reliance on individual
psychology rather than on group and species foundations.

The *supernatural* adaptations controlling, it is believed, man's ultimate
fate, govern those activities and outcomes over which the other two have
insufficient power. Sickness, death, obliteration of the self, social disaster,
and the ill or well being of man are in its compass. Each society has
fashioned its own adaptive controls to meet as best "it" can the terrible
and absolute power of this other world and thereby reduce human anxiety
and dread.

Statuses function to order and coordinate the multiple activities involved in the control of each environment. They assign tasks and socially
locate activities; they include and exclude the members of the society
while placing them in a social universe. The statuses directly involved in
the several adaptive activities, as integral parts of their ordering, possess,
or are attributed, varying power and prestige according to the members
of the society who feel their beneficial or harmful effects. Those with
a high degree of adaptive control are likely to have high ranking; those
believed to exercise low control are often given lower ranking.

Those statuses *not* directly involved in the mechanics of the adaptive processes, but which control those statuses that are, *share* some of their power with them, or they *remove* and *hold* it for themselves. Thus statuses are hierarchically arranged. The problem becomes why these secondary statuses in a rank order exercise control over the others and often accumulate more power and prestige than the primary ones directly involved in the adaptive tasks? This question is closely allied to another. Why do some societies possess specialized and developed rank orders of prestige and power and others only the rudimentary types? These questions will be dealt with in the following section.

The power of an adaptive status, or hierarchy of statuses, may be *intrinsic* and directly applied or *extrinsic* to its activities and functions. In other words, the force it possesses and applies may be an integral and necessary part of its adaptive activity, or it may be ("given") attributed to it by all, or some, members of the society. The power to kill a kangaroo with a spear by a hunter (who does or does not keep its meat for himself, his family, and clan) is at least partly intrinsic, but the man may also be accorded by his group increased power beyond his ability to kill and keep. The first is an intrinsic and integral part of his technical status as a hunter and of his moral status as a member of his family and clan; the latter power, not necessary for the execution of his technical and moral acts, is of course attributed to him.

The prestige of a status, the esteem in which it is held, or the derogation, is attributable and extrinsic. The values of the group, or some part of it, are projected upon the status and determine its social worth. Much of what are popularly and scientifically termed prestige and power are products of the larger group's feelings. The facts of the adaptive actions of a status become evaluated symbols which accumulate and attract other negative or positive social values that may have little to do with the activities of the status.

Since the statuses of adaptation are integral parts of a social system, they are in a position of mutual influence. No one system of adaptation is entirely free from the others. No one at *all* times and *all* places will necessarily dominate the others, the technological, the moral, or the social system, the other two. When the technology is complex the kinds and number of statuses (occupations, for example) are necessarily numerous and highly diverse. Such economic status systems may be scientifically classified into types and arranged along a continuum of simple to complex. In many primitive societies, occupations are largely undifferentiated. Each man performs many productive functions which are not classifiable occupationally. Occupational ranking is therefore not possible. In such a society as ours where the division of labor is exceedingly great, ranking of occupations is one of the principal forms of stratification;

and the accumulation of wealth and the sources of wealth are also ranked
in "separate" systems (257).

The several economic status orders found in different societies may be
closed or open; they may be limited or general rank orders. In any given
society the statuses associated with the technology may dominate the
whole status order and all other types of status be subordinate to one or
more orders of technological status. On the contrary, they may be under
the control of, and subordinate to, the statuses which control the species
or the myths and rituals which regulate the power of the supernatural and
the unknown (32, 123, 165). Or the three may be in conflict (Russia
seems to be a case in point).

The moral order's family, age, and sex statuses control and regulate
some of the most powerful activities and energies of the species environment. The status of the parent, the father particularly, subordinates the
statuses of the sons and daughters. The foundations of authority, its use
by the one and submission to it by the other, are in this universal relation.
The usual superordination of males and subordination of females and the
similar relation of the mature to the young are forms of authority where
social power is exercised. Rudimentary systems of rank are part of all
family, kinship, and age grade systems (13, 139, 140, 178, 200, 263).

By extension or limitation of the usual rules of descent and marriage,
the control of sexual accessibility or its prohibition and of descent of
the offspring (together with economic controls) provides the powerful
foundations for many general systems of rank. Crucial questions for
understanding this problem of the relation of the moral statuses which
control the species environment and rank order are: Are all unmarried
males and females of mature sexuality potential mates, unfettered by any
rules other than those of incest prohibitions (70, 71, 251, 253)? Or is
the choice of mates bounded by, and limited to, sharply defined ranked
categories? The general (inclusive) closed statuses which fix the position
of the individual sharply divide the biological group by social prohibitions
and boundaries. Full access between all members of the sexes for marriage purposes is forbidden. The physical life of the individual is confined within narrow boundaries; mates do not come from diverse but from
socially similar statuses (138). The open, inclusive type provides a
"mating" system where the two members of the marriage pair may come
from most diverse or very similar backgrounds.

Since the children are identified with the social status of the parents,
both the closed and open general systems initially place the child's status
in this system of rank. In the closed system like color caste the child
remains by moral rule at the parents' and his ancestors' level; in the open
he may stay or move out of it.

If the general inclusive type is an open system, the parent-child relation and the sibling relations often assume most diverse forms and are subject to great stress and distortion (68, 182). The son may move to superior position, or the daughter marry into one, thus subordinating the parent and placing the family's superior adult in an inferior position of rank. Some of the siblings may move up, others down, and still others remain at the parents' level. Open systems with free competition disperse the members of many families over distant parts of the rank order. Ordinarily they must if the systems are to continue. Closed fixed systems tend to hold the members of the family together and add their influence to maintaining family solidarity. In an open system the family of orientation quickly yields its maturing young to the larger world and to their own families of procreation; in a closed system the older generations are more likely to be related to the younger ones. The two families, often forming into a *grosse* family, hold together in primary interaction biologically, territorially, and socially. They provide the hard core of fixed position for their members and closure for movement beyond their limits (138).

The families of orientation and procreation are necessary and integral parts of the general, inclusive types of system (251). Their moral power, too, is an integral part of the power of these rank orders. It may be contained and held within the closed ranks of a caste or spread over the several ranks of a class system where there is freedom of movement.

The family may or may not be related to segmentary systems of rank. Political and ecclesiastical and other differentiated forms may derive part or most of their power and their structural form from the family, but such hierarchies can and do exist without the direct use of the family. Certain African political hierarchies are elaborations of superordinate heads of families; ecclesiastical hierarchies may be a scalar system of "fathers," but they may be built without direct use of family relations.

The statuses associated with the control of the unknown which reduce human anxieties about their life chances by the use of myth and ritual are religious and magical. They are ordinarily centered in the church. They include such ritual statuses as priests, magicians, some doctors and psychiatrists, and occasionally other statuses to which such power is attributed.

They, too, may be simple or complex. They, too, may be in societies where the religious life dominates, or is subordinate to, the technological or secular organization. In the simpler societies there may be no more than a temporary ritual leader with little power and prestige, his tenure being only during the ceremony. In many of the complex societies there may be a hierarchy of statuses from local ones up through a hierarchy

that integrates and controls the supernatural activities of a whole nation
or those of many nations.  The vertical height may be exceedingly great
or not, the area of social activity limited, or in a theocracy it may include the whole society.

The powers of the supernatural environment which can harm or benefit men are often dualistically conceived.  The problem confronting the
statuses related to these beings and the forces of sacred good and evil is
to control them and to adapt their power to man's ends.  The forces of
good must be harnessed to assist men; the forces of evil must be diverted, quarantined, or weakened.  When it is believed that the statuses
manipulating myth and ritual accomplish these ends and they "control"
the uncontrollable, the statuses of magicians, priests, and others like them
are attributed some of the power of the environment they control.  They
and their statuses derive power and prestige both from their knowledge
and ability to use the symbols effectively and from the power that comes
from the sacred world itself.  As Durkheim pointed out, supernatural
forces are comparable to physical forces; * the words and objects of the
rites of religion have social force and strength attached to them.  They
have the power to kill or cure.  The priest or magician can benefit man
or the sorcerer can cause sickness and death in his victim.  They control
the forces that can take or give life.  The power that the sacred statuses
possess tends to be absolute.

The generations of individuals arrive and disappear "but (spiritual)
*force* [mana] always remains. . . . This force is an expression of the
social power of the clan [the society]." †  It awakens in all those who
feel its force, all individuals in each society, an idea of an external force.
According to Durkheim, the sign of the totem (the emblem of God) is a
substitute for this abstract social force, allowing the sentiments of the
group to be easily expressed.  Since all religious symbols are signs expressing, and referring to, the forces of group life, the statuses which
control (and manipulate) them exercise their power.

Since all men incorporate some of the society into their persons and
since mana is power socially derived, all men necessarily possess some
mana or social power.  Weber's *charisma* seems to be little more than

---

* The ethnologists early recognized these significant "sacred forces."  Durkheim
took his lead from Codrington, who identified and defined *mana* as he found it
among the Melanesians.  "There is," Codrington said, "a belief in a force altogether
distinct from physical power, which acts in all ways for good and evil. . . . It is a
power or influence . . . it shows itself . . . in any kind of power or excellence which
a man possesses."  (Robert H. Codrington, *The Melanesians,* Oxford, Clarendon
Press, 1891, p. 118.)

† Chapter VI of Emile Durkheim, *The Elementary Forms of the Religious Life,*
New York, Macmillan, 1915, pp. 188, 204.

one form of personal mana. Charisma and mana, as parts of the value and meaning of objects and people, can be forms of attributed power. Ordinarily those in the more lowly statuses have less opportunity to acquire or express power than those advantageously placed in superior statuses. If *mana* (we use this term broadly as applicable to all societies) is largely a felt force deriving from the dominant values of the group being expressed in persons, objects, and actions, then in each society those possessing high mana are likely to be men and women who occupy one or more high-ranking statuses or, if the system be open and free, they will be candidates for achieved higher status. In a fixed and closed system there will be little or no legitimate opportunity (within that system) for those of low status to acquire high mana.

In a society where power primarily is *ritually derived* (attributed to ritual sources), if all men have access to sacred sources it is possible for men of high or low status to gain ritual mana (power and prestige). If the general systems of rank are closed and not open for vertical status movement, then the possessor of such power born to low status may become a very holy man of high spiritual worth, but remain in his same lowly *social* status. He may achieve high status in a formal or informal segmentary hierarchy of sacred significance; at times his increased prestige and power may have such strong social influence that they will threaten the rules and sanctions of the social order. If the status order is open and free the spiritual power may be translated into vertical movement in one or more segmental or general hierarchies (church and association). If the ritual values are ascetic, it may be that lowly organizational and economic status (poor, deprived, and despised) may contribute to the conditions necessary for the acquisition of ritual power (a form of mana).

Since in the simple societies the degree of differentiation among the adaptive statuses is very low, and in the complex ones differentiation is exceedingly great, the powers of the technology and of the moral and sacred orders are accordingly combined and felt as one in the simple societies, and in the more advanced ones they divide into various political, economic, and religious categories and are felt to be many. Among the latter, including Western Europe and America, mana or social power takes on a rational as well as nonrational character. Superordinate statuses appear which often possess great power but which are not directly involved in the immediate adaptive activities.

The sources of power and prestige accordingly are multiple. They derive from all powerful environments and from their adaptive controls. The statuses which function to organize the activities of these controls possess their power. In all societies social power expressed in secular or sacred terms is present and distributed among statuses, persons, and things. Power, like prestige, may not be intrinsic to the activities of the status but attributed by the group to the status and its activities.

### Social stratification, social change, and structural condition

All present research on the very simple societies confirms previous study that stratification there is largely confined to the universal, unspecialized types. However, earlier as well as more recent studies demonstrate that age and sex divisions unequally distribute property, sacred symbols, and other goods and services, and that power and prestige are attributed to certain and not other levels (32). The "advanced" forms of rank more often appear in the complex heterogeneous societies. It is in them that the adaptive statuses are reordered and placed in lineations of super- and subordination and inferiority and superiority (24, 72, 74, 90, 91, 92, 121, 122, 146, 253, 255). Social evolution in its broad sweep moves away from the nonspecialized forms of rank toward the specialized ones which place individuals and families in superior and inferior social orders.

The question is why are these empirically founded generalizations true? Why does rank grow and luxuriate in the heterogeneous societies? We must analyze comparatively the conditions in the several societies which prohibit or contribute to the functioning and presence of rank orders. To do this we must examine within a time perspective the functional statuses, the environments they control, and the societies in which they are found. To guide our inquiry we shall offer an explanation founded on the established fact that greater specialization, heterogeneity, and higher division of labor are associated with a greater development of rank orders. Through the broad, long-term social changes, the emergent complexity of the social parts makes the use of rank orders necessary. If the highly differentiated statuses and activities of contemporary societies are to function properly for the common good, if the necessary social labor is to be performed, and if disorder is to be avoided and unified action among the necessary diverse statuses is to be maintained, hierarchies of segmentary and general types must be present to order and co-ordinate their diverse activities (257). The superordinate and subordinate levels exert power which serves common ends and achieves integration. As the number and variety of statuses among each of the three adaptive types increase and the relations among them become more numerous and complex, the total effect is to produce a society of hierarchies which co-ordinate the variety of statuses and their activities. The need for co-ordination in all complex societies produces rank orders which differentially distribute power and prestige (98). For the social labor of the society to be performed, ordering by co-ordination of the diverse activities must take place. The co-ordinating functions are hierarchically located in positions of power to direct and sanction activity. These positions accumulate actual and attributed power and prestige. Back of many of them is the sanctioned use of force (73). Those which co-ordinate the primary adaptive statuses are re-ordered by superior and superordinate levels (97, 264). Through time, vast hierarchies are often developed. Each may have its own province, political, economic, or ecclesiastical (223, 258).

When the family with its rules of marriage and descent is related to such hierarchies or is an integral part of their development, general types of stratification, open or closed, appear (77, 246). The controls of the family serve to broaden the range of the hierarchy, as well as move the locus of power from the several adaptive primary statuses to one or more superior ones. Power is here inherent; those being controlled have their freedom of choice reduced, and those who control extend the social area of their own choice-making. The ordering of the relations of the statuses of the controlled and controlling takes the form of subordination and superordination (255).

The effect of co-ordination of complex statuses is not only (a) to produce superordinate statuses and subordinate position and (b) to distribute power differentially between them, but (c) to reduce the number of statuses which exercise control within the society, thereby creating a few statuses with more power than the others. This ordering of statuses produces an exclusive few in superordinate relations to an inclusive many. When the *few* exercise power over the many, they establish the foundations for the development of elites and aristocracies with lower rankings beneath them. When social change occurs rapidly the general closed types of rank are not adaptive, since they do not easily accommodate to the movement of individuals vertically or horizontally that is a necessary part of such change. The open system does (251). Color caste and all "fixed" forms are nonadaptive and likely to disappear.

Future research developments on rank, of course, will follow the interests of the investigators. It is certain if important advances are to be made and if we are to use present evidence more fruitfully and future knowledge more purposefully, we must follow MacRae's suggestion. He declares, "The most necessary and I believe the most valuable research open to us in the field of social stratification is synthetic, comparative and genetic" (186).

Many of the obsessive discussions of method, often betraying personal fears rather than scientific acumen, are likely to disappear when the several forms of American rank can be viewed by their investigators without the fear (or presence) of ethnocentrism.

## BIBLIOGRAPHICAL REFERENCES

1. Aberle, D. F., and K. D. Naegele, "Middle-Class Father's Occupational Role and Attitudes Towards Children," *American Journal of Orthopsychiatry*, Vol. 22 (1952), pp. 366–378.

2. Abrahamson, Stephen, "Our Status System and Scholastic Rewards," *Journal of Educational Sociology*, Vol. 25 (1952), pp. 441–450.

3. Abrams, M., *The Condition of the British People*, London, Gollancz, 1945.

4. Adams, S., "Fact and Myth in Social Class Theory," *Ohio Journal of Science*, Vol. 51 (1951), pp. 313–319.

5. Adams, S., "Regional Differences in Vertical Mobility in a High-Status Occupation," *Amer. Soc. Rev.*, Vol. 15 (1950), pp. 228–235.

6. Almond, G., "The Political Attitudes of Wealth," *Journal of Politics*, Vol. 7 (1945), pp. 213–256.

7. Amory, C., *The Proper Bostonians*, Boston, Dutton, 1947.

8. Anastasi, A., and J. P. Foley, *Differential Psychology: Individual and Group Differences in Behavior*, rev. ed., New York, Macmillan, 1949.

9. Anastasi, A., and S. Miller, "Adolescent 'Prestige Factors' in Relation to Scholastic and Socio-economic Variables," *Journal of Social Psychology*, Vol. 29 (1949), pp. 43–50.

10. Anderson, C. A., S. C. Brown, and M. J. Barman, "Intelligence and Occupational Mobility," *Journal of Political Economy*, Vol. 60 (1952), pp. 218–239.

11. Anderson, C. A., and M. Schapner, *School and Society in England: Social Backgrounds of Oxford and Cambridge Students*, Washington, Public Affairs Press, 1952.

12. Anderson, H. D., and P. E. Davidson, *Ballots and the Democratic Class Struggle*, Stanford Univ., Stanford Univ. Press, 1943.

13. Anderson, W. A., "Family Social Participation and Social Status Self-Ratings," *Amer. Soc. Rev.*, Vol. 11 (1946), pp. 253–258.

14. Aron, R., "Social Structure and the Ruling Class," *Brit. J. Sociol.*, Vol. 1 (1950), pp. 1–17.

15. Ashmore, Harry S., *The Negro and the Schools*, New York, Van Rees Press, 1954 (copyright, 1954, Univ. of North Carolina Press).

16. Bailey, W. C., N. Foote, P. K. Hatt, R. Hess, R. T. Morris, M. Seeman, and G. Sykes, *Bibliography on Status and Stratification*, New York, Social Science Research Council, 1952.

17. Baltzell, E. Digby, " 'Who's Who in America' and 'The Social Register': Elite and Upper Class Indexes in Metropolitan American," in Reinhard Bendix (ed.), *Class, Status and Power*, Glencoe, The Free Press, 1953, pp. 172–184.

18. Barber, B., and L. S. Lobel, "Fashion in Women's Clothes and the American Social System," *Social Forces*, Vol. 31 (1952), pp. 124–132.

19. Barnard, C. I., "Functions and Pathology of Status Systems," in W. F. Whyte, *et al.*, *Industry and Society*, New York, McGraw-Hill, 1946.

20. Bascom, William R., "Social Status, Wealth, and Individual Differences among the Yoruba," *American Anthropologist*, Vol. 53 (1951), pp. 490–506.

21. Baudler, Lucille, and D. G. Patterson, "Social Status of Women's Occupations," *Occupations,* Vol. 26 (1947–1948), pp. 421–424.

22. Beales, H. L., "The Labour Party in Its Social Context," *Political Quart.,* Vol. 24 (1953), pp. 90–98.

23. Beals, R. L., "Social Stratification in Latin America," *Amer. J. Soc.,* Vol. 58 (1952–1953), pp. 327–340.

24. Becker, H., "Changes in Social Stratification in Germany," *Amer. Soc. Rev.,* Vol. 15 (1950), pp. 333–342.

25. Becker, Howard S., "Social-Class Variations in the Teacher-Pupil Relationship," *Journal of Educational Sociology,* Vol. 25 (1952), pp. 451–465.

26. Belcher, J. C., "Evaluation and Re-standardization of Sewell's Socioeconomic Scale," *Rural Sociol.,* Vol. 16 (1951), pp. 246–255.

27. Bendix, R., *Higher Civil Servants in American Society,* Univ. of Colorado Studies, Series in Sociology No. 2, Boulder, Univ. of Colorado Press, 1949.

28. Bendix, R., and Seymour Martin Lipset, *Class, Status and Power, A Reader in Social Stratification,* Glencoe, The Free Press, 1953.

29. Bennett, J. W., and M. M. Tumin, *Social Life,* New York, Knopf, 1948.

30. Benney, M., and P. Geiss, "Social Class and Politics in Greenwich," *Brit. J. Sociol.,* Vol. 1 (1950), pp. 310–327.

31. Berent, J., "Fertility and Social Mobility," *Popul. Stud.,* Vol. 5 (1952), pp. 224–261.

32. Bernardi, B., "The Age-System of the Nilo-Hamitic Peoples," *Africa,* Vol. 22 (1952), pp. 316–333.

33. Bonham, J., "The Middle Class Elector," *British J. Sociol.,* Vol. 3 (1952), pp. 222–231.

34. Bossard, J. H. S., "Ritual in Family Living," *Amer. Soc. Rev.,* Vol. 14 (1949), pp. 463–469.

35. Bossard, J. H. S., and E. S. Boll, "Rite of Passage—a Contemporary Study," *Social Forces,* Vol. 26 (1948), pp. 247–255.

36. Bott, Elizabeth, "The Concept of Class as a Reference Group," *Human Relations,* Vol. 7 (1954), pp. 259–285.

37. Bottomore, Thomas, "Social Stratification in Voluntary Organizations," in D. V. Glass (ed.), *Social Mobility in Britain,* Glencoe, The Free Press, 1954, pp. 349–382.

38. Bouriez-Gregg, Françoise, *Les Classes Sociales aux États-Unis,* Paris, Librairie Armand Colin, 1954.

39. Brooks, M. R., "American Class and Caste: an Appraisal," *Social Forces,* Vol. 25 (1946), pp. 201–211.

40. Brown, J. S., "Social Class, Inter-marriage and Church Membership in a Kentucky Community," *Amer. J. Soc.,* Vol. 57 (1951–1952), pp. 232–242.

41. Bultena, Louis, "Church Membership and Church Attendance in Madison, Wis.," *Amer. Soc. Rev.,* Vol. 14 (1949), pp. 384–389.

42. Burt, C., "Family Size, Intelligence and Social Class," *Popul. Stud.,* Vol. 1 (1947), pp. 177–187.

43. Burt, C., "The Trend of National Intelligence," *Brit. J. Sociol.,* Vol. 1 (1950), pp. 154–168.

44. Cantril, H., "Identification with Social and Economic Class," *J. Abnormal Soc. Psychol.,* Vol. 38 (1943), pp. 574–580.

45. Case, H. M., "An Independent Test of the Interest-Group Theory of Social Class," *Amer. Soc. Rev.,* Vol. 17 (1952), pp. 751–754.

46. Cauter, T., and J. D. Downham, *The Communication of Ideas,* London, Chatto and Windus, 1954.

47. Centers, R., "Class Consciousness of the American Woman," *Int. J. Opin. and Attit. Res.,* Vol. 3 (1949), pp. 399–408.

48. Centers, R., "Educational and Occupational Mobility," *Amer. Soc. Rev.,* Vol. 14 (1949), pp. 143–147.

49. Centers, R., "Marital Selection and Occupational Strata," *Amer. J. Soc.,* Vol. 54 (1948–1949), pp. 530–535.

50. Centers, R., "Motivational Aspects of Occupational Stratification," *Journal of Social Psychology,* Vol. 28 (1948), pp. 187–217.

51. Centers, R., "Occupational Mobility of Urban Occupational Strata," *Amer. Soc. Rev.,* Vol. 13 (1948), pp. 197–203.

52. Centers, R., *The Psychology of Social Classes: A Study of Class Consciousness,* Princeton, Princeton Univ. Press, 1949.

53. Centers, R., "Social Class, Occupation, and Imputed Belief," *Amer. J. Soc.,* Vol. 58 (1952–1953), pp. 543–555.

54. Centers, R., "Towards an Articulation of Two Approaches to Social Class Phenomena," *Int. J. Opin. and Attit. Res.,* Vol. 4 (1950), pp. 499–514.

55. Chambers, Rosalind C., "A Study of Three Voluntary Organizations," in D. V. Glass (ed.), *Social Mobility in Britain,* Glencoe, The Free Press, 1954, pp. 383–406.

56. Chen, T. A., "Basic Problems of the Chinese Working Classes," *Amer. J. Soc.,* Vol. 53 (1947–1948), pp. 184–191.

57. Chinay, E., "The Traditions of Opportunity and the Aspirations of Automobile Workers," *Amer. J. Soc.,* Vol. 57 (1951–1952), pp. 453–459.

58. Clark, R. E., "Psychoses, Income, and Occupational Prestige," *Amer. J. Soc.,* Vol. 54 (1948–1949), pp. 433–435.

59. Cole, G. D. H., "The Conception of the Middle Classes," *Brit. J. Sociol.,* Vol. 1 (1950), pp. 275–291.

60. Congalton, A. A., "Social Grading of Occupations in New Zealand," *Brit. J. Sociol.,* Vol. 4 (1953), pp. 45–60.

61. Cox, O. C., *Caste, Class and Race: A Study in Social Dynamics,* New York, Doubleday, 1948.

62. Cox, O. C., "Max Weber on Social Stratification: A Critique," *Amer. Soc. Rev.,* Vol. 15 (1950), pp. 223–227

63. Cox, O. C., "Race and Caste: A Distinction," *Amer. J. Soc.,* Vol. 50 (1944–1945), pp. 360–368.

64. Davies, A. F., "Prestige of Occupations," *Brit. J. Sociol.,* Vol. 3 (1952), pp. 134–147.

65. Davis, A., "Caste, Economy and Violence," *Amer. J. Soc.,* Vol. 51 (1945–1946), pp. 7–15.

66. Davis, A., "The Motivation of Underprivileged Workers," in W. F. Whyte *et al., Industry and Society,* New York, McGraw-Hill, 1946, pp. 84–106.

67. Davis, A., *Social-Class Influences Upon Learning,* Cambridge, Harvard Univ. Press, 1948.

68. Davis, A., and R. J. Havighurst, *Father of the Man,* Boston, Houghton Mifflin, 1947.

69. Davis, A., and R. J. Havighurst, "Social Class and Color Differences in Child Rearing," *Amer. Soc. Rev.,* Vol. 11 (1946), pp. 698–710.

70. Davis, K., *Human Society,* New York, Macmillan, 1949.

71. Davis, K., and W. E. Moore, "Some Principles of Stratification," *Amer. Soc. Rev.,* Vol. 10 (1945), pp. 242–249.

72. Deeg, M. E., and D. G. Paterson, "Changes in Social Status of Occupations," *Occupations*, Vol. 25 (1947), pp. 205–208.

73. de Jouvenal, Bertrand, *Power, The Natural History of Its Growth*, London, Batchworth, 1952.

74. Dobb, M., *Studies in the Development of Capitalism*, London, Routledge, 1946.

75. Dollard, John, "Drinking Mores of the Social Classes," in *Alcohol, Science and Society*, New Haven, Yale Univ. Press, 1945, pp. 95–104.

76. Dotson, F., "Patterns of Voluntary Association among Urban Working-Class Families," *Amer. Soc. Rev.*, Vol. 16 (1951), pp. 687–693.

77. Drake, St. C., and H. Cayton, *Black Metropolis*, New York, Harcourt, 1945.

78. Drucker, P. F., *The New Society*, New York, Harper, 1949.

79. Duncan, O. D., "A Critical Evaluation of Warner's Work in Community Stratification," *Amer. Soc. Rev.*, Vol. 15 (1950), pp. 205–215.

80. Duvall, E. M., "Conceptions of Parenthood," *Amer. J. Soc.*, Vol. 52 (1946), pp. 193–203.

81. Eells, K., *et al.*, *Intelligence and Cultural Differences*, Chicago, Univ. of Chicago Press, 1951.

82. Ericson, M. C., "Child-rearing and Social Status," *Amer. J. Soc.*, Vol. 52 (1946–1947), pp. 190–192.

83. Ericson, M. C., "Social Status and Child-rearing Practices," in T. M. Newcomb and E. L. Hartley, *Readings in Social Psychology*, New York, Holt, 1947.

84. Eysenck, H. J., "Primary Social Attitudes as Related to Social Class and Political Party," *Amer. J. Soc.*, Vol. 57 (1951–1952), pp. 222–231.

85. Fei, Hsiao-Tung, "Peasantry and Gentry: An Interpretation of Chinese Social Structure and Its Changes," *Amer. J. Soc.*, Vol. 52 (1946–1947), pp. 1–17.

86. Fei, Hsiao-Tung, and Chih-I Chang, *Earthbound China: A Study of Rural Economy in Yunnan*, Chicago, Univ. of Chicago Press, 1945.

87. Fei, Hsiao-Tung, and Yung-Teh Chow, *China's Gentry: Essays in Rural-Urban Relations* by Fei with Six Life-Histories of Chinese Gentry Families Collected by Chow, Chicago, Univ. of Chicago Press, 1953.

88. Floud, J., "The Educational Experience of the Adult Population of England and Wales as at July 1949," in D. V. Glass (ed.), *Social Mobility in Britain*, Glencoe, The Free Press, 1954, pp. 98–140.

89. Floud, J., "Educational Opportunity and Social Mobility," *Year Book of Education*, London, Evan Bros., 1950, pp. 117–136.

90. Foote, N. N., "Destratification and Restratification," *Amer. J. Soc.*, Vol. 58 (1952–1953), pp. 325–326.

91. Foote, N. N., "The Professionalization of Labor in Detroit," *Amer. J. Soc.*, Vol. 58 (1952–1953), p. 371.

92. Foote, N. N., and Paul K. Hatt, "Social Mobility and Economic Advancement," *American Economic Review*, Vol. 43, Supplement (May, 1953), pp. 364–378.

93. Foreman, P. B., and M. C. Hill, *The Negro in the United States: A Bibliography*, Oklahoma A. and M. College Bull. 44, Oklahoma A. and M. College, Stillwater, 1947.

94. Form, W. H., "Toward an Occupational Social Pyschology," *Jour. of Social Psychology*, Vol. 24 (1946), pp. 85–99.

95. Friedson, E., "Relation of Social Situation of Contact to the Media in Mass Communication," *Public Opinion Quarterly*, Vol. 17 (1953), pp. 230–239.

96. Friedson, E., "Communications Research and the Concept of the Mass," *Amer. Soc. Rev.*, Vol. 18 (1953), pp. 313–317.

97. Gardner, Burleigh B., "The Factory as a Social System," in Wm. Foote Whyte (ed.), *Industry and Society*, New York, McGraw-Hill, 1946.

98. Gardner, Burleigh B., and David Moore, *Human Relations in Industry*, Homewood, Richard D. Irwin, 1955.

99. Geiger, T., "An Historical Study of the Origins and Structure of the Danish Intelligentsia," *Brit. J. Sociol.*, Vol. 1 (1950), pp. 209–220.

100. Glass, D. V. (ed.), *Social Mobility in Britain*, Glencoe, The Free Press, 1954.

101. Glass, D. V., and J. R. Hall, "A Description of a Sample Inquiry into Social Mobility in Great Britain," in D. V. Glass (ed.), *Social Mobility in Britain*, Glencoe, The Free Press, 1954, pp. 79–97.

102. Glass, D. V., and J. R. Hall, "Social Mobility in Britain: A Study of Inter-Generation Changes in Status," in D. V. Glass (ed.), *Social Mobility in Britain*, Glencoe, The Free Press, 1954, pp. 177–265.

103. Goffman, Irving, "Symbols of Class Status," *Brit. J. Sociol.*, Vol. 2 (1951), pp. 294–305.

104. Gold, Ray, "Janitors versus Tenants: A Status-Income Dilemma," *Amer. J. Soc.*, Vol. 57 (1951–1952), pp. 486–493.

105. Goldhammer, Herbert, and Edward A. Shils, "Types of Power and Status," *Amer. J. Soc.*, Vol. 45 (1939–1940), pp. 171–182.

106. Goldschmidt, W. R., "America's Social Classes: Is Equality a Myth?" *Commentary*, Vol. 10 (1950), pp. 175–181.

107. Goldschmidt, W. R., *As You Sow*, New York, Harcourt, Brace and Co., 1947.

108. Goldschmidt, W. R., "Class Denominationalism in Rural California Churches," *Amer. J. Soc.*, Vol. 49 (1943–1944), pp. 348–356.

109. Goldschmidt, W. R., "Social Class in America: A Critical Review," *Amer. Anthropol.*, Vol. 52 (1950), pp. 483–499.

110. Goldschmidt, W. R., "Social Class in American Sociology," *Amer. J. Soc.*, Vol. 55 (1949–1950), pp. 262–268.

111. Goldschmidt, W. R., "A System of Social Class Analysis" (Drew Univ. Studies, No. 2), Madison, N. J., Drew Univ. Bulletin, 1951.

112. Goodwin, A. (ed.), *The European Nobility in the Eighteenth Century*, London, Adam and Charles Black, 1953.

113. Gordon, M. M., "Kitty Foyle and the Concept of Class Culture," *Amer. J. Soc.*, Vol. 53 (1947–1948), pp. 210–217.

114. Gordon, M. M., "Social Class in American Sociology," *Amer. J. Soc.*, Vol. 55 (1949–1950), pp. 262–269.

115. Gouldner, Alvin, *The Wildcat Strike*, London, Routledge and Kegan Paul, 1955.

116. Gouldner, Alvin, *Patterns of Industrial Bureaucracy*, London, Routledge and Kegan Paul, 1955.

117. Green, A., "The Middle Class Male Child and Neurosis," *Amer. Soc. Rev.*, Vol. 12 (1946), pp. 31–41.

118. Gross, L., "The Use of Class Concepts in Sociological Research," *Amer. J. Soc.*, Vol. 54 (1948–1949), pp. 409–422.

119. Haggard, E. A., "Social-Status and Intelligence: An Experimental Study of Certain Cultural Determinants of Measured Intelligence," *Genetic Psychology Monographs*, Vol. 49 (1954), pp. 141–186.

120. Hall, J. R., and W. Ziegel, "A Comparison of Social Mobility Data for England and Wales, Italy, France and the U.S.A.," in D. V. Glass (ed.), *Social Mobility in Britain*, Glencoe, The Free Press, 1954, pp. 260–265.

121. Hall, J. R., "A Comparison of the Degree of Social Endogamy in England and Wales and the U.S.A.," in D. V. Glass (ed.), *Social Mobility in Britain,* Glencoe, The Free Press, 1954, pp. 344–346.

122. Hall, J., and D. Caradog Jones, "Social Grading of Occupations," *Brit. J. Sociol.,* Vol. 1 (1950), pp. 31–55.

123. Hall, J. R., and D. V. Glass, "Education and Social Mobility," in D. V. Glass (ed.), *Social Mobility in Britain,* Glencoe, The Free Press, 1954, pp. 291–307.

124. Hatt, P. K., "Class and Ethnic Attitudes," *Amer. Soc. Rev.,* Vol. 13 (1948), pp. 36–43.

125. Hatt, P. K., "Occupation and Social Stratification," *Amer. J. Soc.,* Vol. 55 (1950), pp. 533–544.

126. Hatt, P. K., "Social Class and Basic Personality Structure," *Sociology and Social Research,* Vol. 36 (1952), pp. 355–363.

127. Hatt, P. K., "Stratification in Mass Society," *Amer. Soc. Rev.,* Vol. 15 (1950), pp. 216–222.

128. Hatt, P. K., and V. Ktsanes, "Patterns of American Stratification as Reflected in Selected Social Literature," *Amer. Soc. Rev.,* Vol. 17 (1952), pp. 670–679.

129. Havighurst, R. J., "Child Development in Relation to Community Social Structure," *Child Development,* Vol. 17 (1946), pp. 85–89.

130. Havighurst, R. J., and F. H. Broese, "The Relation between Ability and Social Status in a Midwestern Community. III. Primary Mental Abilities," *Journal of Educational Psychology,* Vol. 38 (1947), pp. 241–247.

131. Havighurst, R. J., and R. R. Rodgers, "The Role of Motivation in Attendance at Post-High School Educational Institutions," in *Who Should Go to College,* B. S. Hollingshead (ed.), New York, Columbia Univ. Press, 1952.

132. Havighurst, R. J., and Hilda Taba, *Adolescent Character and Personality,* New York, Wiley, 1949.

133. Henry, W., "The Business Executive: Psychodynamics of a Social Role," *Amer. J. Soc.,* Vol. 54 (1948–1949), pp. 286–291.

134. Hertzler, J. O., "Some Tendencies Toward a Closed Class System in the United States," *Social Forces,* Vol. 30 (1952), pp. 313–323.

135. Hildebrand, George H., "American Unionism, Social Stratification, and Power," *Amer. J. Soc.,* Vol. 58 (1952–1953), pp. 381–390.

136. Hill, M. C., and B. C. McCall, "Social Stratification in a Georgia Town," *Amer. Soc. Rev.,* Vol. 15 (1950), pp. 721–730.

137. Himmelweit, H. T., "Social Status and Secondary Education since the 1944 Act: Some Data for London," in D. V. Glass (ed.), *Social Mobility in Britain,* Glencoe, The Free Press, 1954, pp. 141–159.

138. Hocart, A. M., *Caste: A Comparative Study,* London, Methuen, 1950.

139. Hollingshead, A. B., "Class and Kinship in a Middle Western Community," *Amer. Soc. Rev.,* Vol. 24 (1949), pp. 469–475.

140. Hollingshead, A. B., "Class Differences in Family Stability," *Annals of the Amer. Acad. of Political and Social Science,* Vol. 272 (1950), pp. 39–46.

141. Hollingshead, A. B., *Elmtown's Youth: The Impact of Social Classes on Adolescents,* New York, Wiley, 1949.

142. Hollingshead, A. B., "Selected Characteristics of Classes in a Middle Western Community," *Amer. Soc. Rev.,* Vol. 12 (1947), pp. 385–395.

143. Hollingshead, A. B., "Status in the High School," in W. Lloyd Warner (ed.), *Democracy in Jonesville,* New York, Harper, 1949, pp. 193–213.

144. Hollingshead, A. B., "Trends in Social Stratification: A Case Study," *Amer. Soc. Rev.,* Vol. 17 (1952), pp. 264–285.

145. Hsiao-T'ung Fei, "Peasantry and Gentry in China," *Amer. J. Soc.*, Vol. 52 (1946–1947), pp. 1–17.

146. Hsi-En Chen, Theodore, "The Marxist Remolding of Chinese Society," *Amer. J. Soc.*, Vol. 58 (1952–1953), pp. 340–346.

147. Hsu, Francis L. K., "Social Mobility in China," *Amer. Soc. Rev.*, Vol. 14 (1949), pp. 764–771.

148. Hughes, E. C., "Dilemmas and Contradictions of Status," *Amer. J. Soc.*, Vol. 50 (1944–1945), pp. 353–360.

149. Hyman, H. H., "The Psychology of Status," *Archives of Psychology*, No. 269, 1942, pp. 1–94.

150. Inkeles, A., "Social Stratification and Mobility in the Soviet Union," *Amer. Soc. Rev.*, Vol. 15 (1950), pp. 465–480.

151. Janke, L. L., and R. J. Havighurst, "Relations Between Ability and Social Status in a Midwestern Community. 11. 16-year-old Boys and Girls," *Journal of Educ. Psychol.*, Vol. 36 (1946), pp. 499–509.

152. Jenkins, H., and D. Caradog Jones, "Social Class of Cambridge Alumni of the 18th and 19th Centuries," *Brit. J. Sociol.*, Vol. 1 (1950), pp. 93–116.

153. Kahl, Joseph A., "Education and Occupational Aspirations of 'Common Man' Boys," *Harvard Educational Review*, Vol. 23 (1953), pp. 186–203.

154. Kaufman, H. F., "An Approach to the Study of Urban Stratification," *Amer. Soc. Rev.*, Vol. 17 (1952), pp. 430–437.

155. Kaufman, H. F., *Defining Prestige in a Rural Community* ("Sociometry Monographs," No. 10), New York, Beacon House, 1946.

156. Kaufman, H. F., "Members of a Rural Community as Judges of Prestige Rank," *Sociometry*, Vol. 9 (1946), pp. 71–86.

157. Kaufman, H. F., *Prestige Classes in a New York Rural Community*, Ithaca, Cornell University Agricultural Experiment Station Memoir No. 260, 1944.

158. Kelsall, R. K., *Higher Civil Servants in Britain*, London, Routledge and Kegan Paul, 1955.

159. Kinsey, A. C., *et al.*, *Sexual Behavior in the Human Male*, Philadelphia, Saunders, 1948.

160. Kluckhohn, C., and F. Kluckhohn, "American Culture: General Orientations and Class Patterns," in L. Bryson, L. Finkelstein, and R. M. MacIver (eds.), *Approaches to Group Understanding*, New York, Harper, 1947.

161. Lasswell, H. D., *Power and Society: A Framework for Political Inquiry*, New Haven, Yale Univ. Press, 1950.

162. Lasswell, H. D., D. Lerner, and C. E. Rothwell, *The Comparative Study of Elites: An Introduction and Bibliography*, Stanford, Stanford Univ. Press, 1952.

163. Lastrucci, C. L., "The Status and Significance of Occupational Research," *Amer. Soc. Rev.*, Vol. 11 (1946), pp. 78–84.

164. Lazarsfield, P. F., B. Berelson, and H. Goudit, *The People's Choice*, New York, Columbia Univ. Press, 1948.

165. Leach, E. R., *Political Systems of Highland Burma: A Study of Kachin Social Structure*, London, G. Bell, 1954.

166. Lee, Shu-Ching, "Intelligentsia of China," *Amer. J. Soc.*, Vol. 52 (1946–1947), pp. 489–497.

167. Lenski, G. E., "American Social Classes: Statistical Strata or Social Groups?" *Amer. J. Soc.*, Vol. 58 (1952–1953), pp. 139–144.

168. Lerner, Max, *America as a Civilization* (in press).

169. Lewis, R., and A. Maude, *The English Middle Classes*, London, Phoenix House, 1949.

170. Lewis, R., and A. Maude, *The English,* London, Phoenix House, 1949.

171. Lin, Yueh-Hwa, *The Golden Wing: A Sociological Study of Chinese Familism,* London, Kegan Paul, Trench, Trubner, 1947.

172. Lipset, S. M., and R. Bendix, "Social Mobility and Occupational Career Patterns. 1. Stability of Jobholding," *Amer. J. Soc.,* Vol. 57 (1952), pp. 366–374.

173. Lipset, S. M., and R. Bendix, "Social Status and Social Structure," *Brit. J. Sociol.,* Vol. 2 (1951), pp. 150–168, 230–257.

174. Little, K. L., "Social Change and Social Class in the Sierra Leone Protectorate," *Amer. J. Soc.,* Vol. 54 (1948–1949), pp. 10–21.

175. Little, K. L., "The Study of 'Social Change' in British West Africa," *Africa,* Vol. 23 (1953), pp. 274–284.

176. Loomis, C. P., J. A. Beagle, and T. W. Longmore, "Critique of Class as Related to Social Stratification," *Sociometry,* Vol. 10 (1947), pp. 319–337.

177. Lowie, R. H., *The German People,* New York, Farrar and Rinehart, 1945.

178. Maas, Henry, "Some Social Class Differences in the Family Systems and Group Relations of Pre- and Early Adolescents," *Child Development,* Vol. 22 (1951), pp. 145–152.

179. McCall, Bevode, "Social Status and Social Interaction, A Case Study" (manuscript shortly to be published).

180. MacDonald, M., C. McGuire, and R. Havighurst, "Leisure Activities and the Socio-Economic Status of Children," *Amer. J. Soc.,* Vol. 54 (1948–1949), pp. 505–520.

181. McGuire, C., "Family Life in Lower and Middle Class Homes," *Marriage and Family Living,* Vol. 14 (1952), pp. 1–6.

182. McGuire, C., "Social Mobility: The Rise and Fall of Families," *Democracy in Jonesville,* New York, Harper, 1949, pp. 55–76.

183. McGuire, Carson, "Social Status, Peer Status and Social Mobility" (Memorandum for the Committee on Human Development), Univ. of Chicago, Committee on Human Development, 1949.

184. McGuire, Carson, "Social Stratification and Mobility Patterns," *Amer. Soc. Rev.,* Vol. 15 (1950), pp. 195–204.

185. MacIver, R. M., *The Web of Government,* New York, Macmillan, 1947.

186. MacRae, D. G., "Social Stratification: A Trend Report," *Current Sociology,* Vol. 2 (1953–1954), pp. 5–74.

187. Mannheim, Karl, *Freedom, Power and Democratic Planning,* New York, Oxford Univ. Press, 1950.

188. Marriott, McKim, "Individual Prestige *versus* Caste Ranking in Some Hindu Villages," Unpublished paper read at the AAA meetings, Tucson, 1953.

189. Marriott, McKim (ed.), *Village India,* Chicago, Univ. of Chicago Press, 1955.

190. Marshall, T. H., *Citizenship and Social Class,* Cambridge, Cambridge Univ. Press, 1950.

191. Marshall, T. H., "The Nature and Determinants of Social Status," *The Year Book of Education,* London, Evan Bros., 1953, pp. 30–50.

192. Martin, F. M., "An Inquiry into Parents' Preferences in Secondary Education," in D. V. Glass (ed.), *Social Mobility in Britain,* Glencoe, The Free Press, 1954, pp. 160–174.

193. Meeker, Marchia, "Status Aspirations and the Social Club," in W. Lloyd Warner (ed.), *Democracy in Jonesville,* New York, Harper, 1949, pp. 130–148.

194. Miller, W., "The Business Elite in Business Bureaucracies," in W. Miller (ed.), *Men in Business,* Cambridge, Harvard Univ. Press, 1952, pp. 286–305.

195. Miller, W., "The Recruitment of the American Business Elite," *Quarterly Jour. of Economics,* Vol. 54 (1950), pp. 242–253.

196. Mills, C. W., "The American Business Elite: A Collective Portrait," *J. Econ. Hist.,* 5 (suppl. 5), 1945, pp. 20–45.

197. Mills, C. W., *The New Men of Power: America's Labor Leaders,* New York, Harcourt, 1948.

198. Mills, C. W., *White Collar: The American Middle Classes,* New York, Columbia Univ. Press, 1951.

199. Moser, C. A., and J. R. Hall, "The Social Grading of Occupations," in D. V. Glass (ed.), *Social Mobility in Britain,* Glencoe, The Free Press, 1954, pp. 29–50.

200. Motz, A. B., "Conceptions of Marital Roles by Status Groups," *Marriage and Family Living,* Vol. 12 (1950), pp. 136–162.

201. Mukherjee, Ramkrishna, "A Study of Social Mobility between Three Generations," *Social Mobility in Britain,* London, Routledge and Kegan Paul, Vol. 9 (1954), pp. 266–290.

202. Mukherjee, Ramkrishna, "A Further Note on the Analysis of Data on Social Mobility," in D. V. Glass (ed.), *Social Mobility in Britain,* Glencoe, The Free Press, 1954, pp. 242–259.

203. Mukherjee, Ramkrishna, and J. R. Hall, "A Note on the Analysis of Data on Social Mobility," in D. V. Glass (ed.), *Social Mobility in Britain,* Glencoe, The Free Press, 1954, pp. 218–241.

204. Mulligan, R. A., "Social Mobility and Higher Education," *Journal of Educational Sociology,* Vol. 25 (1952), pp. 476–487.

205. Mulligan, R. A., "Socio-Economic Background and College Enrolment," *Amer. Soc. Rev.,* Vol. 16 (1951), pp. 188–196.

206. Murdock, G. P., *Social Structure,* New York, Macmillan, 1949.

207. Neugarten, B., "The Democracy of Childhood," in W. Lloyd Warner (ed.), *Democracy in Jonesville,* New York, Harper, 1949, pp. 77–88.

208. Neugarten, B., "Social Class and Friendship among School Children," *Amer. J. Soc.,* Vol. 51 (1945–1946), pp. 305–314.

209. Newcomb, T. M., *Social Psychology,* New York, Dryden Press, 1950.

210. Newcomb, T. M., and E. T. Hartley (eds.), *Readings in Social Psychology,* New York, Holt, 1947.

211. North, C. C., and P. K. Hatt, "Jobs and Occupations: A Popular Evaluation," *Opinion News,* Vol. 1 (1947), pp. 3–13.

212. Parsons, T., "The Professions and Social Structure," *Social Forces,* Vol. 17 (1939), pp. 457–467, and in T. Parsons (ed.), *Essays in Sociological Theory: Pure and Applied,* Glencoe, The Free Press, 1949.

213. Parsons, T., "Social Classes and Class Conflict in the Light of Recent Sociological Theory," *Amer. Economic R.,* Vol. 34 (1949), pp. 16–26.

214. Parsons, T., *The Social System,* Glencoe, The Free Press, 1951, pp. 132, 172.

215. Pear, T. H., *English Social Differences,* London, G. Allen, 1955.

216. Pfautz, H. W., "The Current Literature on Social Stratification: Critique and Bibliography," *Amer. J. Soc.,* Vol. 58 (1952–1953), pp. 391–418.

217. Pfautz, H. W., and O. P. Duncan, "A Critical Evaluation of Warner's Work in Social Stratification," *Amer. Soc. Rev.,* Vol. 15 (1950), pp. 205–215.

218. Pope, L., *Millhands and Preachers* (Studies in Religious Education, No. 15), New Haven, Yale Univ. Press, 1943.

219. Pope, L., "Religion and Class Structure," *Annals of the Amer. Acad. of Political and Social Science,* Vol. 256 (1948), pp. 84–91.

220. Prins, A. H. J., *East African Age-Class Systems: An Inquiry into the Social Order of Galla, Kipsigis, and Kikuyu*, Groningen, J. B. Wolters, 1953.

221. Riesman, D., *The Lonely Crowd: A Study of the Changing American Character*, New Haven, Yale Univ. Press, 1950.

222. Rogoff, N., "Recent Trends in Urban Mobility," in P. Hatt and A. Reiss (eds.), *Reader in Urban Sociology*, Glencoe, The Free Press, 1951, pp. 406–420.

223. Rosenstein, Joseph, "Party Politics: Unequal Contests," in W. Lloyd Warner (ed.), *Democracy in Jonesville*, New York, Harper, 1949, pp. 213–235.

224. Ruesch, J., *Chronic Disease and Psychological Invalidism*, Psychosomatic Medicine Monographs, New York, Paul Hoeker, 1946.

225. Ruesch, J., "Social Technique, Social Status, and Social Change in Illness," in H. A. Murray and C. Kluckhohn (eds.), *Personality in Nature, Society and Culture*, New York, Knopf, 1948, pp. 117–130.

226. Ruesch, J., A. Jacobson, and M. B. Loeb, "Acculturation and Illness," *Psychological Monographs: General and Applied*, No. 292, Vol. 62 (1948).

227. Ruesch, J., et al., *Duodenal Ulcer: A Sociopsychological Study of Naval Enlisted Personnel and Civilians*, Berkeley, Univ. of California Press, 1948.

228. Ryan, B. F., *Caste in Modern Ceylon*, New Brunswick, Rutgers Univ. Press, 1953.

229. Schatzman, Leonard, and Anselm Strauss, "Social Class and Modes of Communication," *Amer. J. Soc.*, Vol. 60 (1954–1955), pp. 329–338.

230. Schlesinger, A. M., *Learning How to Behave*, New York, Macmillan, 1946.

231. Schumpeter, J. A., *Imperialism and Social Classes*, New York, Kelley, 1951.

232. Sellars, R. W., V. J. McGill, and M. Faber, *Philosophy for the Future*, New York, Macmillan, 1949.

233. Sewell, W. H., *The Construction and Standardization of a Scale for the Measurement of the Socio-Economic Status of Oklahoma Farm Families*, Oklahoma, Oklahoma A. and M. College Technical Bulletin No. 9, 1940.

234. Sewell, W. H., and B. L. Ellenbogen, "Social Status and the Measured Intelligence of Small City and Rural Children," *Amer. Soc. Rev.*, Vol. 17 (1952), pp. 612–616.

235. Shih, Kuo-Heng, ed. and tr. by Hsiao-tung Fei, and Francis L. K. Hsu, *China Enters the Machine Age*, Cambridge, Harvard Univ. Press, 1944.

236. Shils, E., *The Present State of American Sociology*, Glencoe, The Free Press, 1948.

237. Sjoberg, G., "Are Social Classes in America Becoming More Rigid?" *Amer. Soc. Rev.*, Vol. 16 (1951), pp. 775–783.

238. Smith, Benjamin F., "Wishes of Negro High School Seniors and Social Class Status," *Journal of Eductional Sociology*, Vol. 25 (1952), pp. 466–475.

239. Sorokin, Pitirim, *Society, Culture, and Personality*, New York, Harper, 1947, pp. 277–278.

240. Sorokin, Pitirim, *Social Mobility*, New York, Harper, 1927.

241. Stendler, Celia Burns, *Children of Brasstown* (Univ. of Ill. Bull., Vol. 46, No. 59), Urbana, Bureau of Research and Service of the College of Education, 1949.

242. Stern, Bernhard J., "Some Aspects of Historical Materialism," in R. W. Sellars (ed.), *Philosophy for the Future*, New York, Macmillan, 1949.

243. Stone, Gregory, "City Shoppers and Urban Stratification. Observations on the Social Psychology of City Life," *Amer. J. Soc.*, Vol. 60 (1954–1955), pp. 36–45.

244. Taft, P., *The Structure and Government of Labour Unions*, London, Geoffrey Cumberlege, and Cambridge, Harvard Univ. Press, 1955.

245. Timasheff, N. S., "Vertical Social Mobility in Communist Society," *Amer. J. Soc.*, Vol. 49 (1943–1944), pp. 9–22.

246. Tumin, M. M., *Caste in a Peasant Society*, Princeton, Princeton Univ. Press, 1952.

247. Vogt, E. Z., "Social Stratification in the Rural Middle West: A Structural Analysis," *Rural Sociology*, Vol. 12 (1947), pp. 364–375.

248. Vogt, E. Z., Jr., "Town and Country: The Structure of Rural Life," in W. Lloyd Warner (ed.), *Democracy in Jonesville*, New York, Harper, 1949, pp. 236–265.

249. Warner, W. Lloyd (ed.), *Democracy in Jonesville*, New York, Harper, 1949.

250. Warner, W. Lloyd, "A Methodological Note," in St. Clair Drake and Horace R. Cayton, *Black Metropolis*, New York, Harcourt, 1945.

251. Warner, W. Lloyd, *Structure of American Life*, Edinburgh, The University Press, 1952. (American title: *American Life: Dream and Reality*, Chicago, Univ. of Chicago Press, 1953.)

252. Warner, W. Lloyd, and J. Abegglen, *Big Business Leaders in America*, New York, Harper, 1955.

253. Warner, W. Lloyd, and J. Abegglen, *Occupational Mobility in American Business and Industry, 1928–1952*, St. Paul, Univ. of Minnesota Press, 1955.

254. Warner, W. Lloyd, and William E. Henry, "The Radio Daytime Serial: A Symbolic Analysis," *Genetic Psychology Monographs*, Vol. 37 (1948), pp. 3–72.

255. Warner, W. Lloyd, and J. O. Low, *The Social System of the Modern Factory*, New Haven, Yale Univ. Press, 1947.

256. Warner, W. Lloyd, and P. S. Lunt, *The Status System of a Modern Community*, New Haven, Yale Univ. Press, 1947.

257. Warner, W. Lloyd, M. Meeker, and K. Eells, *Social Class in America*, Chicago, Science Research Associates, 1949.

258. Warner, W. Lloyd, and Marchia Meeker, "The Mill: Its Economy and Moral Structure," in W. Lloyd Warner (ed.), *Democracy in Jonesville*, New York, Harper, 1949.

259. Warner, W. Lloyd, and Leo Srole, *The Social Systems of American Ethnic Groups*, Vol. III, Yankee City Series, New Haven, Yale Univ. Press, 1945.

260. Warriner, Charles K., "Leadership in the Small Group," *Amer. J. Soc.*, Vol. 60 (1955), pp. 361–369.

261. West, J., *Plainville, U.S.A.*, New York, Columbia Univ. Press, 1945.

262. White, Clyde, *These Will Go to College*, Cleveland, Press of Western Reserve Univ., 1952.

263. Whyte, W. F., "A Slum Sex Code," *Amer. J. Soc.*, Vol. 49 (1943), pp. 24–31.

264. Whyte, W. F., "The Social Structure of the Restaurant," *Amer. J. Soc.*, Vol. 54 (1949), pp. 302–310.

265. Williams, Robin M., Jr., *American Society: A Sociological Interpretation*, New York, Alfred A. Knopf, 1951, pp. 78–135.

266. Wray, D., "The Norwegians: Sect and Ethnic Group," *Democracy in Jonesville*, New York, Harper and Bros., pp. 168–192.

267. Wohl, R. Richard, "The Rags to Riches Story: An Episode of Secular Idealism," *Class Status and Power*, Glencoe, The Free Press, 1953.

268. Yang, Martin C., *A Chinese Village: Taiton, Shantung Province*, New York, Columbia Univ. Press, 1943.

# chapter 9

# Social institutions
# and voluntary associations

F. STUART CHAPIN
*University of Minnesota*

Little systematic research and writing on social institutions (5, 36, 94) per se has appeared in the decade 1945–1955.* But there are two active trends of sociological study related to institutional analysis: one concerns the study of voluntary organizations (72), and the other is variously called "group dynamics" and "small group research" (3). The latter development is still in an early stage and yet there are preliminary findings that have at least important implications for institutional analysis. Research in group dynamics and studies of small groups, although scanty in firm substantive results, are nevertheless rich in suggestions for improved techniques of research all the way from operational definitions of basic concepts to experimental tests of hypotheses. Theoretical development built upon or checked by these improved techniques, however

* For books in which social institutions are treated as incidental to some larger purpose, see bibliographical references (58, 66, 69).

trivial or artificial some of the recent findings may be regarded, should
follow in the near future. No adequate synthesis for institutional theory
is yet possible, but convergences of evidence and clarification of some
relationships seem evident.

## VOLUNTARY ASSOCIATIONS

In his recent book (72, chapters 3, 4) Arnold Rose develops a theory
of the function of voluntary associations in contemporary culture, and
then applies it to explain the present ineffectuality of French political
institutions in the recurrent world crises of 1945–1955. Rose identifies
three functions of voluntary associations: (a) they distribute power
over social life; (b) they provide a sense of satisfaction with the modern
democratic process; and (c) they provide a social mechanism for continually initiating social changes. In the United States all these functions
have developed because the conditions of community life have encouraged them. In the frontier days there was weakness of local government
and a tradition of distrust of central government. The increasing mobility of the population and the rapidity of social change were also favoring
trends. Prior to the industrial revolution the expanded family, the
church, and the community met the needs for human fellowship, personal security, and "explanation" of the forces controlling the perceived
world. These needs were not as well satisfied when the industrial revolution weakened the customary social institutions of the local community
which had gratified them, and as a consequence, voluntary associations
developed apace. These filled in the gaps of social structure, formed a
training ground for democratic participation, and provided a structural
network which supported the older political institutions of democracy.
Meanwhile in France this was unfortunately not the case. Here the
tradition of distrust of voluntary social movements, bias against workers'
organizations (72, page 82), and fear (72, pages 98–100) of irresponsible
private social organizations effectively checked the development of voluntary associations. While French voluntary organizations do offer
fellowship, very few provide security or explanation and control. Thus
it came about that the political institutions of contemporary French
democracy became unstable, weak, and lacking in the support of organized workers, who turned to revolutionary activity rather than to reform
within the political system (72, page 115). In this connection it is interesting to note that Durkheim (23) in the 1890's had put his finger on
this same point, when he said, "A nation can be maintained only if, between the state and the individual, there is intercalated a whole series of
secondary groups near enough to the individuals to attract them strongly

in their sphere of action, and drag them in this way into the general torrent of social life."

Voluntary associations in the United States are most numerous in urban areas, but throughout the nation there are thousands of groups which serve the interests of the older social institutions. Early in the decade which concerns us, Mirra Komarovsky (41) described the prevalence of this type of organization and the role that it played in the social class system. More recently, John E. Tsouderos (86, 87) made a study of the formalization process in the social structures of 91 voluntary associations (a random sample of 535 organizations) in Minneapolis in 1951. This is a morphological study concerned with the forms and patterns of structure rather than with the subtler psychological correlates. He began with my hypothesis about formalization and bureaucracy (16), which runs as follows:

Bureaucratic tendencies, usually identified with political institutions only, are also present in all other social institutions, whether business corporations, industry, churches, universities, or school systems. Beginnings of the formalization process may be seen in the history of voluntary organizations of American culture.

A group of citizens meets informally to consider some problem or need. After a few conferences, a chairman is selected. As the problem under discussion is broken down into its elements, various committees are appointed: executive, ways and means, publicity, program, survey, etc. Soon the business of calling conferences and notifying interested persons becomes too arduous for volunteer private citizens and the half-time service of an executive secretary is provided. He soon finds it necessary to have a clerk-stenographer. She needs a typewriter, chair, desk, and filing cabinets. Supplies of stationery and postage, a telephone, and other items of equipment are acquired. As the work of the new organization, branch, section (or whatever the name of the new unit may be) grows in volume, it is systematized by establishing membership requirements and dues. A constitution and by-laws are adopted at some stage of its development. The organization may be incorporated if it is an independent entity and not a department of some larger whole. A full line of officers may be chosen: Chairman of the Board, President, Vice-Presidents, Secretary, Treasurer, etc. As the funds accumulate and a bank account is established, the Treasurer is bonded and an annual audit is required.

Meanwhile the organization finds more office space necessary. A full-time executive secretary is engaged. Additional clerks are needed. Office equipment is increased by additional typewriters, chairs, desks, filing cabinets, and other equipment. Then an office manager is chosen.

As time passes, and the full-time staff grows in size, vested interests in "the job" appear. Some staff persons become more concerned with the perpetuation of their job, and guarding their "rights," than in the function and purpose of the organization. Rules and policies are worked out to cover sick-leave allowances, vacation time, termination pay, and pensions. Along with the expansion of staff hierarchy there goes an expansion of committees of all sorts, so that the dignity and status of office takes on added prestige and social position is sought for by interested persons. As the length of line organization increases, the problems of communication between different status levels become more acute. All these tendencies are signs that point to the formalization of the organization, which was originally quite innocent of bureaucratic trends and characteristics. My hypothesis enlarges the concept of bureaucracy to the process of formalization of any social structure, and hence differs from the treatment of bureaucracy of Von Mises (60), who seems to narrow the concept down to political institutions, and from Max Weber (90), who identifies the phenomenon with "rationalization" of administrative tasks.

Tsouderos' study supplies supporting evidence for the hypothesis on formalization and bureaucracy as stated above. His analysis was done on four structural subtypes; membership-role-group, executive-role-group, representative-role-group, and staff-role-group. A more intensive case history study (19) was made of ten of these associations with a long enough life span to illustrate cycles of growth in social structure, tending to confirm in more detail the results of his larger study.

### Evidence from technical aid programs

The literature on technical assistance programs contains some suggestive material in terms of fact and principle that is relevant to the problem of institutional change. Spicer (78) gives excellent factual illustrations of incidents. When the technology of Western culture is introduced by so-called technical aid programs into areas that are industrially underdeveloped, the impact of power machinery upon the other institutions of the area may be detrimental. Joint family patterns that have existed for centuries are weakened and new and often terrifying problems arise. As Linton (48) says, "They must develop new mechanisms to provide for the economic and psychological needs now taken care of by family organizations." Hoselitz (37) warns of the danger of increase in mental ill health, crime, conflict, and racial discrimination that may accompany industrialization and urbanization in such cases. In this atomic age the need of hasty transformation of local institutions may seem imperative.

Frankel (28) warns that pride in our way of life should not blind us to the social heritage of other and less industrially developed cultures, which may contain devices for solving the problems of their own time and place. Hence it is important to allow time for slower changes to be made. In a UNESCO volume edited by Margaret Mead (57) it is pointed out that in technical aid programs to change local cultures ". . . the very fact of planning itself makes it possible to force through a single line change in disregard of the hundreds of side effects which are taken care of in unplanned change." Leighton (46) stated the principle that no matter how good a plan is, if the people for whom it is made do not feel that it belongs to them, the plan will not work successfully. On the other hand, if the changes are introduced very slowly and the related problems can be discussed and slowly thrashed out, the disruption of old ways of life will be less serious. Then the old and habitual ways of the local institutions may successfully deal with small changes in the slow and traditional methods so that the side effects can be felt and responded to by members of that society. However beneficent the intent, sudden introduction of changes by external agencies such as that designed to give technical assistance, prevent the effective operation of local protective behaviors, and the changes may go much too far in some direction before the compensating measures come into action (57).

Those who have been brought up in an almost blind faith in modern science do not easily realize that peoples of industrially underdeveloped areas have a sense of security in their very insecurity. Insecurity is a condition they know, have lived with, and to which their practices and ideas have been adjusted (57). Alinsky (2) makes the point, "The program can and must come only from the people themselves." In this process of Westernization, the political leadership of Turkey seems to have grasped and applied this principle more effectively than neighboring areas. Hayes (35) stresses, therefore, the need of modification in technical aid programs of development to allow for the influence of local institutions.

It should be evident from this introductory discussion that: (a) voluntary associations develop (sometimes spontaneously, sometimes planned) to satisfy some need; and (b) voluntary organizations having once started on their life career, grow and gain momentum toward formalization of structure. As growth in size of membership proceeds, structure subdivides into subgroups of smaller size and with different functions. Although relatively large in membership, the voluntary association may become a veritable congeries of small constituent groups with mutually supporting or competitive relationships, within the larger system of the over-all group. Attitudes of members then become conditioned to the norms of the groups (often embodied in codes) that stipulate the expected behaviors, to the symbols of the authority and the function of the organization, and to its physical property. An increasing emphasis upon conformity and status develops, and the voluntary organization begins to have traditions. In short, the process of growth and formalization has run its course and the original "voluntary" organization has become a full-fledged institution.

### SMALL GROUPS

If one checks back over the preceding statement it will be noted that certain terms were used in the attempt to describe the process of institutionalization as it began in voluntary association and developed until a social institution emerged. Among the terms and concepts used were: needs, social structure, social function, small groups, attitudes, norms and codes, symbols of authority, conformity, status, etc.

Are these concepts susceptible of objectification? Or are they merely the familiar sounds in the patois of sociologists? Right here we find help from reports of studies in group dynamics and in small group research. Although the conceptual terminology we wish to clarify may have been somewhat changed to sharpen it, or to adapt it to the expediencies of research design, there is sufficient equivalence or similarity in meanings to make a brief survey of the literature of small group research distinctly worthwhile.

The methodologies of small group research range from participant observation of existing social groups, each of which had its own developmental history prior to the date that scientific study of it began, to experimental studies of artificially assembled groups of short duration in a laboratory situation. Whether the work was done by an investigator primarily identified with the field of psychology, or with the subject of sociology, is immaterial to our purpose in this chapter, since in either case it is the phenomena of social psychology with which we are dealing.

It so happens that many results of research reveal the central importance of *need satisfaction* provided by group life. While the relationship of basic social institutions to human need fulfillment in terms of food and clothing (the economic institutions), to shelter and sanctuary (the family and church), etc., has long been recognized, the human organism of today has more than mere creature wants to satisfy. Personality needs of a psychosocial kind are both aroused by and satisfied in small groups, and small groups tend to elaborate in form, grow in size, and become social institutions. What are these subtler psychological needs of personality?

The foregoing description may suffice for an account of some of the macro-processes; we now turn to an account of the micro-processes described in small group research.

### Need satisfaction

What are these needs? Paraphrasing W. I. Thomas' theory of four wishes, we suggest that there are at least four needs: for security; for recognition; for response, the "need to feel needed" by someone; and for new experience.

The need for security is for a stable position, one with a status that persists and supports the individual's morale and his self-confidence. Jenkins (40) found that cliques in the military situation tended to compensate for low morale in the larger organized military group. Zimmerman (93) found that in families, friendship groups tended to be substituted for the security values that used to exist in the older kinship groups. French (29) reports that the position of a person in the friendship structure of the group depended primarily on his ability to satisfy the personal needs of other members.

The second need is for recognition of self as a person, with special abilities or talents or qualities, and of the prestige of one's position (as superior to some others in the group). Ackerman (1) found that the extent to which a role is successfully handled is a function of the degree of overlap between role expectations and the actor's own personality needs. Getzels and Guba (30) found that the intensity of involvement in role conflict varied with certain individual and attitudinal characteristics, which he expects a particular social group to satisfy, whether it be a large and formal group, an informal group, or a mere pair-group; and that the role the actor will usually choose is that role which permits the expression of his specific personality needs. Marquis (53) reports that satisfaction and productivity decrease with self-centered behavior. Thus the extreme form of need for recognition (Hitler) is subject to distortions of ego-manias and self-centered paranoid delusions of grandeur.

The third need is for response of intimates, for close and warm affection, and understanding, the "need to feel needed," and for the reciprocities found in sociability; and these play an important part in group life. E. Gross (32) found that cliques tend to compensate for a feeling of low morale and lack of intimacy in the larger and more impersonal organization of the Air Force. Jenkins (40) reports more numerous friendship choices in small cliques in those Squadrons where morale was

low. Argyris (4) found in a business organization that employees in
a highly mechanized department satisfied their needs for personal contacts by making close friends in the department. Marquis reports that
the position in the friendship structure of a group, in contrast to position
in the hierarchical structure, depended upon ability to satisfy the needs
of others, that satisfaction in the group decreases with incidence of self-
centered or self-oriented behavior on the part of participants, and that
residual disagreements are high when a good deal of self-oriented need
behavior is exhibited. Monachesi *et al.* (61) report that no-task groups,
those which satisfy the need for sociability among university students,
tended to be composed of individuals with higher Minnesota Multiphasic
Personality Inventory (deviate) scores than the average. Winch (91,
92) presents statistical evidence in support of the theory of complementary needs in mate selection, wherein each individual seeks within his
or her field of eligibles that person who gives greatest promise of providing maximum need gratification.

The need for new experience in meeting persons and in seeing new
scenes is often a response to mechanized monotony and the need of a
search for new goals and vistas. All these results suggest that behavior
in groups is better understood if one can discover the needs of the
individuals.

Small group research is beginning to throw some light upon hitherto
obscure processes that go on within voluntary groups to make them
cohesive or to create tensions and conflict; to over-formalize their structures or to provide the flexibility requisite to successful problem-solving;
how divisive clique-formation occurs or hierarchical arrangements of
status and position develop; formal authoritarianism or latent power
structures, etc.

Since the researches we are about to cite were done on groups within
different institutional situations, it may be helpful to indicate in each
particular case the basic social institution involved, i.e., business, education, family, military, religious, etc.

When an individual joins a group which attracts him, he carries with
him certain expectations of the roles of others whom he knew before,
or the roles he looks forward to finding, or fears to find, in the newly
entered group. He brings to the social group compulsions for particular
and personal need fulfillments. He may carry with him the marks of
position and status attained in other groups. His morale may be high
or low. He may or may not have potentialities for leadership roles in
the new group situation, traits which grew out of past experience or
personality integrations in prior group affiliations.

That which the new member brings to the group by way of wishes or desires for personality need satisfactions, we have just considered. Let us now turn to the factor of role expectations. The sociological concept of role is at once an observable form of human behavior in the group situation, whether it be a small group (informal or organized), or a larger organized group. In both situations the role has a dynamic or action function, and contributes as well to the structural aspects of the group system.

## ROLE EXPECTATIONS AND INCOMPATIBILITIES

Linton (49) makes a distinction between two broad types of status and role: (a) that *ascribed* to him by the group in terms of age, sex, caste or class categories, which are determined at birth and which are beyond his control; and (b) that *achieved* by him, based on his own choices or efforts, such as various occupational roles, the military hero, the devout priest, etc. Thus the reciprocal influences of social position, social status and role, appear as a web of social relationships, sometimes one, sometimes another, having priority in time, or as Linton states it, "A role represents the dynamic aspect of status." In another study, Linton (47) notes that at least seven factors appear basic to all systems of age-sex classification: infancy, to boy, to adult, to old man; or to girl, to adult woman, to old woman. While prestige attaches to older age classes, there may be temporary phases in which there is regression to infant or adolescent behavior.

Parsons (67) gives an interpretation of such roles as "bad boy," "glamour girl," "housewife," etc., and offers a rationale (68) for integrating roles into a larger theoretical action-system. Kamarovsky (41) calls attention to the principle that reciprocal actions which are dictated by roles may be at variance with those demanded by the actual social situation. Family role prescriptions may demand a "feminine" daughter, whereas in another situation the same girl should be regarded as a "career girl." Thus the "career girl" versus the "homemaker" is a serious contradiction that may exist between role expectations for the college woman. Girls who are first successful as the "athletic type" are presently faced with the fact that this role is incompatible with expectations of a "feminine" role, with consequent anxiety feelings.

In another setting, the young father finds a conflict between his paternal role of seeking better schools, playgrounds, etc., and his economic role of a citizen who wishes to keep taxes down. Practical problems of behavior thus grow out of group norms in terms of incompatibilities between role prescriptions and role expectations. A comment of Stouffer and Toby (83) is worth consideration: "Study suggests that it is possible

to classify people according to a predisposition to select one or the other
horn of a dilemma in role conflicts."

Seeman (73) has studied role incompatibility of leaders and finds
evidence of a "built-in" role conflict situation with high vulnerability of
leadership positions among school superintendents because of mutually
contradictory demands (role expectations) upon a leader. Ambivalence
becomes the subjective aspect of this conflict. In the status dimension,
the conflict is between a success ideology and an equality ideology. In
social action, the choice is between the obligations of friendship and
one's obligations to the larger society. Then too, there is conflict in the
means-ends dimension between ethics and expediency. Getzels and
Guba (30), in a study of role conflict in two Air Force schools, found
that: situationally, the extent of role conflict varies as a function of incompatibility of role expectations; the intensity of involvement in role
conflict varies with certain individual and attitudinal traits; and a systematic relationship seemed to exist between intensity of involvement in
role conflict and effectiveness in a role. The student officer was faced
with a choice between: (a) the role of a teacher, or (b) the role of a
military officer. Usually the actor (role player) will choose the role
which permits the expression of specific personality needs. When in
a relatively permissive situation he can ignore or neglect the legitimate
role expectations of others. On the other hand, in a more or less rigidly
structural military situation, if he chooses to be a teacher-officer rather
than a military-officer, he is likely to clash with the role expectations of
others, and get himself into a conflict situation. Ackerman (1) stated
the principle, "The extent to which a role is successfully handled is a
function of the degree of over-lap between role expectations and the
actor's own needs." Turning to the military-officer role itself, Davis
(22) found very slight evidence for any association between: (a) the
adjustment of followers, and (b) agreement of officers and followers on
the attributes of the formal officer role, i.e., how the leader *should* act.
Adjustment was measured in four dimensions: job satisfaction, personal
commitment to Air Force goals, military management problems, and Air
Force delinquencies. Military office roles studied were: commanding
officer, generalized officer role, and the non-commissioned officer-in-
charge. Families of men in the Strategic Air Command were much more
often subject to the strain of separation (25). Here the personal desires
of the men and their families were subordinated to military routine requirements. Husbands tended to carry over into the family group an
authoritarian pattern of interpersonal relations from military life. Ma-
triarchal family control often appeared, and premarital background affected the adjustment in families. Wives often feared philandering and

also frequency of transfer which made for uncertainty in family planning. Burchard (10) found that among Army chaplains the incompatibility between expectations of a religious role and the military officer role tended to be resolved in favor of the latter.

Turner (88), in a study of civilian situations, found that there were three ways in which a primary group tended to cope with a member who violated a major norm of the group (in this case, stealing): (a) the norm must be under the governance of the group; (b) the particular "other role" must take precedence in attention; and (c) role prescriptions must not be so internalized by prior experience as to obscure the present situation. The relationships that tended to prevail, in the absence of complications, were those of harmony.

Brown (9), in a well-designed and executed experimental study of adolescents, found: (a) that females perceived most easily the assumption of a female role by a female in a male oriented situation (which contained objects and values customarily associated with male status); and (b) males perceived most easily the assumption of a male role in a female oriented situation (which contained objects and values customarily associated with female status). My explanation of these findings is simply that males get highly conditioned to playing a male role before a female audience; and that females get highly conditioned to playing a female role before a male audience. Thus in role perceptions, male roles are most perfectly defined for the observer in female oriented situations, and vice versa.

Stouffer (5, 82), in a study of role conflict situations, finds evidence for two types of variability in role expectations: "(a) When members of a group agree on the terminal points of a *range* of permissive behavior, but also perceive the range to be large, and (b) when there is lack of consensus among the members as to the terminal points of the range of permissive behavior, even if each perceives a narrow range." Stouffer and Toby (83) state that individuals can be arranged along a scale according to their predisposition to choose personal favoritism as a solution in a variety of role conflict situations which involve legal or contractual obligations. They suggest that if this evidence is widely confirmed, this approach may provide a link between the study of *role* in sociology and of the *trait* in social psychology. Newcomb (63) studied four groups of conservative and four groups of nonconservative students, and within each distinguished between those who were *aware* of their divergence from the prevalent attitude norms of the community, and those who were not aware of their divergences. He concludes, "It is the community role which mediates between social attitudes and total personality organization. . . ."

NORMS, STANDARDS, AND VALUES

Says Newcomb (62), "The degree to which a person's membership group serves also as a reference group, depends upon the degree to which his membership in it brings him satisfaction or dissatisfaction. . . ." Sherif (76) says, "The place and functional meaning of the individual's social attitudes, belongingness (identification), and status aspirations and strivings become more real if they are related to groups from which they are derived. In other words, the individual's standards, attitudes, and status stem from and are related to certain groups. We . . . refer to these groups as the individual's reference groups. . . ."

Merton and Lazarsfeld (59) say, "In general then, reference group theory aims to systematize the determinants and consequences of those processes of evaluation and self-appraisal in which the individual takes the values or standards of other individuals and groups as a comparative frame of reference." Thus attitudes and judgments of men in the Army during World War II (82) were influenced by comparisons with the situations of others: (a) with whom they were in some form of association—married civilian friends, acquaintances, etc., (b) those of the same status—captains with captains, etc., and (c) those of different status or different categories—combat soldiers versus noncombat soldiers. As new group members (replacements, new recruits) are motivated to affiliate they tend to assimilate sentiments and conform with the values of the authoritative and prestigeful stratum of the group.

Gould *et al.* (31) found that morale problems in an Air Base centered on the work situation: that satisfactions with off-duty activities were associated with higher morale, and that dissatisfactions with off-duty activities were associated with low morale and less work efficiency. Men unable to satisfy major recreational and culture interests, such as participation in approved activities of church, school, library, dancing, picnics, etc., showed less work efficiency and lower morale, and engaged in such activities as gambling, going to bars, etc. Wagner (89) found that there were four types of latent functions involved in conflicts between *individual* goals and *system* goals: (a) individuals were subject to tension, role and value conflicts, and reduced morale; (b) groups (Air Force crews) suffered from the effects of inter-crew antagonisms, apathy, and reduced morale; (c) the social system (of the flying Squadron) underwent changes in organization and in power structure, in communications distortions, with decreasing integration; and (d) culture patterns changed and norms were violated.

In civilian groups, Toby (85) found among students in a suburban high school a tendency to overvalue the academic prowess of coreligionists: "The more ethnocentric the chooser, the more likely he will pass over the better student from the religious out-group in order to choose one from his religious in-group." In the civilian community there are multiple membership groups and multiple reference groups. Eisenstadt (24) attempts to bring some order among the facts of such a situation by distinguishing between individuals with a single constellation of undifferentiated reference groups and persons with numerous and differentiated reference group relationships. A single group referent tended to be correlated with: (a) negative identification with the social system, and (b) with deviant tendencies from conformity; while the multiple group referent was connected with positive identification with the larger social system. There tended to be a strong correspondence between the type of individual's status image and his choice of reference groups. Those with a ritual status image (limited, narrow, intense), tended to choose reference groups in such a way as to maximize over-all disintegrative tendencies (deviations from conformity); but those with an open status image (differentiated) tended to choose reference groups so as to spread the risks between different types of dissatisfaction and disintegrative behavior and to maximize possibilities of adjustment within the social system. March (52) found in a study of the League of Women Voters that the more active members tended to exhibit a higher degree of conformity to group norms than did less active members.

## COHESIVENESS AND STABILITY OF INSTITUTIONAL SUBGROUPS

An important characteristic of all groups is *cohesiveness* (as psychologists call it), or *solidarity* (as sociologists call it). Although there are contradictory findings from research on this characteristic, there seems to be some agreement on defining group cohesiveness as the *attractiveness* of a group for its members, sometimes called *valence*.

N. Gross and Martin (33) conclude that attractiveness may mean different things to different members, and hence there is need to recognize such a factor as strength of relational *bonds* among group members as a basis of cohesiveness. Moreover, this added factor is related to the resistance of a group to disruptive forces, which tend to make the group fall apart.

In the business situation, Argyris (4) compared two departments of the same organization: (a) in which workers were isolated, had considerable self-responsibility, were passive, and yet in contact with customers; here employees hardly ever mentioned the *need* to belong to an informal group in the department, and 90 per cent had *no* close friends in the department; and (b) where the work was highly mechanized and organization demands were antagonistic to individual personality requirements—here there *was* a need for group belongingness and informal activities were created to make up for deficiencies in formal relationships; here 85 per cent had made close friends with some fellow employee.

Martin *et al.* (55), using an index of mutuality (number of individual relationships existing within a group) and an index of cohesiveness (extent to which the group members satisfied needs for relationships by choosing other individuals within the group), found little or no association between mutuality and cohesiveness. This result appears to confirm Darley *et al.* (21), who conclude that mutuality and cohesiveness show a high degree of instability of relationship in test-retest situations among 138 college girls in a cooperative housing project. Satisfaction with the total cooperative village experience is probably influenced by some core of membership experience from previous groups, low turnover of group membership, groups which start with reciprocated choices in certain interpersonal relations, but which develop over time higher ratios of in-group to out-group choices in interpersonal relationships of a friendship type. With respect to leadership, N. Gross *et al.* (34) conclude, from another study of the same subjects, that: "The cohesiveness explanation of differential functioning of strong and weak leadership groups must be viewed as inconclusive in view of the contradictory evidence."

Marquis *et al.* (53) report no significant correlation between: (a) satisfaction of group members with its meetings; (b) group productivity; and (c) the amount of residual disagreement after the meeting. On the other hand, the member's satisfaction with the group meeting: (a) *increases* with group cohesion and the amount of procedural structuring; and (b) *decreases* with the incidence of self-oriented behavior on the part of participants. Satisfaction seems to have no relationship to the spread of participation among group members. Group productivity: (a) *increases* with the urgency of the problem, and the power of the group to deal with it; and (b) *decreases* with the incidence of self-oriented need behavior. The productive groups are more orderly in problem-solving behavior and have a more adequate communication process than the less productive groups. Residual disagreements are *high* when there is disagreement on goals, a good deal of self-oriented need behavior, and feelings of inadequacy of power to deal with the problem; they are *low* when members communicate more adequately and are more sensitive to group processes. French (29) studied group productivity and found: (a) the amount of member participation varied inversely with the quantity of the leader's behavior; and (b) there was greater participation for educational activity than for procedural action; (c) an official role (leader, observer, trainee) affects behavior, initiated and received; (d) members of the group were more aware of prestige structure than of friendship structure; (e) position in the prestige structure was determined by the person's contribution to movement toward a goal and his official role in the group. By contrast, the position of a person in a friendship structure depended primarily on his ability to satisfy the personal needs of other members. In general, the personal determinants of productivity of group members were not as influential as (d) and (e) above. In the cooperative group situation, where rewards were equal for all members in solving problems, there was evidence of more coordination of effort, attentiveness to fellow members, mutual understanding, willingness to accept and to agree, orientation to the goal and orderliness of procedure, productivity, better quality of product, quality and friendliness in discussion, favorable evaluation of the group products, and sense of obligation to others to win their respect. The level of production after a change was a function of the degree of participation. Discussion following role playing showed that greater involvement leads to more frequent and more intensive participation in subsequent group discussion. The amount of participation by group members is closely related to their position in the socioeconomic structure of the group.

Informal communication in small groups was studied by Festinger (26) who found: (a) stronger attraction to the group makes for greater pressure toward uniformity in terms of the amount of influence attempted; (b) members of highly cohesive groups tended to report more readiness to change opinion in response to pressures exerted by partner's influence; (c) highly cohesive pairs showed more change which could be attributed to the influence of partners than did low cohesive groups; (d) the volume of communication was higher toward a group member at the extreme of the existing range of opinion in the group; (e) the higher the pressure toward uniformity, the greater the proportion of communications addressed to members of extreme opinions; (f) the greater the pressure the more influence is accomplished; and (g) highly cohesive groups rejected a deviate more than did less cohesive groups. Frequency of communication to the deviate increased among group members who *do not* reject the deviate. For those who *do* reject the deviate, communication increased to a maximum and then dropped off. In another study, Festinger *et al.* (27) found: "There is less attempt to influence others when experts are present or when a correct answer is promised. In the latter condition there is also slightly less tendency to redefine the boundaries of the group to exclude those with divergent opinions. One might summarize as follows: where there are pressures to agree with the correct answer or with an expert, changes in opinion are observed but the other two manifestations of an influence process, namely, influencing others and redefining boundaries of the group, tend to be absent"; and again, ". . . the relative strength of the tendency to redefine the boundaries of the group in response to pressures toward uniformity increases for a member as the discrepancy between his opinions and the modal opinion in the group increases."

Martin *et al.* (56), using sociometric criteria of choices on leaders, followers, and isolates, report:

> Leaders were found to be superior to both isolates and followers with respect to the degree to which they identified with the standards of the middle class (the class with which practically all individuals in the village identified), the frequency with which the families of the respective girls participated as a whole in certain kinds of activities prior to entrance into college, and self-estimates of proficiency in motor skills. It was concluded that a group was more likely to recognize as a leader the individual who conformed most closely to the standards of the group, who had the most experience in the intimate group life of the family, and who regarded herself as proficient in motor skills, presumably by reason of extensive experience and training in that area.

Significant differences were found to show ". . . that an informal leader to be recognized also as a formal leader must have the self-confidence that comes from seeing oneself as emotionally mature, relative to others." They conclude, "The paucity of differences found tends to negate the trait approach to leadership and suggests the utilization of other frames of reference in the study of leadership phenomena." This conclusion is consistent with Bales (44) as cited above.

## PROBLEM-SOLVING AND INSTITUTIONAL ADAPTATION

In the foregoing results, reference was made frequently to the problem-solving process within the group system. Bales (44) has given considerable attention to this process, and suggests that there are three phases: (a) *orientation*, "What *is* it?" which soon passes over to (b) *evaluation*, "How do you *feel* about it?" which passes over to (c) *control*, "What shall we *do* about it?" He finds that departures from this order tend to produce frustration and the process tends to backtrack until the prior problem has been solved. In this context it may be helpful to recall Carr's (11) three-phase definition of the situation that confronts the individual: (a) gestalt awareness, (b) definition of the situation, and (c) assumption of a role. There may also be noted, as relevant to these two formulations of the problem-solving process, my own hypothesis (15, pages 224–237) of the *societal reaction pattern,* based on evidence from legislation and advanced in 1928. When a community faces a serious problem, it tends to react in a three-phase cycle: (a) first it tries to enforce the existing mores; when this reaction fails, it resorts to (b) experimentation, or trial and error, with all sorts of new legislative expedients, until a somewhat chaotic stage of mixed successful and unsuccessful attempts makes it necessary for the community (c) to consolidate its gains from the trial and error efforts and *integrate* the successful experiments into a new pattern or system of codified laws. Since this hypothesis (14) was advanced more than twenty-five years ago, considerable evidence has been collected to support it. It is evident that the congruence from independent origins of these three-phase accounts of problem-solving at different levels is merely a sociological statement of the learning process applied by Bales to small groups, by Carr to social-problem situations, and by Chapin to the larger society, in which collective effort is expressed in statutory law.

Robson (71) in a controlled laboratory experiment attempted to describe the relationship between *valence* (defined as the attractiveness of the group *goal*) and *morale* (defined in terms of productivity, or the number of units of work produced by each member of the group); *persistence,* or willingness to work for the group goal; and *cohesiveness,* or the attractiveness of the *group* for its members. He also used as an intervening variable the factor, "subjective estimate," or the member's estimate of the group's ability to achieve its goal. His conclusions with respect to productivity, persistence, and cohesiveness, as defined by him, were: (a) *productivity* of both high valent and low valent groups increased with running reports of their success at the task, except for groups receiving reports of success followed by failure; (b) *persistence* was greater on reports of failure irrespective of valence, except for the high valent groups which received reports of success followed by failure—these showed reduced persistence—but in general, the high valent groups were more persistent than the low valent groups in this situation; and (c) *cohesiveness* in high valent groups was greater after reports of success than after reports of failure; in low valent groups no difference in cohesiveness was found whether the reports were of success or of failure.

Monachesi, Chapin *et al.* (61), in another experiment on task achievement, group cohesion, and personal satisfaction among university student groups, divided them into: task groups, those engaged in action to achieve goals *outside* the members themselves, and no-task groups with no external goals, but having some "need" of group members for sociability, recreation, etc. Personality profiles of all individuals were obtained from the Minnesota Multiphasic Personality Inventory (MMPI). The results were: (a) task groups and no-task groups showed no significant difference on mean MMPI scores; (b) when, however, effective task groups were compared with ineffective no-task groups, the former had normal MMPI mean score, while the latter tended to have higher scores than average (abnormal); (c) for task groups, the measured sense of personal satisfaction in the group situation correlated $r = +.82$ with estimated effectiveness of group action, whereas for no-task groups the correlation was $r = +.477$. Cohesiveness correlated with mean estimated effectiveness, $r = -.544$ for task groups, and $r = -.079$ for no-task groups. Effectiveness correlated with a measure of group formalization, $r = -.722$ for task groups, and $r = -.192$ for no-task groups. The multiple correlation predicting personal satisfaction from social participation and expansiveness (total within-group choices divided by the number of individuals in the group), was $R = .739$, for task groups.

Bales (44) found that "Different phases of the problem-solving process lead to role differentiation among the participants, both as to the functions they perform and as to their gross amount of participation. Both types of differentiation may threaten the existing order of status among members. Tension tends to rise, especially as the problem passes to the final stage of 'control.' Once a successful solution is reached, however, the group tends to release tension, often by joking and laughter, thus repairing the damage to its social integration in the decision process." Bales's result is not unlike my hypothesis noted above when applied to leadership as differential within the three-phase cycle of the *societal reaction pattern:* Phase I—enforcement of the mores, tends to have titular leaders of a bureaucracy, bound by red tape and precedent; Phase II—experimentation, tends to have leaders who are innovators, experimental executives, and organizing promoters, who may try to do too much themselves; and Phase III—consolidation and integration, is that wherein leaders are great administrators who consolidate gains from the previous phase and organize the "new order" by systematizing social structure and deputizing social functions.

Strodtbeck (44) found, in domestic problem-solving situations, "... that husband or wife whose role is most strongly supported by kinship or economic considerations in the culture will tend to dominate in the discussion."

## STATUS AND STRUCTURAL HIERARCHIES

The manifest structure of larger groups often exhibits a hierarchical arrangement of member's positions or statuses in the group system (the more formal type of structure), and sometimes the existence of a *power structure* (usually latent and more informal). Such factors as authority, leadership, prestige, stereotypes, etc., are also involved. These factors are most easily studied in the relatively large and older institutions, such as military organizations, universities, churches and religious orders, departments of government of long standing, etc.

Shils (77), commenting upon Stouffer's studies of the primary group in the Army, calls attention to the great importance of primary group loyalty for military morale, hence for efficiency in combat; and to the relative unimportance of direct identification with total symbols (total Army, State, political cause, etc.) as compared with feelings of strength and security in primary group comradeship. *The inner cohesion of the military machine is a function of commands that run along a system of overlapping primary groups, rather than of commands that come down from upper levels of the formal hierarchy.* The individual soldier feels the need to protect his primary group of "buddies."

Mack (50) finds support for Parsons' principle that a prestige position throughout a social system is affected by the prestige of the particular part of the system to which the position is attached. He found that Air Force Squadrons ranked (best or worst) according to prestige tended to cluster in groups on the basis of similarity of activity. Personnel in each Squadron tended to rank their own Squadron higher than all other personnel ranked it. This seems to confirm my observation made earlier in this chapter of the "status halo" effect. The conclusion for reference group theory is that men rank their own unit higher than others rank it, and that they tend to identify with the unit having the highest base-wide prestige. Mack also found a relationship between the prestige of a Squadron and the morale of its members. There was a statistically significant relation between morale and personal background factors such as enlisted grade, length of time in the Air Force, membership in the regular Air Force, and intention to re-enlist.

Shartle (75) found that the stereotype of leader behavior in the Navy was of one who: places few demands upon his followers, does not interfere with their freedom, is "one of the boys" himself, and gets things done. The basic conflict of the leader role is between these role expectations, and yet the followers do not want any limitations on themselves. In point of fact, the stereotype of the leader is of the less successful leader. Self-description of leaders is nearer to the subordinates' description of an *ideal* leader than a description of him by his staff. In a hierarchy those superior or subordinate to an intermediate leader are more in agreement than is he with them about his own behavior. Thus administrators tend to perceive themselves quite inaccurately. Leaders who delegate tend to have subordinates who delegate. Hence it is necessary to know the *top* leader to determine the degree of delegation down the "chain of command." Where there are more communications there is less discrepancy between the descriptions of a leader and the ideal stereotype. At a Naval Air Station, Stogdill (80) studied the same leader in one position and then the same leader in different positions. He found the following variables characteristic of *position* rather than the man: level in the organizational structure, time spent with assistants, time spent with superiors, time spent in supervision and coordination and in writing reports. The following variables were characteristic of the *man* rather than of the position: delegation practices, time spent in public relations, evaluation, reading and answering mail, reading technical publications, and time spent with outside persons. Military rank for the same man and the same position correlated .9, even though a two year period elapsed between data collections. For level in the organization the correlation was .8. Both correlations dropped to zero for the same man in different positions. Correlations were raised to .9 and .6 for a different man in the same position. The same position is likely to remain approximately at the same echelon level over a period of time. Mack (50) defined *power* as the ability to determine the behavior of others; then *authority* is that kind of power which goes with position and is legitimized by the *norms* of the position. When power is a right granted by the official organization, we call it authority. *Hierarchy* is then defined as the rank order of positions within each of the elements of a stratification system. Areas of stress occur within and between elements. The Army has a pyramidal system. The Air Force, because of the need of technical skills and knowledge, has a diamond-shaped distribution of rank, when the numbers of individuals at different levels are considered.

### The latent power structure

Thornson (84) states that industrial sociology research shows that the real relationships between members of work groups deviate from the prescribed relationships in regulations and in directives, i.e., the *power* structure deviates from the *authority* structure. After differentiation in an Air Force study between command positions and staff positions, he found that conflicts were built into the system by staff acquisition of power in excess of their nominal authority; staff officers become responsible for activities and command officers responsible for men. The emphasis in the two Wings that were compared was for coordination for immediate production; hence it reinforced the power of specialists, making for deviant behavior which could not be reported. For studies of hierarchical patterns of authority, Stone and Form (81) offer a caution and propose that the notion of status, class, and power arrangements be substituted for the analogous hierarchical conception, and offer several empirical and hypothetical models of status arrangements.

Using data collected by Chapin (17) in 1943 and a follow-up study in 1949 on civilian groups, Olmsted (65) expanded the analysis of the original data of the social participation scores (18) and was able to trace the patterns of participation of 43 community leaders of 1943, and 64 of 1949, of whom 36 were the same persons on each date. He found support for two hypotheses: (a) the social participation scores provided an objective basis for inferences regarding patterns of leadership in voluntary organizations, and (b) "these voluntary-organization leadership patterns constitute an integral part of the power structure or influence system of the social organization of the community studied."

The process of growth and formalization of voluntary organizations in American communities was stated by Chapin (16) as an hypothesis and Tsouderos collected detailed information about scores of such groups to test the hypothesis.

The definitive study of *power structures* in a large city was done by Hunter (38), who defined power as the capacity, influence, or force which commands the movement of goods or services. Hunter is now completing a study of power structures in the national area (39). These references are cited for the use of those leaders who wish to follow the development of the power structure concept beyond its application to small groups.

## THE INFLUENCE OF GROUP SIZE ON FUNCTION

The influence of mere *size* of group has been studied as a separate phenomenon. Bales (44) found that centralizing tendencies increased in a systematic manner as the size of groups increased. A larger proportion of activity is addressed to the top man as size increases and a smaller proportion of activity to other members. The top man tends to address more of his remarks to the group as a whole and to increase his proportionate share of talking. But there seems to be a ceiling for him of around 50 per cent in problem-solving groups. Such a ceiling represents an inherent tendency for the interaction to come to a system-closure. Bales's finding raises the question, "At what size does a group cease to have some intimacy of interaction and tend to react as an *audience?*" While there is at present no completely satisfactory answer to this question, most leaders experienced in committee work and the procedures of conferences contend that a small group (of less than 8 persons) is most likely to achieve results. Although not using sociological concepts, Old (64) studied this problem of group size in relation to boards, committees, and panels in research for the Navy. He obtained results consistent with those previously cited, and his data indicate: (a) the smaller the size of the group (on a scale of 2 to 12), the greater the amount of work done (the drop in effectiveness was sharp at 6 persons and over); (b) technical knowledge of the subject of discussion varied inversely with formal military rank; (c) effectiveness varied directly with the type of chairman—the most effective being one who knows his subject, has a well-prepared agenda which was distributed before the meeting, skillfully keeps the discussion to the subject, requires that action be taken on agreements reached, follows up on such actions, provides for periodic needling of the committee by outside experts, skillfully makes efficient use of the method of task assignment to subcommittees, requires written comment on reports circulated to members, insists on a minimum of six committee meetings per year, and employs an efficient secretariat; and (d) that the heckler-saboteur type of committee member wrecks the average meeting by preventing discussion and agreement. Old presents also some suggestive mathematical models of these social phenomena.

Stephan and Mishler (79), in a study of 81 meetings of 36 student groups of size 4 to 12 members each, derive a mathematical model for their finding that there is a decrease in the rate of participation from the group leader to the highest ranking student as small groups increase in size. Although they do not make the point, it would seem that one explanation of this tendency is that as one passes from smaller to larger groups, there is an increasing tendency for the group members to react as an audience, an explanation made of the results cited above. Since there seems to be evidence even from small groups that as the size of group increases there is a tendency for its members to react as an *audience,* it may be useful to cite here some earlier work which is highly relevant to the psychology of an audience. As long ago as 1920, E. D. Martin (54), an effective leader of rich experience, showed how an audience may become, step by step, an unmanageable crowd, with mob potentialities in which behavior becomes an expression of desires from the unconscious, egotism, hate, and absolutisms, all in conformity with some well-known Freudian concepts.

On conference procedure, Chapin (13) found four categories of purpose in small conferences: (a) to reconcile different opinions by and exchange of information in free discussion; (b) to explore a field by free discussion, using the contributions of members or experts; (c) to make a plan of action that can be agreed upon in discussion; and (d) to act upon a recommendation or report prepared in advance. Other findings of this research anticipate and confirm several of Old's findings noted above.

Bossard (7) reports a study of conference procedures consistent with those of Chapin and Old.

Studies of the number of relationships that could occur within small groups probably began with Graicunas' (20) study of the number of new relationships which an executive experienced because of each assistant that was added to his staff. By the beginning of World War II, the British Army became interested in this matter because of the pressure on general officers that came from the complications of high command. Quite independently of Graicunas' earlier work, Bossard (8) explored the same phenomena in the family situation and concluded that the number of relationships increased in a primary group in the order of triangular numbers with the addition of one person to the group. Beaglehole (6) criticized Bossard's statement as an oversimplification which yielded too small a potential increase. Kephart (43) gave more systematic treatment to the whole problem of increase in the number of relationships that are possible as the size of groups is increased by the addition of one person, and offered a series of exponential functions as appropriate mathematical models descriptive of the phenomena. He presents different models for: (a) the number of potential relationships at the individual level; (b) potential relationships at the subgroup level; (c) potential relationships between the individual and subgroups; and (d) total potential relationships which are intra-group in character. To illustrate the point more concretely: in a pair group there could be two one-way relationships and one reciprocal relationship. When another person is added to this dyad, three self-contained pair-group relationships, or nine relationships, could exist, with the third person not interacting. When the third person interacts with the other pair, there would be $3 \times 3$ additional relationships of a dyad-single kind. Thus we could have a total of eighteen potential relationships. If an additional person is then added, making four individuals in the group, the number of potential relationships increases considerably; and so on. It is evident that the number of potential relationships in small groups is also influenced by the number of reference groups with which each member identifies himself. In any event, the great complexity of interaction in even small groups is evident and this increases in volume with the addition of another in some exponential function.

## SOME INSTITUTIONAL IMPLICATIONS OF SMALL GROUP RESEARCH

Because of the multi-role pattern of individuals in Western culture, the social structure of social institutions is often threatened by internal tensions and even conflicts that arise out of role incompatibilities. Although group membership has often been studied in terms of values, some groups may carry special norms of conduct to which individuals refer, and these are called reference groups. They seem to bear a special responsibility to transmit the norms and values of social institutions. The cohesiveness or solidarity of small groups satisfies a need for intimacy in an otherwise impersonal and fragmented industrial society increasingly composed of secondary groups. The process underlying group flexibility appears in the problem-solving behaviors of individuals in groups. Hierarchical systems of position and status from the humble member participants to top leaders develop and are perpetuated. A latent power structure parallels the formal and manifest pattern of officialdom. The mere size of a group is itself a factor in the volume of personal relationships that develop and the quantitative aspect of size should not blind the observer to the underlying differences in kind that evolve and emerge.

## SUMMARY STATEMENT

Despite these numerous aspects of variability, with resulting flexibility in social structure (mistaken by outside observers as an evidence of disintegration), the institutions of Western culture now extend and penetrate the simpler cultures by way of technical assistance programs. Nevertheless, Western institutions themselves suffer from many disabilities.

A keen analysis of institutional vulnerability in the industrialized mass society of Western cultures is made by Selznick (74). He appraises the capacity of our institutions to preserve their central values and purposes. At one time the mass accepted its proper status, but now it arrogates to itself the right to upset the ideals of attainment established by the traditional culture-bearing elites. Mannheim (51) called attention to this situation in 1940. This situation appears due "to the fact that the social processes which previously favored the development of creative elites, now have the opposite effect, i.e., have become obstacles to the forming of elites because wider sections of the population under unfavorable social conditions take an active part in cultural activities." If it is granted that creative elites are needed for the maintenance and the development of culture, then a mass society which does not permit elites to perform their function "results in the sovereignty of the unqualified." The point is not the quality of the individuals, but rather it is their roles. It is not that the mass itself is so much composed of misfits as that "the nature of the system prevents the emergence of effective social leadership." Hence it happens that educational institutions are under pressure to lower their standards of knowledge. "Elites find it difficult to sustain their own standards," and "mass society threatens to transform them into institutions of specialized training." Emphasis centers on technical specialization. "The student no longer feels his relation to a community of scholarship . . . he expects to retain his commonness and to be distinguished from the multitude only by a certain technical competence. . . ." Other highly sensitive institutions like the church are not immune to this danger. Even the preacher becomes defensive about his role in propagating religious values and deserts his distinctive cultural function. "He finds new security in a feeling of oneness with the common man . . . demagogy may become the characteristic product of our times, the leader reflecting the mood of the mass." Selznick (74) summarizes his views in four principles: (a) Mass behavior results in debilitation of creative and culture-sustaining elites; (b) in superficial adherence to stereotyped values; (c) mass behavior is associated with activist interpretations of democracy and with increasing reliance upon force to resolve social conflict; and (d) social institutions are devalued by subversion of their character-defining functions.

The mass demands narrow utilitarian justification for education and science. Since the cultural elites feel insecure in this situation, they capitulate to the demand for commonness and accept the standards of the mass man, which he insists must be applied to all. "The mass thus joins with other forces in industrial society to transform institutions into organizations. They become technical (and expendable) instruments for the achievement of proximate goals" (74, page 331). If this analysis is accepted, even in part, it suggests an impersonal cycle of change in social structures, beginning with informal and voluntarily organized associations, integrating such groups into more formal and institutional structures, followed in our culture by disintegration into their former group organization patterns, accompanied by loss of older social values as the process completes itself. One is reminded of the phrase, "ashes to ashes, dust to dust."

To abstract from speculative theory and scanty factual evidence the characteristics which are common or equivalent to the properties of *all* institutions in order to recognize the generic traits is a difficult task at best. In an earlier attack (14) on this problem, I defined a social institution as:

> First, a social institution arises out of and as a result of repeated groupings of interacting human individuals in response to elemental needs or drives (sex, hunger, fear, etc.).
> Second, common reciprocating attitudes and conventionalized behavior patterns develop out of the process of interaction (affection, loyalty, cooperation, domination, subordination, etc.).
> Third, cultural objects (traits) that embody symbolic values in material substances are invented or fabricated and become the cue stimuli to behavior

conditioned to them (the idol, cross, ring, flag, etc., are charged with emotional and sentimental meaning).

Fourth, cultural objects (traits) that embody utilitarian values in material substances are invented or fabricated and become the means of satisfying creature wants for warmth, shelter, etc. (buildings, furniture, etc.).

Fifth, preserved in oral or written language, externally stored and handed down from one generation to the next, there is description and specification of the patterns of interrelationship among these elemental drives, attitudes, symbolic culture traits, and utilitarian culture traits (codes, charters, constitutions, franchises, etc.).

. . . We may say that the structure of a social institution consists in the combination of certain related type parts into a configuration possessing the properties of relative rigidity and relative persistence of form, and tending to function as a unit on a field of contemporary culture.

Using the last four items—attitudes and behavior patterns, symbols, real property, and the code (norms), I then differentiated nucleated institutions such as specific families, churches, the state, business, etc., which appeared to possess these four type parts of a nucleus, from more general institutions such as art, language, religion, science, etc. The four type parts of the nucleated institution were ones that were susceptible of objective description and even of measurement.

It should be evident that our brief summary of some of the results of small group research has tended to make definitive the attitudinal and behavioral component; the code component as expressed in norms, standards, and values; to some extent the part played by symbolic representation; and the internal tensions and conflicts that exist.

In a systematic analysis of institutions, Landecker (45) has formulated several hypotheses in which the processes of integration and nucleation may be investigated. Although much research still must be done on the common properties of social institutions in a free society, perhaps the foregoing summary of recent relevant studies may point the way. At any rate one research lead seems to emerge, namely, the identification of at least three irreducible concepts which may serve as aids to further research. These are: the *position* of individuals in a social structure; the social *distance* between their positions; and the *direction* of attitudinal pressures within the system (12).

## BIBLIOGRAPHICAL REFERENCES

1. Ackerman, N. W., "Social Role and Total Personality," *Amer. J. Orthopsychiatry*, Vol. 21 (1951), pp. 1–17.

2. Alinsky, S. D., *Reveille for Radicals*, Chicago, Univ. of Chicago Press, 1946, pp. 78–80.

3. *Amer. Soc. Rev.*, Vol. 19 (1954), pp. 651–781.

4. Argyris, C., "Fusion of the Individual with the Organization," *Amer. Soc. Rev.*, Vol. 19 (1954), pp. 267–272.

5. Barnes, H. E., *Social Institutions*, New York, Prentice-Hall, 1946.

6. Beaglehole, E., "A Critique of Measurement of Family Interaction," *Amer. J. Soc.*, Vol. 51 (1945), pp. 145–147.

7. Bossard, J. H. S., "Experiment in Inter-Group Relations," *Social Forces*, Vol. 32 (1954), pp. 217–225.

8. Bossard, J. H. S., *The Sociology of Child Development*, New York, Harper, 1954, p. 146.

9. Brown, J. C., "An Experiment in Role Taking," *Amer. Soc. Rev.*, Vol. 17 (1952), pp. 587–597.

10. Burchard, W. W., "Role Conflicts of Military Chaplains," *Amer. Soc. Rev.*, Vol. 19 (1954), pp. 528–535.

11. Carr, L. J., *Situational Analysis*, New York, Harper, 1948, p. 20.

12. Chapin, F. S., "A Three Dimensional Model for Visual Analysis of Group Structure," *Social Forces*, Vol. 31 (1952), pp. 20–25.

13. Chapin, F. S., "Conference Procedure for Post-War Planning," *Social Forces*, Vol. 24 (1945), pp. 135–146.

14. Chapin, F. S., *Contemporary American Institutions*, New York, Harper, 1935.

15. Chapin, F. S., *Cultural Change*, New York, Appleton-Century-Crofts, 1928.

16. Chapin, F. S., "The Growth of Bureaucracy—An Hypothesis," *Amer. Soc. Rev.*, Vol. 16 (1951), pp. 835–836.

17. Chapin, F. S., *The Impact of the War on Community Leadership and Opinion in Red Wing*, Minneapolis, Univ. of Minnesota Press, 1945.

18. Chapin, F. S., *The Social Participation Scale*, rev. ed., Minneapolis, Univ. of Minnesota Press, 1952.

19. Chapin, F. S., and John E. Tsouderos, "Formalization Observed in Ten Voluntary Associations: Concepts and Morphology," *Social Forces*, Vol. 33 (1955), pp. 306–309.

20. Columbia University, *International Management Institute*, New York, Columbia Univ., 1933, pp. 181–187.

21. Darley, J. G., N. Gross, and W. E. Martin, "Studies in Group Behavior: Stability, Change and Interrelations of Psychometric and Sociometric Variables," *J. Abn. and Soc. Psy.*, Vol. 46 (1951), pp. 565–576.

22. Davis, F. J., "Conceptions of Official Leader Roles in the Air Force," *Social Forces*, Vol. 32 (1954), pp. 253–258.

23. Durkheim, E., *The Division of Labor in Society*, 1st ed. of 1893, trans. by G. Simpson, New York, Macmillan, 1933.

24. Eisenstadt, S. M., "Reference Group Behavior and Social Integration: An Exploratory Study," *Amer. Soc. Rev.*, Vol. 19 (1954), pp. 175–185.

25. "Family Life in the Air Force," *Research Previews*, Univ. of North Carolina, Vol. 1 (1953), pp. 9–11.

26. Festinger, L., "Informal Communications in Small Groups," in H. Guetzkow (ed.), *Groups, Leadership, and Men*, Pittsburgh, Carnegie Press, 1951, pp. 28–43.

27. Festinger, L., H. B. Gerard, B. Hymovitch, H. H. Kelley, and B. Raven, "The Influence Process in the Presence of Extreme Deviates," *Human Rel.*, Vol. 5 (1952), pp. 327–346.

28. Frankel, S. H., *The Economic Impact on Underdeveloped Societies*, Cambridge, Mass., Harvard Univ. Press, 1953, pp. 94–96.

29. French, J. R. P., "Group Productivity," in H. Guetzkow (ed.), *Groups, Leadership, and Men,* Pittsburgh, Carnegie Press, 1951, pp. 44–54. See also *Annual Review of Psychology,* Annual Reviews, 1954, chapters on social psychology of group processes, industrial psychology, etc.

30. Getzels, J. W., and E. G. Guba, "Role, Role Conflict and Effectiveness," *Amer. Soc. Rev.,* Vol. 19 (1954), pp. 165–175.

31. Gould, R. F., L. Killian, R. E. Freeman, and E. A. T. Barth, "Off Duty Activities and the Air Force Mission," *Research Previews,* Univ. of North Carolina, Vol. 2 (1954), pp. 11–15.

32. Gross, E., "Some Functional Consequences of Primary Controls in Formal Work Organizations," *Amer. Soc. Rev.,* Vol. 18 (1953), pp. 368–373.

33. Gross, N., and W. E. Martin, "On Group Cohesiveness," *Amer. J. Soc.,* Vol. 57 (1952), pp. 546–564.

34. Gross, N., W. E. Martin, and J. G. Darley, "Studies of Group Behavior: Leadership Structures in Small Organized Groups," *J. Abn. and Soc. Psy.,* Vol. 48 (1953), pp. 429–432. See also Albert, R. S., "Comments on the Scientific Function of the Concept of Cohesiveness," *Amer. J. Soc.,* Vol. 59 (1953–1954), pp. 231–234.

35. Hayes, S. B., Jr., "Personality and Culture Problems of Point IV," in B. F. Hoselitz (ed.), *The Progress of Underdeveloped Areas,* Chicago, Univ. of Chicago Press, 1952, p. 209.

36. Hertzler, J. O., *Social Institutions,* Lincoln, Neb., Univ. of Nebraska Press, 1946.

37. Hoselitz, B. F., *The Progress of Underdeveloped Areas,* Chicago, Univ. of Chicago Press, 1952, p. vii.

38. Hunter, F., *Community Power Structure,* Chapel Hill, Univ. of North Carolina Press, 1953.

39. Hunter, F., "Pilot Study of National Power and Policy Structures," *Research Previews,* Univ. of North Carolina, Vol. 2 (1954), pp. 4–10.

40. Jenkins, J. G., "Nominating Techniques as a Method of Evaluating Air Group Morale," *J. Aviation Medicine,* Vol. 19 (1948), pp. 12–19.

41. Kamarovsky, M., "Cultural Contradictions and Sex Roles," *Amer. J. Soc.,* Vol. 52 (1956), pp. 184–189.

42. Kamarovsky, M., "The Voluntary Associations of Urban Dwellers," *Amer. Soc. Rev.,* Vol. 11 (1946), pp. 686–698.

43. Kephart, W. M., "A Quantitative Analysis of Intra-Group Relationships," *Amer. J. Soc.,* Vol. 55 (1950), pp. 544–549.

44. Laboratory of Social Relations, *Report for the Five Years 1946–1951,* Cambridge, Mass., Harvard University, Laboratory of Social Relations, 1952.

45. Landecker, W. S., "The Institutions and Social Integration," in *Papers of the Michigan Academy of Science, Arts, and Letters,* Vol. 39 (1954), pp. 477–493.

46. Leighton, A. H., *The Governing of Men,* Princeton, Princeton Univ. Press, 1946.

47. Linton, R., "Age and Sex Categories," *Amer. Soc. Rev.,* Vol. 7 (1942), pp. 598–603.

48. Linton, R., "Cultural and Personality Factors Affecting Economic Growth," in B. F. Hoselitz (ed.), *The Progress of Underdeveloped Areas,* Chicago, Univ. of Chicago Press, 1952, p. 84.

49. Linton, R., *The Study of Man,* New York, Appleton-Century-Crofts, 1936, pp. 114–115.

50. Mack, R. W., "The Prestige System of an Air Base: Squadron Rankings and

Morale," *Amer. Soc. Rev.*, Vol. 19 (1954), pp. 281–287. See also Carter, L., "Some Research on Leadership in Small Groups," in H. Guetzkow (ed.), *Groups, Leadership, and Men*, Pittsburgh, Carnegie Press, 1951, pp. 146–157.

51. Mannheim, K., *Man and Society in an Age of Reconstruction*, London, Kegan Paul, 1940, p. 85.

52. March, J. G., "Group Norms and the Active Minority," *Amer. Soc. Rev.*, Vol. 19 (1954), pp. 733–741.

53. Marquis, D. G., H. Guetzkow, and R. W. Hays, "A Social Psychological Study of the Decision-Making Conference," in H. Guetzkow (ed.), *Groups, Leadership, and Men*, Pittsburgh, Carnegie Press, 1951, pp. 55–67.

54. Martin, E. D., *The Behavior of Crowds*, New York, Harper, 1920.

55. Martin, W. E., J. G. Darley, and N. Gross, "Studies in Group Behavior: Methodological Problems in the Study of Interrelationships of Group Members," *Educ. and Psy. Measurement*, Vol. 12 (1952), pp. 533–553.

56. Martin, W. E., N. Gross, and J. G. Darley, "Studies of Group Behavior: Leaders, Followers, and Isolates in Small Organized Groups," *J. Abn. and Soc. Psy.*, Vol. 47 (1952), pp. 838–842.

57. Mead, Margaret (ed.), *Cultural Patterns and Technical Change*, Paris, UNESCO, 1953, pp. 315–316. See also Mead, Margaret, "Common Ground in Community Development Experiments," *Community Development Bulletin*, Univ. of London, 2:3:45, June, 1951.

58. Merton, R. K., *Social Theory and Social Structure*, New York, Columbia Univ. Press, 1954.

59. Merton, R., and P. Lazarsfeld, *Continuities in Social Research*, Glencoe, Ill., The Free Press, 1951, pp. 43, 44, 255.

60. Mises, Ludwig Von, *Bureaucracy*, New Haven, Yale Univ. Press, 1944, p. 12.

61. Monachesi, E. D., F. S. Chapin, A. M. Rose, *et al.*, "Group Structure and Function (Task) as Related to Personality Characteristics and Interests of Group Members," Office of Naval Research, Project 101, 1953.

62. Newcomb, T. M., *Social Psychology*, New York, Dryden Press, 1950, pp. 220, 225–232. See also Hartley, E. L., and R. E. Hartley, *Fundamentals of Social Psychology*, New York, Knopf, 1952, pp. 410–424, 466–490, 507–530.

63. Newcomb, T. M., "Community Roles in Attitude Formation," *Amer. Soc. Rev.*, Vol. 7 (1942), pp. 621–630.

64. Old, B. S., "On the Mathematics of Committees, Boards and Panels," *Scientific Monthly* (Aug. 1946), pp. 129–134.

65. Olmsted, D. W., "Organizational Leadership and Social Structure in a Small City," *Amer. Soc. Rev.*, Vol. 19 (1954), pp. 273–281. See also Vaile, R. S., *Red Wing Five Years Later*, Minneapolis, Univ. of Minnesota Press, 1952.

66. Parsons, T., *The Social System*, Glencoe, Ill., The Free Press, 1954.

67. Parsons, T., "Age and Sex Roles in the Social Structure of the United States," *Amer. Soc. Rev.*, Vol. 7 (1942), pp. 604–616.

68. Parsons, T., "Some Comments on the State of the General Theory of Social Action," *Amer. Soc. Rev.*, Vol. 18 (1953), pp. 618–631.

69. Parsons, T., and E. A. Shils (eds.), *Toward a General Theory of Action*, Cambridge, Mass., Harvard Univ. Press, 1951.

70. Read, Margaret, "Common Ground in Community Development Experiments," *Community Development Bulletin*, Univ. of London, Vol. 2 (1951), p. 45.

71. Robson, R. A. H., *An Experimental Study of the Effects of Different Types of Communication on Morale in Small Groups*, Unpublished doctoral dissertation, Univ. of Minnesota, 1951.

72. Rose, A. M., *Theory and Method in the Social Sciences*, Minneapolis, Univ. of Minnesota Press, 1954.

73. Seeman, M., "Role Conflict and Ambivalence in Leadership," *Amer. Soc. Rev.*, Vol. 18 (1953), pp. 373–380.

74. Selznick, P., "Institutional Vulnerability in Mass Society," *Amer. J. Soc.*, Vol. 56 (1951), pp. 320–331.

75. Shartle, C. L., "Studies in Naval Leadership," in H. Guetzkow (ed.), *Groups, Leadership, and Men*, Pittsburgh, Carnegie Press, 1951, pp. 119–133.

76. Sherif, M., *An Outline of Social Psychology*, New York, Harper, 1948, p. 105.

77. Shils, E. S., in D. Lerner and H. D. Lasswell (eds.), *The Policy Sciences*, Stanford, Stanford Univ. Press, 1951, p. 65.

78. Spicer, E. H., *Human Problems in Technological Change*, New York, Russell Sage Foundation, 1952.

79. Stephan, F. F., and E. G. Mishler, "The Distribution of Participation in Small Groups; an Exponential Approximation," *Amer. Soc. Rev.*, Vol. 17 (1952), pp. 598–608.

80. Stogdill, R. W., "Studies in Naval Leadership, II," in H. Guetzkow (ed.), *Groups, Leadership, and Men*, Pittsburgh, Carnegie Press, pp. 134–145.

81. Stone, G. P., and W. H. Form, "Instabilities in Status: The Problem of Hierarchy in the Community Study of Status Arrangements," *Amer. Soc. Rev.*, Vol. 18 (1953), pp. 149–162.

82. Stouffer, S., et al., *The American Soldier*, Princeton, Princeton Univ. Press, Vols. 1–3, 1949, Vol. 4, 1950.

83. Stouffer, S. A., and J. Toby, "Role Conflict and Personality," *Amer. J. Soc.*, Vol. 66 (1951), pp. 395–406.

84. Thornson, J. D., "Structures of Authority and Power in Two Complex Organizations," *Research Previews*, Univ. of North Carolina, Vol. 2 (1954), pp. 6–9.

85. Toby, J., "Universalistic and Particularistic Factors in Role Assignment," *Amer. Soc. Rev.*, Vol. 18 (1953), pp. 134–141.

86. Tsouderos, J. E., *The Formalization Process of Social Structure in Voluntary Associations*, Unpublished doctoral dissertation, Univ. of Minnesota, 1953.

87. Tsouderos, J. E., "Organizational Change," *Amer. Soc. Rev.*, Vol. 20 (1955), pp. 206–210.

88. Turner, R. H., "Self and Other in Moral Judgment," *Amer. Soc. Rev.*, Vol. 19 (1954), pp. 249–259.

89. Wagner, K. C., "Latent Functions of Executive Control: A Sociological Analysis of a System Under Stress," *Research Previews*, Univ. of North Carolina, Vol. 2 (1954), pp. 11–15.

90. Weber, Max, *From Max Weber*, trans. by H. H. Gerth and C. Wright Mills, New York, Oxford Univ. Press, 1946, pp. 212–215.

91. Winch, R. F., "The Theory of Complementary Mate-Selection: An Analytic and Descriptive Study," *Amer. Soc. Rev.*, Vol. 19 (1954), pp. 241–249.

92. Winch, R. F., "The Theory of Complementary Mate-Selection: A Test of One Kind of Complementariness," *Amer. Soc. Rev.*, Vol. 20 (1955), pp. 52–56.

93. Zimmerman, C. C., in Laboratory of Social Relations, *Report for the Five Years 1946–1951*, Cambridge, Mass., Harvard Univ. Laboratory of Social Relations, p. 19.

94. Znaniecki, F., "Social Organizations and Institutions," in G. Gurvitch and W. E. Moore (eds.), *Twentieth Century Sociology*, New York, Philosophical Library, 1945, pp. 172–217.

# chapter 10

# *Industrial sociology*

WILLIAM FOOTE WIIYTE
*Cornell University*

FRANK B. MILLER
*Cornell University*

## HISTORICAL INTRODUCTION

Industrial sociology as a field of scientific inquiry is little more than twenty years old. The selection of any date for its beginning would be arbitrary, but we may take the twelfth period in the Western Electric test room experiment as a convenient starting point (59).

The research team, led by Harvard's Elton Mayo and F. J. Roethlisberger and Western Electric's W. J. Dickson, had been studying the effects of certain changes in conditions of work upon productivity. When experimental variation of lighting showed no clear effects upon output, the researchers turned to the introduction of rest periods and refreshments and changes in the length of the working day.

For the test room experiment, six girls were isolated from the rest of the plant in a special observation room. While their production was measured, the changes in working conditions were introduced, with each change being kept in effect for a long enough period for its presumed effects to be observed.

Through the first eleven experimental periods, the rest pauses and refreshments seemed to be leading to greatly increased production, though there was no indication as to which combination of these conditions was most effective. For the twelfth period, the experimenters returned to the original conditions: no rest periods, no refreshments, and a regular eight hour day. Under these conditions, production reached a new high!

This result forced the researchers to the conclusion that there had been other factors which had not been held constant, and that these other factors had had more impact than the changes of physical conditions of work. As they came to look upon the test room as a social situation, the nature of these factors became evident.

Let us contrast the situation faced by the six test room girls with that faced by other girls on similar jobs in the regular factory departments. Obviously these six girls were singled out for special attention. They were not asked to produce an extraordinary amount, but they were informed that they were playing a part in an important experimental program. They took considerable pride in their part in the experiment.

Furthermore, the girls were removed from the regular channels of factory supervision. In the factory departments, their work had been laid out for them, they had been told what to do and had been closely supervised. No one had consulted them about the conditions of their work. Now, although they were under the constant observation of one of the research team, they were cut off from the regular channels of supervision. They were consulted about each stage of the experiment. The consultation was more than an empty form as eivdenced by the fact that at one point the girls vetoed a research proposal and did not have it imposed upon them. Finally, they were working in the company of an observer who took a friendly, personal interest in them.

The test room girls experienced a marked change in their relations with management and with each other. They built up a tightly knit social group with considerable pride in their membership.

This conclusion applies to the field of productivity but seems to have a much more general relevance that can be stated in this way. In order to change the activities and attitudes of people, change the relations among them.

This aspect of the Western Electric program has been attacked by some scholars as simply being a discovery of the obvious. The researchers discovered that industry is a society in itself, that individuals are not solely concerned with money or with the physical conditions of work. They are also strongly influenced by the relations that grow up among them. In a sense, the criticism has weight, but it fails to recognize the state of knowledge regarding human behavior in industry that existed at the time of the experimental program. At that time, sociologists and social anthropologists who were busily studying primitive and modern industrial communities had not ventured inside the gates of the factory. A few psychologists were active in industry, but most of them were engaged in developing aptitude and other psychological tests concerning the relation between a man's abilities and the physical and mental work required in different jobs. Although it might have occurred to the sociologist that a factory could be looked upon as a social system or community, he did nothing about such an idea until the way had been laid open for him by this experimental program.

Furthermore, at the time of the Western Electric program, popular thinking about human behavior in industry was dominated by certain ideas developed by economists and engineers. The prevailing notion was that man—at least in the factory setting—was an economically motivated individual. He responded as an individual to the financial rewards offered him or to the threats of the withdrawal of such rewards. In such thinking, groups did not exist. Each man responded rationally to his calculations of profit and loss.

The Western Electric experiments exploded these ideas. The studies of the test room and other studies growing out of it demonstrated that it is futile to think and act in terms of these individualistic economic assumptions. Men live in a society when they are in the plant just as when they are in their communities. If we are to understand their behavior in industry, we must therefore study the relations among the men and women who work together in this industrial society. It was that conclusion that opened up our field of study.

While the field work of the Western Electric study had been completed six or seven years earlier, *Management and the Worker* did not appear until 1939. Well before this time, a number of other research men had stepped in to begin shaping the field that was to become industrial sociology—or human relations in industry.

W. Lloyd Warner, a social anthropologist, was one of the first of these. While he was developing his Yankee City study, he was an active consultant on the Western Electric project and must be credited with some influence in turning the attention of the staff toward the detailed examination of the social organization of the "bank wiring room," which followed after the test room experiment.

In the course of field work in Yankee City, the shoe factories were for the time organized by a union. Warner took advantage of this opportunity to develop a study of *The Social System of the Modern Factory* (80).

Meanwhile the interest of other social anthropologists was turning to industry. Eliot Chapple and Conrad Arensberg (20) were setting forth their *interaction* approach to social organization. Chapple (19) developed the first primitive model of his *interaction chronograph,* a machine designed to measure interpersonal relations. Arensberg in collaboration with a social psychologist, Douglas McGregor, carried on a study of morale and social organization in an electrical company (3). Arensberg followed this with his now well-known statement on "Industry and the Community" (2).

The period of the late 1930's was one of great ferment in the field of anthropology. Young men were challenging the established organization of specialties and pushing social anthropology toward application of its methods and theories of the problems of modern, industrialized society. This led to the formation, in 1941, of the Society for Applied Anthropology. Three of the leading figures in this movement, Chapple, Arensberg, and F. L. W. Richardson, Jr., had a strong interest in industrial studies and the Society's journal (*Human Organization,* formerly *Applied Anthropology*) has published a large volume of research reports in this field.

E. Wight Bakke, a sociologist at Yale, began his research studying the problems of the unemployed man first in England (9) and then in New Haven (6, 10). This research led him to recognize that a man's job was not simply the means of earning a living. He found that the job (or lack of job) had important social and psychological effects upon the individual. His interests turned more and more to exploring the meaning of work to the worker.

Another important contribution to the development of the field was provided by Kurt Lewin, refugee social psychologist from Hitler's Germany. After doing pioneering work in the study of small groups (46), he became interested in discovering whether some of the methods of dealing with autonomous groups (45) could be applied to groups of workers within an industrial organization. This led to the development of the Harwood Manufacturing Company's experimental program carried out by Alex Bavelas (14), John R. P. French, Jr., and Lester Coch (21), upon which we shall comment later.

Activity in the field of industrial sociology did not evolve with a steady growth. While the field work on the Western Electric program was being done in the late 1920's and early 1930's, it was not until the 1940's that the great expansion of activity and establishment of industrial sociology as a recognized discipline took place.

In 1943 Burleigh Gardner, Robert J. Havighurst, and W. Lloyd Warner organized the Committee on Human Relations in Industry at the University of Chicago. Gardner, a social anthropologist who had worked with Warner on the Yankee City study and then on other community studies (24), had been research director of the personnel counseling program at Western Electric. The Committee was later expanded to include Allison Davis, Everett C. Hughes, F. H. Harbison, George Brown, and William F. Whyte. Now for the first time there was not just a research project and staff but a continuing research program, with faculty members and graduate students working together on a variety of studies.

E. Wight Bakke followed shortly thereafter (1944) with his Labor Management Center at Yale. Activity also expanded at Massachusetts Institute of Technology under the leadership of Douglas McGregor.

In 1946, Rensis Likert, a social psychologist, set up the Institute for Social Research at the University of Michigan. While the Institute has carried on many activities outside of industry, it has always sponsored an active program of industrial studies. The Institute began as an organization dedicated to making organizational studies primarily by the questionnaire survey method (although experiments were also carried out). Following the death of Kurt Lewin, the Research Center for Group Dynamics moved to Michigan in 1948 as a major part of the Institute.

Meanwhile, there were great organizational changes taking place within universities to make a place for industrial sociology and for the more inclusive field of industrial relations. The New York State School of Industrial and Labor Relations was established at Cornell in 1945, and graduate and undergraduate teaching programs in industrial relations were established at the Universities of Illinois and California, and at many other centers.

Twenty years ago, industrial sociology did not exist as a course in university catalogues. Today there is hardly a sociology department in the country that does not list at least one such course—though the course titles vary considerably. Similarly, twenty years ago the teaching of industrial relations generally just made up a part of a course or courses in labor economics. Today, the economists are more active than ever, but the field of industrial relations has grown beyond the confines of labor economics and has come to be considered an interdisciplinary area of study, where sociologists, anthropologists, psychologists, political scientists, and economists all have legitimate (but often overlapping) jurisdictions.

The volume of activity in industrial sociology has become truly impressive. A new and important area of social organization is being explored. However, the explorers have often plunged into the unknown with more fascination for their data than theoretical and methodological rigor. A rich territory has been opened up, but very little effort has yet gone into the systematic organization of the data found there. Perhaps the stage of systematic development is now beginning. We shall try to make a small contribution in that direction through our review of the field.

It should be the particular function of the sociologist to point out that the industrial organization does not exist in a vacuum but is part of the social network of the larger society. In our eagerness to explore the internal structure of the plant, we have sometimes neglected to note its interconnections with the larger society or have given only lip service to the mutually dependent relations of industry and society. Nevertheless, there now exists a rather substantial body of research which places industry in its social setting, and it is in this area that we shall begin.*

## INDUSTRY AND THE COMMUNITY

Industrial sociologists have been interested in a wide variety of industry-community relationships.

Although there is much disagreement among sociologists as to the methods for determining the statuses of individuals and families in the community, all would agree that social structure has an important bearing upon what happens in the work place.

W. Lloyd Warner explains the unionization of the shoe workers of Yankee City in terms of changes in social structure in plant and in community (80). Within the plant, he points to the breakdown of the craft hierarchy. Technological changes had broken down the pre-existing gradations of craft skills and reduced all the workers to a semiskilled level. In the community, he shows how, as financial control passed outside the city, the shoe factory management people were no longer members of the upper-upper class. The paternalistic relations between the top social group and "their" workers had broken down, so that the workers could no longer look to community leaders in the plant to take care of their needs. Furthermore, when the strike came, management's strength was weakened and the union's strength was increased by a division of sympathies within the upper social levels of the community.

There is also disagreement as to whether the rate of social mobility has been decreasing in the United States, but it is evident that the educational

* In the discussion to follow, space limitations have not allowed us to try to cover every important topic in the field. Some of the more important omissions are: problems of staff-line relations, the role of the specialist (engineer, accountant, personnel man, for example), problems of applying research findings through training or in other ways, and methods of research in industry.

system has been assuming ever-increasing importance in placing people in the social structure. The man without a college education may rise to the level of foreman or general foreman, but his chances of reaching higher management levels are slim. Nevertheless, he may put his son through college, and the son may climb considerably farther in the structure.

Hollingshead (37) has shown that the sorting-out process of employment along class lines tends to begin even before children reach college age. During high school, the more unpleasant and less remunerative tasks usually go to lower class children. Better paying or "cushy" jobs are more often available to youngsters further up in the class system. This is not simply a matter of the "connections" that go with high family status. It also involves language, manners, and style of dress, all of which are related to class position. Thus, by the time the boy reaches the end of high school, he may be already resigned to the positions that go with lesser education. However, we should note that a steadily increasing proportion of the population is going on to college.

Researchers have also sought to explain the level of conflict or cooperation within the plant in terms of plant-community relationships. Thus Harbison and Dubin (35) explain the then harmonious relations between Studebaker Company management and its UAW union *in part* in terms of common worker and management residence in the same community and a recognition that the welfare of the community rested largely upon what happened within this plant.

Kerr and Siegel (41) point out that, on a nation-wide or even world-wide basis, certain industries are more strike-prone than others. They argue convincingly that these differences cannot be accounted for by differences in human-relations skills on the part of management. They propose the hypothesis that the explanation is to be found in the industry-community relationship. In the coal mining industry, for example, the workers generally live close together in communities where they are isolated both from other types of workers and from management people. This isolation is assumed to give rise to a strong in-group feeling, which leads to aggressive, antimanagement behavior.

The world-wide bird's-eye view of Clark and Kerr receives support from a recently published case study by Alvin Gouldner (33). He compares two divisions of a gypsum plant, the mine and the board mill. When the firm installed a new plant manager, he tried to increase the number of rules, and "tighten up" administration of existing rules, thus formalizing what had been informal relations and procedures.

Gouldner found that the mine was able to resist the tendency toward formal, bureaucratic methods quite effectively. The board mill, despite resentment of workers and supervisors, succumbed to bureaucratic pressures rather easily. The reason for differential resistance to bureaucratization is examined on two fronts.

Inside the plant, the technology split mill hands into isolated individuals or loosely organized clusters of three or four men at most. Miners, however, worked in closely knit groups of eight or more, away from close supervision and highly dependent on one another for job performance and personal safety. Thus, the mine had strong, cohesive, informal groups capable of resisting change, while mill workers were disunited and easily subject to management manipulation.

The two groups were characterized by out-of-plant differences, too. Miners lived together in enclaves, forming little brotherhoods of men who drank, gambled, and shared general community disapproval *together*. Mill workers, scattered throughout the area, conformed to the general middle class values. They interacted only weakly with fellow employees in the community setting.

So far we have been observing how the community structure can influence the adjustment of people to each other inside the industrial organization. Philip Selznick has shown how the community structure can affect even the purposes of the organization (67).

One major purpose of TVA was to raise living standards in a depressed area through flood control, electrical power generation, reforestation, distribution of fertilizer, and the improvement of agricultural practices affecting erosion. Certainly, living standards in the area did rise faster than those in many other parts of the nation. Selznick, however, is not concerned with TVA's objective accomplishments. He focuses on the way this new organization adjusted to its regional setting.

Starting with the idea of TVA as a "tool" set up to accomplish certain ends, he examines some of the means necessarily selected, e.g., working through established state agricultural extension services. He finds that the required adjustments to local pressures brought unanticipated consequences and to some extent modified TVA's original goals. Among other things, wealthier, more highly organized, and better educated farmers were the recipients of a disproportionate amount of TVA help. They became the influential local representatives on policy-influencing boards set up by the TVA. This is a necessary consequence of working through the State University extension services that had contacts with exactly this type of farmer. The "trickle down" theory of increasing regional wealth, however, played no part in the original formulation of TVA's social goal.

Interesting ways of focusing on industry and community simultaneously have been applied at the executive level. *Fortune* magazine's William H. Whyte, Jr. (no relation to William F. Whyte) has traced the impact of suburban living, the carefully graded use of status symbols (Don't drive a Cadillac if your boss drives a Buick), the importance of whom you marry, what school you went to, how well you "fit" in the organization (86).

He points out: how the demands of a man's industrial role affect where he can live (the right part of Suburbia for his position in the corporation); how often he must move to gain organizational experience or secure promotions; the kind of acquaintances, hobbies, and vices he and his wife must cultivate in the community in order to fulfill his organizational function most efficiently (or at least more acceptably).

Still another facet of the middle-level, upward-moving executive lies in the social forces which tend to make middle class people what David Riesman (57) calls "other-directed." Both Whyte and Riesman complain (or at least maintain) that the picture of the executive as tough-minded, individualistic, and decisive no longer applies. The executive is still hard working, perhaps even more so than before. But now, he may spend a great deal of his energy mollifying people, smoothing over human relations problems, and getting people to agree to decisions and participate in their formation.

Both authors see this shift in the kind of training upper-middle class children receive. They see the strong emphasis in "progressive education" on cooperation with one's fellows as aiming toward the attainment of a new form of "success." According to this analysis, success has changed from the attainment of competence to be enjoyed for its own sake or because those in authority bestow approval for its attainment. Success now means the "other-oriented" reward of acceptance and popularity from one's associates—*all* of them.

Perhaps the emphasis on "human relations," currently sponsored by many managements, is not just a cold-blooded, mercenary desire to increase productivity through improved morale. Nor is it solely the fullest flowering of humanitarian or ethical impulses. These two elements probably do enter into management motivations. In addition, there may be a very heavy dash of unconscious desire on the part of management individuals to be *loved* by workers.

The relevance of *this* set of motivations to organizational efficiency is extremely interesting. For example, most *workers* probably do not share this strong built-in need for affection from persons with conflicting interests. They may view management overtures with heightened suspicion. The attempt to reconcile or ignore differences of interest is likely to be interpreted as a management trick to exploit workers. And the "courtship" aspect of labor relations may be at least partially self-defeating.

The studies we have mentioned in this section will perhaps give an idea of the variety of work being done here, yet at the same time they

give a very miscellaneous impression of this part of the field. With all
due allowances for our deficiencies in reporting and synthesizing, this is
to some extent a faithful reflection of the current situation. Any industrial
sociologist will argue that the industry-community area is of tremendous
importance, and yet the interrelationships are so many, so varied, and on
so large a scale that the area has so far defied systematic formulation.

## TECHNOLOGY AND HUMAN RELATIONS

Students of society, from Weber and Durkheim to Riesman and Toynbee, have been struck by the relation between social forms and the nature
and uses of tools and machinery. Problems on so broad and inclusive a
level are particularly intriguing to anthropologists examining non-Western societies undergoing change (70), to social philosophers (53), and
to sociologists (28, 54, 61) inspired by one or another or both of these
approaches.

Most industrial sociologists examine social problems of technological
change within a more restricted context than the culture or the national
community. Some prefer to concentrate on the impact of changes in *one*
plant (or industry) on *one* community. We have already mentioned
work by Harbison and Dubin (35) and Warner (80) along these lines,
along with the observation that this kind of study is most feasible in one-
industry or one-plant communities.

Another example involving a one-industry town is Cottrell's study of a
"railroad town" (22). A decision, made in the metropolitan headquarters
of a railroad company, to change from steam to diesel-electric locomo-
tives, had tremendous impact on the life of a town whose main economic
function was to serve as a railroad division point. As the technological
decision rendered previously important skills obsolete, the economic patterns, status systems, and political organization of the community were
thrown out of equilibrium.

This development follows, in a more extreme way, the patterns revealed in Yankee City shoe factories (80) and Steeltown's tubing mill
(78). Highly integrated, supposedly autonomous communities may become socially disorganized as a result of decisions by outsiders based
solely on technical rationale.

Industrial sociologists have been particularly interested in the relation
of technology to the *internal* social systems of work organizations. In a
factory, for example, the kind, number, and location of machines have
immediate impact on the size and membership of work groups ("formal"
or "informal"), the norms relevant to sustaining the group, the relative

prestige of individual members, and clique formation inside a larger group (29, 58).

A "functional" department composed of twenty screw machine operators is quite different from a group of twenty workers, each of whom gets a partially completed piece of work from his predecessor, performs an operation on the piece with his equipment, and passes it on to the next man who, in turn, does something else to the piece with a different machine.

In the first instance, there is no interdependence between neighbors in a technical sense, and status distinctions based on job assignment are minimized. (Status distinctions are likely to depend on newness of machine, or preferred make, seniority, access to windows or vending machines, and perhaps on job competence about which all members are peculiarly capable of making realistic judgments.) Important group "issues" would probably hinge on competence in dealing with supervisors and "outsiders."

In the group characterized by a sequence of operations, social organization tends to be more complex. Internal relationships are quite important, since each man depends on and is depended on by others for product performance. Status distinctions hinge importantly on job assignments, as well as job competence and other factors extrinsic to task performance. Thus, many of the "issues" for which the group must develop norms center around internal relationships, partly in order to get the job done, partly to keep the group socially integrated.*

Workers whose prestige and position in the communications pattern is strategic assume group leadership. Relations with "outsiders," supervisors, the union, and other work groups also require the development of appropriate norms and sanctions for enforcing those norms. Leadership in "foreign relations" is vested in the same persons who are most influential in "internal" group decisions, or in auxiliary leaders.

Quite often, departmental leadership belongs to workers whose jobs allow them in-plant mobility, e.g., machine set-up men or the auto assembly line's relief man. (This does not hold true for mobile workers of very low status, however, e.g., messenger boys or sweepers.) The ability to move from group to group gives great advantage in finding out

---

* In dividing in-group processes into "task-oriented" and "social-emotional" functions, we agree with Bales that these two forms of activity are functional prerequisites of *all* problem-solving groups. See R. F. Bales, *Interaction Process Analysis,* Cambridge, Addison-Wesley Press, 1951. Task-oriented activities correspond roughly to meeting the demands of the "external system," social-emotional activities to meeting the demands of the "internal system" in Homan's typology. See George Homans, *The Human Group,* New York, Harcourt, Brace, 1952.

and communicating "news" and workers' sentiments, not enjoyed by sedentary or immobilized machine tenders. Ordinarily, jobs which allow incumbents to participate in wider interaction systems than their fellows are also high in the organization's job evaluation system. So, informal status is buttressed by formal.

Apropos of spatial mobility, a departmental union representative is usually free to circulate among fellow workers on union business (62). This enhances his opportunity to be an "informal leader" of his fellows. The steward with a fixed work station, who prefers staying conscientiously at his work post rather than circulating through the plant, is rarely as successful as the one whose job allows movement or the one who avails himself of his privileged position to leave his station and talk with the widest possible circle of his constituents.

Many writers have demonstrated the strong social linkage between physical features of the work environment (technology) and individual status and adjustments.

In one restaurant (81) the job status of counterman was found to be higher than that of waitress. The flow of work demanded that waitresses pass customer orders along to counterman. Where this was done orally in a face-to-face contact, the inevitable concomitant was great interpersonal friction between waitresses and countermen. (It is a fairly safe generalization that where subordinates originate activity changes for superiors *more* than they respond to superiors, you will find organizational trouble spots.)

In another restaurant, the physical layout was different. Instead of being waist-high, the counter was so high that face-to-face contact was impossible. Waitresses wrote out order slips and put them on a spindle atop the barrier. Countermen picked up the slips, filled the orders, and placed them in a warming compartment, from which waitresses retrieved them. Here the opportunity for status conflicts was minimized, relations were impersonal, but not bitter, and the men at least were highly enthusiastic about "working conditions." Thus technology-inspired relations must conform to the requirements of the internal status system or trouble follows.

The impact of technological *change* on group relations has been amply documented by sociologists. An interesting example of recent studies along these lines deals with a change in British coal mines (74). The traditional method involved small work teams working together on an entire sequence of activities. They laid track to the seam face, prepared the roof, blasted, and removed coal from one "stall" (10 to 15 yards long) at a time.

"Longwall" mining began in the 1920's and 1930's as an application of mass production methods to mining coal. Mechanical coal cutters and conveyor belts were introduced. The face of a seam was laid bare for a distance of 100 to 180 yards. Individual miners were placed at intervals along the seam. Each miner was responsible for removing the coal from his assigned frontage. Laying of the track, blasting, and so on had been performed by other crews of "specialists" before the "fillers" came to work.

The miners' jobs had been fragmentalized, made into tasks which were monotonously repetitive and required fewer kinds of skills. Furthermore, they were isolated from their accustomed social groupings. Sporadic informal groups emerged, but they were largely powerless to mitigate the pressures on members. The only exception to this process were the second-shift "rippers" who still had a meaningful sequence of operations, which they performed *as a team.*

As a result of these changes, the working life of the average miner became increasingly meaningless and "anomic" as he became further alienated from former sources of pride and support—his skills and his work gang. A great deal of intershift hostility and scapegoating emerged. Under the desperate economic pressures of economic blight during which the Longwall method was introduced, the direct impact of the changed system was masked by side effects attributed to "the depression."

Under postwar conditions of full employment, however, British coal mining emerged as a serious weak spot in the national effort to increase productivity. Without the spur of unemployment and destitution, miners sharply increased absenteeism, recruitment for the mine labor force fell off drastically, and despite nationalization and a Labor government, unauthorized work stoppages spread. "The system" (i.e., the technological system and its attendant social dislocations) became the target for condemnation and investigation by nonminers.

American managements are beginning to question the "scientific" assumption that increasing fragmentation and specialization of worker tasks lead inevitably to higher productivity and lower costs. A realization that there is a point of diminishing returns, at which theoretical increases in efficiency are more than outweighed by losses in worker motivation and responsibility, has led to experimentation with "job enlargement" (42, 77). This is an attempt to reverse the tide of "engineering logic" by recombining a number of related, hitherto separate tasks into a more meaningful cluster of operations, and/or allowing workers to "swap off" jobs with their neighbors in order to become more versatile and less bored.

Charles Walker and Robert Guest have examined the human impact of working on an automotive assembly line (79). They find the process may allow *some* social interaction between workers, but prevents the formation of stable primary groups.

The first assembly line study by Yale researchers was made in a new plant (less than five years old) in a fairly small community, with workers recruited from nonfactory labor. Their outspoken complaints about the monotony and lack of social contact might reflect their "lack of adjustment to factory ways." To check on reactions of people in "the system" for a longer period, a second study was conducted in a different plant, interviewing workers with twelve or more years experience (75).

The only difference found between "veterans of the line" and relative newcomers seemed to be that the former were even *more* frustrated and hopeless than the newcomers. They had been unable to form satisfying informal groups, and they were more keenly aware that opportunities for escaping their plight through promotion were limited. At the same time accumulated pension rights, and other "fringe benefits" related to seniority, tended to "tie" them, however reluctantly, to their jobs. "Time to adjust to the system" does not provide the answer in a "culture" like the mechanically paced assembly line organization, which is geared to machines rather than to men.

Within the ranks of assembly line workers, however, there are degrees of satisfaction and dissatisfaction with jobs. Least satisfying are jobs which have the fewest operations per job cycle, say, less than five. Jobs with five to ten operations are far less monotonous, workers report. Most satisfaction is reported by "relief men" who are moved around the line to substitute for regular workers for brief periods. The relief man may perform a few simple operations on any one job, but he gets a frequent change of pace and a wider range of skills and understanding about the whole process.

The relief man with his wider range of contacts serves as one of the few social integrators in the system and is often personally popular with his mates. The "good foreman" who allows workers to trade off jobs in defiance of "regulations" also functions as a social support. But even the combined presence of good foremen and relief men is not sufficient to compensate for the inability of workers to do meaningful work in a stable, satisfying social system.

One of the aggravating features of this kind of assembly line work is the constant demand for "surface attention." Walker's speculations about job satisfactions are interesting on this score. If you rate jobs on a continuum of how much attention is demanded, he says, you can see three main clusters. Skilled jobs, requiring a complicated series of activities with a need for making critical decisions at key points demand "depth attention." They are the most intrinsically satisfying forms of factory work.

At the other extreme are the simplest jobs, which the experienced worker can perform automatically with little or no conscious attention. His mind is free to indulge in private thoughts or daydreaming—the "reverie" which so disturbed Durkheim and Mayo.

In between are very simple jobs which require the operator to be alert for detail, but entail no decisions or complex activities. This is the "surface attention" demanded of the assembly line worker of the Yale studies. And this is the *least* satisfying form of work, Walker believes. Such workers are denied the "creative" satisfactions of the skilled worker and are not even allowed the privacy or "escape" of daydreaming.

Hand-in-hand with the technical functions of particular industries go related problems of social organization. We now have a wealth of studies on these relationships for a large number of specific organizations.

We still lack a major attempt at generalizing *across* industries about the relationship between technology and work process on the one hand and forms of social organization on the other hand, which takes into account the multiplicity of data in a systematic way. The enormity of the task has made previous attempts at generalization understandably piecemeal, however grandiose the claims of theorists.

It would appear that there is a need in the area of technology and human relations for "upper-middle" generalizations. There is a gap between the vast amount of work done at the small group level and the company level on one side and cosmic theorizing on the impact of "industrialization" or "automation" on Western or United States culture on the other side. We now have enough data to begin to state, tentatively, some uniformities that will apply in comparing one industry with another.

## MORALE AND PRODUCTIVITY

The relationships between morale and productivity have presented a difficult problem to researchers in industry. The layman would like to believe that high morale and high productivity go together, and many people in industry have flatly stated that this is so.

The generalizations we make will depend upon the way in which we define morale. If by "high morale" we mean simply that the workers are contented in their jobs, then there is no necessary correlation. People can be quite content with their jobs and still have no urge to be productive.

Social researchers have not been inclined to accept the *contentment* definition of morale. Although there is no universally accepted definition of morale, we find that students of organization generally think of two points in this connection: the sentiments of members toward each other and toward the organization plus the presence or absence of a group commitment toward an organizational purpose.

Herbert Blumer puts it this way (17): "Group morale exists as a disposition to act together toward a goal." He adds: "All that is basically necessary for morale is that people in a group have a goal which they value highly and seek eagerly in a sense of mutual support in their efforts to attain it."

Alexander Leighton gives this definition (43): "Morale is defined as the capacity of a group of people to pull together consistently and persistently in pursuit of a common purpose."

Leighton states that morale is dependent upon the following five factors:

1. The faith of each member of the group in the common purpose;
2. The faith of each member of the group in the leadership;
3. The faith of each member of the group in the other members;
4. The organizational efficiency of the group;
5. The health and balance of emotions in the individuals of the group.

Following such concepts, we can say that high morale and high productivity necessarily do go together if high productivity is a group goal. The necessity, however, is established by the very nature of our definition of morale, which tells us that Group A, which is strongly determined to reach goal X, is more likely to get there than is Group B, whose members are not interested. We must therefore move on to an examination of the conditions giving rise to high or low morale.

First, let us examine the relationship between group cohesiveness, one aspect of morale, and productivity (65). When we find the members isolated from each other or in conflict with each other, we will not expect to find productivity as high as it would be in a cohesive group that was committed to high production. However, we can have a highly cohesive group which follows a policy of *keeping production down*. Disorganized workers will have no group norm for production. The closely knit group, on the contrary, will have such a norm in terms of which all members will strive to regulate their behavior.

So far we know very little about the conditions making for cohesiveness or disorganization among groups in the work place. Sayles and Strauss (62) have suggested that the degree of homogeneity of jobs is an important influence. That is, workers doing similar jobs at similar rates of pay are more likely to "stick together" than workers representing a wide range of skill and pay. There must, however, be other factors involved also.

If high cohesiveness involves a group norm for production, what factors determine whether the group sets the norm high or low? For the answer to this question, we must examine the relations between the work group and the managerial organization.

We shall look first at the behavior of the supervisor, who is a chief link between a group and the total structure. We now have a rather large volume of research, particularly by social psychologists, which gives us a description of the supervisory process as it affects productivity.

Rensis Likert and his coworkers at the University of Michigan's Institute for Social Research have been distinguishing between the "employee centered" and the "production centered" supervisor (38, 47, 48, 52). The "employee centered" supervisor is seen by subordinates as taking a sincere interest in helping them. The "production centered" supervisor is seen by his workers as just pushing to get the job done. Likert's team has found, in several studies, that the "employee centered" supervisor tends to get more production than the pusher for production (39).

Carroll Shartle (68), John Hemphill (36), and Ralph Stogdill (72, 73), speaking for the Ohio State leadership studies suggest that this dichotomy presents an oversimplified picture (and Likert, in discussion, has been inclined to agree). From questionnaires tapping employee perceptions of supervisors, the Ohio State people have isolated two statistically independent factors which they call "consideration" and "initiating structure." The man rated high on "consideration" is seen as taking a real interest in the problems of subordinates. The man rated high in "initiating structure" is seen as very active in setting goals for his group, in letting them know what is going on and where they stand, and in general, he does what the psychologist speaks of as "structuring the situation."

The Likert and the Shartle and Hemphill conceptions are similar, of course. There seems to be a large overlap between "employee centered" and "consideration." "Initiating structure" includes behavior implied under "production centered," but the term also seems to involve additional aspects such as the giving of information.

The basic difference in the two approaches is that the Ohio State people make no either-or assumption. They hold that a supervisor can be high on both "consideration" and "initiating structure," or low on both, or high on either one and low on the other. In fact, the statement that the two factors are statistically independent means simply that knowing a man's score on one factor does not enable us to predict what he will score on the other.

Shartle and Hemphill are inclined to believe that the most effective supervisor is one who is rated by subordinates as high on both factors.

However, their evidence also suggests that some types of technology and work organization may require for high production a supervisor who is high on "initiating structure," whether or not he scores high on "consideration." Other types of work situations may require for high production a supervisor who is a specialist in "consideration."

While the Michigan and Ohio State conclusions are supported by an impressive weight of survey data and statistical evidence, they are subject to one important limitation. The conclusions are based upon the *perceptions* of supervisors, as reported by their subordinates. These perceptions are, to a large extent, reactions to the behavior of the supervisor, but they do not tell us what behavior is actually going on. Nor do they tell us that supervisor A, who is rated as high on "consideration," is behaving in a similar manner to supervisor B, who is also rated high in that factor by a different work group.

This is not to suggest that we should abandon our interest in getting data upon such perceptions. A good questionnaire in this area will bring in a wealth of material in a highly efficient manner. However, until we have a substantial amount of data upon the *observed* behavior of the same supervisors for whom we are getting worker *perceptions,* our conclusions about supervisory behavior will be on a very shaky foundation.

University of Michigan researchers (39) have been studying the relationship between the closeness of supervision and productivity. There seems to be general agreement that the supervisor who gives general directions and leaves his people a good deal of freedom to exercise their judgment gets better results in morale and productivity than the supervisor who is constantly checking and issuing orders and instructions. Probably future research will refine this conclusion by discovering the ways in which the technology and work flow affect the closeness of supervision necessary for good production. However, there is a good weight of evidence to support the view that management tends to provide closer supervision than is congruent with the production purpose of the organization.

Research begun by Kurt Lewin (46) and continued by Alex Bavelas (14), Lester Coch and John R. P. French, Jr. (21), and others indicates that the involvement of workers in discussion and decision-making regarding matters important to their jobs tends to increase morale and productivity. The Harwood experiments show us cases in which such involvement has led workers more readily to accept technological change and has also influenced them to increase their production.

There now seems no doubt that involvement in this discussion process has an important impact upon the attitudes and behavior of workers—or of anybody, for that matter. However, there has been a tendency in this area for our democratic values to become confused with our scientific work. We would like to believe that "democratic group methods" lead to better results than autocratic action, but "democratic group methods" is a very vague and general term. We have seen people in industry trying to apply such methods, sometimes with very good and sometimes with very poor results. These variations are probably explainable in terms of two main factors:

1. It has not generally been specified, in terms of specific behavior, how the leader acts in such a discussion group. Does he just help the members to reach a decision and go along with that? Or does he just use the group for consultation and, in effect, make his own decision? Many other questions along these lines need to be answered.

2. The possibilities of effective use of group discussion will depend upon the nature of the problem, the organizational level at which decisions are to be made, the speed with which action must be taken, and, no doubt, upon other factors we cannot yet specify.

So far we have been examining supervisor-worker relations on the implicit assumption that the supervisor is free to act in whatever way he thinks best. That is, of course, not the case. The first line supervisor is almost at the bottom of the industrial pyramid, and his handling of employees is strongly influenced both by management's policies and directives and by the "pressures" on him from higher organizational levels.

It has often been observed that the plant manager, or even some higher official, tends to set the pattern of supervision into which the foreman fits. This could lead us to an examination of personality characteristics of executives, a topic beyond the scope of our chapter.

However, these differences in pattern are by no means wholly accounted for by the personalities of top people. We are now finding that the organization structure itself plays an important role in establishing this supervisory pattern.

Gardner and Moore (29) have distinguished between the long, narrow structure and the broad, flat structure. The long hierarchy is based, consciously or unconsciously, upon the span of control theory: that the executive can adequately supervise only a small number of people, perhaps four to eight. At lower levels, with more routine work, it is assumed that the supervisor can handle a larger number, but the theory emphasizes the value of keeping that number down.

The span of control theory is based upon one key assumption: that people need to be closely supervised in order to perform well. If we make the opposite assumption, that people perform best when they are given a large area of freedom to make their own decisions, then we build an entirely different organizational structure. We may then even build our structure by giving the supervisor or executive so many people under him that he cannot possibly supervise them closely. In fact, this seems a much more direct way to lighten supervision than the best supervisory training program.

Management thinking is now shifting away from the span of control theory toward building a decentralized organization: a broad, flat structure. Few studies have as yet been made to show the superior effectiveness of this type of structure, but the scattered evidence is in this direction.

## MEN AND MONEY *

What does money mean to industrial man?

First we must put that question in a cultural perspective. Man is not born loving money. He learns to love it. And the amount of money he feels he needs is in part culturally determined.

By now it is a commonplace observation that workers in many non-industrialized countries do not respond to money wages as do workers in the United States. When they are offered substantially more money than the customary amount for a day's work, they may choose to work fewer days instead of to earn more money. They do not take easily to the discipline of factory life, so they are inclined to prefer more leisure to more money. Only as they learn to value some of the material objects that we associate with a high standard of living does money assume a more commanding position in their scale of values.

How important is money to American workers? As we have already noted, several questionnaire surveys have indicated that they rank "good wages" as seventh or eighth among the items that go to make up a good job. This suggests that not even for the American is money so all-important as is sometimes supposed. Beyond this general statement, however, it is difficult to say what the questionnaire results mean. It is now well recognized that predicting behavior from attitude questionnaires is a very complicated task. When he decides upon his course of action, the worker is not responding to "good wages" in the abstract but to a concrete situation involving a specific rate of pay and many other specific conditions of

* This section summarizes the discussion presented in William F. Whyte, *Money and Motivation* (82).

factory life. When we look at the actual life situation, it is impossible to deny that the worker shows a very considerable concern over the amount of his pay.

### Money as wages

In some parts of the world, men must look upon their pay in terms of whether it enables them to meet the bare necessities of food, clothing, and shelter. The American worker, being in general well above the line of minimum subsistence, uses different standards of judgment.

Bakke (4) has found that the worker tends to evaluate his pay in relative terms. If he is receiving as much as his customary associates in community and factory life, he is able to live as they do, and he tends to feel that he receives a "fair day's pay." He would like to get more, of course, but he does not feel a sense of injustice in this situation.

Gardner and Moore (29) have pointed out that the worker may be more concerned about the fact that a fellow worker gets five cents more an hour than he is about the size of his paycheck in relation to the cost of living. We find that money is an important factor in social prestige or status in the industrial organization. Each job is related to every other job in a scale of prestige as well as in a scale of pay. Workers will agree that job A should be paid more than job B because it requires more skill, carries more responsibility, and so on—or just because they have become accustomed to that differential in the past. Sometimes, in introducing a system of "job evaluation" whereby jobs are rated according to supposedly objective standards, management upsets such established differentials, and runs into stubborn worker resistance. The introduction of an incentive system can also upset these established job relations, as we shall see in the later discussion.

To what extent are high wages an incentive to high production? It is an article of faith among management people and workers alike that high wages and high production go together. It would be exceedingly difficult to test this general proposition, because so many other conditions tend to be associated with high or with low wages.

The problem is that hourly wages are not a *direct* incentive to production. Good wages serve as an incentive for a worker to apply for a job in plant A instead of plant B (although studies by Reynolds and Shister (56) suggest that job-hunting workers do not make nearly as systematic wage comparisons as might be supposed). The wage may also serve as an incentive for the worker to stay on the job and do at least enough work to avoid getting fired, but that is certainly a minimum incentive.

### Incentive pay

If pay based on hours worked offers no direct incentive for increasing production, it is natural to think that basing pay upon amount produced will provide such motivation. Such an approach offers a wide variety of pay systems. Pay can be based upon the performance of the individual worker (individual piecework) or upon that of a group of workers (group piecework). In recent years, there have also developed systems of pay where the performance of an entire plant serves as a basis of rewarding individual workers.

Piece rate plans began to spread in American industry following the pioneering work of industrial engineer Frederick W. Taylor, beginning before the turn of the century. Taylor and his disciples launched what became known as the "scientific management movement."

The movement was based upon certain assumptions about human behavior, which were translated into action as management procedures.

It was assumed that the worker was an acquisitive individual who operated as an isolated unit, relating himself only to his machine. The factory was looked upon not as a society but as a simple aggregation of individuals. According to this adaptation of the "Protestant ethic," the complex problems of motivating workers and increasing productivity were to be solved through standardizing work methods and setting rates of pay per unit of production.

What have been the results of this approach to motivation? Although any generalization must be an oversimplification, we can hazard certain conclusions.

"Other things being equal," the introduction of piece rates does result in higher productivity. On the contrary, it is one of the best demonstrated propositions in social science that, in general, workers do not respond to the incentive to the full extent of their physical and mental capacities. In most instances, they reach a point which they come to consider "a fair day's work" and do not go beyond that point even when they recognize that it would be possible and (in some cases) physically easy to do so. Furthermore, the introduction of piece rates seems generally to be accompanied by increased conflict between workers and management and between union and management. In fact, in some cases the conflict is so severe that one may well wonder whether the piecework system is worth its costs to management even from a narrow economic standpoint.

Why does the system not work as the theories of scientific management hold that it should?

The rationale for restriction of output is generally expressed by workers in terms of a fear of rate cutting. If the workers show management that they can earn more than a certain figure on their job, they fear that management will cut the price per piece so that in the future they will have to work harder to make the same or even less money. There is no doubt that rate cutting has been extensively practiced in American industry, especially in the early days of the development of incentive systems. In the face of such a threat, the response of output restriction is logical, from any point of view.

However, this possibility was recognized at the outset by the theorists of scientific management, who insisted that a rate, once established, must not be changed unless there had been a significant change in machines or work methods. Furthermore, we have cases such as that of the Western Electric Company where no worker of all the thousands interviewed could cite a specific instance of rate cutting practiced by the company and yet where it was widely believed that production beyond a certain point would lead to such a management reaction. Where then did the workers get this fear of rate cutting? Perhaps from the outside world, for in the community workers talk with workers from other companies and perhaps form some generalized impressions of the way management people behave. Still, this seems hardly a full explanation, for research shows that workers respond very strongly to the immediate work situation. There must be some explanation for their behavior to be found within the social system of their own plant.

Roethlisberger and Dickson (59) look upon restriction of output as a group response to occupying the bottom of the industrial pyramid and being constantly subjected to management-initiated innovations. Functioning essentially as a means of protecting the unity of the work group against management pressures, the practices of restriction are seen as nonlogical responses to management's "logic of efficiency." Elton Mayo has also elaborated upon this theme.

The theory implies that workers may act in a manner against their own economic interests in reaction to management controls. While the workers' subordinate position and their resentment of management manipulation certainly suggest part of the answer, the assumption of a worker "nonlogical" response rests upon an oversimplification. It assumes that the only question at issue is whether management will or will not cut rates. If we look at the process of rate administration, we will discover that the problems are a good deal more complex.

On the technical, engineering side of the problem, there are still many disputed points regarding the time and motion study methods that are to be used in setting rates. In fact, experts in the field are beginning to acknowledge that rate setting is, at best, a combination of scientific observation and measurement plus personal judgment. (See critiques of current rate-setting methods by Sol Barkin (12, 13), William Gomberg (32), and Adam Abruzzi (1).)

On the social side of the problem, there are perhaps even greater grounds for friction between workers and management.

The time and motion study man is supposed to observe and time a worker proceeding at a "normal" pace. Suppose the worker tries to slow down—as he nearly always does. Then the time and motion study man is supposed to make an allowance for the reduced pace. In other words, he tries to guess by how much the worker is fooling him.

If a rate proves to be too "tight" (permitting insufficient incentive earnings), management is expected to correct the error. But suppose by mistake the rate has been set too "loose." Has management then the right to tighten the rate? And how will management discover such an error? Presumably only if workers earn "too much"—which suggests that it is a good idea to hold back.

Management assumes the right to set a new rate whenever there has been a "major" or "substantial" change in the machine used or in the method of doing the job. Can the parties agree as to what constitutes such a change? And suppose the worker himself has devised the improved method, as often happens. Does he get anything but a rate cut? Or suppose there has been a series of "minor" changes in the job over a period of months or years. How many "minor" changes equal a "major" change? Assuming everyone agrees that a new rate is to be set on a job that has been yielding high earnings, should the new rate permit approximately the same earnings, or should it bring that job down in line with the plant average?

Such issues as these cannot be resolved on the basis of measurements alone. Whether people will be able to resolve them satisfactorily or not will depend upon the pattern of human relations developed among workers, union officers, and management. We cannot separate worker response to money incentives from the social context.

## INTERGROUP RELATIONS

The study of piece rates provides us with an ideal opportunity to demonstrate what the sociologist means when he says that the industrial plant is a social system, made up of interdependent parts. In setting rates, management is not only dealing with the relations of a particular group of workers to management. Like it or not, management is dealing in intergroup relations.

If workers are very much concerned about the *relative* position of their pay in the pay scale of the plant, it naturally follows that when the earnings of group A are increased, this fact will affect B, C, D, and so on, as well as A.

The intergroup problem appears most prominently in the relationship between production and maintenance workers. Generally maintenance workers receive a higher rate of hourly pay because they are thought to exercise a good deal more skill. Some maintenance workers go through a long apprenticeship before they reach the level of journeymen. It is natural, therefore, for them to look down upon production workers who, in many cases, can step in and do their job with little or no training.

On the other hand, it is difficult to measure the productivity of the maintenance worker. The tendency has been therefore to leave him out of the incentive system. When the incentive is then applied to production workers, we often find that their earnings outstrip those of the maintenance men. This naturally leads to protests on their part. One of the most familiar problems of collective bargaining involves the supposed "inequity" adjustments of maintenance workers. Union and management must agree not only on the amount of the wage increase but upon its distribution between production and maintenance workers.

The "inequity" problem may also crop out in the day-to-day life of the plant. The pieceworkers are dependent upon nonpiece workers for supply of materials, repair of machines, and other activities which can make the difference between good and poor incentive earnings. In such a situation, it is natural for the pieceworkers to complain of the poor service they get from the hourly paid men and to try to hurry them up. It is equally natural for the hourly men to resent being pushed in order to make possible earnings in which they do not share. In some plants, this cleavage leads to a breakdown of cooperation among work groups.

Intergroup problems can also arise between two groups which are both on incentive pay. Let us assume that the hourly pay of group A is $2.00 and that of B is $1.90. Ideally, when both are put on the incentive system, their earnings should be such as to maintain the differential. Actually, almost as often as not, the rates will cancel out or even reverse the differential. Thus group A may find itself faced with a "tight" rate on which earnings run between $2.20 and $2.40 while group B, with a "loose" rate, is able to earn $2.70 or more. Group A members then band together to put pressure on management and union leadership to get them a rate which will re-establish the old differential. Management may also face another problem: the overturn of its system of job progression. Let us assume that in the past men have been promoted from job B to job A. Now no one wants to be promoted to a job that earns him substantially less money.

## THE PLANT WIDE SOCIAL SYSTEM

The picture we have presented may make the reader wonder how workers, managers, and union officials can continue to live with a situation so fraught with conflict. While the sources of conflict described have been real, our focusing on these problems has given a misleading impression. We have also observed situations where the parties are getting along rather harmoniously. What makes the difference?

Research suggests that the difference between conflict and cooperation in piece rate situations is not to be found through examining the methods of work measurement used in rate setting in the contrasting cases. The explanation can be found only through placing the time study activities in the social context of the total organization. If worker attitudes toward management are hostile and suspicious, we can predict that, no matter how highly developed the time study techniques, the incentive system will be a focal point of conflict. If workers react toward management with a degree of good will and an expectation of good faith, then there will still be incentive problems, but the parties will develop ways for resolving those problems to mutual satisfaction.

This has been confirmed in case studies (for example, Whyte's *Pattern for Industrial Peace* [84]) where we have seen worker attitudes and reactions to an incentive system change in response to human relations changes taking place throughout the social system.

The point has also been confirmed through a questionnaire on worker reactions to a piece rate system. The Survey Research Center of the University of Michigan found a close relationship between worker reactions to the incentive system and their reactions to their foreman (38). This did not mean, however, that they liked the system if they happened to have a foreman who listened to them sympathetically and was good at explaining things. It was only if this nice person was also thought to be willing and able to intercede for them and get action from management on their problems that they were really inclined to accept the system. In other words, workers were not just responding to pleasant personal relations between themselves and their supervisors. That relationship was affected by the relationship between foreman and the rest of the management organization. Thus we see that worker attitudes toward incentives have to be interpreted in this broader organizational context.

If, in dealing with the individual worker, we are actually dealing with the social system of the entire plant, why should we not base our approach to incentives upon the plant instead of upon the individual? This is the approach that is being taken by a small but increasing number of experimentally minded people. Joseph Scanlon, former staff member of the United Steelworkers and late lecturer at the Massachusetts Institute of Technology, has been responsible for launching some of the most spectacularly successful plans along this line, although similar plans have sprung up independent of his efforts.

While the new approach varies in detail from plant to plant, the fundamental idea is to base the incentive payoff to the individual upon the performance of the entire plant. This requires establishing a base against which the improved performance of the plant may be calculated and then a formula for the division of the fruits of this improvement.

The Scanlon approach to incentives (26, 63, 64) helps to meet some of the difficult human problems we have observed in piece rate systems. In the first place, it eliminates the intergroup struggle over "inequities." It does not eliminate such "inequities" as workers think exist before introduction of the plan, but since it does not change the relative economic position of work groups, it creates no new "inequities."

The plan also eliminates time study for rate-setting purposes, with all the friction that we have seen accompanying such activities.

The new approach, however, poses an entirely different problem in worker motivation. Under the piece rate system, workers may hate the foreman and the time study man and distrust management and still produce more (within limits) in order to win the individual reward. If, in such a situation, we substitute a plant wide formula for the individual incentive and *make no other changes*, we can expect productivity to go down.

The success of the plant wide system therefore depends upon a radical reorganization of human relations. Men must get their satisfactions from the part they play in a collaborative effort. To accomplish this feat of social organization requires an effective integration of individual with work group and of group with total organization. It also involves developing a new pattern of union-management relations.

While the union retains its grievance procedures, it develops a new set of functionaries responsible for bringing to management the workers' ideas regarding more efficient methods. In order to keep this flow of ideas in motion, management must be willing to accept this apparent invasion of management prerogatives and take action upon the suggestions. At the same time, Scanlon argues that management must be willing to put its problems before worker members of the joint committees.

Where the Scanlon Plan is successful, the suggestions for improved efficiency are not limited to changes in a particular machine or method of work. Those which have the greatest effect upon costs involve changes in the flow of work and in the relations of various parts of the organization to each other. The suggestion involves placing a particular problem in a broad, organizational context. It seems that basing the reward upon the performance of the total organization and stimulating activity toward this goal makes possible the development of efficiency ideas which are not brought forth in other types of incentive programs.

The sociologist may well be happy to find that a new approach to social organization yields results that are not gained through the orthodox individual incentive plan. Nevertheless, he should view with some caution the literature that has grown up around the Scanlon Plan. It is a fact that spectacular results have been achieved in some cases. The results have been documented. However, the social process whereby those results have been achieved has never been documented in a manner that carries the conviction of a good case study. We are given anecdotes illustrating the workings of the new plan, but nowhere do we find a detailed description of how the social system functioned before the plan was introduced, of how the plan was introduced, and of how the social system functioned afterward. Furthermore, we read only about the successful cases. Probably we have as much to learn from examining the cases (and there are some) where the Scanlon approach has been tried without success.

## UNION-MANAGEMENT RELATIONS

### *Why join a union?*

Why do people join unions? It is often assumed that the motivation for such an action is simply economic: alone, the worker has no bargaining power; as a member of an organization, he can get better wages and working conditions.

This is certainly one of the appeals to membership, but it is not the only one. As Bakke (11) and Whyte (85) and unionists Golden and Ruttenberg (31) have pointed out, the worker is at least as much interested in the union as an institution for expressing his thoughts and feelings in such a way that they must be acted upon by management. The worker is at the bottom of the industrial hierarchy. In technical terms, management is constantly initiating action for him. Without a union, he feels that it is difficult, if not impossible, to turn around and do much initiating for management.

If we look upon industrial unions, we find that the members are concerned, in a very real sense, with establishing democratic values in factory life. The advent of the union, then, means a shift from unilateral management control to some sort of sharing of control over the factory community. Such changes are accompanied by friction and, in some cases, by intense conflict.

What is the struggle about? Much of the argument concerns money, and this is a real issue but by no means the only one. In *Mutual Survival* (7), Bakke points out that the leaders on both sides are primarily concerned with establishing and maintaining an organization.

This early period of union-management relations presents management with a difficult problem of social adjustment (66). The manager has been accustomed to making decisions without question and passing them down the line. Suddenly he is faced by challenges to his authority on the part of people with whom he has not been accustomed to dealing. He is accustomed to the give and take of argument among his business associates, but it requires considerable adjusting for him to get used to the sometimes blunt challenges issued him by people whom he has been accustomed to thinking of as his employees. Nor is it easy to adjust to the representative of the international union, who perhaps has never worked in this plant and is therefore not a member of the family—as the boss likes to visualize his organization.

This adjustment is made more difficult by the bitter charges and countercharges that accompany many organizing campaigns. The boss often likes to think of himself as being something of a father to his organization, stern at times, perhaps, but always having the best interests of his people at heart. When he suddenly finds himself characterized as a heartless and insincere exploiter of men, the attack naturally comes as a shock to him. Since no one has spoken openly to him in this manner before, he is likely to assume that these ideas have simply been planted among the good people of his organization by outside agitators. He does not recognize that, however exaggerated the charges may be in the heat of the organizing campaign, no union drive can get very far unless there are very real and strong feelings against certain management individuals or policies. These feelings have never reached the attention of the boss before, because, until the advent of the union, there was no recognized channel whereby complaints and suggestions from the work level could be brought up to high management attention.

Faced by such a situation, it is natural for management people to think in terms of establishing a strong, *defensive* position—of maintaining their organization.

In one approach, management people look upon the union as a watch dog. It is up to management, they feel, to take the initiative on all matters from production methods to employee relations. It is up to the union to police the contract, to challenge management for any alleged violation. With this point of view, management people seek to follow the contract legalistically and allow no concessions to the union except in cases where it can be clearly shown that management is violating the letter of the contract.

When management takes this approach, the union members find they experience many frustrations that are not covered in a narrow interpretation of the contract, and they are happy to support their representatives in exercising pressure upon management at any possible point. Thus the approach of the union becomes not one of solving particular problems but of engaging in a war of maneuver, stepping in to curtail management's powers at any point where management appears vulnerable. With this sort of management approach, the union officers are cut off from taking any part in the creative aspects of operating a factory and can gain satisfaction and support only through successfully attacking management. Managers are constantly on the defensive, trying to hold on to powers they believe are essential to operating the business.

The management people struggle to draw a line separating managerial prerogatives or powers from union rights and from certain matters that they will agree to have jointly determined. They experience constant frustrations in this effort because union-management relations are dynamic. The union will never accept any sharply drawn line limiting the activities of its members and officers. Furthermore, as we survey the union-management scene, we find harmonious relations between union and management in situations that are widely different in terms of the prerogatives maintained by management and in terms of those shared between management and union. Thus there seems no way, on a strictly logical basis, to draw a defensible line.

If the management prerogative approach seems to hold no promise for long run harmonious relations, suppose the management tries to cultivate good relations with the union through giving in to the demands of union officers. Can we expect, if management gives enough to the membership through the officers, that the officers will eventually be satisfied and will not push for further gains? In a few cases this policy has been tried with disastrous results. As the officers go in to management to make demands and take victories back to the membership, the members come to expect a constant succession of victories and the position of the officers in relation to the rank and file comes to depend upon this sort of outcome. Furthermore, workers, like other groups of people in American society, are constantly interested in bettering their lot, so that each new gain leads them only to look ahead for new benefits.

This seems to lead to an impasse: no way out of conflict either through giving in to the union or through establishing a firm, defensive position. But actually people do sometimes resolve the conflict. How do they do it (30)?

The field of union-management relations is unfortunately cluttered up with many explanations that have little relation to observed behavior. We are told that the parties bargain on an "arm's length" basis or enjoy an "armed truce" relationship. These picturesque phrases may tell us something about the attitudes of the parties, but they tell us nothing about what people do, with whom, when, and where. Or we are told that the parties hold a "mutual respect" for each other, without being told how they got to feel that way or what actions go along with the attitude. When we are told about actions, we get anecdotal material, useful for illustrative purposes, but no substitute for a systematic statement of the functioning of the union and management social systems.

While much is yet to be learned regarding the dynamics of union-management relations, research has proceeded far enough so that we can begin to state some uniformities in social structure and patterns of interaction (83).

Let us examine the interpersonal contacts taking place among union and management officers at all levels. Let us give particular attention to observing who is initiating action for whom and how often this takes place. (And here, by "initiating" we do not mean just making a personal contact. We mean that A gets B to do something.)

Where we find that the union officers are always (or nearly always) initiating action for management and management—pursuing the "watchdog" philosophy—never seeks to initiate action for the union, then we can confidently expect to find hostile attitudes on both sides and intermittent conflict taking place. In all the cases so far described of harmonious relations (where workers, union officers, and management people all testify they get along well), we find this one striking uniformity, reciprocity in the initiation of action. The management people do not simply respond to union initiative. They seek also to initiate action for the union. Nor is this reciprocity limited to top level relationships. It can arise at all levels, right down to the foreman-steward relationship. In fact, if we can pick out a level where the reciprocity does not exist, we are also pointing to an area of friction.

The problems on which management seeks to initiate action will vary from case to case and from level to level within the same case. At the foreman-steward level, it may involve a discipline problem. The foreman thinks he has a reason for punishing a worker—absenteeism or coming to work under the influence, for example. Instead of taking direct action, he discusses the matter with the steward and asks the steward to try to "straighten the man out." At the top level, management is planning to introduce extensive, technological changes. The contract gives management exclusive control over this aspect of operations. But instead of acting unilaterally, management calls top union leadership in, explains the plans, asks for help in carrying them out—and offers to try to adjust to any suggestions the union people have to offer.

### Changes within management in response to unionization

Although much attention has been given to a study of the determinants of cooperation or conflict between union and management, this is by no means the only important sociological problem in union-management relations. Whether the parties work together harmoniously or not, we find that unionization tends to introduce certain important changes in the structure and activities of the management organization.

The rise of the industrial relations or personnel department in many large companies has been a direct response to unionization. Where before there was perhaps only an employment office, now we have a large department with records to keep, benefit plans to operate, and personnel procedure systems to administer.

Unionization has also been a strong influence toward centralization of decision making in management. Before the coming of unions, in many companies, the foreman was almost an autonomous manager of his shop. He hired anybody he pleased, and he did his firing with equal freedom.

The first move on the part of a union is to seek to limit this freedom of discharge. Faced with a flood of grievances, management cannot any longer leave this matter in the hands of the foreman. The foreman may still be able to initiate the steps that lead to a discharge, but he is carefully coached on his rights and obligations under the contract and under management policies. Furthermore, he is expected to consult with higher line management or the industrial relations department on all but the most clear-cut cases.

The contract will state that the union steward shall seek to resolve a grievance with the foreman before passing it up to higher management. We find, however, that in most cases the foreman has very little freedom in this area. Management recognizes that a decision in one department can be used by the union as a precedent to justify a grievance in another department. Thus all grievances have at least a potential plant wide impact. Management is therefore inclined to exercise supervision or control over the foremen on this point.

This centralization takes place not only at the plant level. Even where the company does not have a company wide contract with a union, management recognizes that a collective bargaining or grievance decision in one plant can be used by the union to exert pressure in other plants. Where management and union have worked out a company wide contract, with arbitration as the final grievance step, the centralization effect is still greater.

The growth of large scale unionism and company wide bargaining has led some students to believe that all the really important union-management decisions affecting life in the plant are taken at a level far above the plant. This suggests that those who spend their time making case studies of plants are not studying important problems.

Certainly we mislead ourselves if we assume that the plant of a large corporation and the local union of a large international are autonomous social systems. On the other hand, we are equally naive if we assume that the top level industrial relations decisions *determine* union-management behavior in the plant. Certain points, such as wage rates, may, of course, be decided at the top and imposed uniformly. However, as Melville Dalton has shown (23), the local plant has a life of its own, influenced, to be sure, by top level action, but not completely dominated from above.

In Dalton's case study, both local management and local union were presumably bound by a company wide contract. Nevertheless, Dalton observed that the actual day to day handling of union-management problems often involved agreements that were not included in the contract or were actually in violation of certain clauses. He found that local people on both sides had pressing local problems to meet and, in meeting them, tended to develop an exchange of favors: you do something for me and I will do something for you. There was just one limitation: the grievances and other matters discussed were not put in writing. It was only when one or both parties wished the matter to come to the attention of higher officials that the grievance would be put in writing and processed through the formally prescribed channels. By handling matters informally, local plant and union officials were able to adjust to their problems and maintain a considerable degree of independence from controls above the plant level. Thus we have formal rigidity balanced by informal flexibility. And, if the student wants to find out what is going on in industrial relations in the plant, he still has to go into the plant to find out. (Of course, the higher level union-management relations are equally legitimate as an object of sociological study. We are simply pointing out that people have a way of getting around centralized controls so that, while they are influenced by the controls, their reactions may be quite different from those anticipated by higher authorities.)

### Evolution of the union

As the union affects the structure and activities of management, so does the relationship with management affect the structure and activities of the union.

During the organizing period, all union activities are pointed toward conflict with management. This tends to be the period of high drama in which the "colorful" figure (the charismatic leader) emerges to try to solidify worker discontents and give them forceful expression. Membership interest and attendance at meetings is likely to be high at this time. Many workers look upon the union as the "lawyer for the defense" (in the words of Leonard Sayles). Whatever their problems, they see the union fighting for the solution of them.

When management recognizes the union, the role of the union leaders necessarily changes. No longer can they seek to get everything for everybody. They learn that management does not accede to all demands. Furthermore, some of the demands of the members actually conflict with each other, so that the leader must make a decision on internal union problems even before making his demands upon management. The skills of negotiation are quite different from those required for leading a body of men into a new union—and often the two types of skills are not found in the same man.

In the process of dealing with management, the union leader necessarily develops personal relationships with some people in management. This does not mean that he goes out to dinner with them or sees them in their social clubs. But he does see them repeatedly in their offices, and these contacts cannot help but build a relationship that goes beyond the formal requirements of the union contract.

The union leader now has to go in and discuss problems with the same man he used to denounce during the organizational drive. If he uses the same aggressive approach, will the manager cave in and give him what he wants? Or will the manager fight back and refuse to make concessions that might have been won through calm discussion? The union leader learns that there is much that a skillful industrial relations man can do to make him "look good" or "look bad" before his membership. By the same token, the industrial relations man recognizes that a skillful union leader can act so as to either strengthen or weaken his position within management.

Thus there are many forces that push the union leader and the industrial relations man into developing a relationship based upon an exchange of favors. This does not mean that the union leader loses interest in the welfare of his members. He tries to get for them as much as he can, but the process of getting is hedged around with situational limitations that he perhaps never even imagined before he began taking the union's problems into the conference room.

Along with the development of stability (even if not cooperation) in union-management relations seems to go a tendency toward centralization of control within the local union.

Most union contracts provide that a worker or workers in a department who feel they have a grievance against management shall present their case to the steward they have elected to represent them. We often see the steward bypassed in the handling of grievances. If the foreman has little power to make any industrial relations decisions, and the steward can only take the grievance to the foreman, then why bother with consulting the steward?

The union member makes the natural assumption that it is to his advantage to put his problem in the hands of the highest official he can get to. Since higher officials try to get around the plant enough to maintain their contacts, it is not difficult for the worker to appeal directly to the chairman of the grievance committee, the local president, or even the international representative. According to the training manuals, the higher official should meet the situation by asking the worker if he has consulted his steward and, if he has not, advising him to take this step first. However, no officer wants to give the impression that he is "too good" for the rank and file.

The increasing complexity of industrial relations issues also contributes toward centralization. A ten cent an hour wage increase is a simple proposition, but the officers may discover that a change in the plant's incentive system can make more than ten cents an hour's difference in worker earnings, so the union must become involved in these problems too. Few stewards can cope with management's industrial engineers in incentive discussions. Probably not more than one or two top officers of the local union can hold their own in this field, and even they may have to call in help from the international union in order to pit union specialist against management specialist.

The intergroup aspect of many union-management problems also contributes to this centralization. We are accustomed to thinking of a grievance as a problem an individual or work group has with management. Research shows that many, if not most, grievances involve intergroup problems. For example, if group A is entitled to the new XYZ job, then it follows that group B is not entitled to it. Such issues obviously cannot be settled at the level of the union steward. We have found that, in

some union locals, the local officers spend more time in trying to work out
these intergroup problems among themselves than they do in arguing the
cases with management.

The evolution of the union-management relationship requires a role
change from leader of a social movement to head of an organization. It
has been observed both by union men and by students that many officers
are unable to make this transition successfully. The man who keeps up
an aggressive and constant attack upon management finds, in most instances, that he cannot produce the day-to-day results that come from
patient negotiation, and in time he is repudiated by the membership.
There are, however, pitfalls just as serious in the other direction. Some
unions leaders are so flattered by the attention they receive from management that they come to look upon many problems from a management
point of view and allow themselves to be estranged from the rank and
file. Accused of "selling out," they too are then overthrown by more
aggressive or more skillful claimants to leadership. Probably very few
union leaders "sell out" in the sense of taking money bribes from management, but many find that, in building firm ties with management,
they lose the ties that make them accepted as workers' representatives.
The role of union leader is a difficult one to play. He must be able to
keep up the pressure on management without the dramatic attacks that
generally lead just to stubborn resistance. He must be able to understand management people without accepting the management point of
view as representing the "true picture" of the situation. He must be able
to negotiate skillfully and patiently and yet be willing to take drastic
action when negotiations break down.

### The role of the union member

As these changes take place in the institution, the role of the union
member undergoes a corresponding change.

Many observers have noted that the institutionalization process is accompanied by a decline in participation in union activities by the rank
and file members. In the period of struggle for recognition, the members
generally turn out to attend meetings in large numbers. Later on, a
crisis period also brings a large turnout, but as the excitement dies down
meeting attendance tends to drop off to from one to five per cent of the
membership.

The state of excitement is not, of course, the only factor influencing
membership attendance at meetings. There seems also to be inverse
correlation between the size of the local and the percentage of meeting

attenders. Presumably the member of a small local feels a link between himself and his work group and his union that is lost in a large organization.

Noting this low meeting attendance, some are inclined to say that the union is not nearly so democratic as it claims to be, that actually it is controlled by a small clique of officers and their close friends. To weigh this criticism, we must consider what meaning we wish to give to words such as "democratic" and "participation."

Some critics seem to be comparing the local union with their ideal of a community governed by a town meeting. There all the citizens turn out to discuss and decide the issues facing their community.

Actually the town meeting approach to government persists only in a few small communities today. As the town grows larger, the town meeting is abandoned. Furthermore, even where it persists, we do not find town meetings taking place every month, as is the practice in most unions. It is unrealistic, then, to hold up against unions a standard of behavior that is not to be observed in community life today.

It is misleading, also, to measure "participation" entirely in terms of meeting attendance—even though many union officers accept that standard and express guilt feelings about the small number of brothers who turn out. The plant itself is a community, and the officers there run into frequent demands for action, requests for information, and critical comments about their abilities—even about their integrity. Nor do the contacts between officer and member cease when the factory whistle blows. The officer hardly has a chance to pick up his beer at the neighborhood bar before some aggrieved member has buttonholed him. And the officer may be telephoned at home at any hour of the day or night.

If these personal contacts fail to bring action, a group of workers may resort to what Sayles and Strauss call "self-help techniques." If a wildcat strike (a walkout unauthorized by the union) seems too risky in the face of management counteraction, members may call attention to themselves and their problems by instituting a slowdown. Experienced factory workers know how to hold back to a point where it is obvious to everyone that a slowdown is in progress and yet where management will find it difficult to take and defend disciplinary action. Many a union officer has thus found himself precipitated into the leadership of a worker action that he wishes had not started at all.

This is not to claim that, through his contacts outside of meetings, the officer gets a good, cross-sectional view of what the members want. It is only a minority of people who seek him out, and he can only guess at what the less active members want of their union. He cannot afford to ignore the silent majority, however, for the identity of the actives and inactives can change with time. In case studies, we have seen very active groups lapse into inactivity and other groups suddenly spring into action. The union officer's problem of gauging the state of public opinion and pressures is much like that of the politician in community affairs. (When we have said that, we have not explained anything. The determinants of member participation in unions still deserve considerably more study.)

While we as students may recognize that it is misleading to compare the union with an *ideal* political community, we find this democratic ideal wielding a powerful influence among the members. They feel that the union should be almost automatically responsive to the general will. They recognize that the development of a bureaucratic organization has placed the levers of control beyond their direct grasp. They may accept this process as inevitable, and yet they take out their resentment against the officers who operate these controls.

They believe, almost unanimously (as various public opinion polls have shown), that a union is a good thing. They also believe that their officers are, through incompetence, favoritism, dishonesty, and various other vices, perverting this fine thing. In our studies, we have been impressed by the readiness with which members will impute ignoble motives to leaders for actions which can be explained entirely in other terms.

How does the union member feel about management? If he is for the union, does this mean that he must be against management?

That this picture of one-sided loyalty is a misconception is one of the best demonstrated propositions in industrial relations research today. Various students (25, 55, 60, 71) have shown that we must think in terms of a dual loyalty. Questionnaire results do show some individuals as prounion and antimanagement and others as antiunion and promanagement, but, statistically, we find substantial correlations indicating that prounionists tend to be promanagement too, while antiunionists tend to be antimanagement also.

What does this mean? The finding suggests that the workers, who hold the bottom positions in the two organizations, are reacting to the total social system of union and management. They recognize, perhaps unconsciously, that what happens to them is decided in a large measure by union and management officials jointly. They therefore do not discriminate among the leaders of the two parties. They decide either that they have a good union-management system or that they have a bad union-management system. (We should not assume, of course, that these reactions are determined entirely by what happens inside the plant. No doubt the individual comes into the plant predisposed to take certain attitudes toward people in positions of authority.)

## THEORY IN INDUSTRIAL SOCIOLOGY

The only good test of a sociological theory is whether it "works" in the sense of enabling its users to explain, predict, or control human events better than has been possible before. This means that we cannot undertake any very useful evaluation of any theory except in connection with an examination of the data to which it is expected to apply.

Such an evaluation would require a long article in itself for each theory discussed. We have therefore decided to limit ourselves to a brief exposition of the main theoretical tools in use with each "approach" and to the raising of some questions about the utility of these tools.

The first approach for our consideration is that which grows out of the main stream of sociological theory, stemming particularly from Max Weber, but with the influence of other scholars also. With the risk of doing violence to individuals, we might place together here such researchers as Reinhardt Bendix, Herbert Blumer, Robert Dubin, Alvin Gouldner, Seymour Lipset, Robert Merton, Wilbert Moore, and Philip Selznick. They have in common an interest in the study of such broad problem areas as the processes of bureaucracy, power relations, the organization in its "social matrix," and the professionalization process.

The approach lends itself to an examination of important trends in our society. It is not so well adapted toward the prediction or control of behavior in specific, interpersonal situations. In fact, most of those following this approach have not been chiefly interested in observing a particular work group and applying their conclusions to this group first before generalizing to other units. Their interests have been broader from the outset.

Alvin Gouldner is an exception to this statement. For example, he sets out to test some of the Weber ideas about bureaucracy (33), plus certain psychological concepts (34), but he makes the test in a remarkably detailed case study of human relations in a factory. It seems to us that there is a wide gap between Weber and the specific interpersonal data that Gouldner has not quite been able to bridge. However, it is efforts of this sort that can lead to theoretical advance.

Since the work of this group stems from the whole of sociological theory, we cannot here undertake anything so ambitious as a critique of that body of theory. Let us turn to those schemes specifically developed for application to face-to-face relations in groups inside or outside of industry.

Beginning in 1945, E. Wight Bakke has been developing and restating his theory of "adaptive human behavior" (4, 5, 8). Central to Bakke's theory is the concept of the "structure of living" as the pattern whereby (a) *individuals* mobilize (b) the *human, social*, and *natural resources* available to them to attain (c) *desired goals*. Goal attainment is aided and/or channeled by socially or culturally defined (d) *reinforcements*, such as codes, symbols, and rituals, which make features of the structure seem "right and stable."

For the explanation of collective behavior Bakke first analyzed seven social processes, which he called "bonds of organization." The seven "parts of the social system" are the following systems of activities or processes: (a) *workflow*, (b) *authority*, (c) *reward and punishment*, (d) *perpetuation*—i.e., activities required to keep the organization supplied with adequate personnel, ideas, and materials as needed, (e) *communication*, (f) *status*, and (g) *integration*—i.e., "activities which define, express, and symbolize the organization as a whole" and identify it as special and particular.

How do the individual's adaptations and the organizational bonds fit together? Bakke gives his explanation in terms of two major processes (8).

The *fusion process* by which individual and organization work out a *modus vivendi* consists of the simultaneous operation of the *socializing process* and the *personalizing process*. The socializing process consists of the ways in which the individual becomes an *agent* of the organization, while the personalizing process consists of the ways in which the individual attempts to make the organization into an agent of *his*.

The second process basic to individual-in-organizational theory is the *problem-solving process* by which individual agents meet organizational and personal goals. The stages in the problem-solving process (many of which are "internally" quite complicated) are: (a) awareness of stimulus, (b) structuring, (c) simplification, (d) cue observation, (e) anticipatory response, (f) decision and mobilization, (g) responses, (h) experience, judgment, and feeling, (i) fixation or rejection of response, and (j) closure or renewal.

The main question to be directed at Bakke's scheme concerns its great complexity. Certainly Bakke's concepts point at many if not all the important aspects of behavior in organization that should be studied. However, we may point to the "law of parsimony" in this respect: the proposition that scientific advance depends upon building first upon a minimum of concepts. We may wonder whether the complexity of the Bakke system will not prevent its widespread use.

The Lewin field theory approach * is designed to explore the perceptions of the individual of his social world. Lewin represented his system with a diagram of the individual's *life space*. The individual is thought of as occupying one *region* in this life space. At the other end is a region which attracts the individual, or, in Lewin's terminology, has a *positive valence* for him. To reach this goal region, the individual must pass through one or more other regions on the way. Each of these regions may offer some degree of resistance to the individual and thus be thought of as a *barrier*.

A region may also be unattractive to the individual or represent a *negative valence* for him. A conflict exists within the individual when he has to go through a region of negative valence in order to reach the region of positive valence, or when his goal region contains elements of both positive and negative valence for him.

In response to the forces of positive and negative valences, the individual is seen as undertaking locomotion through the regions of his *life space*. To predict his behavior, then, we must know his perceptions of positive and negative valences and the structure of his *life space*—that is, the placement of the regions and barriers he needs to go through in the process of his locomotion.

Field theory has the merit of drawing attention to the importance of understanding the way the individual conceives the world around him. At the same time, it appears to have the corresponding limitation: it is built entirely upon the individual's *perceptions*. Nowhere in the scheme do we have a systematic way of relating perception to the world of action. The term locomotion appears to provide such a link, but that word covers an endless variety of observable behavior plus a similar variety of nonobservable changes in mental or emotional states. Anything an individual does or decides to do, in effect, can be considered locomotion.

When an individual has taken a certain action toward a certain goal, it can be explained that the balance of positive and negative valences was such as to propel him in that direction. However, before the individual acts, can we use the scheme to predict how he is going to act? In other words, how effectively can we use a scheme built entirely upon perceptions in predicting and controlling observable behavior? Further-

---

* For help in condensing the Lewin theory, we particularly depended upon Morris S. Viteles, *Motivation and Morale in Industry* (76). Since ours is a condensation of Viteles' condensation we can hardly claim to do justice to the original. The most complete succinct version of Lewin's theory can be found in his posthumously published papers (44).

more, how effectively can we use a scheme based upon the individual in exploring problems in organization structure?

Another approach goes under the heading of interaction theory. The approach was first stated by social anthropologists, namely, Eliot D. Chapple and Conrad M. Arensberg, and has been used in industry by them and by a number of others, including F. L. W. Richardson, Jr., George C. Homans, and William F. Whyte. These men differ on some points that are beyond the scope of the chapter to explore. The version presented here follows George Homans, as set forth in *The Human Group.**

We shall limit ourselves to the three chief concepts of the Homans statement: *interaction, sentiments,* and *activities.* The aspects of human relations referred to by the concepts are seen as mutually dependent: that is, a change in one will give rise to changes in the other two.

*Interaction* refers to interpersonal contacts. The frequency and duration of these interactions can be observed and quantified. We can also observe initiation and response: when A and B interact, we note whether A initiates a behavior change for B or vice versa.

In an organization, these interactions tend to have a definite pattern. Arensberg has suggested (2) that we look at an organization in terms of the following sets of relations: worker-worker (flow of work), worker-worker (informal), up and down the line of authority, and line and staff. For a unionized situation, we may add interactions up and down the union structure, and union-management interactions at each point of contact. The assumption is that these various sets are not independent of each other. On the contrary, a change in one set is expected to be accompanied by changes in others.

Another aspect of relationships is the kind of *sentiments* associated with certain interaction patterns. *Sentiments* are psychological states about topics or persons, emotionally charged, with some stability through time. They cannot be directly observed or measured, but must be inferred from a person's words or actions. Sentiments and interactions are mutually dependent. That is, my sentiments toward others both *influence* my interactions with them and *are influenced* by our interaction pattern.

The third major component of relationships is *activities*—observable physical actions. Examples would be: amount and kind of work done (reflecting the worker's formal role and the technology of the social system), horseplay, attendance or absenteeism, and punctuality, all of which are quantifiable through observation or organizational records.

* New York, Harcourt, Brace, 1950.

Activities, too, are considered interdependent with the other two components of relationships, both influencing and being influenced by interactions and sentiments. For example, amount of output is both a cause and effect of the interactions a worker has with fellow workers and his foreman, and of the sentiments he and they hold about group solidarity and "a fair day's work."

How useful is this approach? Since the "interactionists" are among those who have been particular targets for critics of research in industrial sociology, our evaluative comments will be reserved for the final section of this chapter.

Our brief review has indicated that we sociologists are far from agreement upon any theoretical scheme in this area. However, the description of concepts is likely to give a more confusing picture than is really justified. Researchers may disagree about the terms they use, but to an increasing degree there seems to be agreement upon what we are observing and, to some extent, even upon the interpretation of these observations. For example, to return to the work of Gouldner in his analysis of a wildcat strike (34), many of us who follow quite different theoretical orientations can agree that he has presented the data we need for our analysis and can even agree with his interpretation up to a point— though each of us would translate Gouldner's terms into our own language. As long as researchers representing different theoretical points of view will present to their colleagues bodies of data that can be subjected to analysis from other points of view, we can expect gradual progress toward a more commonly held and more generally useful scheme.

## HUMAN RELATIONS AND ITS CRITICS

While the field of industrial sociology has enjoyed a remarkable expansion in both teaching and research activity, this growth has been viewed with alarm by many sociologists and economists. No one has questioned that there is a legitimate field of activity for the sociologist among the problems we have described in this chapter. Nor have most industrial sociologists been under fire. Criticisms have been largely directed at those identified with the term "human relations"—particularly Elton Mayo, T. N. Whitehead, F. J. Roethlisberger, Burleigh B. Gardner, George C. Homans, and William F. Whyte. The most active critics have been Herbert Blumer (18), Wilbert Moore (50, 51), C. Wright Mills (49), Daniel Bell (15), Harold Sheppard (69), John T. Dunlop (27), and Clark Kerr and Lloyd H. Fisher (40).

In such a summary chapter, it will not be possible to review all the points made by the critics. Fortunately for our task, however, there has been quite general agreement among them as to the chief points at issue, so that we can undertake to present this main stream of thought.

The critics argue that certain writers on human relations in industry fail to present an adequate description and analysis because of these factors:

1. *An anti-individualism bias.* The writers assume that the individual cannot be happy in isolation and can lead a satisfactory life only in completely submerging himself into the group.

2. *An antirationality bias.* In pointing out that man does not react as a completely rational animal, human relations people have gone overboard to discard rationality altogether. They present a picture of workers as being completely dominated by "sentiments." (Points 1 and 2 are particularly emphasized by economist Clark Kerr.)

3. *Acceptance of stability and harmony as the goals of human relations in industry.* The researchers, beginning with Mayo, have been biased by a nostalgic picture of medieval society in which every man knew his position and relations among men were exceedingly stable. The goal of some researchers is to find out how to provide the closest approximation possible of such stability and harmony under present industrial conditions. This is to be brought about by making the plant manager the leader of the industrial community, by endowing him with the social skills necessary for manipulating the workers so that they will willingly accept management goals.

4. *Subordinating the union to management goals.* At first, critics claimed that human relations researchers failed to consider unions at all. As the volume of human relations studies dealing with union-management relations piled up, the basis of the criticism was changed. The researchers now deal with the union, to be sure, but they see it only as it fits into a framework provided by management. They unwittingly accept the objective that harmony is to be achieved through having the union accept the goals of management: stability in industrial relations, increasing productivity, lowered costs, etc.

5. *Viewing all problems as problems in communication.* The researchers do not recognize any conflicts of interests between workers and management. They assume that conflicts are due to poor communication. Therefore, if the parties can learn to communicate more skillfully, their problems will be resolved. Dunlop (27), for example, says that, "the 'human relations' approach is more or less identified here with the study of communications."

6. *Ignoring the problem of power.* By looking at everything in terms of human relations, the researchers fail to see that who has the power in

any given situation is an important determinant of the course of events.

7. *Ignoring the impact of the larger economic and social environment upon the social system of the factory.* With their interest in small group studies and in face-to-face relations, the researchers tend to look upon the factory as if it existed in a state of isolation.

Since one of the present authors has been a target of these criticisms, we cannot pretend to make an impartial review of the arguments. However, since there has been so much heat generated in these discussions, we shall do our best to avoid a simple counterattack but shall try to utilize the criticisms to point the way toward an improved program of research.

In brief, we feel that some of the arguments raised have merit and should be taken seriously. Others are based upon a misunderstanding of some of the human relations literature—but such misunderstanding is based at least in part upon certain conceptual problems that we shall seek to clarify. Finally, some of the points made are to be explained in terms of the research methodology that has been in use, and this, too, needs further exploration.

The problem of the anti-individualistic, antirationality bias should be seen in terms of a reaction against the economic man theory so prominent in industry around the time of the first human relations studies. While recognizing that their concept did not fully represent reality, economists had been looking upon the worker as an isolated individualist, engaged in the rational calculation of his economic advantages. Many management people had unthinkingly accepted this point of view as reality. Neither in management thinking nor in economic theory was there any systematic way of dealing with groups of men or with anything other than rational economic calculation.

To correct this one-sided view, human relations researchers emphasized the importance of the group and of sentiments or attitudes that are neither based entirely upon intellectual processes nor limited to the economic aspects of life. As often happens in the course of scientific advance, to destroy an existing theory, we have overstated the case against it. We doubt whether much evidence can be mustered to support the charge that human relations researchers really believed that the individual could find happiness only in "complete submergence" in the group. However, we have been so concerned with demonstrating the importance of the human group that we make ourselves vulnerable to the charge of forgetting about the individual.

Similarly, we have been so concerned with discrediting the rational, economic man, that we have given the impression that we do not believe economic considerations are very important or that workers do much thinking about them. Certainly this is a confusing and unfortunate impression. Perhaps the recent research on incentives and human relations, summarized earlier, best demonstrates the point that workers take a very keen interest in money and do some shrewd calculating in this regard.

We need now a better integration of theory about industrial man. This does not mean simply the recognition that the individual and the group are both important, that economic and noneconomic considerations are both important too, or that the individual reacts rationally and nonrationally as well (16). The real problem is how to fit these various aspects together in one coherent scheme for the study of human behavior in industry.

On the individual-group problem, for example, we may quite properly emphasize the importance of the group and of group life for the individual. However, the earliest studies may have given a misleading impression that the informal group in the factory necessarily has a very stable and strong structure. Certainly the informal organization of the "bank wiring room," described by Roethlisberger and Dickson (59), was of that nature. This was such a classic study, representing such a rich vein of observational data and of human relations analysis, that we tended to look upon informal organization on the model of this room, even though the authors made no claim that all groups were like this. In more recent studies (62) we have been finding work groups with this solid, stable structure but others where the ties among the men are relatively weak, where groups form and disintegrate rapidly, and where individuals move in and out of a group. It is misleading, therefore, to think of *the* individual and *the* group. We need instead to seek to discover the factors that lead to a strong or a weak group (in terms of ability of individuals to take concerted action), that lead to changes in group structure, and that lead individuals into and out of groups. This process will lead to an understanding of individuals and groups that is not to be obtained through philosophical arguments over the relative importance of one or the other.

On the question of rational, economic man, similarly, we need to develop out of our studies some scheme that will fit together man's reactions to economic *and* noneconomic aspects of his environment and will encompass his thinking processes along with his emotional processes.

On the question of the stability bias, critics and those criticized have both been trapped by an analogy from the natural sciences: the concept of equilibrium. It is assumed that we are talking about *static equilibrium,* a condition in which any change introduced tends to lead the system to react to restore its pre-existing condition. Actually, we have been thinking in terms of *dynamic equilibrium*, a concept which points to the inevitability of change but focuses upon the magnitude and rate of changes. We shall probably clarify the problem if we abandon the concept of equilibrium altogether, since we have no measures for it and therefore no way of establishing the state of equilibrium or disequilibrium of the organization.

The idea behind the words is important, however, and not to be discarded. Ours is a society characterized by sudden and drastic changes. We cannot return to the stability of the Middle Ages, nor do we know any researchers who are thinking in terms of such a model. At the same time, it has been recognized both by men in industry and researchers that the introduction of change is often accompanied by serious maladjustments and human conflicts. Still, such results do not seem to be inevitable. We have seen cases (14, 21) where significant changes have been introduced without such disorganization and have even been accepted with high morale by workers and management people alike. While it would be going up a blind alley to seek to discover how the factory could become a stable, static organization, it certainly seems a legitimate scientific inquiry to try to determine the effects of change of various sorts upon an organization and the reactions in peoples' attitudes and activities according to the ways in which the changes are carried out.

Is such a study designed to show management how it can succeed in effecting the changes it wants with a minimum resistance from workers and union leaders? Research so far indicates that it is possible to avoid conflict and disorganization in introducing change only if management is willing to relinquish unilateral control over the change process. We are finding that people accept change insofar as they actively participate in the process whereby change is carried out. Nor does participation mean just having the management "sell" workers and union officers with thorough explanations. It means involving the people who are going to be affected in the decision-making process and in the process of carrying out those decisions.

On the harmony question, it is argued that the very choice of union-management cooperation as a problem for study involves a value judgment. Obviously, that is true. We cannot prove scientifically that it is more important to study cooperation than some other possibility. Some of us have just been inclined to think that there is a lot of conflict going on in industry, as well as elsewhere, and that people do not seem to need any scientific guidance as to how to get into a fight but perhaps might benefit from understanding the conditions of cooperation in the work place.

Critics make quite a different point when they say that we have, consciously or unconsciously, accepted a management goal in the study of cooperation. The objective of our study then is assumed to be to show management how to get workers and union leaders to do just what management wants and be happy—or at least uncomplaining—in the process.

Many management people wish they could find the formula for reaching that goal. If they read the research results, however, they are bound to be disappointed, for no such formula has as yet been found.

It is quite correct, as some critics have noted, that in the cases of cooperation described in human relations research, union leaders and many workers, too, have come to take an interest in getting along with management, in increasing productivity, and, in general, have taken a friendlier attitude toward some of management's cherished values. However, that is only one side of the picture. Although the critics have overlooked the point, the research findings make it abundantly clear that cooperation involves important adjustments *on both sides.* The management people, in their turn, have accepted some of the values dear to the hearts of workers and union leaders. In effect, they have agreed that changes having important effects upon workers are not to be subject to management's unilateral decision, that the fruits of increasing productivity shall be shared with workers, and so on to a number of points that will vary from case to case.

It seems to be assumed that harmony to us means an absence of human problems which, in turn, means a passive acceptance by workers of management decisions. This is not borne out in the cases reported. Where we have found cooperation, we have not found an absence of human problems but rather an effective union-management system for resolution of the problems that constantly arise. And the reactions of union leaders are anything but a passive acceptance of management actions. We see the union people taking a very active role in the decisions that are made.

Nor is it correct to assume that top management people are necessarily the leaders in achieving cooperation. Union leaders play an equally important role, in the cases that have been reported (35, 63, 84).

Perhaps, then, what the human relations researchers are really trying to do is show both management and union leaders how to *manipulate* workers toward union-management goals. To this point, there are two answers.

The first involves a scrutiny of the word manipulate, which is loaded with value judgments. We tend to think that if a man influences people in a direction we approve of, he is exercising effective leadership, whereas if he is leading people in the wrong direction, then he is just manipulating them. Whatever our value judgments may be, no one can deny that we live in a society of organizations, in which the behavior of the key people of those organizations has tremendous effects upon the lives of the members. In studying leadership, then, we are studying an important problem. It is true, of course, that in providing leaders with more knowledge of the leadership process we provide them with tools that can be used in the pursuit of goals of which we disapprove. Should we then refuse to study leadership at all?

Such a question cannot be given a scientific answer. At this point in civilization, we seem to be committed to scientific progress, and the knowledge thus gained is always available to a variety of possible uses. If the researcher gets to the point of trying to apply his knowledge to an organization, he must then make the judgment as to what uses of such knowledge he will promote, but that problem in itself does not affect the validity of his research findings.

The second answer involves examining the reactions of the followers in the organization. Research has shown that union leaders do not maintain a cohesive organization with high morale simply through communicating their ideas skillfully to the rank and file. If they do not also respond to the initiation of action on the part of the rank and file, they find that they are no longer able to get the workers to follow their lead, and they may be repudiated at an election of officers. There have been many cases in which a close, cooperative relationship between management and union officers led to an estrangement of the officers from the rank and file and a repudiation of these officers. Thus it cannot be assumed that the workers are mere pawns at the mercy of the maneuverings of management and union leaders (9).

On the questions of communication and interest and power conflicts, the argument has been based largely upon a misunderstanding of the use of certain concepts, and this, in turn, has been partly due to a failure of the researchers to clarify the meaning of the concepts. The problem revolves around the use of the term interaction. Some of us have been interested in observing the *initiation of interaction,* the making of a personal contact. We find that one can learn some significant facts about an organization by determining the frequency and duration of contacts among people and also through noting which individual takes the initiative in making the contact. Let us say that A begins talking to B, asks B to do something, and B responds by refusing to do it. In this sense, we would say that A has initiated interaction for B and B has responded to A.

Such a definition suggests that the important thing in human relations is the pattern of communication among the people. Presumably a leader needs some skill to establish and maintain this pattern of communication, but, given this skill, no conflicts are to be expected.

However, without really clarifying the distinction, various researchers have been using the term interaction in quite a different sense. They speak of the origination or initiation of action or activity (with a confusing lack of uniformity of terminology). In this sense, if A asks B to do something and B refuses to do it, *A has not initiated action for B.* Initiation of action takes place only when B's response is in line with what A is trying to get him to do. This sort of definition involves some difficult and unresolved methodological problems. What A is trying to get B to do is not always obvious, nor is it always easy to determine whether B's action fits in with what A was seeking. It is much easier to observe and measure the frequency and initiation of contacts. However, it clearly does make a good deal of difference in an organization whether B does or does not do what A is trying to get him to do. So, for all the methodological difficulties, we have been dealing with union-management relations in terms of the *initiation of action* (and not simply of the initiation of interaction).

Following this approach, we are not just interested in knowing whether the foreman has listened to the worker and understood him. In other words, communication alone is not enough. Sometimes the worker just wants to express himself and is glad to have somebody listen to him, but, at other times, he wants the foreman to take some action in response to this conversation. If the foreman does not act, then the worker has not initiated action for him—even if the foreman has been most friendly and understanding. Furthermore, on many problems the worker brings up, the foreman will not be able to act without getting approval from higher authority. In effect, then, for the worker to initiate for the foreman, the foreman must initiate action for his boss—and on some problems the initiation must carry through several levels of the organization. If the initiation does not so carry through, then the foreman may perhaps be looked upon by workers as a "nice guy," but the human problems will remain unresolved. In this sense, we are not dealing simply with smooth or rough relations among individuals. We are dealing with the flow of *action* within an organization and between organizations such as union and management.

This brings us to the problem of power. Power is frequently discussed in a very abstract and philosophical sense. We are indeed interested in some of the things people mean by the term, but we are concerned with looking at power in terms that involve the observation of behavior. Here we suggest that when the researcher is examining the initiation of action, he is, in effect, studying the distribution of power. Does A initiate action for B, and how often—and vice versa? What are the conditions under which management official initiates for union officer? What are the conditions under which union officer initiates for management official? And so on for various individual and group relationships. And what happens when there is a great change in the initiation of action between any two points in the social system?

We are also concerned with interest conflicts in industry, but here we see a much more complicated picture than has been suggested by some critics. Some of the critics tend to see workers and management each as homogeneous groups and as having different and sometimes conflicting interests. The interest conflicts are real, to be sure. We can discover through interviewing and observation that workers and managements tend to want different things out of the organization (although there seems to be also a considerable overlapping in what they want). However, as we look at the factory, we do not see a simple division between two camps. On the management side, we see divisions of interest between production and industrial engineering, between production and accounting, among various levels of the production organization, between plant and home office, and so on. On the worker side, we see divisions among workers on the lines of production versus maintenance, day rate versus piece rates, long versus short seniority, low versus high skill, and so on. We are not suggesting that these divisions within management and within the union cancel out any differences of interests between workers and management. We are suggesting that to look at the picture simply in terms of workers versus management is such an oversimplification as to be highly misleading. The industrial organization is a balance (perhaps a precarious balance) of conflicting and congruent interests. We are studying interests in the context of the structure of the industrial organization.

Some years ago, economist John Dunlop charged (27, pages 383–393) that human relations researchers were assuming that the plant was a closed system, unaffected by the economic environment or by the structure of the company of which it made up a part. Whyte replied (27, pages 393–401) that we are indeed interested in the environment, but that the impact of the environment must be studied as it appears in the behavior of the people inside of the plant. The answer is useful in pointing out that we cannot study everything at the same time, that we must focus our attention at some point, and that we can see the impact of the environment reflected in the behavior of people within the plant. However, the answer is not completely satisfactory, for, when we concentrate our attention on behavior within the plant, we are likely to find our explanations for that behavior also within the plant.

The industrial sociologist will agree at once that behavior in the plant is not to be explained solely on an in-plant basis, that plant and community mutually affect each other. However, this affirmation poses methodological problems that highlight some of the difficulties we currently face.

Industrial sociology grew out of the sociological and anthropological study of small groups and of relatively small societies. We have learned to concentrate upon people we personally observe and upon what they tell us. We have learned a good deal about studying, for example, a plant of the U. S. Steel Corporation, but we have not developed the methods to study the U. S. Steel Corporation as a whole. To be sure, our methods would enable us to study the Board of Directors of the Corporation as a small group, but so far it has been much easier to get research access at the plant level than at the top management level.

Similarly, we have given lip service to the industry-community relationship, but so far the task of studying two social systems at once has been beyond our powers.

We must then acknowledge these limitations of our methods and theories. However, let us not throw out what has so far been achieved with them. Through the work of the industrial sociologists we have gained a rich knowledge of how individuals and groups actually do behave in industry, and the nature and functioning of the organizational structure is much better understood than it was when only economists and industrial psychologists were studying industry.

The methods of observation and interviewing developed by the industrial sociologist can now be used against a broader organizational and environmental perspective.

Research of recent years has demonstrated that the state of human relations in an organization is not to be explained entirely in terms of the social skills and attitudes of the members. In fact, these skills may be a relatively small part of the explanation and they themselves may be subject to influence by certain other conditions. Many research men now are inclined to examine human relations against the formal structure of the organization, the flow of work (including paper work), and the technology, as well as in terms of the flow of interpersonal interaction. The assumption is that the nature of human relations is more affected by changes in formal organization, the flow of work, and the technology than by changes in the leadership skills of individuals.

The role of formal organization needs further explanation here. Early research in the field amply demonstrated that the industrial organization does not function according to the ideas of the men who make up the charts of the formal organization. It does not follow from this, however, that the structure of the formal organization is unimportant. We are now convinced that this structure has an exceedingly important impact upon the behavior of people, and it is our task as students of organization to examine systematically this connection between formal structure and behavior.

This does not mean, necessarily, that we must make the richly detailed observational studies characteristic of the field in the past for each case in which we are studying the impact of the formal organization (or the technology) upon human relations. If we can say that with a certain type of organizational structure we can expect to find a certain specified pattern of human relations, then we shall be able to accelerate our progress immensely. Then we can select the case to be studied in terms of the type of structure it represents and select the crucial observations to be made in order to test the hypothesis regarding organizational structure and human relations.

In the industry-community problem area, we can proceed in the same way. Perhaps we shall never learn how to make a community study and a factory case study, side by side, and then relate them effectively to each other. If we take the industry-community relationship as the focus of our interest, we can hypothesize that a certain type of community social structure will be associated with a specified pattern of human relations within the plant—or that a certain type of in-plant social system will be associated with a specified type of community social structure. We can then select our cases and the data necessary to be collected for them in terms of their suitability for hypothesis testing.

A few years ago, it probably would have been unwise to narrow our focus of attention so greatly. We needed the background knowledge obtained from the fully developed case studies in order to formulate hypotheses worth testing. By now we have piled up a rich enough supply of case studies so that we should be able to concentrate our efforts upon more rigorously formulated problems and therefore make more rapid scientific progress.

## BIBLIOGRAPHICAL REFERENCES

1. Abruzzi, Adam, *Work Measurement Principles and Procedures*, New York, Columbia University Press, 1952.

2. Arensberg, Conrad M., "Industry and the Community," *Amer. J. Soc.*, Vol. 48 (1942), pp. 1–12.

3. Arensberg, Conrad M., and Douglas McGregor, "Determination of Morale in an Industrial Company," *Applied Anthropology*, Vol. 1 (1942), pp. 12–34.

4. Bakke, E. Wight, *Adaptive Human Behavior,* New Haven, Yale University Labor and Management Center, 1945, 1948, 1951.

5. Bakke, E. Wight, *Bonds of Organization,* New York, Harper and Brothers, 1950.

6. Bakke, E. Wight, *Citizens Without Work,* New Haven, Yale University Press, 1940.

7. Bakke, E. Wight, *Mutual Survival,* New York, Harper and Brothers, 1946.

8. Bakke, E. Wight, *Organization and the Individual,* New Haven, Yale University Labor and Management Center, 1952.

9. Bakke, E. Wight, *The Unemployed Man,* London, Nesbet and Company, 1933.

10. Bakke, E. Wight, *The Unemployed Worker,* New Haven, Yale University Press, 1940.

11. Bakke, E. Wight, *Why Workers Join Unions,* New Haven, Yale University Labor and Management Center, Reprint No. 1.

12. Barkin, Sol, "Concepts in the Measurement of Human Application," *Industrial and Labor Relations Review,* Vol. 7 (1953), pp. 103–118.

13. Barkin, Sol, "Diversity of Time Study Practice," *Industrial and Labor Relations Review,* Vol. 7 (1953), pp. 537–549.

14. Bavelas, Alex, "Some Problems of Organizational Change," *Journal of Social Issues,* Vol. 4 (1948), pp. 48–52.

15. Bell, Daniel, "Adjusting Men to Machines," *Commentary,* Vol. 3 (1947), pp. 79–88.

16. Bendix, Reinhard, "Compliance and Initiative in Bureaucratic Conduct," in Robert Dubin (ed.), *Human Relations in Administration,* New York, Prentice-Hall, 1951.

17. Blumer, Herbert, "Morale," in W. F. Ogburn (ed.), *American Society in Wartime,* Chicago, University of Chicago Press, 1943.

18. Blumer, Herbert, "Sociological Theory in Industrial Relations," *Amer. Soc. Rev.,* Vol. 12 (1947), pp. 271–278.

19. Chapple, Eliot D., "The Interaction Chronograph," *Personnel,* Vol. 25 (1949), pp. 295–307.

20. Chapple, Eliot D., and Conrad M. Arensberg, "Measuring Human Relations," *Genetic Psychology Monographs,* Vol. 22 (1940), pp. 3–147.

21. Coch, Lester, and John R. P. French, Jr., "Overcoming Resistance to Change," *Human Relations,* Vol. 1 (1948), pp. 512–532.

22. Cottrell, W. Fred, "Death by Dieselization," *Amer. Soc. Rev.,* Vol. 16 (1951), pp. 358–365.

23. Dalton, Melville, "Unofficial Labor-Management Relations," in Robert Dubin (ed.), *Human Relations in Administration,* New York, Prentice-Hall, 1951.

24. Davis, Allison, Burleigh Gardner, and Mary Gardner, *Deep South,* Chicago, University of Chicago Press, 1943.

25. Dean, Lois R., "Union Activity and Dual Loyalty," *Industrial and Labor Relations Review,* Vol. 7 (1954), pp. 526–536.

26. Dreyser, Harold E., "The Scanlon Plan: An Analysis and Case Study," Unpublished doctoral dissertation, Massachusetts Institute of Technology, Cambridge, Mass., 1952.

27. Dunlop, John T., and William F. Whyte, "A Framework for the Analysis of Industrial Relations: Two Views," *Industrial and Labor Relations Review,* Vol. 3 (1950), pp. 383–412.

28. Friedmann, George, *Problemes Humaines du Machinisme Industriel,* Paris, Gallimard, 1946.

29. Gardner, Burleigh, and David Moore, *Human Relations in Industry*, Homewood, Ill., Richard D. Irwin, 1951.

30. Garfield, Sidney, and William F. Whyte, "The Collective Bargaining Process: A Human Relations Analysis—Part I," *Human Organization*, Vol. 9 (1950), pp. 5–10.

31. Golden, Clinton, and Harold J. Ruttenberg, *The Dynamics of Industrial Democracy*, New York, Harper and Brothers, 1942.

32. Gomberg, William, *A Trade Union Analysis of Time Study*, Chicago, Science Research Associates, 1948.

33. Gouldner, Alvin, *Patterns of Industrial Bureaucracy*, Glencoe, Ill., The Free Press, 1954.

34. Gouldner, Alvin, *Wildcat Strike*, Yellow Springs, Ohio, The Antioch Press, 1954.

35. Harbison, Frederick, and Robert Dubin, *Patterns of Union-Management Relations*, Chicago, Science Research Associates, 1947.

36. Hemphill, John K., *Leader Behavior Description*, Columbus, Ohio State University Personnel Research Board, 1950.

37. Hollingshead, August B., *Elmstown's Youth*, New York, John Wiley and Sons, 1949.

38. "Human Relations Research in Large Organizations," entire issue of *Journal of Social Issues*, Vol. 7, No. 3 (1951); eds.: Eugene Jacobson, Robert Kahn, Floyd Mann, and Nancy Morse.

39. Katz, Daniel, Nathan Maccoby, and Nancy Morse, *Productivity, Supervision, and Morale in an Office Situation*, Survey Research Center, Institute for Social Research, Ann Arbor, University of Michigan, 1950.

40. Kerr, Clark, and Lloyd H. Fisher, "Plant Sociology; The Elite and the Aborigines," in Mirra Kamarovsky (ed.), *Common Frontiers of Social Science* (in press), Glencoe, Ill., The Free Press.

41. Kerr, Clark, and Abraham Siegel, "The Inter-industry Propensity to Strike," in Arthur Kornhauser, Robert Dubin, and Arthur Ross (eds.), *Industrial Conflict*, New York, McGraw-Hill Book Co., 1954.

42. Lagemann, John K., "Job Enlargement Boosts Productivity," *Nation's Business*, Vol. 42 (1954), pp. 34–37.

43. Leighton, Alexander H., *Human Relations in a Changing World*, New York, E. P. Dutton and Co., 1949.

44. Lewin, Kurt, *Field Theory in Social Science*, New York, Harper and Brothers, 1951.

45. Lewin, Kurt, "Group Decision and Social Change," in T. Newcomb and E. Hartley (eds.), *Readings in Social Psychology*, New York, Henry Holt and Co., 1949.

46. Lewin, Kurt, Ronald Lippitt, and R. K. White, "Patterns of Aggressive Behavior in Experimentally Graded Social Climates," *Journal of Social Psychology*, Vol. 10 (1939), pp. 271–299.

47. Likert, Rensis, "Motivational Dimensions of Administration," *America's Manpower Crisis*, Chicago, Public Administration Service [n.d.].

48. Likert, Rensis, Floyd Mann, and Nancy Morse, *Employee Attitudes and Output*, Survey Research Center, Institute for Social Research, Ann Arbor, University of Michigan, 1952.

49. Mills, C. Wright, "The Contributions of Sociology to Studies of Industrial Relations," *Industrial Relations Research Association Proceedings*, Vol. 1 (1948), pp. 199–222.

50. Moore, Wilbert, "Current Issues in Industrial Sociology," *Amer. Soc. Rev.*, Vol. 12 (1947), pp. 651–657.

51. Moore, Wilbert, "Industrial Sociology, Status and Prospects," *Amer. Soc. Rev.*, Vol. 13 (1948), pp. 382–391.

52. Morse, Nancy, *Satisfactions in the White Collar Job,* Survey Research Center, Institute for Social Research, Ann Arbor, University of Michigan, 1953.

53. Mumford, Lewis, *Technics and Civilization,* New York, Harcourt, Brace and Co., 1934.

54. Ogburn, William F., *Social Change,* New York, Viking Press, 1950.

55. Purcell, Theodore U., *The Worker Speaks His Mind,* Cambridge, Harvard University Press, 1953.

56. Reynolds, Lloyd G., and Joseph Shister, *Job Horizons,* New York, Harper and Brothers, 1949.

57. Riesman, David, with Reuel Denney and Nathan Glazer, *The Lonely Crowd,* New Haven, Yale University Press, 1950.

58. Roethlisberger, Fritz, *Management and Morale,* Cambridge, Harvard University Press, 1940.

59. Roethlisberger, Fritz, and W. J. Dickson, *Management and the Worker,* Cambridge, Harvard University Press, 1939.

60. Rose, Arnold, *Union Solidarity,* Minneapolis, University of Minnesota Press, 1952.

61. Rosen, S. McKee, and Laura Rosen, *Technology and Society,* New York, Macmillan Co., 1941.

62. Sayles, Leonard R., and George Strauss, *The Local Union,* New York, Harper and Brothers, 1953.

63. Scanlon, Joseph, "Profit Sharing under Collective Bargaining: Three Case Studies," *Industrial and Labor Relations Review,* Vol. 2 (1948), pp. 58–75.

64. Schultz, George P., and Robert P. Crisara, "The Lapointe Machine Tool Co. and the United Steelworkers of America," *Causes of Industrial Peace,* National Planning Association Bulletin No. 10, Washington, 1952.

65. Seashore, Stanley, *Group Cohesiveness in Industrial Work Groups,* Survey Research Center, Institute for Social Research, Ann Arbor, University of Michigan, 1954.

66. Selekman, Benjamin M., *Labor Relations and Human Relations,* New York, McGraw-Hill Book Co., 1947.

67. Selznick, Philip, *TVA and the Grass Roots,* Berkeley, University of California Press, 1949.

68. Shartle, Carroll L., "Leadership and Executive Performance," *Personnel,* Vol. 25 (1949), pp. 370–380.

69. Sheppard, Harold, "The Treatment of Unionism in Managerial Sociology," *Amer. Soc. Rev.*, Vol. 14 (1949), pp. 310–313.

70. Spicer, Edward H. (ed.), *Human Problems in Technological Change,* New York, Russell Sage Foundation, 1952.

71. Stagner, Ross, Theodore Purcell, Willard Kerr, Hjalman Rosen, Walter Gruen, *Dual Allegiance to Union and Management—A Symposium,* Urbana, University of Illinois Bulletin, No. 79, 1954.

72. Stogdill, Ralph M., and Associates, *Aspects of Leadership and Organization,* Columbus, Ohio State University Research Foundation, 1953.

73. Stogdill, Ralph M., and Shartle, Carroll L., *Methods for Determining Patterns of Leadership Behavior in Relation to Organization Structure and Objectives, Journal of Applied Psychology,* Vol. 32 (1948), pp. 286–291.

74. Trist, E. L., and K. W. Bamforth, "Some Social and Psychological Consequences of the Longwall Method of Coal-Getting," *Human Relations,* Vol. 4 (1951), pp. 3–38.

75. Turner, Arthur, "Interaction and Sentiment in the Foreman-Worker Relationship," *Human Organization*, Vol. 14 (1955), pp. 10–16.

76. Viteles, Morris S., *Motivation and Morale in Industry*, New York, W. W. Norton and Co., 1953.

77. Walker, Charles R., "The Problem of the Repetitive Job," *Harvard Business Review*, Vol. 28 (1950), pp. 54–58.

78. Walker, Charles R., *Steeltown*, New York, Harper and Brothers, 1950.

79. Walker, Charles R., and Robert Guest, *The Man on the Assembly Line*, Cambridge, Harvard University Press, 1952.

80. Warner, W. Lloyd, *The Social System of the Modern Factory*, New Haven, Yale University Press, 1947.

81. Whyte, William F., "Social Structure of the Organization: The Restaurant," in Robert Dubin (ed.), *Human Relations in Administration*, New York, Prentice-Hall, 1951.

82. Whyte, William F., *Money and Motivation*, New York, Harper and Brothers, 1955.

83. Whyte, William F., "Patterns of Interaction in Union-Management Relations," *Human Organization*, Vol. 8 (1949), pp. 13–19.

84. Whyte, William F., *Pattern for Industrial Peace*, New York, Harper and Brothers, 1951

85. Whyte, William F., "Who Goes Union and Why," *Personnel Journal*, Vol. 23 (1944), pp. 215–230.

86. Whyte, William H., Jr., *Is Anybody Listening?* New York, Simon and Schuster, 1952.

# chapter 11

# Marriage and the family*

ROBERT F. WINCH
*Northwestern University*

## Introduction

In bygone years dour critics were sounding the death knell of the American family and had been virtually extending invitations to the funeral. During the past decade, however, the vigorous fertility of parents has confounded the gloomy demographers. The fertile type-writers of sociologists, moreover, assure us that the funeral—if it is ever held—will be one of the best-covered stories in history. Despite the fact that the writer makes no claim for the completeness of the bibliography of this article and although the coverage of marginal fields is only fragmentary, the list of references has grown to a magnitude surprising to this author.

* The period of coverage of this chapter is from July 1, 1945, through March 31, 1955.

During the decade two kinds of very useful articles of general interest have been published. One kind is an essay on the state of the American family (46, 151, 284, 310). The other type consists of an assessment of the state of theorizing and research on the family (45, 73, 153, 154, 201, 262, 268, 318). Moreover, from time to time Ellis has been publishing very useful bibliographies in *Marriage and Family Living* (98).

The major part of this article will follow the format of the life cycle. We shall break into the life cycle at the time the adolescent is beginning to date, and we shall carry on with courtship, mate-selection, marriage, and the related topics of love, divorce, and the measurement of marital adjustment. Sex and fertility lead into the cycle of parent-child relations as the offspring grows from infant to adult. After a look at the literature on cultural variation we shall note the general texts that have appeared during the decade. The paper will conclude with an overview of 1945–1955.

### Dating

Among 368 undergraduate students at the University of Colorado, Smith and Monane (313) found that the traits reported as desirable in a date were also those which the subjects saw as characterizing a good mate. W. M. Smith, Jr. (315), has reported that questionnaire responses of Penn State students did not bear out Waller's formulation on "rating and dating" (356). Blood has received similar evidence leading him to discredit the Waller hypothesis (32).

Differing with Waller, Lowrie (227) holds that dating is more educational than it is exploitative or dysfunctional. From data on high school students Crist (74) concurs in this view and says that the basic function of dating in high school is the "heterosexual socialization" of the adolescent. Herman (150) hypothesizes that there are two types of experience denoted by the phrase "going steady"—(a) a relationship of dalliance, and (b) a relationship oriented to and often eventuating in marriage.

It is the reviewer's judgment that the phenomena which Waller had in mind are difficult to tap via the questionnaire method and that we should probably reserve judgment on Waller's ideas until they are tested by some means more direct than the questionnaire. Smith and Monane (313, page 636) seem to support this reservation of judgment:

It is interesting that even when an anonymous questionnaire is used and students are urged to be completely frank in specifying whatever traits they *really* seek, there may still be a tendency for the student to conform to the proprieties, to what he feels he *should* seek, or to what he feels the investigator would like to discover or expects to discover. For example, very few of the male students (and none of the female students) specified such traits as "sexy," "affectionate," or more earthy terms. From observation and interview, however, the authors are led to believe that sex experience is one of the prime dating-values and interests of male college youth.

These authors find that "companionability" is popular as a value in courtship although it diminishes in popularity as the subjects get older (23 years and above). As would be expected, they find that men are interested in the physical appearance of women, and that women are interested in the social graces of men. Winch's hypothesis regarding the progression from a culturally defined ideal to a psychically defined ideal receives support in the finding that younger persons tend to agree more fully on the values which a date should represent, whereas the older subjects show greater variation (377, pages 424–432).\* The poorer students were more modal in their values than those with the higher grades, and the fraternity members were more modal than the "unorganized."

From a nation-wide sample of 2,500 high school students Christensen found that feelings of shyness in the dating situation were common to both sexes, that both boys and girls regarded the boys as more careless, disrespectful, and sex-driven than the girls, whereas they characterized the girls as more inhibited, touchy, and interested in expensive entertainment than the boys (63).

Kirkpatrick and Caplow (185) found among a group of University of Minnesota students that fathers tended to resist the loss of their daughters whereas mothers encouraged them to date, and further that mothers were more disposed than fathers to encourage the dating of offspring, regardless of the gender of the offspring. By an ingenious method of having the subjects report the intensity through time of their love affairs these same authors (186) found that roughly a third deviated from the simple "attraction-love-indifference" cycle in the direction of vacillation between love and hate, or perhaps a "dead-center" mild attraction, or some other pattern.

Nimkoff and Wood (270) found in a sample of college students that those who dated infrequently were "overwhelmingly the socially retiring," but that they were "not particularly emotionally maladjusted." However, "going steady" at an early age—in junior high school—and shifting "steadies" frequently were found to be correlated with emotional maladjustment as measured by the Bell Adjustment Inventory.

\* Perhaps another form of corroboration comes from Strauss's finding of greater correspondence between actual and ideal mates with respect to personality traits than with respect to physical traits (323).

### Courtship

At some variance with the Nimkoff and Wood study just noted is the finding of Winch (372a) of no consistent association between "neuroticism" as measured by the abridged (42-item) Thurstone Neurotic Inventory and progress in courtship for either sex.

Winch's efforts to correlate differential progress in courtship with attachment to parent of opposite sex by means of questionnaire responses from college students led to early corroboration with respect to the mother-son relationship. Only after a variety of attempts was made was he able to discover a father-daughter correlation, and then it was contrary to the hypothesis. In other words, those girls who reported a high degree of attachment to their fathers were overrepresented in the high courtship category. This led Winch to propose a new formulation of the Oedipus hypothesis for the American urban middle class family (372a, 373, 375, 376).*

In an inquiry into characteristics differentiating single and married women Klemer (191) found that over the age range 16–25 the single women had had significantly less culturally approved heterosexual activity † than the married women, but that there was no difference between the two groups with respect to "desire for marriage" or "security-insecurity." (The last finding is consistent with Winch's finding, noted above, on "neuroticism" [372a, 373, 375, 376].) When women are distributed by level of education, Dublin reports a negative correlation between level of education and proportion married (86). And, finally, Koller (195) has concluded that the 200 college-trained married women whom he studied have had about the same moral standards in courtship behavior as did their mothers and their maternal grandmothers.

### Assortative mating

Evidence has continued to pile up that American husbands and wives tend to be similar with respect to race, religion, socioeconomic status, age, previous marital status, education, and location of previous residence.

Burma (50) reports that although the nullification of the California antimiscegenation law did not precipitate a flood of interracial marriages it did make such marriages easier for the sociologist to trace. He found the rates of marriages of whites to other races was only 56 per 10,000.

---

* See page 366. Although they did not emerge with a formal restatement of the Oedipus hypothesis, Kirkpatrick and Caplow laid the groundwork for a somewhat similar reformulation (185, page 115).

† Presumably this refers to dates and not to sexual intercourse.

"Approximately 41 percent of these mixed marriages involved Filipino men; 20.5 percent involved Negro men; 20.4 percent involved Anglo men; 44 percent of these mixed marriages involved Anglo women. Filipino men marrying Anglo women and Anglo men marrying Negro women showed a much higher average age than any other groups" (page 587). Risdon (288) obtained a roughly comparable figure of 0.47 per cent interracial marriages in Los Angeles County in 1948–1949.

Golden's study of Negro-white marriages in Philadelphia (129, 130) concluded that the Negro-white couple usually consisted of a Negro husband and a white wife, that when the husbands were the white individuals they tended to be foreign-born—especially Italian, and that such couples tended to be heterogamous with respect to religion. It was Golden's impression that such marriages did not usually manifest public symbolization of the union, de-emphasized relations with extended family and community, and were low in number of children.

"Next to race," says Hollingshead (159), "religion is the most decisive factor in the segregation of males and females into categories that are approved or disapproved with respect to nuptiality." Hollingshead interviewed 523 couples who were married in New Haven in 1948. He found that 91 per cent of the marriages in his study involved partners who belonged to the same one of the three large religious groupings: Protestant, Catholic, and Jewish. This finding is similar to that reported in two previous studies by Ruby J. R. Kennedy on the same city (174, 175). Thomas (346) believes, however, that these findings should be generalized beyond New Haven only with considerable caution. Using data from the *Catholic Directory* for "132 parishes distributed throughout the East and Middle West," he concluded that the data "reveal a much higher mixed marriage rate for Catholics than the formulators of the triple-melting-pot hypothesis believed . . . The single melting-pot hypothesis is probably as valid as any hypothesis yet advanced."

Certain other studies have produced findings which may contribute to the solution of this dilemma. Lundberg and Dickson (231) find that friendship choices of high school students—both in the majority and in the minorities—increased in ethnocentrism with the size of the out-group. It is conceivable that this principle might explain the difference between the conclusions of Hollingshead and Kennedy on the one hand and Thomas on the other. At any rate it suggests an interesting hypothesis for further study.

Lenski (217) found that in the Milbank-Indianapolis study ". . . the proportion of persons expressing 'much' interest in religion was significantly greater among those whose spouses shared their denominational preference [both Protestant in all couples] than among those married to partners with differing ties."

Barron (15) believes that there is no evidence of any increase in the rate at which Jews are marrying outside their religion either in America or in Europe.* Marcson (240) theorizes that American culture makes interethnic marriages more permissible than interreligious or interclass marriages. Empirically Marcson finds that ethnicity, occupation, and language spoken are crucial factors in predicting intermarriage (241).

Occupation is frequently used as an index of socioeconomic status. So far as urban occupations are concerned Centers (58) has shown on the basis of a Gallup sample that husbands tend to be in the same broad occupational grouping with their fathers-in-law. Where marriages are nonhomogamous, moreover, he found some tendency for women to marry up (and for men, ergo, to marry down). Using residential area as an index of social class and dividing the areas into six classes, Hollingshead (159) found that in 58.2 per cent of his cases in New Haven both partners came from the same class of residential area. In a rather different cultural setting J. S. Brown (43) reports a high degree of marriage within the kin group. Of 107 marriages studied in a Kentucky mountain community he found that 31 involved persons who were third or closer cousins. A good deal of this endogamy he interprets as a desire to avoid marrying into a lower social class.

One of the more obviously homogamous variables is age. Without any systematic evidence it would be almost anyone's impression that the wives of old men are older on the average than the wives of young men. But since things are not always as they seem, it is in order to note some studies which corroborate this impression (128, 160, 329). A greater age-spread of spouses is noted in remarriages than in first marriages (35, 38, 128). Those who are marrying for the second or subsequent time tend to marry persons who have also been married before (126).

In connection with the subject of age at marriage, it is perhaps worth while to make three other more or less unrelated observations. (a) Glick and Landau (128) report a positive correlation between income of husband and his age at marriage. Anderson's sample of college alumni showed a much later average age at marriage than is reported for the general population (7). (b) The Bureau of the Census has been criticized by Monahan for its estimates on average age at marriage. Monahan (258) claims that our data do not enable us to emerge with rational estimates. (c) Registration areas of statistics on marriage and divorce

---

* Concerning Jewish marriages, Bend notes a trend away from explicit emphasis upon economic factors in marital attraction and a trend toward emphasis upon personal qualities in Jewish marriage advertisements in New York (23).

are being set up in this country as of January, 1956, and January, 1957, respectively.

New confirmation for homogamy in education comes from a study of 330 former students of Washington State College (211). Landis and Day corroborate another earlier finding that men tend to marry "down" and women to marry "up" with respect to years of formal education.

Columbus, Ohio, and Duluth, Minnesota, have been added to the cities in which residential propinquity appears to be a determinant in mate-selection (194, 239). Moreover, Koller (194) found that the younger men and those with the higher ranking occupations tended to travel farther to find their wives. In reporting his study of Simsbury, Connecticut, Ellsworth (100) rephrased the proposition on propinquitous selection into the language of Stouffer's "intervening opportunities." Clarke's study—again of Columbus, Ohio—pushed the inquiry back to the "meeting and dating" patterns (68). He found that residential propinquity was present in these patterns also. The Koller and Clarke studies agree on the finding that the higher the occupation of the husband, the greater distance on the average he lived from his bride-to-be. They differed, however, on the correlation between propinquity and age: in Koller's study the younger bridegrooms traveled farther to find their brides, whereas in Clarke's study it was the older who ranged farther afield. Clarke found no correlation between propinquity and educational level, but he did find that Catholics apparently "must extend their courtship range to marry Catholics," a finding supported in substance by Schnepp and Roberts (300).

Winch (377, pages 402–403) has theorized that variables which function homogamously (such as those considered in this section) create a field of eligible spouses by excluding from one's network of associates those whose social characteristics differ from one's own. Since one tends to marry within this network of associates, the process results in homogamy. It seems likely, however, that some selection and rejection also do take place. Fiedler, Warrington, and Blaisdell (109) show that subjects impute similarity in personality traits to themselves and their associates when the latter are positive sociometric choices. (This study involved active members and pledges of a college fraternity.) Notcutt and Silva (271) show that husbands and wives predict each other's self-ratings on expressive behavior best when they *are* similar. Putting these findings together with those of Kirkpatrick and Hobart (188), one may hypothesize that for certain kinds of attitudes the courtship is a process in which those of similar bent select each other, while rejecting eligibles who have inharmonious dispositions.

### Rural-urban differences in marriage

Bogue (34) finds that the recent tendency toward marriage at younger ages appears considerably greater in urban areas than in rural. From data on Denmark, Sweden, Australia, and New Zealand, as well as the United States, Hajnal concludes (141, page 149) that ". . . among women the proportions married are lower in the city than in the country; among men, on the contrary, the proportions are on the whole higher in the city. This pattern reflects the effects of migration on the sex ratio . . . men in agriculture tend to marry later than many urban groups." Over the period 1940–1947, moreover, he found that the proportion of women who are married increased most in the more highly educated groups (cf. 86). In another study (140) Hajnal has found that the "marriage boom" of recent years has been most pronounced, both in Europe and in America, among those groups which seem to "harbor the strongest tendencies toward the postponement and avoidance of marriage—the urban 'white-collar' workers" (page 300). Paul Landis (210) reports that those who migrate from rural to urban areas and those who migrate from urban to rural areas have higher proportions married than those who remain in the same kind of area.

### Love, the nonhomogamous determinant in mate-selection

The decade under review has included some discussion of romantic love and the romantic complex. Stark (320) traces romantic love back, not to courtly life, but to the "primitive consciousness of common country folk." Proceeding from the analysis of de Rougemont, Winch (377, Chaps. 14–15) interprets romantic love in terms of its components of the idealization and inaccessibility of the love-object; from this analysis Winch concludes that romantic love is a symptom of adolescent insecurity and is not an emotional basis conducive to marital stability. Beigel (22) and Kolb (192, 193), on the other hand, speak favorably of romantic love, and the second of these writers regards with disfavor sociologists who would encourage their students not to be romantic.

Many years ago Durkheim observed that "difference, as likeness, can be a cause of mutual attraction" (88, page 55). In mate-selection such attracting differences are in part a function of the sex roles (213). Freud saw dependent persons being attracted to narcissistic ones and vice versa (112). Subsequently various writers in the Freudian tradition have reported cases of husbands and wives who appeared to be complementarily neurotic (26, 252, 273).

A more inclusive theory of complementary mating was formulated on the basis of the personality types of Jung. Statistically, however, the evidence of Gray (133, 134), who offered this hypothesis, was not significant. The effort of Strauss to trace the origin of one's image of the ideal spouse to the parent-image proved inconclusive (324); later Strauss formulated a hypothesis that a person's needs might determine his choice of mate (325).

Pulling these strands together, Winch (203, 377) has defined love in terms of emotional needs and has formulated what he calls the "theory of complementary needs in mate-selection." He finds that his data support his theory and that husbands and wives tend to be unlike and complementary with respect to the intensity of their needs. He suggests that more refined hypotheses as well as classification of marital types will emerge from his research (379, 380).

This writer finds it difficult to rate divergent concepts of "love" as being as scientifically promising as his own. The reader is warned, however, of the partisan nature of the remarks immediately to follow; he is encouraged to read the sources and to form his own more detached judgment. The writer does feel that Foote (110a) with his concept of interpersonal "competence" and Maslow (244) with his idea of the "healthy" lover as a "self-actualizing" person take highly normative theoretical positions. In effect they seem to deny the term "love" to any emotion or relationship which they do not regard as "healthy." For example, it is "love" only when each lover contributes "optimally" to the "development" of the other (110a, page 247). Aside from the fact that we may wax disputatious over the meaning of such words as "healthy" (as over any word rich in connotation but not precise in denotation), the theoretical and logical difficulty of this position may be seen by analogy—as if we were to deny the name "appendix" or "thyroid" to the organs conventionally so designated until autopsy should reveal that organ to have no pathology. Why we should not speak of neurotic (as opposed to "healthy") love just as we may speak of neurotic dependency or whatever, is not clear to this writer.

### The measurement of marital adjustment

Burgess and Wallin offer a review of the major studies of marital adjustment with special emphasis on those of Burgess and Cottrell (47), Terman *et al.* (342), and Burgess and Wallin (49, Chaps. 2, 15). Kirkpatrick (in the appendix to [184]) has summarized findings from the foregoing studies, the researches of Locke (221) and of Karlsson (173), as well as other investigations (see also 182; 357, Chap. 17).

The central question which has occupied Burgess is that of trying to predict the degree of success of marriages. In terms of this objective the Burgess and Cottrell research was a pilot study. The report by Burgess and Wallin gives indication of modest but significant results. From background data gathered before marriage (on parent-child interaction, social participation, economic status, sex attitudes and behavior) these investigators constructed a single score for each person. These scores correlated to .31 for husbands and .27 for wives with marital success three years after marriage (page 519). They also constructed an "engagement success" index (based on such items as satisfaction with engagement partner, whether or not one has regretted the engagement and has considered breaking it, extent of agreement with partner on selected areas—page 305). These scores correlated with marital success scores to .39 for the men and .36 for the women (page 548). It is clear that such values indicate that the unexplained variance in marital success is of the order of 85 or 90 per cent. Yet in the light of the manifest complexity—even ambiguity *—of such a concept as marital success, the mere demonstration of significant correlations is impressive. Kirkpatrick has written a careful and incisive review of this study (183).

The Burgess and Wallin study resembles the Kinsey studies in the sense that it reports a multitude of findings upon which there is some temptation to speculate. In her review of the study Komarovsky (200) commented on one such set of findings. These pertained to the fact that Burgess and Wallin interpreted their data as indicating considerably less idealization of the spouse than the writings of the late Willard Waller had suggested. Professor Komarovsky suggests that this finding be interpreted with caution because the average length of premarital acquaintance (45 months) indicates that Burgess and Wallin might have selected for study the "less impetuously romantic and the more prudent courtships."

Using tests of marital aptitude, of marital happiness, and of sex adjustment on their gifted subjects, Terman and Oden (343) found that the best predictor of marital success six years later (divorce was the negative criterion) was the test of marital aptitude. The authors conclude: "The data, in general, confirm the hypothesis that one's happiness in marriage is largely determined by one's all-round happiness of temperament, and that this trait can be at least roughly measured by a pencil-and-paper test" (pages 262–263).

The central purpose of Locke's study (221) was to validate his scale

---

* Marsh and Humphrey (242) criticize much of the research on marital adjustment and the counseling based thereon because an ethnocentric (middle class) notion of happiness or adjustment is used as a criterion of success.

of marital adjustment by the "known-group" technique. For one end of his continuum he had a divorced group, and for the other end, a group of couples selected on the basis of being regarded as happily married. This scale has many items in common with the Burgess-Cottrell scale and naturally correlates highly with it. One of the findings of this study which has elicited comment and interest is that the development of the ties of affection and common values "begins prior to the marriage ceremony and continues afterwards." In view of the fact that Locke's is a cross-sectional rather than a longitudinal study, such a conclusion is probably not derivable from his data in a rigorously logical sense. Certainly this conclusion seems generally plausible, but it would seem to be more directly inferable from the longitudinal research of Burgess and Wallin.

The study by Karlsson (173), which is based on Swedish data, is most heartening in several respects. In the first place it appears to be the most recently designed of the major studies, and—as might be expected for this reason—it manifests a superiority in design. With respect to sampling the study is especially praiseworthy. Secondly, it is encouraging to see that the general trend of findings in previous studies is corroborated by Karlsson. Although one cannot so argue with impeccable logic, Karlsson's generally similar findings on a somewhat different—but still Western—culture and with a good sampling procedure add plausibility to our belief that the findings of previous studies have validity and generality. (A further increment of support comes from the corroboration provided by King [179] in his study of Negro couples in the South.) The discrepancies between Karlsson's findings and those of American studies are intriguing. For example, is Karlsson's finding that religious participation is either uncorrelated or slightly negatively correlated with marital adjustment a reflection of cultural variation, or does it serve to corroborate the charge that the American studies tended to select conservative and conforming subjects?

Two studies have used older married couples as subjects. Contrary to the surmise of Burgess and Cottrell, Stroup (327) showed that the correlation between the background factors of the couple and their marital adjustment was about as high in later years of marriage as in the earlier. Judson Landis (205) studied the time required by 409 couples to achieve adjustment in sex relations, spending family income, social activities, in-law relationships, religious activities, and mutual friends. The fact that his couples had been married for an average of twenty years meant that (a) his sample was heavily weighted with "successful" marriages (in the sense that they were unbroken), and (b) that his data were necessarily dependent upon the memories of his subjects. Most of his subjects reported satisfactory adjustment from the beginning in all of the studied areas. Sex and income were the areas with the lowest proportions of couples reporting satisfaction from the beginning.

Roth and Peck have arranged the Burgess and Cottrell data into social strata of the Warnerian type, and they have found that "the social class of the spouses' parents *per se* has little relationship to the adjustment of the spouses" (292). They did find, however, that equality of social status of the two spouses is correlated positively with good marital adjustment, whereas inequality—especially where the wife's status is higher—is associated with poor adjustment. This is somewhat at variance with findings from other studies. Williamson found generally positive correlations between high socioeconomic status and good marital adjustment (371, 372). Ogburn (275) reports that the percentage of divorced men in the 30–34 age group of the native white population increases as education increases until the college graduates are reached, when the percentage drops. And, on the basis of his study in Detroit, Goode (132) reports a "rough inverse correlation between economic position and a tendency to divorce." Hollingshead has provided a descriptive rationale for the negative correlation between family stability and social class (158).

Locke and Mackeprang (224) found no difference between the marital adjustment of full-time working wives and of full-time homemaking wives, but Rose (290) reported that "dissatisfied" wives were less likely than "satisfied" wives to have assumed a paying job. Jacobson (166) found that there was a great disparity between the attitudes of married couples. Locke and Klausner (223) reported that remarried wives adjusted better in their second marriages than did the remarried husbands.

Landis (206) finds that children constitute an important factor in the conflicts arising in marriages of mixed religion. From their observations on interethnic marriages in Panama, Biesanz and Smith (30) theorize that three variables pertaining to the intergroup situation contribute to the determination of the level of marital adjustment: relative degrees of (a) prestige, (b) informal-primary organization, and (c) formal-secondary organization.

The research literature seems to be somewhat confusing on the relation between marital adjustment and the presence or absence of children. Landis, Poffenberger, and Poffenberger (209) discovered that more than half of their 212 student couples reported no change in their sexual adjustment as a result of the first pregnancy; about a quarter of both husbands and wives reported an unfavorable effect, and between a fifth and a sixth reported a favorable effect. Jansen (169) found a negative correlation between number of children and "family solidarity." Christensen and Philbrick (67) came out with a negative correlation between family size and marital adjustment, but with the qualification that the value parents placed on their children was more important for marital adjustment than the sheer number. Burgess and Wallin (49, page 712) seem to agree with this formulation. It is possible that where the correlation is negative, a process is operating which was hypothesized by Simmel (309, Chaps. 2–4) and by von Neumann and Morgenstern (355, Chap. 5) and found empirically by Mills (248)—the segregation of a threesome into a pair and an other.

Kirkpatrick and Cotton (187) state that the ages of spouses—both absolutely and relative to each other—do not appear to be consistently related to their marital adjustment, but that a positive relationship does appear with the reported physical attractiveness of the wife.

Wallin (359) hypothesized that students' attitudes toward marriage would be more favorable on the part of those who reported their parents' marriage as happy as contrasted with those with divorced parents. The hypothesis was supported with respect to males; in women the relationship was curvilinear, with those reporting divorced parents registering about as favorable attitudes toward marriage as those rating their parents' marriage happy. The familiar correlation between being married and low incidence of mental illness is reported by Frumkin (116) and by Adler (3). In a well-controlled study Adler also shows that marital status is correlated with rate of recovery.

Annabelle Motz (260) has constructed a questionnaire to reveal the degree to which one's view of the role of husband or wife is traditional or that of companionship. Yi-Chuang Lu (230) used premarital data (*e.g.*, concerning each spouse's relationships to his parents) to predict whether that person would assume a dominant, equalitarian, or submissive role in his marriage.

Finally, Kirkpatrick (182), Ellis (97), and Hill (357) have expressed a variety of criticisms and doubts concerning the value of marital adjustment tests and the studies which have been based upon them (cf. note, page 355). Terman and Wallin have undertaken to rebut Ellis' criticisms (344). While on the subject of data-gathering procedures, we may note that there has been considerable—and in this reviewer's judgment, still inconclusive—discussion of whether procedures in this area should be direct or indirect, disguised or undisguised, structured or unstructured. For arguments and some data, see Ellis (95, 96), Bernard (28), Taves (340), and Frumkin (115).

### Sex

It seems reasonably evident that no other books published during the decade 1945–1955 have created the furor which accompanied the two

Kinsey volumes (180, 181).* Perhaps the most general conclusion to be drawn from the two studies published so far is that the marital relationship seems to account for a surprisingly low proportion of the total "sexual outlet" of both males and females in this country. Beyond this the writer's impression is that the next most noteworthy feature about the two volumes is that the correlation between social stratification and social mobility on the one hand and sexual behavior on the other was quite evident in males, but that such a relationship seemed to be quite absent in the case of the females.

There has been much speculation concerning the effect of the publication of the Kinsey volumes on sex practices in this country. One experimental study of attitudes at two Midwestern universities revealed evidence of change in both directions: some students became more tolerant of nonmarital sexual expression and some students became less tolerant (189). As Kirkpatrick says elsewhere:

> The experiment suggests that the battle lines will be drawn more sharply in America between those who would condemn and repress nonconformist sex behavior and those inclined to greater tolerance. For the present at least, young people are confronted with confusion in regard to the sex code. The female students were especially affected by the Kinsey findings suggesting sex repression and cultural inconsistency differential for the two sexes (184, page 318).

Kirkpatrick regards the culture of the United States as extremely controlling, nonpermissive, and disapproving concerning sexual expression (184, page 47). According to Murdock (263, page 264) it is unlikely that more than five per cent of the peoples of the world condemn all sexual expression outside the marital relationship, as we do.

Julia Brown (44) has done a study of 110 nonliterate societies and has found that incest, abduction, and rape are the forms of sexual behavior which are most frequently tabooed and most severely punished. Adultery

---

* Actually it is very difficult to phrase any perfectly general conclusion from the Kinsey study. The procedure has been questioned from several standpoints, and certainly the sample is one such point. The most exhaustive critique of Kinsey's sampling procedure was performed by a committee of the American Statistical Association, which concluded: "In the absence of a probability-sample benchmark, the present results must be regarded as subject to systematic errors of unknown magnitude due to selective sampling (via volunteering and the like)" (69, page 37). On the other hand, the committee declares (page 39) that the work of Kinsey and his associates is "outstandingly good" in comparison with the nine other leading studies on sex. Numerous critiques have been written of the Kinsey studies on this and other points. If this reviewer's reading is not in error, it seems that one of Kinsey's critics complains that Kinsey's incidence and frequency rates on females are too low because of poor sampling (92), while another critic writing for the same issue of the same journal makes the opposite criticism (207).

is punished less frequently. Premarital sexual expression, especially if with a betrothed partner, is the least frequently and most lightly punished.

Some of the criticisms of the Kinsey studies have come from the psycho-analytic camp and have been based on the argument that it was impossible to study sexuality without studying its psychic correlates and that Kinsey and his associates did not do the latter and were not competent to do so if they had thought of it (27). As this writer has pointed out elsewhere (378), this is the standard criticism of an author for not doing the kind of study in which the critic happens to be interested. In this connection, however, one of the most interesting demonstrations of the link between the psyche and the sexual side of the soma is provided by Benedek (24), who has predicted with remarkable success the hormonal content of menstrual flow in fifteen women on the basis of psychodynamic material revealed in psychoanalytic sessions.

The unmarried mother has been the subject of a couple of investigations. In a clinical, intuitive fashion Leontine Young (385) concludes that the girls who get into this plight are characterized by pre-Oedipal fixations. A more objective study by Clark Vincent (354) reports that the popular conception of the unmarried mother has been distorted because it has been derived largely from social agencies. It is his contention that unwed motherhood is more generally spread throughout the general population.

Christensen (64) estimates that one-fifth of all first births within marriage in Tippecanoe County, Indiana, are conceived before marriage, and that the proportion conceived prior to marriage is higher among those who married young, who had secular wedding ceremonies, and who were in the laboring occupations. It certainly seems probable that such pregnancies are unplanned for the most part. Poffenberger, Poffenberger, and Landis (282) found that where conception took place early in marriage there was a larger proportion of unplanned pregnancies than among couples where pregnancy did not occur early in marriage. And Christensen has shown the existence of a positive correlation between premarital pregnancy and the incidence of divorce (66; cf. also 65).

### Fertility and differential fertility

During the latter part of the 1930's and the early 1940's demographers were predicting that because of a declining birth rate the United States was coming to a time when the population would cease to grow from natural increase; indeed they saw a decline in the population as well within the realm of possibility. From the middle 1930's on there was a gradual increase in productivity and in the proportion of the labor force gainfully employed. Concomitant with economic improvement has come a rise in the birth rate—sometimes referred to as a "baby-boom"—which has upset the predictions noted above.

It appears that perhaps for as long as a century and a half—from the latter part of the eighteenth century to the bottom of the depression in the 1930's—our national birth rate has been declining. While our birth rate was on the wane, there were differences in the fertility of various segments of the population: nonwhites had higher rates than whites; rural than urban; working class than white-collar class, etc. ˙ Now with the upswing in fertility it appears that the less fertile classes are approaching the more fertile in their rates, *i.e.*, the baby-boom is more marked in the white than in the nonwhite population, etc. (34, 190, 364).

One area that has received a good deal of attention from demographers is Puerto Rico, where it has been reported that husbands and wives tend to differ markedly in their concept of ideal family size. The man is characterized as "almost compulsively concerned with sex and procreation, while the woman, at least relatively, is indifferent to birth" (328, page 579; see also 143). It seems likely that we shall continue to learn a good deal from the correlation of attitudinal and demographic data of Puerto Rico.

### Parent-child relations: socialization

In 1955 three trends were visible which seemed to characterize the literature on socialization throughout the preceding decade. (a) Those of a clinical bent, and especially those with a psychoanalytic persuasion, were quite sure that they could see and identify cause-and-effect relationships in the parent-child—especially the mother-child—nexus. (b) Those who sought by means of "hard" or rigorous nomothetic procedures to demonstrate these relationships frequently did not emerge with supporting experimental evidence. (c) Those who advise parents on the rearing of children were, as usual, in the process of developing a new doctrine. Many of the writers of advice tended generally to follow the lead of those noted in (a) above and to ignore the negative evidence of those mentioned in (b).

The range of activities which are subsumable under these three points involves many of the behavioral disciplines outside sociology, and hence a systematic treatment of these points is outside the scope of the present paper. Convenient introductions to these materials exist, however (61; 377, Part 3, especially Chap. 8). Special note may be taken of an annual publication of recent psychoanalytic studies on the child. Reference 71 contains a citation of one of these volumes. Finally, a valuable bibliography on personality and the social development of the child—including, of course, material on parent-child relations—has been produced by Heinicke and Whiting (147).

### Mother and infant

Interaction of parents and children—and especially of mother and children—has long been hypothesized to influence the development of the child. In an earlier generation the thoughts and activities of a pregnant mother were thought to "mark" her yet unborn child. After a period of being relegated to the status of superstition, this general idea has re-emerged with at least a semblance of scientific respectability. Although the evidence is correlational rather than experimental, Lester Sontag (317) has suggested the physiological process by which such influences could pass from mother to fetus. However, an effort to show empirically that individual differences in attitude toward pregnancy and childbirth are correlated with the nature of the experience of pregnancy and childbirth concluded with generally negative findings (282). Since the young mothers-to-be were wives of students on a college campus, it is possible that the reason for the absence of correlation is that the sample studied was too homogeneous.

In the decade before the period under consideration in this volume there was a demonstration of great conviction concerning the effect of the mother's behavior on the psychological development of her infant. A dramatic and apparently influential study was that of Margaret Ribble (287), who held that the lack of proper "mothering" resulted in "infantile atrophy," or "marasmus," as she called it, and sometimes ultimately in death. Although subsequent writers have perhaps failed to match Ribble in dramatic forcefulness, the general theme remains viable—if in a somewhat less extreme and doctrinaire phrasing (71, 104, 172, 291, 319).

Spitz has published some evidence to show that the lack of a mother in the early months of life may seriously inhibit development (319). In carefully controlled studies Sears and associates (304) have found certain behaviors in children related to antecedent practices of mothers. On a cross-cultural basis Whiting and Child (365) were able to support the hypothesis of "negative fixation," *i.e.*, that where childhood training causes anxiety to be associated with a "system of behavior," there will be a tendency in adulthood to attribute illness to that system of behavior. Accepting as established the proposition "that the prolonged deprivation on the part of the young child of maternal care may have grave and far-reaching effects on his character and so on the whole of his future life," Bowlby (39a) has analyzed the conditions which result in maternal deprivation and has reported the experience in various countries with such remedial measures as adoption, foster families, and group care.

The general tenor of the literature of the last decade, however, seems to be one of negative findings and of skepticism regarding readily demonstrable correlations between maternal behavior and general physiological and/or psychological development. One of the more widely remarked studies is that of Sewell (305, 307), who was unable to find that infant training was related to subsequent personality adjustment.[*] Moreover, Anderson (5) has written that children are not nearly as tender and destructible as Ribble supposed, and Pinneau (281) has found many flaws in Ribble's evidence. In a critical review of the literature Orlansky (278) has concluded that there is little evidence that the quality of infant care determines the nature of personality. Sears (302) has presented an able review of literature on a broader set of problems relating personality development to familial influences.

In addition there have been some studies which have appeared to take for granted that there would be differences in the personality development of the child contingent upon whether the parent follows a permissive or nonpermissive regimen, or—with a slight difference in emphasis [†]—the phrasing may be that the parent employs "developmental" or "traditional" practices in child rearing. Davis and Havighurst (78) and others (*e.g.,* 89, 103) working with the Committee on Human Development at the University of Chicago have been concerned with this problem and have sought to relate differences in methods of child rearing to race and social class.

### The content of advice to parents

Despite the fact that the technical literature is far from clear on the nature of the relationship between parental behavior and personality development in children, the level of demand for advice on the "problems" of child rearing seems to remain high, and the output seems generally to keep pace with the demand. Two of the most respectable of

[*] It is advisable to note, however, that the researcher who attempts to sustain a hypothesis by negative findings (*i.e.,* attempts to prove the null hypothesis) must assume the burden of proof on one point not required of the researcher who relies on positive findings. The case of the positive finding is not subject to the possible criticism that it came out that way because of random error—as reflected by unreliability. He who would establish a proposition on the basis of a negative finding should assure himself and his readers that this finding reflects something other than random error—or unreliability—before making a substantive interpretation.

[†] Blood (31) has shown that permissive behavior in parents correlates highly with the "developmental" ideology.

the books on this subject are those by Gruenberg (137) and by Witmer and Kotinsky (382), and within recent times even a salty former editor of the *American Sociological Review* has been dispensing advice to parents (13).

As might be expected, where the advice rests upon such an insecure scientific base, its content swings and vacillates. The spirit of the psychologist J. B. Watson (362) seemed to dominate the latter 1920's and the early 1930's, and parents were counseled to be a bit aloof in relation to their children. The word to be given to parents in the latter 1930's and early 1940's was more consistent with the views of Ribble (287), and it was recommended that parents be permissive, that they fondle and "mother" their children. In the latter 1940's and early 1950's permissiveness seems on the wane; the emphasis is on the rights of parents rather than of infants, and it has been discovered that the child "needs" discipline in order to feel secure. The interpretation seems plausible that these trends in advice-giving are more closely related to social trends and the "needs" of the parents and of teachers than to critical experiments. Several authors have analyzed these trends in advice on child-care (105, 321, 353, 383). Dollard (83) has ably expressed the position of the skeptic, and Brim (41) has reported a set of conditions under which mothers change their approach to "feeding" problems.

### Group differences and positional differences

It has been a truism as far back as the Americanization studies of the 1920's that by virtue of its location in American society a family will impart a "flavor" to the skills and attitudes of its offspring. Sewell and Ellenbogen (306) have found positive correlations between the social status of families (urban, rural farm, or rural nonfarm) and the measured intelligence of their children. MacDonald, McGuire, and Havighurst (233) report that the socioeconomic status of parents tends largely to determine the status of their children's playmates, hence the kind of play the children will engage in, and because of this, the content of the social learning that takes place in play activities of their children. Nye (272) states that upper status adolescents are better adjusted to their parents than are the adolescent offspring at lower levels. Williams has provided frequency distributions of the kinds of problems professed by high school students—including problems with parents (370). Swanson has developed a test for rating parent-child relationships (335). LeMasters (216) reports that higher status college students—in contrast to the lower status students in a small Midwestern coeducational college —did not manifest striving behavior oriented to upward social mobility.

Arnold Green has written an essay purporting to show how the subculture of the middle class builds anxiety into its boys, and in another essay Allison Davis has described a process by which this anxiety is presumably converted into the energy to strive for the goals of social mobility (135, 76). If this formulation is correct, it may account for the higher IQ's shown by Sewell and Ellenbogen for the higher statuses. And finally, the religious orientation of the family seems to have some bearing on whether and how their offspring will drink. The incidence of drinkers is greater in the more permissive religious groups (*e.g.*, Jews and Catholics as opposed to, say, Mormons), but when those who belong to the less permissive groups take up drinking, Straus and Bacon (322) say that they are less apt to be temperate about it.

Position within the family has also been studied. Sears (301) reports that "second children are somewhat less dependent than first." The mothers of second and subsequent children, he says, "tend to be somewhat less frustrating than the mothers of first children." The significance of being a twin is under study by Mowrer (261), and William C. Smith (314) has described the problems of the stepchild. Sheer size of family has intrigued Bossard (36). The children of divorced and estranged parents are subjected to psychological analysis by Louise Despert (81) in the United States and by Haffter (139) in Switzerland.

Reiss (285) has studied the relation between types of delinquents and characteristics of their families. For example: "Delinquents with defective super-ego controls significantly more often come from families where the father is absent but other siblings present," and "where there is open conflict between parents as compared with delinquents with relatively integrated controls" (page 715). Maude Merrill (247) also emphasizes the broken home as a correlate of juvenile delinquency.

McKeown has sought to relate mental disorder in children to the behavior of their parents (238), and by a study reporting a specific predisposing genetic factor for schizophrenia Franz Kallman (171) is keeping the nature-nurture controversy simmering.

In a series of papers (373, 374, 375, 376) Winch has reported that college men who are atypically attached to their mothers and those whose fathers are absent from the home tend to be somewhat retarded in courtship.* This finding has been interpreted as consistent with the Freudian

---

* In a sense Aberle and Naegele (1) provide some content for the correlation noted above by Winch. They observe that middle class fathers are much concerned that their sons should show the traits (*e.g.*, initiative, aggressiveness, competence) thought essential for success in male adult roles. The fathers have only a vague concept of the content of female roles, and hence they are satisfied with the daughter if she is just a "sweet little girl." If the interpretation of these writers is correct, then, it fills in some of the meaning of the loss of a father.

concept of the Oedipus complex. Among women, however, those who appeared closest to their fathers were overrepresented in the "going steady" and engaged categories. (With students at Purdue University as their subjects Andrews and Christensen [8] failed to corroborate Winch's findings with respect to the correlate of the absent parent. They found that sons with missing fathers tended to begin dating earlier, to go steady earlier, to be engaged earlier, and to be involved more often in broken engagements than sons whose fathers were in the home.) Winch concluded this series of studies with a proposal for a reformulation of the Oedipus hypothesis for application to the mother-dominated home of the American urban middle class—the phenomenon of momism.* (That the mother is becoming the more important parent in the hitherto patriarchal German family is suggested in a study by Baumert [18] and in another by Schelsky [297, 298].)

### Emancipation: the adult and his parents

As we move through the cycle until the offspring are becoming adults, we find a study by Wallin and Vollmer (361), which reports that: ". . . the happier the rating of the marriage of parents [by the off-spring], the greater the probability that persons will report the same degree of attachment for both parents . . . the less happy the parents are rated as being, the greater the likelihood that more attachment will be indicated for mother than for father" (page 426). They interpret these findings as indicating that the offspring are more likely to impute major responsibility to the father for whatever marital unhappiness their parents may suffer.†

Sussman holds (332) that parents influence the mate-selection of their children by their choice of location of residence (cf. the concept of residential propinquity) and by registering approval and disapproval as, e.g., through planning recreational activities or withholding financial support.

Parsons (279) sees American girls as having the opportunity to achieve emotional maturity earlier than boys because the adult model (mother) is more readily available for girls.‡ Yet he sees women as frustrated and

---

* For another reformulation see Erich Fromm (114).

† Cupps and Hayner (75) find that university students who rate their parents' marriage as happy date more on the average than those who regard their parents' marriage as unhappy.

‡ But Winch (374) felt that his data led to the opposite interpretation: that by college age daughters do not become emancipated from their parents to the same degree or in the same manner as men, but tend as they marry to transfer their dependence from their families to their husbands.

ambivalent over the conflict of domestic function versus glamour role. Rose (289) believes that middle class American women are confused in their expectations of the adult female role. Hacker (138) feels that the plight of women entitles them to be considered as a minority group. Komarovsky sees the dilemma as the choice between appearing competent in a career orientation and appearing dependent in a marriage orientation (197, 199). She believes that the resolution of this dilemma may be coming with a generation of girls who aspire to be competent wives and mothers but also to have worthwhile interests outside the home. Another intelligent—if indignantly militant—treatment of the woman's dilemma is that of de Beauvoir (80).

In bringing the data of the Burgess and Wallin study to bear on Komarovsky's concept of the functional analysis of the female sex role (198), Wallin (360) found that men tend to dislike their wives' mothers somewhat less than the wives dislike the men's mothers. This finding is, of course, in harmony with Freudian expectations. Wallin's finding is corroborated by Duvall (90) and also by Koller (196), who reports that of the four parents-in-law the wife's mother is the most likely to join the household of the young couple.

Faris (106) has described and analyzed the continuity of generations and some of the conditions which appear to engender discontinuities. Sussman (331) finds that continuity between generations tends to be greater when the offspring marries a spouse of similar cultural background, when the offspring meets parental expectations by having a traditional courtship and wedding, and when the offspring has been reared developmentally (as opposed to traditionally)

### Socialization and social mobility

Ruesch (293) hypothesizes the existence of two kinds of upwardly mobile individuals: (a) those who identify with upwardly mobile parents, and (b) those who rebel against the values of their static or downwardly mobile parents. There are several studies which may be relevant to this formulation. In a study of the leisure activities of children MacDonald *et al.* (233) find a small proportion of lower class children who do not participate in the typical leisure activities of lower class children but rather associate with middle class children in middle class organizations. Such differential association would, of course, provide this small group with social techniques for participating in at least the child-culture of the middle class. We may be seeing some of the consequences of this kind of differential association in the report by Kinsey (180) that males who are going to be upwardly mobile tend to behave sexually during the years of their childhood and adolescence (*i.e.*, prior to having moved upward) in the fashion of the boys who belong to the stratum of their destination.

Henry has reported (149) that men who achieve executive positions in business are probably emancipated from their fathers and have achieved strong positive identifications with their fathers. This description sounds like the first of Ruesch's types.

Evelyn Ellis (99) has conducted a study of sixty "outstanding unmarried women now living in one city, Montgomery, Alabama." As compared with the nonmobile career women, a significantly larger proportion of the mobile respondents report experiences of being rejected by parents and by the community during childhood and being more isolated socially during adulthood. The mobile women, moreover, had a significantly greater incidence of psychosomatic ailments. These women resemble the second of Ruesch's types. From these studies we might conjecture that upwardly mobile individuals of the second type started out as rebellious children with strong negative attitudes toward static or downwardly mobile parents, that they developed substitute associations and activities, and thereby learned the skills and attitudes which are useful in the mobility climb.

### Cultural variation in the family

Cultural variation in the organization of the family continues to fascinate sociologists for it serves to acquaint us with (a) the possible range of variation, and (b) the correlates of various cultural elements—or the functions they fulfill—*e.g.*, the idea that a particular kind of mate-selection is consistent with a particular kind of property system.

During the period under study it appears from the literature that the Chinese was the most popular exotic family system immediately accessible to sociologists. From Olga Lang's fine study at the beginning of the decade (212) the major emphasis has been upon the (telescoped) transition from the traditional extended family to the conjugal family, from obligation to affection as a basis of interpersonal relations, and so forth. According to Lang, the "modernized" Chinese (and especially the women) tend to oppose the patriarchal family, arranged marriages, polygyny, and extensive obligations to kinsmen; they tend to favor affectional attraction as a basis of mate-selection.

Others have noted the functional relation between other aspects of Chinese culture and the mode of selecting mates. For example, in comparing traditional relationships among the Chinese gentry with those among the peasantry, Fei observes (107, page 6):

Marriage has been regarded as a family affair [among the gentry] and has been customarily defined as an alliance of houses. Choice of mate is made on the ground of family status. Through marriage a number of big houses are confederated into a powerful group. But if we turn to the peasants, we shall see that the main consideration in matchmaking is the working ability of the girl.

Two studies published since the Communist conquest of China use the traditional family as a bench mark against which to project the family as it appears to be developing under the People's Republic. Shu-Ching Lee (215) describes the mate-selection pattern in the traditional family as follows:

Since marriage in traditional China means taking a new member into the family rather than simply getting a wife for a husband, marriage is defined in the Confucian Classics as "to make a union between two persons of different families, the object of which is to serve, on the one hand, the ancestors in the temple, and to perpetuate, on the other hand, the coming generation." It must be arranged through "the orders of the parents and the words of the go-between." Among young boys and girls, dating is unknown and romantic love non-existent—both seem to be the devices for a conjugal union, not for an institutional family (page 276).

In the traditional family the three chief qualifications for a wife were: (a) capability of bearing children, (b) compliance with the family's traditions, and (c) ability to endure household drudgery.

Under the revolution, Lee says, the in-group feeling of the family seems to have shifted to the Party. The inconsiderate treatment of wives, concubines, daughters-in-law, and domestic maids, and the low status of women in general have been used by the Party, he continues, to sell the new order, whereby:

Marriage is no longer taken as a matter involving two families as in traditional China, nor between two individuals as in the Western world, but a spiritual union of two comrades of different sexes; and the first task of the couple is to strengthen and cherish their commonly shared belief of communism, and then to engage in production to build a new society (page 280).

Lee concludes that the success of this campaign cannot be estimated.

Chen (60) comes to similar conclusions. He states that according to the doctrine of the Chinese Communists the decision to marry should presumably be contingent upon an affirmative answer to the question as to whether or not the marriage will "result in greater contributions to revolutionary work." The family is charged with the political function of heightening political consciousness. "It is written into the marriage law that husband and wife should love and respect each other, 'engage in production,' and work 'for the building of a new society'" (page 343). Children are expected to report to political authorities any political deviations on the part of their parents. "Filial piety is condemned as a feudal survival; antifilial piety has become a common slogan of the propagandists" (page 343).

The theoretical use to which we have put the traditional Chinese family is to treat it as an ideal-typical formulation of the maximum development and proliferation of a family form under nonindustrial conditions. It seems correct to assert that our lively interest in changes in the Chinese family results from our wishing to witness an accelerated version of the social changes which we assume that occidental family forms have undergone in recent centuries. It is in this same general context of institutional change that Young's study of the Mormons (384) is both fascinating and frustrating. It is uniquely fascinating in reporting the only venture of any magnitude into polygyny by western man in recent centuries. The frustration is not attributable to Young's analysis, but to the subject matter. The Mormons were confronted with the necessity of making numerous adjustments to a polygynous way of life, *i.e.,* of really developing a new family form almost *de novo.* Thus we are able to see a sort of "social origin" *in utero.* Unfortunately for the curiosity of the sociologist the "gentiles" decided that Mormon polygyny was immoral and intolerable, and the frustration arises from the fact that the venture was destroyed before we could see how their adjustive processes would have worked out.

Other writings of the decade on the Chinese family include: 108, 113, 118, 161, 162, 163, 214, 218, 219, 266. Some of the writings on other family forms outside our national borders include: Japan, 10, 102, 219, 245, 336, 338; India, 59, 250, 251; U.S.S.R., 72, 120, 121; Bulgaria, 294; Germany, 18, 20, 40, 226, 296, 297, 298, 347; Italy, 122; France, 57, 117; England (a London suburb), 308; Australia, 274; Brazil, 219, 280, 369; Panama, 29, 30; Mestizo America, 219; West Indies, 148; Egypt, 85. On Puerto Rico there are three studies (143, 155, 328). Descriptions of unusual family forms within our continental borders include those of the Kentucky highlands (42, 43); the Hutterites (91); and the Mormons (265, 384).

In closing this section we may note three publications which have attempted to give something approaching the "wide screen" to a description of family forms. The May, 1948, issue of the *American Journal of Sociology* presents short papers which describe regional (53, 110, 145, 351) and ethnic (51, 111, 170, 363) variation in the American family. The book by Queen and Adams (283) presents ethnographic accounts of a variety of family forms, from the Hopi, Kwoma, and Alorese to the English colonists in America and the contemporary Japanese. And the November, 1954, issue of *Marriage and Family,* under the special editorship of W. F. Ogburn, includes sixteen papers on the family in many sections of the literate world (10, 57, 59, 121, 122, 146, 253, 264, 266, 269, 280, 298, 334, 337, 345, 349).

## Textbooks

During the decade from 1945 to 1955 the writer knows of ten new texts and revisions which have appeared in the field of marriage and the family (11, 48, 55, 101, 136, 184, 267, 350, 357, 377) and of three serious books on marriage (49, 62, 246).*

In 1948 Becker and Hill introduced a new kind of text by editing a book of twenty-six chapters by nearly as many specialists. The book proved to be more coherent than might be thought possible with this format. This book was revised in 1955 (21), and to the revision were added three critiques of the Kinsey studies. Another volume of specially written essays of high quality is that of Anshen (9).

A third type of text to enter the field is the book of readings, *i.e.*, a volume consisting in part or in whole of reprints of previously published articles. Back in 1931 Reuter and Runner had published an excellent book with this format (286), and then little was done with this kind of book for some twenty years. A spate of them began to come off the presses beginning late in 1952 with Landis-Landis (208). In 1953 came works edited by Olsen, Mudd, and Bourdeau (277) and Winch and McGinnis (381); then Sussman's book (333) came along in 1955.

## Overview of 1945–1955

I should like to try to summarize my impressions of the literature on the family produced during this decade under the headings: subject matter, method, and biases.

SUBJECT MATTER. As in sociology in general, the literature on the family has become permeated with a concern with *social stratification*. From the two texts which first gave an appreciable play to this topic—Winch in 1952 and Cavan in 1953—it appears that it was from Lloyd Warner and his associates at the University of Chicago that most of the description and analysis were borowed. I think it is fair to say that this does not necessarily imply that family sociologists have been or are now irrevocably committed to Warner's view—and thereby opposed to the view of Warner's critics—on stratification. It is clear, however, that the type

---

* The writer has made no attempt to cover the field of the so-called "functional" books or of Catholic texts. Sirjamaki has written a book on the American family for the general reader (311).

of analysis which Warner and his group have made (*e.g.*, 156, 157, 234, 235, 236, 237) is easily utilized in family sociology.

Related to the introduction of considerations of social stratification is what we might call the field of *subculture and personality*. Here the work of Allison Davis (76, 77), R. J. Havighurst (78), W. E. Henry (149), Arnold Green (135), and Carson McGuire (234–237) comes to mind. The utility of this kind of analysis is that it points to the different kinds of experiences to which children are exposed who participate in different subcultures; it appears that these experiences result in divergent personality structures and behavior patterns from one social class to another.

The traditional rural-urban dichotomy has not waned in interest for the sociologist, but, perhaps led by *Fortune's* William H. Whyte, Jr. (366, 367, 368), we have come to a very lively interest in *suburbanism* as a way of life. Indeed, one interesting paper (165) professes to see a hitherto unsuspected type of family arising in this milieu. (Cf. also 243, 295.)

The de-emphasis of sociologists on "social problems" is reflected in the relatively little writing of this orientation on the family. Of three problem-oriented titles in this bibliography (152, 202, 232) two had to do with the family problems of the man in military service (152, 232). With the rise in the average age of our national population, however, there has been a concomitant increase in interest in the phenomenon of aging and the problems of *old age* (19, 54, 56, 144, 299, 316, 348). As of the moment of writing, this seems to be the middle of the growing season, and it is too soon to tell exactly how the crop of research on this topic will turn out.

The decade has been lively in the production of *descriptive statistics* concerning family life (79, 87, 94, 123, 124, 125, 126, 127, 128, 140, 141, 164, 167, 176, 177, 254, 255, 256, 257, 259, 329, 339). In particular the literature has been enriched by Glick's articles on the life cycle of the family (124, 127), and by Jacobson's (167) on dissolution of the family; it has been enlivened by a dispute as to whether or not the Bureau of the Census knows what it is doing when it estimates the average age at first marriage (258).

Finally, lest it be thought that the decade has entirely neglected formal consideration of the traditional *institutional* conception, or functions, of the family, 1955 saw publication of a study of the relation between technology and the changing functions of the family by the two familiar names, Ogburn and Nimkoff (276). The major historical work on the family to be published during the decade is also devoted to an explicit institutional analysis with special emphasis on the relation between the family's functions and its power in society. This is the very scholarly but value-laden work of Zimmerman (386).

METHODS. There has not been a great deal of innovation in research methods. The use of *projective techniques* for nomothetic research is illustrated in Sewell's research (305), and this procedure plus the *projective analysis of interview materials* is represented in Winch's study on complementary needs (379, 380).

There has been some disposition to introduce the methods and concepts of *group dynamics* into family studies (39, 110b, 149a, 248, 249, 326).

Finally, there has been some—but all too little—effort at repeat studies (8, 358). This writer would like to offer encouragement to the scholar who will undertake the extremely necessary labor of checking on the results of others. In view of the generally low order of correlations which obtains in sociological research, it seems highly desirable that such studies duplicate just as closely as is humanly possible the details of the initial research. Otherwise, divergent results are subject to ambiguous interpretation.

"BIASES." * One final note concerns what the writer thinks he sees as two more or less characteristic biases of the decade: (a) anti-Kinsey (27, 92, 207), and (b) anti-Waller (32, 150, 315, and see also 200). Some observations have been made above on the work of Kinsey, and here it is sufficient to add that most of an issue of *Social Problems* (April, 1954) has been devoted to this topic.

Having been influenced by Freud, Waller developed formulations which frequently referred to quite covert psychological processes. For this reason it is always difficult to be sure that questionnaire responses pertain to the same order of phenomena. Here the question of validity is crucial. Moreover, as was reasoned above (page 363), the presentation of negative findings is logically not equivalent to disproof. It is this writer's suspicion that in these studies there has been some tapping of the official ideology regarding dating practices rather than of the level which concerned Waller. It may be that Waller, whose formulations and literary style were highly refreshing, was largely wrong, but before this conclusion becomes importunate, we shall need to design studies more indisputably relevant.

* Perhaps "biases" is too strong and too loaded, and therefore possibly "attitudes" or "themes" would be preferable. In any event there is no intent to suggest that such "dispositions" are necessarily "wrong" but merely to note their apparent existence.

## BIBLIOGRAPHICAL REFERENCES

1. Aberle, D. F., and K. D. Naegele, "Middle-class fathers' occupational role and attitudes toward children," *Amer. J. Orthopsychiat.*, Vol. 22 (1952), pp. 366–378.
2. Adams, E. M., "The philosophical approach to marriage and family research," *Social Forces*, Vol. 29 (1950), pp. 62–64.
3. Adler, Leta M., "The relationship of marital status to incidence of and recovery from mental illness," *Social Forces*, Vol. 32 (1953), pp. 185–194.
4. Anderson, C. A., and Mary J. Bowman, "The vanishing servant and the contemporary status system of the American South," *Amer. J. Soc.*, Vol. 59 (1953–1954), pp. 215–230.
5. Anderson, J. E., "Personality organization in children," *Amer. Psychologist*, Vol. 3 (1948), pp. 409–416.
6. Anderson, W. A., "Family social participation and social status self-ratings," *Amer. Soc. Rev.*, Vol. 11 (1946), pp. 253–258.
7. Anderson, W. A., *Marriages and Families of University Graduates*, Ithaca, Cornell University Press, 1950.
8. Andrews, R. O., and H. T. Christensen, "Relationship of absence of a parent to courtship status: a repeat study," *Amer. Soc. Rev.*, Vol. 16 (1951), pp. 541–544.
9. Anshen, Ruth N. (Ed.), *The Family: Its Function and Destiny*, New York, Harper, 1949.
10. Ariga, K., "The family in Japan," *Marriage Fam. Living*, Vol. 16 (1954), pp. 362–368.
11. Baber, R. E., *Marriage and the Family*, 2d ed., New York, McGraw-Hill, 1953.
12. Bain, R., "Needed research in parent-child fixation," *Amer. Soc. Rev.*, Vol. 10 (1945), pp. 208–216.
13. Bain, R., "Making normal people," *Marriage Fam. Living*, Vol. 16 (1954), pp. 27–31.
14. Baldwin, A. L., Joan Kalhorn, and Fay H. Breese, "Patterns of parent behavior," *Psychol. Monogr.*, No. 268, Vol. 58 (1945).
15. Barron, M. L., "The incidence of Jewish intermarriage in Europe and America," *Amer. Soc. Rev.*, Vol. 11 (1946), pp. 6–13.
16. Barron, M. L., *People Who Intermarry*, Syracuse, Syracuse University Press, 1946.
17. Barron, M. L., "Research on intermarriage: a survey of accomplishments and prospects," *Amer. J. Soc.*, Vol. 57 (1951–1952), pp. 249–255.
18. Baumert, G., *Deutsche Familien nach dem Kriege*, Darmstadt, Eduard Roether Verlag, 1954.
19. Beard, Belle B., "Are the aged ex-family? An inquiry into the place of the aged in family life with special reference to the treatment of the aged in sociology textbooks on the family," *Social Forces*, Vol. 27 (1949), pp. 274–279.
20. Becker, H., "German families today," in H. J. Morgenthau (ed.), *Germany and the Future of Europe*, Chicago, University of Chicago Press, 1951, pp. 12–24.
21. Becker, H., and R. Hill (eds.), *Family, Marriage and Parenthood*, 2d ed., Boston, Heath, 1955.
22. Beigel, H. C., "Romantic love," *Amer. Soc. Rev.*, Vol. 16 (1951), pp. 326–334.
23. Bend, E., "Marriage offers in a Yiddish newspaper—1935 and 1950," *Amer. J. Soc.*, Vol. 58 (1952–1953), pp. 60–66.
24. Benedek, Therese, *Psychosexual Functions in Women*, New York, Ronald, 1952.

25. Benson, P., "Familism and marital success," *Social Forces*, Vol. 33 (1955), pp. 277–280.

26. Bergler, E., *Unhappy Marriage and Divorce*, New York, International Universities Press, 1946.

27. Bergler, E., and W. S. Kroger, *Kinsey's Myth of Female Sexuality: The Medical Facts*, New York, Grune and Stratton, 1954.

28. Bernard, Jessie, "Note on: Questionnaire vs. interview methods in the study of human love relationships, by A. Ellis," *Amer. Soc. Rev.*, Vol. 13 (1948), pp. 217–218.

29. Biesanz, J., "Inter-American marriages on the Isthmus of Panama," *Social Forces*, Vol. 29 (1950), pp. 159–163.

30. Biesanz, J., and L. H. Smith, "Adjustment of interethnic marriages on the Isthmus of Panama," *Amer. Soc. Rev.*, Vol. 16 (1951), pp. 819–822.

31. Blood, R. O., Jr., "A situational approach to the study of permissiveness in child-rearing," *Amer. Soc. Rev.*, Vol. 18 (1953), pp. 84–87.

32. Blood, R. O., Jr., "A retest of Waller's rating complex," *Marriage Fam. Living*, Vol. 17 (1955), pp. 41–47.

33. Blum, G. S., and D. R. Miller, "Exploring the psychoanalytic theory of the 'oral' character," *J. of Pers.*, Vol. 20 (1952), pp. 287–304.

34. Bogue, D. J., "Urbanism in the United States, 1950," *Amer. J. Soc.*, Vol. 60 (1954–1955), pp. 471–486.

35. Bossard, J. H. S., "Marrying late in life," *Social Forces*, Vol. 29 (1951), pp. 405–408.

36. Bossard, J. H. S., *Parent and Child: Studies in Family Behavior*, Philadelphia, University of Pennsylvania Press, 1953.

37. Bossard, J. H. S., and Eleanor S. Boll, "Rite of passage—a contemporary study," *Social Forces*, Vol. 26 (1948), pp. 247–255.

38. Bowerman, C. E., "Assortive mating by previous marital status: Seattle, 1939–1946," *Amer. Soc. Rev.*, Vol. 18 (1953), pp. 170–177.

39. Bowlby, J., "The study and reduction of group tensions in the family," *Hum. Relat.*, Vol. 2 (1949), pp. 123–128.

39a. Bowlby, J., *Child Care and the Growth of Love*, London, Penguin Books, 1953.

40. Brandes, O. Jean, "The effect of war on the German family," *Social Forces*, Vol. 29 (1950), pp. 164–173.

41. Brim, O. G., Jr., "The acceptance of new behavior in child-rearing," *Hum. Relat.*, Vol. 7 (1954), pp. 473–491.

42. Brown, J. S., "Social class, intermarriage, and church membership in a Kentucky community," *Amer. J. Soc.*, Vol. 57 (1951–1952), pp. 232–242.

43. Brown, J. S., "The conjugal family and the extended family group," *Amer. Soc. Rev.*, Vol. 17 (1952), pp. 297–306.

44. Brown, Julia S., "A comparative study of deviations from sexual mores," *Amer. Soc. Rev.*, Vol. 17 (1952), pp. 135–146.

45. Burgess, E. W., "The family and sociological research," *Social Forces*, Vol. 26 (1947), pp. 1–6.

46. Burgess, E. W., "The family in a changing society," *Amer. J. Soc.*, Vol. 53 (1947–1948), pp. 417–422.

47. Burgess, E. W., and L. S. Cottrell, Jr., *Predicting Success or Failure in Marriage*, New York, Prentice-Hall, 1939.

48. Burgess, E. W., and H. J. Locke, *The Family: From Institution to Companionship*, 2d ed., New York, American, 1953.

49. Burgess, E. W., and P. Wallin, *Engagement and Marriage*, Chicago, Lippincott, 1953.

50. Burma, J. H., "Research note on the measurement of interracial marriage," *Amer. J. Soc.*, Vol. 57 (1951–1952), pp. 587–589.

51. Campisi, P. J., "Ethnic family patterns: the Italian family in the United States," *Amer. J. Soc.*, Vol. 53 (1948–1949), pp. 443–449.

52. Cannon, K. L., "Marriage and divorce in Iowa (1940–47," *Marriage Fam. Living*, Vol. 9 (1947), pp. 81–83, 98.

53. Cavan, Ruth S., "Regional family patterns: The Middle Western family," *Amer. J. Soc.*, Vol. 53 (1947–1948), pp. 430–431.

54. Cavan, Ruth S., "Family life and family substitutes in old age," *Amer. Soc. Rev.*, Vol. 14 (1949), pp. 71–83.

55. Cavan, Ruth S., *The American Family*, New York, Crowell, 1953.

56. Cavan, Ruth S., E. W. Burgess, R. J. Havighurst, and H. Goldhamer, *Personal Adjustment in Old Age*, Chicago, Science Research Associates, 1949.

57. Ceccaldi, D., "The family in France," *Marriage Fam. Living*, Vol. 16 (1954), pp. 326–330.

58. Centers, R., "Marital selection and occupational strata," *Amer. J. Soc.*, Vol. 54 (1948–1949), pp. 530–535.

59. Chandrasekhar, S., "The family in India," *Marriage Fam. Living*, Vol. 16 (1954), pp. 336–342.

60. Chen, T. H., "The Marxist remolding of Chinese society," *Amer. J. Soc.*, Vol. 58 (1952–1953), pp. 340–346.

61. Child, I. L., "Socialization," in L. Gardner (ed.), *Handbook of Social Psychology*, Vol. II, Cambridge, Addison-Wesley, 1954, pp. 655–692.

62. Christensen, H. T., *Marriage Analysis: Foundations for Successful Family Life*, New York, Ronald, 1950.

63. Christensen, H. T., "Dating behavior as evaluated by high-school students," *Amer. J. Soc.*, Vol. 57 (1951–1952), pp. 580–586.

64. Christensen, H. T., "Studies in child spacing: I—Premarital pregnancy as measured by the spacing of the first birth from marriage," *Amer. Soc. Rev.*, Vol. 18 (1953), pp. 53–59.

65. Christensen, H. T., and Olive P. Bowden, "Studies in child spacing: II—The time-interval between marriage of parents and birth of their first child, Tippecanoe County, Indiana," *Social Forces*, Vol. 31 (1953), pp. 346–351.

66. Christensen, H. T., and Hanna H. Meissner, "Studies in child spacing: III—Premarital pregnancy as a factor in divorce," *Amer. Soc. Rev.*, Vol. 13 (1953), pp. 641–644.

67. Christensen, H. T., and R. E. Philbrick, "Family size as a factor in the marital adjustments of college couples," *Amer. Soc. Rev.*, Vol. 17 (1952), pp. 306–312.

68. Clarke, A. C., "An examination of the operation of residential propinquity as a factor in mate selection," *Amer. Soc. Rev.*, Vol. 17 (1952), pp. 17–22.

69. Cochran, W. G., F. Mosteller, J. W. Tukey, with the assistance of W. O. Jenkins, *Statistical Problems of the Kinsey Report on Sexual Behavior in the Human Male*, Washington, American Statistical Association, 1954.

70. Cohen, Lillian, "Family characteristics of homeowners," *Amer. J. Soc.*, Vol. 55 (1949–1950), pp. 565–571.

71. Coleman, Rose W., E. Kris, and Sally Provence, "The study of variations of early parental attitudes," in *Psychoanalytic Study of the Child*, Vol. VIII, New York, International Universities Press, 1953, pp. 20–47.

72. Coser, L. A., "Some aspects of Soviet family policy," *Amer. J. Soc.*, Vol. 56 (1950–1951), pp. 424–434.

73. Cottrell, L. S., Jr., "The present status and future orientation of research on the family," *Amer. Soc. Rev.*, Vol. 13 (1948), pp. 123–129.

74. Crist, J. R., "High school dating as a behavior system," *Marriage Fam. Living*, Vol. 15 (1953), pp. 23–28.

75. Cupps, Rayanne D., and N. S. Hayner, "Dating at the University of Washington," *Marriage Fam. Living*, Vol. 9 (1947), pp. 30–31.

76. Davis, A., "Socialization and adolescent personality," in *Adolescence, Forty-third Yearbook, Part I*, Chicago, National Society for the Study of Education, 1944, Chap. 11.

77. Davis, A., *Social-class Influences Upon Learning*, Cambridge, Harvard University Press, 1949.

78. Davis, A., and R. J. Havighurst, "Social class and color differences in child-rearing," *Amer. Soc. Rev.*, Vol. 11 (1946), pp. 698–710.

79. Davis, K., "Statistical perspective on marriage and divorce," *Ann. Amer. Acad. Polit. Soc. Sci.*, Vol. 272 (1950), pp. 9–21.

80. de Beauvoir, Simone, *The Second Sex*, New York, Knopf, 1953.

81. Despert, J. Louise, *Children of Divorce*, Garden City, Doubleday, 1953.

82. Dinltz, S., R. R. Dynes, and A. C. Clarke, "Preferences for male or female children: traditional or affectional?" *Marriage Fam. Living*, Vol. 16 (1954), pp. 128–130.

83. Dollard, J., "Do we have a science of child rearing?" in *The Family in a Democratic Society: Anniversary Papers of the Community Service Society of New York*, New York, Columbia University Press, 1949, pp. 41–55.

84. Dotson, F., "Patterns of voluntary association among urban working-class families," *Amer. Soc. Rev.*, Vol. 16 (1951), pp. 687–693.

85. Douglass, J. H., and Katherine W. Douglass, "Aspects of marriage and family living among Egyptian peasants (*Fellaheen*)," *Marriage Fam. Living*, Vol. 16 (1954), pp. 45–48.

86. Dublin, L., "These are the single," in Hilda Holland (ed.), *Why Are You Single?* New York, Farrar Strauss, 1949, pp. 67–85.

87. Durand, J. D., "Married women in the labor force," *Amer. J. Soc.*, Vol. 52 (1946–1947), pp. 217–223.

88. Durkheim, E., *The Division of Labor in Society*, trans. by G. Simpson, Glencoe, Free Press, 1947.

89. Duvall, Evelyn M., "Conceptions of parenthood," *Amer. J. Soc.*, Vol. 52 (1946–1947), pp. 193–203.

90. Duvall, Evelyn M., *In-laws: Pro and Con: An Original Study of Interpersonal Relations*, New York, Association Press, 1954.

91. Eaton, J. W., "Controlled acculturation: a survival technique of the Hutterites," *Amer. Soc. Rev.*, Vol. 17 (1952), pp. 331–340.

92. Ehrmann, W. W., "Non-conformance of male and female reports on premarital coitus," *Social Problems*, Vol. 1 (1954), pp. 155–159.

93. Ehrmann, W. W., "Influence of comparative social class of companion upon premarital heterosexual behavior," *Marriage Fam. Living*, Vol. 17 (1955), pp. 48–55.

94. Eldridge, Hope T., and J. S. Siegel, "The changing sex ratio in the United States," *Amer. J. Soc.*, Vol. 52 (1946–1947), pp. 224–234.

95. Ellis, A., "Questionnaire *versus* interview methods in the study of human love relationships," *Amer. Soc. Rev.*, Vol. 12 (1947), pp. 541–553.

96. Ellis, A., "Questionnaire *versus* interview methods in the study of human love relationships. II. Uncategorized responses," *Amer. Soc. Rev.*, Vol. 13 (1948), pp. 61–65.

97. Ellis, A., "The value of marriage prediction tests," *Amer. Soc. Rev.*, Vol. 13 (1948), pp. 710–718.

98. Ellis, A., "1953 classified bibliography on marriage and family relations," *Marriage Fam. Living*, Vol. 16 (1954), pp. 254–263.

99. Ellis, Evelyn, "Social psychological correlates of upward social mobility among unmarried career women," *Amer. Soc. Rev.*, Vol. 17 (1952), pp. 558–563.

100. Ellsworth, J. S., Jr., "The relationship of population density to residential propinquity as a factor in marriage selection," *Amer. Soc. Rev.*, Vol. 13 (1948), pp. 444–448.

101. Elmer, M. C., *The Sociology of the Family*, Boston, Ginn, 1945.

102. Embree, J. F., *The Japanese Nation*, New York, Farrar and Rinehart, 1945.

103. Ericson, Martha C., "Child-rearing and social status," *Amer. J. Soc.*, Vol. 52 (1946–1947), pp. 190–192.

104. Erikson, E. H., *Childhood and Society*, New York, Norton, 1950.

105. Escalone, Sibylle, "A commentary upon some recent changes in child-rearing practices," *Child Develpm.*, Vol. 20 (1949), pp. 157–162.

106. Faris, R. E. L., "Interaction of generations and family stability," *Amer. Soc. Rev.*, Vol. 12 (1947), pp. 159–164.

107. Fei, H., "Peasantry and gentry: an interpretation of Chinese social structure and its changes," *Amer. J. Soc.*, Vol. 52 (1946–1947), pp. 1–17.

108. Fei, H., and C. Chang, *Earthbound China: A Study of Rural Economy in Yunnan*, Chicago, University of Chicago Press, 1945.

109. Fiedler, F. E., W. G. Warrington, and F. J. Blaisdell, "Unconscious attitudes as correlates of sociometric choice in a social group," *J. Abnorm. Soc. Psychol.*, Vol. 47 (1952), pp. 790–796.

110. Folsom, J. K., "Regional family patterns: the New England family," *Amer. J. Soc.*, Vol. 53 (1947–1948), pp. 423–425.

110a. Foote, N. N., "Love," *Psychiatry*, Vol. 16 (1953), pp. 245–251.

110b. Foote, N. N., "Research: a new strength for family life," *Marriage Fam. Living*, Vol. 16 (1954), pp. 13–20.

111. Frazier, E. F., "Ethnic family patterns: the Negro family in the United States," *Amer. J. Soc.*, Vol. 53 (1947–1948), pp. 435–438.

112. Freud, S., "On narcissism: an introduction," in *Collected Papers*, Vol. IV, London, Hogarth, 1925, pp. 30–59.

113. Fried, M. H., *Fabric of Chinese Society: A Study of the Social Life of a Chinese County Seat*, New York, Frederick A. Praeger, 1953.

114. Fromm, E., "The Oedipus complex and the Oedipus myth," in Ruth N. Anshen (ed.), *The Family: Its Function and Destiny*, New York, Harper, 1949, pp. 334–358.

115. Frumkin, R. M., *The Measurement of Marriage Adjustment*, Annals of American Research, Washington, D. C., Public Affairs Press, 1954.

116. Frumkin, R. M., "Marital status and mental illness," *Sociol. Soc. Rev.*, Vol. 39 (1955), pp. 237–239.

117. Gallagher, O. R., "Looseness and rigidity in family structure," *Social Forces*, Vol. 31 (1953), pp. 332–339.

118. Gamble, S. D., *Ting Hsien: a North China Rural Community*, New York, Institute of Pacific Relations, 1954.

119. Geddes, D. P. (ed.), *An Analysis of the Kinsey Reports on Sexual Behavior in the Human Male and Female*, New York, Dutton, 1954.

120. Geiger, K., "Deprivation and solidarity in the Soviet urban family," *Amer. Soc. Rev.*, Vol. 20 (1955), pp. 57–68.

121. Geiger, K., and A. Inkeles, "The family in the U.S.S.R.," *Marriage Fam. Living*, Vol. 16 (1954), pp. 397–404.

122. Gini, C., and E. Caranti, "The family in Italy," *Marriage Fam. Living*, Vol. 16 (1954), pp. 350–361.

123. Glick, P. C., "Estimates of the future number of families," *Amer. J. Soc.*, Vol. 52 (1946–1947), pp. 235–242.

124. Glick, P. C., "The family cycle," *Amer. Soc. Rev.*, Vol. 12 (1947), pp. 164–174.

125. Glick, P. C., "Family life and full employment," *Amer. J. Soc.*, Vol. 54 (1948–1949), pp. 520–529.

126. Glick, P. C., "First marriages and remarriages," *Amer. Soc. Rev.*, Vol. 14 (1949), pp. 726–734.

127. Glick, P. C., "The life cycle of the family," *Marriage Fam. Living*, Vol. 17 (1955), pp. 3–8.

128. Glick, P. C., and E. Landau, "Age as a factor in marriage," *Amer. Soc. Rev.*, Vol. 15 (1950), pp. 517–529.

129. Golden, J., "Characteristics in the Negro-white intermarried in Philadelphia," *Amer. Soc. Rev.*, Vol. 18 (1953), pp. 177–183.

130. Golden, J., "Patterns of Negro-white intermarriage," *Amer. Soc. Rev.*, Vol. 19 (1954), pp. 144–147.

131. Goode, W. J., "Problems in postdivorce adjustment," *Amer. Soc. Rev.*, Vol. 14 (1949), pp. 394–401.

132. Goode, W. J., "Economic factors and marital stability," *Amer. Soc. Rev.*, Vol. 16 (1951), pp. 802–812.

133. Gray, H., "Jung's psychological types in men and women," *Stanford Med. Bull.*, Vol. 6 (1948), pp. 29–36.

134. Gray, H., "Psychological types in married people," *J. Soc. Psychol.*, Vol. 29 (1949), pp. 189–200.

135. Green, A. W., "The middle class male child and neurosis," *Amer. Soc. Rev.*, Vol. 11 (1946), pp. 31–41.

136. Groves, E. R., and G. H. Groves, *The Contemporary American Family*, Philadelphia, Lippincott, 1947.

137. Gruenberg, Sidonie M., and the Staff of the Child Study Association of America, *Our Children Today: A Guide to Their Needs from Infancy through Adolescence*, New York, Viking, 1952.

138. Hacker, Helen M., "Woman as a minority group," *Social Forces*, Vol. 30 (1951), pp. 60–69.

139. Haffter, C., *Kinder aus geschiedenen Ehen: eine Untersuchung uber den Einfluss der Ehescheidung auf Schicksal und Entwicklung der Kinder nach arztlichen, juristischen und fursorgerischen Fragestellungen*. Bern, Medizinisher Verlag Hans Huber, 1948. (Reviewed by Erna Barschak, *Amer. Soc. Rev.*, Vol. 16 (1951), pp. 416–417. Original not seen.)

140. Hajnal, J., "Analysis of changes in the marriage pattern by economic groups," *Amer. Soc. Rev.*, Vol. 19 (1954), pp. 295–302.

141. Hajnal, J., "Differential changes in marriage patterns," *Amer. Soc. Rev.*, Vol. 19 (1954), pp. 148–154.

142. Hatch, D. L., and Mary A. Hatch, "Criteria of social status as derived from

marriage announcements in the *New York Times*," *Amer. Soc. Rev.*, Vol. 12 (1947), pp. 396–403.

143. Hatt, P. K., *Backgrounds of human fertility in Puerto Rico: a sociological survey*, Princeton, Princeton University Press, 1952.

144. Havighurst, R. J., and Ruth Albrecht, *Older People*, New York, Longmans, Green, 1953.

145. Hayner, N. S., "Regional family patterns: the Western family," *Amer. J. Soc.*, Vol. 53 (1947–1948), pp. 432–434.

146. Hayner, N. S., "The family in Mexico," *Marriage Fam. Living*, Vol. 16 (1954), pp. 369–373.

147. Heinicke, C., and Beatrice B. Whiting, *Bibliographies on Personality and Social Development of the Child*, New York, Social Science Research Council, 1953.

148. Henriques, F., "West Indiana family organization," *Amer. J. Soc.*, Vol. 55 (1949–1950), pp. 30–37.

149. Henry, W. E., "The business executive: the psychodynamics of a social role," *Amer. J. Soc.*, Vol. 54 (1948–1949), pp. 286–291.

149a. Herbst, P. G., "The measurement of family relationships," *Hum. Relat.*, Vol. 5 (1952), pp. 3–35.

150. Herman, R. D., "The 'going steady' complex: a re-examination," *Marriage Fam. Living*, Vol. 17 (1955), pp. 36–40.

151. Hill, R., "The American family: problem or solution?" *Amer. J. Soc.*, Vol. 53 (1947–1948), pp. 125–130.

152. Hill, R., *Families Under Stress: Adjustment to the Crises of War Separation and Reunion*, New York, Harper, 1949.

153. Hill, R., "Review of current research on marriage and the family," *Amer. Soc. Rev.*, Vol. 16 (1951), pp. 694–701.

154. Hill, R., "A critique of contemporary marriage and family research," *Social Forces*, Vol. 33 (1955), pp. 268–277.

155. Hill, R., "Courtship in Puerto Rico: an Institution in Transition," *Marriage Fam. Living*, Vol. 17 (1955), pp. 26–35.

156. Hollingshead, A. B., "Class and kinship in a Middle Western community," *Amer. Soc. Rev.*, Vol. 14 (1949), pp. 469–475.

157. Hollingshead, A. B., *Elmtown's Youth: The Impact of Social Classes on Adolescents*, New York, Wiley, 1949.

158. Hollingshead, A. B., "Class differences in family stability," *Ann. Amer. Acad. Polit. Soc. Sci.*, Vol. 272 (1950), pp. 39–46.

159. Hollingshead, A. B., "Cultural factors in the selection of marriage mates," *Amer. Soc. Rev.*, Vol. 15 (1950), pp. 619–627.

160. Hollingshead, A. B., "Age relationships and marriage," *Amer. Soc. Rev.*, Vol. 16 (1951), pp. 492–499.

161. Hsu, F. L. K., "The family in China," in Ruth N. Anshen (ed.), *The Family: Its Function and Destiny*, New York, Harper, 1949, pp. 73–92.

162. Hsu, F. L. K., *Under the Ancestor's Shadow: Chinese Culture and Personality*, New York, Columbia University Press, 1948.

163. Hsu, F. L. K., and J. H. Hu, "Guild and kinship among the butchers in West Town," *Amer. Soc. Rev.*, Vol. 10 (1945), pp. 357–364.

164. Inter-Agency Committee for the National Conference on Family Life, *The American Family: A Factual Background*, Washington, U. S. Government Printing Office, 1948.

165. Jaco, E. G., and I. Belknap, "Is a new family form emerging in the urban fringe?" *Amer. Soc. Rev.*, Vol. 18 (1953), pp. 551–557.

166. Jacobson, A. H., "Conflict of attitudes toward the roles of the husband and wife in marriage," *Amer. Soc. Rev.*, Vol. 17 (1952), pp. 146–150.

167. Jacobson, P. H., "Differentials in divorce by duration of marriage and size of family," *Amer. Soc. Rev.*, Vol. 15 (1950), pp. 235–244.

168. James, E. O., *Marriage and Society*, London, Hutchinson's University Library, 1952.

169. Jansen, L. T., "Measuring family solidarity," *Amer. Soc. Rev.*, Vol. 17 (1952), pp. 727–733.

170. Jones, R. C., "Ethnic patterns: the Mexican family in the United States," *Amer. J. Soc.*, Vol. 53 (1948), pp. 450–452.

171. Kallman, F. J., "The genetic theory of schizophrenia," in C. Kluckhohn, H. A. Murray, with the collaboration of D. M. Schneider (eds.), *Personality: In Nature, Society, and Culture*, 2d ed., New York, Knopf, 1953, pp. 80–99.

172. Kardiner, A., *The Psychological Frontiers of Society*, New York, Columbia University Press, 1945.

173. Karlsson, G., *Adaptability and Communication in Marriage; a Swedish Predictive Study of Marital Satisfaction*, Uppsala, Almqvist and Wiksells Boktryckeri Aktiebolag, 1951.

174. Kennedy, Ruby J. R., "Single or triple melting pot? Intermarriage trends in New Haven, 1870–1940," *Amer. J. Soc.*, Vol. 49 (1943–1944), pp. 331–339.

175. Kennedy, Ruby J. R., "Single or triple melting pot? Intermarriage in New Haven, 1870–1950," *Amer. J. Soc.*, Vol. 58 (1952–1953), pp. 56–59.

176. Kephart, W. M., "The duration of marriage," *Amer. Soc. Rev.*, Vol. 19 (1954), pp. 287–295.

177. Kephart, W. M., and T. P. Monahan, "Desertion and divorce in Philadelphia," *Amer. Soc. Rev.*, Vol. 17 (1952), pp. 719–727.

178. Kimball, S. T., "Rural social organization and co-operative labor," *Amer. J. Soc.*, Vol. 54 (1948–1949), pp. 38–49.

179. King, C. E., "The Burgess-Cottrell method of measuring marital adjustment applied to a non-white southern urban population," *Marriage Fam. Living*, Vol. 14 (1952), pp. 280–285.

180. Kinsey, A. C., W. B. Pomeroy, and C. E. Martin, *Sexual Behavior in the Human Male*, Philadelphia, W. B. Saunders, 1948.

181. Kinsey, A. C., W. B. Pomeroy, C. E. Martin, and P. H. Gebhard, *Sexual Behavior in the Human Female*, Philadelphia, W. B. Saunders, 1953.

182. Kirkpatrick, C., *What Science Says about Happiness in Marriage*, Minneapolis, Burgess, 1947.

183. Kirkpatrick, C., "Review of Burgess and Wallin's *Engagement and Marriage*," *Amer. Soc. Rev.*, Vol. 18 (1953), pp. 698–700.

184. Kirkpatrick, C., *The Family: As Process and Institution*, New York, Ronald, 1955.

185. Kirkpatrick, C., and T. Caplow, "Courtship in a group of Minnesota students," *Amer. J. Soc.*, Vol. 51 (1945–1946), pp. 114–125.

186. Kirkpatrick, C., and T. Caplow, "Emotional trends in the courtship experience of college students as expressed by graphs with some observations of methodological implications," *Amer. Soc. Rev.*, Vol. 10 (1945), pp. 619–626.

187. Kirkpatrick, C., and J. Cotton, "Physical attractiveness, age, and marital adjustment," *Amer. Soc. Rev.*, Vol. 16 (1951), pp. 81–86.

188. Kirkpatrick, C., and C. Hobart, "Disagreement, disagreement estimate, and non-empathetic imputations for intimacy groups varying from favorite date to married," *Amer. Soc. Rev.*, Vol. 19 (1954), pp. 10–19.

189. Kirkpatrick, C., S. Stryker, and P. Buell, "An experimental study of attitudes towards male sex behavior with reference to Kinsey findings," *Amer. Soc. Rev.*, Vol. 17 (1952), pp. 580–587.

190. Kitagawa, Evelyn M., "Differential fertility in Chicago, 1920–40," *Amer. J. Soc.*, Vol. 58 (1952–1953), pp. 481–492.

191. Klemer, R. H., "Factors of personality and experience which differentiate single from married women," *Marriage Fam. Living*, Vol. 16 (1954), pp. 41–44.

192. Kolb, W. L., "Sociologically established family norms and democratic values," *Social Forces*, Vol. 26 (1948), pp. 451–456.

193. Kolb, W. L., "Family sociology, marriage education, and the romantic complex: a critique," *Social Forces*, Vol. 29 (1950), pp. 65–72.

194. Koller, M. R., "Residential propinquity of white mates at marriage in relation to age and occupation of males, Columbus, Ohio," *Amer. Soc. Rev.*, Vol. 13 (1948), pp. 613–616.

195. Koller, M. R., "Some changes in courtship behavior in three generations of Ohio women," *Amer. Soc. Rev.*, Vol. 16 (1951), pp. 366–370.

196. Koller, M. R., "Studies of three-generation households," *Marriage Fam. Living*, Vol. 16 (1954), pp. 205–206.

197. Komarovsky, Mirra, "Cultural contradictions and sex roles," *Amer. J. Soc.*, Vol. 52 (1946–1947), pp. 184–189.

198. Komarovsky, Mirra, "Functional analysis of sex roles," *Amer. Soc. Rev.*, Vol. 15 (1950), pp. 508–516.

199. Komarovsky, Mirra, *Women in the Modern World: Their Education and Dilemmas,* Boston, Little, Brown, 1953.

200. Komarovsky, Mirra, "Review of Burgess and Wallin's *Engagement and Marriage,*" *Amer. J. Soc.*, Vol. 59 (1953–1954), pp. 513–514.

201. Komarovsky, Mirra, and W. Waller, "Studies of the family," *Amer. J. Soc.*, Vol. 50 (1944–1945), pp. 443–451.

202. Koos, E. L., *Families in Trouble,* New York, King's Crown Press, 1946.

203. Ktsanes, T., and Virginia Ktsanes, "The theory of complementary needs in mate-selection," in R. F. Winch and R. McGinnis (eds.), *Selected Studies in Marriage and the Family,* New York, Holt, 1953, pp. 435–453.

204. Kyrk, Hazel, *The Family in the American Economy,* Chicago, University of Chicago Press, 1953.

205. Landis, J. T., "Length of time required to achieve adjustment in marriage," *Amer. Soc. Rev.*, Vol. 11 (1946), pp. 666–677.

206. Landis, J. T., "Marriages of mixed and non-mixed religious faith," *Amer. Soc. Rev.*, Vol. 14 (1949), pp. 401–407.

207. Landis, J. T., "The women Kinsey studied," *Social Problems,* Vol. 1 (1954), pp. 139–143.

208. Landis, J. T., and Mary G. Landis (eds.), *Readings in Marriage and the Family,* New York, Prentice-Hall, 1952.

209. Landis, J. T., T. Poffenberger, and Shirley Poffenberger, "The effects of first pregnancy upon the sexual adjustment of 212 couples," *Amer. Soc. Rev.*, Vol. 15 (1950), pp. 766–772.

210. Landis, P. H., "Rural-urban migration and the marriage rate—an hypothesis," *Amer. Soc. Rev.*, Vol. 11 (1946), pp. 155–158.

211. Landis, P. H., and Katherine H. Day, "Education as a factor in mate selection," *Amer. Soc. Rev.*, Vol. 10 (1945), pp. 558–560.

212. Lang, Olga, *Chinese Family and Society,* New Haven, Yale University Press, 1946.

213. Langhorne, M. C., and P. F. Secord, "Variations in marital needs with age, sex, marital status, and regional location," *J. Soc. Psychol.*, Vol. 41 (1955), pp. 19–37.

214. Lee, Rose H., "Research on the Chinese family," *Amer. J. Soc.*, Vol. 54 (1948–1949), pp. 497–504.

215. Lee, S., "China's traditional family, its characteristics and disintegration," *Amer. Soc. Rev.*, Vol. 18 (1953), pp. 272–280.

216. LeMasters, E. E., "Social class mobility and family integration," *Marriage Fam. Living*, Vol. 16 (1954), pp. 226–232.

217. Lenski, G. E., "Social correlates of religious interest," *Amer. Soc. Rev.*, Vol. 18 (1953), pp. 533–544.

218. Levy, M. J., Jr., *The Family Revolution in Modern China*, Cambridge, Harvard University Press, 1949.

219. Linton, R. (ed.), *Most of the World: The Peoples of Africa, Latin America, and the East Today*, New York, Columbia University Press, 1949.

220. Locke, H. J., "Predicting marital adjustment by comparing a divorced and a happily married group," *Amer. Soc. Rev.*, Vol. 12 (1947), pp. 187–191.

221. Locke, H. J., *Predicting Adjustment in Marriage: A Comparison of a Divorced and a Happily Married Group*, New York, Holt, 1951.

222. Locke, H. J., and G. Karlsson, "Marital adjustment and prediction in Sweden and the United States," *Amer. Soc. Rev.*, Vol. 17 (1952), pp. 10–17.

223. Locke, H. J., and W. J. Klausner, "Marital adjustment of divorced persons in subsequent marriages," *Sociol. and Soc. Res.*, Vol. 33 (1948), pp. 97–101.

224. Locke, H. J., and Muriel Mackeprang, "Marital adjustment and the employed wife," *Amer. J. Soc.*, Vol. 54 (1948–1949), pp. 536–538.

225. Locke, H. J., and V. A. Snowbarger, "Marital adjustment and prediction in Sweden," *Amer. J. Soc.*, Vol. 60 (1954–1955), pp. 51–53.

226. Lowie, R. H., *Toward Understanding Germany*, Chicago, University of Chicago Press, 1954.

227. Lowrie, S. H., "Dating theories and student responses," *Amer. Soc. Rev.*, Vol. 16 (1951), pp. 334–340.

228. Lu, Y., "Parental role and parent-child relationships," *Marriage Fam. Living*, Vol. 14 (1952), pp. 294–297.

229. Lu, Y., "Parent-child relationship and marital roles," *Amer. Soc. Rev.*, Vol. 17 (1952), pp. 357–361.

230. Lu, Y., "Predicting roles in marriage," *Amer. J. Soc.*, Vol. 58 (1952–1953), pp. 51–55.

231. Lundberg, G. A., and Lenore Dickson, "Inter-ethnic relations in a high-school population," *Amer. J. Soc.*, Vol. 58 (1952–1953), pp. 1–10.

232. McDonagh, E. C., "The discharged serviceman and his family," *Amer. J. Soc.*, Vol. 51 (1946), pp. 451–454.

233. MacDonald, Margherita, C. McGuire, and R. J. Havighurst, "Leisure activities and the socioeconomic status of children," *Amer. J. Soc.*, Vol. 54 (1948–1949), pp. 505–519.

234. McGuire, C., "Social stratification and mobility patterns," *Amer. Soc. Rev.*, Vol. 15 (1950), pp. 195–204.

235. McGuire, C., "Conforming, mobile, and divergent families," *Marriage Fam. Living*, Vol. 14 (1952), pp. 109–115.

236. McGuire, C., "Family life in lower and middle class homes," *Marriage Fam. Living*, Vol. 14 (1952), pp. 1–6.

237. McGuire, C., "Family and age-mates in personality formation," *Marriage Fam. Living*, Vol. 15 (1953), pp. 17–23.

238. McKeown, J. E., "The behavior of parents of schizophrenic, neurotic, and normal children," *Amer. J. Soc.*, Vol. 56 (1950–1951), pp. 175–179.

239. Marches, J. R., and G. Turbeville, "The effect of residential propinquity on marriage selection," *Amer. J. Soc.*, Vol. 58 (1952–1953), pp. 592–595.

240. Marcson, S., "A theory of intermarriage and assimilation," *Social Forces*, Vol. 29 (1950), pp. 75–78.

241. Marcson, S., "Predicting intermarriage," *Sociol. and Soc. Res.*, Vol. 37 (1953), pp. 151–156.

242. Marsh, D. C., and N. D. Humphrey, "Value congeries and marital counseling," *Marriage Fam. Living*, Vol. 15 (1953), pp. 28–32.

243. Martin, W. T., *The Rural-Urban Fringe: A Study of Adjustment to Residence Location*, Eugene, University of Oregon Press, 1953.

244. Maslow, A. H., "Love in healthy people," in Ashley Montagu (ed.), *The Meaning of Love*, New York, Julian, 1953, pp. 57–93.

245. Matsumiya, K., "Family organization in present-day Japan," *Amer. J. Soc.*, Vol. 53 (1947–1948), pp. 105–110.

246. Merrill, F. E., *Courtship and Marriage*, New York, Sloane, 1949.

247. Merrill, Maude A., *Problems of Child Delinquency*, Boston, Houghton Mifflin, 1947.

248. Mills, T. M., "Power relations in three-person groups," *Amer. Soc. Rev.*, Vol. 18 (1953), pp. 351–357.

249. Mills, T. M., "The coalition pattern in three-person groups," *Amer. Soc. Rev.*, Vol. 19 (1954), pp. 657–667.

250. Mitra, D. N., "A Hindu marriage in Bengal," *Amer. J. Soc.*, Vol. 52 (1946–1947), pp. 255–258.

251. Mitra, D. N., "A Hindu wife," *Amer. J. Soc.*, Vol. 52 (1946–1947), pp. 259–262.

252. Mittelman, B., "Complementary neurotic reactions in intimate relationships," *Psychoanal. Quart.*, Vol. 13 (1944), pp. 479–491.

253. Mogey, J. M., "The family in England," *Marriage Fam. Living*, Vol. 16 (1954), pp. 319–325.

254. Monahan, T. P., "One hundred years of marriages in Massachusetts," *Amer. J. Soc.*, Vol. 56 (1950–1951), pp. 534–545.

255. Monahan, T. P., *The Pattern of Age at Marriage in the United States*, 2 Vols., Philadelphia, Stephenson Brothers, 1951.

256. Monahan, T. P., "How stable are remarriages?" *Amer. J. Soc.*, Vol. 58 (1952–1953), pp. 280–288.

257. Monahan, T. P., "Does age at marriage matter in divorce?" *Social Forces*, Vol. 32 (1953), pp. 81–87.

258. Monahan, T. P., and R. Eckler, "Exchange of correspondence re: U. S. Census and calculations of age at marriage," *Amer. J. Soc.*, Vol. 56 (1950–1951), pp. 180–184.

259. Monahan, T. P., and W. M. Kephart, "Divorce and desertion by religious and mixed-religious groups," *Amer. J. Soc.*, Vol. 59 (1953–1954), pp. 454–465.

260. Motz, Annabelle B., "The role conception inventory: a tool for research in social psychology," *Amer. Soc. Rev.*, Vol. 17 (1952), pp. 465–471.

261. Mowrer, E. R., "Some factors in the affectional adjustment in twins," *Amer. Soc. Rev.*, Vol. 19 (1954), pp. 468–471.

262. Mowrer, E. R., and Harriet Mowrer, "The social psychology of marriage," *Amer. Soc. Rev.*, Vol. 16 (1951), pp. 27–36.

263. Murdock, G. P., *Social Structure*, New York, Macmillan, 1949.

264. Nahas, M. K., "The family in the Arab world," *Marriage Fam. Living*, Vol. 16 (1954), pp. 293–300.

265. Nelson, L., "Education and the changing size of Mormon families," *Rur. Sociol.*, Vol. 17 (1952), pp. 335–342.

266. Ni, E., "The family in China," *Marriage Fam. Living*, Vol. 16 (1954), pp. 315–318.

267. Nimkoff, M. F., *Marriage and the Family*, Boston, Houghton Mifflin, 1947.

268. Nimkoff, M. F., "Trends in family research," *Amer. J. Soc.*, Vol. 53 (1947–1948), pp. 477–482.

269. Nimkoff, M. F., "The family in the United States," *Marriage Fam. Living*, Vol. 16 (1954), pp. 390–396.

270. Nimkoff, M. F., and A. L. Wood, "Courtship and personality," *Amer. J. Soc.*, Vol. 53 (1947–1948), pp. 263–269.

271. Notcutt, B., and A. L. M. Silva, "Knowledge of other people," *J. Abnorm. Soc. Psychol.*, Vol. 46 (1951), pp. 30–37.

272. Nye, I., "Adolescent-parent adjustment—socio-economic level as a variable," *Amer. Soc. Rev.*, Vol. 16 (1951), pp. 341–349.

273. Oberndorf, C. P., "Psychoanalysis of married couples," *Psychoanal. Rev.*, Vol. 25 (1938), pp. 453–457.

274. Oeser, O. A., and S. B. Hammond (eds.), *Social Structure and Personality in a City*, New York, Macmillan, 1954.

275. Ogburn, W. F., "Education, income, and family unity," *Amer. J. Soc.*, Vol. 53 (1947–1948), pp. 474–476.

276. Ogburn, W. F., and M. F. Nimkoff, *Technology and the Changing Family*, Boston, Houghton Mifflin, 1955.

277. Olsen, A. R., E. H. Mudd, and H. Bourdeau (eds.), *Readings on Marriage and Family Relations*, Harrisburg, Stackpole, 1953.

278. Orlansky, H., "Infant care and personality," *Psychol. Bull.*, Vol. 46 (1949), pp. 1–48.

279. Parsons, T., "The social structure of the family," in Ruth N. Ashen (ed.), *The Family: Its Function and Destiny*, New York, Harper, 1949, pp. 173–201.

280. Pierson, D., "The family in Brazil," *Marriage Fam. Living*, Vol. 16 (1954), pp. 308–314.

281. Pinneau, S. R., "A critique on the articles by Margaret Ribble," *Child Develpm.*, Vol. 21 (1950), pp. 203–228.

282. Poffenberger, Shirley, T. Poffenberger, and J. T. Landis, "Intent toward conception and the pregnancy experience," *Amer. Soc. Rev.*, Vol. 17 (1952), pp. 616–620.

283. Queen, S. A., and J. B. Adams, *The Family in Various Cultures*, Philadelphia, Lippincott, 1952.

284. Redfield, Margaret P., "The American family: consensus and freedom," *Amer. J. Soc.*, Vol. 52 (1946–1947), pp. 175–183.

285. Reiss, A. J., Jr., "Social correlates of psychological types of delinquency," *Amer. Soc. Rev.*, Vol. 17 (1952), pp. 710–718.

286. Reuter, E. B., and Jessie R. Runner (eds.), *The Family: Source Materials for the Study of Family and Personality*, New York, McGraw-Hill, 1931.

287. Ribble, Margaret, *The Rights of Infants*, New York, Columbia University Press, 1943.

288. Risdon, R., "A study of interracial marriages based on data for Los Angeles County," *Sociol. and Soc. Res.*, Vol. 39 (1954), pp. 92–95.

289. Rose, A. M., "The adequacy of women's expectations for adult roles," *Social Forces*, Vol. 30 (1951), pp. 69–77.

290. Rose, A. M., "Factors associated with the life satisfaction of middle-class, middle-aged persons," *Marriage Fam. Living*, Vol. 17 (1955), pp. 15–19.

291. Ross, Helen, and Adelaide M. Johnson, "A psychiatric interpretation of the growth process in the early years," *J. Soc. Casework*, Vol. 30 (1949), pp. 87–92.

292. Roth, J., and R. F. Peck, "Social class and social mobility factors related to marital adjustment," *Amer. Soc. Rev.*, Vol. 16 (1951), pp. 478–487.

293. Ruesch, J., "Social technique, social status, and social change in illness," in C. Kluckhohn and H. A. Murray, with the collaboration of D. M. Schneider (eds.), *Personality: In Nature, Society, and Culture*, 2d ed., New York, Knopf, 1953, pp. 123–136.

294. Sanders, I. T., *Balkan Village*, Lexington, University of Kentucky Press, 1949.

295. Scaff, A. H., "The effect of commuting on participation in community organizations," *Amer. Soc. Rev.*, Vol. 17 (1952), pp. 215–220.

296. Schaffner, B., *Fatherland: A Study of Authoritarianism in the German Family*, New York, Columbia University Press, 1948.

297. Schelsky, H., *Wandlungen der deutschen Familie in der Gegenwart*, Dortmund, Ardey Verlag GMBH, 1953. (Reviewed by S. Riemer, *Amer. J. Soc.*, Vol. 59 [1953–1954], pp. 272–273. Original not seen.)

298. Schelsky, H., "The family in Germany," *Marriage Fam. Living*, Vol. 16 (1954), pp. 331–335.

299. Schmidt, J. F., "Patterns of poor adjustment in old age," *Amer. J. Soc.*, Vol. 57 (1951–1952), pp. 33–42.

300. Schnepp, G. J., and L. A. Roberts, "Residential propinquity and mate selection on a parish basis," *Amer. J. Soc.*, Vol. 58 (1952–1953), pp. 45–50.

301. Sears, R. R., "Ordinal position in the family as a psychological variable," *Amer. Soc. Rev.*, Vol. 15 (1950), pp. 397–401.

302. Sears, R. R., "Personality development in the family," in R. F. Winch and R. McGinnis (eds.), *Selected Studies in Marriage and the Family*, New York, Holt, 1953, pp. 215–240.

303. Sears, R. R., Margaret H. Pintler, and Pauline S. Sears, "Effect of father separation on pre-school children's doll play aggression," *Child Develpm.*, Vol. 17 (1946), pp. 219–243.

304. Sears, R. R., J. W. M. Whiting, V. Nowlis, and Pauline S. Sears, "Some child-rearing antecedents of aggression and dependency in young children," *Genet. Psychol. Monogr.*, Vol. 47 (1953), pp. 135–234.

305. Sewell, W. H., "Infant training and the personality of the child," *Amer. J. Soc.*, Vol. 58 (1952–1953), pp. 150–159.

306. Sewell, W. H., and B. L. Ellenbogen, "Social status and the measured intelligence of small city and rural children," *Amer. Soc. Rev.*, Vol. 17 (1952), pp. 612–616.

307. Sewell, W. H., and P. H. Mussen, "The effects of feeding, weaning, and scheduling procedures on childhood adjustment and the formation of oral symptoms," *Child Develpm.*, Vol. 23 (1952), pp. 185–191.

308. Shaw, L. A., "Impressions of family life in a London suburb," *Sociol. Rev.*, Vol. 2 (1954), pp. 179–194.

309. Simmel, G., *The Sociology of Georg Simmel*, trans. and ed. by K. Wolff, Glencoe, Free Press, 1950.

310. Sirjamaki, J., "Culture configurations in the American family," *Amer. J. Soc.*, Vol. 53 (1947–1948), pp. 464–470.

311. Sirjamaki, J., *The American Family in the Twentieth Century,* Cambridge, Harvard University Press, 1953.

312. Sjoberg, G., "The preindustrial city," *Amer. J. Soc.,* Vol. 60 (1954–1955), pp. 438–445.

313. Smith, Eleanor, and J. H. G. Monane, "Courtship values in a youth sample," *Amer. Soc. Rev.,* Vol. 18 (1953), pp. 635–640.

314. Smith, W. C., *The Stepchild,* Chicago, University of Chicago Press, 1953.

315. Smith, W. M., Jr., "Rating and dating: a re-study," *Marriage Fam. Living,* Vol. 14 (1952), pp. 312–317.

316. Smith, W. M., Jr., "Family plans for later years," *Marriage Fam. Living,* Vol. 16 (1954), pp. 36–40.

317. Sontag, L. W., "War and the fetal-maternal relationship," *Marriage Fam. Living,* Vol. 6 (1944), pp. 3–4, 16.

318. Spiegel, J. P., "New perspectives in the study of the family," *Marriage Fam. Living,* Vol. 16 (1954), pp. 4–12.

319. Spitz, R. A., "The role of ecological factors in emotional development in infancy," *Child Develpm.,* Vol. 20 (1949), pp. 145–155.

320. Stark, W., "Peasant society and the origins of romantic love," *Sociol. Rev.,* Vol. 1 (1953), pp. 83–92.

321. Stendler, Celia, "Sixty years of child training practices," *J. Pediat.,* Vol. 36 (1950), pp. 122–134.

322. Straus, R., and S. D. Bacon, *Drinking in College,* New Haven, Yale University Press, 1953.

323. Strauss, A., "The ideal and the chosen mate," *Amer. J. Soc.,* Vol. 52 (1946–1947), pp. 204–208.

324. Strauss, A., "The influence of parent-images upon marital choice," *Amer. Soc. Rev.,* Vol. 11 (1946), pp. 554–559.

325. Strauss, A., "Personality needs and marital choice," *Social Forces,* Vol. 25 (1947), pp. 332–335.

326. Strodtbeck, F. L., "The family as a three-person group," *Amer. Soc. Rev.,* Vol. 19 (1954), pp. 23–29.

327. Stroup, A. L., "Predicting marital success or failure in an urban population," *Amer. Soc. Rev.,* Vol. 18 (1953), pp. 558–562.

328. Stycos, J. M., "Family and fertility in Puerto Rico," *Amer. Soc. Rev.,* Vol. 17 (1952), pp. 572–580.

329. Sundal, A. P., and T. C. McCormick, "Age at marriage and mate selection: Madison, Wisconsin, 1937–43," *Amer. Soc. Rev.,* Vol. 16 (1951), pp. 37–48.

330. Sussman, M. B., "The help pattern in the middle class family," *Amer. Soc. Rev.,* Vol. 18 (1953), pp. 22–28.

331. Sussman, M. B., "Family continuity: selective factors which affect relationships between families at generational levels," *Marriage Fam. Living,* Vol. 16 (1954), pp. 112–120.

332. Sussman, M. B., "Parental participation in mate selection and its effect upon family continuity," *Social Forces,* Vol. 32 (1953), pp. 76–81.

333. Sussman, M. B. (ed.), *Sourcebook in Marriage and the Family,* Boston, Houghton Mifflin, 1955.

334. Svalastoga, K., "The family in Scandinavia," *Marriage Fam. Living,* Vol. 16 (1954), pp. 374–380.

335. Swanson, G. E., "The development of an instrument for rating child-parent relationships," *Social Forces,* Vol. 29 (1950), pp. 84–90.

336. Taeuber, Irene B., "Family, migration, and industrialization in Japan," *Amer. Soc. Rev.*, Vol. 16 (1951), pp. 149–157.

337. Talmon-Garber, Yonina, "The family in Israel," *Marriage Fam. Living*, Vol. 16 (1954), pp. 343–349.

338. Tamagi, H., *Nihn Kazoku Seido Ron (A theory of the Japanese family system)*: *Japanese society and Asiatic family system*, Kyoto, Horitsu Bunka Sha, 1953. (Reviewed by Chien-Hsun Huang, *Amer. Soc. Rev.*, Vol. 19 [1954], pp. 510–511. Original not seen.)

339. Tarver, J. D., "Trend in age at marriage of Wisconsin men and women, 1909–1940," *Amer. Soc. Rev.*, Vol. 16 (1951), pp. 246–247.

340. Taves, M. J., "A direct vs. an indirect approach in measuring marital adjustment," *Amer. Soc. Rev.*, Vol. 13 (1948), pp. 538–541.

341. Taylor, C. C., "The family farm in the new society," *Rur. Sociol.*, Vol. 19 (1954), pp. 271–280.

342. Terman, L. M., *et al.*, *Psychological Factors in Marital Happiness*, New York, McGraw-Hill, 1938.

343. Terman, L. M., and Melita H. Oden, *The Gifted Child Grows Up*, Stanford, Stanford University Press, 1947.

344. Terman, L. M., and P. Wallin, "The validity of marriage prediction and marital adjustment tests," *Amer. Soc. Rev.*, Vol. 14 (1949), pp. 497–504.

345. Thamavit, V., and R. Golden, "The family in Thailand," *Marriage Fam. Living*, Vol. 16 (1954), pp. 381–389.

346. Thomas, J. L., "The factor of religion in the selection of marriage mates," *Amer. Soc. Rev.*, Vol. 16 (1951), pp. 487–491.

347. Thurnwald, Hilda, *Gegenwarts-Probleme Berliner Familien*, Berlin, Weidmannsche Verlagsbuchhandlung, 1948.

348. Tibbitts, C. (ed.), *Living through the Older Years*, Ann Arbor, University of Michigan Press, 1949.

349. Tomasic, D. A., "The family in the Balkans," *Marriage Fam. Living*, Vol. 16 (1954), pp. 301–307.

350. Truxal, A. G., and F. E. Merrill, *Marriage and the Family in American Culture*, New York, Prentice-Hall, 1953.

351. Vance, R. B., "Regional family patterns: the Southern family," *Amer. J. Soc.*, Vol. 53 (1947–1948), pp. 426–429.

352. Vedder, C. B., "Lonely hearts clubs viewed sociologically," *Social Forces*, Vol. 30 (1951), pp. 219–222.

353. Vincent, C. E., "Trends in infant care ideas," *Child Develpm.*, Vol. 22 (1951), pp. 199–209.

354. Vincent, C. E., "The unwed mother and sampling bias," *Amer. Soc. Rev.*, Vol. 19 (1954), pp. 562–567.

355. von Neumann, J., and O. Morgenstern, *Theory of Games and Economic Behavior*, Princeton, Princeton University Press, 1944.

356. Waller, W., "The rating and dating complex," *Amer. Soc. Rev.*, Vol. 2 (1937), pp. 727–734.

357. Waller, W., *The Family: A Dynamic Interpretation*, rev. by R. Hill, New York, Dryden, 1951.

358. Wallin, P., "Cultural contradictions and sex roles: a repeat study," *Amer. Soc. Rev.*, Vol. 15 (1950), pp. 288–293.

359. Wallin, P., "Marital happiness of parents and their children's attitude to marriage," *Amer. Soc. Rev.*, Vol. 19 (1954), pp. 20–23.

360. Wallin, P., "Sex differences in attitudes to 'in-laws': a test of a theory," *Amer. J. Soc.*, Vol. 59 (1953–1954), pp. 466–469.

361. Wallin, P., and H. M. Vollmer, "Marital happiness of parents and their children's attitudes to them," *Amer. Soc. Rev.*, Vol. 18 (1953), pp. 424–431.

362. Watson, J. B., *The Psychological Care of Infant and Child*, New York, Norton, 1928.

363. Wessel, Bessie B., "Ethnic family patterns: the American Jewish family," *Amer. J. Soc.*, Vol. 53 (1947–1948), pp. 439–442.

364. Westoff, C. F., "Differential fertility in the United States: 1900 to 1952," *Amer. Soc. Rev.*, Vol. 19 (1954), pp. 549–561.

365. Whiting, J. W. M., and I. L. Child, *Child Training and Personality: A Cross-Cultural Study*, New Haven, Yale University Press, 1953.

366. Whyte, W. H., Jr., "The transients II: the future, c/o Park Forest," *Fortune*, Vol. 47 (1953), pp. 125–131, 186, 188, 190, 192, 194, 196.

367. Whyte, W. H., Jr., "The transients III: the outgoing life," *Fortune*, Vol. 48 (1953), pp. 84–88, 156–158, 160.

368. Whyte, W. H., Jr., "The transients IV: how the new suburbia socializes," *Fortune*, Vol. 48 (1953), pp. 120–122, 186, 188–190.

369. Willems, E., "The structure of the Brazilian family," *Social Forces*, Vol. 31 (1953), pp. 339–345.

370. Williams, M. J., "Personal and familial problems of high school youths and their bearing upon family education needs," *Social Forces*, Vol. 27 (1949), pp. 279–285.

371. Williamson, R. C., "Economic factors in marital adjustment," *Marriage Fam. Living*, Vol. 14 (1952), pp. 298–301.

372. Williamson, R. C., "Socio-economic factors and marital adjustment in an urban setting," *Amer. Soc. Rev.*, Vol. 19 (1954), pp. 213–216.

372a. Winch, R. F., "Primary factors in a study of courtship," *Amer. Soc. Rev.*, Vol. 12 (1947), pp. 658–666.

373. Winch, R. F., "The relation between the loss of a parent and progress in courtship," *J. Soc. Psychol.*, Vol. 29 (1949), pp. 51–56.

374. Winch, R. F., "Courtship in college women," *Amer. J. Soc.*, Vol. 55 (1949–1950), pp. 269–278.

375. Winch, R. F., "Some data bearing on the Oedipus hypothesis," *J. Abnorm. Soc. Psychol.*, Vol. 45 (1950), pp. 481–489.

376. Winch, R. F., "Further data and observations on the Oedipus hypothesis: the consequence of an inadequate hypothesis," *Amer. Soc. Rev.*, Vol. 16 (1951), pp. 784–795.

377. Winch, R. F., *The Modern Family*, New York, Holt, 1952.

378. Winch, R. F., "Review of Bergler and Kroger's *Kinsey's Myth of Female Sexuality: The Medical Facts*," *Marriage Fam. Living*, Vol. 16 (1954), pp. 184–185.

379. Winch, R. F., "The theory of complementary needs in mate-selection: a test of one kind of complementariness," *Amer. Soc. Rev.*, Vol. 20 (1955), pp. 52–56.

380. Winch, R. F., T. Ktsanes, and Virginia Ktsanes, "The theory of complementary needs in mate-selection: an analytic and descriptive study," *Amer. Soc. Rev.*, Vol. 19 (1954), pp. 241–249.

381. Winch, R. F., and R. McGinnis (eds.), *Selected Studies in Marriage and the Family*, New York, Holt, 1953.

382. Witmer, Helen L., and Ruth Kotinsky (eds.), *Personality in the Making: The*

*Fact-finding Report of the Midcentury White House Conference on Children and Youth,* New York, Harper, 1952.

383. Wolfenstein, Martha, "Trends in infant care," *Amer. J. Orthopsychiat.,* Vol. 23 (1953), pp. 120–130.

384. Young, K., *Isn't One Wife Enough? The Story of Mormon Polygamy,* New York, Holt, 1954.

385. Young, Leontine, *Out of Wedlock: A Study of the Problems of the Unmarried Mother and Her Child,* New York, McGraw-Hill, 1954.

386. Zimmerman, C. C., *Family and Civilization,* New York, Harper, 1947.

# chapter 12

# Structure and dynamics of small groups: a review of four variables

ROBERT F. BALES
*Harvard University*

A. PAUL HARE
*Harvard University*

EDGAR F. BORGATTA
*Russell Sage Foundation*

## INTRODUCTION

In this review of research on the characteristics of small groups, we have selected four variables to illustrate the kinds of work being done in the field. The limits of the field itself are still only vaguely defined, and, in general, researchers have extended the boundaries in whatever directions they have thought fruitful. But however defined, the field has been associated with such a flood of research and scholarship that it seems impossible to present more than a sample in this article.

Fortunately, the work of reviewing and republishing materials in this area has kept pace with the research, bringing together from widely dispersed sources findings and theory which cohere into a consistent body of empirical knowledge, and a number of excellent reviews are available. In 1953 Cartwright and Zander (23) edited the first major collection of articles devoted to small group research under the title of *Group Dynamics: Research and Theory*. In 1954 Lindzey (68) edited a *Handbook of Social Psychology* in which several chapters are of direct relevance, particularly Kelley and Thibaut's chapter (62) reviewing the literature on "Experimental Studies of Group Problem Solving and Process," and Riecken and Homans' review (87) on "Psychological Aspects of Social Structure." In 1953 Strodtbeck and Hare (106) published an extensive bibliography of about 1,400 titles, covering the years 1900 through 1953. Using this bibliography as a basis, Hare, Borgatta, and Bales (48) prepared an annotated bibliography of 580 titles, which was published in 1955 with a collection of 55 articles as *Small Groups: Studies in Social Interaction*. In this annotated bibliography 71 articles containing reviews of the literature, major and minor, are indexed. We are indebted to all these sources in the preparation of the present review.

In order to place the present review in perspective, it may be helpful to consider what a more complete review might contain. One suggestion, made by Cattell (24) and based on his factor studies, divides the field according to three classes of variables: population traits, or variables which describe the members of the group; characteristics of internal structure, or variables which describe the relationships among the members of the group; and syntality traits (analogous to personality), or those variables which describe the behavior of the group as a group. The following outline makes another set of distinctions, traditional in sociology, dividing the field into structure, process, and change.

Part I. Conditions which exist initially and can be controlled to some extent prior to the beginning of interaction of the group members, such as:

A. *Size,* the number of members.

B. The *communication network,* that is, the type and degree of contact among members.

C. The *task* and the resources which are provided for its fulfillment, such as equipment, facilities, and information.

D. The *personality characteristics* of the members, such as abilities, values, interests, and habit patterns.

E. The *socially ascribed characteristics* of members, such as age, sex, class, ethnic membership, or status in some other system or organization.

F. The *attitude towards the task,* which may be derived from any of the above, or other sources, particularly from the nature of the relationship to the employer, experimenter, or other agent of some pre-existing organization which holds the group together.

G. The *attitude towards the group* or individual members, which may be derived from any of the above, and may also involve such things as prior acquaintances and friendships, or statuses assigned within the group.

Part II. The nature of the group process and structure that tends to develop as the members interact with each other, such as:

A. The *interaction and decision process.*

B. The *formation of group norms or group culture* and the establishment of social control of members over each other.

C. *Performance characteristics* of the group, evaluated according to the requirements of the tasks and problems which are relevant.

D. The *development of a differentiated internal structure* of modes of task performance, social behavior, perceptions, and affective relations among the members, that is, a system of roles and statuses.

E. The *development of individual feelings of emotional satisfaction and accomplishment,* or their opposites, arising from all the above.

Part III. Problems of change as they may be faced by the members, leaders, or those who have formed the group for a specific purpose, such as:

A. *Problems of training* for improved task performance of the group or individual members.

B. *Problems of therapy* of individuals or the group as a whole, that is, the development of more acceptable social and emotional responses.

C. *Problems of intergroup relations* between the given group and other groups or the larger organization of which it is a part.

The four variables we have chosen to discuss are: *group size, the communication network, the nature of the group task,* and *personalities of the group members.* These are all variables which may be determined or controlled to some extent before the interaction of the group members actually begins. They thus have considerable practical interest. Researchers as well as practitioners may wish to select personnel, to compose groups for specific purposes, to understand limits of group functioning under given conditions and, more generally, to describe or control groups in their process or development. The factors involved in group interaction are many and complex. The four we have chosen are not by any means exhaustive, but they do represent major sources of variance. Knowledge concerning these variables makes it easier to extend research with other variables, as the method of the researcher is to control certain major sources of variance while systematically examining others.

## GROUP SIZE

Although the factor of group size is used by many persons to limit the field under discussion, it is at best a rough and approximate designation. There is no exact specification of how large a group may be before one no longer feels it appropriate to call it a small group. An attempt to name some exact number would actually be misleading. The usefulness of the designation presumably rests on the fact that size is a limiting condition on the amount and quality of communication that can take place among members as individual persons, and hence tends to affect the character of interpersonal orientations that members develop toward each other. But other conditions may also be limiting in the same way. For example, the characteristics of the members and the time available may have a similar limiting effect. Consequently, the effects of size should be considered in conjunction with other relevant variables.

In terms of effective participation in group activity, it may be that certain group sizes are more "natural" and occur more frequently than others under particular conditions. Age seems to be a variable which is related to size in this way. It appears that increasing maturity of the personality associated with age permits effective participation in larger groups. In the early stages of growth the number of children observed in play groups varies with the age of the child. Preschool children tend to play first individually, although in parallel, then in pairs, then in larger groups (44, 82, 83).

Another variable which appears to be associated with "natural" sizes is the rural-urban continuum. Hollingshead (52) reports that rural high school youth form cliques of about three persons, while town youth are more likely to form cliques of four and five persons.

Frequency and duration of contact between members is to some extent conditioned by size, as well as the converse. Fischer (40) finds that among college students as size of group increases, frequency and hours of contact per week and intimacy decrease. From a study of informal groups of sizes two to seven and one of work groups of sizes two to six, James (57) reports that the frequency of occurrence is a negative function of size. The function described appears smooth, and the mean size for both counts is close to 2.4. He concludes that there is a tendency for face to face groups to gravitate to the smallest size, two. The two or three boy relationship is also described by Thrasher (111) as more important to the individual boy than the relationship to the larger group.

As size increases, it presumably becomes more difficult for each member to keep each other group member in mind as a separate differentiated person. Experiments on estimating the number of dots in a visual field with very short time exposures indicate individual subjects can report the exact number up to and including seven with great confidence and practically no error, but above that number confidence and accuracy drop (107). When report time is allowed to vary, time required increases as a function of number of dots up to six or seven dots, and then flattens abruptly and remains about flat, suggesting that the estimation is being done by a different psychological procedure that somehow does not involve a separate discrimination of each dot (58, 60). Observers rating group members face a problem not unlike that of the dot estimators in the sense that they can individually pay attention to only a limited number of persons at a given time. Bass and Norton (9) report maximum agreement on leadership assessment at size six, as compared with sizes two, four, eight and twelve. It may be that leadership tends not to emerge so clearly in the even sizes below six, and that above size six the observer may begin to run into cognitive difficulties. The coincidence of these findings suggests that the ability of the observing individual to perceive, keep track of, and judge each member separately in a social interaction situation may not extend much beyond the size of six or seven. If this is true, one would expect members of groups larger than that size to tend to think of other members in terms of subgroups, or "classes" of some kind, and to deal with members of subgroups other than their own by more stereotyped methods of response.

Possibly a more relevant way of viewing size as a variable is to consider the number of possible relationships in the group by pairs and larger subgroups rather than the number of persons. As the number of individuals increases, it can be simply demonstrated that the number of possible relationships increases much more rapidly than size (17, 33, 63). It may be expected, then, that when there is a desire for intimate and highly developed relationships or need for fine coordination there will also be a tendency toward the restriction of size. It is worth noting in this connection that the appearance of a leader can permit a reduction of the psychological complication of the group to a series of pair relationships of each member with the leader for certain purposes of coordination. The development of leadership is possibly in part an alternative to an actual reduction in size.

A number of investigators associate the emergence of leadership with increasing size of the group. Whyte (114) notes in his study of the restaurant industry that increasing size of the organization is related to increasing difficulty in coordinating activities. On the basis of a large questionnaire study, Hemphill (51) finds that leader behavior differs as size increases, and also that as the group becomes larger (especially above size 31), the demands upon the leader role become more numerous and exacting, and member tolerance for leader-centered direction of group activities becomes greater. Carter *et al.* (22) report that correlations between observer ratings of members on "initiative," "insight," "leadership behavior," and also "authoritarianism" are greater in groups of size eight than those of size four. A similar increase in correlation between predictions of leadership skill made from TAT analysis and the amount of change toward consensus in group discussion when size five was compared with size twelve is reported by Hare (46). He concludes that the larger groups "demand more skill from the leader." Rice (86) in a study of process adjustment in a given group of machine shop workers observes a fluctuation in the underlying emotional tone from an initial period of aggression and withdrawal to a period of dependency on the leader and then back to aggression and withdrawal as size is increased. Hare (46) and Homans (53) note the tendency in larger groups toward the formation of subgroups in which spokesmen represent the opinions of minorities.

The time available per member for overt communication during a meeting of any given length decreases as the group size increases. Thus, each member has a more complicated set of social relationships to maintain and more restricted resources with which to do it. Members of discussion groups are aware of this and report that they have fewer chances to speak in groups of size twelve as compared with size five (46). Gibb (42) also finds that an increased proportion of the members report feelings of threat and inhibition of impulses to participate as size is increased. As the size of kindergarten groups is increased from fourteen to forty-six, not only does the average number of remarks per child and the percentage of the total number of children who participate decrease, but also the total amount of discussion decreases (34). Thus, the effect of increasing size appears to involve not only a mechanical constriction of time per member, but also a feeling of threat or inhibition.

Bales *et al.* (7) report data on distributions of participation in discussion groups of sizes three to eight. Generally, all members address some remarks to the group as a whole, but typically only one member, the top participator, addresses more to the group as a whole than to specific other members. As group size increases a larger and larger proportion of the participators have total amounts of participation under their "equal" share, that is, under the mean for the group. At the same time, at least where a participating leader is appointed, the gap between the top participator and the others tends to grow proportionately greater as size increases. Stephan and Mishler (103) present similar findings and show that when the designated leader of their groups is excluded, the gradient of the remainder of the members tends to follow a simple curve that flattens as the size of the group increases. Carter *et al.* (22) in their comparison of size four and size eight conclude: "In the group of four each individual has sufficient latitude or space in which to behave and thus the basic abilities of each individual may be expressed; but in the larger group only the more forceful individuals are able to express their abilities and ideas since the amount of freedom in the situation is not sufficient to accommodate all the group members."

While size may be viewed as a limiting condition in certain respects, increasing size is obviously not in every respect a constricting factor. Many abilities or resources needed in task performance tend to have an additive character. The kinds of resources which are of this order, in respect to tasks, may include such things as the number of items of information which can be absorbed and recalled, the number of critical judgments available to correct errors of information and inference, the number of ideas or suggestions available for solution of problems, the range of values that are likely to be brought to bear, as well as the range of technical skills, abilities, and amount of muscular power that is available to implement decisions. For example, Watson (112) reports that on a word-building task, the number of words built in a given time increases as the group size is increased from three to ten.

However, the familiar phenomenon of "diminishing returns" tends to set in at some point. The addition of another person to a given group size may not represent a unit addition to task ability. The tendency for difficulty of coordination to increase with size is one factor that may lead to diminishing net returns, but there are other factors also. In audience-like groups of eight sizes ranging from one to ninety-six persons, Gibb (42) finds that the absolute number of volunteered ideas for the solution of a problem produced within a set time follows a negatively accelerated increasing function. The negative acceleration might possibly be due to some limit to the number of solutions available, and reluctance to repeat, or by increasing difficulty of the experimenter in recording all suggestions as they occur. However, the proportion of subjects who report feelings of threat or inhibition of their impulses to participate increases with size. Gibb's design includes a situation which increases feelings of threat by creating a more formal procedure. This situation also leads to a reduction in the number of ideas proposed. One infers then, that increased feeling of threat may reduce participation as size increases, and thus form an interference.

On a task requiring physical pulling power, a four-man group is the most efficient (80). Above that size the pulling power per member decreased by ten per cent with each additional member. One would suppose that difficulty of coordination may be an interfering factor in this case. Marriott (76) reports an inverse relation between output per man and size of work group in motor car factories. It is possible that the formation of norms restricting output or the strength of the group sanctions may have been involved as an interference.

Taylor and Faust (108) find that on a concept formation task (twenty questions) groups of two persons obtain the answer in shorter time, use fewer questions, and fail less often at the task than do individuals. Groups of four fail even less often, but are not otherwise superior to groups of size two. Here we see, apparently, a gain from having available a larger pool of ideas about questions to ask, and a gain from the exercise of critical judgment in eliminating poor ideas or testing closure on the solution, but both sources of gain are subject to diminishing returns. The number of man-minutes required per problem increases with size. This, of course, is typically the case. However, for many practical purposes, where the task is one in which some absolute level of effectiveness must be obtained in a set time to avoid complete failure, the lowered efficiency per unit of time per man may be a secondary consideration.

A number of early experiments include the finding that groups have a lower probability of failure or a greater probability of accuracy in problem solving than individuals since the groups have greater resources for ideas and error checking (32, 96, 101). However, Johnson (59) reviews and analyzes the literature on the superiority of group judgment and concludes that the only clearly demonstrated gain so far is essentially of a statistical sort:

> . . . four judgments are better than one for the same nonsocial reason that four thermometers are better than one. The only consistent finding of significance for social psychology is the trend toward homogeneity or reduction of variance. In a secondary way this usually increases the accuracy of individual judgments, or the size of the majority vote, but it does not by itself increase the accuracy of the group judgment (page 471).

He points out that if the true value of the variable being judged is bracketed by the range of individual judgments, and if the errors are only of a random kind, the tendency to converge toward a group norm of judgments will increase the accuracy of the average individual judgment. If the true value is outside the range of judgments, the average error of the judgments will not change simply by the convergence effect.

The greater variety of opinion available as size increases may give some advantage of critical power, but it has its price in the greater difficulty of reaching consensus. The difficulty is apparently most marked when the task is primarily one of modifying opinion, in the absence of any clear objective criteria for judgment. South (101) finds groups of six take longer on tasks of this sort than groups of three, and Hare (46) finds groups of twelve take longer on a group decision than groups of five. However, if the task is a technical one with clear criteria of correct performance and requires some absolute level of intelligence, speed, or the like, the larger group may have a higher probability of containing some member who can obtain an answer easily acceptable to the others once it is presented. South (101) finds that on what he calls "abstract" tasks his groups of six are faster than his groups of three, possibly for this reason.

The quality of the interaction process tends to vary as a function of group size. Bales and Borgatta (5) present interaction data on groups of sizes two to seven engaged in a group decision problem, where criteria of goodness of solution depend upon values of the members. As size increases, the rate of giving information and suggestion increases, while the rate of asking for opinion, giving opinion, and showing agreement decreases. These changes are consistent with the hypothesis that as size increases there is a tendency toward a more mechanical method of introducing information (by round robin procedure, for example), a less sensitive exploration of the point of view of the other, and a more direct attempt to control others and reach solution whether or not all group members indicate agreement. All these effects are reasonably associated with the increasing constriction of time available per person. Rates of showing tension tend to decrease, but joking and laughter increase, which may indicate a tendency for less direct involvement of members in task success and for tension to be displaced into humor rather than to be reduced directly through serious attempts to resolve opinion differences. In this sense, it is suggested that unresolved differences appear to be more tolerable in larger groups, and they may be handled by compartmentalization and other similar devices rather than by resolution.

In addition to these effects of size which show an increasing or decreasing trend, groups of two appear to show unique characteristics. They tend to have high rates of showing tension, consistently avoid disagreement and antagonism, have high rates of asking for opinion, but avoid giving opinion, and concentrate rather on exchange of information and agreement (or acknowledgment). This pattern of rates is consistent with an interpretation that in groups of two a delicate balance of power exists when, as in *ad hoc* experimental groups, there are few group norms regarded as binding except those to which both members currently assent. In such a case there is no "public opinion," no majority to which either can appeal. Either member can prevent task completion by disagreement or withdrawal. Both members have to proceed within certain limits to avoid this reaction on the part of the other. The task of building a common set of norms in this situation is apparently an anxiety provoking prospect, and it tends to be avoided or in part glossed over by agreement on more specific and superficial matters. In a loose interpretation, the two man group may be viewed as having built into it an implicit agreement that the two members will stay within spheres on which they can agree. In spite of the delicate balance of power, however, there is a strong tendency for two asymmetric roles to develop, that is, for the members to specialize in different types of overt behavior. The differences appear in practically all categories of behavior. Apparently, there is a tendency for one member to gravitate toward a more active role and exercise the power of initiative, while the other tends toward a more passive role and holds the power of veto. In this context, it is difficult to ascribe power or leadership to either role, for the passive person may be construed as defining the permissive range of the active person. In the sense that the group operates toward the achievement of a given task, leadership associated with proper completion of the group task certainly may be associated with both the initiating and control functions.

Strodtbeck (104) studying husband-wife pairs in three cultures finds that the norms in each culture defining the expected power of wife versus husband enable prediction of the tendency of one spouse or the other to take the more active role, and the tendency to win more decisions. A direct relation exists between the amount of participation and number of decisions won. In Strodtbeck's study the more influential spouse tends more frequently to ask questions, give opinions, and make rewarding remarks, while the less influential takes a more reactive role with more acts of agreement, disagreement, and antagonism.

Bales and Borgatta (5) present data which indicate that above size two there are significant differences according to even or odd number of members. Groups of even sizes (four and six) have higher rates of showing disagreement and antagonism, and lower rates of asking for suggestion and possibly in showing agreement, than groups of odd sizes (three, five, and seven). These effects are attributed to the fact that in even sizes a division of the group into two subparts of equal size is possible. Thus, in cases of disagreement in even size groups, the probability of a majority and a minority is lower than in odd sizes, and this in turn may increase the probability that disagreements will remain deadlocked between two subgroups.

The power of majority over minority is especially marked in groups of size three, since in this size any minority must be that of a single person, who is thus left isolated without the support of any other group member, at least in respect to the immediate disagreement. In laboratory groups of size three (78), a relationship in which the two top participators disagree with each other and seek the support of the third low member is unstable through time within a meeting and tends to change toward the end of the meeting to a supporting coalition between the two higher participators with the low man excluded. Bales and Borgatta (5), however, find that member variability from meeting to meeting is particularly high in three man groups, indicating that the coalition pattern may change about from meeting to meeting in *ad hoc* groups, while in more permanent groups of three (father, mother, and son) the tendency toward exclusion of one does not concentrate on a particular one of the three persons in a series of decisions (105).

It may be inferred that the power of a coalition of two in a three person group to force a decision is considerable and is so employed with reference to particular disagreements. Indeed, it may be so powerful that members tend to switch coalitions from disagreement to disagreement simply from a desire to maintain solidarity and avoid the permanent exclusion of one member. The overt interaction should, however, be considered as only one possible indicator of the existence of coalitions. If the coalition pattern in interaction is defined only by the amount of support that is overtly demonstrated between pairs, the fact that where a coalition exists there may be no need for the supporters to demonstrate their agreement to each other is overlooked. In another study, Mills (79) reports that although a third member may be forced to change his behavior pattern completely by two role players who first allow him to form a coalition with one of them, and then combine against him, he changes his opinion less often than his behavior, and he tends to retain his liking for the original partner in spite of the overt desertion. Another complicating consideration is the fact that, as one disagrees, one must also support, or the situation may deteriorate. In terms of interaction scoring, responses in the active support categories covary with those in the negative categories.

In general, these data suggest that the problem of deadlock is most severe in the two person group, but in this instance, each person is also without support in a deadlock, and if the group is to remain in existence, each person must respond to the emergency signs of the other. The level of tension may be high, but the hostility must be controlled since each person *must* face the other. In the four person group, however, in a deadlock situation each person may have a supporter, and the deadlock may continue with each person still having available a source of support and gratification. In the three person group the problem of the overpowerful majority is emphasized. At least some of the idiosyncrasies of extreme small group size may thus be viewed as special cases of the odd and even effects, and these, in turn, may be seen as results of the power of perceived consensus among a majority in persuading the minority (or single person) to change his views, or at least, not to oppose outwardly the resolution of the disagreement. Thus, a number of the important effects of size relate to the ways in which size affects the probability that binding norms based on the perception that a majority of the group is already in consensus may be built in interaction.

A final comment may be made on the relation of size to member satisfaction. Hare (46) finds that members of smaller (five man) groups are more satisfied with the discussion than members of twelve man groups. Bales (4) reports that for discussion groups in his sample the optimal size appears to be five. Below this size members complain that the group is too small, although amount of talking time available to each increases. This may be a reflection of the strains associated with the face to face relationship which have been noted above in the description of the two, three, and four man groups, and the odd and even effects. Above the size of five, members complain the group is too large, and this may be a reflection on the restriction on the amount of participation. Size five combines these characteristics: (a) a strict deadlock is not possible with an odd number of members; (b) the group tends to split into a majority of three and a minority of two, so that being in a minority does not isolate the individual but allows him sources of gratification; (c) the group appears to be large enough for the members to shift roles easily and for any individual to withdraw from an awkward position without necessarily having the issue resolved.

## THE COMMUNICATION NETWORK

The communication network as we define it here refers to the patterns and channels of communication among members and subgroups of the group. In a molar sense, as may be seen with residential groups, spatial location of members relative to each other and probability of contact in the course of daily activity limit in a very tangible way who is likely to interact with whom. Thus, location may be related to the affective relationships among members and to the probability of their building particular group norms and associations. At this level, the study of communication might involve such concepts as the familiar "degree of propinquity," or density of population, which are equally relevant in the study of size.

The spatial arrangement of members in respect to each other and the probability of contact was found by Festinger, Schachter, and Back (38) and Wilner, Walkley, and Cook (116) to be related to persons' liking for each other. In general, the attraction of persons to each other tends to be greater among those who are in spatial locations that promote inter-action, and liking tends to decrease, sometimes turning to hostility, as physical distance increases, and also as lack of interaction contact, and presumably lack of acceptance of each other as members of the same group increase, according to the studies by Merton (77), Danielsson (31), Lundberg, Hertzler, and Dickson (69), Homans (53), Sherif (97), Maisonneuve, Palmade, and Fourment (75), and Simon (98). This generalization involves elements familiar in the discussions of xenophobia and scapegoating. Conversely, once subgroups have formed, there is some tendency to symbolize and maintain social separation by mainte-nance of physical separation, as Hughes (55), for example, observed in the cafeteria of an industrial plant. Liking, however, has complex de-terminants, as does the amount of interactive contact. Neither is a simple function of the other. Particularly in periods of conflict the two may be "out of joint," since interactive contact with deviant members tends to increase in an attempt to influence them, and then to fall off if and when they are given up or rejected (91). In a sense, we may generalize the limiting condition here in terms of the prerequisite of contact before a person may be rejected or accepted into another's sphere of involvement. However, when involvement is not present or forced by contact, a "preju-dice principle" may operate. When prejudice is operative, contact may or may not result in the dissolution or compartmentalization of the preju-dice, depending on the nature and circumstance of the contact as well as on particular persons involved.

In large military and industrial organizations a subsegment of the organization often serves as an information processing center. There the information is collated, displayed, and evaluated, and decisions are made which affect the entire operating organization. Frequently some of the members involved are separated physically from each other and communicate by telephone and other devices in restricted networks. The frequency of concern with problems of communication in restricted net-works has led to experimental exploration of the properties of different sorts of networks.

Leavitt and Mueller (65) explore the effect of one way communication, where the receiver of the information is given no opportunity to "feed-back" acknowledgments, questions, or negative reactions to the sender. They find that accuracy is impaired, as well as confidence, for both sender and receiver. An initial reaction of hostility of the receiver toward the sender tends to appear. Accuracy can improve with time, but not as rapidly as with feedback, and it depends more on the sender than the receiver. An initial period with free feedback appreciably improves sub-sequent communication without feedback. More time is required with the feedback condition, but with experience the amount of time decreases. Thibaut and Coules (110) find that receivers who are permitted to communicate immediately back to a person who has sent them an act of hostility show more postexperimental friendliness to him than those not permitted to communicate. Apparently one way communication prevents not only expressive catharsis, but also the opportunity for building new understandings and norms by which the members manage their social relationships and their process of communication. From this basic impairment other problems may then develop.

A peripheral position in a restricted network in some ways approximates the position of a receiver with no opportunity for feedback. Leavitt (64), in an experiment where members are allowed to communicate only in written form through set channels on a task of assembling information, finds that members in peripheral positions are less well satisfied with their jobs than those in central positions. Centrality, following the procedures described by Bavelas (10), is calculated from location in the various networks used. The man in the position of hub of a five man wheel pattern, the man at the juncture of a Y formation, and the middle man of a linear chain, are central in decreasing degrees, while in a fourth pattern, the circle, no person is central. In general, task efficiency increases with centralization. The wheel allows the fastest trial. The central person tends to receive and send more messages than other members, is regarded as leader by them, and shows higher and increasing satisfaction. But the highest average satisfaction is found in the circle pattern, where members have more independence of action. In the circle network more messages are used, more individual errors are made, members are less likely to know the total structure of their network, and are less likely to recognize one person as a leader. However, in spite of the larger number of errors, they correct a greater proportion of them than in any other pattern, and have a smaller proportion of unanimous, five man errors. Moreover, Smith (100) has shown in a similar experiment that the circle pattern permits members to adapt more readily to a change requiring the breaking and relearning of a previously established set. The greater amount of interaction and feedback which characterizes the decentralized network seems to increase the probability of checking gross unanimous errors, to increase adaptability in the face of new demands for relearning, and to increase average member satisfaction, but at some cost in messages, duplication of effort, and general confusion.

Heise and Miller (50) show that the differences between networks are relative to the type of task and become more pronounced as "noise" is introduced into the communication channels. Random noise is introduced into one and two way telephone circuits connecting three members.

A task calling for individual mental activity where the products are not highly interdependent but simply additive (making the largest possible number of anagrams out of a given word) is little affected by the type of network or amount of noise. An information collection task (completing a list of words, each subject having part of the list) is performed most rapidly in a network where each member is connected to each other, with two way communication. However, a task requiring assembly plus coordination (completing a sentence in proper order, each subject having part of the words) is performed most rapidly in a centralized network where a central person is furnished two way communication with each of the two others, but no connection is provided between the two peripheral members. The one way closed chain (no feedback, no centralization) is in general prone to error, inefficient in terms of time and number of messages, and suffers most with the introduction of noise. Heise and Miller also find that members are most satisfied in the central position and feel "left out and unsure of themselves" when in an isolated position, with no feedback facilities. Christie, Luce, and Macy (28, 72) predict errors from the amount of "noise" in the information theory sense and show that groups use redundant coding as a means of reducing error.

In a series of reports, Shaw (93) systematically examines some features of the communication network. He finds that Bavelas' measure of centrality does not permit measurement of quantitative differences among individuals in the group, and he proposes a measure of independence which takes into account the number of communication channels available to the individual, to the group, and the number of individuals for which a person is a relayer of information. Independence is found to account reasonably for experimental measures of morale (general satisfaction), number of messages used, and recognition of leadership. In another report Shaw (94) explores four man groups in three controlled communication conditions, the wheel, the slash, and the circle, and finds that centrality varies inversely with time required to complete an activity in a position, and directly with individual morale, the number of items transmitted, and the probability that a person will be chosen as the leader. In general, leadership emergence varies with the degree to which the centrality indexes of the persons in the group are widely different. Increasing the amount of information given to a person has an effect similar to increasing his centrality index. Shaw (95) also reports a controlled communication experiment using the wheel, kite, and comcon (all possible channels), where authoritarian (appointed) leadership results in better group performance than nonauthoritarian leadership. Morale is lower in the authoritarian situation, but evidence in terms of errors indicates that the quality of performance is better in the authoritarian situation. Morale is related to the independence of action permitted.

The studies just mentioned show that positions in the communication network, especially those with one way and limited connection restrictions, are related to frustration and antagonism on the part of the disadvantaged members and to satisfaction and leadership status for the central members. Kelley (61) shows that when member perceptions of status and possibilities for upward or downward mobility are experimentally established in a restricted network with apparent but not real feedback, the amount and kind of written communication initiated differs. Persons who are led to believe that their job status is lower are less well satisfied with their job and initiate more conjectures about the nature of the jobs at the other status level. This is interpreted as the result of phantasy about upward mobility, following the ideas of Thibaut (109), and Back, Festinger, Hymovitch, Kelley, Schachter, and Thibaut (1). They also initiate more communication with content irrelevant to the task, which is interpreted as a desire to escape from the position. The members who are led to believe they are in a higher status show evidence of constraint in addressing criticism of their job to lower status members, and constraint in expressing confusion about the job to anyone. Members of control groups where no impression of status differences is established are more free in criticism of other members than are subjects in either of the two status conscious conditions. The perception of possibility of upward mobility for the lower status group increases the attractiveness of the job, and the perception of possible downward mobility for the higher status group decreases the attractiveness. Low status with no possibility of rising or high status with the threat of falling are the variations that are most destructive of interlevel cohesion.

Mechanical constrictions on communication, of course, constitute an extreme and obvious case of conditions that may prevent the full and free interaction of each member with each other. But even in discussion groups where physical conditions of intercommunication are optimized, spatial location still plays some part. For example, Steinzor (102) shows that members tend to address more communication to persons seated opposite to them at a table than to those next to them, presumably because of easier eye contact. Bass and Klubeck (8), however, find little effect of seating position on final leadership ratings received by members. Presumably the difficulties of spatial location and interactive contact tend toward a minimum as size decreases in a discussion situation. In a situation of this kind the communication network is probably constituted more significantly by the expectations of the members than by other more mechanical considerations.

The empirical connection between the amount of liking and amount of interaction found in larger groups also appears to some extent in small discussion groups. Potashin (84) reports that pairs of friends spend more time in spontaneous interactions in a pair discussion situation than do pairs of nonfriends, and also that the members of friendship pairs are more similar in the amounts of interaction initiated to each other. In another study, by Bovard (18), groups set up to encourage intermember interaction (group centered) show a higher average level of liking for each other than leader centered groups where member to member interaction is lower.

In free communication situations a gradient of activity rates among members is the usual thing rather than equal participation (7, 103). Members who talk most generally also receive the most. This is probably in part a result of the tendency for a remark made by one person to be answered by some other, who may then continue to address the person who just spoke. In observations reported by Bales *et al.* (7), about half the remarks are addressed to the group as a whole, and about half to particular other members, that is, in pair relationships. Similarly, in content about half the total content is devoted to substantive contributions while the other half is devoted to positive reactions, negative reactions, and questions. Both of these balances suggest that freely communicating groups devote about as much of their time to feedback as to specific problem solving attempts. Low participators do not talk to each other as much as to high participators. The network of communication is thus in effect restricted more or less spontaneously by the members so that links between low participators tend to drop out increasingly as size increases, especially above size seven. It appears generally true that status distinctions show a high positive correlation with amount of participation, although status in the sense of popularity is not so highly related as status based on task criteria in task oriented groups (3, 6, 56). In free discussion groups the communication network, the liking network, and the hierarchy of status and power are interdependent, but also each is in some degree independently variable so that the congruence is seldom perfect.

In situations where one expects to receive a lecture rather than to participate in a free discussion, two way interaction is more or less drastically limited by common expectations, and yet the results are in some ways similar to forced one way communication. A whole series of studies show that if one wishes to change attitudes and subsequent behavior of a group, discussion and decision where all members participate as directly as possible tend to be more effective than "enlightenment" or "persuasion" by the lecture method, or by an unqualified order from above. Coch and

French (30) report that job and rate changes in a factory setting are accomplished with less quitting by workers, less aggression toward supervision, less drop in production, faster recovery, and higher final rate of production as the method of changeover is experimentally varied toward a total participation method.

The group decision method is also found to be effective in raising substantially the production rate of a group of sewing machine operators on individual piecework, whereas an equal number of meetings in which workers received attention and encouragement from the plant psychologist are not effective, according to Bavelas (reported in Maier [73]). Among college students and housewives group discussion and decision results in substantive change in foods served whereas lectures have little or no effect (66, 115). In all of these cases a change is made to a mode of behavior or performance that presumably is already within the available repertoire of the group members and can be made the chosen response by the development of new group norms to supersede the currently dominant ones. Where learning of new technical content rather than performance or attitude change is required, the results are not so clear. Early studies of the lecture versus discussion method in college courses display contradictory reports (89). Wispe (118) finds that students participate more in permissive class sections and find them more interesting and enjoyable, but prefer directive classes when preparing for examinations. Apparently the purposes and values of the members govern to some degree the reactions they will have to a more or less constricted participation procedure (71). Constrictions adopted freely by the members in order to accomplish a purpose they value are probably less frustrating than those imposed without choice. Nevertheless, an effective change of norms probably requires knowledge of a new consensus which can only be achieved, in the complete sense, by full participation with free feedback.

The attitudes and behavior of the leader apparently can influence the communication network appreciably, even though there are no mechanical constrictions. Indeed, this is one way of looking at the authoritarian-democratic experimental variable employed by Lewin and Lippitt (67) in the study which may be regarded as the classic experiment in the small group field. Maier and Solem (74) find that a "permissive" sort of leadership, which consists mainly in management of the discussion process without interjection of the leader's opinion (as compared to a nonparticipating "observing" leader), operates to protect minorities from social influence and increases the probability that the single member with the correct answer to the problem will be able to convince the majority. As a result the minority members who are wrong tend to stay wrong, but the net effect over all groups is definitely to increase the number of right answers through what amounts to a greater error checking ability.

Preston and Heintz (85) and Hare (47) compare a "supervisory" type of leader, where the leader is instructed to stay out of the discussion, with a "participatory" type, where the leader injects his opinion as well as tries to insure equal participation for all members. Both studies, the first with college students, the second with Boy Scouts, report that participatory leadership results in more group agreement, greater and more permanent influence of the members, and in the first study but not the second, more interest and enjoyment in the task. It appears that members are more satisfied when the leader keeps the communication network balanced and also participates himself. Indeed, in some, if not most situations, the leader who expresses no opinions creates an anomalous and frustrating state of affairs. Lack of leadership is used as a therapeutically intended disturbance in some types of group therapy (12). Berkowitz (11), reporting on a large project study of small decision making conferences in business, industry, and government, indicates that in these groups there appears to be a general expectation that the socially designated leader, the chairman, should be the sole major behavior leader. Leadership sharing by members other than the designated leader tends to be related to a decrease in group cohesiveness and satisfaction, except where problems are urgent. This holds when leaders are more or less permissive and even when the secondary leadership is supportive. It seems definitely indicated that, although the communication network and the gradient of participation set limits on the degree to which new norms can be formed and sensitive regulation of the process can take place, the effects of constriction of communication within a given period are relative to the values and expectations of the members.

## THE NATURE OF THE GROUP TASK

No satisfactory classification of tasks in terms of their behavioral relevance for groups yet exists. Since the task is, in the most pertinent sense, what the group members subjectively define it to be as they respond to the situation in which they find themselves, all of the internal features of the system are likely sooner or later to become relevant to its specification. The task should not be narrowly viewed in terms of what the experimenter intends, or what some objective sense of the situation apparently "demands."

One feature that is particularly dependent upon the definition of the members is the degree and kind of "reality" given to the task. This, in turn, is partly a matter of the kind of consequences that are expected to result from action and also the amount of feedback that actually comes back from the environment. It is suggested that the less feedback or the more delay expected, the lower the degree of reality. In turn the lower the degree of reality, the more the response is determined by internal features and tensions of the system. This, in fact, corresponds with one phase of the theoretical description of the "projective" type test. Horwitz and Cartwright (54) use stories constructed by a group to describe some ambiguous pictures to produce diagnostic information about the group. The set of pictures for group diagnostic use produced by Guetzkow and Henry (45) have received some use by others, but validating materials are absent.

In a comparison of individual behavior through a range of degrees of "reality" from paper and pencil test, to role playing, to actual behavior incidents, Borgatta (13) reports only slight correlation between the performance in the different situations. Moldawsky (81), in an attempt to validate a paper and pencil test in an interaction (role playing) situation, also finds no correspondence. Freedman, Leary, Ossorio, and Coffey (41) take systematic advantage of the discrepancies that appear between various levels of participation and between the different perspectives of subject participants to develop a comprehensive diagnostic system for classification of the individual. Another classificatory system based on discrepancy scores between "levels" arbitrarily chosen in a reality continuum of participation in reference to an act or class of acts of consequence is proposed by Borgatta (13).

A feature of the task that may be thought of as an aspect of the type of feedback from the task environment is the degree to which an "objectively correct" answer is possible, versus the degree to which the answer is simply a matter of agreement with values, or group consensus. Festinger and associates (37) have developed a considerable body of theory centering on motivations to compare oneself with others and to communicate with those more deviant in an effort to achieve uniformity. These motivations are strongest in situations where the main criterion of correctness is agreement with "social reality"—that is, consensus. In general, it is more difficult to achieve consensus when the problem strongly involves values members are likely to hold individually in advance that are different, or believed to be different (39). Deutsch (35) finds that a human relations problem (where there is no objectively correct solution) produces more interaction and more attentiveness to one another's contributions than a mathematical problem. In attempting to build a standard group task for diagnostic use of interaction observations, Bales (2) tried a series of formal problems with objective criteria of success, but finally adopted a case discussion problem with instructions that require assembly of information initially distributed among members, interpretation and evaluation of the information, and eventual group decision on a concrete and detailed plan of action. Several phases of a typical planning-execution cycle are thus included, but not the actual execution of a plan and re-evaluation of results. This task lies somewhere between a highly projective and a highly realistic one.

The type of emergent leadership tends to depend on the task of the group. Carter, Haythorn, and Howell (21) factor analyze the leadership ratings received by subjects in six types of tasks (reasoning, intellectual, construction, clerical, discussion, motor cooperation, and mechanical assembly) and find two factors which they call "intellectual leadership" and "doing things with one's hands leadership." In a factor analysis of ratings of performance made in the OSS assessment program, Sakoda (90) reports two similar factors attributed to situations or tasks that call for verbal intelligence versus those that call for active intelligence. It seems likely that from the point of view of abilities required, the same abilities that can be differentiated from each other by individual testing will also be useful in the description of group tasks, although additional discriminations will probably be required. In addition to abilities, personality characteristics of other sorts will need to be taken in account. Cattell *et al.* (25), using a large number of different tasks, describe 14 different factors in a matrix of 93 personality, task, and derived performance scores associated with a large sample of ten-man groups. Some of these factors are apparently closely related to type of task.

## PERSONALITIES OF THE GROUP MEMBERS

In the initial stages of group formation we may expect the characteristics of the group to be strongly conditioned by the personalities of the members. Cattell, Saunders, and Stice (25) have done the most thorough research in this area, using Cattell's sixteen factor personality test. One of the most interesting distinctions arising from their study is the distinction between personality variables which act in a more or less additive or subtractive way (so that the group *mean* on the personality variable is the best predictive measure to externally defined characteristics of the group), versus those variables which seem to act by some kind of principle of compatibility or lack of it (so that the particular *combination* of values among the members is the best predictive measure). The latter type includes single variables where high or low variance among the members predicts something about the performance of the group, but also may be supposed to include cases where the combination of two or more different types of personality has some predictable effect.

High group *means* on personality characteristics of adventurousness, vigor, dominance, purposefulness, orderliness, willed application, and freedom from anxiety are associated with a congruent kind of group performance; i.e., high performance on tasks requiring vigorous coordinated action and a liking for such tasks as compared to discussion judgment.

High group *means* on personality characteristics of paranoid suspiciousness, nervous tension, emotional immaturity, worrying suspicious anxiety, and lack of self-sufficiency are associated with low observer ratings on degree of leadership, orderliness, we-feeling, level of motivation, degree of group organization and interdependence, and with high ratings of frustration. It is notable, however, that subject ratings do not coincide with those of observers, indicating that defensive mechanisms must be taken into account in evaluating subjects' own estimates of the characteristics and performance of their group.

There is some evidence that high *variances* among members on personality traits of surgency (liking for carefree bustle and excitement), "radicalism" (liking for intellectual and rational examination of issues of convention and authority), and high variance on degree of internalization of social norms, along with high *mean* friendliness, intelligence, and general level of radicalism, are associated with a high level of accuracy on tasks requiring a judgment of facts from inferential grounds. The personality characteristic of surgency is related to a preference for this kind of verbal task, but observers report that groups with high means on this variable suffer from a lack of freedom in the group atmosphere. Possibly this is the observers' reaction to a verbal free-for-all.

High variances on personality measures of tough- versus tender-mindedness, "Bohemian aggressiveness," and paranoid suspiciousness are associated with dislike for a task of resolving opinion and attitude differences, slowness in ranking attitude preferences, and a feeling by members that other members hinder group progress. Of these traits, two are similar to what are probably major factorial dimensions of the attitude universe (see Eysenck [36]): tender- versus tough-mindedness, and "Bohemian aggressiveness." Variance on these traits would be expected perhaps to lead to conflict of values. The other trait in this cluster is paranoid suspiciousness. Apparently what is involved here is an incompatibility of defensive mechanisms for dealing with threat induced by value conflict.

Finally, on the personality variable of emotional maturity (general freedom from defensive mechanisms), *low variance* or uniformity is found to be associated with a certain optimism and confidence in level of aspiration. This seems reasonable in cases where the mean level of emotional maturity is high, but its implications are not clear where the general level is low.

It is important to note that Cattell and associates also locate group characteristics which seem not to be significantly related to any of the personality measures included. Some of these, such as performance on and preference for different tasks (card sorting, construction, planning, resolution of interests), may be more or less directly related to measures of personality characteristics not included in the tests. The authors suggest, however, that certain others arise from "small, accidentally, unintended differences in group experience which have the peculiarity of exaggerating themselves by a feedback mechanism or which for some reason produce, directly, relatively large results." Here they mention a group elation factor, possibly as a success-failure consequence, and a factor related to high general evaluation of the integration of the group by the members which they call intrinsic group synergy. To their suggestions might also be added the factors they find related to observer ratings of high degree of group organization and concern with procedure, a pattern of low absolute but realistic level of aspiration, and a low general level of planning and verbal communication. All of these factors appear to be the result of a complicated synthesis of many small intangible causes, amplified into a general tangible effect through the interaction process. One might expect each of these factors to be the content of developing group norms and subject to normative control.

Using Cattell's personality test in a different approach, Haythorn (49) obtains results generally confirming Cattell's work. Haythorn finds that measured personality traits of members involving emotional maturity, friendly cooperativeness, trustfulness and adaptability, adventurousness, willed application and freedom from anxiety tend to be positively related to smooth and effective group functioning as judged by observers of the group. Conversely, the characteristics of paranoid suspiciousness, eccentricity, and coolness to others as measured by the Cattell Sixteen Personality Factor Test are found to be negatively related to smooth functioning as seen by the observers. In this study observers also rate the behavior of individuals, and group members rate the characteristics of their group. Observer ratings on variables of individual behavior conceptualized as "facilitating the achievement of the group goal," such as cooperativeness, efficiency, and insight, tend to predict the ratings subjects give their groups on such variables as morale, cooperativeness, productivity, motivation, and interest in job completion. Observer ratings of variables of individual behavior grouped as "striving for individual prominence," such as aggressiveness, initiative, confidence, authoritarianism, interest in individual solution, and attempts at leadership, tend to be negatively related to members' own ratings of the cohesiveness and friendliness of their group. Finally, observers' ratings of a third group of variables conceptualized as "sociable behavior" tend to be related to members' own ratings of their group as noncompetitive, friendly, and talkative. In general, subjects choose as coworkers or nominate as best in leadership those members who "facilitate" group functioning and reject those who hinder smooth functioning.

A variable closely related to the concept of "striving for individual prominence" is the tendency of the person to participate at a high rate of interaction. Chapple (26) early posited a tendency toward constancy of interaction rate and later with Lindemann (27) found that amount and patterning of activity and inactivity were related to psychiatric diagnosis of patients. Roberts and Strodtbeck (88) find that paranoid schizophrenic patients have higher rates of interaction, a higher proportion of negative acts, and a higher proportion of acts directed to the leader than do depressed patients. While most studies have taken the gross amount of interaction initiated in a unit of time as their basic measure, Goldman-Eisler (43) reports that long silences (as compared to short silences, short actions, and long actions) are the most characteristic (reliable) indices of the individual's conversation activity.

Significant tendencies toward stability or consistency in both quality and quantity of interaction initiated and received by the individual in both "actual" and role playing situations are found by Borgatta and Bales (14), although certain qualities are more stable than others. In general, the stability for all qualities of interaction over a series of sessions is dependably greater when the individual participates with the same individuals than when the individual participates with different ones, but consistency is shown in either event. Borgatta, Couch, and Bales (16), using an index consisting of interaction rate, sociometric popularity, leadership rating, and intelligence, find that the men identified by simultaneously high scores on all four of these variables often maintain their status in subsequent sessions in which they participate with different persons, and have, according to indirect measures, a significant influence on the satisfaction and effective functioning of the group.

Borgatta and Bales (15) present data which indicate that each individual who is a prospective member of a group may usefully be regarded as having a characteristic rate of interaction, as a personality trait, and a characteristic upper bound (or relative limit on the variability of his performance), with a tendency to increase his rate of initiation in a given group in the direction of the upper bound as a function of the opportunity afforded by the rates and bounds of the other participants. The rate actually achieved by a given person is an inverse function of the characteristic rates of his coparticipators. The total rate achieved by a given group is a positive function of the summed characteristic rates of the participants, but it is also a positive function of the differentiation of the characteristic rates. Why the latter should be the case is not immediately clear. For both individuals and groups, qualitative differences in interaction are associated with differences in gross interaction rates. For individual persons, specialization on the side of activities characteristic of task leadership is generally associated with high gross interaction rate. Persons with relatively lower rates tend to assume roles of supporting, modifying, qualifying, or rejecting. Persons with the lowest rates may be excluded or may withdraw, tend to show high rates of tension, and may not contribute substantially either to the task or to the support of coparticipators.

Bales (3) and Slater (99) find a medium to low and insignificant correlation between amount of participation and amount of liking received, with evidence that the reason for the low correlation is that the relation becomes nonlinear at the top. Presumably, there are some cases where "domination" and "striving for individual prominence" rather than accepted leadership are associated with high participation, with the result that there is some loss of liking received or failure to gain the liking of other members. However, it is apparently not impossible for the same man to combine top participation rank with top ranking on liking received, as noted in Borgatta, Couch, and Bales (16).

The threefold classification we have discussed in detail in regard to the Haythorn study is based on a series of factor analyses made by Carter and Couch (20) of observer ratings made on subjects' behavior. Carter (19) indicates the generality of the factors in reviewing other factor analytic studies, such as those by Sakoda (90), Wherry (113), and Clark (29). Carter conceptualizes the factors as follows: Factor I. *Individual prominence and achievement*—behaviors of the individual related to his efforts to stand out from others and individually achieve various personal goals; Factor II. *Aiding attainment by the group*—behaviors of the individual related to his efforts to assist the group in achieving goals toward which the group is oriented; Factor III. *Sociability*—behaviors of the individual related to the efforts to establish and maintain cordial and socially satisfying relations with other group members. These factors represent underlying dimensions in observer ratings, but it seems likely that the subjects' own reactions to each other involve the same or closely similar factors. It may be that the best way of looking at these factors is not as personality traits, but as frameworks in which personality traits of members are responded to by the perceiver, and which are generalized to a highly consistent degree over a wide range of perceivers.

The hypothesis that particular types of personalities relate uniquely to particular other types of personalities is currently receiving research attention.   Winch (117) reports some success with the hypothesis that marital partners show more than a chance amount of complementarity of needs.   Schutz (92) reports success in composing groups to be compatible and incompatible on the basis of personality tests he constructed to measure degrees of liking for close personal relationships, degrees of need for a dependent, power structured relationship, and various defensive syndromes centering on these variables.   Maas (70) reports an experiment in which leaders who tend to project blame, as a personality characteristic, perceive and behave in a more objective and less biased way when put in informal groups with open membership and activity programs, but less objectively when placed in formal groups.   Leaders who tend to introject blame are more objective in the formal groups and less so in the informal groups.   Several other experiments in this area are known to be under way but not yet reported.

## CONCLUDING REMARKS

The amount of convergence in findings from a number of studies and the cumulative growth of relevant information is encouraging and in some cases impressive.   Rigor in sociological research of group behavior is in its infancy but shows promise.   More comprehensive data gathering researches are greatly needed.   Once an area has been opened by a small study that presents an ingenious and inventive idea, the need appears for larger scale studies which aim at the collection and systematic reduction of data rather than hypothesis testing in the more specific sense.   In the normal meaning of the term, hypothesis testing requires both systematic theory and measures of known reliability and validity.   Hypotheses cannot really be tested in single first studies, no matter how ingenious and useful they may be in other respects.   Nor can maximally useful theory be invented without reference to measured variables.   What passes for theory in the field today is not always empirically based, at least not in the ordinary conception of science.   Generally speaking, even the empirically based theory tends to be top-heavy with necessarily vague and undefined concepts and at the bottom tends to be thin and poorly anchored in operationally defined variables.

It is not enough that a conceptually defined variable has some operational definition in some highly specific situation.   The specificity of the situation being researched or of the method used to measure a given variable may be so great that each such test must stand as a separate case history.   A large amount of research is required to establish the degree of equivalence of various possible measures and thus to obtain conceptualized variables that can be operationally defined over a wide range of applications. The failure to make a sufficient contribution in this direction is one reason why some experimental studies seem thin and even trivial. Comprehensive studies which examine large numbers of variables and attempt to develop measures that are applicable to many empirically different types of groups are an appropriate approach to this problem. Studies of this kind are appearing in increasing number and are an encouraging sign of the increasing maturity of the field.

## BIBLIOGRAPHICAL REFERENCES

1. Back, K. W., L. Festinger, B. Hymovitch, H. H. Kelley, S. Schachter, and J. W. Thibaut, "The methodology of studying rumor transmission," *Hum. Relat.,* Vol. 3 (1950), pp. 307–312.

2. Bales, R. F., *Interaction Process Analysis: A Method for the Study of Small Groups,* Cambridge, Mass., Addison-Wesley, 1950.

3. Bales, R. F., "The equilibrium problem in small groups," in T. Parsons, R. F. Bales, and E. A. Shils, *Working Papers in the Theory of Action,* Glencoe, Ill., Free Press, 1953, pp. 111–161.

4. Bales, R. F., "In conference," *Harvard Bus. Rev.,* Vol. 32 (1954), pp. 44–50.

5. Bales, R. F., and E. F. Borgatta, "A study of group size: Size of group as a factor in the interaction profile," in A. P. Hare, E. F. Borgatta, and R. F. Bales, *Small Groups: Studies in Social Interaction,* New York, Knopf, 1955.

6. Bales, R. F., and P. Slater, "Role differentiation," in T. Parsons, R. F. Bales, *et al., Family, Socialization, and Interaction Process,* Glencoe, Ill., Free Press, 1955.

7. Bales, R. F., F. L. Strodtbeck, T. M. Mills, and Mary E. Roseborough, "Channels of communication in small groups," *Amer. Soc. Rev.,* Vol. 16 (1951), pp. 461–468.

8. Bass, B. M., and S. Klubeck, "Effects of seating arrangement on leaderless group discussions," *J. Abnorm. Soc. Psychol.,* Vol. 47 (1952), pp. 724–727.

9. Bass, B. M., and Fay-Tyler M. Norton, "Group size and leaderless discussions," *J. Appl. Psychol.,* Vol. 35 (1951), pp. 397–400.

10. Bavelas, A., "A mathematical model for group structures," *Appl. Anthrop.,* Vol. 7 (1948), pp. 16–30.

11. Berkowitz, L., "Sharing leadership in small, decision-making groups," *J. Abnorm. Soc. Psychol.,* Vol. 48 (1953), pp. 231–238.

12. Bion, W. R., "Experience in groups: I," *Hum. Relat.,* Vol. 1 (1948), pp. 314–320.

13. Borgatta, E. F., "An analysis of three levels of response: An approach to some relationships among dimensions of personality," *Sociometry,* Vol. 14 (1951), pp. 267–316.

14. Borgatta, E. F., and R. F. Bales, "The consistency of subject behavior and the reliability of scoring in interaction process analysis," *Amer. Soc. Rev.,* Vol. 18 (1953), pp. 566–569.

15. Borgatta, E. F., and R. F. Bales, "Interaction of individuals in reconstituted groups," *Sociometry,* Vol. 16 (1953), pp. 302–320.

16. Borgatta, E. F., A. S. Couch, and R. F. Bales, "Some findings relevant to the great man theory of leadership," *Amer. Soc. Rev.,* Vol. 19 (1954), pp. 755–759.

17. Bossard, J. H. S., "The law of family interaction," *Amer. J. Soc.,* Vol. 50 (1944–1945), pp. 292–294.

18. Bovard, E. W., "The experimental production of interpersonal affect," *J. Abnorm. Soc. Psychol.,* Vol. 46 (1951), pp. 521–528.

19. Carter, L. F., "Recording and evaluating the performance of individuals as members of small groups," *Personnel Psychol.,* Vol. 7 (1954), pp. 477–484.

20. Carter, L. F., and A. Couch, "Factorial studies of the rated behavior of group members," Paper read at meeting of Eastern Psychological Association, New York, March, 1952.

21. Carter, L. F., W. Haythorn, and Margaret Howell, "A further investigation of the criteria of leadership," *J. Abnorm. Soc. Psychol.,* Vol. 45 (1950), pp. 350–358.

22. Carter, L. F., W. Haythorn, Beatrice Meirowitz, and J. Lanzetta, "The relation of categorizations and ratings in the observation of group behavior," *Hum. Relat.,* Vol. 4 (1951), pp. 239–254.

23. Cartwright, D., and A. F. Zander (eds.), *Group Dynamics: Research and Theory,* Evanston, Ill., Row, Peterson, 1953.

24. Cattell, R. B., "Concepts and methods in the measurement of group syntality," *Psychol. Rev.,* Vol. 55 (1948), pp. 48–63.

25. Cattell, R. B., D. R. Saunders, and G. F. Stice, "The dimensions of syntality in small groups," *Hum. Relat.,* Vol. 6 (1953), pp. 331–356.

26. Chapple, E. D., "Measuring human relations: An introduction to the study of interaction of individuals," *Genet. Psychol. Monogr.,* Vol. 22 (1940), pp. 3–147.

27. Chapple, E. D., and E. Lindemann, "Clinical implications of measurements on interaction rates in psychiatric interviews," *Appl. Anthrop.,* Vol. 1 (1942), pp. 1–11.

28. Christie, L. S., R. D. Luce, and J. Macy, Jr., *Communications and Learning in Task Oriented Groups,* Cambridge, Mass., Research Laboratory of Electronics, 1952.

29. Clark, R. A., "Analyzing the group structure of combat rifle squads," *Amer. Psychol.,* Vol. 8 (1953), p. 333.

30. Coch, L., and J. R. P. French, Jr., "Overcoming resistance to change," *Hum. Relat.,* Vol. 1 (1948), pp. 512–532.

31. Danielsson, B., "Some attraction and repulsion patterns among Jibaro Indians," *Sociometry,* Vol. 12 (1949), pp. 83–105.

32. Dashiell, J. F., "Experimental studies of the influence of social situations on the behavior of individual human adults," in C. Murchison (ed.), *A Handbook of Social Psychology,* Worcester, Mass., Clark University Press, 1935, pp. 1097–1158.

33. Davis, R. L., "Structures of dominance relations," *Bull. Math. Biophysics,* Vol. 16 (1954), pp. 131–140.

34. Dawe, Helen C., "The influence of the size of kindergarten group upon performance," *Child Develpm.,* Vol. 5 (1934), pp. 295–303.

35. Deutsch, M., "A theory of cooperation and competition," *Hum. Relat.,* Vol. 2 (1949), pp. 129–152.

36. Eysenck, H. J., *The Psychology of Politics,* London, Routledge and Kegan Paul, 1954.

37. Festinger, L., "Theory of social comparison processes," *Hum. Relat.,* Vol. 7 (1954), pp. 117–140.

38. Festinger, L., S. Schachter, and K. Back, *Social Pressures in Informal Groups: A Study of Human Factors in Housing,* New York, Harper, 1950.

39. Festinger, L., and J. Thibaut, "Interpersonal communication in small groups," *J. Abnorm. Soc. Psychol.*, Vol. 46 (1951), pp. 92–99.

40. Fischer, P. H., "An analysis of the primary group," *Sociometry*, Vol. 16 (1953), pp. 272–276.

41. Freedman, M. B., T. F. Leary, A. B. Ossorio, and H. S. Coffey, "The interpersonal dimension of personality," *J. Pers.*, Vol. 20 (1951), pp. 143–161.

42. Gibb, J. R., "The effects of group size and of threat reduction upon creativity in a problem-solving situation," *Amer. Psychol.*, Vol. 6 (1951), p. 324.

43. Goldman-Eisler, Frieda, "The measurement of time sequences in conversational behavior," *Brit. J. Psychol. (Gen. Section)*, Vol. 42 (1951), pp. 355–362.

44. Green, Elise H., "Group play and quarreling among pre-school children," *Child Develpm.*, Vol. 4 (1933), pp. 302–307.

45. Guetzkow, H., and W. Henry, *Group Projective Sketches*, Ann Arbor, University of Michigan Press, 1949.

46. Hare, A. P., "A study of interaction and consensus in different sized groups," *Amer. Soc. Rev.*, Vol. 17 (1952), pp. 261–267.

47. Hare, A. P., "Small group discussions with participatory and supervisory leadership," *J. Abnorm. Soc. Psychol.*, Vol. 48 (1953), pp. 273–275.

48. Hare, A. P., E. F. Borgatta, and R. F. Bales (eds.), *Small Groups: Studies in Social Interaction*, New York, Knopf, 1955.

49. Haythorn, W., "The influence of individual members on the characteristics of small groups," *J. Abnorm. Soc. Psychol.*, Vol. 48 (1953), pp. 276–284.

50. Heise, G. A., and G. A. Miller, "Problem solving by small groups using various communication nets," *J. Abnorm. Soc. Psychol.*, Vol. 46 (1951), pp. 327–336.

51. Hemphill, J. K., "Relations between the size of the group and the behavior of 'superior' leaders," *J. Soc. Psychol.*, Vol. 32 (1950), pp. 11–22.

52. Hollingshead, A. B., *Elmstown's Youth*, New York, Wiley, 1949.

53. Homans, G. C., *The Human Group*, New York, Harcourt, Brace, 1950.

54. Horwitz, M., and D. Cartwright, "A projective method for the diagnosis of group properties," *Hum. Relat.*, Vol. 6 (1953), pp. 397–410.

55. Hughes, E. C., "The knitting of racial groups in industry," *Amer. Soc. Rev.*, Vol. 11 (1946), pp. 512–519.

56. Hurwitz, J. I., A. F. Zander, and B. Hymovitch, "Some effects of power on the relations among group members," in D. Cartwright and A. F. Zander (eds.), *Group Dynamics: Research and Theory*, Evanston, Ill., Row, Peterson, 1953, pp. 483–492.

57. James, J., "A preliminary study of the size determinant in small group interaction," *Amer. Soc. Rev.*, Vol. 16 (1951), pp. 474–477.

58. Jensen, E. M., E. P. Reese, and T. W. Reese, "The subitizing and counting of visually presented fields of dots," *J. Psychol.*, Vol. 30 (1950), pp. 363–392.

59. Johnson, D. M., *The Psychology of Thought and Judgment*, New York, Harper, 1955.

60. Kaufman, E. L., M. W. Lord, T. W. Reese, and J. Volkmann, "The discrimination of visual number," *Amer. J. Psychol.*, Vol. 62 (1949), pp. 498–525.

61. Kelley, H. H., "Communication in experimentally created hierarchies," *Hum. Relat.*, Vol. 4 (1951), pp. 39–56.

62. Kelley, H. H., and J. W. Thibaut, "Experimental studies of group problem solving and process," in G. Lindzey (ed.), *Handbook of Social Psychology*, Cambridge, Mass., Addison-Wesley, 1954, pp. 735–785.

63. Kephart, W. M., "A quantitative analysis of intragroup relationships," *Amer. J. Soc.*, Vol. 60 (1954–1955), pp. 544–549.

64. Leavitt, H. J., "Some effects of certain communication patterns on group performance," *J. Abnorm. Soc. Psychol.*, Vol. 16 (1951), pp. 38–50.

65. Leavitt, H. J., and R. A. H. Mueller, "Some effects of feedback on communication," *Hum. Relat.*, Vol. 4 (1951), pp. 401–410.

66. Lewin, K., "Group decision and social change," in T. H. Newcomb, and E. L. Hartley (eds.), *Readings in Social Psychology*, New York, Holt, 1947, pp. 330–344.

67. Lewin, K., and R. Lippitt, "An experimental approach to the study of autocracy and democracy: A preliminary note," *Sociometry*, Vol. 1 (1938), pp. 292–300.

68. Lindzey, G. (ed.), *Handbook of Social Psychology*, Cambridge, Mass., Addison-Wesley, 1954.

69. Lundberg, G. A., Virginia B. Hertzler, and Lenore Dickson, "Attraction patterns in a university," *Sociometry*, Vol. 12 (1949), pp. 158–159.

70. Maas, H. S., "Personal and group factors in leaders' social perception," *J. Abnorm. Soc. Psychol.*, Vol. 45 (1950), pp. 54–63.

71. McCurdy, H. G., and H. W. Eber, "Democratic versus authoritarian: A further investigation of group problem-solving," *J. Pers.*, Vol. 22 (1953), pp. 258–269.

72. Macy, J., Jr., L. S. Christie, and R. D. Luce, "Coding noise in a task-oriented group," *J. Abnorm. Soc. Psychol.*, Vol. 48 (1953), pp. 401–409.

73. Maier, N. R. F., *Psychology in Industry*, Boston, Houghton Mifflin, 1946.

74. Maier, N. R. F., and A. R. Solem, "The contribution of a discussion leader to the quality of group thinking: The effective use of minority opinions," *Hum. Relat.*, Vol. 5 (1952), pp. 277–288.

75. Maisonneuve, J., G. Palmade, and Claude Fourment, "Selective choices and propinquity," *Sociometry*, Vol. 15 (1952), pp. 135–140.

76. Marriott, R., "Size of working group and output," *Occup. Psychol.*, Vol. 23 (1949), pp. 47–57.

77. Merton, R. K., "The social psychology of housing," in W. Dennis, R. Lippitt, *et al.*, *Current Trends in Social Psychology*, Pittsburgh, University of Pittsburgh Press, 1948, pp. 163–217.

78. Mills, T. M., "Power relations in three-person groups," *Amer. Soc. Rev.*, Vol. 18 (1953), pp. 351–357.

79. Mills, T. M., "The coalition pattern in three-person groups," *Amer. Soc. Rev.*, Vol. 19 (1954), pp. 657–667.

80. Moede, W., "Die Richtlinien der Leistungspsychologie," *Industr. Psychotech.*, Vol. 4 (1927), pp. 193–209.

81. Moldawsky, S., "An empirical validation of a rigidity scale against a criterion of rigidity in an interpersonal situation," *Sociometry*, Vol. 14 (1951), pp. 153–174.

82. Parten, Mildred B., "Social play among preschool children," *J. Abnorm. Soc. Psychol.*, Vol. 28 (1933), pp. 136–147.

83. Piaget, J., *The Moral Judgment of the Child*, New York, Harcourt, Brace, 1932.

84. Potashin, Reva, "A sociometric study of children's friendships," *Sociometry*, Vol. 9 (1946), pp. 48–70.

85. Preston, M. G., and R. K. Heintz, "Effects of participatory versus supervisory leadership on group judgment," *J. Abnorm. Soc. Psychol.*, Vol. 44 (1949), pp. 345–355.

86. Rice, A. K., "The use of unrecognized cultural mechanisms in an expanding machine shop," *Hum. Relat.*, Vol. 4 (1951), pp. 143–160.

87. Riecken, H. W., and G. C. Homans, "Psychological aspects of social structure," in G. Lindzey (ed.), *Handbook of Social Psychology*, Cambridge, Mass., Addison-Wesley, 1954, pp. 786–832.

88. Roberts, B. H., and F. L. Strodtbeck, "Interaction process differences between groups of paranoid schizophrenic and depressed patients," *Int. J. Group Psychother.*, Vol. 3 (1953), pp. 29–41.

89. Roseborough, Mary E., "Experimental studies of small groups," *Psychol. Bull.*, Vol. 50 (1953), pp. 275–303.

90. Sakoda, J. M., "Factor analysis of OSS situational tests," *J. Abnorm. Soc. Psychol.*, Vol. 47 (1952), pp. 843–852.

91. Schachter, S., "Deviation, rejection, and communication," *J. Abnorm. Soc. Psychol.*, Vol. 16 (1951), pp. 190–207.

92. Schutz, W. C., "What makes groups productive," *Hum. Relat.*, Vol. 8 (1955), pp. 429–465.

93. Shaw, M. E., "Group structure and the behavior of individuals in small groups," *J. Psychol.*, Vol. 38 (1954), pp. 139–149.

94. Shaw, M. E., "Some effect of unequal distribution of information upon group performance in various communication nets," *J. Abnorm. Soc. Psychol.*, Vol. 49 (1954), pp. 547–553.

95. Shaw, M. E., "A comparison of two types of leadership in various communication nets," *J. Abnorm. Soc. Psychol.*, Vol. 50 (1955), pp. 127–134.

96. Shaw, Marjorie E., "A comparison of individuals and small groups in the rational solution of complex problems," *Amer. J. Psychol.*, Vol. 44 (1932), pp. 491–504.

97. Sherif, M., "A preliminary experimental study of inter-group relations," in J. H. Rohrer, and M. Sherif (eds.), *Social Psychology at the Crossroads: The University of Oklahoma Lectures in Social Psychology*, New York, Harper, 1951, pp. 388–424.

98. Simon, H. A., "A formal theory of interaction of social groups," *Amer. Soc. Rev.*, Vol. 17 (1952), pp. 202–211.

99. Slater, P. E., "Role differentiation in small groups," *Amer. Soc. Rev.*, Vol. 20 (1955), pp. 300–310.

100. Smith, S. L., "Communication pattern and the adaptability of task-oriented groups: An experimental study." Cited in A. Bavelas, "Communication patterns in task-oriented groups," in D. Lerner and H. Lasswell (eds.), *The Policy Sciences; Recent Developments in Scope and Method*, Stanford, Calif., Stanford University Press, 1951, pp. 193–202.

101. South, E. B., "Some psychological aspects of committee work," *J. Appl. Psychol.*, Vol. 11 (1927), pp. 437–464.

102. Steinzor, B., "The spatial factor in face to face discussion groups," *J. Abnorm. Soc. Psychol.*, Vol. 45 (1950), pp. 552–555.

103. Stephan, F. F., and E. G. Mishler, "The distribution of participation in small groups: An exponential approximation," *Amer. Soc. Rev.*, Vol. 17 (1952), pp. 598–608.

104. Strodtbeck, F. L., "Husband-wife interaction over revealed differences," *Amer. Soc. Rev.*, Vol. 16 (1951), pp. 468–473.

105. Strodtbeck, F. L., "The family as a three-person group," *Amer. Soc. Rev.*, Vol. 19 (1954), pp. 23–29.

106. Strodtbeck, F. L., and A. P. Hare, "Bibliography of small group research: (From 1900 through 1953)," *Sociometry*, Vol. 17 (1954), pp. 107–178.

107. Taves, E. H., "Two mechanisms for the perception of visual numerousness," *Arch. Psychol.*, Vol. 37 (1941), No. 265.

108. Taylor, D. W., and W. L. Faust, "Twenty questions: Efficiency in problem solving as a function of size of group," *J. Exp. Psychol.*, Vol. 44 (1952), pp. 360–368.

109. Thibaut, J. W., "An experimental study of the cohesiveness of underprivileged groups," *Hum. Relat.*, Vol. 3 (1950), pp. 251–278.

110. Thibaut, J. W., and J. Coules, "The role of communication in the reduction of interpersonal hostility," *J. Abnorm. Soc. Psychol.*, Vol. 47 (1952), pp. 770–777.

111. Thrasher, F., *The Gang*, Chicago, University of Chicago Press, 1927.

112. Watson, G. B., "Do groups think more efficiently than individuals?" *J. Abnorm. Soc. Psychol.*, Vol. 23 (1928), pp. 328–336.

113. Wherry, R. J., *Factor Analysis of Officer Qualification Form QCL–2B*, Columbus, Ohio State University Research Foundation, 1950.

114. Whyte, W. F., "The social structure of the restaurant," *Amer. J. Soc.*, Vol. 54 (1948–1949), pp. 302–310.

115. Willerman, B., "Group decision and request as means of changing food habits," in K. Lewin (ed.), Forces behind Food Habits and Methods of Change. The Problem of Changing Food Habits: Report of the Committee on Food Habits, 1941–43, *Bull. No. 108, Natl. Res. Council*, Washington, D. C., 1943, pp. 35–65.

116. Wilner, D., Rosabelle P. Walkley, and S. W. Cook, "Residential proximity and intergroup relations in public housing projects," *J. Soc. Issues*, Vol. 8 (1952), pp. 45–69.

117. Winch, R. F., "The theory of complementary needs in mate-selection: A test of one kind of complementariness," *Amer. Soc. Rev.*, Vol. 20 (1955), pp. 52–56.

118. Wispe, L. G., "Evaluating section teaching methods in the introductory course," *J. Educ. Res.*, Vol. 45 (1951), pp. 161–186.

# chapter 13

# Racial and cultural relations

ROBIN M. WILLIAMS, JR.
*Cornell University*

## INTRODUCTION

The decade under review was a period of such great research activity that the social science literature on racial and cultural relations has grown far beyond the possibility of adequate coverage in a brief chapter.* In fact the present attempt falls just short of complete hopelessness only because a number of critical reviews and codifications had appeared earlier, to bring some beginnings of order into this active, diffuse, and somewhat chaotic field. There have been research reviews such as those by Christie and Jahoda (38), Harding *et al.* (80), Klineberg (103), Newcombe (146), Rose (163), and Williams (201); recent textbooks include

* For example, in a single year (1953–1954) there were 130 titles listed under "Racial and Cultural Relations" in *Current Sociology: An International Bibliography of Sociology* (Paris, UNESCO).

Berry (15), Brown (27), Davie (49), Hartley (82), Marden (133), McDonagh and Richards (127), Schermerhorn (172), Simpson and Yinger (177), and Walter (194); we have had such critical essays as those by Bradbury (21), Frazier (68), Freedman (69), and Wirth (205); and there have been also many clarifying and organizing influences arising from general sociological and psychological theory.*

The present review will be severely limited in scope to a small sample of recent research, and is intended merely to suggest the range of the available materials. It largely omits the many pertinent anthropological and historical studies. And even within its restricted coverage (reluctantly confined to works in English), it will be possible to present no more than a small portion of the significant hypotheses and findings.

With these drastic disclaimers duly recorded, let us turn to the matter at hand.

It seems bootless here to present still another effort to define or delimit the field in a formal way. At a certain level of development of abstract theory, there would be no point in considering "race and cultural relations" as a special topic of study. It is an acknowledgment of the concreteness, or high degree of empiricism, still characteristic of the present stage of development that we deal with the subject as a special subarea of sociology. Both the pressures of practical concerns in this high-tension subject and unsolved problems of theory and methods have contributed to an empirical-descriptive emphasis. At the same time, there are nevertheless some technical or theoretical justifications for singling out ethnic relations for specialized attention. Such relations constitute one of the primary structural foci of social systems (149). Ethnic collectivities represent ascribed status and relatively abstract social categorization. Continuity and depth of personal involvement are entailed for the individual actor.

Racial and cultural minorities are, clearly, not "groups" in the sense of the small unit of direct interaction to which the term is most properly applied. Racial and cultural *relations* exist wherever persons with recognized physical and cultural differences of a status-defining character come into contact. *Minority* relations, however, appear as a consequence of power relations *within* a larger collectivity in which a given minority has "membership," in some important sense. It is partly because racial and cultural differences are not coincident with systems of social interaction and power relations that our present subject is a focus of special social attention. In the modern world of nations and supranational relations,

* It is impossible to cite all the relevant and important works, and yet some must be cited; it is hoped that no further apologies are necessary.

it is usual rather than unusual to find that racial and cultural categories or collectivities are "minorities." * In the great interminglings of our times, very few "tribal" or "communal" societies have survived (93). Accordingly, relations between individuals or groupings defined as ethnically different are typically minority relations.

Many propositions concerning such relations will not be restricted to that particular phenotypical field but will have a much wider validity. It is essential, therefore, that studies in this subject draw upon concepts, hypotheses, and findings from other content-areas of the social sciences, and that their conclusions be checked against conclusions from other research fields. It would be an edifying but unhappy irony if the sociology of race and cultural relations turned out to be, itself, provincial and isolated.

Although, for purposes of convenient exposition, this chapter brackets together "racial" and "cultural" relations, it is important to stress the existence of well-known and important differences. For quite some time "race" has served as a label for relationships, including conflicts, that were primarily organized around differences in culture and political position. "Race" may be said to be so important because of hereditary quality and high visibility. Yet physical properties can be rendered of little *systemic* importance by cultural compatibility or conflict. And it could be argued with some force that to "resign from one's culture" is, in many circumstances, as difficult as to resign from one's racial category. For many questions of social policy, perhaps one of the most important things we can say is that persons of different racial types can often easily share the same culture, but that many cultural differences as, for example, in religious or nationality minorities, are impressively resistant to change.

With regard to minorities as such, the type-situation is one in which two sets of norms prevail in a social system such that persons who by one set of standards are entitled to the same treatment as members of a different ethnic category are accorded different and "less desirable" responses by virtue of the categorical membership attributed to them by birth or association. A racial or cultural minority may thus be viewed for present purposes as a collection of persons who by token of shared physical properties or cultural characteristics are regarded by other members of some larger collectivity, within whose power-system they live, as different and as an object of out-group sentiments. A minority is in an ambivalent position: it is both in the society and not in it. If an ethnic collectivity is completely outside the physical territory of a given social

* For the distinction between "social category" and "collectivity" see (150, pages 192–193).

system, it is not a minority but an ally, an enemy, a remote people, and so on. If an ethnic population is completely "in" the social system, the whole matter becomes the ordinary one of differentiated statuses within a single system.

Ethnic (racial, cultural, religious) categories, then, refer to aggregates that are ascriptive in origin. Within the category, relations of individuals, so far as these relations are "ethnic," tend toward diffuseness and collectivity orientation. Often ethnic solidarity becomes so attenuated as to appear to be totally absent—only to appear in diffuse mobilization in collective crisis or ceremonial, as sometimes occurs, for example, among Americans of Irish or German descent.*

Enough has been said to hint at the great complexity of the field under consideration here. Problems of definition and taxonomy have been given intensive treatment by the works already cited. The more pedestrian task at hand is to review illustrative propositions drawn from some of the empirical research of the decade. The questions for which we can currently expect some empirical answer, however approximate, are those upon which there has already been expended a considerable amount of prior conceptualization and research specification. Wherever feasible we shall look for research in which it is possible to say fairly explicitly what variables and hypotheses are involved.

Subsequent sections are loosely organized under these headings:

Propositions relating to the properties of ethnic prejudice
Relation of personality to prejudice
Intergroup contacts and situational determinants of intergroup relations
Social structure and group properties of minority ethnic groupings
Social control and the role of power and authority in intergroup relations
Social processes in change in ethnic relations.

### Propositions relating to the properties of ethnic prejudice

In this and the following sections, we shall attempt to state a numbered series of "propositions." This helps us to be brief. The obvious disadvantages are two: (a) the statements will vary greatly in type—they will be at different levels of abstraction and will range from definitional, to descriptive, to correlational, to predictive; (b) the discrete assertions will

* Parsons' definition of ethnic group seems useful here: ". . . an aggregate of kinship units, the members of which either trace their origin in terms of descent from a common ancestor or in terms of ancestors who all belonged to the same categorized ethnic group" (149, page 172). On the phenomena of "ghost nations" see Glazer (72).

not be explicitly organized into a logical system. Nevertheless, let us see what can be done with this rough scheme.*

Early American studies of prejudice were unduly handicapped by a tendency to treat prejudice as an isolated trait of individuals, divorced from enduring social relations and cultural structure, as well as by *ad hoc* one-factor explanations. The last ten years have brought us closer to analysis rather than sheer description, and have resulted in increased sophistication concerning both the methodological and the theoretical aspects of research on prejudice (177, page 3). It is clear that prejudice may be treated as an aspect of cultural, social, and personality systems (150, Allport), and that its place in any one of these three systems is not deducible from a knowledge of its functioning in the other two.

Although a great many somewhat different definitions of prejudice have appeared during the decade, their differences less often represent disagreements than variations in emphasis and in the larger conceptual framework within which the concept is to be used; there seems to be a substantial core of agreement as to the generic qualities of prejudice as a psychological and social phenomenon.

"Prejudice" is, of course, a "sponge word" which has absorbed a wide variety of referents. In examining any particular piece of research it is correspondingly essential to look for the operational specification as well as the formal definition. It does seem to be widely accepted in recent years that prejudices are particular manifestations of social man's universal capacities to form general concepts, to generalize affects attached to these concepts, and to bring thoughts into the service of feelings (cf. 150, Allport).

1. "Prejudice" has two primary characteristics: ". . . the individual is affectively oriented toward an object of regard; and . . . this object of regard is overgeneralized" (150, page 366). Such a generalized (conceptualized) affective disposition is, in one aspect, a value orientation and as such partakes of personality system, social system, and cultural system.

2. As a highly generalized, affective-conceptual prejudgment, prejudice may, or may not, involve conscious hostility. It is perhaps advantageous not to prejudge this question by including hostility as a defining criterion, but rather to leave the degree and kind of hostility as a matter for empirical study. This procedure makes it possible to raise the crucial question as to the specific conditions under which one will predict actively

---

* In the illustrative propositions we shall concentrate upon statements appearing since the compilations by Rose and by Williams in 1947, except for points in those reviews which have undergone major reformulations since that time.

hostile prejudice. It allows for the possibility that definite stereotypes may carry little active or conscious hostility (38, Lasswell, page 214).

3. There is a general tendency for prejudices toward specific outgroups to be linked together into a pattern of prejudice. But there are two important qualifications: (a) there are instances in which one or a few groups are singled out as the primary objects of negative prejudice; (b) individuals may belong to membership-groups which are different from their reference-groups, and thereby manifest positive prejudice towards a social category other than that to which they apparently "belong."

> The research results to date indicate that the concept of ethnocentrism is supported in that (1) individuals who display one form of prejudice toward a specific minority or minorities also tend to display other forms of prejudice, (2) prejudice toward one ethnic minority is usually (although not invariably) accompanied by prejudice toward other ethnic minorities, and (3) that the ethnic ingroup is reified to the extent that patriotic and nationalistic sentiments are related to rejection of ethnic minorities (38, Christie, page 154).

But:

> . . . situational factors which select one group as an especial target of animosity . . . may lead to expressions of hostility toward the culturally selected target . . . without concomitant hostility being directed toward other ethnic groups (38, Christie, page 154). And, there are many known instances of xenocentric attitudes, involving deprecation of one's nominal membership-groups and positive prejudices toward other groups (101, 136).

4. The vague denotation of the word "prejudice" limits its usefulness as a concept to be employed in research. It is, however, a useful term for pointing to a complex area of phenomena; it simply requires further specification for purpose of scientific research. Among the phenomena which we are accustomed to recognize as prejudice are found many different "aspects" or dimensions (80, 106, 201, and many others).

5. Intercorrelations between prejudices toward different outgroups vary widely with (a) the nature of the outgroups being considered, (b) the status-characteristics of the judging population, (c) personality dispositions, and (d) immediate situational influences.

*For example:*

Hatt has shown that intercorrelations between attitudes towards Jews and foreign-born and Negroes and foreign-born were much higher among lower-class than among middle-class persons (83).

Hartley demonstrated that generally high intercorrelations of ethnic attitudes as indexed by a social distance scale did not hold for attitudes toward "Communists" and "Fascists" (82).

6. The total set of outgroup prejudices of any given individual will include areas of high organization and areas of loose structure. Highly structured subsets occur as: (a) clusters of intercorrelations of *different aspects* of orientation toward a *single* group or category, for example, stereotyped beliefs, hostile affect, and unwillingness to accept close social contact with reference to white people; (b) clusters of intercorrelations of attitudes toward several different outgroups (Italians, Negroes, Jews); (c) unidimensional scales of attitudes toward a given social category; and (d) unidimensional scales of attitude toward a set of outgroups.

In short, there are true dimensions of prejudice, represented as a single highly structured aspect of orientation. Other "facets" are more complexly organized, as quasi scales or as "latent structures." Areas of high organization "fade out" into loosely correlated specific attitudes, which seem merely to share some vaguely defined element of manifest content in common with the more tightly organized areas.

As indexed by present research devices, there are found areas of indefinite organization in which it is difficult to determine exactly what is being indexed. A striking statement on this point, indicating our great need for continued work on research techniques, has been given by Christie in his review of the California "F-scale":

> This brief examination of the F-scale leaves us with two conclusions: (1) it captures something common to fascistic philosophy but it is impossible to specify with any precision what it captures, and (2) although there is some evidence that the hypothesized dimensions have some validity the individual items are not related to these in a clearcut way (38, page 140).

It is plausible to suppose that definite organization of a specific prejudiced orientation will be the more likely to appear, the greater the frequency of the prejudice in a given population and the greater the intensity of affect it carries.

7. The content of stereotypes regarding various social categories is only loosely related to the incidence or intensity of hostility toward these groupings.

*For example:*

> . . . we find an almost complete overlap in the proportion of stereotypes most frequently ascribed to . . . (generally liked and generally disliked groups) . . . Both Americans and Jews are described most frequently as aggressive and ambitious, industrious, materialistic, efficient, practical, and intelligent . . . The content of the stereotypes ascribed to Jews . . . fails to explain the hostility directed toward Jews (170, pages 219–222).

8. Specific traits take on different affective loadings in different stereotypes; the same trait may be valued positively when in the context of a

stereotype of one group and negatively when part of the stereotype of another group (170, page 223).

9. A change in feelings toward an ethnic group will involve a change in beliefs, but changes in beliefs may occur without changes in feelings (cf. 80).

10. Stereotypic attitudes held in common in large social aggregates tend to persist through time, changing only slowly except under the impact of major social events—when radical changes can occur in a very short time. The stability of common stereotypes, therefore, appears to be in large part a function of the stability of established relationships between collectivities.

As concerns the special case of mass attitudes between nations, it is indicated by several recent studies that diffusely held stereotypes tend to follow rather than to precede changes in objective power-alignments and the official ideologies and actions of organized groups and governments.

*For example:*

The nine-nation public opinion survey of 1948 showed that generalized attitudes toward other nations were such as would be expected in view of the actual political relations between these countries, and these in turn were rather closely associated with stereotypes. "These stereotypes are not fixed but change with the logic of current events" (29, page 582).

As a broader hypothesis, many suggestive bits of information point to the possibility that the influence of mass propaganda or indoctrination will be the greater, the less the person-to-person interaction across system boundaries. Stereotypic orientations toward socially distant collectivities are likely to be especially subject to the relatively unrestrained operation of such processes as projection and displacement. For a detailed review of research relevant to these problems, see Klineberg (103).

11. The rank-ordering of various ethnic categories ("order-of-preference") tends to be stable through time, changing only slowly in response to major social events.

12. Seemingly different specific attitudes toward a particular ethnic category tend to be more consistent than attitudes toward different outgroups: ". . . attitudes have greater generality as organized around individual minority groups rather than as topically discrete modes of response applied to any and all outgroups" (35).

13. In the case of groupings with which an individual has had little or no direct experience, the acceptance of definite stereotypes often occurs without either high salience or intensity.

It has generally been assumed that stereotyped replies to questions on "national characteristics" indicate stereotyped thinking on the part of the respondents; our results suggest per contra that the majority of respondents have no particular views on the subject at all, and are perfectly aware of the fact that any replies they can make are merely the result of cultural and social indoctrination (56, page 35; see also 23).

14. Direct personal experience with the objects of outgroup stereotypes may either increase or decrease commitment to the stereotypes, and may either increase or decrease generalized hostility and social distance, depending upon other accompanying conditions (see pages 437–447). In so far, however, as the stereotypic orientations are initially affectively weak, nonsalient, and conceptually ill-defined, repeated exposure to direct interaction with members of the outgroup is likely to result in heightened salience, intensity, and complexity of orientation.

The net import of the findings and hypotheses just cited is to re-emphasize the large number of analytically separate problems that have come to be associated with the term prejudice. The conventional attention to an over-all negative or positive direction has been supplemented by analysis of intensity, and by increased conceptual clarity as to other possible dimensions of the phenomena. At long last, there is now some reasonable chance of fitting these phenomena into a framework congruent with a broader body of sociological research and theory.

### Relation of personality to prejudice

In the years since World War II, one of the most prominent lines of research relating to race and cultural relations has been the exploration of the connections between prejudice and various personality structures and processes. Many studies have been made, and the results represent substantial progress.

Additional light has been thrown on the development of outgroup stereotypes and attitudes during the processes of socialization.

*For example:*

15. In our culture, as children grow older their outgroup stereotypes become more complex (differentiated) and more highly organized (74, 187).

16. The intergroup behavior of young children is "variable and inconsistent," and it is likely that with increasing age the "consistency" between behavior and attitudes increases, so long as the relevant social context remains stable (80).

17. Personality development tends to proceed from a low degree of

differentiation, organization, and specificity in earlier life toward greater complexity of organized elements.

> Children grow more consistent in their "moral traits" as they grow older (38, Hyman and Sheatsley, page 58).

> . . . correlations between related attitudes tend to increase with increased exposure to academic influences during college (*idem*).

> Whereas the ethnocentric personality pattern seems quite firmly established in the adult, it appears in the child as incipient, or as a potential direction for development (38, Frenkel-Brunswik, page 244).

Even at very early years, however, definite stereotypes and attitudes of outgroup rejection can be established. There are fundamental psychological dispositions at work in the motivation for this social learning; for example, young children are highly interested in ". . . identifying, describing, classifying, evaluating, and comparing themselves and others . . ." (74).

18. An important variable in the developmental sequence leading to the "hostile personality" is hypothesized to be early deprivation of affectional support.

> From the earliest days the children who hate receive insufficient emotional support and in consequence feel everlastingly alone in an unresponsive and actively hostile world. . . . Egocentricity is most pronounced when early support is weakest (38, Lasswell, pages 205–207).

19. Studies of socialization suggest that prejudices will be the more resistant to change (a) the closer their dynamic connection with the individual's self-conception; (b) the more numerous the need-dispositions gratified by holding, expressing, or behaving on the basis of the prejudiced orientations; and (c) the more strongly reinforced by negative fixation in their developmental history in the personality.

From many sources there has arisen an influential current of research based upon the idea that prejudice is not a set of isolated attitudes but rather a functional part of a total personality system. By all odds the most influential study in this field has been *The Authoritarian Personality* (2). The bold hypotheses of the original study stimulated many partial replications and invited critical analysis. A large amount of relevant research on "intolerance of ambiguity," rigidity, dogmatism, etc., has appeared during the same period. The net result is an impressive increment of both new ideas and empirical findings. A few samples follow.

20. A frequent characteristic of highly prejudiced persons is a generalized "intolerance of ambiguity," which according to the California studies

seems related to ". . . submission to authority, feelings of social marginality, lack of originality, externalization of values, hostility, power-orientation, and rigid social stereotyping" (38, Frenkel-Brunswik, page 246).

21. Researches of K. Goldstein, Rokeach, Block and Block, Cowen and Thompson, Lindzey and Rogalsky, and others suggest that within a given sociocultural context both generalized "rigidity" of personality (persistent use of standardized patterns of action and belief under changing conditions) and outgroup stereotypes are in part functions of incapacity to deal with new and problematic experiences except through "rote" solutions. A poverty of psychological and social resources seems to be an important factor leading to constricted and repetitive perceptions, attitudes, and behavior.

Results consistent with these suggestions have come from studies of so-called social perception. Persons high in prejudice are especially likely to "see" the objects of their prejudice as members of the outgroup category. The prejudiced person is highly sensitive to category membership, but insensitive to variations within it.

22. The dynamic organization of personality is systematically related to specific attitudes toward public objects and symbols. Shils has commented, for example, that *The Authoritarian Personality* has given strong plausibility to the proposition that ". . . there is a determinate relationship between particular attitudes toward public objects and symbols and 'deeper' cognitive and emotional attitudes or dispositions" (38, page 42).

23. However, it has not proved possible to isolate any one unidimensional characteristic of personality that invariably distinguishes between persons who are highly prejudiced against outgroups and those who are not, nor has research shown an invariant clustering of personality dimensions predictive of prejudice. But a large number of studies, in part stimulated by *The Authoritarian Personality,* have shown a loose cluster of "personality" characteristics which tend to go along with hostility toward outgroups. These characteristics include: conventionalism, authoritarian submission, authoritarian aggression, anti-intraception, "superstition" and "stereotypy," emphasis on power and "toughness," "destructiveness" and "cynicism," projectivity, repressed sexuality (38).

24. Among the leaders of organized antiminority movements in the United States, a frequent pattern of personality characteristics includes: low trust of other people, diffuse paranoic trends, instability, diffuse aggressiveness, "intense and self-defeating" demands for affection and response, lack of flexible self-control, low capacity to give affection (38, Shils, pages 45–47; see also 123). Yet these very characteristics render it difficult for such "leaders," or agitators, to meet the systemic require-

ments for building large-scale sustained organizations (38, Shils, page 48). Thus, sociological variables are specifically necessary to account for the organizational outcome.

25. A view of the world as threatening and unpredictable correlates positively with ethnocentric attitudes, although the more passive or depressive personalities who view the world in this way seem to have little hostility toward minorities (38, Christie, page 194).

26. The functional significance of prejudice in the personality system varies widely ". . . between bigotry that is simply stereotyped and bigotry that is saturated with need and necessity" (150, Allport, page 378). For example, compulsive personalities characteristically are highly occupied with the ". . . internal disciplining of incompletely repressed hostility (explosive or continuing rage)" (38, Lasswell, page 205. See also (1)).

27. Studies using measures of "authoritarianism" adapted from the California F-scale show that persons with high (authoritarian) scores tend to have low ability to sense the personality characteristics of others, to be oriented to superiors rather than to peers, to resist scientific investigation, to be "conservative" in political preferences, and to be prone to projective attitudes.

At the same time, it has been shown that such persons have low education, low scores on intelligence tests, low socioeconomic status, and low participation in formally organized groups.*

Thus authoritarianism (which may be a misleading label) is correlated with social location, not only with other personality characteristics. The "bigots" identified by the F-scale tend to be persons of low power and social status (95); there is no guarantee that the bigotry found in influential positions in the social structure will be of precisely the same kind. The actual patterning of responses to items presumed to index personality conforms to social class levels and subcultures in such a way as to suggest: (a) the responses tend to be such as would be expected on the basis of social realities—e.g., for poor and uneducated persons in our present society the world often *is* a threatening "jungle"; (b) many items whose manifest content may appear to refer to deep emotional predispositions are actually so pervasive in the culture as to be accepted by radically different personality types. For some items, at any rate, it appears that variations in responses so closely follow levels of education and social class as to throw serious doubt upon whether personality or culture is being indexed. For example, this is suggested by Hyman and

---

* Based on summaries in (38) of studies by Gough, Scodeland, Mussen, Christie, E. Rosen, O. Milton.

Shcatsley with regard to the value-correlates of ethnocentrism as revealed by projective questions in *The Authoritarian Personality:* "We suspect that what is being scored here are not personality differences but simply the variations in the language of different social classes" (38, page 96).

28. The importance of personality determinants in intergroup behavior will be the greater:

(a) the less the situation of action is already clearly defined for the participants by social norms;

(b) the higher the social rank, authority or power of the individual actor, whose behavior we wish to predict;

(c) the more the personality is "compulsively" organized. (To avoid tautological formulations here, personality organization must be defined by indexes independent of the situation for which predictions of behavior are to be made.) *

(d) the greater the priority-emphasis on functional diffuseness, particularism, and affectivity of the norms held by the participants to define appropriate conduct in the situation;

(e) the more the interaction is an end in itself rather than the means to a further end, e.g., the less the action is task-centered (instrumental);

(f) the more the behavior is oriented to relatively unstructured abstract symbolizations of persons and groups rather than to the immediate actions of the participants themselves.

So ". . . the contribution of internal factors increases as the external-stimulus situation becomes more unstructured, and decreases as it becomes more structured" (176, Sherif, page 211).

29. With regard to the problem of "consistency" in the intergroup behavior of the same personality, there is evidence from many studies that what is ordinarily called inconsistency arises in large part from multiple or changing demands of reference groups. Some inconsistency is a matter of truly idiosyncratic motives, and some results from weak internalization of norms. However, many of the "inconsistencies" that are important in intergroup relations derive from fluctuations in the group-referents which supply the anchoring frames of reference for the individual (176, Sherif).

For example, we might expect that "logical" inconsistency of the norms inferred as directing behavior of the same person in different situations to be the greater: (a) the more widely different the typical behavior patterns in the various groups in which the individual participates; (b)

* Points a–c adapted from Shils (38, page 44).

the greater the difference between publicly accepted and privately toler-
ated behavior; (c) the less the specificity of the norms; (d) the less the
norms to which the actor is oriented in specific situations are linked to
value-orientations accepted by him.  Although these statements can be
taken tautologically, they can be made into predictive hypotheses by
independent definition of the principal terms in research operations.
Clearly, however, the problem of consistency opens up fundamental and
very difficult questions which will require much further work.*

30. The relationships between personality factors and prejudices are
likely to be the greater the more active the participation of the individual in organized groups concerned with social issues.

> It is only to be expected that individuals selected from the ranks of organ-
> ized groups would be more likely to show both some patterning of their
> sentiments and some greater relationship between sentiments and personality
> factors. . . . [For "inert" persons, social and economic issues are more likely
> to be] peripheral and thus not penetrated by more fundamental values and
> energies (38, Hyman and Sheatsley, page 63).

31. The same basic type of personality will react differently toward
outgroups in a social situation with norms of "tolerance" than in a situation in which the norms endorse intolerance.  More specifically, "authoritarian" personalities in which tendencies to accept external authority
are strong will be especially likely to exhibit "conventional" behavior,
tending to move toward even those group norms opposed to their initial
outgroup ideology.

Compare the inconclusive but provocative results of an experiment by
Levinson and Schermerhorn: ". . . when subjected to a social climate
in which ethnic tolerance was the social norm, those relatively high in
initial acceptance of ethnocentric and fascistic statements changed more
in the direction of the social norms than did those who were initially
more receptive to the ideology of the workshop" (38, Christie, page 191).

Christie showed in a study of Army recruits a greater change *toward*
acceptance of F-scale statements by those men who emerged as leaders
in the relatively "authoritarian" military situation.  These leaders were
initially slightly *below* the group mean on the F-scale scores (38, Christie,
page 192).

Perhaps the most essential point here is the impossibility of predicting
from present indexes of authoritarianism how individuals will change
their orientation in test situations.

A NOTE OF EVALUATION.  As compared with ten years ago, there now
exists a more adequate organization of general sociological and psycho-

---

* Interest in the subject is indicated by a large number of articles: see *Journal of
Social Issues,* Vol. 5 (1949), pp. 2–63.

logical concepts with which to grasp the results of observation and experimentation. It is fortunately no longer necessary to debate the importance of "personality" versus "social situation" as a *theoretical* problem in this field; rather, the part played by each set of variables becomes an empirical matter to be answered for each specific problem.

Thus, while personality factors are clearly important in intergroup behavior (in such aspects as differential sensitivity to social situations, rigidity of response, irradiation of affect, etc.), social transactions impose their own demands. Social action is more than any simple unfolding or acting out of personality tendencies. This view is now so widely accepted as to be trite, but generalized acceptance does not always result in specific and detailed recognition in study designs and in the interpretation of findings. To treat the problems of personality and prejudice "in context" does not in the least imply a shapeless merging of anthropology, psychology, and sociology. It involves only a willingness to see specific problems at any one system-level in the context of relevant knowledge of the others. Fruitful possibilities in this direction are suggested by some of the studies of intergroup contacts and relationships, to which we now turn.

### Intergroup contacts and situational determinants of intergroup relations

One of the more encouraging signs of progress in the study of ethnic groupings is the growing emancipation from the "atomistic" approaches which dealt with the members of different racial and cultural categories as unorganized aggregates of separate individuals. For all their shortcomings, it has been one of the great virtues of community studies that they have discerned and highlighted the fact that race and cultural relations are *relations*—that there is organization, recurrence, continuity, pattern in the interactions and sentiments of individuals assigned category-membership in the community. We have abundant and clear documentation of relational qualities that are authentic group properties, not characteristics of individuals taken in isolation from the relational context.

Intergroup relationships, as do any other social interactions, involve opportunity and attraction. The extent of intergroup interaction is partly a matter of sheer opportunity: this is a simple fact but one of high importance because of the role in this particular field of physical separation and pathways of social avoidance. Put schematically, we may say that the extent of opportunity for intergroup contact, where individual choice is nominally possible, varies with: (a) the proportions of various ethnic categories within a given population; (b) the spatial concentration or dispersion of these groupings (spatial segregation is a technically effective way to reduce contact potentialities to a low level even in an aggregate having a high proportion of persons from a given minority category); (c) the degree to which social interactions occur outside of a relatively small kinship group; and (d) given extra-kinship interactions, the number and kind of centers or paths utilized in common by members of the different social categories, e.g., recreational, public services, and commercial establishments.

32. The greater the functional proximity of individuals in physical space, the greater the likelihood of social interaction (51, 58). It appears that this is true even in the presence of quite marked prejudices.

33. A given frequency of interactions of a particular type will have differing effects upon different aspects or dimensions of the content of prejudiced orientations—for example, acceptance of *stereotypes*, generalized *liking-disliking, social distance* (acceptance or exclusion from personal social interaction), *attitude toward public policy* (equality or inequality in economic opportunity, political rights, access to public facilities and accommodations, etc.). Saenger and Flowerman report from a study of college students that living in the vicinity of Jews correlates with lesser acceptance of stereotypes about Jews, but not with willingness to admit Jews to fraternities or sororities.

We may hypothesize that at any level of liking or disliking or sense of social distance, persons with no social contact with members of a racial or cultural outgroup will be more likely than those with contacts to endorse negative stereotypes of that particular outgroup category or collectivity (170, pages 233–234).

34. Given a situation providing opportunities for interaction, but not forcing such contacts, the rate of intergroup interaction will be the lower the greater the initial incidence of hostile orientations; ". . . hostility will be accompanied by relatively low interaction provided that there are no constraints to enforce interaction" (117, Riecken and Homans, page 797).

35. On the other hand: "If there are two groups, the members of each interacting within their own group rather more often than with members of the other group, intragroup friendship with its concomitant, some degree of intergroup hostility, tends to appear" (13, Riecken and Homans, page 797). The phrase "some degree of intergroup hostility" leaves open the possibility of great variation in the degree of hostility, from very mild, joking aggression to the most intense hatreds. The specific conditions associated with these variations are accordingly of the greatest interest.

It has been repeatedly suggested by students of racial and cultural relations that group rivalry or competition is a factor of primary importance in evoking strongly hostile feelings between groups or collectivities. Sherif has recently provided an experimental demonstration of how formerly friendly relations between individuals can be transformed into conflict by inducing group rivalry. Concomitantly, hostile stereotyping appeared, illustrating how stereotypes are produced by conflict, even while furnishing one basis for conflict. And ". . . intergroup conflict produced by incompatible group goals and directions is accompanied by the formation of unfavorable group stereotypes" (175, page 290).

Thus, for predicting the likelihood that friendly relations will emerge from interaction of members of different social categories, we may hypothesize that this outcome is the more likely the less competitive the interpersonal situation. A competitive situation may be characterized, for present purposes, as one in which the achievement of goals by any one individual or subgroup lessens the possibility of others being able to attain their own goals (36, Deutsch, pages 319–353).

American studies of the effects of interracial interaction have largely concentrated upon formalized social situations in which there is a considerable measure of authoritative control over the behavior of the interacting persons—military organizations, public housing projects, schools, factories, boys' camps. Within the United States, the direct study of interaction patterns has been confined almost entirely to areas outside of the South. Within the limits of such coverage, however, there is high consistency in the findings with regard to Negro-white interaction. In the Army (181), in the Merchant Marine (26), in governmental organizations (130), in housing projects (51, 203), in public schools (202), the studies show that the integration of whites and Negroes into the same situations is accompanied and followed by an over-all reduction in the prejudices of whites toward Negroes. Although a portion of the white participants do not change in attitude and although some become more negatively inclined, the net effect is typically found to be "positive."

This conclusion runs directly counter to widely held common-sense assumptions, and it is clearly of very great practical significance. The essential scientific problem here, however, concerns what variables, and relations among them, may be used to explain the varying outcomes of different kinds of interaction in various types of situations. Relevant research has accumulated during the last ten years. For example, MacKenzie (130) found that it was only association of whites in a work situation with Negroes of high occupational status that was effective in breaking down stereotypes.

Now, the question as to the effects of personal interaction between members of differently categorized groupings is a special case of a more general question: *Under what conditions do persons form continuing friendly relations?* Clearly the general question may have nothing directly to do with religious, ethnic and racial classifications, for the generic problem remains even in groups that are homogeneous in these respects; and this fact emphasizes once more that our ultimate scientific interest is in "human relations," not just "ethnic relations." Posing the wider question has the further virtue of implying the futility of any attempt to predict friendship-formation, or the reduction of prejudice or discrimination, without specifying the conditions under which contact occurs.

What have we learned from the studies now available as to the crucial conditions or variables affecting the outcome of intergroup contacts?

36. We may summarize thus:

(a) In the absence of interfering factors, the more frequently persons interact, the more alike they become in their values. And the more alike they are in their values, the more they will interact, in the presence of opportunity, up to some limit. More concretely:

> Persons with hostile (or favorable) attitudes toward a particular group will tend to establish and maintain contact with others who share their attitudes, consequently these attitudes will tend to be maintained and reinforced (58; quoted in 46).

> For those with similar values . . . social contact, because it is rewarding, will motivate them to seek further contact (13, Merton, page 30).

(b) The more frequent the interaction between persons holding the same or similar values, the higher will be their appraisals of the others, and the closer will be the mutuality of appraisals.

(c) The more frequent the interaction between persons holding the same or similar values, the stronger will be the self-identification of the individual with the unit of interaction; ". . . it is the unit of functioning that integrates" (207, page 346).

(d) Unless other conditions mask the effects, intimate social interaction tends to alter the values of the participants in the direction of greater consensus, i.e.: "Not only does intimate social interaction precipitate a deposit of new common values, but it also converts originally disparate values into common values" (13, Merton, page 33).

37. An hypothesis of long standing in this field has been: "Personal contacts between members of different groups are generally most effective in producing friendly relations when the individuals are of the same, or nearly the same, economic and social status . . ." (201, page

69). Yet it has also been apparent for long that equal-status interactions are likely to be competitive, and we assuredly know that equal-status interaction, even within the same racial or cultural category, may be neither rewarding nor productive of positive sentiments. If we take "equal-status contacts" to be those in which it is reciprocally understood by the participants that each has a right to be accorded roughly equivalent consideration, respect, deference, and right to be heard, it would seem that such contacts are especially likely to produce friction if (a) the basis of equality is insecure or uncertain, or (b) the goal-structure of the interaction favors competition.

What does seem likely even under the latter conditions is that the participants tend to become *important* to one another. It is difficult for equal-status contacts to occur repeatedly without some affective involvement: the others become not emotionally neutral but subjects of imperious attention. Thus the relationships are likely to become both affectively charged and affectively and conceptually complex. Both cognitive and affective fields become more dense, more specific, with more discernible facets, and more complex organization. If this hypothesis holds, equal-status contacts may be assumed to change stereotypes, at least in so far as the immediate objects of interaction are concerned.* It is, however, perfectly true that the stereotypes may not be dissolved but rather may become richer, more firmly held ("I know—I have dealt with them"), more intense, and more closely connected with self-conceptions (170, page 236).

In view of these considerations, it is certainly not to be taken for granted that the net resultant of equal-status contacts will be a change toward more friendly or accepting attitudes. The above description of possible effects of this type of interaction fits a duel, a divorce, or a feud as well as a love affair or a lifelong friendship. It is, accordingly, quite impressive to note that a large number of studies of equal-status interracial contacts in America have overwhelmingly reported "positive" attitudinal accompaniments. How is this to be explained?

We may note, first of all, that the findings come almost entirely from *relatively* permissive subcultures of Northern and Western areas. Furthermore, Negroes and whites in these situations already share a broadly similar culture; because they are "American," they have in the beginning a common language and a very large number of shared beliefs, values, and norms. Third, as already noted, many of the studies concern situa-

---

* An "exemption mechanism" often operates in such cases, of course; a generalized stereotypic attitude is retained while the outgroup members one knows well personally become "exceptions to the rule." Nevertheless, this does represent a change in the qualities of the stereotypic orientation.

tions of authoritative control by recognized legal and administrative bodies. Also, the types of interaction involved permit, most commonly, a relatively impersonal, formalized, and functionally specific set of relations—as in military organizations, unions, work groups, or educational institutions. There are probably a number of other important special conditions about which we are ignorant present in some of the situations studied.

To state these speculations is not to detract from the solid finding that "it can be done"—that interracial and intercultural contacts *do* under some conditions lead to increased interpersonal acceptance and friendliness and even to radical alteration of stereotypic orientations. The task is to specify what "other conditions" must be "equal" before we can safely predict "favorable" results from intergroup contact. And the research of the past decade has made it possible to ground hypotheses about the necessary antecedent conditions much more firmly in empirical findings. It appears, for example, that "equal status" is a positive factor only if it indexes common or "compatible" values, norms, or interests. The following paragraphs report some hypotheses which appear to considerably refine the equal-status hypothesis.

38. Interactions are more likely to lead to interpersonal liking when the interacting parties have the same or similar values *relevant to the type of interaction in which they engage*. Merton notes that whites having a consistent personal pattern of values relating to race relations tended, within the setting of an interracial housing project, to name as intimate friends persons who shared the same racial values, whereas persons with ambivalent or inconsistent racial values did not over- or under-select friends according to racial-value pattern (13, pages 27–28). The possibility of a continuing feed-back sequence is implied by much of the recent thinking on this subject, i.e., interaction, liking, and common values interact to lead to increased levels of each, up to limits set by such boundary-conditions as competing group memberships and activities.

39. There is also this hypothesis:

(a) The degree of liking for an "outgroup" member with whom one interacts will be the greater the closer the conformity of the activities of the one participant to the norms held by the other.*

(b) Therefore, given common values and conformity to mutually held norms, the more frequent the interaction the greater, within limits, should be the liking.

(c) On the other hand, conflictful sequences arise in interaction when the participants enter the situation with marked differences in the norms

* Paraphrased from Homans (86).

and values considered by them to apply to the interaction. Especially if the actors initially confront one another as members of different racial or cultural categories, such differences may lead to confusion, disagreement, irritation, and dislike. If such tension-laden interaction is then broken off, it is likely that a residue of antipathies and stereotypes will be left. Even initially friendly interaction can lead to this sequence when it reveals important value-divergences. "Cultural differences indeed increase hostility whenever the insecure person becomes aware of this difference" (170, page 237).

Evidently, further refinement of concepts and hypotheses is called for with regard to cultural differences—many of which are clearly responded to as interesting, challenging, and rewarding. Further progress seems to depend also upon more exact research specification of the generic properties of those cultural differences which are, and those which are not, associated with hostile interaction.

It is perhaps a peculiarity of American sociology that so much research attention has been devoted to *liking,* or friendship-formation, in intergroup contacts. There are certainly other important dimensions of the subject. Thus, we may propose as an illustration, that: The more frequent the interaction between persons of different social categories, the greater their emotional involvement in the relationship, i.e., the stronger their sentiments toward one another.

This result will be accentuated if: (a) the interaction is guided by orientation to functionally diffuse normative standards; (b) the participants expect the relationship to be of long duration; (c) a high proportion of the individual's total interactions is constituted by the intergroup contact.

Illustrative qualifications are: (a) the interaction must have some measure of success in satisfying the goals of the participants; (b) the sentiment will be ambivalent if one participant exercises authority over the other(s).*

40. Given enough commonality of interests or values to permit initial interaction, what properties of the interaction itself are significant in differential outcomes, in terms of attitudes or sentiments concerning the outgroup?

(a) The greatest likelihood of "positive" attitudinal changes attendant upon intergroup interaction is to be anticipated when the relations of the participants are informal, cooperative, noncontrived, and recurrent

---

* These formulations represent adaptations and extensions of general hypotheses presented by Homans (86).

over a relatively long period (183, pages 17–18). Diffuse, personalized relations will have greater effects upon attitudes than will functionally specific, impersonal contacts.

(b) But the likelihood of initial acceptance by prejudiced persons of interaction with outgroup members is less in the former type of situation. As a special case: ". . . it is easier to integrate the Negro or any other outgroup into a secular institution characterized by casual and impersonal contacts than into a sacred institution based upon families and the peculiar cultural traditions of the group" (67, page 8).

In so far as these two propositions are valid, one may hypothesize that in interracial and intercultural relations, those contacts that are easiest to initiate are of the type least likely to lead to important attitudinal changes. A similar "paradox" is generated by our next pair of propositions.

41. The consequences of interpersonal contact are greatly dependent upon the group context in which they occur:

(a) Individuals who are both strongly supported by and identified with a specific social group will be especially amenable to changes accepted by that group.

(b) Group unanimity and the shared awareness of attitude changes serve to reinforce and crystallize the changes in orientations of each individual member.

In so far as these generalizations may be validated by further testing, it may be concluded that piecemeal change is easiest to effect, but most difficult to stabilize. It may perhaps be appropriate to add that in that event the practical dictum would be: if one is able and his values clearly sanction it, divide and persuade—and when change has occurred, recombine into an integral community.

42. We come now to the following special case: what if interpersonal contacts of members of different cultural or racial categories are *not* equal-status, or *not* friendly? Examples of such situations are both important and easy to find.

(a) There is the case in which the interaction is between parties who interact in a relation of super-subordination. Homans has set forth hypotheses which we may summarize thus: When persons interact frequently in a relation of super-subordination, their sentiments toward one another will be ambivalent, and the amount of interaction will tend to be restricted to the minimum necessary for the specific functional roles in question (86, page 116).

(b) It may be further anticipated that relations of this character will be characterized by a relatively high development of "etiquette" or formal conventions which restrict the "intimacy" of the relationship.

James W. Woodward earlier advanced as a general principle of social behavior a hypothesis we may state as follows: In situations in which it is important, for any reason (including constraint), that the interaction of any two or more persons be continued or repeated, maximum conventionalization (formalism) of behavior is to be expected when (a) there is a minimum of initial positive feelings and shared values and (b) a maximum of divergence in interests and values (208).

43. In focusing upon person-to-person interactions across racial and cultural categories, it is essential to keep in view the fact that these contacts do not occur randomly but are themselves channelized by the environing sociocultural system. A special problem meriting intensive research attention is that of the antecedents and consequences of the kind and degree of normative patterning of intergroup contacts. For example:

(a) The less frequently a particular role-intersection occurs in a social system, the more likely it is that those contacts which do, nevertheless, occur will be relatively unpatterned, and will thus be strongly influenced by highly specific situational factors.

(b) If, for any cause, previously infrequent role-intersections increase greatly in frequency *for a given constellation of persons,* the initial ambiguity and conflict will create increased emotional involvement, heightened tension and discomfort, and gropings for a higher degree of normative structure and/or escape from the field.

(c) In so far as escape from the situation is difficult, the more frequently such role-intersections occur, the greater will be the normative patterning.

(d) Stated in terms of cultural similarity and differences, it may be expected that the greater the heterogeneity of beliefs and values represented in status-role behavior within an interacting population, the greater the "need" for explicit and clear definition of expected behavior, if the interaction is to continue. If, in a heterogeneous system, interaction does continue, this need will be felt by individuals in the form of uncertainty, ambivalence, confusion, frustration, and conflict. The deprivational character of these experiences will lead to a diffuse demand for clearer definition. Redefinition, in situations lacking an authoritative center of control, will occur mainly through the resolution of recurring misunderstandings and conflicts; individual solutions will tend to become standardized over time through communication.

44. Along with systematic studies of person-to-contact contacts of members of different cultural and racial categories, the decade has brought a large number of reports describing variations in behavior and attitudes in various concretely different *situations,* or social contexts. In these reports we have accumulated much documentation of the extent to which the conduct of individuals varies accordingly to differences in the complex stage-for-action which we loosely call a "situation." Most of this material can be subsumed under the specific propositions listed elsewhere in this chapter. It seems worthwhile, however, to summarize a few examples of the more generalized findings from this complicated and elusive field of study.

Perhaps the most striking conclusions, well-supported by numerous studies, are:

(a) In a great many important social situations, particularly those in which the situational norms enjoin behavior that is task-oriented (and therefore *tending* toward functional specificity and affective detachment), individuals' generalized stereotypic orientations toward outgroups show very little relation to their overt intergroup behavior. Generalized prejudice is a poor predictor of actual, situationally shaped intergroup conduct (18, 22, 31, 53, 79, 88, 109, 120, 138, 152, 161, 171, and many others).

(b) Previously established ethnic attitudes may be expected to have greatest influence as over against situational factors in those social contexts in which relationships are dominately diffuse, affective, and particularistic.

(c) Specific situational factors have their greatest importance in determining intergroup behavior in new, unexpected, infrequently occurring, or otherwise relatively unpatterned circumstances. Differently stated, a situation in which the participants have clear expectations and are oriented to definite norms of conduct minimizes the role of situationally idiosyncratic factors. Consider this viewpoint: "Intergroup behavior is primarily determined, not by intergroup attitudes, but by other motives in the individual interacting with the circumstances in which he finds himself (80, page 1054).

(d) The specific intergroup attitudes and behavior of the same individuals vary greatly from one institutionalized area of community life to another (114). In a study of industrial union members (white) in Chicago: "It is of particular interest to note that there was no correlation between acceptance or rejection of Negroes on the job and acceptance or rejection of Negroes in their home communities" (157; 120, page 244).

Before leaving the topic of intergroup contacts, it may be appropriate to refer to the insights of a pioneer in sociological study of race and culture. Robert Ezra Park observed that contact between members of different cultural groups initially increases the self-consciousness of the interacting parties as to the characteristics of their own culture as it contrasts with others. Furthermore, such contacts can lead in some measure to *clarification*, of which Park said:

> . . . conflict, and particularly cultural conflict, in so far as it brings into the light of understanding impulses and attitudes of which we would otherwise remain unconscious, inevitably increases our knowledge not merely of ourselves but of our fellows (148, page 50).

This reminder of complexities that still largely elude our research efforts may properly close this review of the accompaniments of intergroup contact.

### Social structure and group properties of minority ethnic groupings

The already enormous body of descriptive studies of ethnic groupings in 1945 has been still further enormously augmented in the years since. In addition to studies within the United States, we have reports on ethnic relations in Brazil (193, 200), Panama (18), Puerto Rico (161), Jamaica (24, 84), Hawaii (33, 37), Switzerland (135), Tristan da Cunha (141), Guatemala (70, 190), Israel (55, 104), Britain (43, 158), South Africa (54, 108, 126, 132, 151), Canada (112, 62), India (71, 143), Ceylon (168), and a number of other areas of the world. If cross-cultural generalizations are not well established in this field, there is at least an increasing coverage of important groups and regions, even if much of the material is, unfortunately, noncomparable.

Of the 101 summarizing propositions listed in a research review published in 1947, exactly four were classified under the heading "Reactions of Minority Groups" (20, pages 60–61), although some other propositions did have something to say on this topic. Today the amount of information available has increased greatly, and there has come about at least moderate progress in conceptualization and codification of the empirical materials.

Although we certainly expect the same general sociological principles to apply to the internal systems of minority ethnic collectivities as to any other social systems, there are particular social and psychological characteristics of such groupings that invest the subject with special interest.

Because ethnic categories or collectivities are groupings that are too large and extended or inaccessible to be perceived at once, they tend to be identified and characterized in such a way as to both simplify and accentuate the qualities apperceived as typical as of the grouping. The derived notion that racial or cultural categories are internally homo-geneous is, of course, repeatedly disproved by serious research. Within every minority are lines of differentiation based upon such factors as social stratification, local or trans-local affiliations and interests, religious participation, place of origin and length of residence, clique membership, stability of life-pattern, ideological convictions, and militancy or accom-modative attitudes toward the majority grouping. A major line of useful future research undoubtedly lies in further specification and analysis of such internal differentiation, especially as it may affect modes of response to the pressure of dominant outgroups.

45. It is well known that suppressed or deprived minorities often show marked lack of ingroup solidarity, and it is equally clear that in other instances there develops high solidarity, morale, and capacity for sus-tained action in concert. We still lack clear explanatory propositions to account for the great variations in responses, but some exploratory formu-lations have begun to appear. For example:

> In general, a relatively weak group, with disorganized institutions and wide internal differences, will tend toward intragroup conflict and a lack of soli-darity in its dealings with the dominant group. A minority with greater resources in income, education, and skill, however, and with well-organized family and community life, is likely to have a strong feeling of group cohesion and identification, at least in those situations that involve contact with the dominant group (177, page 199).

Through greater resources, heightened communication, and greater collective organization, it is possible for an aggregate that originally was merely a status-category to develop into a true minority collectivity. "The derivative minority group of American Negroes has been formed through association of originally heterogeneous elements made homo-geneous by virtue of a common status assigned to them within America's larger society" (64, page 14). See also (164).

46. Minorities, as here treated, live within a "host" society. The degree to which the fundamental social structure of the minority is similar to that of the environing system crucially affects the type of adjustment that is likely to occur.

> . . . isomorphism between parent and host society tends to decrease the like-lihood of the formation of a derivative minority group and to increase the chance of a primary minority group to preserve itself as a functioning social system, and vice versa (64, page 13; see the typology on pages 13–14).

47. The complex reactions of various minorities to deprivation, sup-pression—and "tolerance"—have continued to receive much research at-tention during the period under review. Also, further evidence has

accumulated as to the nature and sources of self-rejection or "self-hatred" among minority members (34, 39, 92).

> Seldom are feelings of inferiority or self-hatred expressed in an unambiguous way. They are more likely to take the form of an ambivalent attitude which shows both antipathy toward and solidarity with one's group. . . . The wholehearted acceptance of inferiority is characteristically a product of isolation—physical and/or social (177, pages 193 and 227).

Another side of this particular problem is the "positive" functional significance for the individual of membership in and identification with a cultural or racial grouping. Lewin, along with others, has stressed the importance for personal security and integration of a "firm social ground" in this respect. Certainly if there are recognized differing social categories, a certain kind of ethnocentrism, in the sense of positive identification and loyalty, is inevitable. The really interesting question arises only, however, when the individual's membership-group is both attractive and unattractive to him, because of the rewards and penalties membership brings and because of the attractiveness of other reference-groups. Analysis of reference-group behavior in this field is in early infancy, but some promising beginnings have been made (126, 165).

48. As one finds ethnic collectivities actually functioning, the character of the social relationships to the dominant majority is affected both by the internal system of the single ethnic grouping and by its external relations to still other groupings.

> . . . the true unit of race and ethnic relations is not the single ethnic group, but the *situation*, embracing all the diverse groups who live in the community or region (90, page 19).

> The character of intergroup relations is determined not only by the character of relations and norms that prevail within the in-groups but also by the process of interaction between groups (175, page 149).

49. The communication and interaction of any minority with the dominant grouping is one side of a two-sided relationship. This truism has been partly overshadowed in recent years by the emphasis on prejudices of majority-group members, but recently there have been several reminders that "minorities" also have prejudices (e.g., 40, 46), that both sets of prejudices emerge from interaction toward a "stimulus," and that the nature of the stimulus-field cannot be ignored in our research (5, page 370; 196).

Studies such as that by Cothran (46) show that the conceptions of a minority group concerning itself and concerning the majority group differ from the parallel conceptions in the majority. The exact role of asymmetry, lack of mutuality, and *systematic* ignorance as these actually become engaged in intergroup relations—contrasting so sharply with the ideal model of full complementarity of expectations—remains as a fascinating and largely unexplored area (177, page 241).

Space does not permit further illustrations from this field. We must leave with the bare mention the problem of the conditions preceding such divergent patterns of interminority relations as conflict, alienation and withdrawal, or a common front against a superordinate majority. And, finally, we must pass over the problems of racial and cultural "marginality," which are currently being reappraised in terms of reference-group concepts and fresh empirical materials. Thus, Leonard Broom (25) has presented a formulation of several different types of marginality; see also Golovensky (73). Research directed toward the "marginal alternative"— in which social locomotion between groups is feasible and is perceived as feasible—will be likely to measurably advance our knowledge of minority-group behavior.

### Social control and the role of power and authority in intergroup relations

The focus of attention in many current works on conditions affecting interpersonal liking or friendship-formation need not, in itself, lead to neglect of the "harder" aspects of the subject. It is evident, although easily forgotten, that many group relations are *objectively* cooperative or conflictful in relative independence of the interpersonal sentiments of the immediately interacting persons. It is probably a special cultural emphasis in America to believe that the primary road to resolving *group* (collectivity) conflicts is through personally friendly interaction of representations of the contending social aggregates. Even the most casual examination of political behavior—domestic or (perhaps especially) international—quickly shows the limitations of this view. With regard to racial and cultural relations, the centrality of problems of social control and power is apparent from the fact that in one important aspect "minorities" are a direct product of power-relations (172). Ethnic categories and collectivities can be defined independently of power-relations, but minorities are defined by their relation to some dominant grouping. Hence comes the significance of research that deals with patterns of social control other than those directly generated in interpersonal relationships.

Some students of race and culture relations in the modern urban environment have come to the conclusion that: ". . . it is more frequently the policy, strategy, and tactics of organized interest groups rather than the folkways, rather than the individual dimensions of personal prejudices or racial amity, which control behavior in specific situations" (120, page 242). It is not necessary to decide what set of factors may be "dominant" in order to accept the importance of taking organized power-groupings into account.

Most of the hypotheses and findings concerning the antecedents and consequences of intergroup contact thus far reviewed have referred to "small group" interaction. We are now calling attention to relations that may transcend the scope of immediately perceivable units of interaction.

A large part of interracial and intercultural relations in modern urbanized societies takes the form of *"mediating" linkages between collectivities as such,* rather than of a diffuse web of immediate personal interactions. Such mediating links are maintained by persons who act as informal or formal representatives, invested with responsibility for a segment of society.

50. Relations of this kind seem to have interesting special characteristics; for example, it seems likely that they are more easily disrupted by forces arising outside the relationship itself than are the internal relations of established small groups, and, on the other hand, that *personal* affinities and repulsions are less important than in the ordinary, "nonrepresentative" types of interpersonal relations.

51. Further, in the absence of constraining factors forcing another pattern of contact, *intergroup* relations will tend to occur between those members from each group who have relatively high ranking within their own group: ". . . two or more groups are linked together at their tops, if at all, and . . . foreign relations are particularly the concern of the head of a state" (117, page 797).

What Jessie Bernard (14) has characterized as the "family and neighbor" technique of accommodating conflicts is often quite far removed from the realities of cooperation, accommodation, or conflict between organized ethnic collectivities. Recognition of this point has been a factor in directing research interest toward the role in racial and cultural relations of legal action, of special-interest groupings, of formal organizations, of power relationships within and between communities, regions, and nations. Frazier has pointedly reminded his sociological colleagues that race relations in present-day urban society are only to a limited extent "in the mores"—regulated by rigid, informally mediated, and unquestioningly accepted social norms. Studies of racial segregation came to attribute crucial importance to power relationships as these determined law, administrative regulations, and formal operating practices—from Washington, D. C. (111) to the Union of South Africa (45, 54, 108).

52. The case for the effectiveness of legal action in shaping intergroup relations found an impressive list of supporters during the past decade.

Older doctrines stressing the slowness of change in the mores and the ineffectiveness of legislation or regulation conflicting with customary practice have been under assault for some time. Latterly, positive appraisals of the effectiveness of legislation, under certain conditions, have come from MacIver, Rose, Berger, Burma, and many others.

"Laws do establish criteria by which actions can be judged . . . a frame of reference within which other necessary processes can be systematized and accelerated" (32, page 423). "Law" is a special manifestation of authoritative normative regulation. The high generality of the subject may help account for the scarcity of rigorous propositions concerning legal factors in ethnic relations. Existing studies, however, already suggest what some of the important variables may be; for example (aside from the obvious factor of the existing intensity and prevalence of prejudicial orientations), the specificity of legal rules, the definiteness of provision for enforcement, the characteristics of the sanctions provided, and the mechanisms for registering complaints or charges. In America as a series of Supreme Court decisions has gradually removed the broadest legal basis for racial segregation in public education, we may perhaps expect increased attention by social science to the behavioral principles underlying legal regulation and responses to it.

### Social processes in change in ethnic relations

Many of the preceding sections of this chapter have dealt by implication with social change in ethnic relations. It is only necessary, therefore, to add a few additional illustrations of problems and findings in this least well-charted portion of our subject.

The period 1945–1955 was one of very rapid major changes in racial and cultural relations in many societies around the world. Such important societal developments could hardly fail to attract the attention of sociologists and other social scientists, and the result has been a large number of new descriptions and analyses.

53. Perhaps the strongest impression left by the conclusions reached by these new studies is the convergence upon the view that *basic changes in ethnic relations can occur in situations of rather strong prejudice as well as those of slight prejudice.* Examples are legion. To cite only a few, for the special case of Negro-white relations in the United States: (a) Marked increases in voting by Negroes have occurred in areas of the South for which there is little reason to suppose that generalized prejudice has been greatly reduced (182). (b) "The attitude of an employer toward Negro workers appears to have very little to do with whether or not he employs them" (31, page 453). (c) Case studies of desegregation in public

schools have noted a lack of close correlation between capacity to change social practice and the apparent prejudice level of the community at large (202).

54. A second recurrent theme in the studies of change may be formulated thus: When major alterations are proposed, demanded, or ordered in an established system of intergroup discrimination, the initial resistance of the dominant group is reinforced by mobilization for defense against an actual threat to vested interests *and* by reactions to projective anxieties. In such instances, if the anticipated change does occur, it is often and perhaps typically experienced as less threatening and traumatic than had been expected. In the specific case of school desegregation: "A direct challenge to customary ways typically arouses anxiety and resistance. The actual change usually removes vague apprehensions, substituting for them concrete problems in operation" (202, page 247).

55. The general sociological problem of reactions of strain under a challenge to vested interests (149, Chap. XI) is well illustrated in racial and cultural relations. New evidence continues to support the hypotheses that.

(a) Hostility of an economically dominant ethnic grouping toward a subordinate group is greatest in incidence and intensity when the subordinate group is rapidly improving its relative position and is actively demanding further improvement (80, page 1041); compare the earlier formulations in (201, pages 57–59).

(b) "Militancy, except for sporadic and short-lived uprisings, is not characteristic of the most deprived and oppressed groups, but rather of those who have gained considerable rights so that they are able realistically to hope for more" (201, page 61).

(c) "A militant reaction from a minority group is most likely when (a) the group's position is rapidly improving, or (b) when it is rapidly deteriorating, especially if this follows a period of improvement" (*idem*).

56. Further, the recent literature points once more to the fact that changes in racial and cultural relations may occur not as the outcome of factors initially "given" in these relationships themselves but rather as the consequence of changes in other aspects of the social or cultural system. Two widely different examples will suggest the rich range of possibilities here:

(a) E. Franklin Frazier (68) has pointed to the possibility that race relations may be determined in large measure by the internal system of the dominant group; for example, segregation and disenfranchisement of Southern Negroes did not occur until twenty-five years after the Civil

War, partly as an outcome of unresolved class conflicts within the white population.

(b) Biesanz and Smith point out (18, page 14) that:

> Whatever makes a specialized (e.g., occupational) status into a generalized status tends to increase racial discrimination. Thus when the external situation of a society requires a high degree of technical skill and discipline, and when these technical requirements happen to be concentrated in one race rather than diffused among several races, racial barriers are raised.

57. An overwhelming number of studies during the decade have dealt with various aspects of attitude-change among individuals exposed to intergroup contact (see pages 437–447) or to educational and informational influences. Much of the scientifically important work that appears relevant here has not directly concerned race or cultural relations (7, 36, 146). Among those researches which have treated changes in attitudes toward racial and cultural categories, the findings seem consistent with the larger body of evidence specifying the significance of immediate group membership, affective involvement, and personal participation as determinants of change and fixation of change (98, 116, 196).

As an instance of the way in which the current hypotheses quickly lead to further implications, we may consider this sequence:

(a) Attitudes and behavior toward outgroup members in a situation of outgroup contact are most easily changed *with reference to that type of situation* if the focus of attention is upon a common interest, task, or group goal, without any explicit reference to racial or cultural membership of the participants.

(b) But under these conditions there is a high probability that processes of "exemption" will occur—either the situation itself or the specific outgroup persons in it, or both, are likely to be defined as exceptions. In so far as this occurs, the changed orientations will not be generalized, and the transfer-value of the experience will be slight.

(c) Implication: if the initial prejudice-level of the participants is low enough to permit it, explicit attention to intergroup relations in the contact situation will heighten the intensity of the experience and increase the probability of generalization to other situations and outgroup members.

CONCLUSION

Nothing could be plainer than that this short overview of a few aspects of the field fails to adequately summarize recent empirical and theoretical progress. It is perhaps encouraging, nevertheless, to see how even a rather limited sampling reveals substantial new knowledge and raises at every turn significant further questions for study. Imperfect and fragmentary as our present knowledge most emphatically is, there is a clear indication that we have moved far, as Wirth has said:

> . . . from an earlier preoccupation with the study of differential traits and capacities of the various racial and cultural components of the human family to the present dominant interest in the processes of interaction between racial and cultural groups and in the development of effective methods for understanding and dealing with the problems of racial and cultural relations (205, pages 118–119).

It is now possible to seriously entertain the possibility of introducing some deductive structure into the body of hypotheses in the field, moving beyond the present *ad hoc* codifications.

It remains true that the field greatly lacks the consistent and clear theoretical framework it requires. A high percentage of the pages printed concerning the subject are so heavily "empiricist" that no analytical propositions can be extracted from them. But in the midst of the continuing flood of description-without-hypothesis we increasingly find studies which focus upon the antecedent-consequent relations of explicitly defined variables and are able to put a clear question to Nature. In 1947 the present writer said, after presenting a rough codification of propositions:

> It is believed that these propositions constitute a reasonably solid base of reference from which future research may depart. It is believed also that they constitute a challenge of the first order to social science and social action in these times (201, page 77).

It is now submitted that the challenge to sociology has been met by a decade's work which, with all its shortcomings, leaves a permanent increment of knowledge of far more than trivial significance for the further development of social science.

## BIBLIOGRAPHICAL REFERENCES

(In this partial listing, priority has been given, first, to works which summarize and evaluate existing research; secondly, to reports of research cited in this chapter and bearing directly on key hypotheses; thirdly, to a sampling of the wide range of special topics within the field.)

1. Ackerman, Nathan, and Marie Jahoda, *Anti-Semitism and Emotional Disorder*, New York, Harper and Brothers, 1950.

2. Adorno, T. W., *et al.*, *The Authoritarian Personality*, New York, Harper and Brothers, 1950.

3. Agnisky, B. W., "The Interaction of Ethnic Groups: A Case Study of Indians and Whites," *Amer. Soc. Rev.*, Vol. 14 (1949), pp. 288–293.

4. Allport, G. W., *The Nature of Prejudice,* Cambridge, Mass., Addison-Wesley Publishing Co., 1954.

5. Allport, G. W., "Prejudice: A Problem in Psychological and Social Causation," in T. Parsons and E. A. Shils (eds.), *Toward a General Theory of Action,* Cambridge, Mass., Harvard University Press, 1951.

6. Allport, G. W., and B. Kramer, "Some Roots of Prejudice," *J. Psych.,* Vol. 22 (1946), pp. 9–39.

7. Asch, S. E., *Social Psychology,* New York, Prentice-Hall, 1952.

8. Banks, W. S. M., II, "Rank Order of Sensitivity to Discriminations of Negroes in Columbus, Ohio," *Amer. Soc. Rev.,* Vol. 15 (1950), pp. 529–534.

9. Barron, Milton L., "Research on Intermarriage: A Survey of Accomplishments and Prospects," *Amer. J. Soc.,* Vol. 57 (1951–1952), pp. 249–255.

10. Barron, Milton L., *People Who Intermarry,* Syracuse, N. Y., Syracuse University Press, 1946.

11. Bayton, J. A., and E. Byoune, "Racio-National Stereotypes Held by Negroes," *J. Negro Educ.,* Vol. 16 (1947), pp. 49–56.

12. Berger, Morroe, *Equality by Statute: Legal Control over Group Discrimination,* New York, Columbia University Press, 1952.

13. Berger, Morroe, Theodore Abel, and Charles H. Page (eds.), *Freedom and Control in Modern Society,* New York, D. Van Nostrand Co., 1954.

14. Bernard, Jessie, "Where is the Modern Sociology of Conflict?" *Amer. J. Soc.,* Vol. 56 (1950–1951), pp. 11–16.

15. Berry, Brewton, *Race Relations: The Interaction of Ethnic and Racial Groups,* Boston, Houghton Mifflin Co., 1951.

16. Bettelheim, Bruno, and Morris Janowitz, *Dynamics of Prejudice: A Psychological and Sociological Study of Veterans,* New York, Harper and Brothers, 1950.

17. Bettelheim, Bruno, and Morris Janowitz, "Ethnic Tolerance: A Function of Social and Personal Control," *Amer. J. Soc.,* Vol. 55 (1949–1950), pp. 137–145.

18. Biesanz, John, and Luke M. Smith, "Race Relations in Panama and the Canal Zone," *Amer. J. Soc.,* Vol. 57 (1951–1952), pp. 7–14.

19. Black, Percy, and Ruth Davidson Atkins, "Conformity versus Prejudice as Exemplified in White-Negro Relations in the South: Some Methodological Considerations," *J. Psych.,* Vol. 30 (1950), pp. 109–121.

20. Bloom, Leonard, and Ruth Riemer, *Removal and Return: The Socio-Economic Effects of the War on Japanese-Americans,* Berkeley and Los Angeles, University of California Press, 1949.

21. Bradbury, W. C., "Evaluation of Research in Race Relations," *Inventory of Research on Racial and Cultural Relations,* Vol. 5, Nos. 2–3 (1953), pp. 99–133.

22. Bray, D. W., "The Prediction of Behavior from Two Attitude Scales," *J. Abn. and Soc. Psych.,* Vol. 45 (1950), pp. 66–89.

23. Brookover, W. B., and J. B. Holland, "An Inquiry into the Meaning of Minority Group Attitude Expressions," *Amer. Soc. Rev.,* Vol. 17 (1952), pp. 196–202.

24. Broom, Leonard, "The Social Differentiation of Jamaica," *Amer. Soc. Rev.,* Vol. 19 (1954), pp. 115–125.

25. Broom, Leonard, "Toward a Cumulative Social Science," *Proceedings Pacific Soc. Society,* 1951.

26. Brophy, Ira N., "The Luxury of Anti-Negro Prejudice," *Pub. Opinion Quarterly,* Vol. 9 (1945–1946), pp. 456–466.

27. Brown, Ina C., *Race Relations in a Democracy,* New York, Harper and Brothers, 1949.

28. Bruner, Jerome S., and Renato Tagiuri, "The Perception of People," in Gardner Lindzey (ed.), *Handbook of Social Psychology*, Vol. II, Cambridge, Mass., Addison-Wesley Publishing Co., 1954, pp. 634–654.

29. Buchanan, W., "Mass Communication in Reverse: The UNESCO International Public Opinion Survey," *Intern. Soc. Sci. Bull.*, Vol. 5 (1953), pp. 577–583.

30. Buchanan, W., and Hadley Cantril, *How Nations See Each Other*, Urbana, University of Illinois Press, 1953.

31. Bullock, H. A., "Racial Attitudes and the Employment of Negroes," *Amer. J. Soc.*, Vol. 56 (1950–1951), pp. 448–457.

32. Burma, John H., "Race Relations and Anti-Discriminatory Legislation," *Amer. J. Soc.*, Vol. 56 (1950–1951), pp. 416–423.

33. Burrows, Edwin G., *Hawaiian Americans: An Account of the Mingling of Japanese, Chinese, Polynesian and American Cultures*, New Haven, Yale University Press, 1947.

34. Campbell, Donald T., and Boyd R. McCandless, "Ethnocentrism, Xenophobia and Personality," *Human Relations*, Vol. 4 (1951), pp. 185–192.

35. Campbell, Donald T., *The Generality of a Social Attitude*, Unpublished doctoral dissertation, University of California, 1947.

36. Cartwright, Dorwin P., and Alvin W. Zander (eds.), *Group Dynamics: Research and Theory*, White Plains, N. Y., Row, Peterson and Co., 1953.

37. Ch'eng-K'un Cheng, "A Study of Chinese Assimilation in Hawaii," *Social Forces*, Vol. 32 (1953), pp. 163–167.

38. Christie, Richard, and Marie Jahoda (eds.), *Studies in the Scope and Method of "The Authoritarian Personality,"* Glencoe, Ill., The Free Press, 1954.

39. Citron, Abraham F., *et al.*, "Anti-Minority Remarks: A Problem for Action Research," *J. Abn. and Soc. Psych.*, Vol. 45 (1950), pp. 99–126.

40. Clark, Kenneth B., "Racial Prejudices among American Minorities," *Intern. Soc. Sci. Bull.*, Vol. 3 (1950), pp. 506–513.

41. Clark, Kenneth B., and Mamie P. Clark, "Emotional Factors in Racial Identification and Preference in Negro Children," *J. Negro Educ.*, Vol. 19 (1950), pp. 341–350.

42. Collins, Orvis, "Ethnic Behavior in Industry: Sponsorship and Rejection in a New England Factory," *Amer. J. Soc.*, Vol. 51 (1945–1946), pp. 293–298.

43. Collins, Sidney, "Social Processes Integrating Coloured People in Britain," *British J. Soc.*, Vol. 3 (1952), pp. 20–29.

44. Colson, Elizabeth, *The Makah Indians: A Study of an Indian Tribe in Modern American Society*, Minneapolis, University of Minnesota Press, 1953.

45. Comhaire, J. L. L., "Urban Segregation and Racial Legislation in Africa," *Amer. Soc. Rev.*, Vol. 15 (1950), pp. 392–397.

46. Cothran, Tilman C., "Negro Conceptions of White People," *Amer. J. Soc.*, Vol. 56 (1951), pp. 458–467.

47. Cox, Oliver C., *Caste, Class and Race: A Study in Social Dynamics*, New York, Doubleday and Co., 1948.

48. Culver, Dwight W., *Negro Segregation in the Methodist Church*, New Haven, Yale University Press, 1953.

49. Davie, Maurice R., *Negroes in American Society*, New York, McGraw-Hill Book Co., 1949.

50. Davis, Arthur K., "Some Sources of American Hostility to Russia," *Amer. J. Soc.*, Vol. 53 (1947–1948), pp. 174–183.

51. Deutsch, Morton, and Mary E. Collins, *Interracial Housing: A Psychological*

*Evaluation of a Social Experiment,* Minneapolis, University of Minnesota Press, 1951.

52. Dingwall, Eric John, *Racial Pride and Prejudice,* London, Watts and Co., 1946.

53. Drake, St. Claire, and H. R. Cayton, *Black Metropolis,* New York, Harcourt, Brace and Co., 1945.

54. Dvorin, Eugene P., *Racial Separation in South Africa: An Analysis of Apartheid Theory,* Chicago, University of Chicago Press, 1952.

55. Eisenstadt, S. N., "The Place of Elites and Primary Groups in the Absorption of New Immigrants in Israel," *Amer. J. Soc.,* Vol. 57 (1951–1952), pp. 222–231.

56. Eysenck, H. J., and S. Crown, "National Stereotypes: An Experimental and Methodological Study," *Intern. J. Opinion and Attitude Research,* Vol. 2 (1948), pp. 26–39.

57. Fairchild, Henry Pratt, *Race and Nationality: As Factors in American Life,* New York, Ronald Press Co., 1947.

58. Festinger, Leon, and H. H. Kelley, *Changing Attitudes through Social Contact,* Ann Arbor, Univ. of Michigan, Research Center for Group Dynamics, 1951.

59. Finkelstein, Louis (ed.), *The Jews: Their History, Culture, and Religion,* 2 Vols., New York, Harper and Brothers, 1950.

60. Flowerman, Samuel H., "The Use of Propaganda to Reduce Prejudice: A Refutation," *Intern. J. Opinion and Attitude Research,* Vol. 3 (1949), pp. 99–108.

61. Foster, Arnold, *A Measure of Freedom,* New York, Doubleday and Co., 1950.

62. Francis, E. K., "The Russian Mennonites: From Religious Group to Ethnic Group," *Amer. J. Soc.,* Vol. 54 (1948–1949), pp. 101–107.

63. Francis, E. K., "The Nature of the Ethnic Group," *Amer. J. Soc.,* Vol. 52 (1946–1947), pp. 393–400.

64. Francis, E. K., "Variables in the Formation of So-Called 'Minority Groups,'" *Amer. J. Soc.,* Vol. 60 (1954–1955), pp. 6–14.

65. Franklin, John Hope, *From Slavery to Freedom: A History of American Negroes,* New York, Alfred A. Knopf, 1949.

66. Frazier, E. Franklin, *The Negro in the United States,* New York, Macmillan Company, 1949.

67. Frazier, E. Franklin, "Race Contacts and the Social Structure," *Amer. Soc. Rev.,* Vol. 14 (1949), pp. 1–11.

68. Frazier, E. Franklin, "Theoretical Structure of Sociology and Sociological Research," *British J. Soc.,* Vol. 4 (1953), pp. 293–311.

69. Freedman, Maurice, "Some Recent Work in Race Relations: A Critique," *British J. Soc.,* Vol. 5 (1954), pp. 342–354.

70. Gillin, John, "Race Relations without Conflict," *Amer. J. Soc.,* Vol. 53 (1947–1948), pp. 337–343.

71. Gist, Noel P., "Caste Differentials in South India," *Amer. Soc. Rev.,* Vol. 19 (1954), pp. 126–137.

72. Glazer, Nathan, "Ethnic Groups in America: From National Culture to Ideology," in Morroe Berger, Theodore Abel, and Charles H. Page (eds.), *Freedom and Control in Modern Society,* New York, D. Van Nostrand, 1954, pp. 158–173.

73. Golovensky, David I., "The Marginal Man Concept: An Analysis and Critique," *Social Forces,* Vol. 30 (1950), pp. 333–339.

74. Goodman, Mary Ellen, *Race Awareness in Young Children,* Cambridge, Mass., Addison-Wesley Publishing Co., 1952.

75. Gordon, Milton M., "Social Structure and Goals in Group Relations," in

Morroe Berger, Theodore Abel, and Charles H. Page (eds.), *Freedom and Control in Modern Society,* New York, D. Van Nostrand, 1954, pp. 158–173.

76. Gordon, Milton M., "The Concept of the Sub-Culture and Its Application," *Social Forces,* Vol. 26 (1947), pp. 40–42.

77. Graeber, Isacque, "An Examination of Theories of Race Prejudice," *Social Research,* Vol. 20 (1953), pp. 267–281.

78. Gremley, William, "Social Control in Cicero," *British J. Soc.,* Vol. 3 (1952), pp. 322–338.

79. Gundlach, Ralph H., "The Effects of On-the-Job Experience with Negroes upon Social Attitudes of White Workers in Union Shops," *Amer. Psychologist,* Vol. 5 (1952), p. 300 (abstract).

80. Harding, John, Bernard Kutner, Harold Proshansky, and Isidor Chein, "Prejudice and Ethnic Relations," in Gardner Lindzey (ed.), *Handbook of Social Psychology,* Vol. II, Cambridge, Mass., Addison-Wesley Publishing Co., 1954, pp. 1021–1061.

81. Harding, John, and Russell, Hogrefe, "Attitudes of White Department Store Employees toward Negro Co-Workers," *J. Soc. Issues,* Vol. 8 (1952), pp. 18–28.

82. Hartley, Eugene, *Problems in Prejudice,* New York, King's Crown Press, 1946.

83. Hatt, Paul, "Class and Ethnic Attitudes," *Amer. Soc. Rev.,* Vol. 13 (1948), pp. 36–43.

84. Henriques, Fernando, *Family and Colour in Jamaica,* London, Eyre and Spottiswoode, 1953.

85. Hollingshead, August B., "Cultural Factors in the Selection of Marriage Mates," *Amer. Soc. Rev.,* Vol. 15 (1950), pp. 619–627.

86. Homans, George C., *The Human Group,* New York, Harper and Brothers, 1950.

87. Hsu, F. L. K., "The Chinese of Hawaii: Their Role in American Culture," *Trans. New York Acad. Sci.,* Vol. 13 (1951), pp. 243–250.

88. Hughes, Everett C., "Knitting of Racial Groups in Industry," *Amer. Soc. Rev.,* Vol. 11 (1946), pp. 512–519.

89. Hughes, Everett C., "Queries Concerning Industry and Society Growing Out of Study of Ethnic Relations in Industry," *Amer. Soc. Rev.,* Vol. 14 (1949), pp. 211–220.

90. Hughes, Everett C., and Helen M. Hughes, *Where Peoples Meet: Racial and Ethnic Frontiers,* Glencoe, Ill., The Free Press, 1952.

91. Ichheiser, Gustav, "Sociopsychological and Cultural Factors in Race Relations," *Amer. J. Soc.,* Vol. 54 (1948–1949), pp. 395–399. (Comment by Louis Wirth and Rejoinder, pp. 399–401.)

92. Ichheiser, Gustav, "Misunderstandings in Human Relations: A Study of False Perceptions," Monograph, *Amer. J. Soc.,* Vol. 55 (1949–1950), No. 2, Part 2, pp. 1–70.

93. International Labour Office, *Indigenous Peoples: Living and Working Conditions of Aboriginal Populations in Independent Countries,* Geneva, International Labour Office, 1953.

94. Irish, Donald P., "Reactions of Caucasian Residents to Japanese-American Neighbors," *J. Soc. Issues,* Vol. 8 (1952), pp. 10–17.

95. Janowitz, Morris, and Dwaine Marvick, "Authoritarianism and Political Behavior," *Pub. Opinion Quarterly,* Vol. 17 (1953), pp. 185–201.

96. Janowsky, Oscar, *Nationalities and National Minorities,* New York, Macmillan Company, 1945.

97. Jones, J. Hardy, Jr., and Vernon J. Parenton, "The People of Frilot Cove: A Study of Racial Hybrids," *Amer. J. Soc.*, Vol. 57 (1951–1952), pp. 145–149.

98. Kagan, Henry Enoch, *Changing the Attitude of Christian toward Jew: A Psychological Approach through Religion*, New York, Columbia University Press, 1952.

99. Kardiner, Abram, and Lionel Oversey, *et al.*, *The Mark of Oppression: A Psychosocial Study of the American Negro*, New York, W. W. Norton and Co., 1951.

100. Katz, Martin R., "A Hypothesis on Anti-Negro Prejudice," *Amer. J. Soc.*, Vol. 53 (1947–1948), pp. 100–104.

101. Kent, Donald P., and Robert Burnight, "Group Centrism in Complex Societies," *Amer. J. Soc.*, Vol. 57 (1951–1952), pp. 256–259.

102. Kiell, Norman, "Attitudes of Foreign Students," *J. Higher Educ.*, Vol. 22 (1951), pp. 188–194.

103. Klineberg, Otto, *Tensions Affecting International Understanding: A Survey of Research*, New York, Soc. Sci. Research Council, Bull. 62, 1950.

104. Koenig, Samuel, "Immigration and Culture Conflict in Israel," *Social Forces*, Vol. 31 (1952), pp. 144–148.

105. Konvitz, Milton R., *The Constitution and Civil Rights*, New York, Columbia University Press, 1946.

106. Kramer, Bernard M., "Dimensions of Prejudice," *J. Soc. Psych.*, Vol. 27 (1949), pp. 389–451.

107. Kramer, Bernard M., *Residential Contact as a Determinant of Attitudes toward Negroes*, Unpublished doctoral dissertation, Harvard University, 1951.

108. Kuper, Hilda, *The Uniform of Colour*, Johannesburg, Witwatersrand University Press, 1947.

109. Kutner, Bernard, *et al.*, "Verbal Attitudes and Overt Behavior Involving Racial Prejudice," *J. Abn. and Soc. Psych.*, Vol. 47 (1952), pp. 649–652.

110. Landis, Judson T., "Marriages of Mixed and Non-Mixed Religious Faith," *Amer. Soc. Rev.*, Vol. 14 (1949), pp. 401–407.

111. Landis, Kenesaw M., *Segregation in Washington*, Chicago, National Committee on Segregation in the Nation's Capital, 1948.

112. La Violette, Forrest E., *The Canadian Japanese and World War II: A Sociological and Psychological Account*, Toronto, University of Toronto Press, 1948.

113. Lazarsfeld, Paul F., and Robert K. Merton, "Friendship as Social Process: A Substantive and Methodological Analysis," in Morroe Berger, Theodore Abel, and Charles H. Page (eds.), *Freedom and Control in Modern Society*, New York, D. Van Nostrand, 1954, pp. 18–66.

114. Lee, Frank F., "The Race Relations Pattern of Areas of Behavior in a Small New England Town," *Amer. Soc. Rev.*, Vol. 19 (1954), pp. 138–143.

115. Leighton, Alexander H., *The Governing of Men*, Princeton, Princeton University Press, 1946.

116. Lewin, Kurt, *Resolving Social Conflicts*, New York, Harper and Brothers, 1948.

117. Lindzey, Gardner (ed.), *Handbook of Social Psychology*, 2 Vols., Cambridge, Mass., Addison-Wesley Publishing Co., 1954.

118. Lindzey, Gardner, "Differences between the High and Low in Prejudice and Their Implications for a Theory of Prejudice," *J. Personality*, Vol. 19 (1950), pp. 16–40.

119. Lippett, Ronald, *Training in Community Relations: A Research Exploration toward New Group Skills,* New York, Harper and Brothers, 1949.

120. Lohman, Joseph P., and Dietrich C. Reitzes, "Note on Race Relations in Mass Society," *Amer. J. Soc.,* Vol. 58 (1952–1953), pp. 240–247.

121. Lohman, J. D., *The Police and Minority Groups,* Chicago, Chicago Park District, 1947.

122. Long, Herman H., "Race Prejudice and Social Change," *Amer. J. Soc.,* Vol. 57 (1951–1952), pp. 15–19.

123. Lowenthal, Leo, and Norbert Gutterman, *Prophets of Deceit: A Study of the Techniques of the American Agitator,* New York, Harper and Brothers, 1949.

124. Luchins, Abraham S., "Personality and Prejudice: A Critique," *J. Soc. Psych.,* Vol. 32 (1950), pp. 79–94.

125. Lundberg, George A., and Lenore Dickson, "Selective Association among Ethnic Groups in a High School Population," *Amer. Soc. Rev.,* Vol. 17 (1952), pp. 23–35.

126. MacCrone, I. D., "Reactions to Discrimination in a Colour-Caste Society: A Preliminary Study of the Race Attitudes of a Dominated Group," *J. Soc. Psych.,* Vol. 26 (1947), pp. 69–98.

127. McDonagh, Edward C., and Eugene S. Richards, *Ethnic Relations in the United States,* New York, Appleton-Century-Crofts, 1953.

128. MacGregor, Gordon, *Warriors Without Weapons,* Chicago, University of Chicago Press, 1946.

129. MacIver, R. M., *The More Perfect Union,* New York, Macmillan Company, 1948.

130. MacKenzie, Barbara K., "The Importance of Contact in Determining Attitudes toward Negroes," *J. Abn. and Soc. Psych.,* Vol. 43 (1948), pp. 417–441.

131. McWilliams, Carey, *A Mask for Privilege: Anti-Semitism in America,* Boston, Little, Brown and Co., 1948.

132. Malherbe, E. G., *Race Attitudes and Education,* Johannesburg, Institute of Race Relations, 1946.

133. Marden, Charles F., *Minorities in American Society,* New York, American Book Co., 1952.

134. Marshall, Douglas G., "Nationality and the Emerging Culture," *Rural Sociology,* Vol. 13 (1948), pp. 40–47.

135. Mayer, Kurt, "Cultural Pluralism and Linguistic Equilibrium in Switzerland," *Amer. Soc. Rev.,* Vol. 16 (1951), pp. 157–163.

136. Merton, Robert K., and Alice S. Kitt, "Contributions to the Theory of Reference Group Behavior," in P. F. Lazarsfeld and R. K. Merton (eds.), *Studies in the Scope and Method of "The American Soldier,"* Glencoe, Ill., The Free Press, 1950, pp. 40–105.

137. Meyers, Henry J., and Leon Yochelson, "Color Denial in the Negro," *Psychiatry,* Vol. 11 (1948), pp. 36–46.

138. Minard, Ralph D., "Race Relationships in the Pocahontas Coal Field," *J. Soc. Issues,* Vol. 8 (1952), pp. 29–44.

139. Minnes, Mhyra S., "Cleavage in Women's Organizations: A Reflection of the Social Structure of a City," *Amer. Soc. Rev.,* Vol. 18 (1953), pp. 47–53.

140. Moon, Henry Lee, *Balance of Power: The Negro Vote,* Garden City, N. Y., Doubleday and Co., 1948.

141. Munch, Peter A., "Cultural Contacts in an Isolated Community: Tristan da Cunha," *Amer. J. Soc.,* Vol. 53 (1947–1948), pp. 1–8.

142. Munch, Peter A., "Social Adjustment among Wisconsin Norwegians," *Amer. Soc. Rev.*, Vol. 14 (1949), pp. 780–787.

143. Murphy, Gardner, *In the Minds of Men*, New York, Basic Books, 1953.

144. Mussen, Paul H., "Some Personality and Social Factors Related to Changes in Children's Attitudes toward Negroes," *J. Abn. and Soc. Psych.*, Vol. 45 (1950), pp. 423–441.

145. Nelson, Lowry, "Speaking of Tongues," *Amer. J. Soc.*, Vol. 54 (1948–1949), pp. 202–210.

146. Newcombe, Theodore M., "Social Psychology and Group Processes," in Calvin P. Stone and Donald W. Taylor (eds.), *Annual Review of Psychology*, Stanford, Annual Reviews, 1953, pp. 183–214.

147. Newcombe, Theodore M., "Autistic Hostility and Social Reality," *Human Relations*, Vol. 1 (1947), pp. 69–86.

148. Park, Robert E., *Race and Culture*, Glencoe, Ill., The Free Press, 1950.

149. Parsons, Talcott, *The Social System*, Glencoe, Ill., The Free Press, 1951.

150. Parsons, Talcott, and Edward A. Shils (eds.), *Toward a General Theory of Action*, Cambridge, Mass., Harvard University Press, 1951.

151. Patterson, Sheila, *Colour and Culture in South Africa: A Study of the Cape Coloured People within the Social Structure of South Africa*, London, Routledge and Kegan Paul, 1953.

152. Pierson, Donald, "Race Prejudice as Revealed in the Study of Racial Situations," *Intern. Soc. Science Bull.*, Vol. 2 (1950), pp. 467–478.

153. President's Committee on Equality of Treatment and Opportunity in the Armed Services, *Freedom to Serve*, Washington, D. C., U. S. Government Printing Office, 1950.

154. Protho, E. Terry, "Ethnocentrism and Anti-Negro Attitudes in the Deep South," *J. Abn. and Soc. Psych.*, Vol. 47 (1952), pp. 105–108.

155. Protho, E. Terry, and O. K. Miles, "A Comparison of Ethnic Attitudes of College Students and Middle Class Adults from the Same State," *J. Soc. Psych.*, Vol. 36 (1952), pp. 53–58.

156. Reid, Ira De A., "The Socialization of the Negro in the American Social Order," *J. Negro Educ.*, Vol. 19 (1950), pp. 780–787.

157. Reitzes, Dietrich C., "The Role of Organization Structures," *J. Soc. Issues*, Vol. 9 (1953), pp. 37–44.

158. Richmond, Anthony H., *Colour Prejudice in Britain: A Study of West Indian Workers in Liverpool, 1941–1951*, London, Routledge and Kegan Paul, 1954.

159. Riley, Matilda White, and Samuel H. Flowerman, "Group Relations as a Variable in Communications Research," *Amer. Soc. Rev.*, Vol. 16 (1951), pp. 174–180.

160. Roberts, Harry W., "The Impact of Military Service upon the Racial Attitudes of Negro Servicemen in World War II," *J. Soc. Problems*, Vol. 1 (1953), pp. 65–69.

161. Rogler, C., "Some Situational Aspects of Race Relations in Puerto Rico," *Social Forces*, Vol. 27 (1948), pp. 72–77.

162. Rokeach, Milton, "The Nature and Meaning of Dogmatism," *Psych. Rev.*, Vol. 61 (1954), pp. 194–204.

163. Rose, Arnold M., *Studies in the Reduction of Prejudice*, Chicago, American Council on Race Relations, 1947.

164. Rose, Arnold M., *The Negro's Morale: Group Identification and Protest*, Minneapolis, University of Minnesota Press, 1949.

165. Rose, Arnold M., and Carolina Rose, *America Divided*, New York, Alfred A. Knopf, 1948.

166. Rose, Arnold M. (ed.), *Race Prejudice and Discrimination*, New York, Alfred A. Knopf, 1951.

167. Ross, Malcolm, *All Manner of Men*, New York, Reynal and Hitchcock, 1948.

168. Ryan, Bryce, *Caste in Modern Ceylon: The Sinhalese System in Transition*, New Brunswick, Rutgers University Press, 1953.

169. Saenger, Gerhart, *The Social Psychology of Prejudice*, New York, Harper and Brothers, 1953.

170. Saenger, Gerhart, and Samuel Flowerman, "Stereotypes and Prejudicial Attitudes," *Human Relations*, Vol. 7 (1954), pp. 217–238.

171. Saenger, Gerhart, and Emily Gilbert, "Customer Reactions to the Integration of Negro Sales Personnel," *Intern. J. Opinion and Attitude Research*, Vol. 4 (1950), pp. 57–76.

172. Schermerhorn, R. A., *These Our People*, Boston, D. C. Heath and Co., 1949.

173. Shapiro, Gilbert, "Myrdal's Definition of the South: A Methodological Note," *Amer. Soc. Rev.*, Vol. 13 (1948), pp. 619–621.

174. Sheppard, Harold L., "The Negro Merchant: A Study of Negro Anti-Semitism," *Amer. J. Soc.*, Vol. 53 (1947–1948), pp. 96–99.

175. Sherif, Muzafer, and Carolyn W. Sherif, *Groups in Harmony and Tension: An Integration of Studies on Intergroup Relations*, New York, Harper and Brothers, 1953.

176. Sherif, Muzafer, and M. O. Wilson (eds.), *Group Relations at the Crossroads*, New York, Harper and Brothers, 1953.

177. Simpson, George E., and J. Milton Yinger, *Racial and Cultural Minorities: An Analysis of Prejudice and Discrimination*, New York, Harper and Brothers, 1953.

178. Sprague, Theodore W., "The Rivalry of Intolerances in Race Relations," *Social Forces*, Vol. 28 (1949), pp. 68–76.

179. Srole, Leo, "Social Dysfunction, Personality and Social Distance Attitudes," Paper delivered before the American Sociological Society, Chicago, 1951.

180. Stone, Calvin P., and Donald W. Taylor (eds.), *Annual Review of Psychology*, Stanford, Annual Reviews, 1953.

181. Stouffer, S. A., *et al.*, *The American Soldier: Adjustment During Army Life*, Vol. I, Princeton, Princeton University Press, 1949, Chap. 10.

182. Strong, Donald S., "The Rise of Negro Voting in Texas," *Amer. Political Science Rev.*, Vol. 42 (1948), pp. 510–522.

183. Suchman, Edward A., *et al.*, *Desegregation: Some Propositions and Research Suggestions—a Memorandum for Discussion Purposes*, Ithaca, Cornell University, 1954.

184. Taft, Ronald, "The Shared Frame of Reference Concept Applied to the Assimilation of Immigrants," *Human Relations*, Vol. 6 (1953), pp. 45–56.

185. Tannenbaum, Frank, *Slave and Citizen: The Negro in the Americas*, New York, Alfred A. Knopf, 1947.

186. Thomas, D. S., and R. S. Nishimoto, *The Spoilage*, Berkeley and Los Angeles, University of California Press, 1946.

187. Trager, Helen G., and Marian Radke Yarrow, *They Learn What They Live*, New York, Harper and Brothers, 1952.

188. Trendley, Mary Bosworth, "The Ethnic Group as a Collectivity," *Social Forces*, Vol. 31 (1953), pp. 261–265.

189. Tuck, Ruth D., *Not with the Fist*, New York, Harcourt, Brace and Co., 1946.

190. Tumin, Melvin M., *Caste in a Peasant Society: A Case Study in the Dynamics of Caste*, Princeton, Princeton University Press, 1952.

191. Useem, John, and Ruth Hill Useem, "Minority-Group Pattern in Prairie Society," *Amer. J. Soc.*, Vol. 50 (1945), pp. 377–385.

192. Vickery, W. E., and Morris E. Opler, "A Redefinition of Prejudice for Purposes of Social Science Research," *Human Relations*, Vol. 1 (1948), pp. 419–428.

193. Wagley, Charles (ed.), *Race and Class in Rural Brazil*, Paris, UNESCO, 1952.

194. Walter, Paul A. F., Jr., *Race and Culture Relations*, New York, McGraw-Hill Book Co., 1952.

195. Warner, W. Lloyd, and Leo Srole, *The Social Systems of American Ethnic Groups*, New Haven, Yale University Press, 1945.

196. Watson, Jeanne, "Some Social and Psychological Situations Related to Change in Attitude," *Human Relations*, Vol. 3 (1950), pp. 15–56.

197. Weaver, Robert C., *The Negro Ghetto*, New York, Harcourt, Brace and Co., 1948.

198. Weaver, Robert C., "The Economic Status of the Negro in the United States," *J. Negro Educ.*, Vol. 19 (1950), pp. 232–243.

199. Weisberg, B., "Racial Violence and Civil Rights Law Enforcement," *University of Chicago Law Review*, Vol. 18 (1951), pp. 768–783.

200. Willems, Emílio, "Racial Attitudes in Brazil," *Amer. J. Soc.*, Vol. 54 (1949), pp. 402–408.

201. Williams, Robin M., Jr., *The Reduction of Intergroup Tensions: A Survey of Research on Problems of Ethnic, Racial, and Religious Group Relations*, New York, Soc. Science Res. Council, Bull. 57, 1947.

202. Williams, Robin M., Jr., and Margaret W. Ryan (eds.), *Schools in Transition: Community Experiences in Desegregation*, Chapel Hill, University of North Carolina Press, 1954.

203. Wilner, Daniel M., Rosabelle P. Walkley, and Stuart W. Cook, "Residential Proximity and Intergroup Relations in Public Housing Projects," *J. Soc. Issues*, Vol. 8 (1952), pp. 45–69.

204. Winder, A. E., "White Attitudes toward Negro-White Interaction in an Area of Changing Racial Composition," *Amer. Psychologist*, Vol. 7 (1952), pp. 330–331 (abstract).

205. Wirth, Louis, "Problems and Orientation of Research in Race Relations in the United States," *British J. Soc.*, Vol. 1 (1950), pp. 117–125.

206. Wood, Arthur L., "Minority-Group Criminality and Cultural Integration," *J. Crim. Law and Criminology*, Vol. 37 (1947), pp. 498–510.

207. Woodward, James W., "Some Implications from Our Present Knowledge of Prejudice," *Amer. Soc. Rev.*, Vol. 11 (1946), pp. 344–356.

208. Woodward, James W., "The Role of Fictions in Social Life," *Trans. New York Academy Sci.*, Vol. 6 (1944), pp. 311–344.

209. Zawadski, B., "Limitations of the Scapegoat Theory of Prejudice," *J. Abn. and Soc. Psych.*, Vol. 43 (1948), pp. 127–141.

210. Znaniecki, Florian, *Modern Nationalities*, Urbana, University of Illinois Press, 1952.

chapter *14*

# The sociology of delinquency and crime

MARSHALL B. CLINARD
*University of Wisconsin*

The early study of criminology emphasized the idea that the criminal was a physical type. At various times since then criminals have been considered as inferior mental types or as products of economic disadvantage. Some criminologists have even adopted an eclectic approach which has included constitutional or psychological, as well as social and economic, factors. There are still remnants of this constitutional and eclectic thinking, but at the present time criminality is increasingly being explained on the basis of more systematic theory.* Present-day controversies in the explanation of delinquency and crime lie chiefly between

---

* An example of the biological approach of a former day was Hans von Hentig's attempt to associate red hair as an important biological factor in the explanation of the behavior of frontier badmen (61). In a reply Rasch showed that not only was the theory unscientific but that the facts failed to support an idea that most frontier badmen were actually red-haired (105).

the psychiatric and psychoanalytic on the one hand and the sociological on the other. The former tend to place emphasis on individual factors, emotions, and personality traits, while the sociologist stresses group factors, social norms, and attitudes.

Sociology and criminology have developed together and each has influenced the other. Research in criminology has been particularly stimulated by sociology, and some developments in criminology, such as certain research techniques, have in turn influenced sociology. The disagreements which exist among sociological writers on criminology reflect in part the confusion in determining a specific sociological approach which still characterizes much of sociological theory and research. While recent research has represented an improvement over the past, many sociologists working in criminology have still not been fully aware of a need for a more systematic approach to deviant behavior called crime which would parallel the developments in social psychological study of behavior in general. The adequate development of criminology will inevitably reflect, in its own research, the main currents of sociology and social psychology.

On a broad scale the sociologist is interested in the relation of criminal behavior to the dynamic processes of social life. He is concerned with the nature and presence of conflicting legal norms in a society, the incidence of delinquent and criminal behavior among certain groups, how social class and occupation may produce or inhibit criminality, and the effect on criminality of larger social processes such as urbanization.

Sociologists are primarily concerned with the socialization process of an offender rather than his heredity, I.Q., glands, or possible Oedipus complex (119). To them criminal behavior is human behavior, since the personality traits and attitudes of all persons are acquired through the learning process (25). To sociologists crime is a product of definitions of situations acquired in life experience. Norms of behavior, ideas, and beliefs are of a group nature, and concepts of right and wrong are acquired from others in the on-going process of living. Accordingly, sociologists are interested in the role that a person plays in groups with deviant norms and the self-conception that such a person secures from others. In general they are skeptical of individualistic explanations.

Sociological research and writing during the past ten years relating to criminology can be analyzed under the topics of the nature of a "crime," criminal behavior and society, behavior systems, the theory of differential association, personality traits, war and crime, the administration of criminal justice, prediction of recidivism, and research techniques which include ecology, analytic induction, control groups, and the need for replica studies.*

### *The nature of a "crime"*

It is encouraging to see increasing interest in more precise concepts not only in sociology but in criminology as well. Upon the definition of the concepts of a "crime" depends obviously the nature of criminal behavior and the "criminal." Many have felt that the mere legal definition of a crime by itself is unsatisfactory for scientific purposes.† A provocative discussion by Hermann Mannheim has sought to clarify those values which should be protected by the criminal law and those left to other agencies (84). He maintains that crime is antisocial behavior and no other human behavior should be so considered. Those values which should be protected are human life, both individual and collective, sexual and family life, property and the infringement of property rights upon persons.

Sutherland's paper in 1940 proposed that the study of civil and administrative penalties be added to the field of criminology (132). During the past ten years the controversy raised by this proposal has continued. Proponents have included chiefly Sutherland, Clinard, and Hartung, while

---

* In preparing this paper most relevant sociological books, articles in the *American Sociological Review, American Journal of Sociology,* and the *Journal of Criminal Law and Criminology* were covered fairly systematically. Some use was also made of certain articles in *Social Forces* and *Federal Probation.* While a few nonsociological writings have been included because of sociological interest in them, psychoanalytic writings have not been discussed. Throughout emphasis has been placed on criminological writings relating primarily to etiology and not the applied area of correctional administration. An earlier and broader discussion of some of the issues presented here is contained in Reckless (107) and Clinard (27). Several articles by sociologists have also appeared in the *Encyclopedia of Criminology* (43) but are not discussed here. This encyclopedia, unfortunately, was on the whole too psychiatric in its emphasis. Among the new and revised editions of textbooks on juvenile delinquency which appeared during this period were those by Carr, Neumeyer, Tappan, and Barron. Texts in criminology included Sutherland, Gillin, Reckless, Taft, von Hentig, Cavan, Elliott, and Barnes and Teeters. Sociologists contributed to a volume on *Contemporary Correction,* edited by Tappan, and Vedder, Koenig, and Clark edited a book of readings in criminology.

† See, for example, Michael and Adler (88). Fortunately, the best statement of the issues and a proposal that sociology study violations of all conduct norms, legal or not, has recently been reprinted (120). Two recent *Annals* publications contain material relating to this broader concept of criminology (2, 3).

the opposition has consisted mainly of Tappan and Burgess, with Cressey offering a partial compromise between the two sides.*

Those who believe that the definition of a crime should be broadened argue that it is necessary to include within the field of criminology all penalties imposed by government, regardless of whether they legally are contained in the criminal law, in order to have a more representative sample of those who violate the law. Differences in the nature of the punishment for given acts actually involve not the act itself but often unorganized public recognition of the extent and consequences of such violations (127). Such a differential public attitude toward white collar crime is a result primarily of the complexity of many economic crimes and their diffused effect over a long period of time as compared to the more overt and often easily recognized nature of many conventional crimes. In addition, white collar offenses seldom receive the same press publicity as do ordinary crimes and thus they do not arouse the same resentment. Recent legislation directed at the antisocial behavior of white collar persons has been characterized, moreover, by greater leniency in enforcement than was the case with laws having a history of several hundred years such as larceny and burglary. These newer laws through being lenient have sometimes avoided antagonizing powerful interest groups, and they have also made it easier to try cases than would be the situation if the criminal law had to be used always.

Most wartime price and rationing violations, according to Clinard (24) should be considered as "crimes" for criminological purposes, despite the fact that only 5 per cent of the violators were punished by a criminal sanction.† Actually there was no uniformity in the sanctions applied by the United States government in black market cases. In thousands of cases, involving almost identical violations, administrative and civil measures were used, and occasionally criminal prosecutions. Cases involving evasive violations where there was definite willfulness, such as falsification of government reports, were sometimes handled with an injunction suit or administrative order suspending the business, and at other times by criminal penalties. In a wartime opinion survey of wholesale businessmen it was found that 88 per cent could not distinguish between criminal fines and civil "fines" since they used the same general term

---

* For a more detailed discussion of these issues see Clinard, "Sociologists and American Criminology" (27), *The Black Market: A Study of White Collar Crime* (24), and Hartung, "White Collar Crime" (57).

† Unless one uses such a broader definition it is impossible, for example, to compare price and rationing violations in the United States with those in Great Britain and Canada, since in the latter two countries nearly all violations were punished as crimes.

to apply to both (24, page 235). A detailed analysis of 122 black market cases in Detroit where different types of penalties were used failed to show any criteria by which the seriousness could be distinguished by the type of sanction (58).

An important issue in this connection has been whether white collar offenders conceive of themselves as "criminals." Burgess (16) has stated that he does not consider black market cases as crimes since such violators do not consider themselves as criminals and the public does not disapprove of such violations.* Tappan has objected to the inclusion of white collar crime within criminology chiefly on the grounds that since the criminal penalty carries public stigma, which is not true of white collar crime, it affects the public's and the offender's conception of an act (136, 137). He has raised other objections. The criminal law follows careful procedural methods; actual or implied intent must be established unless the statute excludes it; guilt is established, except where jury trial is waived, by a unanimous verdict of the jury; and there is protection against the jeopardy of more than one trial for a given crime. Hartung has stated that these objections are contradictory, Tappan believing that white collar crime does not have the legal effects of a crime and Burgess that it is not sociologically a crime (58).

A partial improvement, but at the same time no resolution of the controversy, is Cressey's proposal that part of the artificiality of using legal definitions of crimes in criminological research can be avoided by using more homogeneous categories (37). Although he would restrict the concept of "crime" to behavior defined by the criminal law, he would combine various types of crimes in research so that they would cover similar behavior. An example of this procedure is his own study of "violations of trust," which included many different legal categories besides embezzlement (33).

### Criminal behavior and society

There has been too much preoccupation with changes in the definition of crime, according to Aubert, and too little with the relation of the controversy over white collar crime to the social structure. He maintains that the chief theoretical significance of white collar crime lies in its ambiguous position of being both a crime and not a crime (6). This is symptomatic of the diversity of status systems in present-day social structures. White collar crime differs from ordinary crime in the methods

---

* Clinard did show, however, that public opinion surveys throughout the war showed strong support for price and rationing controls (24).

of dealing with the crime, the status of the offender, the toleration of the public, and the social support of the offenders. White collar crime reflects the structural conflicts and changes in the larger social system in the ambivalence toward it of citizens, businessmen, lawyers, judges, and criminologists. This ambivalence reflects the conflicting nature of the roles and norms of persons who are members of more than one group. The threat of penal sanctions in conformity with legal norms is dependent on group membership, previous norms, and personal interests.*

Analysis of the general society and its relation to criminal behavior has characterized a number of studies. Probably the most provocative statement of the relationship of social structure to criminality is Merton's analysis of *anomie* (87). In this essay he suggested that deviant behavior such as crime was a symptom of the dissociation in a society between culturally prescribed aspirations and socially structured avenues for realizing these aspirations. There are in any culture incentives for success which, in turn, are limited by the culture and social structure. A society which bases achievement on power and material wealth, with opportunities for only limited vertical mobility, puts great pressure on the lower social strata to achieve these ends through means which are not acceptable to other persons in the society, such as ordinary crime, organized vice, and the rackets. Cohen has implied something of the same idea in his view that the behavior of most lower class delinquent gangs represent the logical result of lower class boys being judged in school and other places by middle class standards (31). Both of these studies, while provocative, need to be tested with empirical studies.

Broader approaches to an understanding of delinquency through the study of the values in a society have been suggested by Barron (9). In a subsequent book, with the provocative title of *The Juvenile in Delinquent Society* (10), he has suggested that illegal and unconventional delinquency-provoking patterns of adults in a society serve as behavior models for juveniles. Conflicts of values also exist between those of the juveniles' peer group and the official values of society. There are certain values in a society which are related to delinquent behavior, such as success, status and power ascendance, pecuniary and material wealth, resistance to authority, and toughness. These values are of particular importance in a society characterized by dynamic change, alternative norms, impersonal social relationships, and duality of loyalty and ethics resulting from multi-group membership.

Another writer, Shulman, has stated that at one time the values of a

---

* Aubert and others have made a study somewhat along these lines of an unusual recent Norwegian law carrying penal sanctions which regulated the working conditions of domestic help (7).

society and criminal responsibility were more closely related, but in a modern complex society there are such diverse needs of different groups that resort to criminal values may be the means of a group's survival (125).

In a sociological analysis of gambling Bloch has stated that the opposition to it is caused by gambling's failure to perform normally expected productive functions in a society (13). The degree of antipathy towards gambling varies according to social class. The chance element in gambling is exploited in those societies where status is largely competitive and dependent upon pecuniary standards. Those societies which tend to be stabilized and routinized in their social living tend to be more opposed to gambling.

The relation of secondary influences in society, such as the police and courts, the school and mass media of communication including newspapers, movies, television, radio and "comic books," to juvenile delinquency has been analyzed by Clinard (29). He concluded that so-called "comic books" appear, sociologically, to have little direct relation to delinquency, which is similar to what Cavanaugh believes (19). Wertham, a psychiatrist, in his *Seduction of the Innocent* (148) made a number of claims for the influence of comic books, but he submitted little data, other than a few cases, of a scientifically factual nature, to support this belief. He made no study of the use of comic books by nondelinquents. After examining the news content of four Colorado papers, Davis reports that public opinion about crime reflects trends in the crime news rather than actual crime rates (38).

Other studies have been made of relationships between various aspects of society and delinquent and criminal behavior (1). Wood has studied criminal behavior among minority groups and its relation to cultural integration, but he found the groups too differentiated to reach many general conclusions (152). Compared to the mothers of nondelinquent children, those with delinquent children belong less to organizations (8). Since neighborhoods are a primary area of social participation for the child, according to McKay, an analysis of neighborhood play groups, values, and indigenous institutions is essential in explaining conventional or unconventional juvenile behavior (83). Bloch studied the relation of economic depression to the incidence of criminality in a rural community (12). A correlation was found between offenses known to the police in Minnesota counties and urbanization, educational attainment, and unemployment (122).

Interrelations between suicide and crime have interested some writers. Porterfield has tried to show, on the basis of statistics from cities and states, that suicide and homicide rates have an inverse relationship (101,

100, 103). In Ceylon homicide rates are very high and suicide rates low, a fact which has been explained by the nature of the society (126).

### Behavior systems and crime

Writers in criminology have increasingly recognized that the term "criminal" has little meaning. Instead, there have been recent attempts to describe types of criminals, an interest which was quite common in the early days of criminology. Reckless has suggested the need for analyzing, in a criminal career, the recurrence of and continuation in criminal activities, the way the offenses are committed, the offender's attitude toward his crimes, his criminal connections, and the place crime plays in the total employment and life history of the individual (106). This emphasis on types of careers rather than "criminals" as a group has been reflected not only in research but in a number of recent criminological texts (18, 42, 106). Reckless' classification is an illustration of sociological types of behavior systems when he includes such types as ordinary criminal careers, professional criminals, organized crime, and white collar crime and black markets.

This interest in criminal careers represents an attempt to avoid legal categories and give a more sociological interpretation to criminal behavior. Psychiatrists also classify offenders into types, but their classifications differ sharply from those of sociologists. The former largely utilize broad psychiatric syndromes of personality traits. A single personality type may apply to a variety of careers differing in both the nature and seriousness of the criminal behavior. Consequently, personality classification may have little meaning either for distinguishing types of criminal careers or the behavior of criminals from noncriminals.

Juveniles who steal have been described in most studies as coming from areas of the city where housing is poor and rentals are low, occupations are largely unskilled, populations are more heterogeneous with more recent immigrants, the inhabitants are more mobile, and there is a higher incidence of breakdown of family relationships. Two writers have reported that those delinquents who steal autos have a different pattern.[*] In a study of 230 delinquents involved in auto theft, as compared with 2,774 who had committed other offenses, auto thieves were found to come mainly from economically above average areas of the city where lived on the whole white persons of predominantly Western European origin. In general, they came more frequently from areas which had a more

---

[*] Unfortunately, the authors appear to have depended too much on police reports in their research (144).

homogeneous population, lived in single family dwellings, and had only one parent employed. Indexes of family relationships, school adjustments, and religious training failed to distinguish the two groups. Membership in groups of peers who also stole was common, those delinquents engaging in auto theft representing "definite gangs with a reputation of either being rambunctious or engaging in organized theft" (144, page 577).

What Lemert calls "naive check forgery," an estimated 75 per cent of all forgeries, also does not appear to follow conventional theories of crime based on either culture conflict, delinquency area background, emotional conflict, or differential association with criminal norms.* Analyzing a very small sample of 29 cases he concluded that none had a previous criminal record or previous contact with delinquents and criminals. As an explanation of this rather higher socioeconomic group offense, he suggests that it is a product of certain difficult social situations in which the individual finds himself, a certain degree of social isolation, and a process of "closure" or "constriction of behavior alternatives subjectively held as available to the forger" (70, page 298).

The behavior system involved in embezzlement and other violations of trust appears to be considerably different from more conventional offenses and also different from superficial ideas about such violations (33). Cressey conducted lengthy interviews with 133 trust violators at Joliet, Terre Haute, and Chino, and also used some 200 other case materials. After revising his hypothesis several times, since there were exceptions to it, he finally stated a generalization about the behavior of trust violators, which he claims to be universal.† It consists of three parts, the first being the opportunity to violate a trusted position and the presence of a "non-shareable" financial problem. "Trusted persons become trust violators when they conceive of themselves as having a financial problem which is non-shareable." He found a wide variety of such types of situations, including problems arising from personal failure, business reversals, ascribed obligations, physical isolation, status gaining, and employer-employee relations. In all cases such problems were solved secretly, since the approval of the trust violator's group would have been lost if he had revealed his problem.

Second is the knowledge of how to violate. Those who become trust violators are "aware that this problem can be secretly resolved by violation of the position of financial trust."

---

* Lemert does not always present sufficient facts to support his conceptual framework (70).

† This research method, which is called analytic induction, will be discussed in a later section.

Third is the acceptance of verbalizations or rationalizations "which enable them to adjust their conceptions of themselves as trusted persons with their conceptions of themselves as users of the entrusted funds or property." Among such rationalizations were beliefs that the violation was actually "borrowing," or that their violations of trust were justified by "unusual circumstances."

Although Sutherland in a paper on "White Collar Criminality" (132) in 1940 suggested the need for studying a different type of offender, those businessmen and other similar white collar groups who in connection with their occupations violated the law, it was not until 1949 that he published the first book in this field * (127). In it he analyzed the illegal behavior of 70 of the 200 largest nonfinancial corporations in the United States. He estimated the frequency of violations and classified them into restraint of trade, infringements of patents, unfair labor practices, misrepresentation in advertising, illegal rebates, and other offenses. On the whole, the volume was more a general introduction, with a number of hypotheses, to a broad new area of criminology rather than a detailed study of any one of them.

Sutherland's book was followed three years later by a study of white collar crime, *The Black Market,* by Clinard, a former student of Sutherland (24). It contained a detailed analysis of a single area of white collar crime, price and rationing violations during World War II.† Using a variety of sources, he estimated the extent of the black market and analyzed particularly violations of meat, gasoline, and rent regulations. Clinard maintained that such violations constituted crimes, and should be considered a part of criminology, that they were not a unique phenomenon but were violations of other laws as well, and that their explanation was chiefly but not entirely a matter of differential cultural and ethical definitions.

Hartung made a study of 122 cases of black market violations in the wholesale meat industry in Detroit in a test of Durkheim's thesis that the nature of law is related to social differentiation (58). In this study abstracts of black market cases where civil and criminal penalties were imposed were shown to a stratified sample of the public and to businessmen in order to find out their attitudes toward different legal measures. More recently Lane, a political scientist, analyzed business violations of fair trade and labor laws (68). He interviewed top management of 25 industrial concerns and 7 leaders of government agencies, and analyzed

---

* There have been books by Lincoln Steffens and others dealing in a popular way with this subject, but they were more descriptive and doctrinaire than scientific.

† For a Norwegian study, see Aubert's "White Collar Crime and Social Structure" (6), and also his "Priskontroll Og Rasjonering" (5).

government decisions to try to find out why businessmen violate the law.

Nearly all writings in the past by sociologists about crime have been concerned with some type of variations of theft, and to a limited extent with homicide. However, most studies by sociologists of homicide have tended to be more a description than an analysis of processes. Two studies during the period mentioned were by Gillin (45, 47) and one by Harlan (55). The latter was particularly interested in statistics on the pattern of interpersonal relations between the races and sexes in 500 Alabama homicides. There were few interracial homicides, but one third of all the homicides involved the opposite sex.

Sex offenders have largely been the pre-eminent domain of the psychiatrist and psychoanalyst. Within the past few years there have been a few efforts to subject the writing about, and the offenders in this area, to the scrutiny of a sociological point of view. Gillin has compared the social characteristics of property offenders and murderers with sex offenders in a research study of 486 Wisconsin offenders (45). In two articles dealing with sexual psychopath laws Sutherland raised a number of objections to this concept and criticized the psychiatrists for explaining the behavior of sex offenders almost completely in terms of certain personality trait and family experiences and ignoring the deviant cultural definitions of sexual behavior which are furnished by various subcultural groups (130, 133). He stated that:

> The absurdity of this theory (sexual psychopathy) should be evident to anyone who has an acquaintance with the variations in sexual behavior and sexual codes throughout the history of mankind; practically all of the present sex crimes have been approved behavior for adults in some society or other. Similarly within our society deviant cultures with reference to sex behavior prevail in sub-groups. The manner in which juveniles are inducted into the cultures of these sub-groups in the toilets of schools, playgrounds, and dormitories, as well as in other places, has been shown in many research reports on juvenile sex behavior (130, page 549).

In another article Sutherland has shown how sexual psychopath laws have been diffused from one state to another, the diffusion in part representing public hysteria rather than a rational approach to sex offenses.*
Differences in sentences imposed on sex offenders have been discussed by Tappan (138). Needed research reports on sex offenders were issued in the past few years by New Jersey, Michigan, Illinois, and California (121). The first was directed by a sociologist, the second had major participation by one, while the other two contained information needed by sociologists. The New Jersey report was particularly critical of the

---

* A sociologist and a judge have written a more favorable point of view about such laws (108).

concept of the psychopath, most of them indicated that cultural factors play a role in sex offenses, and all of them showed statistically that, compared to other offenders, sex offenders have a much lower incidence of recidivism.

Among psychiatrists many sexual and other offenses are maintained to be the product of compulsive behavior. Cressey has thoroughly criticized this explanation as being a loose categorization for behavior which is not understood (36). He has suggested a re-examination of "compulsive crimes" in terms of a social psychological framework of motivation, identification, and role playing. Most compulsive crime is motivated and has a developmental history similar to other motivated behavior. It probably has group components and they will become of more concern to sociologists in the future.

Criminological literature has had few references to crime by women, and textbooks have contained little discussion,* in spite of the fact that one of the earliest studies was Lombroso's *The Female Offender* (73). Some twenty-five years ago the Gluecks published a study called *Five Hundred Delinquent Women* (49), and recently Pollak has written a survey but not actually a behavioral analysis of *The Criminality of Women* (99). On the whole, crime among women appears to be much more extensive than the statistics indicate, since much of it is undetected and is indirect in nature. Two types of crime which are most common among women, but often unreported, are abortions and thefts from department stores. Social equality and new occupations seem to be affecting crime among women.

Criminal behavior declines with age, and Moberg has made an analysis of this relationship (89). He found, however, that certain types of crime, such as drunkenness, sex offenses, embezzlement, and fraud, tend to be more important in the older age groups. Statistics indicate that women enter delinquency and crime at a later age than men (99).

### The theory of differential association

Approximately twenty years ago Edwin H. Sutherland formulated the theory of differential association (128) which today is one of the most controversial theories in criminology.† In a revised and more specific

* More discussion is contained in Elliott's recent text than in any others (42, pages 199–255).

† Sutherland's death in 1952 removed the leading sociological criminologist. He was president of the American Sociological Society in 1949, at which time he gave probably one of the best-known of all presidential addresses, "White Collar Criminality" (132).

statement in 1947 he indicated that criminal behavior is learned by a person from those about him. According to the differential association theory, "a person becomes delinquent because of the excess of definitions favorable to violation of law over definitions unfavorable to violation of law. . . . Where persons become criminal they do so because of contact with criminal patterns and because of isolation from anticriminal patterns" (129, pages 6–7). According to him, it is not an offender's constitution or personality traits that explain his behavior, but rather the frequency, priority, duration, and intensity of criminal as opposed to noncriminal associations.

Even today this theory constitutes a major anathema to many psychiatrists working in criminology. Many sociologists, however, have found the theory, while untested, quite acceptable, and there is much evidence to support its general approach (32). Some needed qualifications of this theory, as a result of research, have been developed, however, by other sociologists. Obviously, as stated by Sutherland, the theory does not adequately recognize motivations and the situation as a part of the learning process. Similarly, in having his theory apply to all types of crime, he failed to appreciate that personality traits, rather than attitudes, might be more important in some offenses and should be considered, in any event, in the analysis of all criminal offenders.

After studying trust violators, Cressey concluded that the differential association theory, at least as applied to them, needed revising (35). He reports that it was unnecessary for trust violators to have contacts with others in order to acquire the skill necessary for such a violation. Undoubtedly contacts are necessary for rationalizations, but he states that since it is impossible to observe all prior associations in order to determine contacts with sources of rationalizations the differential association theory needs to be reduced to a learning theory rather than a mathematical ratio of criminal and noncriminal association. Lemert, in his study of naive check forgery, stated that he did not find evidence that differential association was related to this type of offense (70).

After studying price and rationing violations during World War II, Clinard stated that most, but by no means all, violations could be explained by differential association as Sutherland had claimed about all white collar offenses (24, pages 308–313; 127, Chap. XIV). In this connection Clinard pointed out that the theory does not explain why some individuals who were familiar with the techniques and rationalizations of black market violations and associated with those who were did not violate the law. The differential association theory does not allow for the independent invention of a technique. Consequently, in addition to this theory, one must, under certain circumstances, consider the general

personality pattern of the individual in order to explain why some attitudes are accepted while others are rejected.* In failing to do this,
Clinard points out, the differential association theory tends to overempha-
size the more recent developments in the behavior of the individual,
such as a business occupation, rather than the importance of childhood
behavior patterns in the formation of personality. Such early behavior
patterns may well have been enough to counterbalance or play a part
in the acceptance or rejection in adult life of antisocial behavior patterns.
In the differential association theory, moreover, role playing is largely
accounted for in terms of a single social role, which in the case of black
market violations was that of a businessman. Actually, an individual
plays many roles, and whether a person violates the law or not may
depend upon the nature of the integration of these conflicting roles.
White collar offenders probably have less similarity in their several roles
than is true in lower class criminality.

Probably the most frequent criticism of the differential association
theory is that it cannot explain why even in the areas of the worst
delinquency in a city only about one-fourth of the boys have ever appeared before the juvenile court (52). Kobrin has attempted to answer
this criticism by first citing the fact that official delinquency, offenders
brought to the attention of the courts, represents only a small proportion
of actual offenders (67). The more inclusive records of the police show
the number to be at least two thirds. A substantial number of boys engage in delinquency without being apprehended, while those with a
juvenile record may grow up to be law-abiding persons rather than
criminal offenders. The reasons for this are that boys, even in areas of
high delinquency, participate simultaneously in areas of socially approved and disapproved values. This is possible because groups of boys
are not homogeneous. Actually in such areas "nondelinquent" becomes a
meaningless term which is based on middle class standards. Accordingly, Kobrin suggests two types of interacting values in areas of a city.
The first are those areas where the antisocial values are more or less
reinforcing and in which stealing becomes highly developed. In the
second type of area where antisocial values are not integrated, delinquency becomes unrestrained and hoodlum activities result.

Imprisonment represents exposure to differential association with criminal and other antisocial norms, and yet it seems to have little effect on
some persons. In a study of prison as a source of criminality, Clemmer
has indicated some five factors related to prisonization: (a) the inmate's personality and susceptibility to a criminal culture, (b) kind and

---

* Earlier Reckless pointed out that Sutherland's theory did not adequately consider "differential response" (107).

extent of relationships to persons outside the walls, (c) relation to prison primary and semiprimary groups, (d) chance placement on some kinds of prison work, and (e) whether he accepts the dogmas or codes of the prison culture (22).

Sutherland's theory of criminology in general paid little attention to the situation out of which a crime arises and particularly the role of the victim in a crime. In a study of *The Criminal and His Victim,* Hans von Hentig has indicated that the victim plays an important role in crimes (62). In certain cases the victim may actually induce the commission of a crime, and in others the attitude of the victim may play a decisive factor in considering an act a crime.

### Personality traits

Sociologists have continued to emphasize the position that delinquency and criminal behavior are largely a product of the incorporation of deviant norms within the person through group experiences. Increasingly, however, there has been recognition that personality traits play a part in this behavior, particularly in certain types of delinquency and crime.* Monachesi, in a series of articles and later a book with Hathaway, has stressed the importance of research on personality traits using various scales of the Minnesota Multiphasic Personality Inventory (MMPI) to differentiate between delinquents and nondelinquents (59, 92, 93). While they claim that in general there are differences between the groups on several scales the actual relation of these findings to delinquency is not entirely clear.

In one study Monachesi compared two groups of delinquents, one on probation and the other in an institution, with two groups of nondelinquents from different socioeconomic levels (93). While the MMPI distinguished between the delinquents and nondelinquents, he found that those sent to institutions had more extreme personality difficulties such as psychopathy, psychasthenia, and hypomania. These test results add to the general belief among sociologists that institutional populations are not necessarily representative of the majority of offenders.

While sociologists generally do not use psychiatric records in their research, Reiss has used psychiatric data gathered on 1,110 white male probationers at the Institute for Juvenile Research to discover the social

* Not only sociologists but others have criticized the concept of the psychopath as a term which is difficult to define and whose development is largely unexplained. Harrison Gough has suggested a sociological theory of psychopathy in terms of deficiency in role-playing ability. Harrison Gough, "A Sociological Theory of Psychopathy," *Amer. J. of Soc.,* Vol. 53 (1947–1948), p. 365.

correlates of three psychological types of delinquents, the relatively integrated, those relatively defective in super-ego control, and weak ego types of delinquents (110). Those with relatively integrated personal controls will probably become mature, independent adults. Where the super-ego is weak, the delinquents have not internalized social conforming controls of middle class society and experience little sense of guilt. They identify with their peer generation and reject other norms, becoming something like what Hewitt and Jenkins have called the "socialized delinquent" (63). Delinquents with relatively weak ego controls are generally highly insecure persons with low self-esteem or are highly aggressive and hostile persons. Those with weak ego controls appear less often than the other types in areas of high delinquency and are more associated with better economic areas where, however, their families were more mobile than others in the area.

The recognition of the influence of personality traits by no means has meant that sociologists accept any effort to trace primarily all delinquency or crime to such a source. Few books have attracted the criticism of sociologists that the Gluecks received with the publication of *Unraveling Juvenile Delinquency* in 1950 (52). They compared 500 delinquents in a boys' training school with what they felt was a matched group of 500 nondelinquents,* in terms of family and personal background, body types, health, intelligence, temperament, and character. In a number of critiques, sociologists challenged the study. Rubin criticized the research as being eclectic and inadequate in design (114). He also felt that the prediction was invalid. Reiss felt that it was poorly matched on neighborhood and environmental factors, and that the study largely ignored primary group relationships in structuring behavior and enforcing behavior in conformity with a set of norms (111). Sellin claimed that their concept of culture conflict was inadequate (118). Taft criticized it on several issues, suggesting the need for more cooperative research in the future to avoid some of the errors of the Gluecks (135). Clinard felt that it was deficient in social psychological theory, and arbitrary in its attempt to predict delinquency through personality and family factors (30).

This recent research by the Gluecks reflects an inadequate understanding of knowledge of the social psychological processes by which all attitudes are acquired, modified, or changed whether they are delinquent or nondelinquent. Their study was a segmental study of a multitude of factors, many of which were unrelated to a theory of human behavior or the development of attitudes. While they compared the two groups

* This matching will be discussed in a later section.

statistically on a large number of factors, they did not give proper emphasis to the role played by the neighborhood and groups outside the family, the intensity of social contacts, the effects of models on behavior, or the meaning of the delinquency to the self-conception and role playing of the child.

In devising a prognostic instrument to predict delinquency at the age of six, through several family factors and their general emphasis on personality traits, they failed to appreciate fully some other findings of interest to the sociologist. The neighborhood was supposedly experienced in the same way by the delinquent group and the control group. Actually four fifths of the delinquents had moved five or more times more often than the nondelinquents, and half of the delinquents belonged to delinquent gangs, as compared with only 3 out of 500 nondelinquents. In fact, they stated that with few exceptions delinquents went with delinquents, while nondelinquents largely associated together. There were other pronounced differences between the two groups in such behavior as sneaking into movies, running away from home, gambling, hanging around street corners, truancy, amount of time spent at home, and the use of playgrounds.

Still another writer, William H. Sheldon, who has emphasized personality traits but has attributed them to a constitutional basis, attracted the criticism of sociologists (123). What turned out to be Sutherland's last writing was a devastating critique of Sheldon's work (131). Among Sutherland's criticisms of the *Varieties of Delinquent Youth* were the loose definition of delinquency, the manner of selecting cases, the subjective and unreliable method of scoring, the fact that the method did not clearly distinguish types, and, finally, the difficulty of evaluating Sheldon's indexes.

All studies up to 1950 comparing the personality characteristics of delinquents and criminals with those who were not delinquent or criminal have been analyzed by Schuessler and Cressey with what they regard as inconclusive results (117). The 113 studies used tests to measure such factors as differences in emotional stability, emotional maturity, temperament, character, and total personality. Their conclusion was that 42 per cent of the studies showed comparisons in favor of the offenders, while the rest were indeterminate. "The doubtful validity of many of the obtained differences as well as the lack of consistency in the combined results make it impossible to conclude from these data that criminality and personality traits are associated" (117, page 476). This statement may actually be too strong, however, because their summation included some 30 different tests and may partly reflect some differences in the tests themselves.

They indicated several difficulties in making studies of personality trait differences. Generally prison samples were used; these are probably not representative of the general criminal population, the test performances of prisoners may be unreliable, and prison experience may have altered their personalities. Some of the studies did not compare offenders with nonoffenders similar in age, intelligence, and cultural background, but used only a test norm. Most compared the personality characteristics of a heterogeneous group of offenders rather than types of offenders.

### Criminality and war

Primarily during the years immediately after World War II a number of articles appeared about the relation of the war to changes in the nature and extent of delinquency and crime, the effect of military service on criminal behavior, and the characteristics of military and naval offenders. They reflected a contemporary interest in such issues. Lunden published articles showing an increase in wartime juvenile delinquency in England and Wales and in Japan (74, 75). In the United States there was a considerable increase in juvenile delinquency, but a decrease in conventional crime, according to Merrill's analysis (86). A penetrating analysis of wartime increases in juvenile delinquency in Michigan was made by Wiers (150). He concluded that the increase in delinquency during wartime is not due chiefly to a breakdown in moral standards, but rather "population growth and rapid industrial expansion of business activity alone are sufficient to account for 40 per cent of the increase alone since 1939." The nature of white collar crime during war has been analyzed by Clinard and Hartung (24, 58). Several writers, among them Vold, have discussed the significance for criminology of the thousands of conscientious objectors who were imprisoned during the war years (141).

During the postwar years there was much discussion of what was believed to be extensive criminality among veterans. Three studies tended to disprove this idea. Willbach showed statistically that some increase should be expected, without being necessarily disproportionate, because the returned veterans were from the most criminally susceptible age groups (151). Hakeem made the most comprehensive actual study of this relationship (53). Taking two prison groups, 125 ex-servicemen, and 485 others with no military record, he compared them on a number of factors. With the exception of race, where there was a smaller proportion of Negroes among ex-servicemen, he could find no significant differences. There were no more violent crimes in either group than would be expected. A study after the war of 156 servicemen in a reformatory, together with data from other institutions, showed that three fourths of the inmates had a crime record before entering military service (76). In fact, age was a more important factor than military record.

A large group of 24,000 military prisoners have been studied by Austin MacCormick and Victor Fvjen (81).* Among the studies of naval offenders were those by Chappel (20), Richmond and Cain (112), and Boshes and Hermann (14). The antisocial behavior of soldiers has been explained by MacCallum as a way of obtaining those things denied them by conventional society as well as a means of gaining social recognition within the army (77).

### Administration of criminal justice

A number of sociological studies have related to the administration of criminal justice, including the police, the courts, and prisons. To some extent these studies are counterparts of studies of industry made by sociologists. According to a study of Westley, police violence towards criminal offenders is a result of the sanctioning of such violence by other police on the force, as a means of personal status and self-esteem (149). Being an occupational group, the police have their own standards of what ends, such as a forced confession, are not only justifiable but are more important than any laws preventing them. Interaction between white policemen and Negro offenders has been studied by interviews with policemen in Philadelphia (65).† Kephart found that "in general, white patrolmen are inclined to be more strict in their dealings with Negro offenders than in the handling of white offenders. Negro offenders tend to resist arrest more often than do white offenders. These two tendencies fortify each other" (65). The social role played by the county sheriff, in terms of what people think he ought to be and his office as a social control factor against crime in the local community, has been studied by Esselstyn (44).

---

* In one study of ex-juvenile delinquents in the military the majority received honorable discharges, although the bad conduct of some exceeded what might be expected for a comparable group. Peter P. Lejins and Van H. Tanner, "Military Careers of Juvenile Delinquents: A Progress Report," *Proceedings of the 84th Annual Congress of Corrections,* New York, American Prison Association, 1954.

† Lohman has written a manual for the use of policemen dealing with minorities (72). Also see Moses, "Differentials in Crime Rates Between Negroes and Whites Based on Comparisons of Four Socio-Economically Equated Areas" (94).

Two studies have indicated that certain measures do not always have the expected results. Dunham and Knauer reported that the juvenile court does not seem to have as much effect on adult criminality as many people think (40). In their Detroit study they found that over a considerable period of time approximately one third of the juveniles who appeared before the court went on into adult criminality. In the Cambridge-Somerville Youth Study, an experimental group of delinquent boys was assigned counselors, while a control group received no help from the study, but after completion of the research they could find practically no significant difference between the groups on nearly every measure (104). The latter study represents an exception to most published research which reports successful advancement of the hypotheses or objectives.

Persons nominated for grand jury duty presumably represent a cross-section of the population, but a study of persons so nominated in Los Angeles from 1935 to 1947 showed an excess of persons from the upper socioeconomic groups (113). The possibility of using more scientific evidence in securing a change of venue was suggested by a study of community attitudes by an opinion survey group, at the request of the NAACP in a controversial criminal trial (153). Although the judge did not take cognizance of the survey in his decision, he did allow it to be introduced at the trial. A report on several studies of executive clemency, its use and results, has been published by Gillin (46). What would be the result of the punishment of war criminals was suggested by Taft in a paper shortly after the war (134). A study from the inmates' conception of the informal process in felony convictions has been made by Newman (95). He studied the differences between those who pleaded guilty without a lawyer and those who retained one, and the types of informal conviction agreements such as bargaining concerning the charge, sentence, concurrent charges, and dropped charges.

To include all the writings during this period by sociologists about various aspects of correctional institutions would be beyond both the purpose and size of this chapter. The use of the Delaware whipping post, Red Hannah, has been studied by Caldwell, who found that, in general, there was no evidence that whippings prevented recidivism (17). Several sociologists, in an *Annals* issue on "Murder and the Penalty of Death," have examined the extent and trends of capital crimes, the use of capital punishment, the reasons for capital punishment, its deterrent effect, errors in its use, and possible alternatives (4).

Many years ago Clemmer published a book on *The Prison Community* in which he went into prison social structure, an interest which has been carried on by others (23).* McCorkle and Horn have examined the social system of the prison and how the inmate social system enables prisoners to cope with problems of living in an institution (80). This social system has several characteristics: (a) it cannot be avoided except by psychological withdrawal, (b) it is rigidly hierarchical with little mobility, (c) it is authoritarian, (d) there is coercive power, and (e) this coercive power produces a pattern of evasion of inmate codes termed "informing." Weinberg has indicated how stereotyped opinions of inmates are transmitted in prison from officer to officer and about officers from old inmates to new inmates (147).

Inmate leadership appears to be associated with a criminal career and institutional adjustment, according to a study by Shrag (124). The inmate in a woman's prison who defines her own goal and does not conform to any group, termed a "fringer," consists of several types, according to Ida Harper (56).

Emerging interest in small group research has led in criminology to studies of group therapy or what has been termed sociologically "guided group interaction." This work may result not only in contributions to correctional work but to social psychological theory in general (26). While many papers have been published by psychologists and psychiatrists, McCorkle has been the chief sociological writer in this area. His papers have described what goes on in guided group interaction sessions and its effect upon the social roles, status, and self-conception of inmates (11, 78, 79).

Tests of the results of group therapy have been limited. Weeks has given a preliminary evaluation of one of them, the Highfields Project (146). One writer has felt that most group therapy work in correctional institutions has been based on an individual theory of criminology with too much emphasis on personality traits (34). Cressey has suggested, instead, that this work should be based on a group theory of criminality and be directed mainly at changing attitudes and establishing more adequate relations with the norms of conventional groups.

### Prediction of recidivism

Approximately twenty-five years ago Burgess, and shortly thereafter the Gluecks, tried to predict recidivism and nonrecidivism among a group

* Suggestions for a more theoretical approach to informal inmate relations, in terms of values and status systems, have been made by Foreman in order to bring these studies together with research on the prediction of personal adjustment. Paul B. Foreman, "Guide Theory for the Study of Informal Inmate Relations," *Southwestern Sociological Society Quarterly*, Vol. 34 (1953), pp. 34–46.

of prisoners, in two pioneer studies (15, 50). Others since then have tried to predict adjustment of juvenile delinquents and probationers, as well as those on parole. There has been a disproportionate interest in this type of work in criminology, perhaps reflecting the statistical emphasis in general sociology, the use of easily available data, and the possibility of a significant contribution by criminology to the more applied area of correctional administration.

It is impossible here to give more than a brief summary of some of the recent developments.* Several studies have suggested the use of more significant factors in such studies.† Schnur has reported a positive relationship between prison conduct and recidivism and education in prison, if the education is for more than six months (115, 116). Clark found that those paroled to a community of similar size had a lower violation rate than those who were not and suggested that this is related to adjustment to a familiar or unfamiliar environment (21).

In his study of 1,110 white, male, juvenile delinquent probationers, Reiss isolated a set of personal and social controls related to recidivism and evaluated them as prognostic devices (109). He suggested that more efficient items in prediction are those which measure the adequacy of personal controls in terms of acceptance or submission to social control rather than items which merely measure the strength of social controls. Monachesi has suggested that case record information is generally inadequate and feels instead that more standardized items should be used, such as the Minnesota Multiphasic Personality Inventory (90). In a number of studies he and Hathaway have attempted to predict delinquency with the MMPI (59).

A major criticism of prediction studies has been the comparative absence of a basic theory behind the statistical manipulation of factors. Glaser has suggested a theory of "differential identification" in which success on parole would tend to vary directly (a) with the identification of the parolee with persons whose influence supports conventional values, (b) with the parolee's probable economic opportunities and acceptance of conventional associations, and (c) inversely with the parolee's identification with conventional persons (48). Using 4,448 paroled inmates, he applied specific indexes which he believed represented this theory. He reported that a table based on his factors was better than the one which he was then using. Ohlin and Lawrence compared the use of objective factors found in records with the more

---

* For other more detailed statements see Ohlin (96), Monachesi (90), and Clinard (27).

† For two general studies see De Stephens (39) and Zuckerman (154).

attitudinal response of inmates, as suggested by Laune, and found that objective factors are more discriminating but less stable than attitudinal factors (97).

Improvements in statistical techniques have been of more concern to others than theoretical factors. Ohlin and Duncan have suggested that an instrument is needed to test whether so-called prediction studies actually predict better than less rigorous methods (98). They suggested three types of error in applying prediction tables to samples to measure actual outcome: (a) lack of association between the predictive factors and outcome in the population, (b) sampling fluctuation, and (c) errors correlated with time in which there are marked changes in the probabilities associated with outcome. The instrument they proposed, the percentage reduction in the error of prediction, is a way of measuring the efficiency of various prediction methods. It is the ratio of the error in prediction based upon any method of scoring predictors to the ratio of the error in predictions, made on the basis of total over-all rates of favorable or unfavorable responses of offenders to specific forms of treatment. After applying their instrument to a number of previous studies, they found that only two tables went beyond a predictive capacity of 25 per cent and some were zero. The prediction on individual factors in some cases was so inadequate that they were not better than a prediction based on over-all rates. Kirby has used multiple correlations in a study of 445 federal parolees and refined the 19 items he used (66).

Few follow-ups of prediction studies have been made. Instead, each prediction study has been assumed to rest on its own merits. Two such follow-ups, however, have been made, one by Monachesi and the other by Hakeem. The former made a follow-up prediction of those on probation using factors derived from 896 juvenile cases in 1923–1925 to predict the behavior of 120 juveniles from the period 1939–1940 (91). Monachesi found that there was accurate prediction for the extreme scores but not for the middle scores. Hakeem's study was a more ambitious one, using 1,861 burglary cases from 1939–1940, which enabled him to hold the offense constant (54). After making some adjustments to handle differences in violation rates between this experimental group and the other group of 9,729 cases from the same prison during the period 1925–1935, he found that prediction and actual behavior coincided. In his follow-up he found psychiatric prognosis, social type, previous criminal record, work record, type of offenders and preinstitutional community to have a particularly important relationship. Ohlin and Duncan, however, claim that neither the predictions of Monachesi nor Hakeem were much better than the over-all rate (98).

It is possible that improvements in theory, factors, and techniques will result in future scientific contributions from prediction studies which will be different from the disappointing emphasis so far given to this work in criminology. On the whole these prediction studies have not as yet demonstrated general improvement over prediction based on over-all rates. Part of this difficulty lies in the preoccupation with techniques rather than with the theory of human and criminal behavior which is being predicted. The items used in the prediction scores must have meaningfulness to a science of criminology. In general, the items have been mechanistic and restricted to experience before institutionalization and to a large extent have given a static rather than a dynamic picture of the on-going process of adjustment to social norms and interpersonal relations in society.

### Research techniques

None of the techniques used in criminological research are peculiar to this field. Some of the emphasis on certain techniques in criminological research is of importance, and among them are the use of ecology, analytic induction, control groups, and replica research.

ECOLOGICAL TECHNIQUES. While the location of data in space and its analysis has not been limited to criminology, in few fields of investigation has this technique been so widely used. Beginning with the studies of Shaw and McKay in Chicago in the late 1920's, great interest has developed in such work. The past ten years has seen perhaps some diminution, but probably more careful usage, of ecology in criminology. Probably the largest study during this period was that of Lander in Baltimore (69). He analyzed the residences of 8,464 cases of delinquency, using factor analysis which gave him more precise results than in most previous studies. Although his findings were in general agreement with Shaw and McKay's, he felt that the processes of city growth do not provide the basic explanation of the wide variations in delinquency rates. He found no *real* association between housing and delinquency, nor between race and delinquency, since those areas of the city with more than 50 per cent Negro population had less delinquency. Factor analysis indicated that poverty, bad housing, room density, and location near the center of the city are merely superficial relations. The only factors actually related to delinquency were home ownership and Negro population density. On this basis, he claims delinquency is related to *anomie*. "When the *group norms* are no longer binding or valid in an area or for a population sub-group, insofar is an individual's behavior likely to lead to deviant behavior" (69, page 89). Provocative as is this idea, the indices used and the almost completely statistical nature of the investigation make it doubtful whether there is sufficient support for this explanation.

Areas with high suicide rates and low crime rates in Fort Worth are high in social status and residence of native whites (100). In a study of an English city Mannheim found that wards with 50 per cent of the population had 73 per cent of the delinquent sample, but that delinquent gangs had little permanence (85). Ecological patterns have been studied in Mexico City by Hayner with a concentration of conventional juvenile delinquency and crime in the central part similar to American cities (60). He suggests, however, that there is a high incidence of unreported white collar crime in the city's periphery.

There appear to be ecological differences in gang membership and juvenile delinquency. In a Detroit study of 5,878 boys contacted by the police, it was reported that the gang boys came from "easy-going" homes in low socioeconomic areas (145). Nongang boys come from "tense or depriving families" located generally in good socioeconomic neighborhoods.

Jonassen has challenged both the logic and some of the methods used by Shaw and McKay (64). He has questioned the limitations of the data, methodology, and internal consistencies. On this basis he stated that they have not demonstrated that "All nationality groups evidence the same rate of juvenile delinquency in the same urban areas and that nationality is not vitally related to juvenile delinquency" (64, page 614).

ANALYTIC INDUCTION. Two studies have used Znaniecki's technique of analytic induction, Lindesmith's *Opiate Addiction* (71) and the newer research by Cressey, *Other People's Money* (33). Both have attracted considerable interest among sociologists not immediately interested in these areas (140). It seems doubtful that analytic induction, at least as already used, will offer much as a research technique in criminology.

While Cressey's study represented a substantial addition to criminological literature dealing with behavior systems, it does not have, nor is it claimed to have, much predictive capacity. The generalizations are so broad that they have little meaning. On closer inspection a nonshareable problem turns out to be almost any serious difficulty in which a person finds himself and which he must resolve secretly. As for knowledge of techniques and rationalizations, it is unlikely that persons who have long been in a position of trust would be unfamiliar with them, anyway, through the nature of the position and association with others. Since the generalizations lack predictive capacity, one can say almost nothing about a trust violation until the total act has been completed, since the presence of one or two parts of the generalization would not mean that the other parts would necessarily follow. Unfortunately, the study neither indicates what offenders with what characteristics are more likely to violate, nor what situations are likely to be more productive of viola-tion.  As he himself stated, "the theory we have presented has few practical implications either for prevention or detection of trust violators or for treatment of apprehended violators" (33, page 153).

Actually, the proof of the final universal generalization depends on whether violators do not violate when all the factors in the generalization are not present.  To prove this, Cressey uses the violator's own statements that there were previous occasions when they did not violate because all factors were not present.  Trust violators reported how they conceived of themselves, whether they had a nonshareable problem, and whether their rationalizations were adequate.  Some of the difficulties in this study might have been avoided if an actual control group, consisting perhaps of a sample of persons who were at the time in a position of trust, had been interviewed to ascertain whether all parts of the generalization were present without violation.

As in the Lindesmith study, there seems also to have been some other lack of precision.  Practically nothing is reported about the characteristics of the sample.  Some might suggest that it was immaterial to the hy-pothesis whether the cases were representative or not, since all were trust violators.  On the other hand, the claim of establishing a generali-zation without exceptions is not a modest one, and it is difficult to make further studies, using different samples, to test it without knowing the characteristics of the one used by the originator.

CONTROL GROUPS.  In most cases data about the characteristics of criminals do not constitute valid scientific knowledge until they have been compared with the frequency of such data in the noncriminal popu-lation.  Whom to use for this noncriminal control group presents a difficult problem, particularly when there are indications that undetected or unprosecuted delinquency and criminal behavior are fairly extensive in the general population.  When compared with 2,049 delinquent boys who appeared before the juvenile court, a group of 337 college boys were found to have committed more offenses (102).  In another study Waller-stein and Wyle found that 91 per cent of a supposed sample of the general population had committed offenses after the age of 16 for which they could have received a penal sentence (142).  This means that the re-search on a control group of nonoffenders must be, to ascertain this fact, nearly as complete as that on a group of offenders.  Gillin used brothers as control, as have several other studies, but this controls only the family and not the companions and other neighborhood influences (45).  Powers and Witmer used a somewhat more refined method of matching (104).  They did not use the usual method of matching on certain isolated characteristics because they wanted to recognize the dynamics of personality aspects. Both the experimental and the control groups were studied statistically and configurationally, and variables such as personality and delinquency prognosis were used.

To compare delinquents who have been brought before juvenile courts with those who have not is an unsatisfactory procedure, according to Wattenberg, because juvenile court delinquents are often the product of socioeconomic selection (143). Instead he compared a group of repeaters and nonrepeaters who had contact with the police.

Few control groups have attracted so much attention from the sociologist as the one used by the Gluecks in their most recent work (51, 52). They attempted to match a group of 500 boys in institutions for delinquents with 500 nondelinquents. They were matched according to similar areas of the city, age, ethnic or racial derivation, and general intelligence. This control group was far from adequate. In the first place, the homes of the nondelinquent boys were explicitly approached as ones where "good boys" in these families would be compared with others who were not. This knowledge may have tended to make the families present more favorable information. Since the delinquent group was institutionalized, it was less difficult to obtain knowledge about them. One group's being institutionalized and the other not could have had a different effect on their personality traits. Finally, in matching the group on a neighborhood basis it was fallaciously assumed that a neighborhood is experienced in the same way because a person lives in it.

Studies attempting to isolate personality factors of delinquents and nondelinquents, criminals and noncriminals, have generally used ex post facto designs and are open to such criticism of this reliability as (a) records for control groups are rarely as adequate as for the delinquent group, (b) there is necessity for recall and subjective evaluation by subjects, their associates, and the investigators, (c) individuals with a delinquent history have had experiences which cannot be matched by most control groups. In order to overcome some of the difficulties in securing adequate control groups, information needs to be secured prior to delinquency or criminality on a sample of the general population. This information would help to avoid the differential effect of arrest, court procedures, or institutionalization on those who have experienced this treatment as compared with those who have not. Something like this procedure on a more limited scale has been done by Hathaway and Monachesi (59). They collected data by testing the entire ninth grade in Minneapolis, securing 4,048 completed tests which they followed up two years later. At that time they found 591 had appeared before the police; these individuals were then classified as to whether their misbehavior occurred before the testing, after the testing, or continuously both before and after the testing.

REPLICA STUDIES.  Characteristically both in criminology and sociology in general there have often been only a single and at most only a few studies in a specific area.  Where there have been additional studies they have seldom been repeated in the same way with similar samples, hypotheses, and questionnaires.  Under these circumstances each study becomes to a certain extent a finding which is unique, even though the results may have been statistically significant.  To establish a generalization similar studies must be repeated by different persons in a similar way on different samples in another time and place * (82).

Such replica studies have been rare in general sociology, but even more rare in criminology.  Recently such a study was made by Eastman, repeating some ten years later a study made by Clinard of the relation of the process of urbanization to criminal behavior (41, 28).  He used almost identical hypotheses, design, questionnaire, tabular presentation, and statistical techniques.  Similar techniques were used to select a sample in the same reformatory that had been used in the previous study.  Such replica research presents many problems.  Among them are whether the person in the original and in the replica study should have, on the whole, a similar theoretical background and whether improvements in research techniques during the intervening period should be used in the replication.  Most important of all is what constitutes validation of a study.  If in the intervening years, for example, there has been social change in the society, should this change also be reflected in any validation by the replica study.

## BIBLIOGRAPHICAL REFERENCES

1. *Annals of the American Academy of Political and Social Science,* "Juvenile Delinquency," Vol. 261 (January 1949), pp. 1–179.

2. *Annals of the American Academy of Political and Social Science,* "Ethical Standards in American Public Life," Vol. 280 (March 1952), pp. 1–157.

3. *Annals of the American Academy of Political and Social Science,* "Ethical Standards in Professional Conduct," Vol. 297 (January 1955), pp. 1–124.

4. *Annals of the American Academy of Political and Social Science,* "Murder and the Penalty of Death," Vol. 284 (November 1952), pp. 1–166.

5. Aubert, Vilhelm, *Priskontroll Og Rasjonering* [Price Control and Rationing], Oslo, Institute for Social Research, 1950.

6. Aubert, Vilhelm, "White-Collar Crime and Social Structure," *Amer. J. Soc.,* Vol. 58 (1952), pp. 263–271.

* For a discussion of the need for replica studies in sociology, see Arnold M. Rose, *Theory and Method in the Social Sciences* (Minneapolis, University of Minnesota Press, 1954).

7. Aubert, Vilhelm, Torstein Eckhoff, and Knut Sveri, *En Lov I Skelyset* [*A Law in the Searchlight*], Oslo, Institute for Social Research, 1952.

8. Barker, Gordon H., "Parent Organizational Affiliation and Juvenile Delinquency," *Journal of Criminal Law, Criminology and Police Science,* Vol. 44 (1953), pp. 204–207.

9. Barron, Milton L., "Juvenile Delinquency and American Values," *Amer. Soc. Rev.,* Vol. 16 (1951), pp. 208–214.

10. Barron, Milton L., *The Juvenile in Delinquent Society,* New York, Alfred A. Knopf, 1954.

11. Bixby, F. Lovell, and Lloyd W. McCorkle, "Guided Group Interaction in Correctional Work," *Amer. Soc. Rev.,* Vol. 16 (1951), pp. 455–461.

12. Bloch, Herbert A., "Economic Depression as a Factor in Rural Crime," *Journal of Criminal Law and Criminology,* Vol. 40 (1950), pp. 458–470.

13. Bloch, Herbert A., "The Sociology of Gambling," *Amer. J. Soc.,* Vol. 57 (1951–1952), pp. 215–221.

14. Boshes, Louis D., and Phillip J. Hermann, "Study of Naval Delinquents by Questionnaire," *Journal of Criminal Law and Criminology,* Vol. 38 (1947–1948), pp. 218–231.

15. Bruce, A. A., A. J. Harno, E. W. Burgess, and J. Landesco, *The Workings of the Indeterminate Sentence Law and the Parole System in Illinois,* Springfield, Ill., State of Illinois, 1928.

16. Burgess, Ernest W., "Comments on Frank E. Hartung, 'White-Collar Offenses in the Wholesale Meat Industry in Detroit,'" *Amer. J. Soc.,* Vol. 56 (1950–1951), pp. 32–33.

17. Caldwell, Robert G., *Red Hannah: The Delaware Whipping Post,* Philadelphia, University of Pennsylvania Press, 1947.

18. Cavan, Ruth Shonle, *Criminology,* New York, Thomas Y. Crowell Co., 1948.

19. Cavanaugh, John R., "The Comics War," *Journal of Criminal Law and Criminology,* Vol. 40 (1949), pp. 28–35.

20. Chappel, Richard A., "Naval Offenders and Their Treatment," *Federal Probation,* Vol. 9 (1945), pp. 3–7.

21. Clark, Robert E., "Size of Parole Community, as Related to Parole Outcome," *Amer. J. Soc.,* Vol. 57 (1951–1952), pp. 43–47.

22. Clemmer, Donald, "Observations on Imprisonment as a Source of Criminality," *Journal of Criminal Law and Criminology,* Vol. 41 (1950), pp. 311–319.

23. Clemmer, Donald, *The Prison Community,* Boston, Christopher Press, 1940.

24. Clinard, Marshall B., *The Black Market: A Study of White Collar Crime,* New York, Rinehart and Co., 1952.

25. Clinard, Marshall B., "Criminal Behavior Is Human Behavior," *Federal Probation,* Vol. 13 (1949), pp. 21–28.

26. Clinard, Marshall B., "The Group Approach to Social Reintegration," *Amer. Soc. Rev.,* Vol. 14 (1949), pp. 257–262.

27. Clinard, Marshall B., "Sociologists and American Criminology," *Journal of Criminal Law and Criminology,* Vol. 41 (1951), pp. 549–577.

28. Clinard, Marshall B., "The Process of Urbanization and Criminal Behavior," *Amer. J. Soc.,* Vol. 48 (1942–1943), pp. 202–213.

29. Clinard, Marshall B., "Secondary Community Influences and Juvenile Delinquency," *Annals of the American Academy of Political and Social Science,* Vol. 261 (1949), pp. 42–55.

30. Clinard, Marshall B., "Review of the Gluecks 'Delinquents in the Making,'" *Federal Probation*, Vol. 17 (1953), pp. 50–51.

31. Cohen, Albert K., *Delinquent Boys: The Culture of the Gang*, Glencoe, Ill., Free Press, 1955.

32. Crawford, Paul L., Daniel I. Malamud, and James R. Dumpson, *Working with Teen-Age Gangs, A Report on the Central Harlem Street Clubs Project*, New York, Welfare Council of New York City, 1950.

33. Cressey, Donald R., *Other People's Money: A Study in the Social Psychology of Embezzlement*, Glencoe, Ill., Free Press, 1953.

34. Cressey, Donald R., "Contradictory Theories in Correctional Group Therapy Programs," *Federal Probation*, Vol. 18 (1954), pp. 20–26.

35. Cressey, Donald R., "Application and Verification of the Differential Association Theory," *Journal of Criminal Law and Criminology*, Vol. 43 (1952), pp. 43–52.

36. Cressey, Donald R., "The Differential Association Theory and Compulsive Crimes," *Journal of Criminal Law and Criminology*, Vol. 44 (1954), pp. 29–41.

37. Cressey, Donald R., "Criminological Research and the Definition of Crimes," *Amer. J. Soc.*, Vol. 56 (1950–1951), pp. 546–552.

38. Davis, James F., "Crime News in Colorado Newspapers," *Amer. J. Soc.*, Vol. 57 (1951–1952), pp. 325–330.

39. De Stephens, William P., "Initial Failures in Rehabilitation Among 16,965 Ohio State Reformatory Inmates," *Journal of Criminal Law, Criminology, and Police Science*, Vol. 44 (1954), pp. 596–603.

40. Dunham, H. Warren, and Mary E. Knauer, "The Juvenile Court in Its Relation to Adult Criminality," *Social Forces*, Vol. 32 (1954), pp. 290–296.

41. Eastman, Harold D., "The Process of Urbanization and Criminal Behavior: A Restudy of Culture Conflict," Unpublished doctoral dissertation, University of Iowa, 1954.

42. Elliott, Mabel A., *Crime in Modern Society*, New York, Harper, 1952.

43. *Encyclopedia of Criminology*, ed. by Vernon C. Branham and Samuel B. Kutash, New York, Philosophical Library, 1949.

44. Esselstyn, T. C., "The Social Role of the County Sheriff," *Journal of Criminal Law and Criminology*, Vol. 44 (1953), pp. 177–184.

45. Gillin, John L., *The Wisconsin Prisoner*, Madison, University of Wisconsin Press, 1946.

46. Gillin, John L., "Executive Clemency in Wisconsin," *Journal of Criminal Law, Criminology, and Police Science*, Vol. 42 (1952), pp. 755–765.

47. Gillin, John L., "Murder as a Sociological Phenomenon," *Annals of the American Academy of Political and Social Science*, Vol. 284 (1952), pp. 20–25.

48. Glaser, David, "A Reconsideration of Some Parole Prediction Factors," *Amer. Soc. Rev.*, Vol. 19 (1954), pp. 335–341.

49. Glueck, Sheldon, and Eleanor Glueck, *Five Hundred Delinquent Women*, New York, Alfred A. Knopf, 1934.

50. Glueck, Sheldon, and Eleanor Glueck, *500 Criminal Careers*, New York, Alfred A. Knopf, 1930.

51. Glueck, Sheldon, and Eleanor Glueck, *Delinquents in the Making*, New York, Harper, 1952.

52. Glueck, Sheldon, and Eleanor Glueck, *Unraveling Juvenile Delinquency*, Cambridge, Harvard University Press, 1950.

53. Hakeem, Michael, "Service in the Armed Forces and Criminality," *Journal of Criminal Law and Criminology*, Vol. 37 (1947), pp. 120–131.

54. Hakeem, Michael, "Glueck Method of Parole Prediction Applied to 1,861 Cases of Burglaries," *Journal of Criminal Law and Criminology*, Vol. 36 (1945), pp. 87–98.

55. Harlan, Howard, "Five Hundred Homicides," *Journal of Criminal Law and Criminology*, Vol. 40 (1950), pp. 736–752.

56. Harper, Ida, "The Role of the 'Fringer' in a State Prison for Women," *Social Forces*, Vol. 31 (1952), pp. 53–60.

57. Hartung, Frank, "White Collar Crime," *Federal Probation*, Vol. 17 (1953), pp. 31–36.

58. Hartung, Frank, "White Collar Offenses in the Wholesale Meat Industry in Detroit," *Amer. J. Soc.*, Vol. 56 (1950–1951), pp. 25–32.

59. Hathaway, Starke, and Elio Monachesi, *Analyzing and Predicting Juvenile Delinquency with the MMPI*, Minneapolis, University of Minnesota Press, 1953.

60. Hayner, Norman S., "Criminogenic Zones in Mexico City," *Amer. Soc. Rev.*, Vol. 11 (1946), pp. 428–438.

61. Hentig, Hans von, "Redhead and Outlaw: A Study in Criminal Anthropology," *Journal of Criminal Law and Criminology*, Vol. 38 (1948), pp. 1–6.

62. Hentig, Hans von, *The Criminal and His Victim*, New Haven, Yale University Press, 1948.

63. Hewitt, L. E., and R. L. Jenkins, *Fundamental Patterns of Maladjustment*, Springfield, State of Illinois, 1946.

64. Jonassen, C., "A Re-Evaluation and Critique of the Logic and Some Methods of Shaw and McKay," *Amer. Soc. Rev.*, Vol. 14 (1949), pp. 608–617.

65. Kephart, William, "The Negro Offender: An Urban Research Project," *Amer. J. Soc.*, Vol. 60 (1954–1955), pp. 46–50.

66. Kirby, Bernard C., "Parole Prediction Using Multiple Correlation," *Amer. J. Soc.*, Vol. 59 (1953–1954), pp. 539–550.

67. Kobrin, Solomon, "The Conflict of Values in Delinquency Areas," *Amer. Soc. Rev.*, Vol. 16 (1951), pp. 653–661.

68. Lane, Robert E., "Why Business Men Violate the Law," *Journal of Criminal Law, Criminology, and Police Science*, Vol. 44 (1954), pp. 151–165.

69. Lander, Bernard, *Towards an Understanding of Juvenile Delinquency*, New York, Columbia University Press, 1954.

70. Lemert, Edwin M., "An Isolation Closure Theory of Naive Check Forgery," *Journal of Criminal Law, Criminology, and Police Science*, Vol. 44 (1954), pp. 296–307.

71. Lindesmith, Alfred R., *Opiate Addiction*, Bloomington, Principia Press, 1947.

72. Lohman, Joseph, *The Police and Minority Groups*, Chicago, Chicago Park Police, 1947.

73. Lombroso, Cesar, *The Female Offender*, London, T. F. Unwin, 1895.

74. Lunden, Walter A., "War and Juvenile Delinquency in England and Wales, 1910–1943," *Amer. Soc. Rev.*, Vol. 10 (1945), pp. 390–393.

75. Lunden, Walter A., "Juvenile Delinquency in Japan: Prewar, War, and Postwar Years," *Journal of Criminal Law and Criminology*, Vol. 44 (1954), pp. 428–432.

76. Lunden, Walter A., "Military Service and Criminality," *Journal of Criminal Law and Criminology*, Vol. 42 (1952), pp. 766–773.

77. MacCallum, Malcolm R., "The Study of the Delinquent in the Army," *Amer. J. Soc.*, Vol. 51 (1945–1946), pp. 479–482.

78. McCorkle, Lloyd W., "Group Therapy," in Paul W. Tappan (ed.), *Contemporary Correction*, New York, McGraw-Hill Book Co., 1951, pp. 211–223.

79. McCorkle, Lloyd W., "Group Therapy in Correctional Institutions," *Federal Probation*, Vol. 13 (1949), pp. 34–37.

80. McCorkle, Lloyd, and Richard Horn, "Resocialization within Walls," *Annals of the American Academy of Political and Social Science*, Vol. 293 (1954), pp. 88–98.

81. MacCormick, Austin, and Victor Evjen, "Statistical Study of 24,000 Military Prisoners," *Federal Probation*, Vol. 10 (1946), pp. 6–11.

82. Mack, Raymond W., "The Need for Replication Research in Sociology," *Amer. Soc. Rev.*, Vol. 16 (1951), pp. 93–94.

83. McKay, Henry D., "The Neighborhood and Child Conduct," *Annals of the American Academy of Political and Social Science*, Vol. 261 (1949), pp. 32–41.

84. Mannheim, Hermann, *Criminal Justice and Social Reconstruction*, New York, Oxford University Press, 1946.

85. Mannheim, Hermann, *Juvenile Delinquency in an English Middletown*, London, Kegan Paul, Trench, Trubner and Co., 1948.

86. Merrill, Francis E., *Social Problems on the Home Front*, New York, Harper, 1948.

87. Merton, Robert K., *Social Theory and Social Structure*, Glencoe, Ill., Free Press, 1949, pp. 125–150.

88. Michael, Jerome, and Mortimer Adler, *Crime, Law and Social Science*, New York, Harcourt, Brace and Co., 1933.

89. Moberg, David O., "Old Age and Crime," *Journal of Criminal Law, Criminology, and Police Science*, Vol. 43 (1953), pp. 764–776.

90. Monachesi, Elio D., "American Studies in the Prediction of Recidivism," *Journal of Criminal Law and Criminology*, Vol. 41 (1951), pp. 268–289.

91. Monachesi, Elio D., "A Comparison of Predicted with Actual Results of Prediction," *Amer. Soc. Rev.*, Vol. 10 (1945), pp. 26–31.

92. Monachesi, Elio D., "Personality Characteristics and Socio-Economic Status of Delinquents and Non-Delinquents," *Journal of Criminal Law and Criminology*, Vol. 40 (1950), pp. 570–583.

93. Monachesi, Elio D., "Personality Characteristics of Institutionalized and Non-Institutionalized Male Delinquents," *Journal of Criminal Law and Criminology*, Vol. 41 (1951), pp. 167–179.

94. Moses, E. R., "Differentials in Crime Rates Between Negroes and Whites Based on Comparisons of Four Socio-Economically Equated Areas," *Amer. Soc. Rev.*, Vol. 12 (1947), pp. 411–420.

95. Newman, Donald R., "A Study of Informal Processes in Felony Convictions," Unpublished doctoral dissertation, University of Wisconsin, 1954.

96. Ohlin, Lloyd E., *Selection for Parole: A Manual of Parole Prediction*, New York, Russell Sage Foundation, 1951.

97. Ohlin, Lloyd E., and Richard A. Lawrence, "A Comparison of Alternative Methods of Parole Prediction," *Amer. Soc. Rev.*, Vol. 17 (1952), pp. 268–274.

98. Ohlin, Lloyd E., and Otis D. Duncan, "The Efficiency of Prediction in Criminology," *Amer. J. Soc.*, Vol. 54 (1948–1949), pp. 441–452.

99. Pollak, Otto, *The Criminality of Women*, Philadelphia, University of Pennsylvania Press, 1950.

100. Porterfield, Austin L., "Suicide and Crime in the Social Structure of an Urban Setting: Fort Worth, 1930–1950," *Amer. Soc. Rev.*, Vol. 17 (1952), pp. 341–349.

101. Porterfield, Austin L., "Suicide and Crime in Folk and Secular Society," *Amer. J. Soc.*, Vol. 57 (1951–1952), pp. 331–338.

102. Porterfield, Austin L., *Youth in Trouble,* Fort Worth, Leo Potishman Fund, 1946.

103. Porterfield, Austin L., and Robert H. Talbert, *Crime, Suicide and Social Well-Being in Your State and City,* Fort Worth, Leo Potishman Foundation, 1948.

104. Powers, Edwin, and Helen Witmer, *An Experiment in the Prevention of Delinquency,* New York, Columbia University Press, 1951.

105. Rasch, Philip J., "Red Hair and Outlawing," *Journal of Criminal Law and Criminology,* Vol. 38 (1948), pp. 352–356.

106. Reckless, Walter C., *The Crime Problem,* New York, Appleton-Century-Crofts, Inc., 1950.

107. Reckless, Walter C., *The Etiology of Delinquent and Criminal Behavior,* New York, Social Science Research Council, Bull. No. 50, 1943.

108. Reinhardt, James M., and Edward C. Fisher, "The Sexual Psychopath and the Law," *Journal of Criminal Law and Criminology,* Vol. 39 (1949), pp. 734–742.

109. Reiss, Albert J., "Delinquency as the Failure of Personal and Social Controls," *Amer. Soc. Rev.,* Vol. 16 (1951), pp. 196–207.

110. Reiss, Albert J., "Social Correlates of Psychological Types of Delinquency," *Amer. Soc. Rev.,* Vol. 17 (1952), pp. 710–718.

111. Reiss, Albert J., "Unraveling Juvenile Delinquency, II, An Appraisal of the Research Methods," *Amer. J. Soc.,* Vol. 57 (1951–1952), pp. 115–120.

112. Richmond, Mark S., and Leo F. Cain, "Success and Failure of 926 Naval Offenders," *Journal of Criminal Law and Criminology,* Vol. 37 (1947), pp. 390–407.

113. Robinson, W. S., "Bias, Probability and Trial by Jury," *Amer. Soc. Rev.,* Vol. 15 (1950), pp. 73–78.

114. Rubin, Sol, "Unraveling Juvenile Delinquency, I, Illusions in a Research Project Using Matched Pairs," *Amer. J. Soc.,* Vol. 57 (1951–1952), pp. 107–114.

115. Schnur, Alfred C., "Prison Conduct and Recidivism," *Journal of Criminal Law and Criminology,* Vol. 40 (1950), pp. 36–42.

116. Schnur, Alfred C., "The Educational Treatment of Prisoners and Recidivism," *Amer. J. Soc.,* Vol. 54 (1948–1949), pp. 142–147.

117. Schuessler, Karl F., and Donald R. Cressey, "Personality Characteristics of Criminals," *Amer. J. Soc.,* Vol. 55 (1949–1950), pp. 476–484.

118. Sellin, Thorsten, in Symposium of Reviews on *Unraveling of Juvenile Delinquency, Journal of Criminal Law and Criminology,* Vol. 41 (1951), pp. 738–742.

119. Sellin, Thorsten, "The Sociological Study of Criminality," *Journal of Criminal Law and Criminology,* Vol. 41 (1951), pp. 406–422.

120. Sellin, Thorsten, *Culture Conflict and Crime,* New York, Social Science Research Council, Bull. No. 41, 1938.

121. Sex Offender Reports: (a) *The Habitual Sex Offender,* Report and Recommendations of the Commission on the Habitual Sex Offender as formulated by Paul W. Tappan, Technical Consultant, State of New Jersey, 1951. (b) State of Michigan, *Report of the Governor's Study Commission on the Deviated Sex Offender,* 1951. (c) *Report of the Illinois Commission on Sex Offenders,* to the 68th General Assembly of the State of Illinois, Springfield, March 15, 1953. (d) *California Sexual Deviation Research,* January, 1953 (printed by the Assembly of the State of California).

122. Shaw, Van B., "Relationship Between Crime Rates and Certain Population

Characteristics in Minnesota Counties," *Journal of Criminal Law and Criminology*, Vol. 40 (1950), pp. 43–49.

123. Sheldon, William H., with Emil M. Hartl and Eugene McDermott, *Varieties of Delinquent Youth: An Introduction to Constitutional Psychiatry*, New York, Harper, 1949.

124. Shrag, Clarence, "Leadership Among Prison Inmates," *Amer. Soc. Rev.*, Vol. 19 (1954), pp. 37–42.

125. Shulman, Harry, "Cultural Aspects of Criminal Responsibility," *Journal of Criminal Law and Criminology*, Vol. 43 (1953), pp. 323–327.

126. Straus, Murray A., and Jacqueline H. Straus, "Suicide, Homicide and Social Structure in Ceylon," *Amer. J. Soc.*, Vol. 58 (1952–1953), pp. 461–469.

127. Sutherland, Edwin H., *White Collar Crime*, New York, Dryden Press, 1949.

128. Sutherland, Edwin H., *Principles of Criminology*, 3d ed., New York, J. B. Lippincott Co., 1939.

129. Sutherland, Edwin H., *Principles of Criminology*, 4th ed., New York, J. B. Lippincott Co., 1947.

130. Sutherland, Edwin H., "The Sexual Psychopath Laws," *Journal of Criminal Law and Criminology*, Vol. 40 (1950), pp. 543–554.

131. Sutherland, Edwin H., "Critique of Sheldon's *Varieties of Delinquent Youth*," *Amer. Soc. Rev.*, Vol. 16 (1951), pp. 10–13.

132. Sutherland, Edwin H., "White-Collar Criminality," *Amer. Soc. Rev.*, Vol. 5 (1940), pp. 1–12.

133. Sutherland, Edwin H., "Diffusion of the Sexual Psychopath Laws," *Amer. J. Soc.*, Vol. 56 (1950–1951), pp. 142–148.

134. Taft, Donald, "Punishment of War Criminals," *Amer. Soc. Rev.*, Vol. 11 (1946), pp. 439–444.

135. Taft, Donald, "Implication of the Glueck Methodology for Criminological Research," *Journal of Criminal Law and Criminology*, Vol. 42 (1952), pp. 300–316.

136. Tappan, Paul, "Crime and the Criminal," *Federal Probation*, Vol. 11 (1947), pp. 41–44.

137. Tappan, Paul, "Who Is the Criminal," *Amer. Soc. Rev.*, Vol. 12 (1947), pp. 96–103.

138. Tappan, Paul, "Sentences for Sex Criminals," *Journal of Criminal Law, Criminology, and Police Science*, Vol. 42 (1952), pp. 332–337.

139. Thompson, Richard E., "A Validation of the Glueck Social Prediction Scale for Proneness to Delinquency," *Journal of Criminal Law and Criminology*, Vol. 43 (1953), pp. 451–470.

140. Turner, Ralph H., "The Quest for Universals in Sociological Research," *Amer. Soc. Rev.*, Vol. 18 (1952), pp. 604–611.

141. Vold, George B., "Criminology at the Crossroads," *Journal of Criminal Law and Criminology*, Vol. 42 (1952), pp. 155–162.

142. Wallerstein, James S., and Clement J. Wyle, "Our Law-Abiding Law-Breakers," *Probation*, Vol. 25 (1947), pp. 107–112.

143. Wattenberg, William W., "Juvenile Repeaters from Two Viewpoints," *Amer. Soc. Rev.*, Vol. 18 (1953), pp. 631–635.

144. Wattenberg, William W., and James Balistrieri, "Automobile Theft: A 'Favored-Group' Delinquency," *Amer. J. Soc.*, Vol. 57 (1951–1952), pp. 575–579.

145. Wattenberg, William W., and James Balistrieri, "Gang Membership and Juvenile Misconduct," *Amer. Soc. Rev.*, Vol. 15 (1950), pp. 744–752.

146. Wccks, Ashley, "Preliminary Evaluation of the Highfields Project," *Amer. Soc. Rev.*, Vol. 18 (1953), pp. 280–287.

147. Weinberg, S. Kirson, "Aspects of the Prison's Social Structure," *Amer. J. Soc.*, Vol. 57 (1951–1952), pp. 717–726.

148. Wertham, Frederic, *Seduction of the Innocent*, New York, Rinehart and Co., 1953.

149. Westley, William A., "Violence and the Police," *Amer. J. Soc.*, Vol. 59 (1953–1954), pp. 34–41.

150. Wiers, Paul, "Wartime Increases in Michigan Delinquency," *Amer. Soc. Rev.*, Vol. 10 (1945), pp. 515–523.

151. Willbach, Harry, "Recent Crimes and the Veterans," *Journal of Criminal Law and Criminology*, Vol. 38 (1948), pp. 501–508.

152. Wood, Arthur Lewis, "Minority-Group Criminality and Cultural Integration," *Journal of Criminal Law and Criminology*, Vol. 37 (1947), pp. 498–510.

153. Woodward, Julian L., "A Scientific Attempt to Provide Evidence for a Decision on Change of Venue," *Amer. Soc. Rev.*, Vol. 17 (1952), pp. 447–452.

154. Zuckerman, Stanley, B., Alfred J. Barron, and Horace B. Whittier, "Follow-Up Study of Minnesota Reformatory Inmates," *Journal of Criminal Law, Criminology, and Police Science*, Vol. 43 (1953), pp. 622–636.

# The sociology of education

C. WAYNE GORDON
*University of Rochester*

In the last ten years the social organization of educational institutions has become the primary focus of attention in the field of educational sociology. Contributions have come from many fields in the behavioral sciences, and the literature is found in a wide range of books and journals. Three major influences have helped determine the criteria of selection in the following bibliography. The first was the 1949 article by Wilbur Brookover on "The Sociology of Education" and his subsequent text of 1955 on this subject, which delimited the field to the study of the school as a social institution, its relation to the community, and to society, and the impact of such institutions on the participants. The second emphasis to this orientation was furnished by W. W. Charters' summary in 1952 of trends in educational research within the framework of "The School as a Social System" comparable to other developments of specialized disciplines of study in the field of social organization. The third emphasis for selecting research studies based primarily on the social structure of educational institutions resulted from the author's research on the high school as a social system. Empirical research studies, articles summarizing research, general works, and theoretical articles which include hypotheses for the formulation of studies are included.

An attempt has been made to select those items which dealt more specifically with school organization as distinguished from those which present material of a more general nature. Also those items were selected which had the major purpose of advancing the scientific analysis of groups within a framework of educational organizations. It is hoped that the bibliography will be useful for those interested in recent developments in this significant field.

Anderson, Harold, *et al.*, *Studies of Classroom Personality*, I, II, III, Applied Psychology Monographs of the American Psychological Association, Stanford, Calif., Stanford University Press, 1945–1946.

This is a report of an extensive investigation of the roles of elementary school teachers and their pupils. On the basis of classroom observation, teachers were classified as dominative or integrative in varying degrees. Dominative types were found to make decisions about activities of children and to expect conformity to a greater degree: integrative types permit the child to decide concerning his interest in activities suggested by the teacher.

Association for Supervision and Curriculum Development, *Forces Affecting American Education*, Washington, D. C., National Education Association, 1953.

This yearbook presented an over-all analysis of certain forces affecting American education. Chapter II, "The Culture Affecting Education," is especially significant.

Barker, R. G., *et al.*, "There is no Class Bias in Our School," *Progressive Education*, Vol. 27 (1950), pp. 106–110.

This is a study of the impact of social class upon child development in a small Midwestern town. The social acceptance of children differed in age, sex, social class, and ability. Social class did not overwhelmingly influence personal development.

Barr, A. S., *et al.*, "The Measurement of Teaching Ability," *Journal of Experimental Education*, Vol. 14 (1945), pp. 321–344.

An examination of the factors related to effective teaching ability indicates that the ratings which administrators, supervisors, and students give the teachers which are assumed to be valid measure of the teacher's effectiveness may have little correlation with objective measures of pupil changes.

Barzun, Jacques, *Teacher in America*, Boston, Little, Brown and Company, 1945.

A critical appraisal of teaching and the passive adaptation of students in American education is presented.

Bassett, R. E., "Cliques in a Student Body of Stable Membership," *Sociometry*, Vol. 7 (1944), pp. 290–302.

A study of clique structure, leadership, and role differentiation by sex.

Beck, H. P., *Men Who Control Our Universities*, New York, King's Crown Press, 1947.

This study analyzed the governing boards of thirty leading American universities (nongovernmental and state) with reference to age, sex, occupations, income, business, officers, directorships, residence, type of board membership, and length of service of board members.

Becker, Howard S., "The Career of the Chicago Public School Teacher," *Amer. J. Soc.*, Vol. 57 (1952), pp. 470–477.

This is a case study of the careers of Chicago public school teachers. They were found to exhibit "horizontal" movement among positions at one level of the status hierarchy, rather than vertical movement between several such levels. Teachers sometimes adapt their values to their students, but generally they use every possible means to transfer to middle class schools, failing which they often leave teaching altogether. After having settled in a school, the teacher may be upset by changes in neighborhood structure or in the administrative personnel with whom she must deal.

Becker, Howard S., "The Teacher in the Authority System of the Public School," *Journal of Educational Sociology*, Vol. 27 (1953), pp. 128–141.

This article deals with the authority problems of the metropolitan public school teacher. She is concerned with maintaining legitimate authority over pupils and parents. In her view the principal and other teachers should help her in building a system of defenses against challenges to her authority.

Becker, Howard S., "Social Class Variation in Teacher-Pupil Relationship," *Journal of Educational Sociology*, Vol. 25 (1952), p. 463.

This article on social-class and teacher-pupil relationship reports an analysis of the teacher role in the institutional complex of the school. It treats the teacher as a functionary in relation to the pupils as clients or customers. The analysis is based on sixty interviews with teachers in the Chicago system. Three problems are analyzed that loomed largest in the teachers' discussion of adjustment to their students: (1) the problem of teaching itself, (2) the problem of discipline, and (3) the problem of the moral acceptability of the students. The variation in the form and adjustment to the problem by the characteristics of the children of the various class groups distinguished by teachers is discussed in relation to each of the three above problems.

Biber, Barbara, Lois B. Murphy, Louise P. Woodcock, and Irma S. Black, *Life and Ways of the Seven to Eight Year Old*, 2d ed., New York, Basic Books, 1952.

A case history is presented for each of ten seven year olds in a school situation centering around regular school activities, test situations, and experimental situations. Patterns of social behavior are described.

Bidwell, Charles E., "The Administrative Role and Satisfaction in Teaching," *Journal of Educational Sociology*, Vol. 29 (1955), pp. 41–47.

An empirical investigation was made of the relationship between the administrative role and satisfaction in teaching.

Bledsoe, Joseph C., "Analysis of the Relationship of Size of High School to Marks Received by Graduates in First Year of College," *Journal of Educational Sociology*, Vol. 27 (1954), pp. 414–418.

Students from Georgia high schools who are members of large graduating classes were found to make significantly higher average marks during the first year of college than students who attended small and middle-sized high schools.

Bonney, M. E., "A Sociometric Study of the Relationship of Some Factors to Mutual Friendship on the Elementary, Secondary, and College Level," *Sociometry*, Vol. 9 (1946), pp. 26–34.

Pairs of mutual friends in elementary and secondary schools and college were compared with pairs of children in which friendship was not reciprocated. No relationship was found between mutual friendship and academic achievement, intelligence, interests, and personality. Between mutual friendship and socioeconomic background and with a friendship scale some positive relationship was found.

Bonney, M. E., R. E. Hoblit, and A. H. Dreyer, "A Study of Some Factors Related to Sociometric Status in a Men's Dormitory," *Sociometry*, Vol. 16 (1953), pp. 287–301.

Acceptance by peers was found to be due to responnses to total personalities rather than to certain traits. Some traits are more characteristic of highly chosen personalities.

Bonney, M. E., and J. Powell, "Differences in Social Behavior Between Sociometrically High and Sociometrically Low Children," *Journal of Educational Research*, Vol. 46 (1953), pp. 481–495.

In five of twenty-five areas, differences were found between ten sociometrically high and ten sociometrically low children in the first grade. Children who were highly acceptable were more conforming, smiling, and cooperative and less likely to play alone.

Brameld, Theodore, *Minority Problems in the Public Schools*, New York, Harper and Brothers, 1946.

This report analyzes sources of discrimination in public schools in relation to separate schools, administrative practices, proportion of teachers from minority groups, school placement and transfer problems of minority members, district boundaries, transportation, and distribution of Negro and white teachers.

Brookover, W. B., *A Sociology of Education*, New York, American Book Company, 1955.

This outstanding text delimits the field to the study of an analysis of the school as a social institution, its relation to the community and to society, and the impact of such institutions on the participants.

Brookover, W. B., "America Needs a New Social Class Theory of Education," *Education Digest*, Vol. 17 (1951), pp. 1–4.

This article treats social stratification as it challenges educational theory and practice and the social matrix in which education operates.

Brookover, W. B., "The Relation of Social Factors to Teaching Ability," *Journal of Experimental Education*, Vol. 83 (1945), pp. 191–205.

This study presents evidence on the problem of social distance and teaching ability. Sixty-six history teachers and their 1,270 pupils were studied. Students' views of teacher participation in student activities were elicited. Two teacher roles were delineated: authoritarian, and friendly or sympathetic teacher. Either role may be equally effective, but failure to demonstrate capacity in either may be the basis for disqualifying the teacher by pupils, patrons, and supervisors.

Brookover, W. B., "Research on Teacher and Administrator Roles," *Journal of Educational Sociology,* Vol. 29 (1955), pp. 2–13.

This is a theoretical discussion which seeks a clarification of the usages of the role concept as applied to teachers and administrators. A conceptual schema is developed showing the relationship between several aspects of role phenomena. The framework is then employed to examine some of the research dealing with teachers' and administrators' behavior.

Brookover, W. B., "The Social Roles of Teachers and Pupil Achievement," *Amer. Soc. Rev.,* Vol. 8 (1943), pp. 391–400.

This article examines the teacher's role in relation to his pupils. It is found to be a significant part of the learning situation. A quantitative analysis of the relationship between a controlled sample of 66 history teachers and their pupils shows that those teachers who maintain congenial democratic relationships teach significantly less history information than those who assume more autocratic roles. This may result from the fact that students in American schools expect dictation and do not respond effectively to democratic patterns.

Brookover, W. B., "Sociology of Education: A Definition," *Amer. Soc. Rev.,* Vol. 14 (1949), pp. 407–415.

The author defines educational sociology as "the analysis of the human relations in the educational system and between the educational system and other aspects of society." He also includes the impact of such human relations on the behavior of the individuals.

Brookover, W. B., "Teachers and Stratification of American Society," *Harvard Educational Review,* Vol. 23 (1953), pp. 257–267.

A critical examination is made of the research evidence on the teacher's position in the stratification system of the community and the impact of various "social class" teacher models on the level of aspiration, the personality, and the behavior of students. He finds the evidence concerning the social position of teachers not sufficiently established to allow conclusive generalizations about them. He also cautions on the difficulties of "class placing" the large portion of teachers who stay in one community.

Brown, Douglass, "Some Factors Affecting Social Acceptance of High School Pupils," Unpublished doctoral dissertation, Indiana University, 1952.

Factors related to social acceptance and status in the high school were studied. Girls were found to be somewhat more conscious of social class differences in the choice of friendship than boys. Clearly defined clique structures were present centering around elite and "nobody" groups. Students most frequently rejected by schoolmates tended to be those who were not members of formally organized groups.

Byrd, E. A., "Study of Validity and Constancy of Choices in a Sociometric Test," *Sociometry,* Vol. 14 (1951), pp. 175–181.

A fourth grade class of 27 children were given a sociometric test, then a life situation test for acting in a play. They were later retested with the sociometric test. Change from test to life situation was not significantly greater than from test to retest. Status from condition to condition did not change.

Charters, W. W., Jr., "The School as a Social System," *Review of Educational Research,* Vol. 22 (1952), pp. 41–50.

This chapter summarizes a trend in research toward a theory of organization relevant to educational systems. Educational research is placed within a framework of organization theory dealing with role, leadership and authority relations, communication, mobility of personnel, informal groups, and theories of organization. A bibliography is included.

Charters, W. W., Jr., "Social Class Analysis and the Control of Public Education," *Harvard Educational Review,* Vol. 23 (1953), pp. 268–283.

Dr. Charters explores the generalization that "American public school systems support the values of the 'dominant' social class of their constituent communities. The focus is on the administrative and policy forming aspects of the school in relation to social stratification. Four basic assumptions are designated as necessary to the support of the above proposition. The evidence for the dominant class control of the school is analyzed, as well as the adequacy of social class analysis. The conclusion is drawn that "dominant class control has not been demonstrated."

Clark, R. A., and C. McGuire, "Sociographic Analysis of Sociometric Valuations," *Child Development,* Vol. 23 (1952), pp. 129–140.

A sociograph is described which places members systematically by cliques and shows cleavages in group structure.

Conrad, Richard, "The Administrator Role: A Sociological Study of Leadership in a Public School System," Unpublished doctoral dissertation, Stanford University, 1951.

People tend to support the actions of the leader when there is a consonance of the educational leader's role definition and definitions by people inside and outside the school system. The data were of a variety in nature: interviews with public school officials and others, observation, content analysis of documents and newspapers.

Conrad, Richard, "A Systematic Analysis of Current Researches in the Sociology of Education," *Amer. Soc. Rev.,* Vol. 17 (1952), pp. 350–355.

An assessment was made of the current level of research in the sociology of education through a systematic analysis of a sample of published research papers. Three journals were examined. The data showed an absence of studies containing formally stated hypotheses, an absence of a variety of research methods, and the absence of concepts and theories. The author concludes that there is little distinction between common sense and scientific knowledge.

Cook, Lloyd Allen, *et al., College Programs in Intergroup Relations,* Washington, D. C., American Council on Education, 1950.

This is the first volume of a two-volume report of the College Study in Intergroup Relations, a project on teacher education conducted by the American Council on Education. It reports the various projects in a large number of colleges and universities.

Cook, Lloyd Allen, "Experimental Sociographic Study of a Stratified 10th Grade Class," *Amer. Soc. Rev.,* Vol. 10 (1945), pp. 250–261.

An experiment was designed to democratize pupil attitudes and behaviors through the use of group processes. The group was stratified with a view to determining the relationship of social stratification to friendship structure.

Cook, Lloyd Allen, *Intergroup Relations in Teacher Education*, Washington, D. C., The American Council on Education, 1951.

This is a final report on a four-year project in teacher education, the College Study in Intergroup Relations. The focus is on majority-minority relations seeking to combine theory and practice for improvement of intergroup education in colleges and schools. It is a study in school and community relations.

Cook, Lloyd Allen, *A Sociological Approach to Education*, New York, McGraw-Hill Book Company, 1950.

This is a revision of *Community Background of Education*. It is a problems approach to the study of the American community as it bears on school practice and public relations. It is somewhat oriented to teacher training and educational method. The institutional analysis is minimized.

Cunningham, Ruth, *et al.*, *Understanding Group Behavior of Boys and Girls*, New York, Bureau of Publications, Teachers College, Columbia University, 1951.

Sociometric methods were used to analyze differences in group structures by grade levels and to show changes in group structures over time periods.

Dahlke, H. Otto, "Determinants of Sociometric Relations Among Children in the Elementary School," *Sociometry*, Vol. 16 (1953), pp. 327–338.

For grades 2 to 8 in an elementary school sociometric choice was related to sex and personality adjustment. Social class structure was found within class groups with members preferring same occupational classes, i.e., those of semiskilled and clerical parentage.

Dahlke, H. Otto, and Thomas Monahan, "The Application of Sociometry to Schools," *The School Review*, Vol. 57 (1949), pp. 223–234.

A review of literature on the application of sociometry to schools.

Darley, J. G., N. Gross, and W. E. Martin, "Studies of Group Behavior: the Stability, Change, and Interrelations of Psychometric and Sociometric Variables," *Journal of Abnormal and Social Psychology*, Vol. 46 (1951), pp. 565–576.

Thirteen groups were studied for homogeneity on personality and sociometric variables. Tests and retests were compared. Satisfaction of girls with dormitory life was related to stability of population, high-in-group choices, and high mutual choices.

Davie, James S., *Education and Social Stratification*, Unpublished doctoral dissertation, Yale University, 1951.

A significant relationship between the position of the family in the social class structure of the community and the educational pattern of attendance of the children was found. Social class indices were based on ecological data.

Davie, James S., "Social Class Factors and School Attendance," *Harvard Educational Review*, Vol. 23 (1953), pp. 168–174.

Dr. Davie presents in this article his major findings from his doctoral dissertation, "Education and Social Stratification," Yale University, 1951. He shows that there is a significant relationship between the position of the family in the social class structure of the community and the educational pattern of attendance of the children. He analyzes some of the factors which he thinks operate to produce these differences.

Davis, Allison, "American Status Systems and the Socialization of the Child," in C. Kluckhorn, and H. A. Murray, *Personality in Nature, Society and Culture,* New York, Alfred Knopf, 1949.

Basic significance of age, sex, class instigations, and goals in the socialization of the human organism are examined.

Davis, Allison, *Social-Class Influences upon Learning,* Cambridge, Harvard University Press, 1948.

The central problem of the book was to describe the basic socialization of the human character and intellect as guided in middle-class and lower-class culture.

Davis, Allison, "Some Basic Concepts in the Education of Ethnic and Lower Class Groups," in Hilda Taba and William Van Til (eds.), *Democratic Human Relations,* Washington, D. C., National Education Association, 1945 (Sixteenth Yearbook, National Council for Social Studies).

"Race" and "culture" concepts were outlined, as well as the three systems of culture in America. Included is a discussion of acculturation of ethnic and lower class groups.

Dymond, Rosalind F., Anne S. Hughes, and Virginia L. Raabe, "Measurable Changes in Empathy with Age," *Journal of Consultative Psychology,* Vol. 16 (1952), pp. 202–206.

More popular children have better insight into empathetic response according to sociometric test.

Eells, Kenneth, "Some Implications for School Practice of the Chicago Studies of Cultural Bias in Intelligence Tests," *Harvard Educational Review,* Vol. 23 (1953), pp. 284–383.

An example of the meaning of cultural bias is presented. In view of this type of bias, implications are drawn for school administrators, classroom teachers, and guidance counselors. A case is made for caution in the use of results of traditional intelligence tests, the need for new culture-free tests, and the development of individual aptitudes.

Epley, Dean G., "Adolescent Role Relationships in the Dynamics of Prejudice," Unpublished doctoral dissertation, Michigan State University, 1953.

This is a study of prejudice in relation to the associations between students and between students and teachers. The author found that students who had positive relations with teachers were more likely to grow tolerant over a period of three years than students who were negative in their reactions to teachers.

Ericson, M. C., "Child Rearing and Social Status," in T. M. Newcomb, and E. L. Hartley, *Readings in Social Psychology,* New York, Henry Holt Company, 1947.

The inquiry was based on the proposition that, since social classes represent different learning environments, systematic differences could be found in child-rearing practices.

Feidler, F. E., W. G. Warrington, and F. J. Blaisdell, "Unconscious Attitudes as Correlates of Sociometric Choice in Social Group," *Journal of Abnormal and Social Psychology*, Vol. 47 (1952), pp. 790–796.

Fraternity men were found to perceive members they liked best as more like themselves than members they liked least.

Festinger, L., "The Role of Group Belonginess in a Voting Situation," *Human Relations*, Vol. 1 (1947), pp. 154–180.

Both Catholic and Jewish girls favor their own religious group in the election of a leader in small experimental groups. Catholics tend to vote for Catholics when religion is identified. Jews are more likely to be identified.

Fischer, P. H., "An Analysis of the Primary Group," *Sociometry*, Vol. 16 (1953), pp. 272–276.

According to a questionnaire given to 75 college students, frequency of contact and hours of contact per week of members of the group were the best predictors of group intimacy.

Flanders, N. A., "Personal-social Anxiety as a Factor in Experimental Learning Situations," *Journal of Educational Research*, Vol. 45 (1951), pp. 100–110.

Teacher-supporting group climate creates student hostility while student-supportive climate decreases anxiety from students and improves problem orientation.

Gardner, B. B., *et al.*, "Social Status and Education in a Southern Community," *School Review*, Vol. 50 (1942), pp. 179–191.

This study demonstrated that the school board, the school superintendent, the largest group of graduating pupils, the largest number of graduates attending college, and most of the teachers were upper middle class although they did not constitute the largest part of the community.

Getzels, J. W., "A Psychosociological Framework for the Study of Educational Adminstration," *Harvard Educational Review*, Vol. 22 (1952), pp. 235–246.

A structural-functional framework for formulating theory of school administration is proposed. Within the administrative relationship as the basic unit for inquiry three dimensions are described: (a) the authority dimension, (b) the role dimension, (c) the affectivity dimension. Empirical and research considerations of these dimensions are discussed.

Getzels, J. W., and E. G. Guba, "Role, Role Conflict and Effectiveness: an Empirical Study," *Amer. Soc. Rev.*, Vol. 19 (1954), pp. 164–175.

This investigation was concerned with examining the relationships existing in the military situation between two highly organized roles, those of officer and of teacher; the conflict between these roles when held by a single person; and the results of the conflict for the management of one of the roles. The study is primarily methodological.

Gordon, C. Wayne, "The Role of the Teacher in the Social Structure of the High School," *Journal of Educational Sociology*, Vol. 29 (1955), pp. 21–29.

This article is an analysis of the teacher role in the context of three aspects of school organization: (1) formal, (2) informal, (3) semi-formal, student organizations.

Gordon, Wayne C., *Social System in the High School,* Glencoe, Illinois, Free Press, 1957.

An analysis of the student social structure of one secondary school.

Gough, H. G., "Relationship of Socio-economic Status to Personality Inventory and Achievement Test Scores," *Journal of Educational Pychology,* Vol. 37 (1946), pp. 527–540.

Data are presented using socioeconomic status, age, intelligence, vocabulary, arithmetic, reading ability, language ability, health information, and personality adjustment. A slight positive relationship was found between socioeconomic status and academic achievement.

Berenda, Ruth M., *The Influence of the Group on the Judgments of Children,* New York, Columbia University Press, 1950.

This study reports an extended observation of children in school.

Grambs, Jean D., The Sociology of the 'Born Teacher,'" *Journal of Educational Sociology,* Vol. 25 (1952), pp. 532–541.

The teacher role is examined in relation to the elements of the "born teacher." The future teacher, it is suggested, learns to view the role from a negative cultural viewpoint, prevented from genuine insight. Social processes isolate the future teacher from any trying out of the teacher role, taboo on association with teachers and exclusive adult and peer influence over children. Born teachers are those who have escaped the typical cultural process of insulation, and have through informal teaching relationships and leadership positions moved into teaching.

Greenblatt, E. L., "Relationship of Mental Health to Social Status," *Journal of Educational Research,* Vol. 44 (1950), pp. 193–204.

The study examined the relationship between social status and mental health. No significant relationship was found.

Gronlund, Norman E., "Relationship Between the Sociometric Status of Pupils and Teachers' Preferences For or Against Having Them in Class," *Sociometry,* Vol. 16 (1953), pp. 142–150.

This study examined the relationship between teachers' preferences for or against having certain pupils in class and the number of choices those pupils receive on a sociometric test. Teachers tend to prefer those pupils that are highly chosen and least prefer those least chosen.

Gross, Neal, "A Critique of Social Class Structure and American Education," *Harvard Educational Review,* Vol. 23 (1953), pp. 298–329.

A critique of the special issue of the *Harvard Educational Review* volume devoted to the problems of social class and education. A tandem examination of the assumptions, methodology, and the propositions of the various articles is combined with a critical evaluation of issues raised.

Gross, Neal and Ward Mason, "Some Methodological Problems of Eight-hour Interviews," *Amer. J. Soc.,* Vol. 59 (1953–1954), pp. 197–204.

This is a methodological report of interview problems in the study of the occupational role of school superintendents. An unstructured question approach failed to reveal role-conflict situations. A combination of structured check-list questions and probes was followed by an open-ended series of questions. This succeeded. A role-within-a-role procedure for the interviewer was conducive to effective rapport.

Hallworth, H. J., "Sociometric Relationships Among Grammar School Boys and Girls Between the Ages of Eleven and Sixteen Years," *Sociometry*, Vol. 16 (1953), pp. 39–70.

By use of sociometric techniques the mode of development of hierarchical structures in children's groups and the value-systems associated with those structures were studied. Data were from English grammar schools.

Harrocks, J. E., and Mae E. Buker, "A Study of the Friendship Fluctuations of Pre-Adolescents," *Journal of Genetic Psychology*, Vol. 78 (1951), pp. 131–144.

A correlation was found among greater stability in friendship and increasing age and grade among pre-adolescent boys according to sociometric tests over a period of time.

Hartley, Ruth, *et al.*, *Understanding Children's Play*, New York, Columbia University Press, 1952.

Play activities are described as a prime factor in personality development in nursery school and kindergarten.

Havighurst, R. J., "Child Development in Relation to Community Structure," *Child Development*, Vol. 17 (1946), pp. 85–89.

Five studies are presented which investigated child development in a midwestern community, child rearing practices in relation to social stratification.

Havighurst, Robert J., and Allison Avis, "Child Socialization and the School," *Review of Educational Research*, Vol. 13 (1943), pp. 29–37.

Research is reviewed concerning socialization of children in and out of school.

Havighurst, R. J., and Mary Russell, "Promotion in the Armed Services in Relation to School Attainment and Social Status," *School Review*, Vol. 53 (1945), pp. 202–211.

Progress in rank in the armed forces was studied in relation to previous schooling in a sample of a "typical group of young men from a typical midwestern town." Positive relations were found between promotion and educational attainment before entering the services.

Havighurst, Robert J., and Hilda Taba, *Adolescent Character and Personality*, New York, John Wiley and Sons, 1949.

This volume reports a group of studies of factors related to the character and personality formation of adolescents. The relationship between community structure and its impact on the school as an agency of primary importance is the central focus which unifies the studies. Institutions other than the school are examined. The central thesis is that adaptation to school is dependent upon the ability to meet expectations of the school which is dominated by middle class values. Five modalities of character and personality types are described and illustrated with case studies. Implications are drawn for character education, and the various methods of studying character and personality are described.

Hayes, Margaret, *A Study of Classroom Disturbances of Eighth Grade Boys and Girls,* Contributions to Education No. 871, New York, Bureau of Publications, Teachers College, Columbia University, 1943.

An analysis of the types of behavior teachers expect in the classroom in relation to maintaining the conditions for learning activity. In her study of classroom disturbances, Hayes developed a list of types of behavior that constituted interference with the teacher's requirements for orderly classroom procedures.

Herrington, George Squires, "The Status of Educational Sociology Today," *Journal of Educational Sociology,* Vol. 21 (1947), pp. 129–139.

This survey of trends noted the decline in the institutions offering courses in educational sociology and the increase in the number of courses in general sociology taken by persons in education. Greater maturity and evidence of agreement regarding the nature and functions in the field have developed since 1926.

Hieronymus, A. N., "Study of Social Class Motivation: Relationships Between Anxiety for Education and Certain Socio-Economic and Intellectual Variables," *Journal of Educational Psychology,* Vol. 42 (1951), pp. 193–205.

Differences in social and economic expectancies of children from different socioeconomic groups and of the variations in their outlook on education were examined. Socialized anxiety was considered a factor in the selectivity of education.

Holland, John B., "Attitudes Toward Minority Groups in Relation to Rural Social Structure," Unpublished doctoral dissertation, Michigan State University, 1950.

This study examined the relationship between the amount of formal education and prejudice in a Midwestern rural community. People with more education expressed more tolerant attitudes than those with less education. Those with college education were most tolerant.

Hollingshead, A. B., *Elmstown's Youth,* New York, John Wiley and Sons, 1949.

The behavior of adolescents is a function of the positions that their families occupy in the social structure of the community. Clique membership was primarily of students in the same school grade and the same prestige class or adjacent one. Dating occurred within the same social class and adjacent classes. The social system of the high school operates as a reflection of the social class system of the community. Differentials in rewards and punishments, school dropouts, and participation in school activities are correlated with position in the community prestige structure.

Jackson, W. M., "Interaction in a College Fraternity," *Applied Anthropology,* Vol. 3 (1944), pp. 16–21.

Only the actions originated by the president of the college fraternity achieved satisfactory group action. Conclusion was based on a case study of leadership and communication patterns.

Jenkins, D. H., and R. Lippitt, *Interpersonal Perceptions of Teachers, Students and Parents,* Washington, D. C., National Education Association, 1951.

Three themes were drawn from interview and questionnaire data of children, their teachers, and parents: teachers are most interested in friendliness in all the relationships; power and control are primary in teacher-student and parent-child relations; and both teachers and parents have a common interest in social and extracurricular activities with the children.

Jennings, Helen H., *Leadership and Isolation,* 2d ed., New York, Longmans, Green, 1950.

This is a new edition of the classic study using sociometry as an approach to social structure and personality. Patterns of sociometry choice are analyzed in relation to leadership and isolation.

Jennings, Helen H., "Leadership and Sociometric Choice," *Sociometry,* Vol. 10 (1947), pp. 32–49.

Leadership patterns are analyzed from a sociometric study of a community of 400 individuals. Leaders were found to be highly chosen. Difference between socio (work group) and psyche (friendship group) are discussed.

Jennings, Helen H., "Sociometric Differentiation of the Psyche Group and the Socio Group," *Sociometry,* Vol. 10 (1947), pp. 71–79.

The work group and the friendship group are compared in a further analysis of the data for leadership and isolation.

Jennings, Helen H., "Sociometric Grouping in Relation to Child Development," in Caroline Tryon (ed.), *Fostering Mental Health in Our Schools,* Washington, D. C., Association for Supervision and Curriculum Development, National Education Association, 1950.

The author reviews the findings in sociometric research on the operation of groups, and draws implications for classroom situations.

Kahl, Joseph A., "Educational and Occupational Aspirations of 'Common Man' Boys," *Harvard Educational Review,* Vol. 23 (1953), pp. 186–203.

This study explored the social influences which account for differences in motivation to go on to college among high school boys of similar background, age, and intelligence level. It is an interview study of 24 boys of the "common man" or "working" class. Included is a report that indicated that IQ and family status were useful predictors of educational and occupational ambitions of high school boys. A further level of analysis was undertaken to examine the great variability in the percentage of boys with high IQ's going to college, dependent on father's occupation. A third level of analysis sought to explain the variability in percentage going to college, holding occupation of father constant. This analysis uncovered family pressure as possibly the important factor to explain differences in level of aspiration for high IQ boys whose fathers had lower-middle status occupations.

Kelley, Janet A., *College Life and the Mores,* New York, Bureau of Publications, Teachers College, Columbia University, 1949.

A description is given of the social organization on the campus and the cultural factors which influence it.

Kinney, Elva E. A., "A Study of Peer Group Social Acceptability at the Fifth Grade Level in a Public School," *Journal of Educational Research,* Vol. 47 (1953), pp. 57–64.

Fifth grade children using three groupings (entire grade, ability groups, and informal flexible groups) were studied. Use of informal groups increased the acceptance of isolates and created more cohesion.

Lemann, T. B., and N. Solomon, "Group Characteristics as Revealed in Sociometric Patterns and Personality Ratings," *Sociometry*, Vol. 15 (1952), pp. 7–90.

This study investigated certain group characteristics by means of data obtained from sociometric tests and rating scales, using as subjects the members of three small dormitories at a girls' college. On the basis of cohesiveness, the houses were ranked in the same order as the amount of insight.

Lenn, T. I., "Social Class: Conceptual and Operational Significance for Education," *Journal of Educational Sociology*, Vol. 25 (1952), pp. 51–61.

The article surveyed the major findings of a number of studies on social class covering a period of twenty-five years. A parallel is demonstrated between studies of "social class" by social scientists and the consideration educators have given the same subject.

Loeb, Martin B., "Implications of Status Differentiation for Personal and Social Development," *Harvard Educational Review*, Vol. 23 (1953), pp. 168–174.

The concept of the "core culture" is used in this discussion to view the American class system. Loeb finds that this culture is taught in our school, and the teacher is the mediator between the learner and the established culture. He draws implications of this point of view for education, child rearing, and social mobility. Propositions concerning status and social development are drawn from empirical studies of social class.

Loomis, C. P., and Harold B. Pepinsky, "Sociometry, 1937–1947: Theory and Methods," *Sociometry*, Vol. 11 (1948), pp. 87–103.

A survey of the method of sociometry. This review presents a summary of sociometric studies with special reference to the varying degrees of reliability in sociometric choice over short periods.

Mangus, A. R., "Effect of Mental and Educational Retardation on Personality Development of Children," *American Journal of Mental Deficiency*, Vol. 55 (1950), pp. 208–212.

The author studied retardation and its effect on elementary school children. He found one in six children to be retarded. They were found to be lacking in self-confidence, self-esteem, and a sense of personal worth. They were also considerably below par with respect to withdrawing tendencies, neurotic symptoms, family and school relations.

Mitchell, J. C., "A Study of Teachers' and Mental Hygienists' Rating of Certain Behavior Problems of Children," *Journal of Educational Research*, Vol. 36 (1943), pp. 292–307.

A restudy of E. K. Wickman's earlier evaluation of teachers' codes of desirable and problem behavior as determined by the mental hygienists' concepts of wholesome child behavior.

Moore, Clyde B., and William E. Cole, *Sociology in Educational Practice*, Cambridge, Houghton Mifflin Company, 1952.

In this general text educational sociology is viewed as the application of sociological knowledge to education. The result is a diffuse treatment of sociological aspects of education in relation to major social institutions.

Moreno, J. L., *Sociometry, Experimental Method and the Science of Society,* Boston, Beacon House, 1951.

Moreno summarizes data on methods and uses of sociometry.

Moreno, J. L., *Who Shall Survive?* rev. ed., New York, Beacon House, 1953.

This is a revision of the classic printed in 1934. Major revisions have been made bringing the material up to date.

Moreno, J. L., and Helen H. Jennings, "Sociometric Methods of Grouping and Regrouping; With Reference to Authoritative and Democratic Methods of Regrouping," *Sociometry,* Vol. 7 (1944), pp. 397–414.

Seating arrangements in a training school for girls, when guided by sociometric tests increased reciprocation of first choices and a decrease in the number of isolates.

Murray, W. I., "Measuring the Social-Class Status of Negro Children in the Elementary and High School," *Journal of Educational Sociology,* Vol. 25 (1951), pp. 102–111.

The article described the development of an instrument for measuring social-class status among Negroes.

Neugarten, Bernice L., "Social Class and Friendship Among Children," *Amer. J. Soc.,* Vol. 51 (1945–1946), pp. 305–313.

This study of friendship among children as related to social class revealed that in grades five and six the child from a family of upper status occupied an enviable position among his peers. On three grade levels children tended to choose friends from a class higher than their own and from their own social class. In grades ten and eleven upper status was a sure indicator that the adolescent would become the center of attention among his peers.

Phillips, E. L., "Intellectual and Personality Factors Associated with Social Class Attitudes Among Junior High School Children," *Pedagogical Seminary,* Vol. 77 (1950), pp. 61–72.

Phillips studied the relationships between class attitudes and measures of intelligence, personality, and socioeconomic status.

Pohlman, Vernon C., "Relationship Between Socioeconomic Status and Choice of High School," Unpublished doctoral dissertation, Washington University, 1953.

The author examines socioeconomic status of family as related to choice made by the student of type of high school (e.g., technical, commercial, etc.), in the city of St. Louis. Given consideration are the value systems of teachers in encouraging students to select type of school. Besides the factor of socioeconomic status, variables such as IQ and grade achievement are also incorporated for study.

Potashin, Reve, "A Sociometric Study of Children's Friendships," *Sociometry,* Vol. 9 (1946), pp. 48–70.

Persons who have mutual relationships were found to be chosen more often than persons in one-sided relationships.

Queen, Stuart A., William N. Chambers, and Charles M. Winston, *The American Social System,* Boston, Houghton Mifflin Company, 1956.

This volume on social control includes a chapter, "Education: A Social System

Within a System," which treats education in the United States in relation to social control.

Raths, Louis E. (ed.), "Emotional Needs and Teacher Training," *Journal of Educational Sociology,* Vol. 24 (1951), pp. 369–380.

Experimental programs seeking to assess emotional needs in teacher training are described.

Raths, Louis E. (ed.), "Social Class and Teacher Training," *Journal of Educational Sociology,* Vol. 25 (1952), pp. 437–492.

Four papers are included: "Our Status System and Scholastic Rewards," "Social Class Variation in Teacher-Pupil Relationship," "Wishes of Negro High School Seniors and Social Class Status," and "Social Mobility and Higher Education."

Raths, Louis E., and E. F. Schweickart, "Social Acceptance Within Interracial School Groups," *Educational Research Bulletin,* Vol. 25 (1946), pp. 85–90.

In the upper elementary grades in an Ohio school system social acceptance was found to cut across sex and race and seemed to be independent of both factors.

Rickey, H. G., and Nicholas Pastore, "Larger Social Context of Education," *Review of Educational Research,* Vol. 22 (1952), pp. 14–24.

Part of the review is devoted to research on social class, class mobility, and education. Class and IQ and other psychological, educational, and social factors are considered.

Robbins, Florence G., *Educational Sociology,* New York, Henry Holt and Company, 1953.

The author of this text views educational sociology as a special "sociological area which deals with the structural and dynamic aspects of the educative process." Following this definition, the materials are organized around three different topics: (a) social and cultural orientation of the child encompassing primarily the problem of socialization in child development; (b) social and cultural aspects of the school, which treats the school as an institutional system with its internal differentiations and their relationship to society; (c) integration of child, school, and community, which embraces the community approach to education.

Rose, Arnold, *Studies in Reduction of Prejudice,* 2d ed., Chicago, American Council on Race Relations, 1948.

A summary of studies in the reduction of prejudice.

Seeman, Melvin, "Role Conflict and Ambivalence in Leadership," *Amer. Soc. Rev.,* Vol. 18 (1953), pp. 373–380.

This report is a study of role conflict in the institutional position of the school superintendent. The analysis is in terms of four dimensions of the total cultural situation from which types of role conflict are derived. The four dimensions are: (a) the status, (b) authority, (c) institutional (particularistic-universalistic), and (d) means-ends. Three types of role conflict are analyzed from data collected bearing on the four dimensions of culture.

Sims, V. M., "Social Class Affiliations of a Group of Public School Teachers," *School Review,* Vol. 59 (1951), pp. 331–338.

Teachers and the relation of their social position. A positive relationship was found between social-class identification and conservatism. The large majority of teachers were from the "middle and upper-middle classes."

Sims, V. M., "Some Correlates of Social Class Identification Among High School and College Students," *School Review*, Vol. 60 (1952), pp. 160–163.

Data on social-class identification among college freshmen, high school seniors, and vocational students in a large urban high school are reported. Self-assignment is to social classes closely related to their projected college attendance and ability to do college work. Particular aptitudes were not related to self-assignment to social class status.

Smith, H. P., "A Study of the Selective Character of American Secondary Education: Participation in School Activities as Conditioned by Socio-economic Status and Other Factors," *Journal of Educational Psychology*, Vol. 36 (1945), pp. 229–246.

Extracurricular activities tended to be highly selective in terms of socioeconomic status.

Smucker, Orden, "Near-sociometric Analysis as a Basis for Guidance," *Sociometry*, Vol. 12 (1949), pp. 326–340.

Smucker discusses the advantages of using sociometric indices of peer acceptance for personal problems in a college.

Smucker, Orden and Lucille Nick, "A Sociometric Study of Dormitory Cleavages on Michigan State College Campus," Unpublished master's thesis, Michigan State University, 1949.

Clique patterns in a girls' dormitory were analyzed by use of a sociometric test. Number, size, and degree of closure were studied. The clique is more influential than the larger dormitory or larger campus unit; the clique is the focus of socialization to campus culture, the restraint on academic achievement, and the family away from the family.

Stendler, Celia Burns, *Children of Brasstown*, Urbana, University of Illinois Press, 1949.

Stendler's study of a Midwestern community shows at what age levels and grades children become aware of social class differences and suggests that the value system of the school can inhibit social class evaluation within the school. First grade shows no awareness of social class symbols; fourth grade shows some awareness and eighth grade pupils are very much like adults. Implications for education are drawn.

Stendler, Celia, Dora Asmrin, and Aleyne C. Haines, "Studies in Cooperation and Competition; I. The Effects of Working for Group and Individual Rewards on the Social Climate of Children's Groups," *Journal of Genetic Psychology*, Vol. 79 (1950), pp. 173–197.

Second grade children showed more positive interaction when working for a group prize than when working for individual prizes. Group size studied was eight.

Taba, Hilda, *et al.*, *Curriculum in Intergroup Relations*, Washington, D. C., American Council on Education, 1949.

This is a manual of curriculum practices and techniques for intergroup education using sociodramatic or role-taking techniques.

Taba, Hilda, *et al., Diagnosing Human Relations Needs,* Washington, D. C., American Council on Education, 1951.

Techniques are described for the study of social interaction in the classroom.

Taba, Hilda, *et al., Intergroup Education in Public Schools,* Washington, D. C., American Council on Education, 1953.

This is the final report of a five-year experimental program in cooperating schools.

Taba, Hilda, Elizabeth Hall Brady, and John T. Robinson, *Intergroup Education in the Public Schools,* Washington, D. C., American Council on Education, 1952.

This is a general report on the work of the Project in Intergroup Education in Cooperating Schools sponsored by the American Council on Education. It is a statement of the principles and theories that guided the project.

Taba, Hilda, and Deborah Elkins, *With Focus on Human Relations,* Washington, D. C., American Council on Education, 1950.

A case study of an eighth grade class is reported.

Taba, Hilda, and William Van Til, *Democratic Human Relations,* Washington, D. C., National Council for the Social Studies, 1945.

This is a summary of practices in intergroup and intercultural education in the social studies. It is based on an inquiry made among teachers throughout the United States.

Terrien, Frederick W., "The Behavior System and Occupational Type Associated with Teaching," Unpublished doctoral dissertation, Yale University, 1950.

A study of the behavior system of teaching with reference to the channeling of behavior into patterns and the existence of occupational type.

Terrien, Frederick W., "The Occupational Roles of Teachers," *Journal of Educational Sociology,* Vol. 29 (1955), September, pp. 14–20.

This article reports part of an extensive study undertaken in 1949 in an Eastern city to test the hypothesis that an occupation could act to channel the behavior of its incumbents into an identifiable system both on and off the job. The inquiry sought further to determine whether occupational types are correlated with these systems. Data were obtained from interviews of a randomly selected 10 per cent sample of 1,000 teachers. Extensive inquiry was directed toward activities, attitudes, goals, patterns of life organization, and beliefs of these teachers. The major proposition that behavior is channeled into systems, and that an occupational type is determined was substantiated. This paper reports only part of the larger study; it is concerned with the forces in the community which combine with the process of behavior-system formation and occupational typing in the profession of teaching which defines the occupational role.

Trow, W. C., A. E. Zander, W. C. Morse, and D. H. Jenkins, "Psychology of Group Behavior: The Class as a Group," *Journal of Educational Psychology,* Vol. 41 (1950), pp. 322–338.

Findings from the field of group dynamics are considered in relation to the problems of the teacher and the classroom.

Warner, W. Lloyd, *et al., Democracy in Jonesville,* New York, Harper and Brothers, 1949.

Warner's study shows that teachers belong to middle class almost without exception and this profoundly affects the behavior patterns which are emphasized in the schools.

Warner, W. Lloyd, R. J. Havighurst, and M. B. Loeb, *Who Shall Be Educated? The Challenge of Unequal Opportunities,* New York, Harper and Brothers, 1944.

Evidence is presented regarding social class influences in the distribution of unequal educational opportunities, and the schools are indicted for continuing to serve the social system by keeping down many who might aspire to higher status.

Washbourne, Chandler, "Involvement as a Basis of Stress Analysis: A Study of High School Teachers," Unpublished doctoral dissertation, Michigan State University, 1953.

The study is a part of a larger study conducted by the Social Research Service of Michigan State University. It examined the nature of stress in the general situation of the teacher status as well as situational aspects of teaching.

West, James, *Plainville,* New York, Columbia University Press, 1945.

This study of social stratification in a small Midwestern community has general significance for understanding the role of the school in the community. A section on the school deals with some cultural discontinuities between school and community.

Willerman, B., and L. Swanson, "An Ecological Determinant of Differential Amounts of Sociometric Choices Within College Sororities," *Sociometry,* Vol. 15 (1952), pp. 326–329.

Those living together in the sorority tend to choose each other more frequently than those living outside tend to choose each other.

Williams, Robin M., Jr., *The Reduction of Intergroup Tensions; a Survey of Research on Problems of Ethnic, Racial and Religious Group Relations,* New York, Social Science Research Council Bulletin 57, 1942.

Williams provides a twofold classification of the techniques used for controlling intergroup relations: one approach which seeks a modification of the situation in which the person acts or redefines the situation without changing it overtly; a second approach that appeals to the values and attitudes of individuals without changing the situation for action.

Withall, J., "The Development of a Technique for the Measurement of Social-emotional Climate in Classrooms," *Journal of Experimental Education,* Vol. 17 (1949), pp. 347–361.

A system of categories was developed to distinguish learner-oriented from teacher-reoriented statements.

Withall, J., "The Development of the Climate Index," *Journal of Educational Research,* Vol. 45 (1951), pp. 93–100.

An index for classifying teacher statements is presented as a tool to examine social-emotional climate in the learning situation.

Wrightstone, J. W., "Measuring the Social Climate of a Classroom," *Journal of Educational Research*, Vol. 44 (1951), pp. 341–351.

A scale for describing the social climate of a classroom in terms of teacher-pupil rapport is described.

Zeleny, Leslie D., "New Directions in Educational Sociology and the Teaching of Sociology," *Amer. Soc. Rev.*, Vol. 13 (1948), pp. 336–341.

In a note on teaching and research the author examines the current condition of educational achievement and points out the distinctive role of educational sociologists who by training are specialists best equipped to guide educators in the development of curriculum. Also he finds in sociometry a technique best suited to measure the degree of progress in personality development.

Zeleny, Leslie D., "Status, Its Measurement and Control in Education," *Sociometry*, Vol. 4 (1941), pp. 193–204.

The author hypothesized that status, defined as the "average intensity of the attitudes expressed toward a person by his associates in a group," was measurable. He explained how social status indices were computed and wrote that these indices have been "shown to be both a reliable and a valid measure of status defined."

# The sociology of politics

JOSEPH R. GUSFIELD
*University of Illinois*

The sociology of politics studies political institutions with the perspectives and concepts which sociologists have found useful in studying other institutions. It views the State as susceptible to study by general theories of human groups and human behavior.

This bibliography emphasizes the growing interpenetration between sociological theory and the study of specific institutions. The works selected include significant efforts during the 1945–1955 period to apply sociological categories and theories to political behavior. The selections were chosen both for their intrinsic merit and for the contribution they make to the development of a body of findings sufficiently related to constitute the application of sociology to politics.

That political institutions cannot be completely understood by formal analysis of legal structure and chronological history has long been understood. Plato's discussion of the relation between political structure, social stratification, and personality type represents a detailed theory of politics. The writings of the social contract theorists—Hobbes, Locke, Rousseau, and Kant—are based on their judgment of the limits and possibilities of attaining social order without great use of force. The social group, with articulate interests, is the key actor in the political analysis of *The Federalist Papers*. One finds in the writings of perceptive travelers, such as Herodotus or de Tocqueville, a great many hypotheses on the relation between the culture of the society and its governmental system.

The systematic approach of a political sociology, however, may be said to begin with the writings of Karl Marx. The interpretation of political conflict as a manifestation of the conflict between economic and social groups, the relation of ideology to social structure, and the impact of technological and economic change on politics all resulted from Marx's influence. The European sociologists, Karl Mannheim, Max Weber, and Roberto Michels have built on or reacted against the writings of Marx. From the work of these sociologists has emerged the major theoretical problems of political sociology, such as class conflict, bureaucratization, mass democracy and irrationality, and the careers of political movements. It is worth noting that the impact of such work has not been narrowly political but has had general sociological influence.

Within American political sociology, the empirical spirit has been manifest since World War I. The great concern with political corruption in American politics led to many studies of machine politics, which stressed the "natural" development of this institution. Political scientists such as Lasswell and Gosnell utilized the findings of clinical psychology, the concepts of social stratification, and the findings of social psychology to understand such phenomena as political leadership and voting behavior. Quantitative methods, first developed in sociological studies, were drafted for the study of public opinion and propaganda.

It should be clear that the sociology of politics is not a substitute for traditional political science. American government, for example, cannot be easily analyzed without an understanding of the American Constitution. Sociology of politics attempts to get beyond and behind legal and historical analysis to the structural and dynamic elements of the society which bear upon its governmental institutions. As such, it has produced some of the most fruitful results of the growing interdisciplinary character of American social science.

This bibliography is divided into six major categories, each of which refers to a general body of sociological theories and findings. Thus the category "Collective Behavior" illustrates the application of collective

behavior hypotheses and theories to political behavior. The notations
are intended to give a clearer picture of the contents and to point out
cross references.

## I. THEORETICAL AND GENERAL

This category includes works which attempt to state the major concepts and ideas of political sociology.

• Davis, Kingsley, *Human Society*, New York, The Macmillan Co., 1949, Chap. 18,
"Political Institutions."

> An attempt to define the major functions of government. Rich in materials
> drawn from primitive and Oriental cultures.

Lasswell, Harold, and Abraham Kaplan, *Power and Society*, New Haven, Yale University Press, 1950.

> Written by a political scientist and a philosopher, this work attempts to state
> the major hypotheses of the field of political study in systematic propositional
> form.

MacIver, Robert, *The Web of Government*, New York, The Macmillan Co., 1947.

> A general work on bases, forms, and transformations of governments. Devotes
> attention to the cultural basis of political authority.

Weber, Max, *From Max Weber: Essays in Sociology*, trans. by H. Gerth and C. W.
Mills, New York, Oxford University Press, 1946.

> The translation of Weber's writings into English is perhaps the most significant
> development in political sociology during the past ten years. See Part I, "Science
> and Politics," for a discussion of the nature of political action.

Weber, Max, *The Theory of Social and Economic Organization*, trans. by A. M.
Henderson and Talcott Parsons, New York, Oxford University Press, 1947.

> Weber's treatment of legitimacy and authority has had great influence. See
> pp. 87–158, 324–362, 412–423.

## II. GROUP BEHAVIOR

Political institutions have often been seen as areas in which various
social groups—economic, ethnic, social class, and others—seek representation. The sociologist studies the structure of the major groups within
the society, changes affecting such groups, and the associational structures through which such groups are organized politically.

In these works, the interests influential in the analysis of political behavior are related to concrete groups and to their position in the social
and economic structure.

The "pressure group" and other organizations by which social groups attempt to function politically are also foci of sociological interest. Such studies are more interested in the internal structure and dynamics of the organization than in the tactics of influence. They explore the nature of representation through private associations in a pluralistic society.

Bailey, Stephen, *Congress Makes a Law*, New York, Columbia University Press, 1950.

A study of the passage of the Full Employment Act of 1946.

Bendix, Reinhard, "Social Stratification and Political Power," *Amer. Pol. Sci. Rev.*, Vol. 46 (1952), pp. 357–375.

An analysis of the Marxian approach to the study of politics. Bendix casts doubt on the adequacy of the approach in studying modern political movements.

Berelson, Bernard, Paul Lazarsfeld, and William McPhee, *Voting*, Chicago, University of Chicago Press, 1954.

A study of the 1948 presidential election based on data from Elmira, N. Y. Group affiliation is treated specifically in Chaps. 3 and 4.

Centers, Richard, *The Psychology of Social Classes*, Princeton, Princeton University Press, 1949.

A study of public opinion data which relates political opinion to socioeconomic status and to self-perception of status. The author argues for a theory of class consciousness among American occupational groups.

Clark, S. D., "The Religious Sect in Canadian Politics," *Amer. J. Soc.*, Vol. 51 (1945), pp. 207–216.

An unusual study of the political role of evangelical sects and churches. Clark examines the sect-church transition as an explanation for the political opportunism of the evangelical churches in Canada.

Cleveland, Alfred, "National Association of Manufacturers—Spokesman for Industry?" *Harv. Bus. Rev.*, Vol. 26 (1948), pp. 353–369.

A study of a "pressure group" which questions their claim to representativeness. Analyzes the sources of disunity in the N.A.M.

Gusfield, Joseph R., "Organizational Change: A Study of the Woman's Christian Temperance Union," Unpublished doctoral dissertation, University of Chicago, 1954.

A study of the changes in social composition and internal structure of one "pressure group." Contains data on internal conflicts and their relation to the policies of the group.

Heberle, Rudolf, *Social Movements*, New York, Appleton-Century-Crofts, 1950.

Heberle analyzes social movements and political parties largely as manifestations of group aims.

Key, V. O., *Politics, Parties and Pressure Groups*, New York, Thomas Y. Crowell, 1947.

A far better than average text. Part I is a description of the most significant groups in American politics.

Latham, Earl, *The Group Basis of Politics,* Ithaca, Cornell University Press, 1952.

A study of basing-point legislation and the role of the Cement Institute. Contains a valuable theoretical chapter on the role of the "group" concept in political theory.

Lubell, Samuel, *The Future of American Politics,* New York, Harper and Brothers, 1952.

A brilliant analysis of contemporary American politics. Lubell analyzes the impact of changes in American social structure on economic, religious, racial, and ethnic groups. Using voting returns, he finds these changes reflected in voting trends. Includes a theory of American political parties based on their functions as "brokers of political interests."

Mannheim, Karl, "The Sociological Problem of Generations," in Paul Keckameti (ed.), *Essays on the Sociology of Knowledge,* New York, Oxford University Press, 1953.

One of the most significant writings in the sociology of politics, now available in English. Mannheim here analyzes the consequences for political life of the fact that society contains groups whose socialization has occurred at different points in time.

Riesman, David, and Nathan Glazer, "The Intellectuals and the Discontented Classes," *Partisan Rev.,* Vol. 32 (1955), pp. 47–72.

An insightful analysis of current shifts in American politics as they reflect changes in American social structure and culture since World War II.

Seidman, Joel, Jack London, and Bernard Karsh, "Political Consciousness in a Local Union," *Pub. Opin. Quart.,* Vol. 15 (1951–1952), pp. 692–702.

A study of the opinions of members of a local union in a union town. Indicates the narrow conception of union political interests held by members.

Truman, David, *The Governmental Process,* New York, Alfred A. Knopf, 1951.

An excellent and significant discussion of government from the interest group viewpoint. Summarizes a great deal of current research on political behavior. Part II is an excellent summary of existent studies on the cohesion of organized interest groups.

## III. INSTITUTIONAL BEHAVIOR

This category includes works which study governmental institutions through the general understanding of social organization. Bureaucratization, for example, constitutes a body of theory which has been applied to labor unions, businesses, and other institutions as well as to government. The emphasis of these materials is not on the representational character of political institutions, as it is in the materials using the group as central concept. These materials treat governmental institutions as patterns of behavior with their own traditions, habits, systems of stratification, and other features of organized behavior. The structure of public administration and its social context, the informal organization of legislative bodies and the operation of political parties are described and analyzed in the materials listed below.

Bendix, Reinhard, *Higher Civil Servants in America,* Boulder, Colorado, University of Colorado Press, 1949.

A study of the social and educational backgrounds of civil servants. Valuable both for its data on social backgrounds and for its analysis of recruitment channels.

Clinard, Marshall, *The Black Market,* New York, Rinehart and Co., 1952.

A study of one form of white-collar crime. Illustrates the relation between administration and community values and norms.

Esman, Milton, "Administrative Stability and Change," *Amer. Pol. Sci. Rev.,* Vol. 44 (1950), pp. 872–885.

A discussion of ways by which administrative groups accommodate to political and social changes.

Garceau, Oliver, and Corrine Silverman, "A Pressure Group and the Pressured," *Amer. Pol. Sci. Rev.,* Vol. 48 (1954), pp. 672 601.

An unusual study of the legislator's knowledge and use of pressure groups in one session of the Vermont legislature. Casts much doubt on many stereotypes of "pressure group government."

Heberle, Rudolf, *Social Movements,* New York, Appleton-Century-Crofts, 1950.

Heberle treats political parties as social movements. Part V analyzes much material on the structure of American and European parties.

Key, V. O., *Southern Politics,* New York, Alfred A. Knopf, 1949.

A thorough study of a one-party system.

Lipset, Seymour, "The Political Process in Trade Unions," in Morroe Berger, Theodore Abel, and Charles Page (eds.), *Freedom and Control in Modern Society,* New York, Van Nostrand, 1954.

Although this is a study of trade unions, its conclusions are stated in a manner general enough to be applicable to other situations. Many of the organizational and leadership crises discussed are clearly analogous to the structure of legislative bodies.

Merton, Robert, *et al.* (eds.), *A Reader in Bureaucracy,* Glencoe, Ill., The Free Press, 1952.

A collection of articles and excerpts from larger works on the general problem of bureaucracy. Contains many readings on governmental bureaucracy.

Michels, Roberto, *First Lectures in Political Sociology,* trans. by Alfred de Grazia, Minneapolis, University of Minnesota Press, 1949.

A group of papers by one of the leading thinkers in the sociology of politics. See especially Chap. 7, 'The Sociological Character of Political Parties."

Page, Charles, "Bureaucracy's Other Face," *Social Forces,* Vol. 25 (1946), pp. 88–94.

Emphasizes the informal structure which develops parallel to formal organization. Based on the author's experiences in the U. S. Navy.

Rossi, P., *A Communist Party in Action,* New Haven, Yale University Press, 1949.

A study of the French Communist party. Rossi describes the organization and appeals of the party.

Selznick, Philip, *TVA and the Grass Roots,* Berkeley and Los Angeles, University of California Press, 1949.

An excellent study of a governmentally operated enterprise. Emphasizes the role of internal structure in the determination of policy.

Selznick, Philip, *The Organizational Weapon,* New York, McGraw-Hill Book Co., 1952.

A study of the Communist Party in democratic countries. Based on written documents. Contains a stimulating chapter on mass society and political manipulation.

Truman, David, *The Governmental Process,* New York, Alfred A. Knopf, 1951.

Truman's analysis of the legislative process includes the role of the group life of the legislature itself as a factor in its behavior. See Chap. 11, "Dynamics of Access in the Legislative Process," and Chap. 12, "The Techniques of Interest Groups in the Legislative Process."

Weber, Max, *From Max Weber: Essays in Sociology,* trans. by H. Gerth and C. W. Mills, New York, Oxford University Press, 1946.

The most influential discussion of bureaucratization in sociological literature. See pp. 196–241, 253–265. The essay "Politics as a Vocation" is a profound analysis of the implications for mass democracy of political party structure and political leadership.

## IV. POLITICAL STRATIFICATION

Gouldner, Alvin (ed.), *Studies in Leadership,* New York, Harper and Brothers, 1950.

A collection of writings, many of them new, on the topic of leadership. The focus is on leadership in large-scale organizations. Many of the papers are relevant to political leadership and authority.

*Hoover Institute Studies in Elites,* Palo Alto, Stanford University Press, 1951, 1952.

A group of studies on the composition of political elites in various countries. Daniel Lerner, *The Nazi Elite* and Robert C. North, *Kuomintang Chinese Communist Elites* present considerable data on the social backgrounds of elites. Also see Harold Lasswell, *The Comparative Study of Elites.*

Hunter, Floyd, *Community Power Structure,* Chapel Hill, University of North Carolina Press, 1953.

A unique study of the elite of a city. The setting is local and the author traces the relation between informal power and the operation of the political system. A good instance of the relation between economic and political elites.

Sanford, Fillmore, "Public Orientation to Roosevelt," *Pub. Opin. Quart.*, Vol. 15 (1951), pp. 189–216.

An analysis of leadership appeals, based on a study of attitudes toward Franklin Roosevelt. The author argues that acceptance or rejection of leadership depends on psychological factors in the follower, such as material dependency, need for warm appeal, and need to submit to strong authority.

Seligman, Lester, "The Study of Political Leadership," *Amer. Pol. Sci. Rev.*, Vol. 44 (Dec. 1950), pp. 904–915.

A summary of leadership studies, with emphasis on the need for studying political leadership in situational contexts.

Weber, Max, *From Max Weber: Essays in Sociology*, trans. by H. Gerth and C. W. Mills, New York, Oxford University Press, 1946.

See Chap. 9, "The Sociology of Charismatic Authority."

## V. COLLECTIVE BEHAVIOR

The semiamorphous and often spontaneous rise of social movements has always interested the historian and the sociologist. Democratic mass society has made us more concerned with these phenomena and with the impact of the "public" in political affairs. Materials listed below are concerned with the sociological study of social movements and with analysis of public opinion and voting.

Almond, Gabriel, *The American People and Foreign Policy*, New York, Harcourt, Brace, 1950.

An analysis of the role of public opinion in the determination of foreign policy. Contains a valuable discussion of different types of publics.

Arendt, Hannah, *The Origins of Totalitarianism*, New York, Harcourt, Brace, 1951.

A stimulating analysis of the roots of German Fascism and Russian Communism in the conditions of contemporary Western society. The author shows great originality in tracing the relations between nineteenth century experience and the present.

Berelson, Bernard, Paul Lazarsfeld, and William McPhee, *Voting*, Chicago, University of Chicago Press, 1954.

A voting study that adds greatly to our understanding of the social process within which voting decisions are made.

Bruner, Jerome, and Sheldon Korchin, "The Boss and the Vote," *Pub. Opin. Quart.*, Vol. 10 (1946), pp. 1–23.

A study of voting and voter opinion in the Boston mayoralty election of 1945. One of the few studies of local elections.

Campbell, Angus, and Robert L. Kahn, *The People Elect a President*, Ann Arbor, Mich., Survey Research Center, Institute for Social Research, 1954.

Campbell, Angus, Gerald Gurin, and Warren Miller, *The Voter Decides*, Ann Arbor, Mich., Survey Research Center, Institute for Social Research, 1954.

These are studies of the 1948 and 1952 presidential elections. Based on surveys of a national sample.

Egbert, Donald, and Stowe Persons (eds.), *Socialism and American Life*, 2 Vols., Princeton, Princeton University Press, 1952.

A collection of lengthy essays on various aspects of the American Socialist movement. The second volume is an exhaustive bibliography.

Green, Arnold, and Eleanor Melnick, "What Has Happened to the Feminist Movement?" in Alvin Gouldner (ed.), *Studies in Leadership*, New York, Harper and Brothers, 1950.

The woman's movement collapsed after the attainment of suffrage. This article analyzes the reasons for this collapse, emphasizing the class cleavages in the movement.

Katz, Daniel, *et al.* (eds.), *Public Opinion and Propaganda*, New York, The Dryden Press, 1954.

A collection of readings prepared by the Society for the Psychological Study of Social Issues. Contains a useful section on methods, as well as materials on most phases of public opinion.

Lipset, Seymour, *Agrarian Socialism*, Berkeley and Los Angeles, University of California Press, 1950.

An analysis of the rise to power of the C. C. F. in Saskatchewan. Particularly good for its discussion of conditions giving rise to agrarianism.

Mannheim, Karl, "Conservative Thought," in Paul Kecksmeti (ed.), *Essays on Sociology and Social Psychology*, New York, Oxford University Press, 1953.

One of Mannheim's early and important writings, at last available in English. Mannheim traces the role of social position as a source for the idea systems of political conservatism.

Messinger, Sheldon, "Organizational Transformation," *Amer. Soc. Rev.*, Vol. 20 (1955), pp. 3–10.

This is a study of a declining movement, the Townsend Clubs. It indicates the strength of organizational values over ideology.

Saenger, Gerhart, "Social Status and Political Behavior," *Amer. J. Soc.*, Vol. 51 (1945), pp. 103–113.

This study is representative of many which relate group affiliations to political opinion. Emphasizes the dilemma of "cross-pressures" when the voter has contradictory affiliations.

Shils, Edward, "Authoritarianism: Right and Left," in Richard Christie and Marie Johoda (eds.), *Studies in the Scope and Method of the Authoritarian Personality*, Glencoe, Ill., The Free Press, 1954.

A critical examination of some propositions in *The Authoritarian Personality*. In the course of the discussion the author presents some valuable hypotheses concerning recruitment into movements.

Weber, Max, *Theory of Social and Economic Organization,* trans. by A. M. Henderson and Talcott Parsons, New York, Oxford University Press, 1947.

See pp. 363–407, "The Routinization of Charisma."

## VI. THE PERSON

We must not lose sight of the fact that political behavior is one phase of human behavior. The individual brings to it his particular personal makeup. It may involve his loyalties and interests at different levels of identification. Clinical and social psychology have greatly enriched our understanding of human beings. They have also been a rich source for theory and hypothesis in political sociology. The materials listed here discuss political leadership, movements, public opinion and other areas of politics as influenced by factors of personality.

Adorno, T. W., E. Frenkel-Brunswik, *et al., The Authoritarian Personality,* New York, Harper and Brothers, 1950.

This is an elaborate study of the relation between anti-Semitic attitudes, personality type, and political opinion. The study is based on a variety of methods and instruments.

Almond, Gabriel, *The Appeals of Communism,* Princeton, Princeton University Press, 1954.

A study of former Communist Party members in Europe and the United States. Tries to discover why they joined and why they left.

Berelson, Bernard, *et al., Voting,* Chicago, University of Chicago Press, 1954.

Contains much material on social characteristics of active participants in political campaigns.

De Grazia, Sebastian, *The Political Community,* Chicago, University of Chicago Press, 1948.

An examination of the relationship between political authority and the citizen which rests on certain insights of psychiatric theory.

Goldhamer, Herbert, "Public Opinion and Personality," *Amer. J. Soc.,* Vol. 55 (1950), pp. 346–354.

Takes issue with many current theories of personality and politics.

Kornhauser, William, "Liberal and Radical Political Careers," Unpublished doctoral dissertation, University of Chicago, 1953.

An excellent study of the amateur political activist. Based on extensive interviews.

Lasswell, Harold, *Power and Personality,* New York, W. W. Norton and Co., 1948.

A systematic treatise by a political scientist closely associated with the use of personality theory in political science. The concern is with the power-seeker rather than the public.

Orwell, George, *A Collection of Essays*, Garden City, N. Y., Doubleday Anchor Books, 1954.

Anyone interested in political sociology should have an acquaintance with Orwell's essays as well as his novel *1984*. In this volume see "Raffles and Miss Blandish," "Politics and the English Language," and "Inside the Whale."

Parsons, Talcott, *Essays in Sociological Theory*, Glencoe, Ill., The Free Press, 1949, pp. 298–322.

A discussion of the major socialization agencies and institutions of modern industrial society. Parsons relates frustrations arising from structural sources to their displacement in political areas. Emphasizes the disorganizing consequences for traditional security systems of the rise of science.

Riesman, David, *The Lonely Crowd*, New Haven, Yale University Press, 1950.

A unique book of great perception. Riesman presents a theory of change in American character type. He discusses the consequences of this change for the uses of politics in American life. The book also contains a penetrating discussion of shifts in American ruling classes. Also see Riesman's *Faces in the Crowd*, New Haven, Yale University Press, 1952, for an essay on the relation of character to politics.

Riesman, David, and Nathan Glazer, "Criteria for Political Apathy," in Alvin Gouldner (ed.), *Studies in Leadership*, New York, Harper and Brothers, 1950.

A stimulating discussion of the uses of politics in American life.

Rosenberg, Morris, "The Meaning of Politics in the Mass Society," *Pub. Opin. Quart.*, Vol. 15 (1951), pp. 5–15.

Some reasons for political indifference. Contains a useful typology of functions of political discussion.

# Culture change

JUNE MACKLIN
*Connecticut College*

Phenomena of permanence and change in human history have long enjoyed much attention of a speculative nature. More systematic approaches to cultural change, as a part of the problem of cultural stability, have been possible with the development of sociology and anthropology.

Studies of the last half of the nineteenth century were couched in terms of unilinear evolution: extant peoples were arranged hierarchically according to sociocultural "stages" of development, and there was a corollary concern with social and cultural origins.

Early twentieth century work stressed empirical research and resulted in the accumulation of ethnographic data which served to force recognition of the fact of diffusion, thus outmoding nineteenth century evolutionism. Diffusionist and historicalist approaches assumed the conservatism of culture, and reconstructed culture history by studying the temporal and spatial distribution of specific traits and trait complexes.

Starting in the early 1920's, theoretical orientation was avowedly non-historical, with emphasis on structure, pattern, personality analysis, cultural dynamics, and the functioning of each aspect of a given culture in relation to every other aspect.

During the past fifteen years, cultural dynamics have been examined in connection with culture contact situations, especially those in which European peoples have influenced nonliterate groups. It is often felt that the *processes* involved in change can be more clearly perceived by studying such acculturation.

Despite a plethora of culture change studies, most recent reviews of the field reveal the need for terminological clarification, developing theoretical structures, and a reappraisal of objectives and methods. Certain problem areas of common interest do emerge, however, and have been used here as the categories for organizing some representative studies of culture change from January 1, 1945, to December, 1955.

Since this bibliography purports to look at how change has been handled on the cultural rather than the social level, anthropological works predominate. Works have been included in the bibliography which were considered to have theoretical or methodological significance.

## CULTURE CHANGE: GENERAL

Barnett, Homer G., *Innovation,* New York, McGraw-Hill, 1953.

The first modern book-length study of culture change theory, this treatment focuses on innovation itself as the crux of the problem.

Gillin, John, *The Ways of Men,* New York, Appleton-Century-Crofts, 1948, pp. 532–569.

These pages of Gillin's book offer a concise, systematic analysis of change and the conditions and processes involved in acceptance or rejection of innovation.

Gluckman, Max, *An Analysis of the Sociological Theories of Bronislaw Malinowski,* Capetown, Rhodes-Livingstone Papers, 1949.

Pertinent here for the critical review of Malinowski's functional analysis of change.

Hallowell, A. I., "Personality Structure and the Evolution of Man," *American Anthropologist,* Vol. 52 (1950), pp. 159–173.

This article systematically formulates the way in which psychological characteristics are combined with the physiological to form man's psychobiological nature.

Herskovits, M. J., *Man and His Works: The Science of Cultural Anthropology,* New York, Alfred A. Knopf, 1948, pp. 459–608.

These sections on cultural dynamics and variation state the problem of change as seen by a worker long interested in the field.

Hodgen, Margaret T., *Change and History*, Viking Fund Publications in Anthropology, No. 18, New York, Wenner-Gren Foundation for Anthropological Research, 1952.

Only after she has thoroughly examined the detailed historical data attendant to technological change in England is historian-anthropologist Margaret Hodgen willing to venture certain generalizations about the dynamics of change. Discussion of social scientific methodology is also included.

Keesing, Felix M., *Culture Change: An Analysis and Bibliography of Anthropological Sources to 1952*, Stanford, Stanford University Press, 1953.

Following a tightly packed ninety-page summary of how culture change has been handled within anthropology up to 1952, Keesing presents an exhaustive, chronologically arranged bibliography.

Kluckhohn, C., H. A. Murray, and D. M. Schneider, *Personality in Nature, Society, and Culture*, New York, Alfred A. Knopf, 1954.

Many of the selections in this volume, plus the introductory chapters presenting a theoretical framework, are relevant to culture process.

Kroeber, A. L., *Anthropology: Race, Language, Culture, Psychology, Prehistory*, New York, Harcourt, Brace and Co., 1948.

Kroeber devotes a third of his *Anthropology* to developing a frame of reference for understanding total culture growth.

Kroeber, A. L. (ed.), *Anthropology Today: An Encyclopedic Inventory*, Chicago, University of Chicago Press, 1953.

This volume includes survey papers on how problems of change have been handled in all areas of anthropology. *An Appraisal of Anthropology Today*, a companion volume, edited by Sol Tax and others, presents discussions of these papers.

Kroeber, A. L., *The Nature of Culture*, Chicago, University of Chicago Press, 1952.

Some of these collected papers are pre-1945, but 17 are recent amplifications of Kroeber's view of culture and his method of understanding it.

Kroeber, A. L., and C. Kluckhohn, *Culture: A Critical Review of Concepts and Definitions*, Peabody Museum of American Archaeology and Ethnology, Papers, Cambridge, Harvard University Press, 1952.

An exhaustive, analytical survey of the culture concept and how it has been variously used.

Linton, Ralph (ed.), *The Science of Man in the World Crisis*, New York, Columbia University Press, 1945.

Linton has brought together the contributions of 21 authorities in the behavioral sciences. Particularly relevant for general treatment of change are Herskovits' paper, in which he addresses himself to a statement of the "processes of cultural change"; and Linton's paper, in which archaeological and other evidence is used in surveying the development of culture.

Malinowski, Bronislaw, *The Dynamics of Culture Change: An Inquiry into Race Relations in Africa*, New Haven, Yale University Press, 1945.

Published posthumously, these papers on culture contact and change deal mainly with "the contact conflict and co-operation, and of compromise and passive resistance." Malinowski shows how new composite forms evolve, members of both cultures participating.

Rouse, Irving, "The Strategy of Culture History," in A. L. Kroeber (ed.), *Anthropology Today,* Chicago, University of Chicago Press, 1953.

This article discusses the complementary roles of archaeology and ethnology in culture-historical research.

Thomas, William L., Jr. (ed.), *Yearbook of Anthropology,* New York, Wenner-Gren Foundation for Anthropological Research, 1955.

In reporting on major accomplishments and trends during the period from 1952 to 1954, this volume brings *Anthropology Today* (A. L. Kroeber, ed.) up to date. Of special interest are articles by A. L. Kroeber, Julian Huxley, Oscar Lewis, Gordon Macgregor, and Wilhelm Koppers.

Wilson, G. and M., *The Analysis of Social Change, Based on Observations in Central Africa,* Cambridge, Cambridge University Press, 1945.

The Wilsons formulated a set of hypotheses about the nature of society and societal change, which were then tested against data gathered in the field.

## ACCULTURATION: GENERAL

"Acculturation: An Exploratory Formulation," *American Anthropologist,* Vol. 56 (1954), pp. 973–1001. The Social Science Research Council Summer Seminar on Acculturation.

As stated by the authors, this paper represents their "conception of an orderly approach to the study of cultural change as it is generated by culture contact." Bibliography.

Beals, Ralph, "Acculturation," in A. L. Kroeber (ed.), *Anthropology Today,* Chicago, University of Chicago Press, 1953.

Following an historical survey of acculturation studies, Beals discusses confusions centering around the definition and use of the concept. He reviews critically various methodological approaches, and concludes by suggesting areas toward which future acculturation studies might profitably be directed.

Hallowell, A. I., "Culture, Personality, and Society," in A. L. Kroeber (ed.), *Anthropology Today,* Chicago, University of Chicago Press, 1953.

A comprehensive survey of works resulting from the recent interest in the culture-personality area, including discussion of those concerned with change.

Kardiner, Abram, *The Psychological Frontiers of Society,* New York, Columbia University Press, 1945.

A further application of the concept of basic personality, this sequel to *The Individual and His Society* (1939) includes neo-Freudian analyses of three additional societies.

Mead, Margaret, "Character Formation and Diachronic Theory," in M. Fortes (ed.), *Social Structure: Studies Presented to A. R. Radcliffe-Brown,* London, Clarendon Press, 1949.

In this study, Mead deals with what happens to the character structure of individuals in societies which are changing at different rates and experiencing differing degrees of contact.

Meggers, Betty, "Recent Trends in American Ethnology," *American Anthropologist,* Vol. 48 (1946), pp. 176–214.

Among other things, Meggers questions the theory that social process can be observed more readily in cultures undergoing rapid change, as in contact situations.

Powdermaker, Hortense, "Communication and Social Change, Based on a Field Study in Northern Rhodesia," *Transactions of the New York Academy of Sciences,* Series 2, XVII, No. 5, 1955, pp. 430–440.

This study is concerned with how the moral order is affected by the *ways* and by *whom* new symbols are communicated in situations of culture contact.

Spiro, Melford E., "The Acculturation of American Ethnic Groups," *American Anthropologist,* Vol. 57 (1955), pp. 1240–1252.

Spiro opines that both culture theory and acculturation theory have suffered because anthropologists have neglected to study American ethnic groups.

Tax, Sol (ed.), *Acculturation in the Americas: Proceedings and Selected Papers of the XXIXth International Congress of Americanists,* Chicago, University of Chicago Press, 1952.

Following Herskovits' introductory discussion of modern trends in cultural anthropology, these thirty-three papers dealing with the processes of culture change in the Americas cover (1) acculturation and culture change; (2) Afroamerican studies; (3) modern Indian, mixed, and Creole cultures; and (4) aspects of colonial America.

Tax, Sol (ed.), *Heritage of Conquest: The Ethnology of Middle America,* Glencoe, Ill., Free Press, 1952.

Particularly relevant in this collection of papers is Beals' scheme for understanding contemporary acculturation, suggesting analysis on the basis of content, structure or organization, and ethos.

Thompson, Laura, *Culture in Crisis, A Study of the Hopi Indians,* New York, Harper and Brothers, 1950.

Thompson concludes from her research that problems of acculturation are in general problems in the dynamics of culture structure, and that administrative problems may be "reduced to scientific problems in culture structure analysis."

## LONG-RANGE CULTURAL REGULARITIES

Bidney, David, *Theoretical Anthropology,* New York, Columbia University Press, 1953, pp. 182–285.

These pages are concerned with cultural dynamics, specific discussion directed to how problems of long-range regularities have been approached. Bidney considers culture history with especial reference to the positions of A. L. Kroeber, E. E. Evans-Pritchard, L. A. White, and M. Herskovits.

Bock, Kenneth E., "Evolution and Historical Process," *American Anthropologist,* Vol. 54 (1952), pp. 486–496.

Bock re-examines the "history-as-unique-events" versus "evolutionism-as-the-generalizing-science-of-man" controversy, and concludes that "knowledge of the universal and knowledge of the particular are inseparably intertwined."

Childe, V. Gordon, *Social Evolution,* London, A. Watts and Co., 1951.

Basing his discussion on European and Near Eastern prehistory, archaeologist Childe relates his data to the evolution of economy and social organization.

Elkin, A. P., "Reaction and Interaction: A Food Gathering People and European Settlement in Australia," *American Anthropologist,* Vol. 53 (1951), pp. 164–186.

Elkin traces the history of European-Australian aborigine contact and emerges with a sequence of phases of interaction which might be comparable to other such contact situations during the past 150 years.

Leacock, Eleanor, *The Montagnais "Hunting Territory" and the Fur Trade,* American Anthropological Association, Memoir No. 78.

This monograph discusses the shift in Montagnais social organization as it relates to the shift in socioeconomic base, a process found to some extent among Arctic hunters as a whole, where white influence has been felt.

Lesser, Alexander, "Evolution in Social Anthropology," *Southwestern Journal of Anthropology,* Vol. 8 (1952), pp. 134–146.

Lesser asserts that anthropologists do accept the historical fact of sequential relations and make use of them constantly in their interpretations.

Murdock, G. P., *Social Structure,* New York, Macmillan Co., 1949.

Through consideration of inherent limitations, or limited possibilities, Murdock presents here a developmental approach to change in kinship systems, which he refers to as the "evolution of social organization."

Patai, Raphael, "The Dynamics of Westernization in the Middle East," *The Middle East Journal,* Vol. 9 (1955), pp. 1–16.

This paper examines the specific ways in which westernization has affected the Middle East and finds corroborative evidence for Redfield's contention that the technical order is the destroyer of the moral order, and sees indications that the technical order may effect new moral orders.

Redfield, Robert, *The Primitive World and Its Transformations,* Ithaca, Cornell University Press, 1953.

With particular emphasis on values, Redfield considers the changes in human life resulting from the rise of cities.

Siegel, Bernard J., "The Meaning of History in Anthropology as Exemplified by Near Eastern Culture Materials," *Southwestern Journal of Anthropology,* Vol. 3 (1947), pp. 50–56.

Siegel considers the history versus function dilemma, and concludes that in order to do full justice to the organized meaning of the "acts and artifacts" of a culture, both synchronic and diachronic materials are desirable.

Steward, Julian H., "Evolution and Process," in A. L. Kroeber (ed.), *Anthropology Today*, Chicago, University of Chicago Press, 1953.

Commenting on the renewed interest in cultural evolution in the past two decades, the author distinguishes three ways such data may be handled: evolution may be regarded as unilinear, universal, or multilinear. He finds multilinear evolution to be widely accepted and considers this a useful concept in the search for cultural regularities or "laws." Bibliography.

White, Leslie A., *A Science of Culture: A Study of Man and Civilization*, New York, Farrar, Straus and Co., 1949.

To neo-evolutionist White, culture is to be conceived as an objective, autonomous reality, *sui generis,* which must be explained as if it were independent of man.

## SOCIOLOGICAL DIMENSIONS OF CHANGE

### A. General

Goldschmidt, Walter, "Social Class and the Dynamics of Status in America," *American Anthropologist*, Vol. 57 (1955), pp. 1209–1217.

This article reviews anthropological contributions to the subject of social class and suggests that attention now be directed toward an examination of the dynamics of status.

Homans, George C., *The Human Group*, New York, Harcourt, Brace and Co., 1950.

Homans is able to deal with a culture change situation by regarding it as one in which people are no longer *interacting* as they formerly did. Acculturation, on this level, is what happens when certain people meet new people.

Mead, Margaret, *Male and Female*, New York, Wm. Morrow and Co., 1949.

Drawing on her extensive field work for cross-cultural perspective, Mead writes about the roles of men and women in America's changing society.

Mead, Margaret, "Social Change and Cultural Surrogates," in C. Kluckhohn, H. A. Murray, and D. M. Schneider (eds.), *Personality in Nature, Society, and Culture*, New York, Alfred A. Knopf, 1954, pp. 651–662.

Mead discusses the relationship between the developing individual and those mediating the culture to him, as it is influenced by the stability or change exhibited by the total social structure.

Warner, W. Lloyd, *American Life: Dream and Reality*, Chicago, University of Chicago Press, 1953.

For the most part, this concise, readable summary of research on American society covers the work which Warner and his associates have published in the Yankee City series, and various other books and papers.

West, James, *Plainville, U.S.A.*, New York, Columbia University Press, 1945.

This study examines the impact of the commercialized, urbanized national mass culture as it affects an isolated and backward community in the central United States.

## B. Social organization

Brown, Paula, "Changes in Ojibwa Social Control," *American Anthropologist*, Vol. 54 (1952), pp. 57–70.

Lacking a tradition of formal authority and formal means of social control, loss of the economic and social basis of informal authority and social control leaves the Red Lake Ojibwa without solutions to modern dilemmas.

Collins, June M., "Skagit Intragroup Conflict During Acculturation," *American Anthropologist*, Vol. 54 (1952), pp. 347–355.

The breakdown in social organization (resulting from White contact) permits the display of physical aggression in those relationships which were traditionally regarded as potentially troublesome, even in pre-White times.

Fortes, M., "Time and Social Structure: An Ashanti Case Study," in M. Fortes (ed.), *Social Structure: Studies Presented to A. R. Radcliffe-Brown*, London, Clarendon Press, 1949.

Fortes uses Ashanti case material in this concise demonstration of how the British handle the time dimensional aspect of change.

Schmitt, Karl and Iva O., *Wichita Kinship, Past and Present*, Norman, Oklahoma, University Book Exchange, 1952.

The authors use both comparative and historical methods to reconstruct the 1850–1875 Wichita kinship system and to show the changes by which it reached the modern reservation system.

Tumin, M. M., *Caste in a Peasant Society: A Case Study in the Dynamics of Caste*, Princeton, N. J., Princeton University Press, 1952.

Tumin brings sociological theory and techniques to the field of ethnography in this detailed case study of the stratified social system in a Guatemalan village.

Useem, John, "The Changing Structure of a Micronesian Society," *American Anthropologist*, Vol. 47 (1945), pp. 560–589.

Whether it is the urbanization of rural life or the modernizing of non-literate peoples, the impact of the larger society on local cultures can be profitably regarded as part of the same social process.

## SOCIOPSYCHOLOGICAL DIMENSIONS OF CHANGE

Benedict, Ruth, *The Chrysanthemum and the Sword: Patterns of Japanese Culture*, Boston, Houghton Mifflin Co., 1946.

This pioneer national character study discusses Japanese culture and personality, including comments on stability and change.

Caudill, W., *Japanese American Personality and Acculturation*, Genetic Psychology Monographs, Vol. 45 (1952), pp. 3–102.

Resulting from interdisciplinary group research concerned with the wide acceptance and upward social mobility of Japanese Americans coming from federal relocation camps to Chicago, this monograph presents the Thematic Apperception Test materials which were gathered.

Devereux, George, *Reality and Dream Psychotherapy of a Plains Indian,* New York, International Universities Press, 1951.

Based on psychotherapeutic interviews with a young adult male Plains Indian patient, this book is methodologically important. Devereux presents evidence corroborating Hallowell's contention that, regardless of apparent acculturation, many "Indian" personality features persist in the contemporary reservation-bred Indian.

Dollard, John, "The Acquisition of New Social Habits," in Ralph Linton (ed.), *The Science of Man in the World Crisis,* New York, Columbia University Press, pp. 443–464.

The Yale learning approach is demonstrated with economy, as Dollard applies the theory to various situations in which the habits of individuals may change.

Erikson, Erik H., *Childhood and Society,* New York, W. W. Norton and Co., 1950.

Relying on comparative cross-cultural data as well as clinical experience, Erikson is concerned with historical process in this study of ego development.

Firth, Raymond, *Religious Belief and Personal Adjustment,* Henry Myers Lecture, London, Royal Anthropological Institute of Great Britain and Ireland, 1948.

Firth finds that the functionalism of Malinowski and Radcliffe-Brown provides no framework for understanding change and suggests that change can result from the action systems of individuals.

Hallowell, A. I., *Culture and Experience,* Philadelphia, University of Pennsylvania Press, 1955.

The final section of Hallowell's book includes four papers which deal with the "psychological dimension of culture change."

Hallowell, A. I., "Sociopsychological Aspects of Acculturation," in Ralph Linton (ed.), *The Science of Man in the World Crisis,* New York, Columbia University Press, 1945, pp. 171–200.

Using learning theory formulations, Hallowell systematically approaches acculturation in sociopsychological terms.

Havighurst, R. J. and Neugarten, B. L., *American Indian and White Children: A Sociopsychological Investigation,* Chicago, University of Chicago Press, 1955.

The sixth volume in a series of studies on the development of children in six American Indian tribes, this book compares and contrasts the tribes among themselves and with children from a typical American community in the Midwest. Other studies in this series include: L. Thompson and A. Joseph, *The Hopi Way* (Chicago, University of Chicago Press, 1944); C. Kluckhohn and D. Leighton, *The Navaho* (Cambridge, Harvard University Press, 1946); Gordon Macgregor, *Warriors Without Weapons* (Chicago, University of Chicago Press, 1946); D. Leighton and C. Kluckhohn, *Children of the People: the Navaho Individual and His Development* (Cambridge, Harvard University Press, 1947); and A. Joseph, R. Spicer, and J. Chesky, *The Desert People* (Chicago, University of Chicago Press, 1949). These studies are of tribal units, including the Hopi, Navaho, Sioux, and Papago, and analyze persistence and change in these groups by means of various ethnological and psychological approaches.

Joseph, A., and V. F. Murray, *Chamorros and Carolinians of Saipan,* Cambridge, Harvard University Press, 1951.

Both ethnographic and psychological data are used to report on the past and present life of these Micronesian people, who were subjected to Japanese evacuation and early American occupation.

Mead, Margaret, "The Implications of Culture Change for Personality Development," *American Journal of Orthopsychiatry*, Vol. 17 (1947), pp. 633–646.

After discussing the effects of culture change, Mead finds that rapidly changing American society has developed techniques for strengthening human beings so that they can cope with such cultural strain.

Riesman, David, *The Lonely Crowd: A Study of Changing American Character*, Glencoe, Ill., Free Press, 1951.

Using neo-Freudian concepts, Riesman sees changing American "social character" moving from "tradition-directed" people, where shame is the means of social control, through "inner-directed" character, with guilt the principal means of control, to the typical members of today's American society who are "other-directed": these anxiously seek to conform to expectations and preferences of others.

Spindler, George, *Sociocultural and Psychological Processes in Menomini Acculturation*, University of California Publications in Culture and Society, Vol. 5, Berkeley, University of California Press, 1955.

The author isolated the sociocultural and psychological aspects of acculturation, and then demonstrated the relationship between these two variables.

Spiro, M. E., "Culture and Personality: The Natural History of a False Dichotomy," *Psychiatry*, Vol. 14 (1951), pp. 19–46.

Spiro contends that culture and personality are both part of a unified process, and that the dichotomy between them in our thinking is a function of our own highly disorganized cultural heritage.

Wallace, A. F. C., "Some Psychological Determinants of Culture Change in an Iroquoian Community," in William N. Fenton (ed.), *Symposium on Local Diversity in Iroquois Culture*, Bureau of American Ethnology, Bulletin No. 149, Washington, D. C., Smithsonian Institution, 1951, pp. 55–76.

Establishing a base line from early eighteenth century historical documents, Wallace shows how the dominant psychological characteristics of the Tuscarora may serve either to facilitate or to inhibit acculturation.

Holmberg, Allan R., *Nomads of the Long Bow: The Siriono of Eastern Bolivia*, Institute of Social Anthropology, Publications, No. 10, Washington, D. C., Smithsonian Institution, 1950.

A relatively unacculturated and perenially hungry group, the Siriono are analyzed in the psychological framework of basic and learned drives, change being interpreted in the same frame of reference.

## CHANGE AND CULTURAL STRESS

Eaton, Joseph, and Robert J. Weil, *Culture and Mental Disorders*, Glencoe, Ill., Free Press, 1955.

This sociological and psychiatric survey of the Hutterite religious communities in the United States and Canada demonstrates the influence of society on the rate of mental disorders. Data on the variations in types of disorders from one society to another are also included.

Fromm, Erich, *The Sane Society*, New York, Rinehart and Co., 1955.

Fromm continues the theme developed in *Escape from Freedom* (New York, Farrar and Rinehart, 1941), considering the adverse effect of contemporary industrial society on man, and offering suggestions for a society more conducive to mental health.

Goldhamer, Herbert, and Andrew Marshall, *Psychosis and Civilization: Two Studies in the Frequency of Mental Illness*, Glencoe, Ill., Free Press, 1953.

On the basis of available official records, Goldhamer and Marshall conclude that, in spite of changes in social structure in the United States between 1840 and 1940, there have been no significant changes in the rate of serious mental illness.

Halliday, James, *Psychosocial Medicine: A Study of a Sick Society*, New York, W. W. Norton and Co., 1948.

Halliday brings case material to support his hypothesis that a sick society can develop if, as a result of change, its psychological and social needs are no longer met.

Ruesch, Jurgen, Annemarie Jacobson, and Martin B. Loeb, *Acculturation and Illness*, Psychological Monographs, General and Applied, Vol. 62, No. 5, 1948.

Primarily concerned with immigrants or their children and grandchildren, this monograph studies the dynamics of culture change in relation to illness, indicating the ramifications for therapeutic and preventive procedures in cases where culture change is responsible for unusual stress.

## CHANGE AND VALUES

Du Bois, Cora, "The Dominant Value Profile of American Culture," *American Anthropologist*, Vol. 57 (1955), pp. 1232–1239.

Du Bois hypothesizes that there is a strain for consistency among the apparent contradictions inherent in any value system. This, then, may be one of the forces accounting for changes in the American value system over the last three hundred years.

Goldfrank, Esther S., "The Different Patterns of Blackfoot and Pueblo Adaptation to White Authority," in Sol Tax (ed.), *Acculturation in the Americas: Proceedings and Selected Papers of the XXIXth International Congress of Americanists*, 1952, pp. 74–79.

Relating Pueblo "conservatism" to theocratic control, as contrasted with the fluid, secular control found among the Blackfoot, the writer raises the question of the negative as well as the positive aspects of cultural integration.

Hallowell, A. I., "Values, Acculturation and Mental Health," *American Journal of Orthopsychiatry*, Vol. 20 (1950), pp. 732–743.

In this paper, Hallowell emphasizes the integrative role of the value system in relation to the functioning of the total personality.

Kluckhohn, C., *et al.*, "Values and Value-Orientations in the Theory of Action: An Exploration in Definition and Classification," in T. Parsons and E. A. Shils (eds.),

*Toward a General Theory of Action,* Cambridge, Harvard University Press, 1951, pp. 388–433.

Of the limited anthropological analyses of values, Kluckhohn's is perhaps the most extensive and systematic, although emphasis here is primarily on stability.

Mandelbaum, David G., *Change and Continuity in Jewish Life,* Glencoe, Ill., Library of North Shore Temple Israel, 1955.

Mandelbaum contends that, while many of the behaviors peculiar to Jewish life are apparently being "chipped" away, the core of American Judaism shows more cohesion.

Siegel, B., "Currents of Anthropological Theory and Value Concepts," *Southwestern Journal of Anthropology,* Vol. 4 (1948), pp. 199–210.

This paper traces how the anthropological attitude toward value judgments developed and then sets forth the problems relating to value systems which are of concern to social science.

Thompson, Laura, "Attitudes and Acculturation," *American Anthropologist,* Vol. 50 (1948), pp. 200–215.

Thompson concludes that once basic attitudes (such as an orientation regarding the nature of the universe, man's relation to it and its nonhuman component) become entrenched in tribal culture, they tend to endure in spite of changes in culture content and emphasis.

Vogt, Evon Z., *Navaho Veterans, A Study of Changing Values,* Peabody Museum of American Archaeology and Ethnology, Papers, 41, No. 1, Cambridge, Harvard University Press, 1951.

Vogt's research found that a given veteran's reactions were influenced more by his early experiences than by the situations he encountered in the war. Of further interest is Vogt's thesis that values controlling social organization are more resistant to change than are religious values.

## ON METHOD

Bagby, Philip H., "Culture and the Causes of Culture," *American Anthropologist,* Vol. 55 (1953), pp. 535–554.

Having defined culture as "regularities of behavior among the members of a single society," Bagby attempts to sharpen the "conceptual weapons" with which anthropologists may attack the problem of elucidating the flux of history.

Beals, Ralph L., "Urbanism, Urbanization and Acculturation," *American Anthropologist,* Vol. 53 (1951), pp. 1–10.

Beals urges the need for a unified body of sociological and anthropological theory, necessary for understanding the similar processes of change involved in urbanization and acculturation.

Broom, L., "A Measure of Conservatism," *American Anthropologist,* Vol. 47 (1945), pp. 630–635.

Broom feels that until students of acculturation isolate elements from a given segment of the cultural space and quantify these data, results will remain noncomparable.

Du Bois, Cora, "The Use of Social Science Concepts to Interpret Historical Materials: Comments on the Two Preceding Articles," *Far Eastern Quarterly*, Vol. 21 (1951), pp. 31–34.

Du Bois issues the caveat to those handling problems of contact that the levels of generalization must be observed and critically related.

*Ethnohistory*, Bloomington, Indiana, Indiana University Press.

This new journal represents a recent emphasis in anthropology on the use of documentary evidence of interpreting the cultures and movements of primitive peoples, especially the American Indian.

Foster, George, "What Is Folk Culture?" *American Anthropologist*, Vol. 55 (1953), pp. 159–173.

Questioning the assumptions underlying Redfield's folk-urban dichotomy, Foster suggests criteria for a distinction between "folk society" and "folk culture," the distinction being useful for both descriptive and theoretical purposes.

Gillin, John, "Parallel Cultures and the Inhibitions to Acculturation in a Guatemalan Community," *Social Forces*, Vol. 24 (1945), pp. 1–14.

Gillin shows that, despite much overlapping of traits, the two configurations of American Indian and Ladino cultures are distinguishable, and that the amount and kind of acculturation can be conveyed by objective, statistical procedures.

Hallowell, A. I., "The Rorschach Technique in the Study of Personality and Culture," *American Anthropologist*, Vol. 47 (1945), pp. 195–210.

Hallowell delineates the problems which can be approached by the Rorschach technique and further suggests that this test can give insight on the actual process of readaptation which individuals undergo before any new sociocultural equilibrium is reached.

Holmberg, Allan, "Adventures in Culture Change," in R. F. Spencer (ed.), *Method and Perspective in Anthropology: Papers in Honor of Wilson D. Wallis*, Minneapolis, University of Minnesota Press, 1954.

This paper has been included because it reports a self-conscious attempt by an anthropologist to introduce innovations into a nonliterate group, describing both expected and unexpected results.

Kardiner, Abram, "The Concept of Basic Personality Structure as an Operational Tool in the Social Sciences," in R. Linton (ed.), *The Science of Man in the World Crisis*, New York, Columbia University Press, 1945, pp. 107–122.

This article traces the insights out of which the concept of basic personality has been developed as a technique of operational value for understanding the correlations between the institutions of a culture and personality.

Redfield, Robert, *A Village that Chose Progress: Chan Kom Revisited*, Chicago, University of Chicago Press, 1950.

Redfield demonstrates the methodological importance of documenting stability and change by revisiting a group periodically.

Rose, E., "Innovations in American Culture," *Social Forces*, Vol. 26 (1948), pp. 255–272.

Rose stresses the importance of using dated materials on the introduction of new features into American culture, rather than the undated selections of ethnographical data frequently used in postulating (as opposed to demonstrating) culture centers.

Spindler, George E., and Walter Goldschmidt, "Experimental Design in the Study of Culture Change," *Southwestern Journal of Anthropology,* Vol. 8 (1952), pp. 68–83.

Stressing the importance of rigorous method to the further study of acculturation, the authors suggest a design for isolation, definition, and the relating of variables to problems and hypotheses.

Steward, Julian H., "Levels of Sociocultural Integration: An Operational Concept," *Southwestern Journal of Anthropology,* Vol. 7 (1951), pp. 374–390.

Steward illustrates how the problems in culture change can be approached meaningfully from a structural-functional viewpoint.

Taylor, Walter W., *A Study of Archaeology,* Menasha, Wisconsin, American Anthropological Association Memoir, No. 69, 1948.

This monograph is relevant as being perhaps the most comprehensive study to date of the methodology of American Archaeology, and the most explicit statement of how archaeology can contribute to an understanding of culture change through time.

Warner, W. Lloyd, Marcia Meeker, and Kenneth Eells, *Social Class in America,* Chicago, Science Research Associates, 1949.

The Warner method for studying the American social system is clearly set forth in this volume.

Watson, James B., "Four Approaches to Culture Change," *Social Forces,* Vol. 32 (1953), pp. 137–145.

Watson discusses and illustrates diagrammatically the ordered relations which exist among culture change studies and examines their position in the larger field of fact and theory.

## MISCELLANY

Beals, R. L., "Acculturation, Economics and Social Change in an Ecuadorean Village," *Acculturation in the Americas: Proceedings and Selected Papers of the XXIXth International Congress of Americanists,* 1952, pp. 67–73.

Beals suggests possible outcomes to this village's major problems of an increasing population and diminishing land base. He further predicts the direction of concomitant social changes.

Ewers, John C., *The Horse in Blackfoot Indian Culture,* Bureau of American Ethnology, Bulletins, No. 159, Smithsonian Institution, Washington, D. C., U. S. Government Printing Office, 1953.

Such a meticulously detailed study of one factor in change, the influence of the horse on a Plains Indian tribe, allows for more valid generalizations about the process of acculturation.

Fried, M. H., "Land Tenure, Geography and Ecology in the Contact of Cultures," *American Journal of Economics and Sociology,* Vol. 2 (1952), pp. 391–412.

When the invading culture is of far greater economic complexity than the indigene, the results of the contact depend upon the ways in which the exploitative rights to strategic resources are distributed in the two societies.

Kimball, Solon T., "Diversity and Change in the Culture of Nonliterate Peoples," in E. DeS. Brunner (ed.), *Farmers of the World*, New York, Columbia University Press, 1945, pp. 8–18.

Addressing himself primarily to extension workers, Kimball emphasizes the need for knowledge of the principles of cultural anthropology, if one is concerned with effective social engineering.

Mead, Margaret (ed.), *Cultural Patterns and Technical Change* (from the "Tensions and Technology Series"), Paris, UNESCO, 1953.

Five descriptions of whole cultures are followed by a survey of the effects and implications of technical change in many areas of daily life. Selected and master bibliographies appended.

Meggers, Betty J., "Environmental Limitation on the Development of Culture," *American Anthropologist*, Vol. 56 (1954), pp. 801–824.

Having distinguished four types of environment in terms of agricultural potentiality, Meggers suggests that "definite limitations and possibilities for cultural development" are associated with each.

Shimkin, D. B., "Industrialization, A Challenging Problem for Cultural Anthropology," *Southwestern Journal of Anthropology*, Vol. 8 (1952), pp. 84–91.

This paper defines problems in the cultural study of industrialization, emphasizing the importance of the historical and acculturative aspects.

Siegel, B. J., "Suggested Factors of Culture Change at Taos Pueblo," in Sol Tax (ed.), *Acculturation in the Americas: Proceedings and Selected Papers of the XXIXth International Congress of Americanists*, 1952, pp. 133–142.

To understand processes of culture change at Taos, Siegel presents data on such variables as communication, population increase, subsistence economy, and patterns of authority and leadership.

Spicer, Edward H. (ed.), *Human Problems in Technological Change: A Case Book*, New York, Russell Sage Foundation, 1952.

Concerned primarily with the sociocultural dynamics attendant on technological changes, the data from these fifteen case studies are organized in a standard framework: (1) the problem; (2) the course of events; (3) relevant factors; (4) the outcome; and (5) analysis.

# The sociology of religion

DAVID J. PITTMAN

*University of Rochester*

Religion, the existence of which has been noted for all human societies, is a basic social institution which fulfills both manifest and latent functions and dysfunctions on the individual and societal level. The sociology of religion employs the scientific method to view religion as a product of human social interaction and as an expression of cultural, group, and individual needs and activities. It explores religion as a basic social institution which affects and is affected by other institutions in the society and as an integral part of the social structure in any society.

In viewing the period 1945–1955, a major generalization emerges: the scientific study of the religious institution is not a primary focus in the field of sociology as is the recent run of attention given to social stratification and the small group. Many scholars in their book reviews, prefaces to works in this area, or in commentaries on introductory textbooks in sociology keep referring to the "neglected" field of the sociology of religion. A second generalization emerges concerning the magnitude and significance of the publications during this period. The decade saw no massive intellectual contributions on the order of the classic studies of religion such as Durkheim's *The Elementary Forms of Religious Life*, Weber's *The Protestant Ethic and the Spirit of Capitalism*, Tawney's *Religion and the Rise of Capitalism*, or Malinowski's essays on magic, science, and religion. In summary, few sociological man-hours of work are employed in the mines of religion, and we can expect few returns of the magnitude of the works mentioned earlier.

Perhaps one way of explaining the decline of interest in the sociology of religion is found in the history of the development of American sociology. Many of the early recruits to sociology were seminarians, theologians, or ministers who were either uncomfortable in their former background or completely rejecting it; others were seeking answers and ways of obtaining a more equitable social order through sociology. Despite their motivations, religion was an area of both personal and professional concern because of the changing intellectual climate in reference to religion in the society. The shift from a sacred to a secular society in America during the nineteenth and twentieth centuries has been noted by many historians and sociologists. The secular trend became victorious, at least in academic circles, to be replaced by the new trinity of scientific method, statistics, and research. Religion was no longer viewed as being the ultimate or sole authority and itself was to be subject to the same scientific scrutiny as other areas of human activity.

Whatever the reasons, the focus of attention in American sociology is not on the study of religion, and there are few indications that this basic trend will be reversed in the next decade. However, no competent sociologist can deny or dismiss the pervasive role that religion plays in the life activities of many individuals as is exemplified in evangelistic crusades, sect and cult groups, and congregate church activities. Individuals in the secular society still enter rigorous religious orders and engage in demanding and taxing missionary endeavors. One need only to view the political arena to note that political parties still "balance the ticket" in terms of religious affiliation, and legislative action is delayed on crucial issues such as federal aid to education because of religious considerations. That human behavior scientists tend to ignore or treat cursorily an area does not mean that the area does not have pregnant significance for individual and group behavior.

This annotated bibliography has been drawn from the major journals in the field of sociology and closely allied areas and from monographs and books published in this area. Works published before 1945, a necessarily arbitrary date, have been eliminated from consideration. The general criterion which governed the selection of a work was its general relevancy to the field of the sociology of religion.

After the bibliographical items were selected, a classification scheme was devised to group the works into seven divisions. The scheme is in no way viewed as being definitive. When difficulty was engendered in the classification of an item, it was placed in what was deemed the most closely allied category. The bibliography is arranged in the following divisions:

1. General and Theoretical Works on the Sociology of Religion
2. Selected Studies in Comparative Religion (this category does not attempt to include all the massive number of studies from anthropological sources)
3. Religious Organization (the emphasis is both on the structural features of organized religion and its functions)
4. Studies of Individual Religious Groups (the major focus in this area is on the study of sects and cults)
5. Studies of Religious Personnel
6. Studies of Religious Attitudes and Participation Related to Behavior
7. Studies of the Relationship of the Religious Institution to Other Institutional Areas

## GENERAL AND THEORETICAL WORKS ON THE SOCIOLOGY OF RELIGION

Barnett, James H., "The Easter Festival: A Study in Cultural Adjustment," *Amer. Soc. Rev.*, Vol. 14 (1949), pp. 62–70.

A study in the sociocultural changes in a festival, Easter, which is both a holy and secular holiday, with emphasis upon the United States since 1870.

Bryan, G. McLeod, "The 'Kingdom of God' Concept in Sorokin and Toynbee," *Social Forces*, Vol. 26 (1947), pp. 288–292.

A critique of the use of the concept "Kingdom of God" by Sorokin and Toynbee in their social and historical theories.

Dynes, Russell R., "Toward the Sociology of Religion," *Sociology and Social Research*, Vol. 38 (1953), pp. 227–232.

An excellent discussion of the neglected field of the sociology of religion, which delineates six major areas of investigation and points out the many existent gaps in our knowledge.

Grafton, Thomas Hancock, "Religious Origins and Sociological Theory," *Amer. Soc. Rev.*, Vol. 10 (1945), pp. 726–739.

Religious origins should not be sought in the evolutionary scheme of early anthropologists but in human nature itself.

Hertzlcr, J. O., "Religious Institutions," *Annals of the American Academy of Political and Social Science,* Vol. 256 (1948), pp. 1–13.

A general essay on the religious institution organized in terms of the nature, institutionalization, functions, and sociological significance of religion.

Hudson, R. Lafton, "The Social Context of Religion," *Sociology and Social Research,* Vol. 31 (1946), pp. 43–47.

The author presents a definition of religion as composed of "frames of reference" which are culturally transmitted and arc functional to the individual in giving meaning to actions and meeting crises.

Hughes, Everett (ed.), "Sixtieth Anniversary Issue—Part Two," *Amer. J. Soc.,* Vol. 60 (1954), pp. 1–90.

This anniversary issue is devoted to the republication of classic articles from the files of the *Journal* that deal with the sociology of religion. The issue contains a foreword by Everett Hughes on "The Early and Contemporary Study of Religion." Republished are the following six papers: (1) "A Contribution to the Sociology of Religion" (1905), Georg Simmel; (2) "Religion and the Mores" (1910), William Sumner; (3) "The Passing of the Saint" (1919), John M. Mecklin; (4) "The Church and Class Conflicts" (1919), Albion W. Small; (5) "The Sect and the Sectarian" (1928), Ellsworth Faris; (6) "Some Phases of Religion That Are Susceptible of Sociological Study" (1929), Ellsworth Faris.

Nottingham, Elizabeth K., *Religion and Society,* Garden City, New York, Doubleday and Company, 1954.

A short booklet prepared especially for students of sociology and laymen analyzes in a lucid fashion the interrelationships of religion and society from a functional point of view.

Parsons, Talcott, *Religious Perspectives of College Teaching in Sociology and Social Psychology,* New Haven, Edward W. Hazen Foundation, 1951.

A valuable essay which deals with some theoretical aspects of the sociology of religion.

Smith, William C., "Sociology and the Social Gospel," *Sociology and Social Research,* Vol. 32 (1948), pp. 609–615.

A brief analysis of the reasons for the lack of success of the social gospel movement in America, and an evaluation of its present status.

Wach, Joachim, *Sociology of Religion,* Chicago, University of Chicago Press, 1944.

An only partially successful attempt by this German scholar to bring organizational concepts to bear on the confused field of the sociology of religion. The scope of materials covered is broad in an historical sense, but narrow in terms of sociological relevancy.

Yinger, J. Milton, *Religion in the Struggle for Power: A Study in the Sociology of Religion,* Durham, N. C., Duke University Press, 1946.

An excellent examination of Weber and Troeltsch's theories as they particularly apply to religious groupings in America and also to historical situations.

## SELECTED STUDIES IN COMPARATIVE RELIGION

Goode, William J., *Religion Among the Primitives: The Web of Religion and Sex, Economics, Politics,* Glencoe, Illinois, The Free Press, 1951.

A sociological theory of religion utilizing structural-functional analysis and data from five carefully selected nonliterate societies.

Patai, Raphael, "Religion in Middle Eastern, Far Eastern, and Western Culture," *Southwestern Journal of Anthropology,* Vol. 10 (1954), pp. 233–254.

An extremely ambitious attempt to present the differential roles religion has played in these major world areas.

Wach, Joachim, *Types of Religious Experience, Christian and Non-Christian,* Chicago, University of Chicago Press, 1951.

A collection of lectures and articles dealing with comparative religions and presenting a definition of religion cast in a nonsociological framework.

Weber, Max, *The Religions of China: Confucianism and Taoism,* trans. and ed. by Hans H. Gerth, Glencoe, Illinois, The Free Press, 1951.

The translation of the brilliant study on Chinese religion by one of the masters of the sociology of religion.

## RELIGIOUS ORGANIZATION

Abrams, Ray H., "The Churches and the Clergy in World War II," *Annals of the American Academy of Political and Social Science,* Vol. 256 (1948), pp. 110–119.

The analysis of the attitude of the churches and clergy before and after World War II toward intervention in the world situation and adjustment to war.

Bultena, Louis, "Church Membership and Church Attendance in Madison, Wisconsin," *Amer. Soc. Rev.,* Vol. 14 (1949), pp. 384–389.

A religious census of Madison, Wisconsin, in 1944 of 24,489 individuals 18 years of age and over in terms of church membership and attendance.

Clark, S. D., *Church and Sect in Canada,* Toronto, University of Toronto Press, 1948.

An excellent study on the development of the religious institution in Canada from 1760–1900, with a consideration of the basic sociocultural forces of urbanism, industrialization, and the frontier as they impinged on the religious structure. The internal social organization of the churches is also considered.

Culver, Dwight, *Negro Segregation in the Methodist Church,* New Haven, Yale University Press, 1953.

A thorough descriptive account of the intensity and changes in the segregation practices of the Methodist Church. Based on a study of church records and documents and questionnaires from 785 people.

Fichter, Joseph H., *Dynamics of a City Church: Southern Parish,* Vol. 1, Chicago, University of Chicago Press, 1951.

An excellent study in the social organization of a religious institution—a Southern Catholic parish—by a Catholic priest.

Fichter, Joseph H., "Conceptualizations of the Urban Parish," *Social Forces*, Vol. 31 (1952), pp. 43–46.

A typical large urban parish may be viewed as a "legal corporation, a super-imposed association, an institutionalized association, a communal group, and a cluster of sub-groupings."

Francis, E. F., "Toward a Typology of Religious Orders," *Amer. J. Soc.*, Vol. 55 (1949–1950), pp. 437–449.

An excellent sociological and historical account of the evolution of Roman Catholic religious orders. The movement has been from the *gemeinschaft* type of religious community represented by monasticism to the *gesellschaft* type of order represented by the Jesuits.

Furfey, Paul Hanly, "The Churches and Social Problems," *Annals of the American Academy of Political and Social Science*, Vol. 256 (1948), pp. 101–109.

The role of social thought, social action, and social work in the church's approach to social problems is considered.

Garrison, Winfred, "Characteristics of American Organized Religion," *Annals of the American Academy of Political and Social Science*, Vol. 256 (1948), pp. 14–24.

A review of the differentiating features of organized religion in this country from the establishment of the federal government to the present.

Hoult, Thomas Ford, "Economic Class Consciousness in American Protestantism," *Amer. Soc. Rev.*, Vol. 15 (1950), pp. 97–100.

The ecological patterning of denominational churches of Protestant groups in Los Angeles (1940) is related significantly to average denominational per capita wealth of churches. Churches of lower economic areas have low denominational wealth.

Kane, John L., "Protestant-Catholic Tensions," *Amer. Soc. Rev.*, Vol. 16 (1951), pp. 663–672.

The article concludes that Protestant-Catholic tensions have increased in the last decades as measured by a content analysis of *America* and *Christian Century*, religious publications, for the first six months of the years 1939, 1944, and 1949.

Landis, Judson T., "Social Action in American Protestant Churches," *Amer. J. Soc.*, Vol. 52 (1946–1947), pp. 517–522.

An analysis of social action programs of Protestant denominations obtained through questionnaires reveals that though such programs are in operation, they are still in the formative stage as measured by financing, personnel, and scope.

Lee, Alfred McClung, "The Press and Public Relations of Religious Bodies," *Annals of the American Academy of Political and Social Science*, Vol. 256 (1948), pp. 120–131.

A study of the religious press in America dealt with in terms of its publications and their coverage, impact on the public, and characteristic themes.

Loescher, Frank, *The Protestant Church and the Negro*, New York, Association Press, 1948.

A review of the policies and practices of the major Protestant churches in reference to the integration of the Negro into church membership and activities.

Nuesse, C. J., and Thomas J. Harte (eds.), *The Sociology of the Parish: An Introductory Symposium,* Milwaukee, Bruce Publishing Company, 1951.

An analysis by fifteen contributors of the Catholic parish as more than an ecclesiastical unit but also as a unit in an institutional structure—as a social system which is a proper focus for sociological study.

Pope, Liston, "Religion and Class Structure," *Annals of the American Academy of Political and Social Science,* Vol. 256 (1948), pp. 84–91.

An excellent summary of the scant data relating to religious affiliation (Catholic, Jewish, and Protestant denominations) to class position in American society

Spencer, Robert F., "Social Structure of a Contemporary Japanese-American Buddhist Church," *Social Forces,* Vol. 26 (1947–1948), pp. 281–287.

The social organization of an unassimilated group of Japanese-Americans as viewed by the congregation of a Buddhist church in a university town in California.

Sullenger, T. Earl, and Gwen Lindevall, "The Urban Church in a Changing Social Scene," *Sociology and Social Research,* Vol. 30 (1945–1946), pp. 196–200.

A survey of sixty-one Protestant churches in Omaha to determine the role of the church in meeting problems occurring with social change in an urban setting.

Wilson, Charles Lee, "A Social Picture of a Congregation," *Amer. Soc. Rev.,* Vol. 10 (1945), pp. 418–422.

This article presents a brief analysis of the social class composition and power structure of a New England Protestant congregation.

Tubeville, Gus, "Religious Schism in the Methodist Church: A Sociological Analysis of the Pine Grove Case," *Rural Sociology,* Vol. 14 (1949), pp. 29–39.

An analysis of the Methodist unification conflict in 1939 as represented by the Pine Grove Church in Turbeville, South Carolina. The analysis is in terms of the decisive influence of the community and its power structure as it impinges on the religious institution. The impact of conflict is viewed as it affects community integration.

## STUDIES OF INDIVIDUAL RELIGIOUS GROUPS

Brewer, Earl D., "Sect and Church in Methodism," *Social Forces,* Vol. 30 (1951–1952), pp. 400–408.

An application of the sect and church concept typologies to Methodism, especially as it occurs in the United States.

Brown, James Stephen, "Social Class, Intermarriage, and Church Membership in a Kentucky Community," *Amer. J. Soc.,* Vol. 57 (1951–1952), pp. 232–242.

The system of class stratification in an isolated Kentucky mountain settlement is utilized to explain intermarriage and participation in the Holiness sect The functions of the Holiness group for lower class individuals is clearly presented.

Collins, June McCormick, "The Indian Shaker Church: A Study of Continuity and Change in Religion," *Southwestern Journal of Anthropology,* Vol. 6 (1950), pp. 399–411.

An analysis of the reasons for the acceptance of the Shaker Church by a group of Coast Salish Indians in western Washington in the latter nineteenth century and the reasons for its stability through change.

Eister, Alan W., *Drawing Room Conversion: A Sociological Account of the Oxford Group Movement,* Durham, N. C., Duke University Press, 1950.

A descriptive account of the Oxford Group Movement until the present time, with a consideration of its history and a relating of some of the events of its meeting. However, many sociological questions involved in the group's formation are not discussed.

England, R. W., "Some Aspects of Christian Science as Reflected in Letters of Testimony," *Amer. J. Soc.,* Vol. 59 (1953–1954), pp. 448–453.

The membership and the dynamics of the appeal of the Christian Science sect are analyzed through an examination of a sample of five hundred letters of testimony appearing in the group's publications. Psychological functions of the Christian Science practitioner's role are discussed.

Frances, E. K., "The Russian Mennonites: From Religious to Ethnic Group," *Amer. J. Soc.,* Vol. 54 (1948–1949), pp. 101–107.

The transformation of a homogeneous religious though ethnically heterogeneous group, the Russian Mennonites, into an ethnic group over time through isolation on the American continent is presented in this excellent study.

Hawley, Florence, "The Keresan Holy Rollers: An Adaptation to American Individualism," *Social Forces,* Vol. 26 (1947–1948), pp. 272–280.

The acculturation of some members of the Pueblo of the Sun to a Negro Holy Roller cult is presented in an analytical case study.

Hershberger, Guy F., *The Mennonite Church in the Second World War,* Scottdale, Pennsylvania, Mennonite Publishing House, 1951.

Although not cast in a sociological frame of reference, this story of the reactions and planning of the Old Mennonite Church and its members to the wartime situation in view of their pacifist position provides more data on religious sects in this country.

May, L. Carlyle, "The Dancing Religion: A Japanese Messianic Sect," *Southwestern Journal of Anthropology,* Vol. 10 (1954), pp. 119–137.

An excellent account of the origin, leadership, belief system, and functions of the new religious sect, Odoru-Shūkyō, in Japan after World War II.

O'Dea, Thomas F., "Mormonism and the Avoidance of Sectarian Stagnation: A Study of Church, Sect, and Incipient Nationality," *Amer. J. Soc.,* Vol. 60 (1954–1955), pp. 285–293.

An excellent discussion of the particular factors which prevented Mormonism from becoming a stagnant sectarian movement. The Mormons by their formation of a subcultural area and the acquisition of many of the traits of a nationality group do not lend themselves to classification according to any of the traditional typological schemes.

Opler, Marvin W., "Two Japanese Religious Sects," *Southwestern Journal of Anthropology,* Vol. 6 (1950), pp. 69–78.

A report on two minor Japanese religious sects, the Gedatsu-Kyo-Kai cult, a development from Buddhism, and the Kon-Kwo-Kyo cult, an offshoot of popular Shinto, studied at the Tule Lake wartime relocation center.

Stroup, Herbert Hewitt, *The Jehovah's Witnesses,* New York, Columbia University Press, 1945.

An analysis of a religious sect group which has received considerable public attention.

## STUDIES OF RELIGIOUS PERSONNEL

Burchard, Waldo W., "Role Conflicts of Military Chaplains," *Amer. Soc. Rev.,* Vol. 19 (1954), pp. 528–535.

A study of the role conflict of the military chaplain engendered by the divergent ends of the religious and political institutions, based on interviews with less than seventy present and former chaplains in the San Francisco Bay area.

Comfort, Richard O., "Survey of Activities and Training of Selected Rural Ministers in the United States," *Rural Sociology,* Vol. 12 (1947), pp. 375–387.

An article based on a survey of 231 town and country ministers who are described in terms of education and their present activities. The analysis shows the ministers received inadequate training in seminary for their present activities.

Goldstein, Sidney I., "The Roles of an American Rabbi," *Sociology and Social Research,* Vol. 38 (1953–1954), pp. 32–37.

A presentation of the multiplicity of roles which the rabbi is expected to enact and the conflicts engendered by the incompatibility of the roles.

Gregory, W. Edgar, "The Chaplain and Mental Hygiene," *Amer. J. Soc.,* Vol. 52 (1946–1947), pp. 420–423.

Both manifest and latent functions of the military chaplain's role as it relates to the mental hygiene of service personnel are considered in this rather impressionistic article.

Roberts, Harry W., "The Rural Negro Minister: His Work and Salary," *Rural Sociology,* Vol. 12 (1947), pp. 285–295.

A survey of 141 Negro ministers in Virginia (117 of whom are rural pastors) in terms of types of activity and salary scales.

Roberts, Harry W., "The Rural Negro Minister: His Personal and Social Characteristics," *Social Forces,* Vol. 27 (1948–1949), pp. 291–300.

This presents the results of a survey of the personal and social characteristics of 141 rural Negro ministers who were in attendance at the Summer School for Ministers at Virginia State College from 1943–1946.

Rodehaver, Myles, "Ministers on the Move: A Study of Mobility in Church Leadership," *Rural Sociology,* Vol. 13 (1948), pp. 400–410.

A study using 196 ministers of a small liberal denomination as the sample of the frequency and causes of the minister's mobility. The high mobility of the rural minister is examined.

Smith, Luke M., "The Clergy: Authority Structure, Ideology, Migration," *Amer. Soc. Rev.,* Vol. 18 (1953), pp. 242–248.

A study of the influence of the type of church social organization (episcopal type versus congregational type) upon the migration and consequences of migration of the clergy.

Zeitlin, Joseph, *Disciples of the Wise. The Religious and Social Opinions of American Rabbis,* New York, Columbia University Press, 1945.

Based on a 1937 questionnaire, a picture is presented of the attitudes of the Reform, Conservative, and Orthodox Jewish clergy toward such matters as peace, civil liberties, racial discrimination, and so forth.

## STUDIES OF RELIGIOUS ATTITUDES AND PARTICIPATION RELATED TO BEHAVIOR

Eister, Allan W., "Some Aspects of Institutional Behavior with Reference to Churches," *Amer. Soc. Rev.,* Vol. 17 (1952), pp. 64–69.

A study of freshmen students at Southern Methodist University, which relates attitude toward and participation in an institutional structure, *i.e.,* the church.

Fichter, Joseph H., "The Marginal Catholic: An Institutional Approach," *Social Forces,* Vol. 32 (1953–1954), pp. 167–173.

This research cast in the theoretical framework of marginality and institutional inconsistency examines the role of the white marginal or fringe Catholic living in the three ecclesiastical parishes of a Southern city.

Fichter, Joseph H., "The Profile of Catholic Religious Life," *Amer. J. Soc.,* Vol. 58 (1952–1953), pp. 145–149.

Based on censuses of religious participation in three white urban Catholic parishes, religious observance as related to sex and age categories is used to obtain religious profiles.

Kelly, George A., *Catholics and the Practice of the Faith: A Census Study of the Diocese of Saint Augustine,* Washington, Catholic University of America Press, 1946.

A survey of the diocese of St. Augustine, Florida, which relates practice of Catholicism to selected social factors.

Kitay, Philip Morton, *Radicalism and Conservatism Toward Conventional Religion,* New York, Teachers College, Columbia University, 1947.

An investigation through life histories of the background factors of 139 Jewish students at the College of the City of New York who are divided into those positive and those negative toward the church. An attempt is made to discriminate the disagreements of religious radicals and conservatives on specific political and economic issues.

Lantz, Herman, "Religious Participation and Social Orientation of 1000 University Students," *Sociology and Social Research,* Vol. 33 (1948–1949), pp. 285–290.

A study of a group of Ohio State University students to test the hypothesis that religious participation and activities are correlated with personal satisfaction concerning social conditions. Results are negative.

Lenski, Gerhard E., "Social Correlates of Religious Interest," *Amer. Soc. Rev.*, Vol. 18 (1953), pp. 533–544.

A systematic analysis of data obtained from Indianapolis in the early 1940's of the correlations between degree of interest in religion by selected Protestants and social variables such as sex, parenthood, financial status, and so forth.

Moberg, David O., "The Christian Religion and Personal Adjustment in Old Age," *Amer. Soc. Rev.*, Vol. 18 (1953), pp. 87–90.

An experimentally designed study of the adjustment of institutionalized oldsters as related to religious faith. Significant correlations were obtained between good adjustment in old age with formal participation—past or present—in church activities.

Nimkoff, Meyer F., and Arthur L. Wood, "Effect of Majority Patterns on the Religious Behavior of a Minority Group," *Sociology and Social Research*, Vol. 30 (1945–1946), pp. 282–289.

An excellent study of the religious participation of Catholics as represented by attendance at Mass when they are the minority group participating in a Protestant and secular dominated social system.

Porterfield, Austin L., "The Church and Social Well-Being: A Statistical Analysis," *Sociology and Social Research*, Vol. 31 (1946–1947), pp. 213–219.

A discussion of the negative correlations as they are found between indices of social well-being and religious activity as measured by churches per 100,000 population, number of ministers, and church members.

Smith, Philip M., "Organized Religion and Criminal Behavior," *Sociology and Social Research*, Vol. 33 (1948–1949), pp. 362–367.

A partial review of the literature to discern the relationship of religious affiliation and criminal behavior. Organized religion, on the basis of present evidence, did not significantly reduce the crime rate.

Vernon, Glenn M., "An Inquiry into the Scalability of Church Orthodoxy," *Sociology and Social Research*, Vol. 39 (1954–1955), pp. 324–327.

An application of the Guttman Scalogram Technique to church orthodoxy in a ward of the Church of Jesus Christ of Latter Day Saints in Lewiston, Idaho.

Zetterberg, Hans L., "The Religious Conversion as a Change of Social Roles," *Sociology and Social Research*, Vol. 36 (1951–1952), pp. 159–166.

A study of the rapid shifts in social roles and attitudes occurring with religious conversions, based upon data from a youth group of a fundamentalist church in Sweden.

## STUDIES OF THE RELATIONSHIP OF THE RELIGIOUS INSTITUTION TO OTHER INSTITUTIONAL AREAS

Baber, Ray E., "Religion and the Family," *Annals of the American Academy of Political and Social Science*, Vol. 256 (1948), pp. 92–100.

A discussion of the tremendous role which religion, especially the Christian faith in American society, has played in shaping the family institution.

Clark, S. D., "The Religious Sect in Canadian Politics," *Amer. J. Soc.,* Vol. 51 (1945–1946), pp. 207–216.

The assumed fact that the evangelistic religious groups such as the Baptists in Nova Scotia, the Methodists in Ontario, and Aberhart's followers in Alberta have supported the growth of liberal political thought in Canada is based on superficial analysis which overlooks the effects of the sects before they emerged into the evangelical church.

Cronin, John F., *Catholic Social Principles: The Social Teachings of the Catholic Church Applied to American Economic Life,* Milwaukee, Bruce Publishing Company, 1950.

The use of church encyclicals and other authoritative sources from which are deduced the Catholic positions in reference to socioeconomic life in the United States.

Dall, Eugene E., "Social and Economic Organization in Two Pennsylvania German Religious Communities," *Amer. J. Soc.,* Vol. 57 (1951–1952), pp. 168–177.

A keen sociological analysis of two historical Pennsylvania German communities, Ephrata and Bethlehem, whose web of social and economic life was organized around religious values. The disintegration of these two eighteenth century communities and the factors producing the decay are only superficially treated.

Ebersale, Luke, *Church Lobbying in the Nation's Capital,* New York, Macmillan Company, 1951.

The efforts of Protestant, Catholic, and other religious groups to mold the governmental process and public opinion are treated. A short consideration of the factors producing increased church activity in this particular area is presented.

Hunt, Chester L., "Religious Ideology as a Means of Social Control," *Sociology and Social Research,* Vol. 33 (1948–1949), pp. 180–187.

The struggle between the German Protestant Church and the National Socialism of Hitler is recounted.

Johnson, Alvin W., and Frank H. Yost, *Separation of Church and State in the United States,* Minneapolis, University of Minnesota Press, 1948.

An historically oriented study of the relationship of the religious to the political institution viewed particularly through legal statutes in the United States.

Jonassen, Christen T., "The Protestant Ethic and Spirit of Capitalism in Norway," *Amer. Soc. Rev.,* Vol. 12 (1947), pp. 676–686.

A case study of Norway which posits that Weber's thesis of the Protestant ethic is applicable to this country.

Marshall, Douglas G., "The Decline of Farm Family Fertility and Its Relationship to Nationality and Religious Background," *Rural Sociology,* Vol. 15 (1950), pp. 42–49.

An excellent study of fertility declines in Minnesota rural areas between 1875 and 1940 which shows differential declines in terms of religious and ethnic groups. Religious affiliation such as Roman Catholicism shows a more significant relationship to fertility rates than nationality status.

May, Henry F., *Protestant Churches and Industrial America*, New York, Harper and Brothers, 1949.

A study of the shifts in orientations of Protestant church leaders in the period, 1861–1895, that led to the development of the social gospel philosophy that characterizes twentieth century Protestantism.

Monahan, Thomas P., and William M. Kephart, "Divorce and Desertion by Religious and Mixed-Religious Groups," *Amer. J. Soc.*, Vol. 59 (1953–1954), pp. 454–465.

A short summary of research relating to religious affiliation and divorce and desertion rates. In the data analyzed for Philadelphia, the Protestants show the highest incidence of divorce, although the Catholic proportion is sizable. For the white population the Catholic rate for desertion and nonsupport cases is disproportionately higher than that of Protestants, while the Jewish group is the least represented.

Rutland, Walter B., "Church-State Relations in America: Status and Trends," *Social Forces*, Vol. 28 (1949–1950), pp. 83–86.

A summary of selected events in the 1940's that provides a case for the existence of tensions between the religious and political institutional agents.

Schnepp, Gerald J., and Louis A. Roberts, "Residential Propinquity and Mate Selection on a Parish Basis," *Amer. J. Soc.*, Vol. 58 (1952–1953), pp. 45–50.

An empirical study of the propinquity rate of marriages occurring in a Catholic parish in St. Louis shows a rate lower than that for other studies of propinquity. The hypothesis that the parish unit acts as a cohesive force for mate selection is rejected.

Thomas, John L., "Religious Training in the Roman Catholic Family," *Amer. J. Soc.*, Vol. 57 (1951–1952), pp. 178–183.

An assessment of the amount of preschool religious training obtained by Roman Catholic children, from data received by questionnaires, is presented. The results are that the children obtain less religious training than is expected by religious authorities, and that there are regional and urban-rural differences.

Thorner, Isidor, "Ascetic Protestantism and Development of Science and Technology," *Amer. J. Soc.*, Vol. 58 (1952–1953), pp. 225–233.

This excellent reanalysis of Sorokin's data on inventions and discoveries supports the hypothesis of the positive influence of ascetic Protestantism on the development of science and technology. Affective neutrality is viewed as one of the important variables of ascetic Protestantism in this relationship.

Ward, Harry F., "Organized Religion, the State, and the Economic Order," *Annals of the American Academy of Political and Social Science*, Vol. 256 (1948), pp. 72–83.

A brief account of both historical and contemporary relations of organized religion in the United States to the political and economic institutions.

# The sociology of art

DAVID J. PITTMAN

*University of Rochester*

Art in each society is a social product deriving from the social forces operating in a particular society. Although artistic creation occurs in a social context and influences and is influenced by the social environment, sociologists have almost completely ignored the relationships which exist between art and society, leaving the problem to the scholars in the humanities.

No one can deny the general proposition of the crucial role of the social structure and organization of society and the cultural environment in affecting artistic creation. The above statement, along with the frequently stated proposition that art reflects or mirrors the society, is much too broad in scope to be really meaningful to the critical social scientist. An artistic creation is the product of three interacting factors. First, the broad framework in which the artistic creation occurs is set by the social structure and cultural environment of the total society. Of concern to the scholar is the existence of what kind of cultural ethos, what type of social structure, the value attached to artistic endeavor, and so forth. For example, the total social organization and cultural values become of relevance in considering the intense concentration on religious themes for artistic endeavors in the Medieval Period in Western Europe. Second, artistic creations are the products of societal members who react to more than the general social framework. The artist in his socialization process was exposed to the influence of specific subcultural groupings as a result of his position in the social hierarchy. The influence of such relevant facts as social class position, racial background, religious affiliation, and nationality status will materially influence his perception of the socio-cultural organization and the attitudes and interests he possesses. Third, the artist perceives the world as do all individuals in unique ways. In the final analysis the structuring or organizing of external reality occurs in the individual as a product of not only cultural and group factors but also as expressions of individual wants, needs, and desires that are balanced in unique personality combinations. Thus the artistic creation represents a synthesis of personal, group, and cultural factors in a creative product.

The student of the sociology of art is concerned not only with the influence of society on artistic creation but with the reverse, which is the question of the influence of artistic creations on society in general and groups in particular. Basic to this consideration of influence is the receptivity of the groups toward the artistic creation. As Karl Schuessler has demonstrated in his study of the positive relationship between musical taste and cultural background, group membership, and position in the social hierarchy will influence the selection of artistic creations. The receptiveness toward innovations in techniques also is anchored in socio-cultural factors. But the exact effect which artistic creations will have on behavior and social organization is one that remains to be explored by the investigator.

In reviewing the period 1945–1955, the general fact emerges that sociologists have generally ignored the field of art with the exception of the Indian sociologist, Radhakamal Mukerjee, who has concentrated on many theoretical problems involved in the sociology of art; Albrecht and Duncan, who have been concerned with the sociology of literature; and Mueller, who has done empirical investigations in the area of the sociology of music.

In the compilation of this annotated bibliography on the sociology of art, the major journals in the field of sociology have been consulted along with the major monographs written in this area. In arranging the bibliography the following subclassifications have been used:

## SOCIOLOGY OF ART

Mukerjee, Radhakamal, "Social Disguise as the Principle of Art," *Sociology and Social Research*, Vol. 30 (1945–1946), pp. 3–10.

Art represents a compromise between the unconscious and conscious as conceptualized by Freud. Art through the use of social disguises represented by phantasies, sublimation, and symbolization on the conscious level gives expression to the pressing forces of the unconscious.

Mukerjee, Radhakamal, "The Meaning and Evolution of Art in Society," *Amer. Soc. Rev.*, Vol. 10 (1945), pp. 496–503.

An essay by the noted Indian sociologist which makes a case for the view that art is created through social forces and acts as a way of social control.

Mukerjee, Radhakamal, *The Social Function of Art*, New York, Macmillan Company, 1950.

Art is viewed by the author as "the autobiography of a culture." A statement of theoretical importance relating to the function of art in society is included.

Mukerjee, Radhakamal, "The Sociological Approach to Art," *Sociology and Social Research*, Vol. 30 (1945–1946), pp. 177–184.

The type and pattern of artistic creation in a society is dependent not only upon its social organization and cultural history but upon the synthesis of the milieu by the creations of individual personalities. Art acts as a unifying force in a society and transcends all other cultural forms.

## SOCIOLOGY OF LITERATURE

Albrecht, Milton C., "The Relationship of Literature and Society," *Amer. J. Soc.*, Vol. 59 (1953–1954), pp. 425–436.

A thorough investigation of the major empirical studies and writings involved in various theories of the relationship of literature and society.

Barnett, James H., and Rhoda Gruen, "Recent American Divorce Novels, 1938–1945: A Study in the Sociology of Literature," *Social Forces*, Vol. 26 (1947–1948), pp. 322–327.

This brief article is based on the comparative analysis of twenty-five divorce novels to determine how the theme of divorce is treated in fiction as compared with actual research studies of this phenomenon.

Bogardus, Emory S., "Social Distance in Greek Drama," *Sociology and Social Research*, Vol. 33 (1948–1949), pp. 291–295.

A short analysis of the Greek drama, *Medea*, is presented to illustrate the use of social distance by authors of Greek tragedies.

Bogardus, Emory S., "Social Distance in Poetry," *Sociology and Social Research,* Vol. 36 (1951–1952), pp. 40–47.

A cursory look at the use of the social nearness and farness concept as a theme by poets.

Chartier, Barbara, "The Social Role of the Literary Elite," *Social Forces,* Vol. 29 (1950–1951), pp. 179–186.

A brief glance at the personal and social role characteristics of the "producers of ideas" for public consumption, reviewed both in an historical and contemporary light.

Deegan, Dorothy Yost, *The Stereotype of the Single Woman in American Novels,* New York, King's Crown Press, 1951.

A study which abstracts from 125 American novels published between 1851 and 1935 the qualities attributed to the adult single woman by the novelists. The work is marked by a strong value orientation that single females have been incorrectly presented in the novel according to cultural stereotypes.

Dinkel, Robert M., "The Influence of Nursery Literature on Child Development," *Sociology and Social Research,* Vol. 31 (1946–1947), pp. 285–290.

The author makes the assumption that nursery literature does have an influence upon the socialization of the child. The article is not concerned with the extent of the literature's influence, but with the ideal types of nursery literature that should be selected by parents as a socialization aid.

Downer, Alan S., *Fifty Years of American Drama,* Chicago, Henry Regnery Company, 1951.

A historical account of the developmental trends in American drama during this century. The sociological implications must be obtained by the reader himself.

Duncan, Hugh, *Language and Literature in Society. A Sociological Essay on Theory and Method in the Interpretation of Linguistic Symbols with a Bibliographical Guide to the Sociology of Literature,* Chicago, University of Chicago Press, 1953.

A brilliant analysis of the general field of communication and the role of literature and symbols in society.

Hoffman, Frederick J., *Freudianism and the Literary Mind,* Baton Rouge, Louisiana State University Press, 1945.

An attempt to show the influence of Freudian writings and interpretations on major literary figures such as Joyce, Lawrence, Kafka, Mann, and others.

Hoffman, Frederick J., *The Modern Novel in America, 1900–1950,* Chicago, Henry Regnery Company, 1951.

An examination of the movement of the American novel in this period toward an interest in the social problems of society and in the internal mechanics of art with only an implicit sociological frame of reference.

Larsen, Cecil E., "Social Elements in Norwegian Poetry," *Sociology and Social Research,* Vol. 37 (1952–1953), pp. 169–174.

A brief review of the social determination of certain themes in Norwegian poetry. The article is superficial in its coverage.

Larsen, Cecil E., "The Family in Norwegian Fiction," *Sociology and Social Research*, Vol. 36 (1951–1952), pp. 97–101.

This brief article based on a survey of eighty-nine novels authored by Norwegians from 1870 to 1940 places its emphasis upon the novel as an invaluable source from which the sociologist may gather data.

Larsen, Cecil E., "The Race Problem in Contemporary American Negro Poetry," *Sociology and Social Research*, Vol. 38 (1953–1954), pp. 162–167.

A dominant theme of Negro poetry in the twentieth century has been a protest against the prejudice and discrimination that Negroes experience.

Le Coq, J. P., "Dynamic Social Forces of Literature," *Sociology and Social Research*, Vol. 31 (1946–1947), pp. 117–126.

The author has two propositions: (1) literature has reflected through the centuries the social systems of humans, and (2) literature contains dynamic social forces that influence society. These are illustrated through a brief review of many works through the centuries. From this is deduced the third proposition that in the future literature will mirror society as it has done in the past. The empirical support for these propositions is at the present time inadequate.

Simmons, Ernest J. (ed.), *Through the Glass of Soviet Literature*, New York, Columbia University Press, 1953.

Soviet society is viewed through its literature by a group of scholars at the Russian Institute of Columbia University.

Vincent, Melvin, "Fiction Mirrors the War," *Sociology and Social Research*, Vol. 30 (1945–1946), pp. 101–111.

A review of the major works of fiction that used World War II as their focus, with a partial classification of the themes that have sociological and psychological relevance.

## SOCIOLOGY OF MUSIC

Mueller, John H., "Methods of Measurement of Aesthetic Folkways," *Amer. J. Soc.*, Vol. 51 (1945–1946), pp. 276–282.

By use of statistical techniques, an analysis is made of the aesthetic folkways in musical taste as documented by trends in the repertoire of symphony orchestras.

Mueller, John H., *The American Symphony Orchestra: A Social History of Musical Taste*, Bloomington, Indiana, Indiana University Press, 1951.

A presentation of the historical background and the sociocultural forces impinging on the development of the symphony orchestra. A mature and lucid case is made for the fact of the sociopsychological determination of preferences and opinions about music.

Schuessler, Karl F., "Social Background and Musical Taste," *Amer. Soc. Rev.*, Vol. 13 (1948), pp. 330–335.

This is a study of the music preference of over 1,200 people in Evansville, Indiana, as related to the respondents' socioeconomic background, sex, age, and musical background. The conclusion is that there is a positive relationship between the individual's musical taste and his particular cultural background.

## THE MOTION PICTURE

Fearing, Franklin, "Influence of the Movies on Attitudes and Behavior," *Annals of the American Academy of Political and Social Science,* Vol. 254 (1947), pp. 70–79.

An insightful presentation of various theories of the impact, especially psychological but also cultural, of movies on human behavior.

Wolfenstein, Martha, and Nathan Leites, "An Analysis of Themes and Plots," *Annals of the American Academy of Political and Social Science,* Vol. 254 (1947), pp. 41–48.

An excellent article on the treatment of the love themes in American movies.

Wolfenstein, Martha, and Nathan Leites, *Movies: A Psychological Study,* Glencoe, Illinois, The Free Press, 1950.

An outstanding study utilizing the cultural-psychoanalytic method of analysis of the major themes in American motion pictures.

# Index

# Date Due

| | | |
|---|---|---|
| APR 17 1958 | | |
| MAY 19 1958 | OCT 3 1966 RESERVED | |
| MAY 15 1958 NOV 7 | 6 P.M. Soc 339 | |
| DEPARTMENT NOV 13 | 6 P.M. | |
| MAR 8 1960 | | |
| MAY 30 '60 NOV 14 | 1 P.M. | |
| NOV 3 1960 6 P.M. APR 25 | | |
| NOV 3 1960 JAN 30 | 4 P.M. | |
| Carrel JAN 30 | 5 P.M. | |
| FEB 1 1961 | | |
| MAY 24 1961 | | |
| DEC 11 '61 | | |
| NO 6 '63 | | |
| AP 9 '64 | | |
| AP 7 '65 | | |
| NO 24 '65 | | |
| MY 11 '66 | | |
| OC 25 '66 | | |
| | PRINTED | IN U. S. A. |